RUSSIA

A HISTORY AND AN INTERPRETATION

IN TWO VOLUMES

VOLUME I

By MICHAEL T. FLORINSKY

TOWARDS AN UNDERSTANDING OF THE U.S.S.R.

FASCISM AND NATIONAL SOCIALISM

THE SAAR STRUGGLE

WORLD REVOLUTION AND THE U.S.S.R.

RUSSIA: A HISTORY AND AN INTERPRETATION

RUSSIA

A HISTORY
AND
AN INTERPRETATION

IN TWO VOLUMES

BY

MICHAEL T. FLORINSKY

VOLUME I

THE MACMILLAN COMPANY

❋

NEW YORK · 1953

PREFACE

✳

The present study is an attempt to encompass within the relatively brief space of two volumes the history of Russia from the earliest days to March, 1918. In dealing with a subject as vast and unwieldy as a thousand years of Russian history, the most difficult problems, perhaps, are those of selection and organization. Both the choice of the "facts" and their presentation necessarily reflect the predilections and beliefs of the author. To make my position clear I could do no better than to quote the statement by H. A. L. Fisher to which I fully subscribe: "Men wiser and more learned than I have discerned in history a plot, a rhythm, a predetermined pattern. These harmonies are concealed from me. I can only see one emergency following upon another as wave follows upon wave, only one great fact with respect to which, since it is unique, there can be no generalizations, only one safe rule for the historian: that he should recognize in the development of human destinies the play of the contingent and the unforeseen." [1]

The recognition of "the play of the contingent and the unforeseen" has determined the plan which I have adopted. It was relatively easy to decide on the division of Russian history into four main parts which, by a historical accident, coincide with the change of capital. Part I, "From Kiev to Moscow," deals with the uncertainties of the formative period of the Russian state; Part II, "The First Moscow Period," describes the territorial consolidation of Muscovy and the growth of monarchical absolutism; Part III, "The St. Petersburg Period," presents an account of Russia as a European Power, from the beginning of the eighteenth century to the transfer of the capital to Moscow in March, 1918. Part IV, "The Second Moscow Period," was to deal with the Soviet phase of Russian history, but for reasons

[1] H. A. L. Fisher, A *History of Europe* (Houghton Mifflin Company, Boston, 1935), I, vii.

v

given in a Note at the end of this study its execution has been indefinitely postponed. This scheme, I believe, is not open to serious objections. It proved more difficult to devise a satisfactory arrangement within each of the three periods with which I have dealt. Careful consideration has led me to the conclusion that the personalities of the tsars and emperors had a greater part in determining the course of Russian history than I was at first inclined to believe. I have accordingly followed the somewhat unimaginative plan of making my chapters coincide with the reigns of the successive monarchs, except where the insignificance of the rulers or the brevity of their tenure of office made this inexpedient (the first Romanov in the seventeenth century, the successors of Peter I, 1725–1761). I have not neglected, however, the broad economic and social factors, and have endeavored to bring out their significance.

My discussion of the political and social evolution of Russia in the tenth to the fifteenth centuries owes much to the excellent monographs of Professor A. S. Presniakov, whose studies have revolutionized the traditional view of the Russian Middle Ages. It is a minor tragedy of the revolution, and a major tragedy of Russian historiography, that Presniakov's volume on the formation of the Muscovite state, published in 1918, has passed almost unnoticed, especially abroad. As late as 1952 his major books were not available in the Library of the British Museum. In recent years, however, Presniakov's work has gained wide recognition in the Soviet Union. I must also acknowledge my indebtedness to Professor B. H. Sumner, whose admirable volume *Russia and the Balkans, 1870–1880* (The Clarendon Press, Oxford, 1937), has been invaluable to me, especially in writing my Chapter XXXVI.

Mention must be made of the vexed questions of calendar, transliteration, and sources. Dates in this study are given in accordance with the Russian calendar used at the time, except when stated otherwise. Prior to February 14, 1918, Russia adhered to the Julian, or Old Style calendar, which was superseded, first in the Catholic and later in the Protestant countries, by the Gregorian, or New Style calendar introduced by Pope Gregory XIII in 1582. In the sixteenth and seventeenth centuries the Julian calendar was ten days behind the Gregorian. On March 1, 1700, the spread had increased to eleven days; on March 1, 1800, to twelve days; and on March 1, 1900, to thirteen days. A decree of the Soviet government of January 26, 1918, adopted the Gregorian calendar; February 1, 1918, Old Style, became February 14, and the difference between the Russian and the western calendars disappeared.

As E. H. Carr notes, "No system of transliteration is satisfactory except to the philologist who has invented it"—and even this may well be an overstatement. I have followed, as a rule, the transliteration of the Library of Congress, subject to some simplifications. For instance, I have written Solovev (not Solov'ev or Soloviev) and Zinovev (not Zinov'ev or Zinoviev). The most troublesome point, perhaps, is the soft Russian *a*, which is rendered in English as *ia* or *ya*. I have used in most cases the *ia* form and have written Ianzhul (not Yanzhul), but in a number of cases, to conform with what I believe to be the prevalent practice, the *ya* form has been used, for example, *boyar* (not *boiar*), Yaroslavl (not Iaroslavl). The inconsistencies, to which I plead guilty, resulting from these and other departures from uniformity may be justified on the ground that they minimize the element of the odd and the bizarre, but inconsistencies they remain.

The scholarly-minded reader will be disappointed by the smallness of the number of references to sources. Most of my references would be to Russian publications, and as this study is addressed to English-speaking readers it appeared undesirable to burden it with footnotes which few would use, especially since the books to which I refer are available in but a small number of libraries outside the Soviet Union. Another consideration I had in mind was the high cost of manufacturing, which would be greatly increased by the inclusion of references to Russian sources. To soothe the pangs of my academic conscience, I have inserted in parentheses, or otherwise noted, in some instances, the names of the authors from whom the information is taken, a weak compromise which nevertheless may be of use to those who would wish to pursue the subject further. The more significant references, especially in chapters dealing with foreign relations, have been retained.

In connection with this study I have used the Staatsbibliotek in Berlin, the Bibliothèque Nationale in Paris, the Russian Historical Archives in Prague, the libraries of the British Museum, the London School of Slavonic and East European Studies, the League of Nations and the International Labor Office in Geneva, the Osteuropa Institut in Breslau, the New York Public Library, and above all the excellent Russian collection of Columbia University. A. F. Meyendorff and the late B. E. Nolde gave me on many occasions valuable advice on the sources to consult, and I have greatly benefited by my discussions with them of the obscure and debatable issues of Russian history. I owe an even greater debt of gratitude to S. A. Bolan, of the library staff of Columbia University, who has generously put at my disposal his unique knowledge of Russian bibliography and who has taken infinite trouble in securing the books I needed.

My interest in Russian history goes back to 1920 when it was my good fortune to become associated with the late Sir Paul Vinogradoff, F.B.A., Corpus Professor of Jurisprudence in the University of Oxford, in planning and editing twelve volumes of the Russian Series of the Economic and Social History of the War published by the Carnegie Endowment for International Peace. Sir Paul's wisdom, insight, and keen historical sense have greatly contributed to the elucidation of my own views, and, indirectly, this book owes him much.

The initiative of my writing a history of Russia came from The Macmillan Company of New York, more specifically from its former President, the late George P. Brett, Sr., whom I never had the privilege of meeting but who knew my first book, *The End of the Russian Empire*, which was published in 1931. I accepted the offer in 1934, expecting to complete the study within two or three years. It took two decades. Thus whatever its shortcomings are, they should not be ascribed to hasty workmanship. The patience and interest in my work displayed by The Macmillan Company, and their understanding of my problems, were essential to the completion of my task.

Mrs. C. P. Killien has given me valuable assistance in preparing for the press Chapters I–XLIV, and Miss Grace H. Gerberich Chapters XLV–XLVIII. I gratefully acknowledge their help.

For years my wife has borne with fortitude and good humor my, at times, excessive absorption in the history of Russia, and her encouragement and penetrating criticisms have greatly helped the progress of this work. My gratitude to her is here affectionately recorded.

M. T. F.

April 15, 1953

CONTENTS

❋

VOLUME I

ix

VOLUME II

PART III. THE ST. PETERSBURG PERIOD (Cont'd.)

Contents

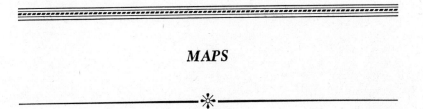

MAPS

---- ✳ ----

VOLUME I

VOLUME II

RUSSIA

A HISTORY AND AN INTERPRETATION

VOLUME I

INTRODUCTION

THE LAND

The historical destinies of nations, like the lives of individuals, are determined largely by their environment.

It was no mere historical accident that the immense plain occupying one-sixth of the land surface of the globe became gradually absorbed within the political frontiers of the Russian state. The vast territory that stretches from the White Sea and the Arctic Ocean to the Black and the Caspian seas, to Persia, Afghanistan, India, and China, and from the Baltic Sea to the Pacific Ocean, presents remarkable features of unity that seem to have predetermined its political future. The boundless expanse of Russia comprises a wide range of climatic and botanical conditions, from the bleak tundra in the extreme north to the luxuriant orange and lemon groves of the Crimea and the Caucasus and the cotton plantations of Turkestan. But the transition from one climatic zone to another is gradual, by slow and hardly perceptible stages, without any abrupt changes. Unlike western Europe, the monotony of the Russian plain is not broken by ranges of mountains. Lofty mountain chains such as the Caucasus, the Altai, the Tian Shan, and the Saian, and high plateaus like those of Armenia and Pamir, are to be found only on the outskirts of the Russian state. The Verkhoiansk range in eastern Siberia is situated in an outlying district that has never played an important role in national history. The Urals, which are traditionally regarded as the dividing line between Europe and Asia, are hardly more than a glorified chain of hills rising merely some fifteen hundred feet above sea level. They never offered anything like a natural barrier to the expansion of the Russian state, nor do they seriously interfere with the fundamental unity of the Russian plain. The division of Russia into two parts—

1

European and Asiatic—would seem to be artificial, and it can hardly be justified on any topographical grounds. The absence of natural barriers was an important element, favoring both Russia's political expansion and internal migration. Not unlike the United States, although for different reasons, Russia had her "frontier," which in her case has continuously been shifted. This process has not yet been brought to a close. The absence of natural barriers also greatly facilitated the invasion of Russian territory by the nomadic tribes of the steppes. The struggle against these invaders, which heavily overcast the life of the nation until near the end of the eighteenth century, left a deep and lasting imprint upon the development of the country.

Another geographical feature that exercised a vast influence upon the course of Russia's history is the character and the distribution of her rivers. The great rivers of European Russia—and it is with European Russia alone that we are concerned while discussing the early history of the future empire—originate in the central region, at the foot of the Valdai tableland, a plateau which rises to the modest altitude of some one thousand feet. The Volga, the Dnieper, and the Western Dvina have their beginnings in the lakes and marshes of this part of the Russian plain. Their leisurely and winding course takes the first to the Caspian, the second to the Black, and the third to the Baltic seas. In the north, access to the Gulf of Finland was gained through the waterway formed by the Neva, Lake Ladoga, the Volkhov, Lake Ilmen, and the Lovat. The level surface of the country, the close geographical proximity of the issues of the main rivers, and their wealth of tributaries created a complex and almost interlocking system of waterways that is unique on the European and Asiatic continents. The waterways were the main roads of the ancient world, greatly facilitating the process of internal migration. They emphasized the unity of the Russian plain, worked against the establishment of independent political states, and thus contributed to the eventual triumph of a centralized political system. It was along the rivers that the population settled in the early stage of the country's history, and it was the highly ramified network of waterways that brought to the inhabitants of the territory that later became Russia their first contacts with western nations. The enterprising Scandinavians used the Russian rivers for their trade and for their plundering expeditions to the eastern countries and Byzantium. It is believed that the natives participated in eastern trade long before the Russian state came into being. This international intercourse, modest as it probably was, could not but have a profound influence upon the social structure and economic conditions. The existence of foreign trade at this early date leads one to believe that the inhabitants of the Russian plain in those remote centuries had already emerged from the purely pastoral and nomadic stage and were producing certain commodities that were of value to the eastern and the Scandinavian traders.

Rivers, again, played a by no means unimportant part in favoring the eastward march of the Russian state. The Kama, a tributary of the Volga, extends its ramifications eastward, coming into close proximity with the water system of the Ob, in western Siberia. It was largely along the water routes that the restless Cossacks penetrated behind the Ural Mountains in the reign of Ivan IV, an adventurous enterprise that gradually brought the whole of Siberia under the rule of the tsars.

But if the Russian state, from the very first days of its existence, controlled the sources of its main rivers, it was not until many centuries later that it succeeded in annexing the territories where these rivers gained access to the seas. This fact and the relative insignificance of Russia's shore line in proportion to the vast expanse of her territory have undoubtedly influenced the course of her national development. Moreover, the Arctic Ocean and the White Sea are of but little importance from both the political and the economic point of view; the Caspian is a closed sea, and it was not until the eighteenth century that Russia gained a firm foothold on the shores of the Baltic Sea and the Black Sea. A continental nation, her ventures on the high seas have been relatively few, and they have seldom brought her laurels.

One more geographical factor of great historical importance must be mentioned—the division of the Russian territory from the botanical point of view into the broad belt of forests in the north and the steppes in the south. There was no hard and fast frontier between the two zones. The somewhat uncertain line dividing them shifted more than once in the course of the eleven centuries of Russia's history. In the earlier period forests stretched northward from a line passing through Kiev and south of the present cities of Moscow and Kazan; the forest belt then turned around the southern slope of the Ural Mountains and followed their eastern slope, coming down again to the Saian Mountains and from there extending solidly to the Pacific Ocean. The steppes of European Russia comprised the entire territory south of the line of forests, and through the wide gateway left open between the Urals and the Caspian Sea merged with the steppes of eastern Siberia. It was probably through this gate that the Asiatic hordes descended upon southern Russia. Until the middle of the eighteenth century the forest belt remained the principal stage of Russia's history. The Asiatic invaders felt at home in the steppes and seldom made any attempt to penetrate within the forest belt that to them was foreign. For centuries, therefore, the southern steppes, with their fertile black soil, remained a negative factor in the political history of the country. Although they were the hiding place of a powerful enemy and were therefore to be carefully watched, they were also a haven for all those—and they were many—who sought to escape from the heavy yoke and the many burdens the Russian princes, and later the Muscovite state, imposed upon their people. It was in the southern steppes that the free and unruly communities of the Cossacks came into being. To the Russian state as an organized political body, and to the bulk of its population—landlords, artisans, merchants, and farmers—the steppes remained for centuries a deadly menace. But to those who were driven to despair by domestic oppression, and to those adventurous souls who cherished the dream of a perhaps somewhat anarchistic freedom—a dream that has never been realized in the course of Russia's history—the steppes were a hope and a promise.

THE PEOPLE

The early history of the land that eventually became Russia presents many elements of uncertainty. The thick curtain of oblivion that covers bygone centuries is only occasionally lifted to allow a glimpse of the boundless expanse of the steppes alive with milling thousands of nomadic horsemen and their wagons, irresistibly moving westward from the mysterious and threatening uplands of central Asia. The reasons for these great migrations of peoples, the origins of the nomadic tribes, and sometimes their very names are the subject of more or less successful and learned conjectures. One of the few certain things known about the nomads is that they sojourned sometimes as long as two or three centuries in the steppes north of the Black Sea, until they were forced to make place for new invaders from the east. In the early centuries of this era the territories east of the Danube were to western civilization what the southern steppes were to the Russian state of the Kiev and Moscow period.

The earliest mention of the present Russian territory goes back to the seventh century B.C., when a number of Greek colonies were founded on the northern shores of the Black Sea. The Greeks made no attempt to annex the adjoining hinterland, but carried on a profitable trade with the local barbarian population, whom they called Scythians. The Scythians sold to the Greeks grain, fish, and amber, and they bought from them wine, oil, textiles, and articles of luxury. It would seem that the Scythians were not entirely unresponsive to the influence of Greek art and culture, but before the beginning of the Christian era the Scythians had already disappeared from the map and their place had been taken by the Sarmathians. In the second and third centuries after Christ, the Sarmathians were overcome by the Germanic tribes of the Goths who descended upon them from the southern shores of the Baltic Sea. The Goths kept in a state of terror the eastern territories of the Roman empire, frequently invaded Asia Minor and the Balkans, and formed in the middle of the fourth century a unified state under the leadership of Hermanaric. It was not long, however, before they themselves became the victims of foreign invasion. The hordes of the Huns, moving irresistibly westward from the plains of Asia, defeated the Goths, who were forced to abandon the Black Sea steppes and overrun the Roman empire. The Huns established a huge state stretching from the Volga to the Danube. In the fifth century they expanded farther west and reached the zenith of their power under Attila, who transferred the center of his empire to the plains of the present Hungary, where he threatened practically the whole of Europe. After Attila's death, however, the Hunnish empire disintegrated and its territory fell under the control of another Asiatic tribe, the Avars, who emerged from Asia in the second half of the ninth century. But even earlier, in the middle of the seventh century, the domination over the Black Sea steppes passed to the hands of the Khazars and somewhat later to the Magyars, who formed an alliance with the Khazars. The Khazar empire was overthrown in the tenth century by a new Asiatic tribe, the Patzinacs (Pechenegs); and the Magyars, under the pressure of the same invaders, were gradually pushed westward, first to the plains of the Don, then to the lower Danube, and finally into the territory of the present Hungary. The Patzinacs were followed by the Torks and the Cumans and—in the thirteenth century—by the Tartars. Thus for nearly a thousand years southern Russia remained in the highroad of nomadic intruders and sustained the first shock of the tidal waves of the great migrations originating in the confused economic and social upheavals and obscure political turmoil of the Asiatic continent and fed by its seemingly inexhaustible reservoir of humanity. It was fortunate for the Slavic and Finnish population of the forest belt of European Russia that the Asiatic invaders, faithful to the nomadic tradition of the steppes, seldom ventured beyond the protective line of the forests. It is in these woodlands that are to be found the ethnographic and political elements from which was built the Russian state.

The distant origin of the Slavic tribes is as obscure and uncertain as is that of the Asiatic nomads who swept over the steppes. They, too, came presumably from Asia, and their early European settlement would seem to have been the territory along the northern slope of the Carpathian Mountains. They were first described as Slavs (*Sclaveni, Sclavini, Sclavi*) in the writings of the Greek and Latin authors of the sixth century, but references to the same tribes under different names have been identified in earlier documents. The Slavic tribes shared the destinies of the other populations of that part of Europe in the eventful era when Asiatic empires rose and fell in the plains of southeastern Europe. The Slavs themselves crossed the Danube and organized military expeditions against the Byzantine empire in the sixth and seventh centuries. It was probably in the seventh century that the heterogeneous mass of the Slavic tribes became subdivided into three definite groups: the southern or Balkan Slavs, the western Slavs, comprising the Czechs, the Moravians, and the Poles, and the eastern Slavs, who later became known as Russians. It is believed that the downfall of the Hunnish empire and the invasion of the Avars may have had something to do with the gradual shifting of the masses of the Slavs from the Carpathian Mountains. The eastern Slavs reached the Dnieper, probably in the seventh century, and gradually spread along the great rivers of the Russian plain. In the middle of the ninth century they occupied both shores of the Dnieper except for a narrow strip at the mouth of the river. In the northwest they controlled the upper course of the Western Dvina and in the north reached the southern shores of Lake Ladoga. In the northeast the Slavic settlements extended as far as the upper course of the Volga, of the Moscow River, and of the Oka; in the southeast they reached a point east of the Dnieper rapids. They failed, however, to establish themselves on the shores either of the Black Sea or of the Sea of Azov.

In their expansion over the Russian plain the eastern Slavs occupied the territories formerly held by Lithuanians, who in the middle of the ninth century were pushed back into a relatively restricted area on the Baltic Sea, in the basin of the Nieman and the lower Western Dvina. The Slavs also invaded the land populated by various Finnish tribes and forced them to withdraw to the north and the east. The Finns, however, retained the shores of the Gulf of Finland.

The Lithuanians and the Finnish tribes were, if possible, even more primitive than the eastern Slavs, and the contact of the newcomers with the natives seems to have had no effect upon the social organization and the pursuits of the Slavs. The very fact, however, that they found themselves largely in control of the ancient waterway connecting the Baltic Sea with the Black Sea and the Caspian Sea had important repercussions upon the future course of their development, for they became involved in the trade carried over the water routes of European Russia. The transformation of a primitive people into a trading community was facilitated by the appearance in the southern steppes in the seventh century of the Khazars, a tribe differing in many respects both from the Asiatic nomads who preceded and from those who followed them. While preserving the nomadic mode of life, the Khazars were interested in trade, an interest that may be partly explained by the considerable influx of Arabs and Jews in their midst. The influence of the Jews was sufficiently strong to induce the Khazar ruler and many of the chieftains to embrace Judaism. Itil, a city on the lower Volga, was the capital of the Khazar state, and in the middle of the eighth century it became the center of animated trade relations between the Baltic countries and the Arabic east. The Bulgars, who lived along the upper Volga and the Kama, were also active participants in the trade exchange between east and west. A number of Slavic tribes that had settled in the territories adjoining the southern steppes were conquered by the Khazars and were compelled to pay them tribute. Some of the Slavs, nevertheless, benefited by this conquest, through which they gradually became involved in the trade operations of their new masters. The mighty waterway of the Western Dvina and the Volga brought the Slavic traders to the Caspian Sea, and their presence in Bagdad early in the ninth century was reported by an

Arab author. It is this eastern trade route, made relatively safe by the protection of the Khazars, that seems to have been of particular importance in the eighth and ninth centuries.

The articles of export contributed by the Slavs to this international commercial exchange were slaves, amber, salt, and products of the forest—furs, honey, wax. The Slavic merchant princes exacted their export merchandise from the local people through the imposition of tributes and also by reducing some of the natives to slavery. This two-fold aspect of their trade operations played a part in the establishment of the early cities, which were the military strongholds of the early Russian rulers, the depots for goods, and the meeting place of the merchants. All the ancient cities—Kiev, Novgorod, Chernigov, Liubech, Smolensk, Polotsk—located on important trade routes, gradually became the political centers from which grew the Russian state. This process was accelerated by an external event. The power of the Khazars collapsed in the first half of the ninth century under the pressure of new intruders from Asia, the Patzinacs. The merchant princes, confronted with a danger that menaced their commerce, found it necessary to organize in defense. The leadership in this task sometimes fell into the hands of another foreign element, the Norsemen, or Varangians.

The Varangians were Scandinavian adventurers who in the eighth century began to appear in various parts of Europe. They probably came upon the great waterway of the Western Dvina and the Volga, which linked the Baltic Sea with the Caspian Sea, a route that made possible trade between the western European countries and the Arabic east. It is today considered certain that the Western Dvina-Volga route was known and widely used at an earlier period than that of the Neva-Volkhov-Dnieper, which played so important a part somewhat later and brought the Norsemen to the gates of Constantinople. This statement is based on the overwhelming preponderance of Arabic over Byzantine coins in the numerous treasure troves in Sweden and on the Island of Gotland. Archaeological data seem to indicate that trade relations between Sweden and the Khazars probably began at the end of the eighth century.

The Norsemen were traders, pirates, and above all soldiers of fortune. Attracted by the profits offered by the eastern trade, they came to Russia in large numbers. They mixed freely with the Slavs and contributed to the formation of the upper stratum of the young society, a group that consisted of merchants and soldiers just emerging from a primitive stage. The Norsemen sometimes merely joined the local merchants as co-partners in commercial and military expeditions, the two elements being by no means easily distinguishable in those days. Not infrequently, however, they came in large and well armed bands and succeeded in imposing themselves as rulers to whom the local population was forced to pay tribute. It then became the interest and also the duty of the conquerors to organize the defense, from the attacks of other intruders, of the territories over which they had control. With the downfall of the Khazars and the appearance of the Patzinacs, the necessity of such defense became strongly felt. It was in 862 that, according to tradition, Riurik, the first Nordic ruler of Russia and the founder of the dynasty, established himself in Novgorod.

Although the commercial and military activities of the Scandinavians were an important element in framing the developments that led to the creation of the Russian state, there is no evidence that they left any particular imprint upon the political and social structure of the country. They tended, on the contrary, to become assimilated by the Slavs.[1] In one repect only did the Norsemen leave behind them an ineffaceable trace, one which the Soviet Government has attempted —and so far without success—to obliterate: they gave to the country the name under which it has been known for over a thousand years. The term *Ros*, or *Rhos*, was originally applied to the bands of Norsemen who operated along the water routes of the Russian plains. The exact meaning of the term is uncertain, like so many other things belonging to this beclouded period. It became gradually accepted, however, as denoting, first, the upper class, then the entire population, and finally, the country itself. The name "Russian state" was not officially adopted until the fifteenth or sixteenth century. The foreign origin of the nation's name is not altogether inappropriate, for foreign influences have played an unusually large part in Russia's destiny. It may have been fitting, therefore, that one of the largest nations of the world should have made its appearance on the historical stage under a name borrowed from shady adventurers from a tiny country on the northern fringe of Europe.

[1] The last reference to the Varangians appears in the Chronicle under the year 1043.

PART ONE

FROM KIEV TO MOSCOW

"It may be imagined that the poorer the sources the easier is the task of the student. Actually the opposite is true. On abundant sources he can draw freely and if he has the gift of a historian he may create real history. The situation is very different when the sources are inadequate. To achieve anything at all the writer of history must become a kind of assiduous rag-picker (*triapichnik*) who diligently turns over dozens of times all sorts of rubbish (*khlam*) in order not to miss a single scrap or bit of evidence which may serve his purpose or be used; he must become a meticulous research worker while preserving from being dried up the living man every historian should be; and he is continuously pursued by a lingering feeling of dissatisfaction and disappointment."

—E. GOLUBINSKY, *Istoriia russkoi tserkvi* (History of the Russian Church) (2nd ed., Moscow, 1901), Vol. I, Pt. I, p. xviii.

CHAPTER I

THE RISE AND FALL OF KIEV

———————————————————— ✳ ————————————————————

THE CHRONICLE

The opaque veil of oblivion that conceals the early history of the territory that later became Russia is only partly lifted during the early centuries of the existence of the new state. The student's chief source of information is the Russian Chronicle, supported by an important body of valuable but necessarily fragmentary evidence supplied by foreign historical records and writings, especially Byzantine and Arabic, by archaeological, ethnographic, and linguistic data, and by whatever has been preserved of popular tradition in songs and folklore. But the Chronicle remains the most important and comprehensive source for the study of the early centuries of Russia's history. Unfortunately, the inestimable value of these records was not realized until the middle of the eighteenth century, and their systematic collection and publication did not begin until the second quarter of the nineteenth. In the meantime many valuable manuscripts had been destroyed or lost.

The Chronicle is a monumental work which covers, with a varying degree of completeness, a long line of centuries, from the middle of the ninth to the sixteenth and, in some of the later copies, even the seventeenth and the eighteenth centuries. Some of the chronicles comprise a compilation dealing with the origins of the Russian state and written at the beginning of the twelfth century, presumably in 1110 or 1112. Unfortunately, the earliest Chronicle in existence containing this compilation—the so-called Laurentius Chronicle—was prepared by a monk of that name as late as 1377. The ancient scripts used by Laurentius and his predecessors have all disappeared. A. A. Shakhmatov, fellow of the Russian Academy of Science and a leading authority on the subject, has analyzed the early compilation and has

13

restored the text of a still earlier Chronicle which he believes was written in 1039. This still leaves a wide gap between the year 854, the first year mentioned in the Chronicle, and the period in which its unknown author may have lived. The Chronicle therefore belies its name, especially in so far as it deals with the period previous to the eleventh century, Shakhmatov's restored text notwithstanding. It is not merely a record of events of which its authors were eyewitnesses or contemporaries, but also a comprehensive collection of general information drawn from all available sources. One finds in it, side by side with the description of current happenings, biblical stories and a varity of excerpts borrowed from Greek chronicles, the lives of the saints, legal documents, popular tradition, and so on. The chronology of the Chronicle is often defective, and it is generally accepted that the grouping of the earlier material under definite years was the work of a later writer. It must also be remembered that in those remote days every copyist regarded the result of his work as his private property and felt at liberty to change the text according to his taste. To this must be added the unintentional but inevitable errors that will find their way into a text that has been copied by hand a great many times in the course of centuries, as well as linguistic and paleographic obstacles of the most baffling nature. No wonder, therefore, that the information provided by the Chronicle is far from lucid, comprehensive, or reliable. Russian historians have often found it necessary to depend on the texts of the later copies of the chronicles in order to interpret, explain, and amplify the numerous obscure and unintelligible passages that occur in the earlier scripts. The danger inherent in such a procedure is self-evident.

The business of keeping chronicles was, moreover, in the hands of the Church, and the introduction of a definite and pronounced theological point of view, the representation of the whole course of history as a struggle between the forces of good and evil, could not but distort the narrative and thus further aggravate the task of the student who attempts to untangle the elusive thread of historical development. Beginning with the twelfth century, the Chronicle reflects local sympathies and dislikes which, inspired by the partisan feelings of their authors, preserve something of the flavor of the political struggles of bygone ages. But the light it sheds on the early period of the country's history is necessarily dim and uncertain.

THE BEGINNING OF THE RUSSIAN STATE

The traditional account of the establishment of the Russian state is based on the entry in the Chronicle under the year 862. According to this statement the Slavic and other tribes centering around Novgorod, having ejected the Varangians to whom they were paying tribute, found themselves confronted with so much internal discord and confusion that they were soon forced to invite new rulers from Scandinavia. Riurik, the founder of the future dynasty, who arrived with his two brothers and the usual military retinue, became the prince of Novgorod. This romantic legend is no longer accepted as an adequate explanation of the formation of the Russian state, and much of the story, including the very existence of Riurik, is open to the gravest doubts. Nevertheless the traditional version contains an element of truth. It points to the existence in the northwest of Russia of an earlier state controlled by the Norsemen. This conclusion is supported by a considerable body of evidence from non-Russian sources. The Varangians, it will be remembered, had been roving along the Russian rivers since the beginning of the ninth century, or perhaps even earlier. By the year 862 they were a familiar and well established element in the upper layer of the trading and military communities that had sprung up along the water routes of the Russian plains.

The appearance in Constantinople of a mission representing a people who called themselves *Rhos* is reported in the *Annales Bertiniani* in the year 839. The newcomers described themselves as Swedes (*comperit eos gentis esse Sueonum*), offered the Byzantine emperor a treaty of friendship in the name of their ruler (*Chacanus*), and asked for protection and facilities to return home, since the route by which they had come was in the hands of fierce and barbaric tribes. The Scandinavian origin of *Rhos* seems thus reasonably well established, but it is less easy to identify the state they represented. It has been suggested (Kliuchevsky) that they were the emissaries of the *Kagan* of the Khazars. A more recent investigation (Shakhmatov) places the state of the *Rhos* in the northwest of Russia, a conclusion supported by evidence from Arabic sources. The apprehensions expressed by the members of the mission as to the safety of their returning home by the route they had used to reach Constantinople—presumably the Dnieper—is given as an indication of the fact that the Norsemen, while entrenched in the north of Russia, had not yet succeeded in imposing their rule over the territories along the Dnieper. The reference of the emissaries to their ruler as the *Kagan* has been interpreted—perhaps not very convincingly—as proof of the fact that the state of the Norsemen had already reached a somewhat advanced stage of political organization and was no longer a colony of mere marauders and pirates. The desire of this new state to obtain access to the fertile regions of southern Russia and to gain control over the important waterway leading to the Black Sea might well have been the reason for the treaty of friendship the emissaries of the Russian *Kagan* offered to Byzantium.

In 860 the Russian army appeared for the first time at the gates of Constantinople. This venture, it is now believed, was by no means such a complete failure as it was made to appear by some of the Byzantine sources. The very magnitude of the enterprise suggests that the new Russian state had already reached a certain degree of cohesion. The Norsemen, before they reached Constantinople, had to overcome the resistance of the Slavic tribes dwelling along the Dnieper as well as that of the Patzinacs and the Magyars, unless one assumes —as some historians do—that the invaders of Byzantium came from the region of the Sea of Azov. Whatever the truth may be, the existence of a Russian state long before the events described by the Chronicle under the year 862 may be considered as reasonably certain.

The romantic legend of the invitation issued by the tribes of Novgorod to Riurik, when stripped of the ornate phraseology in which it was dressed by the author of the Chronicle, is by no means incompatible with the somewhat brutal facts of Russia's history, facts that the learned and God-fearing chronicler preferred to gloss over or of which he was perhaps ignorant. The basic elements in the structure of the early Russian state were the commercial and military cities. They controlled the adjoining territories, either because the latter were vitally interested in the trading ventures of these small metropolises, or—and this is more plausible—because the more enterprising, better armed and organized trading and military groups in the cities succeeded by measures of coercion in imposing themselves upon regions within their easy reach. The Norsemen played an important part both in the promotion of trade and in the creation of the city-states. Since the slave trade and the collection of tributes were among the functions of the new ruling group, it was only natural that relations with the populations under its control should lead to conflicts. The leadership of the merchant soldiers in the struggle against the neighboring tribes and the nomads of the steppes might, however, have made their harsh rule more palatable. Moreover, the Varangians not infrequently made their first appearance as hired defenders against the outside enemy. Nevertheless the abuse of power of which the Norsemen and their Slavic fellow merchant soldiers were undoubtedly guilty, several references to which are to be found in the Chronicle, could not but result in occasional popular uprisings against the oppressors. It is probable that it was one of these occurrences that led to the expulsion of the Varangians from Novgorod and to the subsequent arrival of a new group of Norsemen reported by the Chronicle in the year 862. Whether the new ruler of Novgorod was Riurik and whether he actually came on the invitation of the tribes centering around Novgorod, or whether he merely succeeded in imposing himself by force, remain uncertain, although the contractual character of the origin of his rule is usually admitted by historians. Riurik, if he existed at all, was one of the several Scandinavian *konungr* (Russian *kniaz*) or princes of the city-states. According to the Chronicle two more princes, brothers of Riurik, arrived simultaneously with him and became the rulers of other city-states. Their family ties with Riurik are, however, sometimes challenged even by those historians who do not deny the latter a place in Russian history. The chief function of the Scandinavians, however, was not internal administration and maintenance of order, as stated by the Chronicle, but the defense of the frontiers of the territories under their control.

It was the performance of this all-important duty that probably led to the shifting of the center of the future Russian state from Novgorod to Kiev. According to the Chronicle two of the members of Riurik's retinue, Askold and Dir, moved down the Volkhov and the Dnieper, occupied the city of Kiev, and engaged in successful warfare not only against the local Slavic tribes, whom they reduced to obedience, but also against the Patzinacs and the Bulgars. These activities of Askold and Dir were typical of those of the Scandinavian rulers of this period. They pursued a double object: the maintenance of their eastern and southern trade and the defense of the land and of the chief waterways from the Asiatic tribes. The collapse of the Khazar kingdom in the middle of the ninth century and the appearance of the Patzinacs in the Black Sea steppes served as a strong stimulus to the consolidation of the Slavic tribes behind their rulers. Common interest and common danger made the Slavs overlook, at least for a time, the hardships they themselves suffered only too frequently at the hands of the Norsemen.

The geographical position of Kiev on the main trade route to the Black Sea and Byzantium and its importance as a bulwark against the invasion of the southern and eastern nomads probably explains the leading part it played in the first three centuries of Russia's history. During that period the vital interests of the land, or at least of its most influential groups, were intimately bound up with the fate of Kiev. The rulers of the other principalities, therefore, were gradually induced to acknowledge the leadership of the Kievan prince. He acted in their name in the negotiations with the Greeks in 907 and eventually assumed the title of grand duke (*velikii kniaz*), while the heads of the other principalities continued to use the title of prince (*kniaz*).[1] The new state was in the making, even though it was still lacking in most of the essential characteristics of a modern state.

THE EARLY KIEVAN PRINCES

The early Kievan princes are semi-legendary, semi-historical figures. Popular tradition and the Church have collaborated in surrounding them with the romantic aura of national heroes. The first Scandinavian rulers of Kiev, Askold and Dir, were murdered by one of their countrymen, Oleg, who came to Kiev from Novgorod in 879. The story of Oleg's life bears unmistakable resemblance to those of the heroes of the Nordic sagas. In 912 Oleg was succeeded by Igor, who was killed in 945 while attempting to exact particularly heavy tribute from one of the Slavic tribes. Igor's son, Sviatoslav, became his father's successor, with Olga, Igor's widow, acting as regent. In 957 Olga visited Constantinople, where she was received by the Emperor Con-

[1] The propriety of employing the term *velikii kniaz* while dealing with the Kievan period has been questioned. According to Prof. Hrushevski it was unknown in the earlier chronicles. Prof. Presniakov maintains that *velikii kniaz* was never used to denote "seniority" among the princes in Kievan Russia. I have nevertheless retained the term (which somewhat illogically, but in conformity with modern usage, I translate as "grand duke," and not "great prince") partly because it seems desirable to adhere to the accepted practice, and partly because of the extreme difficulty of finding an English equivalent to convey the meaning of the Russian term *stareishenstvo* with its peculiar connotation of "seniority." The expressions "grand duke of Kiev" and "grand duchy of Kiev," if not strictly accurate, are not really misleading, since until the latter part of the twelfth century "seniority" among the princes was invariably associated with the possession of Kiev.

stantine Porphyrogentius. It was during her stay in Constantinople that, according to the Russian Chronicle, Olga embraced eastern Christianity. This version, contradicted by the Byzantine sources, is made all the more dubious by the assertion of the Russian chronicler that Olga's clever ruse interfered with the emperor's intention of marrying her. In 957 Olga was over sixty and Constantine Porphyrogentius was already married, his empress duly taking part in Olga's official reception. It is more likely that Olga became converted to Christianity some time before she went to Constantinople (Golubinsky). Her son, Sviatoslav, was killed in 972 in the course of an unsuccessful war against the Patzinacs, and the Kievan throne passed to his son, Yaropolk I, who lost his life in the struggle against his brother, Vladimir I (978–1015). Vladimir, one of the most picturesque figures of this period of Russia's history, repudiated heathenism, became converted to Christianity, and established Greek Orthodoxy as the official Church of Russia. Vladimir and Olga were both canonized, although such information as can be gathered about their lives does not disclose any striking devotion on their part to the Christian virtues of humility, charity, chastity, and abstinence.

Information regarding the conditions prevailing in Russia in the ninth and tenth centuries is uncertain and fragmentary. It would seem that the two great forces that shaped the history of the country were, as it has already been pointed out, the interest of the ruling military and merchant group in the trade with the east and Byzantium and the more general interest of the Slavic tribes in the defense from Asiatic invaders of the shifting frontiers of their settlements. It was these forces, to repeat, that are believed to account for the rise of Kiev to a position of leadership among the other city-states. And the same motives may be detected behind the policies of the early Kievan princes.

The character of the trade relations between the Russians and Byzantium is well known from the much-quoted description by Constantine Porphyrogentius of the Russian trade caravans to Constantinople. Although these relations were regulated by a number of trade agreements, the text of which has been preserved and the earliest of which was concluded in 907, commercial intercourse did not always proceed smoothly, and between the ninth and eleventh centuries the Russians undertook six or seven military expeditions against Byzantium.

Wars and international trade were so closely interwoven in the first two centuries of Russia's history that one hesitates to draw a hard and fast line between the two. Until almost the end of the tenth century the Russian princes continued the struggle with the Slavic and other tribes, which they conquered one after another. The bringing together under a unified rule of the heterogeneous elements that populated the Russian plain, weak and imperfect as the union was, may rightly be regarded as an important step towards the creation of the Russian state. At the same time the conquered populations, or at least a large section of them, were reduced to slavery, and the slaves thus secured were the chief article with which the Russian merchant princes supplied the foreign markets. The internal administration of the country was largely concerned with the collection of tributes, which were either levied by the princes and their representatives in the course of annual expeditions to the conquered territories or were delivered by the populations themselves to Kiev and other cities. It was during one of these expeditions for the collection of tribute that, according to the Chronicle, Igor lost his life. Tributes were usually paid in kind, especially in furs, but they were sometimes collected in Arabic coins, which were widely circulated in Russia during this period.

The purely military aspects of the policies of the Kievan princes were at least as important as, if not more important than, their trading and commercial ventures. The question whether international trade actually played as decisive a part in the creation of the Kievan state as is believed by some historians (Kliuchevsky) is one of the much disputed problems of Russia's history. There is evidence in the Chronicle and other sources that Oleg and his immediate successors were deeply concerned with the territorial expansion of their realm and with the defense of its frontiers. It is these military activities, and not foreign trading, that are believed by other historians to have been the real reason for the rise of Kiev (Shakhmatov). In view of the inconclusive evidence on which all such generalizations are based, one may accept the broader view that foreign trading and military expansion together engrossed the attention of the early Kievan rulers and contributed to the temporary supremacy of Kiev.

It may be questioned whether the use of the term "state" is justifiable with reference to the political body headed by the early Kievan princes. To begin with, the geographical frontiers of the territory over which they ruled were uncertain. The Slavic tribes that they had conquered were still in a condition of flux and had not yet completely abandoned their nomadic habits. The powers of the grand dukes of Kiev were, moreover, anything but precise and well defined. In the treaty of 907 with the Greeks, Oleg was represented as speaking not only in the name of the principality of Kiev but also in the name of all the Russian princes "under him." It would be unwise, however, to attach too much significance to a purely formal title. The Kievan state of the ninth and tenth centuries was hardly more than a very loose federation of autonomous city-states which were themselves in process of expansion. The efforts of the Kievan princes were directed largely to the consolidation of political ties within the vast realm. This policy found expression in the delegation of control over the principalities and cities that were brought under the sway of the grand duke of Kiev to the members of his family or of his immediate military retinue, his *druzhina*. The representatives of the prince in the local centers were known as *possadnik*, or governors. In addition to their chief function of collecting tribute, the governors also served as judges, the two activities being not entirely unrelated since the administration of justice generally took the form of the imposition of fines in the proceeds of which both the prince and his representative shared. The office of governor was thus a lucrative one, and the princely families were often large. According to the Chronicle, Riurik, Oleg, and Vladimir inaugurated their respective reigns by appointing men of their immediate entourage as their representatives in the main cities. Vladimir had twelve sons, and each of them was appointed *possadnik* of some part of the country. This policy of Vladimir had important political repercussions, since his family thus became associated with the seats of power throughout the land and created a *de facto* foundation for future dynastic claims by the descendants of Riurik. The legal unity of the state was expressed in the appointment of the rulers of the cities and principalities by the grand duke of Kiev, to whom they paid tribute. In practice, however, local interests and allegiances were not infrequently stronger than the somewhat nominal acceptance of the supremacy of Kiev. The fact that the majority of the princes were interrelated not only failed to ensure a close and harmonious cooperation among them, but on the contrary almost immediately became the source of discord and violent internal struggle.

Until the death of Yaroslav I (1054) no definite rule seems to have governed the succession to the principality of Kiev, except, perhaps, the rule that it was to be maintained in the same family. The newly acquired political unity of the state was precarious and lacking in any real foundation. It was based on the extension to the political field of the traditional paternal authority. The supremacy of the grand duke of Kiev was generally, although by no means uniformly, recognized as long as that position was held by the elder member of the family, father of the local princes. But at his death the fragile link that united the various principalities and cities with Kiev was apt to disappear, and the entire political structure was in danger of collapse.

THE POLITICAL STRUCTURE OF
THE ELEVENTH AND TWELFTH CENTURIES

Uncertainty as to the right of succession was one of the causes of the frequent feuds among the princes. After the death of Vladimir a war broke out between his sons, the opposing parties making a liberal use of Poles and Cumans in their struggle for their father's succession. Sviatopolk, who established himself in Kiev after Vladimir's death and who was finally defeated by Yaroslav, formerly prince of Rostov and later of Novgorod, died—presumably from wounds—while fleeing to Bohemia in 1019. Yaroslav was immediately confronted with a new struggle—with his younger brother Mstislav. After a protracted and bloody feud, the two brothers finally agreed in 1025 on the partition of the land, Mstislav retaining control of the territories east of the Dnieper, including Chernigov, while Yaroslav ruled the territories west of the Dnieper, including Kiev. In 1035, after Mstislav's death, Yaroslav took possession of his brother's former domain and the two parts of Vladimir's succession were reunited.

Yaroslav was the last grand duke of Kiev to exercise direct control over the entire realm. His successors no longer attempted to govern the whole country through appointed representatives, nor is there any evidence that the local princes continued to pay tribute to Kiev as in the tenth and the first half of the eleventh century. The quasi-patriarchal rule of the early Kievan princes was breaking down. The explanation of the change must be sought partly in the fact that the legal supremacy of the grand duke of Kiev during the earlier period was based on the application to the constitutional sphere of the principles of customary law governing the administration of family property. These principles were the recognition of paternal authority and the indivisibility of the property of the clan. Russia was looked upon as the joint property of the princely family of which the grand duke of Kiev was the natural head. Feuds among the princes were the logical consequence of the then prevailing legal theory and practice, which knew of only two methods of administering joint property: the patriarchal rule of the father or, at his death, the indivisibility of the estate, under joint management, co-heirs having no individual shares in any part of the succession.

The first practical step towards the breaking up of the single political authority of the head of the state—the appointment of the sons as their father's representatives and *de facto* rulers of the principalities and cities—confronted the realm, after the death of the patriarch, with the choice of one of the following alternatives: the preservation of the unity and integrity of the country through the ruthless extermination of those relatives and descendants who challenged the supremacy of the new grand duke of Kiev, or the division of the national territory into a number of independent principalities. It was the first of these alternatives that was usually followed until the middle of the eleventh century, but the tendency towards complete emancipation from the rule of Kiev manifested itself on several occasions, for instance, in the attempt of Vladimir's son Yaroslav to repudiate the authority of his father and to become the independent ruler of Novgorod, which he had governed in his father's name. It is perhaps not an unwarranted generalization to say that the Russian princes of the tenth and eleventh centuries thought of Russia in terms of the customary law governing the property of the clan. What we may call today a trend towards political separatism appeared to them as an issue of family versus clan ownership. The tendency towards emancipation from the authority of the clan and its head and the resulting threat to the unification of the country under the leadership of Kiev found itself in conflict with the vaguely recognized need for national unity, a need dictated by political considerations, the most pressing of which were defense and the protection of trade routes. In the reign of Yaroslav the separatist tendencies became strongly manifest, and this may explain his abortive attempt to find a way out of the dilemma and to reconcile the conflicting national and family-dynastic interests.

Yaroslav's road to power, as we have seen, was not an easy one. During his long reign he fought the Poles and the Finnish tribes. He is also reported to have inflicted an important defeat upon the Patzinacs (1036). A few years later, in 1043, Yaroslav organized the last Russian expedition against Constantinople, an expedition that ended in the rout of his armies. These military activities were not essentially different from those of the Kievan princes who preceded and followed Yaroslav. It was his disposition of the future political control of the country that is regarded by historians as an important landmark in the political organization of Kievan Russia.

Just before his death in 1054, Yaroslav divided his realm among his five surviving sons and a grandson whose father had died in Yaroslav's lifetime, the principality of Polotsk remaining under the rule of the descendants of Iziaslav, Vladimir's eldest son. This partition presented an important departure from the policy of unification followed by the earlier Kievan princes. It was accompanied by two recommendations which were intended to counteract its disruptive effects upon the somewhat precarious unity of the state. Handing over Kiev to his eldest son, Iziaslav, Yaroslav enjoined Iziaslav's younger brothers to obey him as they had obeyed their father—to "let him be in my place." And warning his children against fratricidal feuds, the unhappy consequences of which he knew only too well from personal experience, Yaroslav begged Iziaslav to come to the assistance of any of his brothers who might suffer injustice at the hand of other brothers. Such, in brief, was the content of Yaroslav's "testament" reported in the Chronicle in the form of an appeal made by the dying Yaroslav to his assembled children.

These testamentary dispositions of Yaroslav are of considerable importance to an understanding of the events that followed. On the one hand, the partition of the territory among his heirs meant the abandonment of the former attitude towards the Kievan state as the indivisible patrimony of the patriarchal princely family headed by the grand duke. On the other hand, Yaroslav, by enhancing the authority of his eldest son, attempted to mitigate the inevitable consequences of territorial partition and the threat it represented to the unity of the country and to the clan rule. Iziaslav was to be *in loco parentis* to the other princes. This authority, however, was now largely moral. Iziaslav was not, like his father, the natural head of the princely house, but merely one of the several brother princes and therefore merely *primus inter pares*. Yaroslav, with his bitter experience of family feuds and foreign wars, realized the necessity of saving the clan from complete disruption in order to preserve peace at home and to maintain a united front against the external enemy. These presumably were the considerations that inspired his appeal to his sons. In the eleventh century, however, moral authority was no better a foundation for building up the machinery of government than it is today. If Kievan Russia succeeded in preserving a certain degree of national unity for several generations after Yaroslav's death, it was because the forces working for its disruption had not yet gained sufficient momentum. Yaroslav's "testament" was in the nature of a compromise between the idea of national unity and that of local separatism. The dynastic, or family (as opposed to clan), ambitions of the princes eager to escape from the supremacy of Kiev were important, but they were by no means the only factor that fostered separatist tendencies.

The political organization of the Kievan state after Yaroslav's death was extraordinarily involved and obscure. It has provoked a passionate if somewhat inconclusive debate among historians. An influential school (Solovev) has taken the view that the testamentary dispositions of Yaroslav were the starting point of a mode of succession among princes, to be determined by their lineage and their respective positions among Yaroslav's descendants. The seniority rule, it is held, applied not only to the grand duchy of Kiev but also to all the other principalities. The death of the grand duke of Kiev therefore necessitated the transfer of all princes from one principality to another, the principalities themselves being arranged in a hierarchical order. The rotation of the members of the dynasty, who in turn occupied the various princely seats, embodied, according to this theory, the idea of the indivisible right of Yaroslav's descendants to rule Russia.

Professor Kliuchevsky injected new blood into Solovev's venerable theory. In his opinion the respective seniority of Yaroslav's descendants determined not only their place in the order of succession but also the respective economic importance of the principalities over which they ruled. Close correlation between the genealogical position of the princes and the economic value of their domain existed during the period immediately following Yaroslav's death. In the following generations, with the multiplication of princely families, the practical application of the seniority rule became more and more difficult; the understanding of the principle itself became blurred (which is perhaps not surprising), and the whole system collapsed amidst family feuds.

The seniority, or "clan," theory did not pass unchallenged. A number of eminent Russian scholars (Chicherin, Sergeevich) denied the very existence of the "seniority" rule. According to this school the relations between the princes and, consequently, the political structure of the state were determined by considerations of self-interest which had nothing to do with the genealogical position of the princes. The instruments they used to achieve their aims were agreements into which the princes entered among themselves, as well as agreements between the princes and the *veche*, or popular assemblies. The idea of national unity based on family ties, which plays so important a part in the scheme of Solovev and Kliuchevsky, was declared by the other school of historians to have been utterly non-existent. The supporters of this theory pointed out that Yaroslav's "testament" contained no reference to the "seniority" rule except the very vague remark that Iziaslav was to be *in loco parentis* to his brothers. And they also emphasized the fact that Yaroslav dealt merely with the division of the country among his immediate heirs, and made no attempt to lay down a general law of succession.

These conflicting views—and the above statement barely touches the surface of a controversy that fills volumes—must suffice to indicate the complexity of the problem. The reason for the wide range of theories concerning so vital a question is explained not merely by the legitimate divergences in the approaches of the Russian scholars, but primarily by the regrettable inadequacy of the basic sources with which they have to deal. All attempts to give a comprehensive account of the political structure of Russia during this period must be considered, therefore, as purely tentative. They cannot claim any degree of finality.

I have already pointed out that both the forces working for the unity of the Kievan state and those working for its disruption were in existence even before the reign of Yaroslav and that his "testament" was merely an attempt to find a working compromise. The vastness of the country and the perfunctory nature of the unification of the Slavic tribes under the early Kievan princes would suggest the existence of strong centrifugal tendencies. This fact has, of course, been duly noted by Russian historians and has been elaborated in the writings of Kostomarov, who saw in the Kievan state a federation of autonomous principalities which gradually evolved from the former tribal organization and were united by common origins, language, religion, and dynasty. The elements both of diversification and of unity were also emphasized in the works of Ilovaisky. The more recent and extremely well documented monographs of Professor Presniakov have done much to elucidate the history of this period and also to bring out the artificiality and often the lack of real foundation of some of the widely accepted historical schemes.

The element of dualism, which was apparent in the early political history of Russia, continued to color its development after Yaroslav's death. The partition of the country among Yaroslav's heirs duly took place according to the provisions of his "testament," but Iziaslav, the new grand duke of Kiev, found it difficult to impose his authority as the head of the princely house. Until 1068 a certain degree of national unity was maintained through the cooperation of Iziaslav with two of his brothers—Sviatopolk, prince of Chernigov, and Vsevolod, prince of Pereiaslavl. They ruthlessly suppressed by joint efforts two attempts of other princes to challenge their supremacy. In 1068, however, Iziaslav, Sviatopolk, and Vsevolod suffered a terrible defeat at the hands of the Cumans. The people of Kiev rebelled against Iziaslav, and he was forced to flee to Poland. He returned with the assistance of the Polish troops, but found himself confronted with a coalition of his younger brothers and was soon again obliged to seek refuge in Poland. Looking for foreign allies, Iziaslav approached the German emperor, Henry IV, and the pope, Gregory VII, but failed to gain their assistance. Kiev in the meantime was held by Sviatoslav, and it was only after his death in 1076 that Iziaslav, with the support of the Poles, succeeded in taking possession of the city and making peace with his brother Vsevolod. In 1078, in a new princely feud in which his opponents were supported by the Cumans, Iziaslav was killed and was succeeded by his brother Vsevolod.

The rule of Vsevolod I (1078–1093) and the years immediately following his reign were a critical period in the development of the Kievan state. The partition of the land among Yaroslav's heirs had strengthened the disruptive tendencies. Until the death of Yaroslav, to repeat, Russia was considered as the joint and indivisible patrimony of his princely house. After the partition of 1054 this attitude underwent an important change. Yaroslav's sons and their descendants were inclined to look upon the principalities and cities over which they ruled, not as an integral part of a somewhat abstract entity, such as the Kievan state, but as the property of their family, that is, of themselves and their issue, to the exclusion of the other branches of the clan. This attitude found support among the peoples over whom they ruled, since they had little to gain by the frequent change of princes. A definite link between the branches of the princely families and the principalities was being forged. This link, needless to say, was not merely the result of loyalty or of legal and dynastic considerations. The princes as well, and their *druzhina*, were being gradually transformed from roving vikings and soldiers of fortune into landed proprietors and administrators. They were now united with the territories they controlled by numerous economic ties which, as time went on, it became more and more difficult to sever. The *veche* had an important voice in deciding who should rule over them, and they were more apt to make their selection from among the candidates whom they knew and who were familiar with local conditions and needs than from among outsiders, irrespective of their dynastic claims.

Vsevolod, like his predecessors, attempted to counteract these separatist tendencies and to strengthen the political unity of the country, not so much by enhancing the moral authority of Kiev, as by gaining control over new territories. This was achieved by imposing his sons and nephews as rulers of principalities formerly held by weaker princes. Such a policy, of course, could not pass unchallenged, and Vsevolod's reign was filled with endless internal strife.

When Vsevolod died he was succeeded, not by his son, Vladimir Monomakh, but by his nephew Sviatopolk, son of Iziaslav. According to the Chronicle the people of Kiev wanted Vladimir. The latter, however, realizing that he could not obtain Kiev without a struggle with his cousin whose father had occupied the Kievan throne before Vsevolod, supported the candidacy of Sviatopolk, who was duly installed. This did not prevent the revival of princely feuds. Sviatopolk, moreover, in spite of the fact that he was the first of the Russian princes to marry the daughter of one of the Cuman khans, had to fight the Cumans, who frequently invaded Russia. Fighting their relatives, however, was a very usual occupation for the Russian princes, nor were the Cumans averse to the practice.

An attempt to bring about some cohesion in the relations between the princes was made in 1097, when representatives of the main branches of the dynasty met at Liubech. The conference decided that in the future the princes should rule over the territories that their respective fathers had received in 1054 from their own father, Yaroslav. It thus sanctioned the principle of patrimonial succession (*otchina*) by granting official recognition to a system that was already in existence. It was significant that the decisions of the Liubech conference made no reference to the sole and indivisible right of Yaroslav's descendants to the Russian land, nor did it mention the "seniority" of Kiev. Even Sviatopolk's right to Kiev was confirmed, not because Sviatopolk was the "senior" member of the princely house, but because his father, Iziaslav, had held the city. The Liubech decisions conformed to the then prevailing idea of clan and family ownership to which I have already referred: indivisibility of the right of ownership as long as the clan was kept together, and complete severance of all common property ties the moment the clan was broken up into a number of independent families. The system prescribed the partition of the grandfather's estate into several separate estates which were inherited by the grandsons from their respective fathers. The bloody strife among Yaroslav's heirs, which started with the expulsion of Iziaslav from Kiev in 1068, dealt a severe blow to the policy of unification pursued by Yaroslav's predecessors.

Although separatist tendencies were thus gaining ground, the idea of a united realm was not dead. The dangers of internal strife and foreign invasions were more pressing than ever, and the tradition of national unity was in the minds of the princes who congregated at Liubech. Characteristically enough, the conference entrusted the function of maintaining domestic peace and of organizing the external defense of the country not, as had Yaroslav in 1054, to the eldest brother, who would be *in loco parentis*, but to all the princes who "kissed the cross," that is, took the oath faithfully to observe the terms of the agreement. The former rule of the clan was thus being transformed into a union of independent princes loosely held together by political exigencies and by a vague and fading tradition of national unity cemented by family ties. This tradition was kept alive throughout the eleventh and twelfth centuries not so much by the grand dukes of Kiev as by the conferences of princes which met at irregular intervals and played a decisive part in the enterprises—chiefly the defense of the frontiers and the suppression of internal dissensions—in which the interests of the entire land were involved.

Important as were the decisions of the Liubech conference, they did not solve the problem confronting the Russian princes. The pledges given at Liubech were almost immediately broken. Internal feuds continued unabated, and Sviatopolk became involved in a most callous attack on Prince Vasilko, who was treacherously blinded. After Sviatopolk's death in 1113, Kiev passed, not to his son, but, in violation of the rules laid down at Liubech, to Vsevolod's son, Vladimir II, Monomakh. According to the Chronicle Vladimir surrendered to the insistence of the Kievan *veche*. Internal strife continued under Monomakh's rule; but he was successful in fighting both his domestic and foreign enemies, and his victories over the Cumans added much to his popularity. It was under his rule that Kiev reached the zenith of its political influence, a development that must be ascribed to Monomakh's outstanding personality and shrewd political sense. The Chronicle gives a most glowing account of Monomakh's rule, and according to the same source his death, in 1125, caused a flood of tears and lamentations. The chroniclers, however, were never conspicuous for moderation in bestowing either blame or praise.

Vladimir Monomakh was succeeded by his son Mstislav, who, like his father, was represented by the Chronicle as a great ruler. He held the upper hand in domestic feuds and won victories over the Cumans and the Lithuanians. With his death in 1132 began the decline of Kiev. The reign of his brother and successor, Yaropolk, was filled with internal conflicts, and the Cumans, who had been kept in check since the days of Vladimir Monomakh, again invaded the Russian land. Yaropolk's death in 1139 was followed by years of violent domestic disturbances in the course of which Kiev was at the mercy of various pretenders, each claiming an ancient and unchallengeable right to rule the first principality of the land. Vsevolod, prince of Chernigov, seized Kiev after Yaropolk's death and, in spite of the protracted struggle he was forced to wage against the other princes, retained control of the city until his death in 1146. He was succeeded by his brother Igor, who was less fortunate, his rule lasting only a very short time. The citizens of Kiev, who had promised Vsevolod to support Igor, failed to keep their word and offered Vsevolod's succession to Iziaslav, son of Mstislav and grandson of Vladimir Monomakh. Iziaslav defeated Igor and took possession of Kiev, but was confronted by a protracted struggle with Yuri Dolgoruky, prince of Rostov. Kiev changed hands several times. Even more confusion prevailed after

Yuri's death in 1157. Ambitious princes, with or without the support of the Kievan *veche*, came and went amidst much disorder and torrents of blood. The final blow to the supremacy of Kiev was dealt by Andrew Bogoliubsky, son of Yuri and prince of Rostov and Suzdal. In 1169 his armies took Kiev by storm, the city was sacked and pillaged, churches and monasteries were burned, the population was massacred, and not a few men and women were driven away and reduced to slavery. This was an unprecedented disaster, for never before had Kiev been treated by a victorious Russian prince as a conquered foreign city. Andrew, moreover, did not transfer his residence to Kiev, but continued to live in the north and established his capital in Vladimir, which became the new political center of the land. Kiev, put under the rule of Andrew's young brother, Gleb, rapidly sank into political insignificance. The Kievan chapter of Russia's history was closed.

One should not imagine that the eclipse of Kiev was due to princely feuds alone. Internal strife was not limited to Kiev; it was by no means unknown in the other parts of the land. The position of Kiev, however, was particularly vulnerable; its reputed wealth and the prestige derived from a century-old tradition of "seniority" amidst the other principalities made it an especially coveted prize and a focal point of princely feuds. This was why it failed to obtain a firmly established dynasty, as was the case with the other principalities (with the exception of Novgorod), and why it had an exceptionally large share of frequent and bloody conflicts.

Kievan Russia, viewed as a whole, was a loose and informal federation of independent states of which Kiev was merely one. The other important politico-territorial subdivisions of the eleventh and twelfth centuries were the principalities of Novgorod, Rostov, Suzdal, Pereiaslavl, Smolensk, Polotsky, Chernigov, Volynia, Galicia, Murom-Riazan. These principalities originated in the city-states that came into existence along the water routes at the dawn of the country's history. Their unification under the rule of the early Kievan princes, it will be recalled, was largely perfunctory. From the middle of the eleventh century these principalities, with the exception of Kiev and Novgorod, acquired their own dynasties. This does not mean that they were exempt from the plague of princely feuds. Far from it. Nevertheless the local dynasties, while claiming a common descent from Riurik, looked upon their domains as something to which the other branches of the house of Riurik had no right. This was the principle sanctioned by the Liubech conference. On the other hand, in agreement with a familiar principle of customary law, each member of the dynasty was considered as entitled to a share of the land his family controlled. In due time a new principality was accordingly carved for him. The application of this rule inevitably led to the breaking up of the territory into a continuously increasing number of political units whose size was naturally getting smaller. Over the political fortunes of the princes and princelets the head of the local dynasty exercised an uncertain but nevertheless real quasi-patriarchal authority. This authority, however, was not infrequently challenged, and the princes missed few opportunities to increase their domains at the expense of their relatives and neighbors. The people, through the *veche*, showed little reticence in interfering with political life; they often expelled the princes they did not like and invited new ones, displaying sometimes the scantiest respect for lineage or dynastic claims. The state of confusion and continuous internal strife we have observed in Kiev repeated itself on a somewhat smaller scale throughout the entire length and breadth of the country.

The absence of a definite central organ of government and the distressing picture of dismemberment and discord one finds in Russia during this period suggests the question of whether Kievan Russia was a state at all. Was it not rather a chaotic aggregation of independent political bodies fighting each other tooth and nail according to the law of the jungle? Some historians have given an affirmative answer to this question, and there is much evidence to support their contention. It may be argued, on the other hand, that they have undervalued the significance of the unifying elements, which were not completely lacking and which found their external expression in the conferences of princes. These conferences voiced, not always very distinctly, the recognition of the need for national unity. Kievan Russia, undoubtedly, was not a state in the modern sense of the term. And yet it was something more than a haphazard assemblage of antagonistic political units. Kliuchevsky was nearer to the truth than are some of his critics when he described Kievan Russia as "a federation based on the fact of the kinship of the rulers, a union involuntary in its origin and not really binding in its effect—one of those medieval social formations where political relationships have evolved from the norms of private law." A certain basic unity of the country is, moreover, suggested by the surprising similarity of the fundamental institutions of that period and the uniformity of social conditions throughout the land.

SOCIAL AND ECONOMIC CONDITIONS

The economic and social history of Kievan Russia is almost as confused and uncertain as is its political history. One of the chief sources for the reconstruction of the economic and social relationships of this period is the legislative collection *Russkaia Pravda* (Russian Truth), which is based largely on the Byzantine models *Ecloga* and *Procheiron*. *Russkaia Pravda* is known in two chief versions, the long one and the short one. The earliest available manuscript of the former dates back to the end of the thirteenth century, that of the latter to the end of the fifteenth century. *Russkaia Pravda* was once believed to have been an official code issued by Yaroslav, grand duke of Kiev in 1019–1054. This view is no longer accepted, and students of the problem are divided into those who maintain that *Russkaia Pravda* was an official collection containing legislation issued not only by Yaroslav but also by his successors, and those who think that it was merely a private collection of legislative enactments with no official standing.[2] Professor Kliuchevsky expressed the opinion that not only was *Russkaia Pravda* the work of several generations, but also that it had a limited jurisdiction: the jurisdiction of the Church in non-ecclesiastical questions. He described it somewhat too optimistically as "a good but broken mirror of the Russian law of the eleventh and twelfth centuries." To sort out these scattered and tarnished fragments and to piece them together into a comprehensive picture requires the hand of an expert and the imagination of an artist.

The composition of Russian society at the time of the arrival of the Varangians—about which no real information exists—was presumably very simple. The population was divided into free citizens and slaves, the latter being drawn largely from among the conquered tribes. By the end of the twelfth century a more complex structure came into

---

[2] Prof. Sergeevich, for instance, writes: "Who, in the old days, would care to learn how to read *Russkaia Pravda?* Everyone profited by reading the Holy Scriptures; they were read and even committed to memory. But *Russkaia Pravda?* Who needed it? It had no practical significance and it is therefore doubtful whether anyone tried to learn how to read it. It interested no one but professional copyists." V. Sergeevich, *Russkaia Pravda v chetyrekh redaktsiiakh* (Russian Truth in Four Versions) (St. Petersburg, 1904), p. xx.

being. At the top of the social pyramid were the princely dynasties, all claiming lineal descent from Riurik, yet from the middle of the eleventh century jealously defending their patrimony from infringements by members of other princely houses. The unwritten law that entitled every member of the dynasty to participate in the business of governing the principality was largely responsible for the extraordinary mobility of the princes during this period, and for their continuous shifting from one city to another. This mobility, which was a distinct feature of the Kievan era, cannot be wholly ascribed to the mechanics of the "seniority" rule. The Chronicle, no doubt, frequently referred to the genealogical claims of the princes in order to explain conflicts between them, but there is little indication that the "seniority" rule was often observed in practice. The usual method of deciding the fate of the disputed cities and lands was armed force, the most brutal and also the most effective way of cutting the Gordian knot of political complications. On several occasions territorial grievances were discussed at conferences attended by a number of princes, and the settlements arrived at were embodied in agreements which the participants solemnly promised—but frequently failed— to observe. It also happened that the princes disposed of their succession by testament which, however, invariably followed the rules of customary law. Extremely important in determining the fate of the principalities were the decisions of the *veche*, which played an active part in the political life of the eleventh and twelfth centuries, freely expelling reigning princes and inviting new ones. The *veche* also entered with the princes into agreements defining the scope of the latter's powers, particularly the amount of tribute to which they were entitled.

Originally the chief function of the princes was military leadership, especially the defense of the territory and of trade routes. They also administered justice, both directly and through appointed representatives. Their revenue consisted of tributes levied on the people, judicial fines, proceeds of trade operations, and military booty. It would also seem that as early as the tenth century the princes began to appropriate large tracts of land and whole villages, which became their private estates. The decline of foreign trade after the appearance of the Cumans on the southern steppes in the middle of the eleventh century, combined with the increase in the number of princes, gave a strong stimulus to the development of this new source of revenue.

The princes were gradually transformed from soldiers of fortune into landed proprietors, a development that gained momentum in the twelfth century and acted as a check on their freedom of movement from one city to another. Thus came into being an economic factor that contributed to the final abandonment of the practice of princely transfers, which were discontinued in the thirteenth century.

The power of the early princes rested on the support of their *druzhina*. Originally the majority of the *druzhina*, like the princes themselves, were Varangians, whose duties consisted of assisting the prince in his manifold activities—military, trading, administrative, judicial. Gradually the *druzhina* lost its former complexion and began to include the upper stratum of the native Slavic society as well as various foreign elements other than the Norsemen—Poles, Lithuanians, and others. The *druzhina* thus formed a privileged group or an aristocracy. At the outset an aristocracy of the sword and commercial capital, it derived its political influence either from princely favors and the tenure of high offices or from its wealth. At an early stage this new ruling class became subdivided into several groups of which the boyars (a term of uncertain and disputed origin) were the most influential. There was, again, considerable stratification among the boyars themselves, with no rigid caste and no hard and fast line dividing them from the rest of the free population. "Aristocracy" is therefore really a misnomer when applied to the boyars.

In the earlier days of the *druzhina* the members depended on the prince for their income, just as he depended on them for the raising of his own revenue. Sometimes they received direct maintenance and money payments; sometimes they were sent as representatives of the prince to the more remote parts of the country, and they were then entitled to a part of the tributes and judicial fines they collected from the people. This practice, known by the succulent term "feeding" (*kormlenie*), was later used on an even larger scale. It was also customary for the prince to share with his *druzhina* the proceeds of his military and trading ventures, to the success of which the latter contributed in no small degree.

It was usual for the *druzhina* to follow the prince in his frequent peregrinations from city to city. This, however, was not a legal duty, and the decision of each member of the prince's retinue, aside from questions of personal loyalty which could not be completely disregarded, was determined by considerations of self-interest. There are indications that beginning with the eleventh century the boyars' practice of following the prince was becoming less common. They, like the princes, were turning to landownership as a source of revenue. With the decline in foreign trade and the multiplication of the number of princes and boyars, the sources on which the boyars had depended were no longer adequate. With the development of the domestic market, land value was increasing; land, moreover, was a less uncertain source of income than were princely favors. The resulting link between the boyars and the soil naturally weakened their desire to follow their master in his uncertain political progress. In the twelfth century the boyars, like the princes, were no longer merely soldiers of fortune. The aristocracy of the sword, slowly transformed into a landed aristocracy, was growing into an element of stability in the unsteady world of Kievan Russia.

The higher state officers were drawn from the ranks of the boyars, whose opinion counted for much in the conduct of the affairs of state. They formed a council known as the boyar duma, over which the prince himself presided. Apparently the duma had neither a formal constitution nor a definite membership, but it included the most trusted and influential members of the ruling class. Consultation with the duma was nevertheless a practical necessity for the prince, as those rulers who attempted to disregard it were not slow in learning from bitter personal experience. Consequently the jurisdiction of the duma was as broad as it was ill defined, and covered all important questions, both foreign and domestic.

Below the boyars and the other ruling groups was the multitude of free townsmen—merchants, small artisans, and tradesmen—and a free peasantry. The merchants were often wealthy and exercised considerable influence in public affairs, especially through the *veche.* Little, however, is known about the free peasantry, although presumably they comprised a majority of the taxpayers and it is probable that they provided men for the army. Their chief pursuits were hunting, beekeeping, and agriculture, in which they engaged either on the land they owned or on the estates of the princes and boyars. There are indications that, with the development of large estates between the eleventh and thirteenth centuries, the boyars and the Church not infrequently encroached on the property of the small farmers, depriving them of their holdings, with the result that the number of tenants increased at the expense of the free peasantry. Economic dependence brought personal dependence in its wake. The tenant farmers came to form part of a large group of people who were on the border line between personal freedom and slavery. The exact legal position of this group, as well as its origin, remains uncertain, although it is believed that the relationship between creditor and debtor had something to do with it. The plight of the peasantry is suggested by the fact that they often described themselves as the "prince's orphans" (*gosudarevy siroty*). The princes, however, had neither the means nor, perhaps, the desire to defend them against the arbitrary actions of the powerful local lords. This may explain why the peasant farmers sometimes found it advantageous to trade their precarious freedom for the protection of the local magnate (Diakonov). The suggestion has been advanced by a recent author (Grekov) that the private estates both of the princes and of the boyars were cultivated largely by the labor of this group.

At the bottom of the social pyramid were the slaves (*kholopy*). This unhappy status was the normal fate of prisoners of war, but it could be acquired also by birth, bankruptcy, voluntary agreement, and in some other ways.

The politically influential element in the eleventh and twelfth centuries was not the agricultural community, but the cities. The old city-states were the political units from which the principalities had grown. The rural districts and the minor urban centers were still largely dependent on the regional capitals such as Kiev, Novgorod, Polotsk, Chernigov, Smolensk, Rostov, Suzdal, Riazan. The *veche* was the institution through which the urban populace expressed its will and took part in public affairs. Like the boyar duma, the *veche* was an ancient institution and, again like the duma, an effective and essential part of the machinery of government, even though it had no definite constitution or jurisdiction. The *veche* was an assembly of the adult male population of the cities and their dependencies. There were no franchise requirements and no fixed rules of procedure. The *veche* could be summoned either by the prince or by a high officer, such as the *possadnik*, or by any citizen. Its decision was required on every occasion when the prince was in need of effective popular support, for instance, in the declaration of war. The influence of the *veche* increased in the second half of the eleventh and during the twelfth century largely because of the brief tenure of office of the princes and the destructive effects of internal feuds upon general welfare. Several instances of the expulsion of the princes by the *veche* have already been noted. It will also be remembered that the *veche* sometimes endeavored to limit the powers of the princes by entering into agreements with them. Crude, ruthless, passionate, anarchistic, and often bloody as were the meetings of the *veche*, it was the nearest approach to a democratic institution Russia has ever experienced. The influence of the *veche* did not last long, for it declined with the decline of the commercial cities, with the notable exception of Novgorod and Pskov. Rooted in immemorial customs, a successor perhaps of the ancient assembly of the clan elders, the *veche* did not disappear at once. It survived until the fourteenth century, a mere shadow of its former robust self. The events of the second half of the twelfth century and the Tartar invasion had dealt a death blow to its political influence.

THE FALL OF KIEV

From the very beginning of the Kievan state, and especially under Yaroslav in the middle of the eleventh century and, again, under Vladimir Monomakh in the first quarter of the twelfth, Kiev occupied a position of unchallenged leadership among the Russian cities. The see of the head of the Russian Church, it was the most magnificent of Russian urban centers and a coveted prize for the possession of which the Russian princes considered no sacrifice too great. The supremacy of Kiev, however, was built on a shifting foundation and contained the germs of its own destruction. The unification of Russia under the early Kievan princes was, as we have seen, largely illusory. Regional interests were more powerful and more pressing than the demands resulting from a somewhat unwilling allegiance to the national capital. The attempt to control the country directly from Kiev lapsed with the death of Yaroslav. Regional capitals exercised a stronger power of attraction than did the distant residence of the Kievan prince, which, moreover, was frequently changing hands in the midst of almost uninterrupted princely feuds. The disruptive tendencies found expression in the attempts of the local princes to emancipate themselves from the authority of Kiev and in the ascendancy of the *veche*.

The advantages derived by Kiev from its position on the great water route leading from the Baltic to the Black Sea and from its commercial relations with Byzantium gradually became impaired, and new commercial ties were established, especially between northern

Russia and western Europe. The great water route "from the Varangians to the Greeks" was, moreover, no longer safe. The Cumans, from the middle of the eleventh century, exercised an ever increasing pressure upon the shores of the Dnieper. Vladimir Monomakh and his son Mstislav succeeded in keeping the Cumans in check; but after Mstislav's death in 1132 the Cuman hordes, descending upon southern Russia with unprecedented frequency and violence, met with little resistance from the Russian princes, who were absorbed in domestic quarrels. The proximity of Kiev to the steppes and the inability of its princes to organize defense were probably the chief reasons for its gradual decline, impoverishment, and final eclipse. Kiev's geographical position, its greatest asset in the ninth and tenth centuries, proved its undoing two hundred years later.

The political system of the country underwent a curious evolution through the customary law regulating the administration of clan property: paternal authority and indivisibility of ownership as the starting point, and severance of property ties after the breaking up of the clan into independent families. This led to the partition of the country into political areas controlled by independent branches of the dynasty and a further analogous process within each territorial subdivision. Opposed to these separatist tendencies was the attempt to preserve a certain unity through a more or less nominal acceptance of the supremacy of Kiev and the conferences of the princes, an attempt rooted in the tradition of the former unified rule of the clan and in the needs of national defense. But the economic and social conditions for the strengthening of national ties were lacking. The former economic bases—the political hegemony of the commercial cities and their common interest in the preservation of foreign trade—had disappeared. The regional capitals, while no longer united by any common interest, continued to exercise a powerful influence over the territories which historically and economically gravitated towards them. The transformation of the princes and the boyars from merchant soldiers into a landed aristocracy contributed to the strengthening of local ties. And there is discernible the regrouping of the principalities around new political centers, the forerunners of future political formations—the Moscow state in the northeast and the Lithuanian-White-Russian-Ukrainian state in the southwest.

But this process of national reconstruction proved slow and painful. In the meantime much of the land and cities of southern Russia had been laid waste and bare, an easy prey to the Asiatic horde.

CHAPTER II

THE PARTING OF THE WAYS

The Southwest and the Northeast

———————————— ✳ ————————————

NEW POLITICAL CENTERS

The decline and fall of Kiev, dubious and unstable as had been its leadership in the past, proved to be an event of extreme political importance. Her economic supremacy gravely impaired by the dwindling and the final disappearance of her eastern and Byzantine trade, her population harassed by the Cumans, her internal peace at the mercy of princely feuds—feuds in which Russia's foreign enemies often appeared as the allies of the competing princes—Kiev, "the mother of Russian cities," was after the middle of the twelfth century no longer in a position to protect the rights or even the lives of her peoples. The sacking of Kiev by the troops of Andrew Bogoliubsky in 1169, the first of several such occurrences, and Andrew's retention of his residence in Vladimir after assuming the title of grand duke, were telling proofs of the decline of the former capital. The men and women who lived on the banks of the Dnieper were hardy, long-suffering, and patient, virtues they have transmitted to their descendants. But there is a limit to all endurance. When the people of southern Russia were threatened with almost certain extermination, they did what every living being does in face of an imminent peril that it is powerless to combat—they fled. It was not, of course, a sudden exodus like the biblical flight of the Jews from Egypt, but a protracted and gradual process of migration, which brought about a drastic decline in the population of the territories along the Dnieper. The Chronicle and foreign travelers have given vivid pictures of the decay and ruin of the formerly prosperous cities of southern Russia. The countryside, too, appeared abandoned and deserted. Both rich

40

and poor gave up their old places of settlement and moved westward and northward where they might hope to escape from at least the immediate prospect of being robbed, raped, reduced to slavery, or massacred.

The principalities of Kiev, Chernigov, and Pereiaslavl, then among the most populous territories of Kievan Russia, were particularly affected by the process of migration. All of the adjoining principalities received their share of the settlers escaping from domestic turmoil and Asiatic invaders, who were first the Cumans and later the Tartars. Some of the settlers fled to Smolensk, which at the end of the twelfth and the beginning of the thirteenth century showed signs of increased activity; others went still farther to the northeast, to Rostov and Suzdal. And a great many moved west to Volynia and especially to Galicia, which for a time became the successor of Kiev as the political center of southern Russia. Kiev, however, still retained its leading position as the see of the head of the Russian Church, but in 1300 the Metropolitan Maxim transferred his chair to Vladimir in the principality of Rostov-Suzdal. The somewhat superficial unity of the country was thus definitely broken. Its history for the succeeding three or four hundred years followed two separate channels. The southwestern Russian territories gradually became absorbed in the grand duchy of Lithuania, which was incorporated at the end of the fourteenth century with the kingdom of Poland. These principalities took no immediate part in the building up of the Muscovite state that grew to maturity under a different political sky in the northeast of the country. The two main streams of Russia's history account for the evolution from a common source and for the territorial distribution of the three chief divisions of the Russian people, although the process of this evolution has not yet been sufficiently studied. Presumably the parting of the ways took place between the fourteenth and sixteenth centuries and was largely the result of the influence exercised upon the eastern Slavs by their immediate neighbors—the Finns, Tartars, Lithuanians, and Poles. In the west, within the frontiers of the Lithuanian-Polish state, the eastern Slavs formed the White Russian group of the Russian people; in the south, under the strong influence of Lithuania and Poland, the Little Russian or Ukrainian group came into existence; in the northeast, on the territory of the future Muscovy, the Great Russian group made its appearance.

THE SOUTHWESTERN PRINCIPALITIES AND LITHUANIA

The cleavage of Russia into two political bodies living their own independent lives did not occur at once. It was the continuation of the process of disintegration that we have observed in the earlier period, a process that was undoubtedly influenced by external factors such as the appearance of the Cumans and, later, the Tartars, in the south, and the establishment of the grand duchy of Lithuania in the west. In the twelfth and thirteenth centuries the people in the southwest and the northeast still had a number of political and economic interests in common, but these were outweighed by regional considerations which proved to be the more powerful.

One of the consequences of Kiev's political eclipse was the rise of its western neighbors, Galicia and Volynia. They had suffered less than Kiev from the invasion of the Cumans. The ascendancy and the growing spirit of independence of Volynia found expression in frequent conflicts with the powerful northern princes, Yuri Dolgoruky, Andrew Bogoliubsky, and Vsevolod III. At the end of the twelfth century the principalities of Galicia and Volynia were merged into one under the rule of Roman, formerly prince of Volynia, who enjoyed great prestige and influence. This position was maintained for a while by Roman's successors, in spite of frequent internal strife in which the boyars, who formed a powerful group, played a conspicuous part. Although the Tartar invasion did not spare Galicia and Volynia, they were at first less affected than were the territories east of their borders. In 1283, however, Volynia and Galicia were again overrun by the Tartars, and this time they suffered a devastation from which it took them a long time to recover. They were obviously not in a position to offer further resistance to the Mongols.

The southwestern principalities, moreover, had to fight on two fronts. While the Tartars were pressing them from the south, a new and rather formidable power appeared on their western border. The Lithuanian tribes, in the basin of the Nieman and the Western Dvina, were old neighbors, and in the earlier centuries the Russians had had no great difficulty in dealing with them. But in the middle of the thirteenth century the Lithuanians formed a strong state under the leadership of Mindowh. The grand duchy of Lithuania, as the new state came to be known, embarked almost immediately on a policy of eastward expansion. Political and economic penetration was soon followed by outright annexation. The first Russian principality to be formally absorbed by Lithuania was Polotsk (1307); it was followed by a number of other ancient Russian regions—Smolensk, Chernigov, Kiev, Volynia. At the beginning of the fifteenth century the grand duchy of Lithuania embraced a vast territory, including the basin of the upper and middle Western Dvina, the Nieman, the Southern Bug, the Dnieper, and the upper Oka. The rapid territorial expansion of Lithuania cannot be ascribed solely to the military victories of its armies. At least as important a factor was the lack of resistance on the part of the Russian princes. Many of the economic interests of the Russian southwestern principalities were in the west. For instance, their trade with Germany was carried over the water routes controlled by Lithuania and Poland. The Russia of the thirteenth and fourteenth centuries, weakened as it was by internal dissensions and the weight of the Tartar yoke, fell an easy prey to its neighbor, an energetic, vigorous, and ambitious young state. Both Lithuania and the territories of southwestern Russia, moreover, were subject to common pressure from the outside. In the south the Tartars were spreading desolation and death. In the northwest the Teutonic knights, who appeared on the shores of the Baltic Sea early in the thirteenth century, displayed fanatical zeal in bringing, by fire and sword, the light of Roman Catholicism alike to the Lithuanians, who were heathens, and to the Orthodox Slavs, while in the west there was strongly felt the pressure of a militant Roman Catholic Poland. In the northeast the growing power of Muscovy was forcibly advancing its expansionist claims and policies that were often opposed to the interest of the Russian southwest. Under these conditions it was not surprising that the harassed south Russian princes ranged themselves behind the determined leadership of the Lithuanian grand dukes, a leadership that the latter were prepared to enforce by the use of arms. Professor Liubavsky maintains that the annexation of the southwestern Russian principalities by Lithuania was a process essentially similar to that of the unification of the early city-states under the rule of the Kievan princes at the dawn of Russia's history.

But there were also important differences. The capital of Lithuania was Vilna, not Kiev. The dominating influence was western, not Russian. At the end of the fourteenth century (1385–1386) the grand duchy of Lithuania was incorporated in the kingdom of Poland, but it almost immediately regained its independence. Nevertheless the link between Poland and Lithuania was maintained, with but brief intervals, through a personal dynastic union until 1569, when, by the Act of Liublin, the grand duchy, while still retaining its identity as an administrative unit, was finally merged with the Polish Crown. Polish influence was strong in Lithuania, and this also meant the dominant position of the Roman Catholic Church. All things Russian were regarded as being inferior, and western ideas and institutions found a fertile soil. Roman Catholicism became, not without a struggle, the religion of the upper classes, while Greek Orthodoxy, the creed of the masses of the Russian peasantry, was looked upon as a definite mark of social inferiority. The institutions of the Polish-Lithuanian state were essentially western institutions, different in many respects from those of Russia. The aristocratic constitutional monarchy of Poland and Lithuania had but little in common with the autocratic form of government that had been evolved in Moscow. From a great many points of view the cleavage between the Russian southwest and the northeast was complete.

The Russian lands annexed by Lithuania in the fourteenth century did not return to Russian rule until much later. They therefore did not play any direct part in the formation of the unified Russian state. This historical task was performed in the northeast, where a centralized Muscovy eventually emerged from the political confusion of the thirteenth and fourteenth centuries.

ROSTOV, SUZDAL, AND VLADIMIR

Kiev's immediate successor as the national capital, however, was not Moscow—in the twelfth century still an obscure minor city—but Vladimir, in the principality of Rostov-Suzdal. The unexpected appearance of the princes of Rostov-Suzdal in the center of the political stage, and the part they played in paving the way for the eventual unification of Russia under the rule of Moscow, are not easy to explain. Both have greatly puzzled historians. The most popular and generally accepted theory is the one advanced by Kliuchevsky,[1] who ascribed to geographical, topographical, ethnographical, and social reasons a determining influence in the ascendancy of the Rostov-Suzdal princes. According to this view the decay of southern Russia

---

[1] The basic ideas of this theory are found in the works of Pogodin, Solovev, and Chicherin.

resulted in a wide movement of population to the northeast, where it concentrated in the triangle formed by the upper Volga and the Oka, that is, the territory of the principality of Rostov-Suzdal. The new-comers, it is maintained, completely changed the complexion of this area, which in the past had been occupied largely by Finnish tribes. It was the mixture of the Slavic settlers with the Finns that eventually brought into existence the Great Russian branch of the Russian people. The growth of the political influence of Rostov-Suzdal was concurrent with this ethnographical process. Topographical condi-tions in the northeast prevented the creation of large villages and settlements such as were common in southern Russia. The country was covered with virgin forests and marshes, wild and difficult to conquer. Primitive methods of agriculture favored eastward migra-tion. The princes of Rostov-Suzdal directed much of their energies to the building of new cities and lent assistance to the settlers in their endeavor to wrest from a reluctant and hostile nature parcels of arable land on which they could make a meager living. The general environ-ment, entirely different from that of southern Russia, gave rise to princes of a new type, to a new social structure. The princes of Rostov-Suzdal were "frontiersmen"; they looked upon the domain they had built for themselves by the sweat of their brow as their private prop-erty, their patrimony (*otchina*), and felt that they could dispose of it as they pleased. The boyars became a class of tenants who received their land by virtue of the services they rendered the princes. The result of these new conditions was the breaking up of the territory into innumerable small independent principalities as the first stage in the process of the creation of a unified national state. The division of the country into autonomous political units, considered as the private property of the princes and disposed of by them without any reference to the rule of seniority or national considerations, was of course the very opposite of the ideal of national unification. It proved, nevertheless, an important steppingstone towards the latter. It pre-pared the ground for the activities of the Moscow princes who even-tually succeeded in reassembling the scattered bits of the national ter-ritory and in building them into the highly centralized Muscovite state.

According to Kliuchevsky the fall of Kiev and the transfer of the capital to Vladimir were more than a mere landmark in Russia's history, more than a simple turn of the road. It was the beginning of an entirely new chapter. The developments that followed had no connection with the Kievan period and must be explained by the new conditions that had developed on the arid soil of northeastern Russia.

Kliuchevsky had not only a vast knowledge of historical sources but also a literary genius unique among Russian historians. His interpretation, therefore, was presented in a manner so convincing and attractive that few have found it possible to free themselves from the spell of the fascinating and lively visions that came so naturally from his pen.[2] Nevertheless the theory of a clear breach between Kievan Russia and the Russia of Rostov-Suzdal, and of the emergence of an entirely new set of political, economic, and social conditions as the result of the migration north of the population of southern Russia, could not but cause the gravest doubts. The artificiality of this theory and the inadequacy of the evidence on which it was based have been pointed out by various scholars (Sergeevich, Spitsin, and especially Presniakov). A somewhat different interpretation of the sources than the one followed by Kliuchevsky would seem to reveal that the breach between Kievan Russia and Rostov-Suzdal was not quite so wide and complete as he would have us believe. As a matter of fact it is argued that there was no breach at all, but on the contrary a continuation of the same or a similar process of historical development, with inevitable minor variations resulting from a different geographical and physical environment and changing political conditions.

It would be indeed strange if this were not the case. Rostov in the twelfth century was in no sense a newcomer to the family of Russian cities. Its origins are lost in the darkness of the ages. It was mentioned for the first time in the Chronicle in the year 862 as one of the cities distributed by Riurik to the members of his military retinue on his arrival in Novgorod. In the early part of the tenth century Rostov was already the capital city of an independent territory and had its own prince. In the middle of the twelfth century the city of Suzdal came to the fore as Rostov's competitor, and in the second half of the same century the city of Vladimir made a strong bid for political supremacy. Following the changing fortunes of its three leading cities, as well

---

[2] The remarkable literary abilities of Kliuchevsky form an essential part of his performance. It is therefore a source of particular regret that the English translation of his lectures on Russian history, which appeared under the title *A History of Russia*, does not do justice to the outstanding literary merits of his work.

as their own predilections, the chroniclers referred to the principality as the principality of Rostov, Suzdal, Rostov-Suzdal, Suzdal-Vladimir, or, finally, as the grand duchy of Vladimir. The land of Rostov was not only an ancient member of the loose confederation known as Kievan Russia but also an active participant in the life of the country, in spite of its geographical remoteness from Kiev. It had had its own bishop since the days of Vladimir I. According to the Chronicle, Gleb, son of Vladimir I, was prince of Rostov. Vladimir II, Monomakh, absorbed as he was in his struggle with the Cumans, displayed considerable interest in Russia's northeastern outpost and visited Rostov several times. He was the founder of the city Vladimir-on-Kliazma, which eventually became the capital of the principality and of northeastern Russia. His son, Yuri Dolgoruky, was prince of Rostov for some forty years, and it was under his rule that Suzdal, his favorite city, came into prominence. There seems to be no real ground, therefore, for considering Rostov as having been outside the big political currents of Russian life before the middle of the twelfth century.

The assumption that Rostov, judged by the standards of southern Russia, was a wild and undeveloped country is supported by no direct evidence but is based on the scarcity of information concerning the conditions prevailing in that ancient land. Presniakov observed judiciously that lack of historical information should not be taken as indicating the absence of "historical life." Indirect evidence would tend to show that Rostov was a participant in the foreign commerce of the ninth, tenth, and eleventh centuries. I have already pointed out that the Volga trade route linking the Baltic Sea with the Caspian Sea, the Khazar empire and Arabia, was presumably known and widely used before the Dnieper-Volkhov route, probably as early as the eighth century. The Volga trade route passed through the Rostov territory. It is no wonder that the Russian princes from the days of Riurik and Vladimir I were by no means indifferent to the fate of Rostov. The political ascendancy of Rostov in the twelfth century would itself suggest a fairly well advanced stage of economic and social development. This assumption is supported by the fact that the Rostov-Suzdal princes of the twelfth century were great church builders. The chief building material used was a white stone that came from the state of the Bulgars, on the Kama. The Rostov-Suzdal-Vladimir church edifices rank among the greatest achievements of early Russian art, achievements that would have been artistically and economically impossible in a land just entering upon an early stage of colonization.

The political history of Rostov-Suzdal offers little support for the view that its social and economic structure was essentially different from that of southern Russia. The predilection of Yuri Dolgoruky, prince of Rostov, for Suzdal, where he established his capital, and the transfer of the political center of the principality from Suzdal to Vladimir by Andrew Bogoliubsky were due to the same cause. Rostov, like the ancient cities of Kiev, Volynia, Chernigov, and Galicia, had already in the first half of the twelfth century a strong and influential aristocracy, the boyars, who derived their power from tenure of political offices and from the ownership of landed estates. This aristocracy very largely controlled the affairs of the land, either independently or with the concurrence of the *veche*, which it dominated. The boyars and the princes often found themselves in conflict. The influence of the boyars was too strong for the princes to break down; and as the aristocracy was particularly powerful in the older cities the princes of Rostov-Suzdal tried to escape its immediate authority by transferring their capital to smaller and younger cities. That was why Yuri Dolgoruky went from Rostov to Suzdal. In the middle of the twelfth century Suzdal had already developed its own aristocracy, and Andrew Bogoliubsky moved his capital from there to Vladimir. How bitter was the opposition of the older aristocracy to the princes who, refusing to bow to its will, surrounded themselves by newcomers was well illustrated by the fate of Prince Andrew, who became the victim of a boyar conspiracy. His death was the signal for a massacre of his appointees and the pillaging of their houses. The struggle between the Rostov-Suzdal princes and the boyars discloses a state of affairs similar to the one observed in other parts of Russia: the twelfth century was a period of the growth of boyar wealth, boyar influence, and boyar privileges. In this respect Rostov-Suzdal was in no way different from the rest of the country.

POLICIES OF THE ROSTOV-SUZDAL PRINCES

The policies of Yuri Dolgoruky (1120–1157) and his immediate successors were largely inspired by a desire to retain control of Rostov-Suzdal within their family and at the same time to ensure its leading position among the Russian principalities. The broader national aspect of their policies was subordinated to the better understood and more pressing interests of Rostov-Suzdal. The struggle of Yuri Dolgoruky and his son Andrew Bogoliubsky (1157–1174) for the strengthening of their influence in southern Russia was not, as has often been stated, an endeavor to win for themselves the somewhat abstract and platonic recognition of "seniority" among the Russian princes. It was inspired by concrete and practical considerations. Rostov-Suzdal had trade and cultural ties with the other Russian lands. Its position on the ancient trade route made it essential to maintain these connections, which extended to Chernigov, Kiev, Galicia, and Novgorod. Caravans carrying valuable goods came to Rostov-Suzdal from the south, west, and east. Western craftsmen and German merchants were familiar figures on the streets of Rostov, Suzdal, and Vladimir. The transit trade of the Russian northeast facilitated the exchange of German woolen cloth for wax from Bulgaria. This trade and cultural intercourse was an important element in the policies of the Rostov-Suzdal princes and in the growth of their political influence.

The defense of these varied interests was by no means foreign to Yuri Dolgoruky's struggle for Kiev, nor was the attention of the Rostov-Suzdal princes entirely absorbed by the south. Even more vital from the point of view of the regional interests they represented was the control of Novgorod, the great trading center of northwestern Russia, and of the routes leading from Novgorod to the upper Volga. In pursuance of this policy Yuri Dolgoruky fought the Kama Bulgars in 1120 and forced the acceptance of his sons as princes by Novgorod, with which he later engaged in frequent conflicts, sparing no effort to undermine its independence and to control its trade routes. A similar policy, based essentially on the promotion of the specific Rostov-Suzdal regional interests, was followed by Andrew Bogoliubsky and Vsevolod III (1176–1212). Andrew, like his father, fought the Kama Bulgars in 1164 and 1172 and, again like his father, imposed upon Novgorod his sons and nephews. The war between Andrew and Mstislav, prince of Kiev, a war which ended in the pillage of Kiev in 1169, originated in a contest over Novgorod.

Vsevolod III continued the policy of his predecessors. He, too, fought the Bulgars in 1184 and 1186, but it was with the control of Novgorod that he was particularly concerned. The freedom-loving boyars and people of Novgorod, alarmed by the increasing pressure of the Rostov-Suzdal princes, tried to find a support against them in Smolensk and Chernigov, but with little success. Novgorod itself was passing through a difficult period. The growth of its western trade brought it into frequent conflict with Sweden, Lithuania, and the Teutonic knights for the control of the Baltic trade routes. Novgorod was also endeavoring to expand its domination over the neighboring Finnish territories. In these many enterprises it needed allies and military leaders. The princes of Rostov-Suzdal were naturally indicated for this task; they were united with Novgorod by many economic and political ties, they had at their disposal military experience and were in a position to offer Novgorod the military assistance it so badly needed. But this assistance was purchased at a price: the princes of Rostov-Suzdal, beginning with Yuri Dolgoruky, firmly and consistently pursued the policy of making Novgorod dependent on themselves and their appointees. Their efforts were crowned with success under Vsevolod III, when Novgorod definitely accepted the leadership of "the grand duke of Vladimir" and asked him for the appointment of a prince of his own choice. Vsevolod, accordingly, sent to Novgorod his sons and nephews.

The defense of the regional Rostov-Suzdal interests involved Yuri Dolgoruky and his successors in a number of protracted and costly wars. Their success depended on the ability of the Rostov-Suzdal princes to enlist the support of other princes, a fact that largely determined their policies towards the principalities of central and southern Russia. Yuri Dolgoruky, who waged a long struggle for the possession of Kiev, for a short time held the city. His son Andrew Bogoliubsky, however, broke the old tradition of Kiev's "seniority" and remained in Vladimir with the title of grand duke. Nevertheless the Rostov-Suzdal princes found it useful to continue to control Kiev through their appointees in order to prevent the competing princely houses from establishing themselves in the former capital. An attempt at the revival of Kiev's traditional supremacy might have proved a useful weapon in the hands of an ambitious challenger of Vladimir's only too recent leadership.

However, despite a bold stroke by Andrew, which brought about a separation between Kiev and "seniority" among the princes, the idea of "seniority" was not abandoned. Vsevolod III attached it to the grand duchy of Vladimir. The princes of Rostov-Suzdal continued to speak of themselves as "the senior in the brotherhood of Russian princes." The content of the ancient formula, however, had undergone a significant change. The notion of "seniority" in Kievan Russia had its historical justification and practical meaning in a certain community of national interests, primarily the struggle against the Cumans. It was principally the recognition of the necessity of a common action against the foreign invaders that had kept Kievan Russia from breaking up into independent political units. The Rostov-Suzdal princes put the venerable idea of "seniority" to a very different use. It served them as a protective screen behind which they concealed the selfishness of their policies, an undertaking in which the chroniclers have given them their support. The idea of brotherly cooperation under the leadership of the grand duke of Vladimir was dragged in every time the powerful princes of Rostov-Suzdal desired to force the hand of weaker rulers in the south and attempted to make them participate in conflicts which not only had nothing to do with the interests of the latter princes but were sometimes detrimental to them. Thus, for instance, Andrew and Vsevolod induced the princes of Smolensk to fight the battle of Rostov-Suzdal against Novgorod and Chernigov. Vsevolod acted on the same principle in his dealings with the princes of Riazan-Murom. Southern Russia, as such, made no special appeal to the grand dukes of Vladimir, and their sporadic interference in southern affairs, inspired by narrow regional considerations, merely added to the political confusion and disintegration of the south.

The internal policies of Yuri Dolgoruky, Andrew Bogoliubsky, and Vsevolod III were not essentially different from those of the other princes of the same period. The principle of "patrimonial" (*otchina*) succession, that is, of the association of a princely family with a particular territory and the right of all the male descendants to a share in the succession, led in Rostov-Suzdal, as in other principalities, to the subdivision of the land into a number of quasi-independent political units which remained under the general control of the grand duke of Vladimir. The principle itself, as I have pointed out, was evolved in the course of the eleventh century in Kievan Russia and was officially sanctioned by the Liubech conference. The growth of the population and the increase in the number of princes were accompanied by the building up of a more elaborate administrative machinery. The Rostov-Suzdal princes, especially Andrew Bogoliubsky, took much interest in the advancement of colonization and in the founding of new cities. It is a mistake to believe, as do Solovev and Kliuchevsky, that the latter activity was peculiar to Rostov-Suzdal. It was also in evidence in

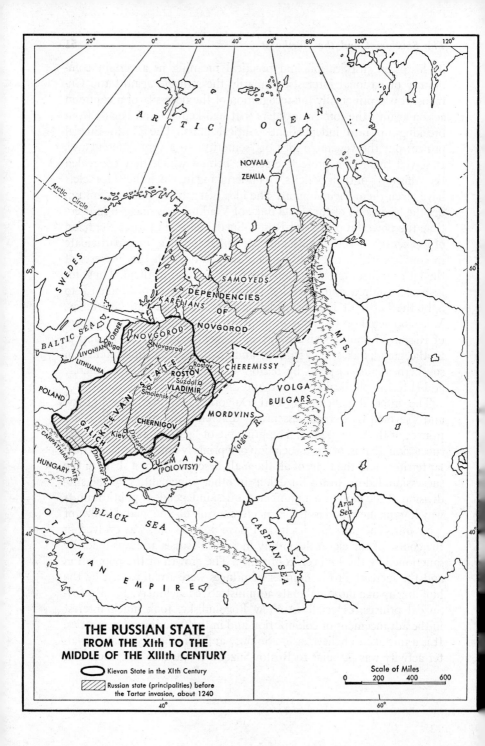

THE RUSSIAN STATE
FROM THE XIth TO THE
MIDDLE OF THE XIIIth CENTURY

⬭ Kievan State in the XIth Century

▨ Russian state (principalities) before
the Tartar invasion, about 1240

Scale of Miles
0   200   400   600

southern Russia, for instance, in Galicia and Volynia, when the general conditions there were not yet too seriously disturbed by such external events as the invasion of the Cumans or the Tartars.

The dynastic and family policies of the Rostov-Suzdal princes were not always in harmony with the interests of the boyar aristocracy, whose influence, it will be remembered, continued to increase during the twelfth century. The history of Rostov, Suzdal, and Vladimir was full of clashes between the princes and the boyars. Yuri Dolgoruky attempted to provide that, after his death, his domain should be divided between his sons Michael and Vsevolod. This arrangement, although sanctioned by the people in Yuri's lifetime, was not carried into effect. The boyars opposed the partition of the principality, and Andrew, Yuri's eldest son, was accordingly elected as his father's sole successor. In the eighteen years of his rule he lost his popularity with the upper classes and fell victim to a boyar conspiracy (1174). Andrew's death was followed by confusion and civil war in which the boyars played an important part. In 1177 Vsevolod, Andrew's brother, emerged from the struggle as grand duke of Vladimir. His death in 1212 was the signal for a fresh outburst of princely strife. In the grim and obscure events of this period a certain inconsistency appeared to exist in the relationships between the princes and the boyars. The latter disliked and actually dreaded any changes in the ruling dynasty, which meant the arrival of a new prince accompanied by new boyars. Such changes led to a weakening of the political influence of the local aristocracy and sometimes brought about its ruin. The local boyars therefore supported the dynastic ambitions of their princes in so far as they were concerned with the retention of the territory under the control of the local dynasty. But the princes were also getting in the habit of looking upon the principality over which they ruled as family property, and they often attempted to divide it among their heirs. This tendency the boyars resisted, not only because the division of the principality interfered with their economic interests but also because it was usually accompanied by civil war, which the boyars had every reason to avoid. The boyar aristocracy thus became an element of political stability and contributed to the building up and the preservation of the somewhat precarious leadership of the grand duchy of Vladimir.

The strengthening of the power both of the boyars and of the princes—with the resulting frequent clashes between the two—and the decline of the influence of the *veche* were among the chief characteristics of this period. In the northeast, even more than in Kievan Russia, regional interests were overshadowing the vaguely felt need for national unity. The inner ties holding together each political subdivision were getting looser. In all these respects the land of Rostov-Suzdal-Vladimir followed in the twelfth and thirteenth centuries a trend that was already apparent in the preceding period. Nor were these developments vastly different from what was taking place in the southwest. And just as Kievan Russia, in spite of increasing chaos in the interprincely relations and the success of the separatist tendencies, retained a degree of national unity that eludes exact definition, so the grand duchy of Vladimir was preserved from division into independent political units. The seniority of the grand duke of Vladimir was generally recognized by the princes, and the occupants of the Vladimir office followed policies that largely reflected the interests of northeastern Russia as a whole. In this respect the tradition of Yuri Dolgoruky, Andrew Bogoliubsky, and Vsevolod III was carried on by Vsevolod's son, Yuri II, who, after a struggle against his brother Constantine and the death of the latter, reigned in Vladimir until 1238, when he was killed in the Tartar invasion.

It was unfortunate that the prestige and power enjoyed by the grand dukes of Vladimir should have been used, as I have pointed out, for the advancement of the narrow regional interests of northeastern Russia, often to the detriment of those of the other principalities. Under these conditions the traditional and almost ritualistic phrase referring to the "brotherhood" of Russian princes was a euphemism. Bitter rivalries and bitter antagonisms were rampant in the Russian land. There was much suspicion and hatred among the princes and no real cooperation between the princes and the boyar aristocracy on which the former had so largely to depend. The vigorous and ruthless democracy of the *veche* was at a low ebb, and with the development of the princely and boyar landed estates an ever increasing section of the rural population had been reduced to slavery or near-slavery. Thus was sown the evil seed of future social upheavals.

Such was the political and social complexion of Russia when she was faced with the acid test of the Tartar invasion.

CHAPTER III

THE TARTAR DOMINATION

THE INVASION

The course of Russia's history was deeply affected by an event that occurred far beyond her frontiers, in distant Mongolia. Early in the thirteenth century the Mongolian tribes in central Asia were united under the leadership of Temuchin, who eventually assumed the name of Chingis Khan. His troops conquered North China and the Turkestan and proceeded to move west, following the route used by so many Asiatic peoples during the preceding centuries. A few years before the death of Chingis Khan in 1227 the first Tartar horsemen, forerunners of the great invasion, appeared in the south Russian steppes then occupied by the Cumans. The Cumans appealed to the Russian princes for assistance, and several princes, among them Mstislav of Galicia, who was married to the daughter of a Cumanian khan, joined arms with their enemies of yesterday against the new invaders. The enterprise proved a disaster. The Cumans and their allies suffered an overwhelming defeat in a battle on the river Kalka (1223). Many of the Russian princes were taken prisoner and brutally put to death. But the Tartars were not yet ready to gather the fruit of their victory. They withdrew behind the Urals as suddenly as they had arrived. To the Russians the invasion seemed almost uncanny, and the chronicler probably expressed the general feeling when he described the Tartars as an emanation of the Unclean Spirit. Nothing was heard of them for a few years, but in 1229 and 1232 came further rumors of a Tartar attack on the Volga Bulgars. Then followed a few more years of ominous silence. The reprieve, however, was of but short duration.

Chingis Khan was succeeded as the great khan by his son Ugedei. The territories between the Urals and the Dnieper had been given by Chingis Khan to his son Djuchi, who died in his father's lifetime.

The conquest of the new domain then became the task of Djuchi's son, Batu. In 1236 Batu crossed the Urals and invaded the state of the Volga Bulgars. The force under his command was different from the flying detachment of horsemen that had defeated the Cumans and the Russians on the Kalka. Batu, whose troops were accompanied by women and children, had no intention of returning to his native Mongolia. He had come to conquer and to stay. The invasion of 1236 was not merely the advance of an army; it was the migration of a nation.

It seems reasonably certain that no organized resistance by the Russian princes could have stopped the victorious advance of the Asiatic hordes. But it is also clear that the lack of unity among the Russian rulers, absorbed in their petty quarrels, facilitated the fulfillment of Batu's plan. Having inflicted a defeat on the Volga Bulgars, their first victims, the Tartars crossed the Volga and late in 1237 invaded the Russian principality of Riazan. The Riazan princes asked Yuri II, grand duke of Vladimir, for assistance, but were given none. The city of Riazan was taken and burned, and the invaders continued their advance into northwestern Russia. They captured, pillaged, and burned Kolomna, Moscow, Suzdal, Vladimir, Rostov, Yaroslavl, and Tver. Detachments of the invading army swept along the Volga and conquered the adjoining territories. During February, 1238, alone the Tartars occupied not less than fourteen cities.

The grand duke Yuri II left his sons to defend his capital city of Vladimir and withdrew to the Volga region, where he awaited the arrival of the Tartars. In the meantime his wife, sons, daughter, and grandchildren, as well as the local bishop and many boyars and citizens, were all murdered or perished in the conflagration that accompanied the seizure of the capital by the Tartars. Yuri's reasons for abandoning Vladimir at a moment of extreme danger would seem to have been honorable: he was attempting to raise a new army for the defense of his realm. Nevertheless he set an unfortunate example that was followed, unconsciously no doubt, by a great many Russian princes in the years of the subsequent struggle against the Tartars. It is noteworthy that the Russian rulers of that period only too often deemed it necessary to depart from a besieged city at the very time when their presence there would seem to have been particularly needed, not infrequently leaving their wives and families at the mercy of the assailants. The army of Yuri, which met the Tartars on the shores of the river Sit on March 4, 1238, was routed and the grand duke himself was killed.

The Tartars then turned to the southwest, pillaged the city of Torzhok, and advanced towards Novgorod, but before reaching the metropolis of northern Russia they changed their course to the southeast and invaded the Black Sea steppes. The Cumans suffered an overwhelming defeat and fled, the majority of them to Hungary, where they were permitted to settle. They thus ceased to be an active factor in Russia's history.

In 1239 Batu, continuing his conquest of the northwest and of the south, captured and burned Chernigov, and in December, 1240, occupied Kiev. Some cities fought bravely for their independence and offered a stubborn resistance to the Tartars. But the princes all too often continued their domestic feuds even in the face of supreme peril. Not a few of them died on the battlefield or were murdered by the Tartars, others fled to Hungary, Poland, and Galicia. From Kiev, Batu moved farther west, invading Volynia and Poland, and in the spring of 1241 he crossed the Carpathian Mountains and penetrated into Hungary. He won several victories over the Poles, the Germans, and the Hungarians, devastated Silesia and Moravia, but met with some reverses at the hands of the Czechs. The driving force of his army seemed to have worn itself out in the continuous fighting of the preceding years. The Tartars, somewhat suddenly turned back, retreated along the Danube and returned to the Russian steppes. It is possible that news of the death of Ugedei, the great khan of Mongolia, which reached Batu in the middle of his European campaign, might have influenced his decision to abandon further conquests. The burden of the Tartar "yoke" now rested squarely on Russian shoulders. Central Europe escaped with nothing worse than a bad scare and relatively insignificant damages.

THE GOLDEN HORDE

The Mongol empire of the thirteenth century was a complex political organism, the very vastness of its expanse precluding the possibility of a centralized administration. The new state established by Batu west of the Ural Mountains became known as the Golden Horde. Batu and his successors acknowledge their dependence on the great khan, but the nature of this relationship changed in the course of years. In the period immediately following the conquest of Russia, the great khan took an effective part in the conduct of Russian affairs; and sometimes the Russian princes, after having been confirmed in office by the khan of the Golden Horde, had to journey to Mongolia in order to obtain the final sanction of the great khan. Internal dissensions, however, weakened the Mongol empire, and from the end of the thirteenth century the allegiance of the khans of the Golden Horde to their supreme ruler became more or less nominal, disappearing altogether three-quarters of a century later. The Golden Horde, however, continued to play a leading part in the destinies of Russia for another hundred years.

There has been a tendency among Russian historians to underestimate the importance of the Tartar domination. Kliuchevsky, for instance, discussing the political organization of northeastern Russia during this period, suggests that one "should forget for a time . . . that Russia was conquered by the Tartars." There are, however, some illuminating observations in the latter part of his book on the effects of the Tartar rule upon the country's political structure. Kliuchevsky's point of view is firmly rooted in Russian historiography, in spite of the criticisms to which it has been subjected by some eminent authorities, among them Kostomarov and Sergeevich. The nature of the sources on which they have to depend is one of the reasons for the tendency among historians to underestimate the effects of the Tartar rule. The only Russian chronicles dealing with this period now available are copies written after the unification of Russia under the leadership of Moscow. The Moscow princes of the end of the fifteenth century and those of the sixteenth century displayed eagerness in trying to justify their rule by reference to "immemorial tradition." In this enterprise they had the support of the Church, with which, indeed, originated some of the crudest falsifications of history. The tsars and the Church together controlled the business of keeping the chronicles. The result was that in their later versions the earlier scripts (which are no longer available) were submitted by the copyists to careful editing in order to eliminate much of the information that either made the princely rulers appear in an unfavorable light or contradicted the recently espoused autocratic tradition. Solovev remarked on the inadequacy and the often incomprehensible inconsistencies and omissions of the official texts. More recently Presniakov, who submitted the chronicles to a searching analysis, arrived at the conclusion that the ancient texts have been the object of a highly tendentious revision. In spite of this unfortunate tampering with the sources, the chronicles and other contemporary documents contain sufficient information to indicate the far-reaching effect of the Tartar domination.

The khans of the Golden Horde looked upon the conquered Russian principalities as integral parts of their domain, mere provinces, or *ulus*. The will of the khans became the fountain of all power, and the grand dukes of Vladimir and Moscow and the other grand dukes —for several other grand duchies rose and fell during this period— as well as the princes of the minor principalities, had to seek a *yarlyk*, or decree of the khan, confirming them in office. The same rule applied to the higher Church dignitaries, who became the appointees of the Tartar rulers. The khans were usually content with approving the candidates who were entitled to this or that principality according to the Russian customary law, and they also displayed in religious matters a broad tolerance which the Christian churches might well envy. Unfortunately, Russian immemorial customs were anything but clear. Kliuchevsky goes so far as to maintain that at the beginning of the Tartar rule "no order of any kind might be observed in the relations between the princes" of northern Russia, a statement that seems somewhat exaggerated. There is no doubt, however, that the confusion was great. Sarai, the capital of the Golden Horde, became the center of princely intrigues as a result of which not a few of the candidates lost their lives. The chief weapon of this internal struggle was money. Presents to the khans, as well as promises to pay more tribute than the rival candidate paid—the surest methods of winning favor with the Golden Horde—were freely used. The *yarlyk*, conferring the control of a grand duchy or a principality, went to the highest bidder. Other and even less savory methods, such as the denunciation of rival candidates, were not unknown, but the details of cases of this nature have been largely expunged from the records. How close was the dependence of the Russian princes on the khans will appear from the fact that Ivan I, of Moscow (1325–1341), journeyed to Sarai nine times, and his son Simeon (1341–1353) five times. On such pilgrimages the princes were occasionally accompanied by their boyars and their wives and children. The ceremony of the enthronement of the princes was performed in the name of the khan and in the presence of his envoy, a stern reminder of the watchfulness and reality of the Tartar rule.

The chief interest of the Golden Horde in the conquered Russian territories was the exaction of revenue through the imposition of direct and indirect taxes. The assessment was based on a population census, the last of which took place, according to Russian sources, in 1275. The collection of taxes was originally in the hands of Tartar officials stationed throughout the land and supported by a body of police officers. Information on the working of this system is slight and fragmentary, although there is ground for believing that it led to much abuse, with resultant discontent and revolt. The latest references to Tartar tax officials are to be found in the Chronicle of the end of the thirteenth century. In the fourteenth century the Russian princes acted as Tartar agents for the collection of taxes. The most important of the direct taxes, called *vykhod*, was assessed by the local grand duke among the princes and was collected by them from the population of the territories under their control. Offers to increase the amount of the *vykhod* became a powerful means of obtaining from the khan the grant of a coveted territory. The consolidation of power and land in the hands of certain dynasties—and this was particularly true of the Moscow princes—was therefore often purchased directly at the expense of the people, whose tax burden was further increased as a result of intrigues at the khan's court. This aspect of the situation is not unimportant, since it introduced a new source of friction between the princes and the people they governed. The former frequently appeared in the part not only of Tartar agents but even of defenders of Tartar interests against those of the people they were supposed to represent.

Of the many indirect taxes and extortions, the most onerous perhaps was the obligation of providing transportation and maintenance for the Tartar officials and envoys with their large retinues. Equally burdensome were the frequent journeys of the Russians to the Golden Horde and the obligation to present gifts to the khan, his family, and Tartar dignitaries.

MONGOL INFLUENCE

The absence of information concerning the presence of permanent Tartar officials in Russia after the end of the thirteenth century and the collection of taxes and tributes by the princes themselves is often given as a proof of the relatively slight influence exercised by the Mongols on the course of internal Russian affairs. It is difficult to agree with this opinion. The interference of the Golden Horde with the life of the conquered territory was not limited to the issue of the *yarlyks* and the levy of tributes and taxes. According to Solovev, Russia suffered forty-eight Tartar invasions between 1236 and 1462. Some of these expeditions were punitive and were the result of revolts against the oppressors. But on many occasions the Tartar armies entered the country on the invitation of the Russian princes themselves. For instance, Alexander Nevsky, grand duke of Vladimir and one of Russia's national heroes canonized by the Church, denounced his brother Andrew to the khan for failing in his duty to the Golden Horde and interfering with Alexander's right of succession. In 1252 the Tartars invaded the grand duchy of Vladimir, Andrew was defeated and fled to Novgorod and then to Sweden. He was succeeded by Alexander Nevsky. Ivan I *Kalita*, grand duke of Moscow, another outstanding historical figure of this period, brought with him in 1327 a Tartar army estimated at fifty thousand men to suppress an anti-Tartar rebellion in the grand duchy of Tver. In this invasion, according to the Chronicle, the Russian land "was laid bare," although Moscow and Novgorod were spared. Other examples of direct Tartar interference in Russia's domestic affairs will be found in the following pages.

The records have also preserved a number of instances of cooperation between the Russians and the Tartars, even in the early period of the Tartar rule. The Russian troops participated in the military ventures of their conquerors, and the presence of Russian regiments was reported in the Mongol army fighting in South China at the end of the thirteenth century. On the other hand, the Tartars sometimes lent their support to Russia in her struggle against the enemies on her western and southern frontiers. In 1275, for instance, the Russian princes with the support of the Tartar troops fought a successful war against Lithuania. In 1287, however, when the Golden Horde attempted to organize a joint Russo-Tartar expedition against Poland, the Russians displayed little enthusiasm for the enterprise, and in spite of their friendly attitude towards the Tartars the Russian land suffered considerable devastation.

The eastern trade, which played an important part in the period preceding the Mongol invasion, was disorganized during the early period of the Tartar rule. Eventually, however, this trade regained some of its former importance. The Tartars, although not abandoning their nomadic habits, established a number of commercial cities which became centers for the exchange of goods between east and west. Sarai, the capital of the Golden Horde, was situated on a tributary of the lower Volga, on the ancient trade route. The Tartar commercial settlements, benefiting by the advantages of their geographical position, attracted merchants from many lands. Russia sent furs; Greece, brocades; Persia, silks and rugs; India, articles of luxury and precious stones. The Tartars themselves took an active part in this international exchange, to which they contributed horses, hides, and leather goods. The peaceful intercourse between the Russians and the Tartars could not have been entirely without effect. The marks of the Mongol domination were not all inflicted by the fire and sword.

Tartar influence was particularly noticeable in the social group that had intimate connections with the invaders, that is, the princes and the boyars. Many of them, it will be recalled, had to pay frequent and protracted visits to the Golden Horde and, in turn, had to receive Tartar dignitaries who arrived uninvited with large retinues and remained as long as they pleased. Some of the Russian princes married Tartar princesses. For instance, Fedor, later prince of Yaroslavl, married in the middle of the thirteenth century the daughter of the khan, and Yuri III, grand duke of Moscow (1303–1325), was married to the sister of the khan. By a strange paradox Mongol influence in the domestic affairs of Russia increased rather than decreased with the decline of the power of the Golden Horde. The severe crisis that developed in the Mongol state in the second half of the fourteenth century and brought about the collapse of that state a century later had among its consequences the influx into Russia of Tartar princes and high officials, accompanied by numerous servants and armed detachments. The growing power of Moscow offered them better opportunities than did the Golden Horde, torn as it was by internal dissension. This process of migration assumed mass dimensions after 1445, when Vasili II of Moscow was defeated by the Tartars and made prisoner. He recovered his freedom by paying an exorbitant ransom and by assuming certain mysterious obligations which the chronicler preferred to leave in the dark: "And the other [obligations] are known to God, and also to them" (that is, the grand duke and the Tartars). Vasili returned to Moscow accompanied by a large number of Tartar notables and soldiers. Many of them remained in his service, were appointed to important administrative offices, and received large estates—presumably in fulfillment of Vasili's mysterious undertaking. This mass infiltration of the Tartars was resented at the time, and contributed to the outbreak of a severe political crisis. The grand duke was blinded and for a time exiled from Moscow. He regained control later, however, and brought with him on his return his Tartar supporters, who had proved faithful friends in adversity.

The Mongol element continued to play an important part at the Moscow court. According to the avowedly approximate computations of Kliuchevsky, at the end of the seventeenth century about 17 per cent of the Moscow upper class was of Tartar or eastern origin. With the passing of the years the Tartar princes became assimilated, and merged with the upper class of Russian society. Yet nearly two and a half centuries of Mongol domination could not but leave an ineffaceable imprint on Russia. Curiously blending with the Byzantine tradition, represented and sponsored by the Russian Church, Mongol ideas and administrative usages paved the way for the establishment of the semi-oriental absolutism of the Muscovite tsars. The "window on Europe," which might have admitted the refreshing breeze of western influences, was still tightly shut, while the deadening storms from the Asiatic steppes swept freely through the length and breadth of the land. The Moscow autocracy of the sixteenth century was not essentially different from the absolute rule of the khans which the ancestors of the Russian tsars had once learned to dread and which they were later eager to imitate. The landed aristocracy, after a struggle, was forced to surrender the independence it had enjoyed in earlier centuries and was reduced to the position of servants of the Moscow grand dukes and tsars, a position involving an ever increasing element of dependence on the sovereign's pleasure and reminiscent in some of its aspects of the despotic tradition of the Mongols. The *veche*, whose influence was on the decline even before the Tartar invasion, lost under the rule of the Golden Horde two of its most important functions: the right both to choose and to expel the princes, this right passing into the hands of the khans. The *veche* itself then sank into insignificance. The great masses of the people, harassed by almost uninterrupted wars, princely feuds, and foreign invasions, and bending under the double burden of domestic taxation and of the tributes extorted by the Tartars, drifted away from the position of precarious freedom they had enjoyed in the past into that of a still greater dependence on the landlords, precursor of the coming serfdom. The effects of the Tartar domination in Russian history were felt long after the Golden Horde had ceased to exist.

"LIBERATION FROM THE TARTAR YOKE"

If Russian historians have a tendency to under-estimate the actual influence of the "Tartar yoke"—as the rule of the Golden Horde is traditionally called—they sin as freely in the direction of over-dramatizing the events that led to the liberation of Russia from the Mongols.

The process of disintegration and schism which, as I have pointed out, made itself felt in the Mongol empire at the end of the thirteenth century and eventually led to the emancipation of the Golden Horde from the great khan had its counterpart in the history of the Golden Horde itself. While a unified Muscovite state was gradually and painfully emerging from the chaos of the interprincely feuds, the Tartar invaders, as if contaminated by the political debility of their Russian vassals, a condition that had contributed to their own triumph, became involved in a long series of domestic crises which started at the end of the fifties of the fourteenth century. The struggle among various pretenders to leadership weakened the grasp of the Golden Horde over the outlying parts of its vast domain and encouraged separatist tendencies. A number of minor secessions took place in the early part of the fifteenth century, although the definite breakup of the rule of Sarai did not occur until somewhat later, when the two new Tartar kingdoms came into existence. In 1445 the kingdom of Kazan was established on the Volga, and in 1446 the Crimean Tartars, with the support of the Polish king Casimir IV, formed the Crimean kingdom. These two states proclaimed their independence from the Golden Horde, whose power and influence were on the wane. Akhmad, the last khan of the Golden Horde to invade the Russian territory, was assassinated early in 1481 by one of his own countrymen, and the final blow to Russia's secular enemy was dealt in 1502 by the Crimean Tartars, who defeated the Golden Horde and wiped it off the map.

The direct contribution of Russia towards bringing about these events was surprisingly small. There had been, of course, a great many uprisings against the Tartars, uprisings followed by punitive expeditions. The Russian princes, in order to reduce the burden of the tributes or even escape them altogether, took advantage of the internal dissensions that were weakening the Tartar rule. These, however, were sporadic and short-lived attempts. The Russians, conscious of their own weakness, relied on submission, ruse, and inaction rather than on open organized resistance.

Against the bleak, drab, and uninspiring background of Russia's half-hearted policies under the Tartar domination, the events of the seventies of the fourteenth century stand out in sharp relief. The Golden Horde was living through a severe inner crisis. Dimitry, grand duke of Moscow (1359–1389), secured his confirmation in office by the new khan Mamai in 1371 and also obtained a reduction of the customary tribute. It seems likely that even this reduced tribute was not paid after 1375, when Dimitry succeeded in winning over the grand duchy of Tver, thus bringing to an end its former alignment with the Golden Horde and Lithuania. Frictions between Mamai and Moscow multiplied and assumed dangerous dimensions. In August, 1378, Dimitry, in an encounter that took place on the river Vozh (a tributary of the Oka, in the principality of Riazan), inflicted a defeat on a Tartar army that was moving towards Moscow. This reverse, although of purely local significance, determined Mamai to teach a severe lesson to his rebellious vassal. He concluded an alliance with Yagailo, grand duke of Lithuania, and in the summer of 1380 crossed the Volga. Simultaneously he sent envoys to Dimitry demanding the resumption of the payment of the tribute on the scale that was in force before the agreement of 1371. These negotiations, however, failed to produce an agreement.

Dimitry's appeal for a crusade against the oppressors was given a mixed reception. Many of the Russian lands were not represented in the huge army at the head of which the grand duke of Moscow moved to the Don. Novgorod, Pskov, Nizhni-Novgorod, and Tver failed to respond to the call to arms. Oleg, grand duke of Riazan, whose principality had been the scene of the recent clash between the Tartars and Dimitry, maintained an ambiguous attitude and attempted to save his land from devastation by carrying on underhand negotiations with both sides. This too clever policy brought its reward, and Riazan was eventually invaded and pillaged, first by the Tartars and later by Dimitry.

The Russian army met the Tartars in the Kulikovo plain on September 8, 1380, before Yagailo had had time to join his ally. The battle was of extraordinary violence, and resulted in the rout of Mamai and his legions. The Russian victory was the more striking since it was unexpected. According to a recent historian (Presniakov) the general feeling in the country on the eve of the Kulikovo encounter was not unlike that of Greece on the eve of Marathon: one of deep despondency and apprehension. No wonder, therefore, that the first and only major Russian victory over the Golden Horde produced a great impression both on contemporary and on later generations and had, undoubtedly, important political repercussions. The career of Mamai had been brought to an end. On his return to the Golden Horde, and while preparing for a new attack on Russia, he was defeated by Tokhtamysh, who became his successor. Of greater significance was the effect of the Kulikovo victory upon the position of the grand duke of Moscow as the national leader of Russia. This result of Mamai's defeat, however, did not become manifest until considerably later.

Solovev, commenting on the world significance of the Kulikovo victory, compares it to the epic encounters that took place in western Europe at the beginning of the Middle Ages, during the great migration of peoples, battles that saved western civilization from destruction by the Asiatic hordes. He maintains that Dimitry's defeat of Mamai was "a sign of the triumph of Europe over Asia," a statement that has been reproduced in a somewhat modified form in innumerable history books. Even leaving aside the pertinent question as to what extent the Russia of the fourteenth century may be considered to have been a European Power, Solovev's evaluation of the significance of the Kulikovo victory would seem to be belied by the subsequent course of the Russo-Tartar relations, of which he himself has given a candid account.

The awe with which Russia looked at the Tartars before September 8, 1380, was, if anything, intensified by Dimitry's victory. The general apprehension that retribution was near at hand proved only too well justified. In 1382 the army of the new khan, Tokhtamysh, invaded Russia and plundered Moscow, which was abandoned by the grand duke, as well as a number of other cities. One after another the Russian princes hastened to pledge their allegiance to the Golden Horde. Dimitry Donsky, too, sent to Sarai his son, who was duly confirmed in office by the khan, and remained a vassal of the Golden Horde until his death in 1389. His son, Vasili I, received his throne from the hands of a khan's envoy. Confusion at Sarai after the defeat of Tokhtamysh by Tamerlan (Timur) in 1395 was followed by an attempt by Vasili I to evade the Tartar control and to suspend the payment of tributes. In spite of the resulting friction there was a definite tendency in Moscow to look to the Tartars for support in the struggle with Lithuania. In 1406 the Tartar troops took part on the Russian side in the war against Vitovt of Lithuania. But two years later Amir Edigei besieged Moscow. The city was abandoned by Vasili, but Edigei withdrew after the payment of an indemnity. Minor Tartar invasions continued throughout the reign of Vasili I—in 1410, 1414, and 1424— and this in spite of the fact that the grand duke, bringing rich presents, visited the Golden Horde in 1412 accompanied by his court. Vasili I died in 1425 and was succeeded by his son, Vasili II, still in his teens. His rights were contested by an uncle, Yuri, and in 1432 the question finally was left to the decision of the khan. The case was won by Vasili on the plea of his representative, Vsevolozhsky, who maintained that the ancient customs on which Yuri based his claim were null and void since the only fountain of princely power in Russia was the will of the khan. This thesis had the backing of the Church. The Moscow Metropolitan, Photius, had from the very beginning attempted to settle the feud between Yuri and Vasili by inducing the former to accept the khan's verdict as final. Vasili was inducted into office by the khan's representative. In the course of Vasili's stormy reign the Tartars continued to play an important part. The disintegration of the Golden Horde led to the severance from the rule of Sarai of separate hordes led by adventurous Tartar princes who sometimes invaded the Russian territory. One of them, Ulu Mehmet, brother of the reigning khan, sought in 1438 the support of Vasili against his brother, and promised in return to defend the Russian frontier, to waive the Golden Horde's traditional claim to tributes, and to stop other extortions. But the fear inspired in Russia by Sarai had not yet been lived down. Ulu Mehmet's offer was rejected, and a Russian army sent against him was defeated. Ulu Mehmet occupied Nizhni-Novgorod and remained there until 1445. From this stronghold he sent out expeditions to various parts of Russia, even besieging Moscow. Riazan suffered from a Tartar invasion in 1425, again in 1437, and in 1444 and 1445. Galicia was devastated by the Tartars in 1428. As I have already pointed out, Vasili, who in 1445 was made prisoner by Ulu Mehmet, recovered his freedom by paying the Golden Horde a large ransom and by entering into obligations about which the Chronicle maintained a discreet silence. The financial commitments assumed by Vasili further increased the burden of taxation borne by all classes, especially the peasants. Vasili's return to Moscow with a large number of Tartar notables, to whom he distributed land and offices, precipitated a domestic crisis. Early in 1446 Prince Dimitry Shemiaka, son of Yuri, and an old antagonist, seized Vasili, who was blinded and sent into exile. His struggle against Shemiaka nevertheless continued, and ended in Vasili's victory and Shemiaka's death by poisoning in 1453. The Tartars, supporters of Vasili, participated actively in the obscure and unhappy events of this period. Among Vasili's innovations was the creation on the lower Volga of a semi-dependent state for Kasim, son of Ulu Mehmet. The origins of the new state, known as the kingdom of Kasimov, as well as the exact time of its organization remain uncertain. Presumably the establishment of this state was among the undisclosed obligations assumed by Vasili as the price of his liberation. On this question, too, the Chronicle is silent.

The formation in 1445 of the Kazan kingdom complicated the situation still further. Dimitry Shemiaka, in his struggle with Vasili, sought the support of the Kazan Tartars and on several occasions instigated their invasions of Russian territory. The kingdom of Kasimov, it is believed, served as a barrier against the growing strength of Kazan, although reliable information on the relations of the latter with Moscow is lacking. From the time of Vasili's victory over Shemiaka to the death of the former in 1462 Moscow was practically independent of the Golden Horde. Tartar invasions, however, continued throughout the reign of Vasili. These clashes would indicate that Moscow was not eager to meet its obligations towards Sarai. Nevertheless the testament of Vasili, prepared shortly before his death, contained detailed provisions concerning the method of collecting the Tartar tributes.

The exact nature of the relations between Vasili's son, Ivan III (1462–1505), and the Golden Horde is difficult to determine. There is no question that towards the end of the previous reign the power of Moscow increased while that of Sarai waned. The Tartars, however, had not yet formally renounced their claim to the Russian tribute. In 1472 the troops of Khan Akhmad invaded the Russian territory and pillaged and burned some of the cities, and in 1474 Moscow received a large Tartar embassy composed of several hundred people and accompanied by over three thousand traders with some forty thousand horses for sale. In 1476 a khan's envoy came to Moscow and urged Ivan to appear in person at Sarai. The grand duke sent instead a representative with a message which presumably displeased Akhmad. Little is known about subsequent negotiations except that no agreement was reached. Akhmad concluded an alliance with Casimir, grand duke of Lithuania and king of Poland, and in 1480 proceeded to move his troops against

Moscow. Ivan showed no enthusiasm for the coming struggle. Lending a willing ear to his advisers, who revived the unpleasant memories of the capture of Vasili II by the Tartars in 1445, he was reluctant to assume personal command of the army. He was, moreover, suspicious —and probably not without reason—of his own brothers, whose cooperation in the struggle against the Mongols was not obtained without protracted and tortuous negotiations. Only the strong pressure of an influential group led by Vassian, bishop of Rostov, induced Ivan to join the troops while he was still negotiating with Akhmad for the latter's withdrawal. The Russian and the Tartar armies found themselves face to face on the two banks of the river Ugra, which formed the boundary between Muscovy and the grand duchy of Lithuania. Ivan kept prudently in the background and refrained from any aggressive moves. Akhmad followed similar tactics, waiting for the arrival of his Lithuanian ally, who, however, failed to appear. The two armies spent the entire summer gazing at each other across the narrow stream. Nothing happened until November, when Akhmad suddenly retreated. The Russian sources ascribe his flight to the panic that spread among his troops when they learned that the Russians had moved their positions somewhat back from the river. This maneuver, the chronicler believed, was interpreted by the Tartars as an attempt to lure them into a trap. The explanation, although ingenious, is hardly convincing. Solovev has wisely observed that armies do not usually flee merely because their opponents are retreating. Probably the failure of Lithuania to send troops, and also the reported attack by a Tartar chieftain upon the encampment occupied by Akhmad's wives and family, had something to do with his retreat. It was on his return march to Sarai that he was assassinated by a Tartar prince. I have already referred to the destruction of the Golden Horde by the Crimean Tartars some twenty years later.

The year 1480 is usually given as the date of Russia's "liberation from the Tartar yoke," although earlier dates are sometimes suggested. The question as to when the Tartar domination was actually brought to an end cannot be definitely answered.[1] The history of Russo-Tartar relations after the Kulikovo battle contains little to justify Solovev's

---

[1] Curiously, the testament of Ivan III, who died in 1505, contained provisions concerning the assessment of the tribute due the Tartars among his heirs. This tribute, however, went no longer to the Golden Horde but to the ruler of the Mongol kingdom in the Crimea.

enthusiastic panegyric upon "the triumph of Europe over Asia." As a matter of fact Asia, as represented by the Golden Horde, was never actually defeated by Russia, whom, moreover, it is not easy to force into the shining armor of the European knight, defender of western civilization. For a century after Dimitry Donskoy turned back the armies of Mamai, the Russian princes continued as vassals of the Tartars, and probably at no time was this dependence greater than in the first half of the fifteenth century. Like so many of the Asiatic empires, the Golden Horde fell victim to its own inner weakness, a process that was an important contributing factor, although not itself the direct cause, of the rise of Muscovy. The heroic but, from the point of view of Russo-Tartar relations, futile episode of the Kulikovo battle stands in sharp contrast to the real success that crowned the pusillanimous policies of Ivan III on the Ugra River. The grand duke's "bloodless victory" may be considered as symbolic of the spirit in which Russia for two and a half centuries endeavored to free herself from the "Tartar yoke."

CHAPTER IV

THE GROWTH OF MOSCOW ABSOLUTISM

---※---

DIFFICULTIES OF THE PROBLEM

The history of Russia from the thirteenth to the fifteenth centuries is, if possible, even more obscure, confused, and controversial than that of the preceding period. I have sufficiently emphasized the limitations of the Chronicle, the chief source on which the historian has to depend. The tendentious editing to which the earlier records have been subjected in the copies of the fifteenth and sixteenth centuries— the earliest available—is particularly regrettable so far as the unification of the country under the rule of Moscow is concerned, since the efforts of official commentators were largely concentrated on this process. It was their object to provide a firm genealogical and historical basis for the dynastic claims of the Moscow princes. "When in the last [eighteenth] century Russian historiography gradually began to master its sources," writes Professor Miliukov, "these sources met the students with their own established point of view formed in the course of ages. No wonder that the interpretation offered by the sources led the student along the beaten roads and arranged for him historical facts in the same order in which they took root in the minds of contemporaries. The result was that while the student imagined that he was making discoveries and interpreting history, in actual fact he was merely following in the footsteps of the philosophers of the fifteenth and sixteenth centuries." These lines, written by Miliukov in 1897, offer an apt characterization of the traditional attitude of Russian historiography, not only in the eighteenth century but even to this very day.

The Chronicle is not, however, the only source for the study of the political and social history of this period. Two other important sources are the testaments of the princes (*dukhovnyia gramoty*), of which

71

sixteen have been preserved, and a large number of interprincely agreements (*dogovornyia gramoty*). The interpretation of these documents,
which are of great value, demands extreme caution. Russian princely
chanceries were eminently conservative, a trait common to all bureauc-
racies. They invariably referred to "immemorial customs" even when
dealing with developments that were distinctly novel, a procedure
inspired perhaps in certain cases by considerations of political expediency and not merely by conservatism or ignorance. On the other hand,
venerable traditional formulas continued to be used to describe relationships which, while reminiscent of those of the past, had undergone important changes. Each of the testaments and interprincely
agreements, therefore, must be interpreted in the light of the conditions of its own time. The acceptance of the traditional phraseology on
its face value, a very common practice, leads to erroneous conclusions.
Needless to say, this situation is by no means peculiar to Russia. For
instance—to take a crude example—it is a fact of common knowledge
that party government and a cabinet responsible to Parliament are
not provided for by any English statute and that in law the ministers
of the British Crown are merely heads of government departments and
personal appointees of the queen. No one, however, would dream of
writing the constitutional history of modern England in these legalistic
and antiquarian terms. The real difficulty with Russian history of the
thirteenth to the fifteenth centuries is that it is anything but easy to
obtain an even approximate idea of the conditions that would offer
a firm ground for a sound interpretation of the ancient documents.
Moreover, although the historians invariably refer to the testaments
and interprincely agreements, the scientific analysis of these texts—
strange as this may appear—has been much neglected, the only special
study being that of B. N. Chicherin, published in 1858, and this can
no longer be accepted as adequate.

The unenviable task of the historian who ventures into the wilderness of the Russian Middle Ages is further aggravated by the depressing
and dreary nature of the conditions and events he has to investigate.
The feeling of bewilderment and despondency experienced by the
student has been eloquently stated by Kliuchevsky. "In studying history," he writes, "it is only reluctantly that one turns to those periods
that give too little food to both intelligence and imagination. It is
difficult to evolve a great idea from unimportant events; colorless developments do not lend themselves to the creation of a vivid picture;

there is nothing interesting, nothing inspiring." And Kliuchevsky quotes a telling characteristic of the period as given by Solovev. "The actors perform silently," writes the dean of the Russian historians, "they make war and they make peace, but they will not say, nor will the chronicler explain, why they make war and why they make peace; in the city, at the court of the prince, all is quiet, all is still; everyone keeps behind closed doors and thinks his thoughts all by himself; the door is open, the actors walk on the stage and do something, but they do it in silence." This reticence of the chronicler is, no doubt, to a certain extent the result of the later editing to which I have already referred, but the general dreariness of the period is well conveyed by Kliuchevsky and Solovev. The former adds, however, that epochs so tedious from the point of view of the student and, on the surface, so barren from the point of view of history are nevertheless of great significance as epochs of transition.

THE TRADITIONAL SCHEME

In spite of Kliuchevsky's stern and sound appraisal of the general character of the Russian Middle Ages, no other historian has done more than he to dramatize the uninspiring events of this period and to compose them into a lively and coherent picture, one that has captured the imagination of his contemporaries and left a lasting imprint on Russian historiography. Few elements of his historical scheme are entirely new. It is rooted, indeed, in the officially inspired views of the "philosophers of the fifteenth and sixteenth centuries," views which color so heavily the Chronicle subsequent to the unification of Russia under the rule of Moscow. The historians of the nineteenth century, as I have already pointed out, have followed the lead of their less distinguished predecessors. Kliuchevsky has restated the familiar arguments in a form brilliant and convincing; he has filled the time-honored and somewhat scholastic formulas with a wealth of details, and he has provided them with the appropriate economic and social background. It is generally and rightly considered, therefore, that he has practically re-created the widely accepted theory of Russia's development from the earlier days to the rise of Moscow. A brief summary of his historical scheme seems imperative, not only because of its popularity, but chiefly because its claim to validity has been grievously impaired by recent investigations.

Kliuchevsky's theory, in so far as it deals with the migration in the

twelfth century of the population of southern Russia to the northeast
and its political and social consequences, has been summarized above.[1]
It will be recalled that according to this view the Russia of Suzdal-
Vladimir had but little in common with Kievan Russia. The geographical, topographical, and ethnographical factors, it is argued, all
combined to produce a social and political structure fundamentally
different from that of the preceding period. The princes of Suzdal-
Vladimir, who were representative of the new type of northeastern
princes, had occupied and colonized a virgin country, and looked upon
it as their personal property. There were no organized social groups,
such as existed in the ancient cities of Kievan Russia, to offer them any
resistance. In the austere physical environment of the northeast and
under the pressure of the day-to-day struggle for existence, the tradition
of national unity characteristic of the Kievan era had been forgotten.
The principalities were divided by the princes among their descendants
without any regard for the tradition of the past, a tradition that had
succeeded to a certain extent in preserving the unity of the nation.

Kliuchevsky's interpretation of Russia's history in the thirteenth to
the fifteenth centuries is the logical development of his generalizations
concerning the earlier period. The political evolution of the country
was dominated by the multiplication of small independent principalities, *udel* (appanage), over which the princes exercised complete
control, including freedom of testamentary disposition, a privilege
that was not enjoyed by them, according to Kliuchevsky, during the
earlier period. The consequences of this process were of extreme importance. The territory of northeastern Russia was broken up into
innumerable small principalities, and the political ties between these
groups, never too strong, tended to disappear altogether. The decrease
in the size of the principalities led to the impoverishment of the
princes, who, gradually transformed into small landlords, abandoned
all ambitions of political leadership, and had but little contact with
one another. The national ideal was at a low ebb. This process of disintegration of the nation, however, paved the way for its approaching
unification. When in the midst of the weak and impoverished princes
there appeared a strong dynasty determined to expand its political
influence, there was little resistance on the part of the other princes,
who had lost the habit of collective action. The local people, moreover, had no reason to take the side of their contemptible rulers and

[1] See pp. 44 *et seq.*

showed no inclination to resist the annexationist tendencies of the rising power. "All this determines the significance of the *udelni* order in our history," writes Kliuchevsky; "by its consequences it facilitated its own destruction."

The new force, which gathered the scattered bits of Russia and unified them under its rule, was Moscow. The reason for the rise of Moscow is one of the significant features of Kliuchevsky's theory. It is explained first of all by Moscow's geographical position at the crossroad of two important currents: the current of immigrants fleeing to the northeast and the current of transit trade along the Moscow River, which connected the upper Volga with the middle Oka. The growth of the population caused by the arrival of the settlers, as well as the profits derived from the transit trade, greatly increased the financial resources of Moscow. The second important element was the genealogical position of the Moscow princes. They belonged to the younger branch of the descendants of Vsevolod III and, according to Kliuchevsky, could not hope to obtain the position of grand dukes of Vladimir in a legitimate way. They therefore did not feel bound by any restrictions imposed by considerations of seniority and boldly embarked on a policy dictated by expediency and dynastic ambitions. The ample resources at their disposal were used by them to increase their domain through purchases of new territories and also through purchase of the favors of the Tartar khans. Particularly important was the granting in 1328 by the khan to Ivan I of a *yarlyk* which made him grand duke of Vladimir as well as prince of Moscow, a position his descendants retained. The good relations that existed most of the time between Moscow and the Golden Horde enhanced the political influence of the former. The fact that Ivan I acted as the Tartar agent for the collection of the tribute added, according to Kliuchevsky, to his prestige among the princes and put into his hands an effective means by which to exercise pressure. The accumulation of new territories by Ivan and his successors was thus accompanied by the growth of their political influence. The victory over the Tartars won by Dimitry Donskoy on the Kulikovo plain established the Moscow princes as the national leaders in the struggle against the secular enemy. The transfer, in the second quarter of the fourteenth century, of the see of the metropolitan from Vladimir to Moscow further strengthened the position of the new capital by bringing together the two principal forces that were working for the unification of the country. The relative peace enjoyed by the grand duchy of Moscow endeared its princes to their subjects, who grew accustomed to look upon them as model administrators and defenders of the vital interests of the people.

The grand duchy of Moscow, like the other grand duchies that existed in Russia during this period, consisted of a group of smaller principalities quasi-independent of the rule of the Moscow grand duke. Beginning with Ivan I, whose death occurred in 1341, it became customary for the grand dukes of Moscow to leave an ever increasing share of their domain to the son who inherited the grand-ducal title. The resulting accumulation of financial and material means in the hands of the grand duke assured his supremacy among the Muscovite princes. The *udelni* order, therefore, which according to Kliuchevsky was based on the complete freedom of testamentary disposition, provided the Moscow grand duke with a weapon for the destruction of that order. A concurrence of fortunate circumstances made it possible for the grand-ducal title to pass from father to the eldest son almost without interruption for a hundred years after the death of Ivan I. Thus the dynastic position of the grand duke of Moscow was strengthened. It survived, undamaged, the trials and tribulations that had filled the reign of Vasili II. What was even more important, the dynastic and often selfish policies of the Muscovite grand dukes gradually acquired a much broader and a truly national significance. The masses of Russian settlers who drifted from the south to the northeast were assimilated in the course of two hundred years by the local population and in the middle of the fifteenth century emerged as a new ethnographic formation, the Great Russian branch of the Russian people. They had suffered much from feuds, foreign invasions, and innumerable calamities. They had long been waiting for a leader, and this leader had at last appeared. "As soon as the population of northern Russia felt that Moscow was capable of becoming the national center around which could unite all the forces ready to struggle against the foreign enemy," writes Kliuchevsky, "that the Moscow prince could be the leader in this struggle, a drastic change took place in the minds of the people and in their relations, a change that decided the fate of the *udelni* order. All the suppressed and inarticulate national and political aspirations of the Great Russian nation, aspirations that had so long and so unsuccessfully sought means of self-expression, then met with the dynastic ambitions of the grand duke of Moscow and carried him to the exalted height of the sovereign of Great Russia."

The above necessarily sketchy and fragmentary account of Kliuchev-sky's noble vision in no way does justice to the original, which must be read in the author's own delectable prose in order to be properly appreciated and enjoyed. The summary, nevertheless, contains the essence of his conception of the formation of the Muscovite state, a conception to which it is impossible to deny real grandeur. Seldom has the inner logic of the fascinating process of the birth of a nation been brought out with greater force and clarity. In Kliuchevsky's presentation the various stages of this process are sharply defined and delimited, while its continuity is emphasized by a logical derivation of each stage from the preceding one. One may well wonder how Kliuchevsky could describe as uninteresting and uninspiring a period characterized by such inner consistency and crowned by so momentous a development. He has certainly triumphed over all obstacles and has succeeded in evolving "great ideas from unimportant events" and in composing "colorless developments" into a "vivid picture."

The very logical perfection and consistency of Kliuchevsky's theory cannot but suggest grave apprehensions and doubts, for history can seldom be fitted into a well rounded scheme without suffering grievous distortions. Less romantically minded historians would hesitate to use such a metaphysical concept as that of a new ethnographical formation —in this case Great Russia—"waiting for a leader" and, when the leader was somewhat suddenly discovered, carrying him "to the exalted heights of the sovereign of Great Russia." Acceptance of this concept is especially difficult when the leader was so unprepossessing a figure as Vasili II, center of one of the worst of the interprincely feuds, who had returned to Moscow from Tartar captivity burdened with heavy commitments and surrounded by Tartar nobles and soldiers. His return was followed by a new round of bloody internal strife. Nor did Vasili's heir, Ivan III, both timorous and ruthless, qualify better as a national leader. Even more questionable is Kliuchevsky's method of dividing history into sharply defined periods, in spite of his truly remarkable ability to endow them with an economic and social content that gives these periods a most pleasing inner unity. I have already pointed out how dubious was the opposition between Kievan Russia and the Russia of Suzdal-Vladimir which provides the foundation for Kliuchevsky's generalizations about the thirteenth to the fifteenth centuries. Still more disturbing is his tendency to divorce the fundamental trend of Russia's history from the general setting in which it unfolded, and this in spite of his own detailed and often illuminating study of the immediate economic and social environment. I have quoted in a different connection Kliuchevsky's statement that in studying the political organization of northeastern Russia one "should forget for a time . . . that Russia was conquered by the Tartars." As a matter of fact, this organization cannot be properly understood unless one keeps continuously in mind not only the ever present Tartar influence but also Russia's almost uninterrupted struggle with her neighbors—Lithuania, Poland, Sweden, the Teutonic knights, and the Finnish tribes.

The historical school, of which Kliuchevsky is the most eminent and brilliant representative, has been attacked from many sides without, however, losing popularity. Sergeevich has challenged its views and has emphasized the influence of the Tartars and of the boyar aristocracy in bringing about the unification of Russia. Pokrovsky, an outstanding representative of Marxism in pre-revolutionary Russia, has given a very different interpretation of the country's history. Presniakov, in a relatively recent study, has provided by far the best and the most devastating analysis of the traditional interpretation of the Russian Middle Ages, an interpretation based on "legalistic and sociological dogmatism." The unfortunate result of this approach, according to Presniakov, has been that Russian historiography has contented itself with selecting from the sources what has fitted in with its preconceived ideas and has brushed aside all evidence that would disturb the sacrosanct historical tradition.[2] Presniakov's own exhaustive and critical study

[2] A striking example of this attitude will be found in a bulky volume by Alexandre Eck, Le Moyen Âge russe (Paris, 1933). M. Eck disposes of Presniakov's views on the evolution of northeastern Russia in the twelfth and thirteenth centuries in a brief footnote (p. 30). In his opinion Presniakov's exposition has in no way shaken the theories expounded by the two "illustrious scholars," Solovev and Kliuchevsky, and, moreover, is in contradiction with the "irrefutable" (irrécusable) evidence provided by the Chronicle, by archaeology, and by the monuments of the period. As a matter of fact, Presniakov's conclusions—with which, of course, one is at liberty to disagree—are based on the most thorough study of the sources to be found in any of the works on this period, including those of Solovev and Kliuchevsky. M. Eck should also be aware that the evidence both of the Chronicle and of archaeology, far from being "irrefutable," is questionable, and had lent itself to conflicting interpretations long before Presniakov entered the field. M. Eck uses against Presniakov another and this time truly "irrefutable" argument: "The venerable S. Platonov, fellow of the Russian Academy of Science, does not seem to have been impressed by Presniakov's presentation." Unless I am mistaken, there are no other references in M. Eck's volume to Presniakov's views, and he ignores completely Presniakov's illuminating analysis of the forma-

of the sources led him to significant conclusions that differ from the accepted textbook version rooted in the writings of Solovev and Kliuchevsky.

THE DECLINE OF THE GRAND DUCHY OF VLADIMIR

The history of Russia in the thirteenth, fourteenth and fifteenth centuries unfolded itself against a background of almost uninterrupted warfare. Solovev has stated that between 1228 and 1462 northern Russia suffered 133 foreign invasions, including forty-eight by the Tartars. To this number must be added ninety interprincely feuds, which brings the total of warlike disturbances to 223. The armed conflicts were, of course, distributed unevenly both in time and in space, and it was the frontier territories that naturally suffered most. Solovev judiciously observes that statistics in history should be used with caution. Nevertheless the figures just quoted bring out clearly the important part played by international wars and domestic strife in the history of this period.

The conquest of Russia by the Tartars worked far-reaching changes in the position of northeastern principalities and especially in the position of the grand duchy of Vladimir. Russian eastward expansion and colonization suffered a lasting check. The former ties with southern Russia were practically severed, although relations with the southwestern principalities were maintained. The Bulgar trade was gone, and the drying up of the financial resources of the grand dukes of Vladimir contributed to the decline of their former power. The sphere of their influence was narrowed, and this encouraged a strong movement in Novgorod for its emancipation from the authority of Vladimir. The conditions that made it possible for the grand duchy of Vladimir to build up its supremacy among the Russian principalities in the hundred years preceding the Tartar invasion were now rapidly disappearing, and with them went the influence of its grand dukes, who no longer represented the broader interests of northeastern Russia. This change, however, was gradual.

Yuri II, grand duke of Vladimir, was killed in 1238 in a battle with the Tartars, and was succeeded by his brother Yaroslav I (1238–1246). Even in the midst of the Tartar invasion Yaroslav continued the tra-

---

tion of the Muscovite state, although the two monographs written by Presniakov are duly noted in the bibliography. M. Eck, needless to say, laboriously expounds in some five hundred pages the familiar theories of official Russian historiography.

ditional policies of his predecessors, policies that were inspired by the community of interests in northern Russia. In 1239 he repulsed a Lithuanian advance on Smolensk. Yaroslav's son Alexander, prince of Novgorod, defeated the Swedes in 1240 on the Neva River, a victory that won him the surname of Nevsky. In 1242 Alexander triumphed over the German knights who had entered the territory of Pskov, and three years later an army drawn from many parts of the country and headed by Alexander defeated the Lithuanians. In the autumn of 1242 Yaroslav journeyed to the Golden Horde and was duly confirmed in office by the khan. The other princes of northern Russia, following suit, also received their appointments from the khan's hands. This procedure, however, was merely formal, and the Tartars did not at first interfere with the customary right of succession. Vladimir retained its position as the "senior" city, and the relations between the grand duke and the other princes remained very much what they had been before the Tartar invasion. The death of Yaroslav was followed by an outburst of princely feuds and the grand-ducal throne was occupied for short periods by his brother Sviatoslav, and then, in turn, by his sons Michael I and Andrew II (1249–1252). The latter attempted to revolt against the Mongols, but had to flee before a Tartar army. He was succeeded by his brother, Alexander Nevsky (1252–1263), who was a frequent visitor to the Golden Horde and had won the favors of the khan.

Alexander's policies bear the imprint of a pronounced dualism: he appears, on the one hand, as the true representative of the interests of northern Russia, on the other, as a tool and agent of the khan. The defense of the country against its western neighbors continued to be one of Alexander's chief preoccupations. In 1253 his son Vasili repulsed the Lithuanians who had invaded the territory of Novgorod, and in 1256 the grand duke himself led his army against the Swedes. In 1262 he sent his troops, this time in alliance with Lithuania and supported by Novgorod, to fight the Germans. These activities were distinctly in line with the grand-ducal tradition inherited from the Kievan days. There was, however, another side to the picture. In domestic affairs Alexander took his orders from the Golden Horde, to whom he owed his tenure of office, and suppressed the anti-Tartar movements in Novgorod and other cities. This policy was probably wise since it saved the country from punitive expeditions whose outcomes were foregone conclusions. It temporarily strengthened the position of the grand duke, and Alexander was the last occupant of the office whose authority was not seriously challenged. He was the acknowledged commander of Russia's military forces, her leader in the struggle against her western enemies, her chief representative at the khan's court. This superficial success could not disguise, but on the contrary, rather emphasized, the change that had taken place: the supreme arbiter of the destinies of Russia was no longer the grand duke of Vladimir, but the khan and the Tartar troops on whose support Alexander had to lean so heavily and whose policies he had to enforce. A new and formidable power—the Golden Horde—had entered the field of Russia's domestic politics. Alexander's submissive attitude towards the Tartars provoked resentment and left much bitterness in Novgorod and in the minds of the local princes, boyars, and the common people. Popular tradition and the Church, who canonized Alexander, have done much to silence the echoes of contemporary criticisms, but they have not succeeded in expunging them from the record. Inevitable as the policies of Alexander might have been, they contributed to the impending decline of the grand duchy of Vladimir.

The eclipse of the political influence of the grand duchy of Vladimir was a slow and gradual process. Its chief elements were the loss of control by the grand dukes over the country's defense, which came more and more within the purview of the local princes, and the growing tendency on the part of Novgorod to shake off its traditional close ties with Vladimir. The association between Novgorod and Vladimir, it will be remembered, was an essential factor in the political and financial supremacy of the latter. It was Novgorod's long-established policy to accept princes from the dynasty that was able to give it the surest guaranties of protecting its far-flung commercial interests. Since the appearance of the Golden Horde, Vladimir was no longer in a position to offer such protection, and Novgorod took advantage of this weakness to loosen the ancient ties. In the reign of Alexander's brother and successor, Yaroslav II (1263–1272), Novgorod and its dependency, Pskov—which was rapidly achieving independence—began to appear as mighty political factors, and proved unwilling to bow to dictations from Vladimir. In 1269–1270 Novgorod rebelled against Yaroslav, who attempted to interfere too much with the internal affairs of the "free city," and through Yaroslav's brother Vasili appealed to the Golden Horde. The khan decided the dispute in favor of Novgorod, and against Yaroslav. The wealth of Novgorod put into its hands powerful means of persuasion to which the khans were particularly susceptible. The check suffered by Yaroslav was a clear evidence of the decline of his authority and indicated the road, followed since by so many Russian princes, of seeking the solution of their disputes at the khan's court. Although Yaroslav's effective control over the principalities that formed part of the grand duchy was weakened, his general policies were still in conformity with the grand-ducal tradition. Little is known about the reign of Yaroslav's brother and successor, Vasili (1272–1276), except that it brought about a new and this time bloody conflict with Novgorod in which the Tartar troops sided with the grand duke.

The history of Vladimir in the last quarter of the thirteenth and in the beginning of the fourteenth century is not only confused but is filled with the struggle of the occupants of the grand-ducal throne, supported by some of the princes and nobles, against coalitions of other princes and their boyars, with Novgorod playing an important and often decisive part. The central figures in these fratricidal wars were the two sons of Alexander Nevsky, Dimitry and Andrew III, who intermittently occupied the throne of Vladimir from 1276 to 1304. The contesting parties frequently appealed to the khan, and Tartar troops were freely used. The inevitable result of the feud was the further weakening of the grand-ducal authority. The defense of the northern frontier passed almost entirely into the hands of Novgorod and Pskov, who also assumed very largely the control of their relations with the Swedes, the Dutch, the Germans, and the Tartars. The conflict between the contesting princes and the boyar interests behind them was fundamentally similar to the interprincely feuds of the earlier period. It was primarily a struggle between the pretenders to the grand-ducal throne. Weakened as it was, Vladimir had not yet lost the whole of its prestige and economic and political influence. Still traditionally associated with the control of Novgorod and Pskov with their vast resources, Vladimir retained its claim to act as the chief representative of northern Russia at the Golden Horde. The aspirations of the grand dukes to national leadership were not forgotten and were revived whenever the opportunity presented itself. For instance, in spite of the conflicts with Novgorod, the Grand Duke Andrew participated in 1293 in a war against Sweden and, again, in 1301 led against her an army in which several Russian lands were represented. The means at the disposal of Vladimir, however, were no longer adequate to enforce its leadership. Nevertheless, there seems to be little ground for drawing a sharp distinction between the princes of the pre-Mongol era and those of the second half of the thirteenth century, or for representing the latter as mere landlords engrossed in the expansion of their private domains.

THE ASCENDANCY OF MOSCOW

Moscow made a somewhat sudden and dramatic appearance on the historical stage at the beginning of the fourteenth century. It is first mentioned in the Chronicle of the year 1147, but little is known about its history for the next one hundred and fifty years, and there is no information as to the exact time it reached the status of a principality. The first definitely Muscovite prince was Daniel, son of Alexander Nevsky. Daniel died in 1303, and his son and successor, Yuri (1303–1325), immediately entered the broader arena of Russian politics.

It is difficult to discover a satisfactory explanation for Moscow's rapid rise. The reasons usually given—the trade advantages of its geographical position and the exceptionally large influx of settlers from the south—are not convincing. There is probably more truth in the opinion (Platonov) that during the thirteenth century the role of Moscow was largely that of a military outpost on the southern boundary of the principality of Suzdal-Vladimir. This "strategic" position of Moscow—but in a much broader sense—may account for its ascendancy in the fourteenth century (Presniakov). In the struggle for the succession to Vladimir's failing leadership, Moscow became the center of the forces that were anxious to prevent the dismemberment of the country. It was better equipped for the task than its chief competitor, Tver, which was too absorbed in the complex relationships on its western frontier to aspire seriously to national leadership. Moscow's interests were both more universal and more national: in the west they comprised Novgorod, Tver, Lithuania, the Baltic countries; in the south and east, the Golden Horde and the colonization and trade movements along the Volga. This historical significance of Moscow, however, did not appear until much later. Two more immediate considerations may help to an understanding of the activities of Yuri of Moscow. With the death of Andrew III of Vladimir, Yuri was the only direct surviving descendant of Alexander Nevsky, and he therefore had reasons to consider himself entitled to the grand-ducal throne. Moreover, his father, Daniel, obtained in 1302 the control of the ancient principality of Pereiaslavl, an action which was contested by the grand dukes of Vladimir on the ground that Pereiaslavl was a part of their domain. The desire to make safe the possession of Pereiaslavl was probably not altogether foreign to Yuri's claim to the grand-ducal title.

The death of Grand Duke Andrew in 1304 was the starting point of a particularly bloody and devastating feud. The two pretenders to the vacant throne were Prince Michael of Tver, a nephew of Alexander Nevsky, and Prince Yuri of Moscow. The emergence of these principalities in the national arena indicated a shifting westward of the center of political activity. The change has been ascribed (Liubavsky) to the movement in that direction of the population of the southeastern territories which were particularly affected by repeated Tartar invasions in the second half of the thirteenth century. It was another sign of the decline of the supremacy of Vladimir.

Michael and Yuri both went to the Golden Horde and laid their competing claims before the khan. In the meantime Yuri made an unsuccessful attempt to impose his representatives on Novgorod, Kostroma, and Nizhni-Novgorod, while Michael launched an attack against Pereiaslavl. The rival boyar parties actively participated in these ventures and sometimes even took the initiative. The very broad and comprehensive character of these attempts suggests that what Michael and Yuri were seeking was not merely the aggrandizement of their respective domains, but the establishment of an effective political control over northeastern Russia. The proceedings at the Golden Horde showed the Russian princes at their worst. It was a case of open and shameless bargaining, the khan cynically holding out the coveted *yarlyk* to the highest bidder, that is, the grand-ducal appointment was to go to the prince who was prepared to extract the highest tribute from his unhappy countrymen. From this sordid competition Michael emerged the victor and returned to Vladimir with the title of grand duke. He was duly installed in office in a ceremony at which Metropolitan Maxim officiated. Yuri, however, did not accept his defeat, and the reign of Michael (1304–1318) was filled with intermittent conflicts with the Moscow prince.

These events could hardly add to the prestige of grand-ducal power; if anything, they contributed to the disintegration of Russia. There were, however, two forces which energetically and stubbornly fought the separatist tendencies. These forces were the boyars and the Church. It would, of course, be a mistake to picture the boyars of the fourteenth century as conscious "empire builders" (Sergeevich). Their immediate and selfish interests demanded the preservation of the grand-ducal authority, which offered them opportunities through lucrative offices for the acquisition of wealth, especially in the form of landed estates often scattered throughout several principalities. Princely feuds and the weakening of the central authority spelled heavy losses for the landed aristocracy, whose members were the first to be massacred in the civil wars and whose properties were frequently confiscated. It is also likely that the old boyar families, especially those associated with the grand-ducal court, were not altogether unaffected by the "Great Russia" tradition of Vladimir and that they not unnaturally considered their private interests as identical with those of the country at large.

The attitude of the Church was even clearer. Like the boyars, the Church was a large landlord with far-flung economic interests, and therefore it was an immediate sufferer from the disturbed conditions of the land. It had, moreover, inherited from Byzantium the tradition of universality ("Catholicism") and had consistently maintained the position that there must be only one Russian metropolitan as the sole head of the Russian Church and the great unifying influence in the turmoil of interprincely strife. The alarming decay of the grand-ducal authority at the turn of the thirteenth century spurred both the Church and the boyars to rally around the shaking throne. An important step was the transfer in 1300 of the metropolitan see from Kiev to Vladimir. Maxim, the then titular head of the Church, was the first to assume the title of metropolitan of "All Russia." It was also no mere coincidence that Michael was the first to style himself "Grand Duke of All Russia."

Michael proved incapable of taking advantage of the support offered to him by the Church and the boyars. After the death of Maxim in December, 1304, the grand duke became involved in an obscure intrigue which had for its purpose the appointment of a metropolitan of his own choice. The patriarch of Constantinople, with whom the decision rested, disregarded Michael's candidate and nominated Peter to the Russian see. Peter did not reach Vladimir until 1310, when he was duly installed, but at the instigation of Michael his fitness to hold office was challenged. An influential party, including Yuri of Moscow, supported the metropolitan, and at a trial by a representative of the patriarch Peter was cleared of the charges brought against him.

The net result of this unhappy affair was that Michael lost a potential powerful ally, since Peter became an ardent partisan of Moscow. The Church canonized both Peter and his antagonist Michael, thus displaying an admirable impartiality which, unfortunately, had been only too often wanting in more worthy cases.

The relations of Michael with Novgorod, that pillar of the grand-ducal authority, were just as disastrous. Earlier friction with the freedom-loving northern metropolis was renewed in 1312 and in the years immediately following. Novgorod sought the support of the khan and of Moscow against the grand duke, but for a time the latter had the upper hand. Yuri of Moscow, who, on Novgorod's invitation became its prince, was forced to withdraw. Michael, backed by Tartar troops, inflicted on Novgorod a humiliating defeat, followed by ruthless repressions and drastic interferences with the city's "ancient liberties." In 1316, however, Novgorod ejected Michael's representatives and successfully defended itself against his army. Yuri, in the meantime, was living at the khan's court, had married the khan's sister, and had been appointed grand duke of Vladimir. He returned to Russia at the head of Tartar troops. Michael's attempt to organize resistance proved a failure and he was induced to appear at the Golden Horde, where Yuri had also returned. Michael was tried for insubordination to the khan, convicted, and executed (1318).

The triumph of Yuri was complete but it was also short-lived. The new grand duke was besieged with many difficulties. The obligations he had assumed towards the Golden Horde as the price of his elevation were heavy and were resented by the people. The defense of Novgorod claimed much of his time in 1322–1324, while his relations with Tver were highly strained and the support of the Tartars uncertain. Dimitry of Tver, Michael's son and successor, was not reconciled to Yuri's victory and to the diminished importance of his own position. He took advantage of Yuri's insistence to act as the sole agent for the collection of the Tartar tribute, and after the grand duke's failure to surrender to a Tartar emissary the sums paid by Tver, Dimitry went to the Golden Horde, where he denounced Yuri and obtained a *yarlyk* for the grand duchy. Yuri's endeavor to rally the country to his support met with no success, and when at the end of 1324 he appeared at the Golden Horde he was assassinated by Dimitry. His death was avenged by the stern ruler of Sarai, who several months later ordered

Dimitry's execution. Alexander of Tver became the successor to his brother Dimitry as grand duke of Vladimir.

Moscow recovered from this shattering blow in a remarkably short time. Yuri's brother, Ivan I, known as *Kalita*, or "Moneybag," probably had become prince of Moscow even before his brother's death. When in 1327 a Tartar emissary and his suite were massacred in Tver, Ivan went to the Golden Horde and headed a punitive Tartar expedition against the rebellious city. The Grand Duke Alexander fled to Pskov and later to Lithuania, and in 1328 Ivan became grand duke of Vladimir while retaining his principality of Moscow. The association of these two cities had been maintained with but brief interruptions until the final unification of the Muscovite state.

The position of Ivan was complicated by the strengthening of the grand duchy of Lithuania, which under the rule of Gedimin (1316–1341) became a powerful factor in the politics of eastern Europe. The western territories of Russia were showing strong pro-Lithuanian sympathies, and Smolensk and Chernigov, which were definitely within the Lithuanian sphere of influence, were soon annexed by that Power. Tver, Novgorod, and Pskov displayed similar leanings, which were strengthened by Moscow's close dependence on the Golden Horde and Ivan's zeal in his capacity as the khan's agent. The western Russian lands harbored the hope of freeing themselves from the Tartar domination with the assistance of Lithuania and, if necessary, under its leadership. This situation cemented the ties between Moscow and the Tartars, the latter being anxious to preserve intact their Russian possessions. The extortions of the Golden Horde which it was Ivan's unenviable task to enforce led to many serious conflicts with Novgorod and the other lands. The return of the former Grand Duke Alexander to Tver in 1335 and his reconciliation with the khan presented a real menace to Ivan's political supremacy, especially since Alexander continued to maintain close relations with Lithuania. Ivan used against his enemy the familiar and trusted weapon of denunciation and intrigue. Alexander, lured to visit the Golden Horde, was assassinated there, together with his son, in 1338, and, as a consequence, the dependence of Tver on Moscow was increased.

Ivan is often represented as the founder of Moscow's future greatness through his expansion of its territory by purchase. The very fact of such purchase has been declared by Sergeevich to be questionable, and the same author has maintained that Ivan's policies prepared the dismemberment rather than the unification of the country. The question of the purchase of territories is not really important, for the growth of the Muscovite state was the result, not of the territorial expansion of the principality of Moscow, but of the acquisition of political power by the Moscow grand dukes. Ivan I had done much to strengthen the grand-ducal authority. He achieved this objective, however, not by wise economies but by the unscrupulous use of Tartar forces and by his docile compliance with Tartar orders. Such policies had their reverse side. The familiar picture of the relative prosperity and peace enjoyed by Moscow in the reign of Ivan is the result of wishful thinking and is based on the slightest historical evidence. An important factor in the ascendancy of Moscow was its close alliance with the Church. Metropolitan Peter spent much of his time in the new capital, where he died in 1325. He was buried in the Moscow Uspensky Cathedral and, after his canonization, became Moscow's patron saint. His successor, Theognostus, transferred the metropolitan see from Vladimir to Moscow.

POLITICAL RELATIONS IN THE FOURTEENTH AND FIFTEENTH CENTURIES

The grand duchy of Vladimir and the principality (later grand duchy) of Moscow were merely two of the several political units into which Russia was divided during the Mongol era of her history. Nor was Moscow the only one to reach such a status. Tver continued to be known as a grand duchy after it lost its control over Vladimir, and remained for over a century a small political world of its own. Three more grand duchies emerged from the turmoil of the fourteenth century —those of Riazan, Yaroslavl, and Nizhni-Novgorod, although information about them is regrettably fragmentary and confused. There is also mention in the Chronicle of the grand duchy of Pronsk, one of the component parts of the grand duchy of Riazan. Novgorod the Great and Pskov, as we have already seen, were by no means merely tools in the hands of Vladimir or Moscow, for they continued to display a spirit of independence that created serious difficulties in the path of the centralization of authority. The whole history of this period bears the deep imprint of the struggle between centripetal and centrifugal tendencies, and there were many moments when the final outcome appeared problematical. The situation was reminiscent of the one we found in Kievan Russia and in the northeastern Russia of the pre-Mongol era.

The same pronounced dualism permeated the relations within the several political subdivisions of the country during this period. It can best be traced in the case of Moscow and, to a lesser degree, in that of Tver. Ivan I of Moscow died in 1341, and his testament (he really left two testaments which are subject to varying and often contradictory interpretations) provided for a political organization essentially similar to the one we have observed as operating in the past. Conforming to tradition, Ivan entrusted his widow, daughters, and young sons to his eldest son, Simeon, as the head of the joint family to whose members he was to be in *loco parentis*—the familiar principle of "seniority." The idea of joint family ownership regulated the distribution of the estate among the heirs. The resulting relationship was somewhat complex. Although Ivan's heirs received definite territorial shares from the estate, these shares were not their individual property to be disposed of at will, but component parts of the family-owned estate—the principality of Moscow. The right of enjoyment was made subject to the possibility of reapportionment of the shares among the heirs in case the estate itself suffered diminution. Ivan specifically provided for such a redistribution should the Tartars force the severance of some of its territory from the principality. The city of Moscow and the collection of revenue from the tax-paying population—which provided the bulk of the Tartar tribute—were left to the joint administration of Ivan's three surviving sons. The term *udel* was not used by Ivan to describe the territorial share of his heirs, but made its first appearance in an agreement concluded by Ivan's eldest son, Simeon, with his two brothers.

Ivan's testament contained no provision for the disposition of the territorial shares after their holders' death. Such provisions were not really necessary, since, after the days of the Liubech conference of 1097 and even earlier, the idea of "patrimonial" succession (*votchina, otchina*), that is, the right of the descendants to a share in the principality held by their father, was an accepted principle of Russian customary law. This principle, which led to the breaking up of the principalities into an ever increasing number of quasi-independent territorial units, was, as we have seen, in irreconcilable contradiction to the equally recognized principle of "seniority," which demanded a degree of unification under the rule of the "senior" prince. The two resulting policies and the conflict between the two ideas formed an essential element in the eventful and unhappy history of Kievan Russia and in that of the grand duchy of Vladimir. Moscow and the other Russian lands of the fourteenth and fifteenth centuries inherited this conflict from the past. Hence the profound dualism that colored their development. The political structure was continuously torn by the clash between the forces working for its unification and those that would bring about its disruption. Unification won in Moscow, as it did in Tver, but the process was slow, painful, and often uncertain.

The vacillating course of Moscow's political development was reflected in the testaments of its grand dukes and in the interprincely agreements. The latter had for their object to define the powers of the "senior" prince, that is, the occupant of the Moscow throne, and at the same time to protect the junior princes from the arbitrary interference of the grand duke and, especially, to safeguard the rights of their issue in the principalities they held. Such, for instance, was the agreement concluded by the Grand Duke Simeon (1341–1353) with his two brothers. The grand-ducal prerogatives usually (there were some exceptions) included the command of all the armed forces as well as the right of collecting the Tartar tribute. Moscow was thus interposed as an intermediary in the relations between the other princes and the Golden Horde. It was these "political" functions of Moscow that made possible the growth of its effective control over the smaller principalities. The separatist tendencies inherent in the *udelni* order were further checked by the traditional right of the boyars to own estates in various principalities and to move freely from one to another, a right that was safeguarded by interprincely agreements. The strengthening of Moscow, which was due to its "strategic" position in the broad political sense, brought a gradual change in its relations with the junior princes. The element of grand-ducal power asserted itself under the time-honored phraseology of the interprincely agreements. The once clear distinction between the hereditary princes and the boyar nobles holding estates in service tenure tended to become blurred and to disappear altogether. The Grand Duke Dimitry (1359–1389) gave his cousin Vladimir, prince of Serpukhov, the cities of Dimitrov and Galich, to which Vladimir had no hereditary claim. This transfer, sanctioned by the agreement of 1389, was a novel departure, and created a new source of princely territorial rights—grand-ducal grant. The venerable institution of "seniority" was thus undergoing a significant transformation: the grand dukes of Moscow were showing a tendency to look upon themselves as the sovereigns of the entire principality and were displaying only the scantiest respect for the rights of the junior princes, even though they still continued to adhere to the traditional formulas in official documents. The former clear-cut distinction between the "patrimony" of the Moscow dynasty, that is, the principality of Moscow, and the grand duchy of Vladimir also tended to disappear. While Dimitry, in his testament, was the first "to bless" his son Vasili with the grand-ducal throne as his "patrimony," he at the same time somewhat weakened the future grand dukes by including parts of the grand-ducal domain in the share he assigned to his younger sons. This was another instance of the devious course that led to Moscow's unification.

Kliuchevsky's attractive scheme, which ascribes the ascendancy of Moscow's "senior" prince, among the other Moscow princes, to his larger share in the common inheritance, cannot be accepted. Such an increase applied merely to the principality of Moscow, and the accretion was small when compared with the resources of the grand duchy of Vladimir, which, since the days of Ivan I, were controlled by the occupant of the Moscow throne. It was the association of the "senior" see of Moscow with the throne of the grand duchy of "All Russia" (Vladimir) which put at the disposal of the Moscow grand dukes the powerful economic and political means they freely used both in overcoming the separatist tendencies among the weaker junior Moscow princes (Presniakov) and in their struggle for supremacy among the other Russian lands.

THE EBB AND FLOW

The process of Russia's unification comprised two distinct and yet closely interdependent developments: (1) the unification of the principality of Moscow under the rule of its "senior" princes, the merging of their powers with those of the grand dukes of Vladimir and the resulting creation of the "grand duchy of Moscow, Vladimir and All Russia," precursor of the state of the Muscovite tsars, and (2) the bringing of other Russian land under the sway of the new grand duchy.

In the fourteenth century and the first half of the fifteenth these two processes followed an eventful course. In the reign of Ivan I the position of Moscow was considerably strengthened. His son Simeon (1341–1353) was confirmed in office by the khan, who put "under his hand" all the Russian princes. Nevertheless his reign, as well as those of his brother Ivan II (1353–1359) and the latter's son, Dimitry

Donskoy (1359–1389), was filled with stormy developments that threatened to jeopardize both the supremacy of Moscow and the process of unification. It was during this period that the grand duchy of Nizhni-Novgorod came into existence, while the Riazan princes assumed the title of grand dukes and showed a tendency to emancipate themselves from the authority of Moscow. The success attained by Simeon at the Golden Horde was purchased at the usual high cost— heavy tributes and other payments to the Tartars. The collection of funds to meet these commitments led, as it had in the past, to friction not only with Novgorod, that treasure house on which the grand dukes of Vladimir and Moscow never failed to draw, but with other lands as well. The separatist tendencies of Novgorod, Pskov, Tver, and Riazan were fostered by Lithuania, whose influence in Russian affairs was increasing. Pskov, for a time, accepted a son of Olgerd, grand duke of Lithuania, as its prince, but in 1348 resumed its former relations with Novgorod and Moscow. A decline of Moscow's power set in during the 1360's. When control over the foreign relations of northeastern Russia escaped from the hands of the Moscow grand dukes, the component elements of "the Grand Duchy of All Russia" sought to solve their pressing international problems by entering into direct negotiations with the Golden Horde and Lithuania. The Russian princes were not reconciled to Moscow's all too recent leadership. After Simeon's death in 1353, Constantine, prince of Nizhni-Novgorod and Suzdal, made a strong though unsuccessful bid for the throne of "All Russia." His son Dimitry, prince of Suzdal, repeated the attempt after the death of Ivan II of Moscow in 1359, and obtained the khan's *yarlyk* for the grand duchy. It was a period of political confusion in the Golden Horde, khans rapidly succeeding one another. Dimitry Donskoy, son of Ivan II, also obtained a *yarlyk*, and the struggle between the two Dimitries, who both relied on the support of the antagonistic Tartar rulers, continued until 1365, when it ended with the victory of the Moscow prince. Around 1370 and again in 1375 the throne of Vladimir was given by Mamai to Michael of Tver. The latter never succeeded, however, in making his title effective, a failure that was due in part to the defection of his ally Lithuania and to the change of mind at the khan's court, a development influenced, no doubt, by Michael's inability to meet his heavy financial obligations to the Tartars.

In their domestic and foreign policies Ivan II and Dimitry Donskoy were ably seconded by Metropolitan Alexis (1354–1378), the actual ruler during the minority of Dimitry, who had succeeded his father at an early age. Alexis, a member of an old Moscow boyar family, was an ardent partisan of the dynastic ambitions of the Muscovite princes. His local patriotism broadened by assimilation with the tradition of "universality" of the Byzantine Church, he fought not only for the restoration of the unity of the metropolitanate of "All Russia," temporarily broken by the appointment of a separate metropolitan for the Russian lands under the Lithuanian rule, but also for the "unification of the temporal power." In his hands the ecclesiastical weapon of pastoral blessings, interdicts, and excommunications was generously put at the service of the Moscow grand dukes. Alexis looked upon a breach of allegiance to Dimitry Donskoy as a crime against the Church (although in 1360 he himself recognized Dimitry of Suzdal as grand duke of Vladimir), and he acted accordingly. In his administration the interests of the Church were identified with those of the Moscow throne, a departure resented by many as an infringement on the "ancient liberties" to which the Russian lands had grown accustomed. The assistance of the metropolitan was of inestimable value to Dimitry, especially in his fight against Lithuanian sympathies. Alexis and the patriarch of Constantinople, presumably at the former's instigation, branded the Lithuanians as "enemies of the cross" and "godless fire worshipers" and threatened with excommunication their Russian supporters. The patriarch, however, soon reversed his attitude and hastened to make peace with Lithuania. The services rendered by Alexis to the national cause received recognition in his canonization. Unfortunately, he must be considered also as one of the founders of that tradition of subservience of the Russian Church to the state that found so full a development in later years and proved, in the long run, equally fatal to the Church and to the monarchy it endeavored to serve.

A lasting conflict between Moscow and Lithuania continued throughout the reigns of Ivan II and Dimitry and resulted in the annexation by Lithuania of a number of territories along Russia's western frontier. It was only internal dissensions in Lithuania, following the death of Olgerd in 1377, that somewhat relieved the pressure exerted by Lithuania. Dimitry had also to fight Riazan and to carry on a protracted war with Tver, a war that started in 1366 and lasted until 1375. The agreement that ended this conflict was favorable to Moscow. Michael of Tver recognized the "seniority" of Dimitry and agreed to refrain from direct negotiations either with the Tartars or with Lithu-ania. In spite of the wording of this agreement, which would seem to indicate a submission of Tver to Moscow, the former continued to enjoy a large degree of independence both in its domestic affairs and in its foreign relations. How precarious was the control exercised by the grand duke over the Russian lands was made clear by the absence from the army he led against the Tartars in 1380 of the troops from Novgorod, Pskov, Nizhni-Novgorod, and Tver, while Oleg of Riazan tried in vain to save his principality from devastation by serving both Moscow and the Tartars. The Russian victory over the Tartars on the Kulikovo plain, it will be remembered, had no direct influence upon Russo-Tartar relations, although with the passing of years the legend that had grown around the exploits of Dimitry Donskoy added to the prestige of his descendants. The Tartar invasion of 1382 restored the relations between Moscow and the Golden Horde to very much the same basis as before the Kulikovo victory, but that invasion was fol-lowed by a conflict between Moscow and Riazan. This conflict, in which Moscow had the upper hand, was ended in 1385 by an agree-ment similar to the one signed by Tver ten years earlier. The fact that Dimitry succeeded in inducing Tver to break its allegiance to Lithuania and in strengthening the ties between Moscow, on the one side, and Tver, Nizhni-Novgorod, and Riazan, on the other, would seem to indicate that the authority of the grand-ducal throne had been en-hanced. The events of the following years, however, demonstrate that Dimitry's success was largely illusory.

The lack of unity among the Russian princes displayed during the struggle with the Tartars in the early eighties had significant reper-cussions on the position of Moscow. In spite of their sworn agreements with Moscow, Riazan, Nizhni-Novgorod, Novgorod the Great, and Tver resumed direct negotiations both with Lithuania and with the Tartars. Michael of Tver made a new bid for the Vladimir grand-ducal throne in violation of the terms of the agreement of 1375. Vasili I of Moscow (1389–1425) succeeded his father and was confirmed in office by the khan, while the Tartars continued, as in the past, to be one of the chief pillars of Moscow's precarious supremacy. One of the first important steps of Vasili was the acquisition by pur-chase of the khan's *yarlyk*, which gave him direct control over Nizhni-Novgorod, Gorodets, and several minor principalities along Russia's eastern and southeastern frontier.

Internal dissensions in the Golden Horde at the end of the fourteenth century temporarily weakened Moscow's dependence on the Tartars. Vasili drew closer to Lithuania, and in 1391 married the daughter of Vitovt, grand duke of Lithuania in 1392–1430, and a defender of his country's independence against impending assimilation by Poland. The Russian princes and boyars in the lands under Lithuanian rule were divided in their sympathies. On the one hand, they gravitated towards Moscow, with which they were united by bonds of a common language, culture, and religion; on the other, their ties with Lithuania and the western territories were both numerous and strong, and they favored Vitovt's endeavor to resist the encroachment of Poland. The influence of Lithuania in Novgorod, as well as Novgorod's independence from Moscow, was increased. Vitovt, who was under the nominal suzerainty of the Polish king Yagailo, harbored vast plans for a crusade against the Tartars. His schemes came to nought, and his army was defeated by the khan on the river Vorskla in the summer of 1399. This defeat of Vitovt, his aggressive policies in Novgorod, the annexation of Smolensk (1404), and the suspicious hospitality offered by Vitovt to the former khan Tokhtamysh, who took refuge in Lithuania after his defeat by Tamerlan, were among the causes that brought about the revision of Vasili's Lithuanian policy. Vitovt no longer appeared to be a desirable ally against the Tartars. Once more Vasili sought the support of the Golden Horde, and in 1406 the Tartar troops were his allies in a war with Lithuania. This reversal of Vasili's attitude did not, however, prevent the repeated invasion of his realm by the Tartars in the following years.

The reign of Vasili I was a period of severe trial for northeastern Russia. The grand duke, hampered by the inadequacy of the means at his disposal and continually vacillating between different policies and alliances, exercised only the slightest control over the nation's destinies. In the second decade of the fifteenth century Vasili succeeded, it is true, in consolidating his rule over Nizhni-Novgorod. On the other hand, his hold over Riazan was notoriously weak. Novgorod the Great displayed much independence, especially in its relations with Lithuania, Sweden, Pskov, and the Teutonic knights. Tver, which achieved internal unification in the first quarter of the fifteenth century, had also largely emancipated itself from Moscow. The later years of Vasili's reign brought about a new *rapprochement* with Lithuania, and in his testament he put his widow and son under the protection of Vitovt.

The position of Moscow was further weakened by the death in 1378 of Metropolitan Alexis, supporter of Russia's unification. His successor, Cyprian, a Bulgarian and a former metropolitan of Kiev and Lithuania, became the center of a violent conflict between Moscow and Constantinople, a conflict that lasted for ten years. When Cyprian was finally installed in Moscow, he showed no desire to continue the policies of his predecessor. He considered his office, not as a mere subsidiary to that of the Moscow grand duke, but as an independent organ of the eastern Church. On many important questions his attitude was far from being identical with that of Vasili. He carefully avoided giving offense to Lithuania and was even not averse to the idea of a union between the eastern and western Churches. When he died in 1406 he was succeeded by a Greek, Photius, who, like his predecessor, had to sustain a long struggle for unified ecclesiastical control over the whole of Russia, including the lands under Lithuanian rule. Again, like his predecessor, Photius kept away from political complications and endeavored to maintain the independence of the Church from the state.

The crisis experienced by the authority of Moscow at the end of the fourteenth century and in the first half of the fifteenth was not due entirely to external factors. The political structure of the grand duchy was itself a source of grievous complications. It rested, as we have seen, on the shifting foundation of two ancient principles of customary law: (1) the traditional "seniority" of the grand dukes, which included the command of all the armed forces and the control of the financial administration in such matters as the collection of the Tartar tribute; and (2) the "patrimonial" rights of descendants in the principality held by their father. The testament of Dimitry Donskoy extended the application of the latter principle to the formerly indivisible territory of the grand duchy of Vladimir, thus creating the danger of its breaking up into small quasi-independent political units. The forcible imposition of the "seniority" of the Moscow grand dukes upon the lands outside their traditional patriarchal jurisdiction provoked from the local princes resistance which all but destroyed the recognition of the community of Russia's interests that formed the very essence of this complex, contradictory, and archaic system. The introduction by Dimitry of a new source of princely territorial right—grand-ducal grants —offered vast possibilities for a further dismemberment of the country. The death of Dimitry was followed by much disagreement among the members of his house, and their conflicting claims were usually settled by exchange and redistribution of territories. In this confused process the former not too clear idea of the patriarchal family as the basis of the political system tended to disappear altogether. It was replaced by bargaining among the parties officially sanctioned by the grand-ducal grants. There was a loosening of the ancient bonds which kept together the patriarchal princely family; the authority of the local "senior" prince, overshadowed by the much stronger authority of the Moscow grand duke, lost its former significance. The consequence was that the once sovereign principalities became divided into mere landed estates, held in service tenure by their princely owners. Eventually they were merged in the mass of the boyar landowners.

There are indications of considerable friction between Vasili I and two of his brothers, Yuri and Constantine. After Vasili's death Yuri was the senior member of the dynasty. As such, he considered himself entitled to the throne of the grand duchy of Vladimir. Under the terms of the testament of Dimitry Donskoy, however, the grand duchy was made subject to the application of the principle of "patrimonial" succession. The son of Vasili I, Vasili II (1425–1462), accordingly, became his father's successor. In actual fact Moscow and not Vladimir was the capital of the country. Since the days of Ivan I it had been the residence of the grand dukes of "All Russia" and the see of the metropolitan. In the fifteenth century the severance of Moscow from the "All Russian" grand-ducal throne was outside the realm of possibility. According to the ancient principle of "patrimonial" succession, Vasili II was entitled to Moscow. But Yuri was not prepared to surrender his claims derived from the equally ancient right of dynastic "seniority." The two basic principles of Russian customary law, which thus found themselves in conflict, were finally wiped out in the bloody feud that raged during the first twenty-five years of Vasili II's reign.

Vasili II, who ascended the throne as a boy in his teens, ruled first under the guardianship of Metropolitan Photius and the boyars. Yuri, until his death in 1434, then his son Vasili, until he was blinded by Vasili II two years after Yuri's death, and finally Yuri's son Dimitry Shemiaka, until his death by poisoning in 1453, carried on a savage struggle for the possession of Moscow. I have already related the chief events of this fratricidal war and the part played in it by the Tartars.[3] In the course of this struggle the political influence of Moscow was practically destroyed. Vitovt resumed in 1426 and again in 1428 his

[3] See pp. 62, 67.

advance on Novgorod and Pskov, while Novgorod, Riazan, and Tver took advantage of the confusion to recover much of their former independence from Moscow. The very gravity of the situation rallied the Church and the boyars under Vasili's banner. The Tartar supporters, who came to Moscow with Vasili after his capture in 1445 and whose presence was partly responsible for the short-lived triumph of Dimitry Shemiaka, remained faithful to Vasili in adversity. The joint effort of these elements proved sufficient to overthrow Shemiaka's unpopular rule. His armies suffered a severe reverse in 1450, and Vasili II, blinded but not broken, returned to Moscow.

THE MUSCOVITE STATE

The short period of twelve years between Dimitry Shemiaka's defeat and Vasili's death in 1462 stands out as a definite landmark in the history of the Russian Middle Ages. It brought to a close an era dominated by the patriarchal structure of the princely family, with its inherent and insoluble contradictions. Vasili II, with the same grim and ruthless determination that had characterized his struggle against his uncle Yuri and his cousins Vasili and Dimitry Shemiaka, proceeded with the liquidation of a political system, the absurdity of which had been more than proved by past history and had been forcibly impressed upon him by bitter personal experience. The process of liquidation was as bloody and harsh as the events that led to it. Its consequences—the birth of a national Russian state under the stern rule of Moscow—were of momentous importance to Russia and to the world at large. This was not a romantic and roseate picture, like the one so skillfully drawn by Kliuchevsky. But Nature itself has ordained that the act of birth is neither aesthetic nor pleasing.

Vasili's purpose was the concentration in his own hands and in those of his descendants of the scattered bits of political power unevenly distributed among the many suzerains of Russian principalities, large and small. The successful accomplishment of this task laid a firm foundation on which developed the autocracy of the Muscovite tsars. The methods were those of Vasili's own time and of the social milieu in which he was brought up. There was, however, one important innovation. Vasili was the first to make an extensive use of a hired Tartar force, on which he leaned heavily in his policy of liquidation. With somewhat terrifying impartiality, the blows of the grand duke fell upon the princes who supported Dimitry Shemiaka, for instance, the prince of Mozhaisk and some of the princes of Suzdal, and those who faithfully served his own cause, such as Vasili, prince of Serpukhov. The chroniclers are suspiciously reticent about the details of the liquidation of the Shemiaka affair, and only a few passages have escaped the vigilance of the Muscovite censors. These, nevertheless, speak in no uncertain terms of the feeling of bewilderment and horror experienced by the boyars, merchants, priests, and common people at the sight of the savage cruelty displayed by Vasili II in dealing alike with his former and with his potential enemies. "No such things have ever been heard of or seen," one chronicler added, although it seems difficult to imagine tortures and savagery to which the Russians had not become accustomed during the course of the preceding centuries. Whatever the methods, the net result was that Vasili achieved his purpose and established himself as the undisputed master of the territories of the grand duchies of Vladimir and Moscow. He then turned to the other Russian lands. In 1456 a large Muscovite army invaded Novgorod in retribution for its disobedience and to punish it for harboring traitors. Although Novgorod hastened to make peace by paying a heavy indemnity and by extending the grand-ducal powers in the administration of its internal affairs, and although both Novgorod and Pskov still retained many of their "ancient liberties," they were incorporated within the Muscovite state. The dying grand duke of Riazan, hard pressed by Lithuania, simplified Moscow's task by putting his young son under Vasili's protection. Riazan continued to rank as a grand duchy but became for all practical purposes a dependency of Moscow. Of the political formations of northeastern Russia, Tver alone remained for a while on a footing of equality with its threatening neighbor. In an agreement concluded by Vasili and Boris of Tver, the latter acknowledged "the grand-ducal throne, Moscow and Novgorod the Great," as the "patrimony" of Vasili and his issue and pledged Tver's support against the Tartars, Poles, Lithuanians, and Germans. This was no mean success since Tver had until shortly before that time been under the strong influence of Lithuania. It will also be remembered that during the last ten years of his reign Vasili was practically independent from the Golden Horde and that the Tartar kingdom of Kasimov created by Vasili proved useful in defending the eastern frontier.

Such was the truly remarkable revival of Moscow's political authority. It is reasonably certain that Vasili's policy could not have succeeded had not the way been thoroughly prepared by the earlier course of

Russia's history. Yet there was no clear breach with the past. The wide powers consolidated in the hands of the grand duke of Moscow were not fully protected against the possibility of future dismemberment by the terms of Vasili's testament, and much remained to be done in this direction. That testament has been aptly described as a typical document of the period of transition. Vasili, who did not hesitate to break away from secular tradition in his practical policies, had neither the vision nor the ability to free the internal organization of the grand duchy of Moscow from the obsolete dogma of the patriarchal family. His testament adhered strictly to the sacrosanct phraseology and ancient formulas used by his predecessors. He entrusted his widow and sons to the protection of Casimir, king of Poland and grand duke of Lithuania, assigned definite territorial shares to each of his five sons, and followed in his other testamentary dispositions the pattern set by Ivan I and Dimitry Donskoy. But there was new wine in the old bottles. Ivan III, Vasili's eldest son, received as his "patrimony" the grand duchy, whose territory was defined in a manner that completely disregarded the former rigid delimitation between the grand duchy of Vladimir and the share of the "senior" Moscow prince. The two were now merged into a single domain, the hereditary property of the Moscow grand duke. The Muscovite state, as a territorial unit, had come into existence.

Vasili, inspired probably by Byzantine examples, enhanced the position of his eldest son and heir by making him—a boy in his teens —his co-ruler. But the internal structure of the grand duchy was still entangled in the tenets of the old concept of the patriarchal family. Vasili did not openly attempt to do away with it. His aim was merely the retention by his issue of the succession to "the grand-ducal throne, Moscow and Novgorod the Great." I have pointed out that the recognition of this claim was specifically written into his agreement with Tver. Similar provisions were made in agreements with other lands. In spite of the possibility of future dismemberment, which was not eliminated by Vasili, he had built a solid foundation for the edifice of Moscow autocracy which Ivan III proceeded to erect along the lines laid down by his father.

SOCIAL AND ECONOMIC CONDITIONS

The consolidation of political power in the hands of the grand dukes of Moscow had its fitting counterpart in the evolution of the social structure, as far as the latter process can be reconstructed from the fragmentary and controversial evidence scattered through the ancient documents. It will be remembered that towards the end of the Kievan period the principal division of the population was into free men and slaves, with a presumably fairly large group of people occupying a somewhat uncertain and precarious position in the borderland between freedom and slavery. The chief economic development towards the end of the Kievan era was the decline of the commercial cities and the acquisition of landed estates by the princes, the Church, and the boyars. These trends continued in the thirteenth to fifteenth centuries; but under the pressure of new conditions they assumed a character different from that of the past.

The original source of landownership was, presumably, occupation and purchase. The land thus acquired became the unrestricted property of its owners, who had complete freedom of enjoyment and could dispose of it as they pleased. Such estates were known as *votchina*, and carried no obligations to the state except the payment of taxes. The owners frequently obtained from the princes special privileges, including the right to administer justice among the people living on their land. Since the middle of the fifteenth century these "manorial" courts had no jurisdiction over the more serious criminal offenses—larceny (only if the accused was caught in the act), robbery, and murder. The privileges also extended to the field of taxation. The owner of an estate might be given the right to collect the taxes and deliver them to the appropriate government office, thus relieving the tenants on his estate of the onerous and vexatious duty of dealing directly with the tax officials. This privilege might include the consolidation of the taxes in a payment known as *obrok*, which offered considerable advantages, since taxes were many and displayed a tendency to increase at a distressing rate. Finally, the estate might be freed from some or all of the taxes and services, usually for a specified period of time. The privileges granted were stated in letters patent issued by the prince to the owner of an estate. It is believed that this was an ancient and common practice, although it can be traced definitely only to the first half of the fourteenth century. Among the chief beneficiaries were the Church and the boyars, but there are indications that letters patent conferring privileges were also issued to landowners of modest means and of humble social standing (Sergeevich).

It remains uncertain when grants by the princes became a source of landownership, a source the importance of which rapidly increased. In the thirteenth and fourteenth centuries land was still plentiful, but the central authority was too weak and helpless to organize colonization. The princes were vitally interested in the economic development of the country. Private owners and monasteries to whom estates were granted converted waste land into agricultural settlements and thus created new sources of revenue for the hard-pressed princely treasuries. Land, however, was not always granted unconditionally, as a *votchina*. There developed another, conditional, form of tenure later known as *pomestie*, or service tenure. The enjoyment of the estates that fell in this category was granted on condition that the tenant and his heirs should perform certain duties, usually military service. The granting of a *pomestie*, like that of a *votchina*, might be accompanied by the conferring of privileges with regard to taxation and administration of justice. The exact origin of this form of tenure is unknown, but it is believed (Diakonov) that it grew out of a regime that had developed on the estates owned by the princes. Such estates were cultivated and administered not only by slaves but also by free men. The latter, like the members of the old *druzhina*, either received maintenance from the prince or were given, in return for their services, the use of a specified area of land. With the strengthening of some of the princely dynasties and the expansion of their landholdings, employment by the princes became a desirable profession which attracted even members of the upper class, the boyars. Reference to the junior members of this group (*deti boyarskiia*) employed under the *dvorskii*, manager of the princely estates, is found as early in the records as the thirteenth century. The first instance of the granting of an estate in service tenure to a person presumably not employed under the *dvorskii* appears in the testament of Ivan I of Moscow (1341), but it is believed that the practice was in existence long before that date. It received wide application in the second half of the fifteenth century and became the general rule in the sixteenth, when the once sharp line dividing the *votchina* from the *pomestie* disappeared and government service became compulsory for all landlords.

Another important method of rewarding deserving supporters and winning new ones was the appointment by the princes of their trusted boyars as administrators of cities and provinces. This practice, known as *kormlenie* ("feeding") and familiar in Kievan Russia, was widely used in the fourteenth century. The appointee, an officer of the central government, performed the functions of a governor, and administered justice. For the exercise of these duties he retained for his private use judicial fees, fines, and other revenue that would normally have gone to the treasury. The nature of the revenue to which the appointee was entitled was usually defined in the letters patent issued to him. Sometimes he received, not the whole, but only a part, of the revenue he collected. The appointment was generally made for a short time, a year or more, but there were cases when the privilege, conferred not only on the holder of the office, but also on his issue, became hereditary (Sergeevich). These cases, however, were exceptions. The avowed purpose of *kormlenie* was to provide the appointee with the means of accumulating a comfortable fortune so that he might retire to his estates and make room for other servants of the prince or grand duke. Although the zeal displayed by some of the holders of *kormlenie* imposed no small burden upon the people over whose destinies they presided, the practice was continued in the fifteenth and sixteenth centuries and survived in the seventeenth, although it had by then become less common.

There was considerable stratification in the upper class of the free population. This group consisted of landowners, loosely known as boyars, who exploited their estates by employing servile or semi-servile labor. It is necessary, even if it may seem redundant, to insist on the fact that the basic and most precious privilege of the freeman is his freedom. The economic independence of the boyars rested on their vast landholdings, while their personal independence was safeguarded by the ancient rule inherited from the old *druzhina*, according to which rule the boyars were under no obligation to serve the prince within whose domain they resided and owned estates. The boyars entered the service of a prince, usually for army duty, but they were free to choose their master. The agreement between a prince and a boyar could always be denounced in favor of service with another prince. The interprincely agreements invariably safeguarded this ancient privilege by providing immunity for the estates owned by any boyars who broke their agreement with the local prince to enter the service of another ruler. The scattering of boyar estates through the various principalities, which were frequently at war, presented obvious disadvantages from the point of view of the princes. Some of the interprincely agreements contained provisions prohibiting the acquisition of estates by the princes and their boyars within the territory of the other contracting party. But the right of the boyars to enter the service of whatever prince they preferred was not openly challenged, much as the princes disliked it. The landed aristocracy rightly cherished this privilege as the only real guaranty of its independence, and boyars seldom hesitated to desert their master and enter the service of even his worst enemy at the very time when their assistance was particularly needed.

The princes, since they were too weak and too dependent on the support of boyars to withdraw openly the distasteful privilege, accepted it in theory, although they often prevented its exercise. They were, of course, always glad to receive wealthy and influential boyars from the enemy camp, while they showed some tolerance in the case of their own boyars who deserted them in favor of an allied prince. But the solemn promises of immunity were not infrequently forgotten in the case of those boyars who went over to the enemy. The estates of such boyars were burdened with ruinous taxes, plundered, or confiscated. The Moscow grand dukes displayed particular severity in dealing with the boyars whose activities, though legally unimpeachable, they considered as treasonable. This policy found much support from the pulpit. It will be remembered that Metropolitan Alexis enunciated the doctrine that made a breach of allegiance to the Grand Duke Dimitry of Moscow a crime against the Church. With the growth of the authority of Moscow the persecution of the departing boyars became more frequent and more ruthless. Under these conditions the right of free service could not be expected to survive very long.

The exercise of the privilege of free service was subject to few legal restrictions. In the fourteenth century, however, Novgorod ordered the confiscation of the estates of the boyars who left its service. The Grand Duke Vasili II of Moscow made similar provisions in his agreements with his uncle Prince Yuri, with Tver and Lithuania, but these provisions applied merely to the estates owned by former sovereign princes who had entered the service of Moscow. The restriction did not affect the holdings of the boyars. Vasili's action has been attributed to a desire to strengthen his control over the vast estates belonging to the former sovereign princes (Diakonov). The legal fiction of free service was maintained until 1531, when, dressed in the traditional phraseology, it appeared in the last interprincely agreement. After the second half of the fifteenth century, however, little opportunity was left for the exercise of the ancient right, and it finally disappeared with the consolidation of the power of Moscow. The privilege of free service was never formally abolished; it simply went out of existence. In the sixteenth century compulsory service was extended to all the landlords. The change was of immense significance: the members of the former independent landed aristocracy, free to choose their masters and to change them at will, had been converted into the servants of the Muscovite state.

The other groups of the free population suffered a fate not unlike that of the boyars. The rebellious and democratic institution of the *veche*, or popular assembly, which was already on the decline in the second half of the twelfth century, ceased to exist under the Mongol domination. Its fate was sealed by the dwindling of foreign trade and by the interference of the Golden Horde in the domestic affairs of its Russian vassals. Trade, of course, continued and was carried on by merchants drawn from every social class, from the boyars to the slaves, but, with the exception of Novgorod, the corporate organizations of merchants did not develop until the sixteenth century. There were artisans also, but next to nothing is known about them. Many of the so-called cities, moreover, were still merely military outposts or rural settlements.

By far the largest group of freemen were the peasants, presumably once independent farmers, who eventually came to live as tenants on the land owned by the princes, the Church, and the boyars. The nature of this evolution, however, is obscure. There is evidence that in a number of instances the powerful ecclesiastical and secular landlords annexed outright the land of their weaker neighbors. A more general reason was probably the weakness of the central government and its inability to offer sufficient protection to the small landowners. The privileges conferred upon the Church and boyar estates by the princes, especially in matters of taxation, created a real inducement for the small farmers to exchange their precarious independence for the protection of a powerful local lord. This inducement must have acquired added importance under the Mongol domination with its exorbitant tributes, a burden that necessarily rested largely on the shoulders of the farmers. The landlords were vitally interested in colonizing their estates, for in those days land was abundant and labor relatively scarce. Slavery, it is believed, never played a prominent part in the exploitation of landed estates, especially since its chief source—prisoners of war—had disappeared after the conquest of the national territory had been completed. Moreover, large estates frequently consisted of scattered strips that did not lend themselves to direct exploitation by the owner. Tenancy, of course, had many disadvantages, since the former independent farmer had to give a part of his time or surrender a part of his produce to the landlord. Nevertheless, under this system the farmer stood a better chance of having something left for himself and his family than he did when confronted with the rapacious officers of the treasury. It is generally accepted that in the fourteenth century tenant farming was much more common than was independent small farming.

The economic interests of the tenant were safeguarded in the earlier days by the fact that he was a freeman, that is, he enjoyed the unrestricted right of leaving the landlord on whose land he was working and moving to another place. The relations between the tenant and the landlord were regulated by an agreement which specified the reciprocal duties of the contracting parties; namely, the exact area of land to which the tenant was entitled and the services and payments he was to make to the landlord. At the expiration of the term of the contract, and sometimes even earlier, the tenant was free to move away. The landlord had the corresponding right to dismiss his tenant. It is easy to overrate the importance of the tenant's personal freedom, since a farmer, especially a well-to-do farmer, was not likely to abandon his establishment and run away. The landlords, one may surmise, were not oblivious of the fact, and must have exploited it to their own advantage. On the other hand, the shortage of labor at that time should not be completely disregarded. The gradual curtailment of the right of the tenants to give up their tenancy is in itself a revealing evidence that the safeguard offered by the right to leave was not entirely ineffective. In many essential respects the relationship between the tenants and the landlords was similar to that between the boyars and the princes, and it suffered a like fate.

The object of the first legal restrictions was not to deprive the free tenants of their right to leave, but to limit the opportunities for the exercise of this right. Every prince was anxious to prevent his taxpaying population from escaping the reach of his fiscal officers. The Moscow grand dukes, therefore, concluded agreements with other princes which mutually bound them not to accept free peasants leaving the domain of the contracting parties. In the letters patent conferring privileges or granting land, the grand dukes of Moscow sometimes included provisions which prohibited the beneficiaries from settling on their land free tenants coming from the grand-ducal estates. These restrictions, it will be noted, did not directly affect the freedom of the tenant, but, by imposing definite limitations on the freedom of the landlords themselves, reduced the tenant's opportunity of finding a new landlord. This was merely the first step. The free tenants traditionally enjoyed the right to change their landlords at any time of the year. In the middle of the fifteenth century the Moscow grand dukes and some of the local princes decreed that the tenants living on specified estates belonging to certain monasteries should not be permitted to leave except during the fortnight preceding and the fortnight following Saint George's day (November 26). While this was a purely local measure, it was indicative of the general trend, and its general application in the sixteenth century played an important part in the establishment of serfdom. Moreover, in 1455–1462 Vasili II of Moscow prohibited the free tenants living on certain monastic estates from abandoning their tenancy. No reason for the drastic decision was given.

Even more significant than legal restrictions were the financial and economic ties between the landlord and his free tenants. The latter were often in need of funds, and their landlords, both secular and ecclesiastical, were usually willing to come to their assistance. Indeed, funds were essential to start a new establishment, with the success of which both the tenants and the landlords were concerned. Such loans paid handsome interest and created an extra bond between the tenant and the landlord. It appears that in the earlier days the existence of an outstanding debt did not authorize the landlord to prevent the tenant from leaving, although the creditor retained his claim and could enforce it through the courts. The efficacy of this safeguard is open to doubt since the debtor was seldom in a position to repay the loan and the bankrupt debtor was turned over to the creditor, for whom he had to work until the debt was repaid, which in practice meant life slavery. As early, perhaps, as the thirteenth century, the debtor-creditor relationship became an important source leading to the *de facto* enslavement of people who were *de jure* free. In the second half of the fifteenth century the grand duke of Moscow decreed that the tenants of a certain ecclesiastical estate should not be permitted to leave until they had repaid the money they owed their landlord. It is likely that there were other similar cases, the records of which have not been preserved. Although this measure was local, it was an ominous precursor of the impending doom of the free peasantry.

"RUSSIAN FEUDALISM"

It has been frequently advanced by both Marxian and non-Marxian historians that medieval Russia was living under feudalism. There are many aspects of the political, economic, and social relationships of this period that are closely reminiscent of those of feudal Europe: the weakness of the central government, the prevalence of large estates, the existence of a hierarchy among the landlords, the delegation to them of judicial and fiscal powers, the contractual nature of the services of the boyars and of the free tenants. It is argued, on the other hand, that the element of hereditariness essential in feudal institutions was generally absent in Russia and that some of the most important offices, such as *kormlenie*, were held—with but rare exceptions—for only a brief period. Privileges in the matter of taxation were also usually granted to secular landlords for a specified term of years. The absence of definitely crystallized feudal institutions in Russia is sometimes conceded by even the Marxian historians (Liashchenko). The answer to the question whether Russia had a feudal system depends on whether one chooses to put the chief emphasis on the elements of similarity or of difference. Surely the latter cannot be entirely disregarded. To describe the Russian structure of the pre-Muscovite era as "Russian feudalism" may give some satisfaction to the pedantic minds that firmly believe in the universality of historical and sociological schemes. Outside this limited objective "Russian feudalism" serves no useful purpose, for it is merely another way of saying that the situation in Russia was different from that in western Europe. It is only fair to observe, however, that in the feudal organization of the various western European countries there was no uniformity. In the case of Russia the differences seem to have been so pronounced and fundamental as to make use of the term "feudalism" a source of confusion rather than of enlightenment.

At the end of the reign of Vasili II (1462) the evolution of Russia's political, social, and economic structure was entering a new stage. The survivals of the past were many. Moscow had not yet definitely emancipated itself from the Mongols, and the political unification was still incomplete. Both the boyars and the peasantry continued to enjoy *de jure* the ancient right of choosing their own masters. The secular tradition of local independence had not yet surrendered to the policy of centralization enforced by Moscow. Nevertheless, it seems reasonably clear that the Muscovite absolutism was already born. It needed merely time and favorable conditions to grow to manhood.

CHAPTER V

EXPERIMENT IN DEMOCRACY

Novgorod and Pskov

---------------------------- ❋ ----------------------------

SURVIVAL OF DEMOCRATIC INSTITUTIONS

The decline of the influence of the *veche* at the end of the twelfth century and its final eclipse under the Tartar rule was one of the factors that contributed to the rise of Muscovite absolutism. Democracy, however crude and imperfect, had been replaced over the entire territory of Kievan Russia and beyond by no less crude and ruthless authoritarian governments. To this movement there was, however, one exception: Novgorod the Great retained its popular institutions until the end of the fifteenth century. The reason for the preservation of the *veche* in Novgorod was the absence there of the conditions that precipitated its downfall in other parts of the land.

The origins of Novgorod are lost in the darkness of the ages. Situated within easy reach of the Gulf of Finland, on the Volkhov, which formed a part of the ancient trade route linking the Baltic Sea with Byzantium and the Arabic east, Novgorod was presumably one of the earliest military and trading outposts established by the Varangians and the Slavic merchant princes at the dawn of Russia's history. It was the people of Novgorod who, according to the Chronicle, invited Riurik to be their ruler. Novgorod's geographical position explains many of the peculiarities of its subsequent development. Protected by its remoteness from the southern steppes, it escaped the fate of Kiev and other cities and was spared the costly and painful experience of frequent invasions by the Patzinacs, the Cumans, and the Tartars. The powerful enemies against whom Novgorod had to fight did not appear until later: the Teutonic knights at the beginning of the thirteenth century, and the grand duchy of Lithuania in the second half of the same century. Possibly even more fortunate was the fact that Novgorod maintained as early as the twelfth century animated trade relations with Gotland and later became the Russian outpost of the Hanseatic League. Trade with Germany replaced the former commercial intercourse with the Arabs and the Greeks at the very time when the latter commerce was going through a severe crisis from which it never recovered. Novgorod's international trade became one of the chief interests of its upper class, and, because of the relative security that it enjoyed until the end of the thirteenth century, this trade contributed to the preservation of the institutions of popular government. Commercial interests also determined in large measure the relations between Novgorod and the other Russian principalities, and were behind the territorial expansion of Novgorod, presumably begun in the eleventh century or perhaps earlier. This expansion was generally carried on by armed bands of traders who ventured farther and farther north and east, conquering the Finnish tribes, from whom they exacted furs and other products of the forest—the principal articles of Novgorod's export trade. The Novgorod government sanctioned these acquisitions and in the thirteenth century exercised a somewhat vague jurisdiction over a vast territory which comprised the whole northern part of European Russia, including the shores of the White Sea and the upper Volga, and a region beyond the Ural Mountains.

THE GERMAN TRADE

Although information regarding the relations between Novgorod and the Germanic countries during the earlier period of its history is slight, there is some documentary evidence to be found in the records of the twelfth century. The chief sources for a study of trade between Germany and Novgorod are the agreements between that city and the associations of German merchants. The first of these agreements was concluded towards the end of the twelfth century with the German merchants of Wisby, on the Island of Gotland. Although Wisby continued to play a part in the commerce of Novgorod even before the formation of the Hanseatic League, leadership had passed into the hands of Lübeck. Still later, at the end of the fourteenth and during the fifteenth century, some of the eastern German cities—Dorpat, Reval, and Riga—had become dominant.

The German merchants who came to Novgorod formed a closed

corporation, organized along the lines of a medieval guild. The rules governing the internal life of the corporation were embodied in charters known as *skra*. The earliest available charter was drawn up in the thirteenth century, but there is evidence that there had been a guild of foreign merchants in Novgorod in the middle of the twelfth century. Authorities differ, however, as to whether this was a German guild or a guild controlled by the native merchants of Gotland. The preponderance of the Germans in the commerce of Novgorod during the subsequent period is generally admitted. The charters and agreements give a comprehensive picture of the position of the German merchants in Novgorod and of their relations with local traders and authorities. The activities of foreign merchants were strictly limited. They were permitted to reside only within the German Settlement, an autonomous corporation governed by elected officials headed by an alderman. The alderman had wide powers over the visiting German merchants and exercised jurisdiction over any disputes that might arise among them. Litigations between foreigners and Russians were tried by a mixed tribunal consisting of Novgorod officials and representatives of the Germans. The Germans were exempted from arrest, a valuable privilege which, however, was more honored in breach than in observance. There were elaborate provisions for the protection of the German Settlement and of the property of the merchants. The church attached to the Settlement was the object of detailed regulations rather in regard to its use as a warehouse for merchandise than as a place of worship. The Germans were specifically prohibited from trading with the Russians in the church, an edifice usually filled with valuable cargoes, with barrels of wine occasionally placed around the altar. The German priest, in addition to his ecclesiastical duties, had to attend to less exalted matters, such as the business correspondence of the members of the guild, many of whom were illiterate. The Germans were allowed to remain in Novgorod only during the time required to dispose of their wares, and were not to settle there indefinitely. They were forbidden to bring merchandise valued at more than one thousand silver marks, a rule which was often disregarded. Although the regulations prescribed a barter exchange of goods between the Russian and the German traders, cash transactions were by no means unknown. Credit transactions, however, were specifically prohibited and the non-observance of this provision was the source of much friction. A similar interdict was placed on the formation of partnerships between Germans and Russians and on the sale by the Germans of Russian goods on a commission basis. The German merchants were not permitted to deal with other foreigners—Poles, Lithuanians—except through the intermediary of a native trader. It is believed that foreigners were excluded from the retail trade (Kulisher) although some historians deny the existence of the restriction (Nikitsky). It remains uncertain whether the Germans enjoyed the right to carry on their commercial activities within the territory of Novgorod outside the city itself. Such a privilege would necessarily have led to competition with the Novgorod merchants by making it possible for foreigners to exchange their wares directly for local products. It is highly unlikely—and the evidence to the contrary is inconclusive—that the Novgorod merchant aristocracy was induced to give up its monopolistic position as the sole intermediary between the domestic and the foreign markets.

Novgorod's participation in western trade was somewhat one-sided, that is, the Russian city did not take an active part in international commerce. Its merchants seldom went abroad, although they visited the near-by Baltic trading centers of Dorpat, Riga and Reval. The absence of a seagoing fleet handicapped the Novgorod traders and effectively prevented them from expanding the sphere of their operations, for Novgorod, a continental city, was unable to avail itself of the many economic advantages enjoyed by a seaport. The resulting loss was only partially offset by the exclusive right reserved to the Novgorod boatmen to transport foreign goods on the Volkhov. At the mouth of the river incoming cargoes were trans-shipped from German to Russian boats which the Russians piloted down the Volkhov, an arrangement that may have had some justification in the fact that the current of the stream was cut by rapids with which the natives were more familiar than were the Germans. The profits made on this monopoly, to which the Germans unsuccessfully objected, could not have been great. Since the Germans resided within the German Settlement, the good people of Novgorod suffered further from the loss of such legitimate earnings as are derived from the renting of lodgings and warehouses, innkeeping, and the like.

Novgorod's western trade was large and was the chief source of the city's wealth. The intercourse with the Germans did not always proceed smoothly, in spite of elaborate rules and numerous agreements. The constant violation of these provisions by both parties led to much mutual recrimination and sometimes to violent conflicts. The principal articles of Russian exports were furs and wax, while imports consisted chiefly of woolens, but also included wine, beer, salt, sweets, metal goods, linen, needles, thread, yarn, and grain. The bulk of the exported furs and wax came from Novgorod's own vast domain, but the city also acted as intermediary in the trade between Germany and the adjoining Russian territories. There is evidence that in the thirteenth and fourteenth centuries Novgorod maintained commercial relations with Tver and Suzdal. The upper classes of Novgorod society —the prince, the boyars, and the higher clergy, including the archbishop—were actively engaged in trading side by side with the merchants. After 1270, however, the prince was compelled to accept an important restriction: all his commercial dealings with the Germans were to be carried on through the intermediation of a representative of Novgorod.

In the thirteenth to fifteenth centuries German trade with Russia was no longer exclusively in the hands of Novgorod. The German merchants of Riga were also using the trade route of the Western Dvina, and maintained warehouses in Polotsk, Vitebsk, and Smolensk. However, this trade never reached the importance of that of Novgorod, and was, moreover, centered in cities which for most of this period remained under the rule of Lithuania.

THE PRINCE AND THE VECHE

The early political history of Novgorod, so far as it can be ascertained, was in no way different from that of the other Russian lands. Novgorod paid tribute to the grand duke of Kiev and was governed by a prince, usually a near relative of the grand duke, assisted by a *possadnik* over whose appointment the *veche* had no control. The *veche*, here as elsewhere, took an active part in the conduct of public affairs but enjoyed no special powers. In the twelfth century the situation had changed. It will be recalled that by that time the various principalities into which Russia was divided obtained their own dynasties. This, however, was not the case in Novgorod, which continued to be a dependency of Kiev and to receive its prince through appointment by the grand duke. With the fall of Kiev, Novgorod transferred its allegiance to Vladimir and, with the latter's decline, to Moscow. At times, however, Novgorod broke away from its somewhat nominal suzerain and invited princes from dynasties which had been in conflict with its former ruler. The control of Novgorod appeared to be a necessary condition of the supremacy of the grand-ducal throne. The princes of Suzdal-Vladimir, beginning with Yuri Dolgoruky and Andrew Bogoliubsky, fought stubbornly for possession of the metropolis of northwestern Russia, and the Moscow grand dukes followed a similar policy. In spite of the fact that Novgorod was in frequent conflict with its Russian neighbors, there were vital interests which dictated a policy of cooperation with Vladimir-Moscow. Novgorod, whose trade routes were largely at the mercy of the latter, depended on the territories south and east of its frontier for its supply of grain, a weakness well known in Moscow and used occasionally as a weapon to bring it to terms. Novgorod needed leadership and assistance in its many military ventures—against the Finns, and later against the German knights, the Swedes, and the Lithuanians. Friendly relations with Vladimir-Moscow were also essential for the protection of the eastward movement of Novgorod's colonization, on which its export trade was largely dependent. All these considerations made imperative some arrangement with Vladimir and Moscow, arrangements which were not facilitated by the fact that Novgorod, in its internal organization, followed an independent course.

Although the *veche* in the twelfth century was rapidly losing ground throughout Russia, in Novgorod, on the contrary, it was steadily encroaching on the traditional powers of the prince. This was probably due not only to the growth of the urban community, for which the expansion of Novgorod's commerce was responsible, but also to the frequent changes of the Kiev-appointed princes and *possadnik*. After the death of Vladimir Monomakh (1125), the occupants of the Kievan throne succeeded one another at short intervals, and because each new grand duke sent his representative to Novgorod the tenure of office of the appointees was of but brief duration. This, combined with the general decline of Kiev's authority, strengthened the tendency towards autonomy. Presumably Novgorod during this period made considerable progress towards self-government. It was customary for the documents dealing with Novgorod's ancient liberties to refer to a charter granted to the city by Yaroslav of Kiev (1019–1054). Since the text of the charter has not been preserved, the extent of the privileges it conferred upon Novgorod has been the subject of learned conjectures. During the twelfth century the administrative powers were passing into the hands of elected officials. The first reference to a *possadnik* elected by the people of Novgorod occurs in the Chronicle of the year 1126. Election instead of appointment eventually became the rule for higher officials and applied not only to the officers of the administration, the *possadnik* and the *tysiatskii* (leader of the thousand), but also to the bishop. The latter was originally appointed by the metropolitan of Kiev, but beginning with 1156 the *veche* elected its own candidate, who was then consecrated by the metropolitan. This change of procedure was of extreme importance: the Novgorod administration, both secular and ecclesiastical, was put under the effective control of the local elements. It was no longer an agency of the prince in dealing with Novgorod but, on the contrary, an agency of the ruling group of Novgorod in dealing with the prince. The powers of the latter, therefore, suffered important curtailments.

The practice of defining by agreement the relations of the prince with the local *veche* was common in Kievan Russia. The little that is known of these agreements would seem to indicate that they dealt chiefly with the revenue to which the prince was entitled, and had for their object the safeguarding of the people from excessive exactions. In Novgorod the agreements with the princes introduced many more far-reaching restrictions. The earliest agreement available is dated 1265, but there are indications that some of the limitations on the powers once enjoyed by the prince were in effect before that date. The agreements, indeed, worked a fundamental change in the former relationship between the *veche* and the prince by transforming him into a constitutional ruler.

Although the prince remained the chief magistrate of Novgorod and the head of its administration, he could not exercise his judicial powers without the participation of the elected *possadnik*, nor could he hold court outside the territory of Novgorod. The appointment of the provincial administrators was made subject to the approval of the *possadnik*, and no elected official could be removed without a public trial. The revenue rights of the prince were made subject to meticulous regulations. He received the income from definite territories but he was to administer the outlying provinces by leasing them out to natives of Novgorod. Novgorod was anxious to prevent the prince from entering into direct personal contact with the people of its provinces, fearing that this might eventually lead to the severance of these territories. Even the rights of the prince to hunt, fish, and keep bees were carefully delimited and made subject to various restrictions. The prince, his family, and the boyars and servants who accompanied him were prohibited from holding mortgages or acquiring land within the principality of Novgorod. The Novgorod aristocracy was particularly anxious to safeguard its position with reference to its German trade. The prince therefore could not interfere with the German Settlement, was prohibited from dealing with the German merchants directly, and was compelled to use the services of a Novgorod intermediary.

The position of the prince in Novgorod offered a certain analogy with that of his predecessors, the Varangian rulers of the early city-states. He was primarily the hired leader of the Novgorod military forces, and his chief duty consisted in defending the country and in organizing its military expeditions. The separation between the prince and the broad currents of local affairs was emphasized by the fact that he did not reside in the city, but with his retinue occupied a castle or estate known as *Gorodishche*, outside the city limits.

SELF-GOVERNMENT

The structure of the Novgorod government was of great complexity. This may be traceable to the city's growth through the fusion of several once independent settlements. For military and policy purposes the city constituted a *tysiacha* (thousand); this unit was subdivided into *sotnia* (hundreds), a military organization that was to be found in other Russian towns. For administrative purposes Novgorod was divided into five *konets* (ends), each comprising two *sotnia*. These administrative subdivisions had their own elected *starosta* (elder) and their own *veche*. The *sotnia* was further subdivided into *ulitsa* (streets) which also elected their elders and enjoyed a degree of self-government. It is believed that each *konets* exercised independent control over certain provincial territories acquired, presumably, through conquest by its residents, but the evidence available on this question is admittedly inadequate.

Although the all-Novgorod *veche* was in theory the central organ of the government and continued until the end of the fifteenth century to play an important part in the life of Novgorod, it failed signally to develop into an orderly and workable institution and to establish definite rules of procedure. Participation in the deliberations of the *veche* was open to all the citizens of Novgorod, and while usually only the residents of the city exercised this right occasionally representatives from other parts of the territory were also present. The initiative in calling the *veche* generally came from the prince or the high officials, but there were instances when the assembly was summoned by private citizens. All that was necessary to call a meeting was to strike the *veche* bell. The *veche*, whose jurisdiction was not precisely defined, tried the most serious offenses and dealt with all questions of legislation, foreign relations, and internal administration. A sovereign body not bound by even its own decisions, the *veche* frequently paid but the slightest attention to the prince, and settled in his absence questions which, according to the agreements, were to be decided jointly by the prince and the *possadnik*. The unruly and passionate character of Novgorod's popular assembly and the very number of its participants precluded the possibility of orderly discussion, to say nothing of voting. The *veche* was susceptible not so much to the eloquence of the orators and the logical perfection of their arguments, as to brute force. Every important issue was decided by a free-for-all fight. Sometimes the rival parties would call two separate *veche*, one on each bank of the Volkhov, which traversed the city. They would then meet on the bridge that spanned the river and stage a battle. To give one's opponents a sound thrashing and then to throw them down into the chilly waters of the Volkhov was the customary and effective method of settling political and religious issues.

The anarchistic character of the *veche* suggests that it could not have been the effective organ of government in a large commercial city, one which, moreover, controlled extensive territories. The business of administration was concentrated in the hands of the two higher officials, the *possadnik* and the *tysiatskii*, who were elected by the *veche* at first for an indefinite term, but in the fifteenth century for a year. They were assisted by a body of judicial and administrative officers. The legislative and other functions, which in theory belonged to the *veche*, were in practice exercised by the Council of Notables (*soviet gospod*, the German *Herrenrat*). The existence of this body, which had not been suspected by historians until the second half of the nineteenth century (Nikitsky), throws much light on the actual working of the machinery of the government. The Council of Notables consisted of some fifty or more members, including the archbishop, the present and former higher officials, and the leading representatives of the *konets*. It is believed that the prince and his retinue, who had once been in the council, were no longer among its members during the latter part of Novgorod's history. The Council of Notables had thus become the organ of the local aristocracy. Its jurisdiction, like that of the boyar duma in the other parts of Russia, was as broad as it was indefinite. Although in theory the council was a servant of the *veche,* in practice it was a supreme body to whose decisions the *veche* merely gave its tumultuous approval. Sometimes the *veche* was ignored altogether and the council acted independently of the popular assembly. In spite of the spectacular and stormy outbursts caused by the ruthless vitality of the *veche,* a closer scrutiny of the institutions of the "free city" discloses that its democracy was an empty shell and that actual power was in the hands of a small group of the landed and commercial aristocracy.

SOCIAL CONDITIONS

The political organization of Novgorod was a by-product of its social structure. Unlike the other Russian cities in the thirteenth, fourteenth and fifteenth centuries, Novgorod had a powerful, wealthy, and ambitious urban class. It was headed by the boyars, who, as in the other parts of the country, owed their supremacy to accumulated wealth and to the tenure of high offices. The boyars owned large estates which provided furs, wax, timber, and other articles of export. They also seem to have largely monopolized credit and banking operations, which increased their hold over the other social groups and thus strengthened their authority. Next to the boyars came a class known as *zhityi liudi,* whose position is not quite clear. Presumably they did not differ essentially from the boyars, since they owned estates and took part in business activities, but they were not members of the Novgorod aristocracy. As early as 1135 the upper stratum of the merchants, who were numerous and influential, was organized into a guild which enjoyed important privileges. Their political influence was somewhat weakened by the fact that many of them were operating with funds borrowed from the boyars. The lower groups of the urban community consisted of small tradesmen, artisans, and laborers. The rural population was composed of free peasants and slaves (*kholopy*). The free peasants either farmed their own land or lived on land belonging to the state or to private owners—the Church, the boyars, and others. For the use of the land they performed certain services for their landlords or surrendered to them a part of the produce. The free tenants living on private estates were known as *polovniki.* In the thirteenth to fifteenth centuries the curtailment of the free tenants' personal rights was a general process that was taking place all over Russia. Novgorod not only was no exception to the rule but even showed particular eagerness to tear down the fragile barrier that separated the free tenants from the slaves (Kliuchevsky). It is noteworthy that the factual enslavement of men who were legally free was proceeding with utmost energy at the very time when the "free city" had proudly emancipated itself from the prince and when the *veche* was nominally supreme. Under these conditions the equality of all citizens before the law proclaimed by the Statute (*sudebnaia gramota*) remained an empty phrase, devoid of real meaning. The benefit of freedom from the arbitrary rule of the prince was reaped by merely a thin layer of the Novgorod magnates and the upper group of the urban population. The masses of the people in Novgorod were no better off than if they had been under the heavy hand of the Muscovite grand dukes.

PSKOV

The complexity that characterized the municipal organization of Novgorod was reflected in the administrative structure of its colonial domain. The more ancient parts of Novgorod's territorial dependencies formed units known as *piatina*, which, presumably, were controlled severally by the five chief subdivisions of the capital city (*konets*). Each *piatina* was divided into *volost* which had their administrative center in the local city, or *prigorod* (suburb). The *volost* and *prigorod* enjoyed a certain degree of self-government which found expression in the *veche* held in the *prigorod*. The sovereign privileges of Novgorod manifested themselves in the widely exercised right of collecting tribute from the *volost*, in appointing the *possadnik* of the *prigorod*, and in final jurisdiction in all civil, criminal, and religious cases. The semi-autonomous dependencies, which were also under obligation to provide troops for Novgorod's military ventures, were sometimes given as *kormlenie* to the deserving citizens of the capital city whose finances needed repletion. Other parts of Novgorod's colonial domain had no self-governing institutions and were administered by permanent officials sent from Novgorod. Among these were the important territories of Zavoloche and Dvinsk. Still other territories, especially the outlying districts in the extreme north, had no permanent administration at all and were merely visited annually by military detachments for the collection of tributes.

The stormy domestic history of the city of Novgorod had its counterpart in its relations with its dependencies. The latter were in a state of almost continuous ferment and frequently displayed a strong tendency to break away from the metropolis. Novgorod's exactions and the state of turmoil prevailing in the political life of the city strengthened these separatist tendencies. Pskov, an important *prigorod* of Novgorod, had been since the sixties of the thirteenth century under the strong influence of Lithuania. Lithuanian princes occupied the throne of Pskov, whose ties with Novgorod were getting looser. Early in the fourteenth century the Pskov *veche* began to elect its own *possadnik*, who administered public affairs side by side with the *possadnik* sent from Novgorod. Numerous conflicts between the metropolis and Pskov were finally resolved in the Treaty of 1347, which recognized the independence of Pskov and of the adjoining territories. Novgorod then withdrew from any participation in the internal affairs of its former dependency. Described by the chronicler as Novgorod's "junior brother," Pskov had a form of government similar to that of its former metropolis. This consisted of a *veche*, a prince invited by the *veche* and enjoying limited powers, a Council of Notables (known in Pskov as *gospoda*), two elected *possadnik*, and other officers. The municipal and territorial administration of Pskov was modeled largely on the Novgorod pattern. Its social structure was also analogous, and the actual conduct of public affairs was in the hands of the boyar aristocracy, who, as in Novgorod, derived their influence from the tenure of high offices and from wealth based on landownership and the control of commercial activities. It would seem that the internal life of Pskov was somewhat more peaceful and less subject to violent political disturbances than was that of its "elder brother." This was perhaps due to the fact that social and political antagonisms in a smaller community, like Pskov, were not quite so sharp as they were in the much larger and wealthier state of Novgorod. The widely held view that the lot of the agricultural population in Pskov was much happier than it was in Novgorod (Kliuchevsky) cannot be accepted. The *izornik*, as the free tenant in Pskov was called, shared the fate of his brethren in Novgorod and elsewhere, and was becoming enslaved *de facto*, a process that was the consequence of his economic dependence on the landlord (Diakonov). It would have been, indeed, surprising if this had not been the case.

THE FALL OF THE SELF-GOVERNING
COMMUNITIES

The history of Novgorod, which in many aspects has not been adequately studied, presents a maze of conflicting tendencies. There was a fundamental contradiction between the democratic institution of the *veche* and the oligarchical rule of a small minority of wealthy and aristocratic families. The true nature of Novgorod's government is disclosed by the preponderance of the members of a few families among the holders of the higher offices. There was a no less fundamental contradiction between the theoretical equality of all the citizens before the law and the process of enslavement of the free tenants. The aristocracy itself was divided into antagonistic factions which used the *veche* as a tool for achieving narrow political ambitions or personal advantages. This cleavage was based partly on the differentiation of the economic interests of the opposing boyar families. Some of them gravitated towards Kiev or Smolensk, others towards Vladimir or Moscow, still others towards Lithuania or Poland. The prince in Novgorod, who was in the precarious position of a hireling of the party in control, also served as a link between the "free city" and those of its neighbors whom this party favored at the time. Novgorod needed him as the leader of its army, as the traditional symbol of its unity as a state. At the same time the ruling clique kept the prince under close supervision and turned him out in a most unceremonious fashion when this was deemed necessary to meet the exigencies of a capricious and rapidly changing political situation. The relations of the metropolis with its colonial domain were an odd mixture of centralization and self-government, of autonomy and ruthless exploitation.

The position of Novgorod in the community of Russian principalities was complicated by its geographical proximity to western countries —Lithuania, Poland, the German knights, Sweden—and its close commercial and other relations with them. Western trade was one of the pillars of Novgorod's economic supremacy, but the Russian lands, especially the grand duchy of Vladimir-Moscow, were no less essential elements in its far-flung activities, and it was on Muscovy that Novgorod depended for its supplies of grain. Although Novgorod was spared the experience of the Tartar invasion, it had to pay tribute to the Tartars, and the grand dukes of Vladimir-Moscow never failed to enforce the claims of the Golden Horde. Moscow's subservient attitude towards the Mongols and its desire to free itself from continuous exactions contributed to the pro-Lithuanian sentiment that sometimes gained the upper hand and threatened to bring Novgorod and Pskov within the orbit of its western neighbors. Hence the frequent shifts in the orientation of Novgorod's policies and her conflicts with Moscow.

It is hardly possible to evaluate the actual part played by each of these conflicting factors in Novgorod's eventful history. The evidence of the Chronicle, somewhat retouched perhaps by the later Muscovite editors in order to make the destruction of the ancient liberties of the "free cities" most palatable, presents a distressing picture of political turmoil and glaring social and economic inequalities. That these conditions existed cannot be reasonably doubted. Exploitation of the masses by a small and divided minority cannot but have resulted in a condition that would be described in modern terminology as class war. The *veche* contained elements which, on a different soil, might have developed into a democratic form of government. But in Novgorod, to repeat, this institution was hardly more than a tool in the hands of the ruling clique, except when it occasionally escaped from the control of its instigators and, like Frankenstein's monster, swept them away in an orgy of mob rule.

The consolidation of political power in the hands of Moscow towards the end of Vasili II's reign marked the beginning of Novgorod's impending doom. In 1456, when Vasili sent a punitive expedition against Novgorod, the city proved incapable of organizing its defense and hastened to sue for peace. Under the terms of the peace agreement Novgorod paid a large indemnity and, although still preserving its traditional form of government, was incorporated within the Muscovite state. At the same time the powers of the grand duke of Moscow in the internal affairs of the "free city" were increased, and Novgorod gave a pledge to refrain from harboring Moscow's enemies. This pledge, however, was not kept, and an influential party headed by the Boretsky, an ancient boyar family, carried on underhand negotiations with Lithuania. A Lithuanian prince was appointed by Casimir, grand duke of Lithuania and king of Poland, to rule over Novgorod "according to the will of its free men." Although the full support of Lithuania was promised in the approaching clash with Moscow, the plan proved a failure. Sharp dissensions developed in Novgorod, and the Lithuanian help failed to materialize. Vasili's successor, Ivan II of Moscow, met with little resistance when, under the pretext of a holy war against traitors to Russia and to the Orthodox Church, he invaded Novgorod in 1470 with a large army in which Pskov was represented. Novgorod, although it paid a heavy indemnity, still retained its self-government under the terms of the agreement of 1471, which was similar to that of 1456. The leaders of the pro-Lithuanian party were executed. Taking advantage of the dissensions that developed in Novgorod in the following years, Ivan gradually expanded the field of his authority. In 1477 he made on Novgorod new demands which clearly indicated his intention to abolish its free institutions. These demands created consternation in the territory, the pro-Lithuanian party came again to the fore, and the supporters of Moscow had to flee. Ivan raised a new army, besieged the city, and Novgorod's defense collapsed. Negotiations followed, but Ivan, confident in his strength, refused to make any concessions. In January, 1478, Novgorod accepted the inevitable: the *veche*, the elected *possadnik*, and other elected officials were abolished. The *veche* bell, symbol of the city's ancient liberties, was carried away to Moscow, and Novgorod was to be governed in the future just as was any other part of the Muscovite state. The leaders of the anti-Moscow party, headed by Martha Boretsky, widow of a former *possadnik*, were deported. Ivan made these harsh terms somewhat more palatable by adding the oral promise not to deport the Novgorod boyars, not to interfere with their estates, and to preserve the traditional methods of administering justice.

These promises were not fulfilled, however. In the years following Ivan embarked upon a policy designed to wipe out the possibility of a revival of opposition. In 1479 Archbishop Theophilus of Novgorod was accused of treasonable activities and incarcerated in a Moscow monastery. Many notables suspected of anti-Muscovite sympathies suffered a similar fate. In 1484 and 1489 large numbers of Novgorod boyars and other landlords were forcibly removed to other parts of the realm, where they received estates in service tenure, while land belonging to the deportees was confiscated and distributed, also in service tenure, to men foreign to Novgorod's tradition. The German Settlement was closed in 1494, and the German merchants, as well as their merchandise, were seized. Although relations with the Hanseatic League were resumed later, they never regained their former importance.

Pskov shared the fate of its "elder brother." With the strengthening of Moscow it was forced to abandon the ancient practice of inviting its own princes and had to accept instead the representatives sent from Moscow. The self-governing institutions and elected officers continued to function, but they gradually lost control over public affairs, which passed into the hands of the Muscovite appointees. Just as in Novgorod, internal dissensions and mutual recriminations of the opposing political parties precipitated the *dénouement*. The final blow came in 1510, when the leaders of Pskov were summoned to Novgorod and arrested there. In their absence the Pskov *veche* obediently accepted Moscow's demands, which included the abolition of the elected *possadnik* and of the *veche* itself. As in Novgorod, the *veche* bell was taken down and the "free city" became an administrative subdivision of Muscovy, while the bulk of the boyars and other landed proprietors were deported, together with their families, and their confiscated estates were distributed in service tenure to newcomers alien to the autonomous tradition of Pskov. In the task of eradicating every vestige of potential opposition, Moscow has displayed throughout the ages unerring insight and stern efficiency.

The fall of the self-governing communities of medieval Russia was the logical consequence of the growth of Muscovite absolutism. Their fate was nevertheless prepared by the inadequacy of their own social and political structures. There was no reason why the masses of the people should rally to the defense of the "ancient liberties" of Novgorod and Pskov, "liberties" that meant nothing to them except ever increasing burdens and exploitation. With characteristic indifference they exchanged the near slavery that had been their lot in the northern "democracies" for the serfdom the Muscovite tsars had in store for them.

CHAPTER VI

THE CHURCH, LETTERS, AND THE ARTS

※

INTRODUCTION OF CHRISTIANITY

Very little is known of the early beliefs and religious practices among the Slavic tribes that dwelt on the Russian plain. Before their conversion to Christianity they were heathens and, like so many other primitive peoples, presumably deified the forces of nature and worshiped crude images. Although the installation of Greek Orthodoxy as the national creed occurred towards the end of the ninth century, it is believed that Christianity was not unknown in Kiev long before that date. It was probably introduced to the Russians by the roving Norsemen, and its progress is indicated by Grand Duchess Olga's conversion towards the middle of the ninth century. Vladimir I, according to the Chronicle, was a robust and seemingly insatiable pagan, inordinately devoted to drinking and carnal pleasures. The reasons that induced him to embrace Christianity cannot be determined, but the romantic tale of an embassy sent abroad by him to discover the best religion must be rejected (Golubinsky) as the invention of a later writer. Vladimir's inclination towards Christianity has sometimes been ascribed to the fact that four of his five legitimate wives were Christians. It must not be overlooked, however, that he is also reported to have maintained a harem of some eight hundred women, an establishment that proved inadequate to satisfy his gargantuan sexual appetite. Thus the four legitimate Christian wives were hardly more than a drop in the bucket. Whatever the causes may have been, Vladimir joined the Greek Orthodox Church in 987 or 988. One may surmise that his conversion did not materially affect his mode of living, though this has been vigorously denied by the official apologists for one of Russia's first national saints. The selection of eastern Christianity was presumably based on the old established ties with Byzantium and the geographical remoteness of Rome. Although the official breach between Rome and Constantinople did not occur until 1054, the *de facto* parting of the ways between the western and the eastern Churches, necessitated by their conflicting political and cultural traditions, took place as early as the ninth century.

Vladimir, the first Christian ruler of Kievan Russia (Olga became converted after she had ceased to be regent), soon embarked upon an extensive campaign for the spreading of the true faith among his subjects. Information as to the form that his missionary zeal took is scarce, but there is little doubt that methods other than those of persuasion were freely used. The effective preaching of the Christian doctrine was an impossibility not only because its dogma was beyond the grasp of the Russian masses but also for the reason that there was no one to explain the new creed to a bewildered population. All the higher clergy and, in the early days, some of the lower clergy were Greeks, and their command of the Russian language, if they knew it at all, was inadequate. The number of clergy, at the time the Christian religion was introduced, was far too small. The progress of Christianity was slow. Centuries passed before it reached the remote corners of the ever expanding realm, and the process has not been completed to this day. What Vladimir's missionaries could not achieve by persuasion and eloquence they succeeded in imposing by force, at least in the most important centers. The horrified Russians saw the effigies of their pagan gods pulled down and destroyed. There was much resistance, which sometimes, as in Novgorod, developed into uprisings against the crusaders. Some of the people accepted the new faith because they recognized its superiority, but there were many who merely bowed to the inevitable and became Christians in name, against their will and convictions. In Russia, as in so many other countries, the religion of brotherly love was imposed by fire and sword. The inevitable result was that in the early centuries Russia's conversion to Christianity was nominal. When in the eighties of the eleventh century the bishop of Novgorod, challenged by a pagan magician, asked the people to choose between their former gods and the religion of Christ, the good citizens of the "free city" went as one man to the magician's side, and only the prince and his immediate entourage took the side of the bishop. This revealing incident occurred in one of Russia's greatest commercial cities almost one hundred years after its official conversion to Christianity. Old beliefs and old religious loyalties were still very much alive behind the official acceptance of a faith the meaning of which only a few understood and which had been imposed by government fiat.

As time went on and the number of churches and clergy increased, a working compromise between hidden heathenism and official Christianity came into being. The old pagan beliefs were preserved under the cloak of Christian observances. The traditional celebrations were maintained in the guise of Christian holidays, a process by no means peculiar to Russia. The outer form of the festivities was somewhat modified, but their inner meaning and associations remained the same as before the days of Vladimir. The Reverend Golubinsky, the eminent and penetrating historian of the Russian Church, has aptly described the resulting situation as that of a "double-faith," that is, heathenism and Christianity existed side by side in the observances and beliefs of the Russian masses. The transition to this mixed form of religion was facilitated by the peculiarities of the Russian Church organization. The lower clergy and not a few members of the higher hierarchy were just as ignorant of Christian dogma as were their parishioners. The village priests were almost all illiterate and incapable of understanding the Gospel; they were far from being fitted to preach it. They were not teachers of the religion of Christ in those remote centuries, and they seldom have been later. Their ministry was reduced to the commitment to memory and the more or less mechanical repetition of the sacred formulas, or so much as they remembered of them. The Church-Slavonic language in which the services were conducted was a peculiar vernacular which not only the masses but even the educated people found it difficult to comprehend and to follow. Mystery and religion are intimately associated, especially in the minds of primitive people. The unintelligible utterances mumbled by the *pop* took the place of the equally awe-inspiring incantations of the pagan priests. The flowing robes and sacred vestments of the Christian clergy, the complex and obscure ritual of religious services, and the threat of eternal damnation reserved for the delinquent members of the congregation were reminiscent in more than one way of customary practices and beliefs. Far from denouncing pagan and semi-pagan observances, the clergy encouraged them, partly because of ignorance and partly because they were a source of revenue on which the village priests largely depended. The survival of heathenism was apparent, as in other Christian countries, in the multiplication of local cults.

Every city and every monastery of any importance had its miracle-working icons and its equally miraculous "imperishable" remnants of its patron saint. The discovery of such holy relics and the advertising of their miracle-working powers were in the interest of the local clergy, since they brought pilgrims and donations. Adoration of the sacred objects can hardly be considered as a manifestation of Christian faith, nor was even this form of worship quite as common as has often been imagined. The external piety that has so deeply impressed many foreign and Russian observers and has contributed to the legend of "Holy Russia" was notoriously lacking during the earlier period. According to Golubinsky, the strict observance of the Church ritual—genuflections, constant performance of the sign of the cross, and so on—goes back no further than to the middle of the seventeenth century, when it was enforced by police measures in the reign of the very pious Tsar Alexis. Contrary to the widely held assumption, the indifference of the masses towards religion is one of the characteristics of Russia's history. This was a consequence of the inability and, later, of the neglect on the part of the clergy to instruct their congregations in the principles of Christianity. Among those, both clerics and laymen, who took an active interest in religious questions—and their number was not insignificant—piety found its expression in devotion to the letter and the form of religious observances, the ritual and the formulas obscuring the deeper and real meaning of Christianity. It was this attitude, and not any divergence of opinion about dogmas or the principles of Christian morality, that became the source of the violent conflicts that shook the Russian Church in the sixteenth and seventeenth centuries.

THE ADMINISTRATION AND THE SOCIAL ACTIVITIES OF THE CHURCH

The nature of the Church administration and its social complexion had much to do with its failure to live up to the higher ideals of Christianity. The whole of Russia constituted a single metropolitanate whose titular head, until the middle of the fifteenth century, was nominated, as well as consecrated, by the patriarch of Constantinople. The metropolitanate was subdivided into a number of dioceses which usually comprised several principalities. The large size of the dioceses effectively prevented the bishops from performing their sacerdotal duties. The bishops appear to have resigned themselves to their less exacting and more profitable activities as administrators of Church properties and as supervisors of the lower clergy. The lack of zeal displayed by the bishops for their apostolate may, perhaps, be explained by the fact that during the earlier period they were all Greeks and that Byzantium was naturally reluctant to send to a savage and little known country like Russia the more high-minded representatives of its clergy. The elevation of Russian priests to the bishopric does not seem to have improved the situation. Although, according to the canons, the candidates were to be elected by a council of bishops, they were in practice nominated by the local prince and then consecrated by the metropolitan. In Novgorod and Pskov the selection of candidates soon passed into the hands of the *veche.*

The bishopric was both honorable and lucrative. It attracted representatives of the upper class, the boyars, and was a coveted prize reserved by the princes for their favorites. The bishops were entitled from the days of Vladimir to the proceeds of a special tax which was originally imposed on certain groups only, but under the Mongol domination this levy was extended to the entire lay population, as well as to the lower clergy. The lower clergy, moreover, had to pay their bishops a variety of fees for consecration, the right to perform marriages, and several other privileges and dispensations. Judicial fees were another important source of revenue, since the Church exercised a wide jurisdiction not only in matters within the purview of the ecclesiastical courts but also in the case of all offenses committed by those residing on estates owned by the Church. The collection of the taxes to which the higher clergy were entitled and the administration of justice were in the hands of an unwieldy and complex administration. The expenses of its officers were defrayed largely by the levy on the lower clergy of special taxes and fees. The laity also contributed to the maintenance of the princes of the Church in various ways in addition to the payment of the general tax. There was, for instance, a fine on widows and on unmarried women who gave birth to illegitimate children or who were known to "live in sin." There is no doubt at all, according to Golubinsky, that the collection of Church taxes and fees was accompanied by gross abuses.

Although information on the estates owned by the higher clergy in the pre-Mongol era is fragmentary, it is generally believed that the metropolitan and the bishops were large landowners. It is impossible, however, to determine what proportion of their revenue came from this source. Some of the members of the higher hierarchy, including the metropolitans, are known to have supplemented their incomes by lending money at advantageous rates. They lived in great luxury, kept expensive establishments, and displayed marked interest in increasing the earthly possessions of the Church and in defending them against temporal power. Some of the princes of the Church were men of intellectual distinction and were well educated according to the standards of the time. They were, however, rare exceptions.

The position of the lower clergy, especially in the case of the village priests, was very different. Throughout history the lower clergy have enjoyed none of the economic and social advantages of their superiors; they have not only had no share in the tax levied for the benefit of the Church but have, in many ingenious ways, been called upon to contribute to the treasuries of the bishops and the metropolitan. In the early days the priests received a small stipend (*druga*) which was probably paid in cash and in grain. Such payments were necessary to attract into the ranks of the priesthood anyone except the few who felt a call to the ministry. For some time after the introduction of Christianity the people felt no need of the services of their priests and could not be counted upon to provide for their support. When, with the spread of Christian observances, the payment of the stipend was discontinued, voluntary donations and the fees collected for the performance of masses, weddings, christenings, funerals, and other services became the chief sources of revenue of the lower clergy. This meager income was sometimes supplemented by proceeds from the cultivation of small parcels of land. The only privilege enjoyed by the lower clergy was exemption from payment of land and other taxes. The desire to escape the ever increasing burden of taxation not only furnished a stimulus among the unprivileged groups to join the ranks of the priesthood but also contributed to the creation of a hereditary clerical class. Humble and trying as was the position of the lower clergy, it was nevertheless a step up the social ladder for those whose only other alternative was dire poverty and semi-slavery. It is believed that the number of priests increased rapidly. The bishops collected fees for each consecration and had every reason to encourage an increase in the number of clerics, especially since this could justifiably be interpreted as the advancement of the cause of Christianity. The rather formidable obstacle to the attainment of priesthood—the requirement of literacy—was overcome by reducing it to a bare minimum. Only a minority of the lower clergy was fully literate, the majority was half literate, and some could not read at all but merely committed to memory the most important prayers and services. The low educational level of the priests in the sixteenth century is established by available documents, and presumably the situation was worse, and not better, in the earlier period. The social status of the lower clergy may be inferred from the fact that the priests in charge of private chapels maintained by many wealthy people were actually nothing but servants and as late as the thirteenth century sometimes continued to remain in a state of slavery even after their elevation to the priesthood. Such was the economic and social position and the intellectual standard of the group on whom rested largely the responsibility for the enlightenment of the Russian people in the dogmas of Christianity. It is no wonder that the result was far from satisfactory.

The monasteries and the "black clergy," or monks, had an important part in the molding of Russia's religious life. It is believed that they made their appearance at the same time as Christianity, that is, before Vladimir I. The first monasteries referred to in the Chronicle were established in the reign of Yaroslav, in the middle of the eleventh century. Some of them, like the Monastery of the Caves in Kiev, were founded by men of ascetic disposition who tried to escape from the turmoil of a sinful world; others were built by the princes and, less frequently, by wealthy boyars who were anxious to have private establishments that would minister to their spiritual needs and pray for the eternal rest of their souls after the monastery's benefactor (or, rather, owner) had died. The practice of founding such "private" monasteries was borrowed from Byzantium.

During the pre-Mongol period of Russia's history monasteries made but little progress. Gradually the situation was changed, and the number of monasteries, as well as their wealth, proceeded to increase at an amazing pace. The reasons for the transformation are common both to the eastern and to the western Churches, but in the case of Russia the effect of the change was strengthened by the character of Russian Christianity. The obscure fear of the beyond, from which no one is free, combined with the predominance of ritual and external observances characteristic of Russian piety, led to the spreading of the general belief that the surest way of achieving eternal salvation was to secure in perpetuity the prayers of the Church. The continuity of the monasteries was assured by their organization, and they were obviously fitted for the task, which they were willing to undertake in return for generous gifts. The Church itself did its best to popularize this doctrine. After the end of the twelfth century it also became fairly customary among the princes and wealthier classes to seek eternal peace by the rather simple method of taking monastic vows at the close of an eventful life, sometimes only a few hours before death. The growing demand for the services that the monasteries alone could render led to a large increase in the number of these institutions. Their popularity was enhanced by the possession of holy relics which attracted masses of pilgrims. Pious people and repentant sinners made it a practice at their death to leave estates to the monasteries in return for their holy prayers. The princes granted to the monasteries large tracts of land, which they developed, thus providing new sources of revenue for themselves and for the treasury. It is believed that in the middle of the thirteenth century the holdings of monasteries were relatively modest, but three hundred years later the Church owned about one-third of the entire area under cultivation. The monastic estates were exploited in the same manner as those of other landlords. It will be recalled that the first known measures suspending the right of the former free tenants to move away were enacted for the benefit of certain monasteries.

The growth of monastic wealth—and political influence went with it—was, as always, purchased at a price. In the early monasteries, especially those established by the monks themselves, attempts were made, with a varying degree of success, to live up to monastic vows: equality of all members of the order, poverty, charity, chastity, strict discipline. These principles were never repudiated, but they were no longer enforced. The monasteries began to attract people whose objectives had nothing in common with monastic ideals. Many saw in monasticism an easy way of leading an idle and relatively comfortable life at the expense of the believers. It became customary for the monks to retain their private property, to have their meals prepared for them, to enjoy the prestige attached to their status without accepting any of the restrictions imposed by this calling. The admittance to the holy orders became largely a question of wealth, and not of personal merit. The doors of the monasteries were open only to those who could afford to make a suitable donation, while impecunious aspirants were limited to the number necessary for the performance of the more laborious and unpleasant tasks. Since the taking of vows was a prerequisite for the bishopric, monastic cells were invaded by ambitious boyars, with their retinues, awaiting consecration. Others were forced into the holy orders against their inclination and will: defeated political opponents and the spouses of princes and influential boyars determined to free themselves from their consorts were compelled to take the vows. Under these conditions not much was left of the monastic ideal. "Nothing has led to greater abuses in the Christian world than monasticism," writes Golubinsky, and he adds that nothing is more difficult than to live up to its principles. To this rule Russia was no exception.

One of the consequences of the general loose attitude towards monastic vows was the growth of a class of "errant monks" who were not attached to any monastery but traveled from place to place, living on charity. These "holy fathers," who were not infrequently mere imposters, enjoyed great popularity and should be included among the teachers of religion of the Russian people. Although the kind of Christianity they preached had often but little to do with the Gospel, they survived throughout the centuries. The most recent and famous specimen of this strange breed was Rasputin, favorite of the last empress of Russia.

There were, of course, pious men and women who continued to cherish the higher ideals of monastic life, but they could not hope to realize them in the wealthy and popular monasteries and convents. The reaction against prevailing conditions found its expression at the end of the fifteenth century in the movement of the so-called Volga "hermits" (startsy), who sought salvation in the wilderness of the forests of eastern Russia. Even earlier, in the second half of the thirteenth century, there came expressions of protest against the prevailing practice of charging fees for the consecration of the clergy, a practice that was interpreted as simony. At the end of the fourteenth century a small sect of the so-called strigolniki (a term of obscure and disputed origin) appeared in Novgorod and Pskov. This sect rejected the Church hierarchy, repudiated sacraments, and denied the necessity of prayers for the dead. Their teachings, as far as can be ascertained, were those of the early Christian Church, headed by the apostles, and they would seem to have had certain elements in common with the later evangelical movement of western Europe. The execution of the leaders of the strigolniki failed to discourage their followers, who formed the nucleus from which grew the minor movements of the dissenters of the later period.

Much has been written by the apologists for the Russian Church to prove that from the beginning it has exercised a strong humanizing influence. There is evidence that the Church preached a more humane attitude towards the slaves, that it encouraged the freeing of slaves by churchmen in their testaments, and that it attempted to discourage the slave trade. On the other hand, in the earlier days the clergy were permitted to own slaves (Diakonov), and it is evident that later the position of the tenants on the ecclesiastical estates was in no way better, and sometimes worse, than on the estates of secular landlords. The procedure of the ecclesiastical courts was just as barbaric as that of the other courts: trial by iron and water, high fines, flogging, and torture. The Church has jealously guarded its vast holdings from encroachment by the temporal power on the ground that "the Church's wealth is the beggars' wealth." This principle, however, received a peculiar interpretation. Russian churches and monasteries failed to establish, as was the custom in Byzantium, hospitals and hospices for the poor. Golubinsky was able to discover in the pre-Mongol period only one Church institution (with the exception of the libraries) that could possibly be classified as being of public utility: this was, of all things, "Greek baths" built in Pereiaslavl by a wealthy local bishop. It was only later that hospitals and hospices began to appear in the monasteries. The chief application of the principle that the wealth of the Church belongs to the poor found its expression in the distribution of alms to the beggars who congregated in church yards, especially on holidays. This form of charity gained remarkable popularity and contributed to the creation of a class of professional beggars that survived up to the twentieth century. The inadequacy of this form of relief is only too obvious. It is highly unlikely that the Church divested itself of much of its wealth through the distribution of alms, especially since laymen generously participated in giving to the beggars. Oddly enough, the beggars even became a source of Church revenue: it was customary in the earlier centuries to allow them to put up shacks on Church property in consideration for a small payment (Golubinsky).

There is a tendency in Russian historiography to over-emphasize the part of the higher clergy in smoothing out political and social frictions. We have seen that the political history of the country before its unification under the rule of Moscow was filled with an uninterrupted series of fratricidal wars. The very nature of these events indicates that the pacifying influence of the higher clergy could not have been great. In contravention of the Church canons the bishops were appointees of the princes and, again in contravention of the canons, the princes dismissed them in the rare cases when the bishops attempted to oppose their policies. It is indicative of the then prevailing opinion that the chroniclers, who themselves were clerics, reported the known instances of the arbitrary removal of bishops by the princes not only without indignation, but on the contrary with approval.

THE CHURCH AND THE STATE: BYZANTINE INFLUENCE

While the humanizing influence of Christianity was slight, the Church played an important part in the unification of the Russian state and in the advancement of Muscovite absolutism. At the end of the tenth century, when Russia embraced Greek Orthodoxy, Byzantium had already entered upon a period of political decadence that was further accentuated by the events following the separation of the Churches in 1054. Yet the cultural and religious standards of Byzantium, even in this era of decline, were still beyond the grasp of the Russians, and the gradual substitution of Russian higher clergy for the Greeks led to a further lowering of these standards. Nevertheless, the link with Constantinople and its political and cultural tradition remained a factor of paramount importance.

No information has been preserved on the actual installation of the Russian Church administration. At the dawn of her Christian era Russia appeared as a metropolitanate under the rule of the patriarch of Constantinople. The patriarch selected and consecrated the metropolitans, acted as the higher court in ecclesiastical matters and in cases bearing on Church administration, and exercised the general right of supervision over the Russian Church. In the pre-Mongol period only two metropolitans were Russians, and the appointment of foreigners to the highest office in the Russian Church continued, with intervals, until the final breach with Constantinople in 1448. Although this dependence on Constantinople had obvious political disadvantages, especially since the Byzantine emperors often brought strong pressure upon the patriarchs, it did help to keep alive the idea of national unity in the midst of the interprincely feuds. To the patriarchate, Russia was an important source of revenue, and Byzantium looked towards a united Russia as a potential ally in the struggle with the many enemies who finally brought about its downfall. In principle Constantinople considered all the Russian principalities as a single metropolitanate. In practice the patriarchate, under the pressure of the grand dukes of Galicia and Lithuania and the kings of Poland, found itself compelled in the fourteenth century to appoint from time to time separate metropolitans for the southwestern Russian territories which were no longer under the rule of Vladimir and Moscow. These appointments were, however, merely measures of expediency, and after a few years the unity of the Russian metropolitanate was in all cases restored. It was not until 1458, ten years after the breach with Constantinople, that a definite split between the Russian and the Lithuanian Churches took place. The fact that until 1448 the Russian metropolitans were appointed by the patriarch gave them a certain degree of independence from the Russian princes and saved the Church from much confusion during the periods of acute struggle for political supremacy. The principle of the unity of the Russian metropolitanate made the Church a champion of political unification, a policy also dictated by the economic interests of the Church, which had suffered heavy losses in the civil wars.

The Mongol invasion did not materially affect the position of the Russian Church. It will be recalled that the rulers of the Golden Horde displayed in religious matters a truly admirable tolerance. The khans installed in office metropolitans and bishops and issued to the higher clergy special *yarlyk* confirming their old privileges and, perhaps, conferring new ones. The earliest known *yarlyk* was issued in 1267 or 1279. It is possible that the still earlier *yarlyk* have not been preserved, and it is believed that the practice of issuing them was discontinued in the second half of the fourteenth century, probably because of the political uncertainties prevailing at the Golden Horde (Golubinsky). The privileges granted by the khans to the Church were of vital importance. The Christian faith was safeguarded from insults, and special protection was given to the objects of the cult; the clergy were freed from all taxes and tributes; the estates owned by the Church were declared inviolable, and the servile population living on such estates was freed from the performance of any services except those imposed by their masters. The infringement of these privileges was punishable by death. The Church was, moreover, given jurisdiction over criminal and other offenses committed by the population under its control. In return for these favors the Church accepted the obligation to pray publicly for the khans. The tolerance of the Golden Horde was not entirely disinterested: the khans wished to exploit their Russian possessions without interference, and they enlisted the services of the Church just as they had enlisted those of the grand dukes of Vladimir and Moscow. The privileges granted to the Church were probably encroached upon both by the Russian princes and by the Mongol officials themselves. It is sometimes argued that the protection offered by the Mongols to the Church weakened the dependence of the Church on the princes. This was hardly the case since the princes not only continued to select bishops, just as they had done before the invasion, but occasionally failed to show any respect for the sacrosanct Church properties. Both the temporal and the ecclesiastical authorities leaned heavily on the support of the real masters of the country, the Golden Horde. It was probably the desire to be nearer to the fountain of power and its chief Russian agents—the grand dukes of Vladimir and Moscow—that induced the metropolitans to transfer their see from Kiev, first to Vladimir (1300), and then to Moscow (Sergeevich). The interlocking interests of the Church and of the state imperatively demanded their close cooperation, although there have been significant departures from that policy, especially when the holders of the metropolitan chair happened to be non-Russians who were more concerned with the maintenance of the unity of their ecclesiastical domain, even at the price of a compromise with the Church of Rome, than with the promotion of the national and dynastic ambitions of the Russian grand dukes. The metropolitans and some of the bishops, like the grand dukes and princes, were frequent visitors to the Golden Horde. It will be recalled that after the death of Vasili I of Moscow in 1425, the Metropolitan Photius urged Vasili II and his uncle Yuri to settle their impending dispute by accepting the decision of the khan as final. In the subsequent conflict between the Church and the state over the secularization of the ecclesiastical estates, the defenders of the Church's interests invariably cited as an argument against the Muscovite grand dukes and tsars the privileges granted to the Church by the khans.

The intimate cooperation between the Church and the state, in spite of occasional conflicts and divergence of interests, was facilitated and indeed prepared by the political tradition of Byzantium. Having started as a persecuted and illegal sect, Christianity with the conversion of Constantine the Great became the official religion. Emperor Justinian's constitution of 530 proclaimed that "what is prohibited by the holy canons is also prohibited by our laws." The legal structure of the Byzantine empire assumed the character of a theocracy (Sergeevich). The emperor was "the Lord's Anointed," but in theory his powers were limited by the obligation of observing Church dogmas and canons. His title described him as "holy" and "lord of the Christian universe." Although the Church claimed that the spiritual power was above the temporal one, its ambition failed of realization. The Byzantine emperors were the successors of the Roman emperors, and for the most part they were not prepared to bow to the commands of the Church. The conflicts between the patriarchs and the emperors were frequent and ended in the defeat of the Church. After the separation of the Churches in 1054 the supreme power in ecclesiastical affairs was concentrated in the eastern Church, in the hands, not of the patriarch, but of the emperor. As a Catholic historian has put it, "The Greek Church, in flagrant disregard of its tradition, has proclaimed this position of dependence and subjugation as normal and in accordance with the laws." The idea of the subservience of the Church to the state and of the "universality" of eastern Christianity, that is, the recognition of Greek Orthodoxy as the only true Christian faith, had been transplanted from Byzantium to Russian soil.

For centuries the dependence of the Russian Church on Constantinople served as an effective bar to the full development of the first of the above tendencies. Although the right of supervision over the internal affairs of the Russian metropolitanate remained largely a dead letter and was reduced in practice to the collection of a subsidy, the patriarch's power to appoint the Russian metropolitan and to act as the higher court in disputes affecting the Russian Church was jealously safeguarded by Constantinople. The patriarch and the emperor looked askance at the elevation of Russians to the metropolitan see. The ardent partisanship of Metropolitan Peter (1308–1326) and Metropolitan Alexis (1354–1378), both of them native Russians and untiring champions of the grand dukes of Moscow, was rightly taken in Constantinople as a warning. With the consolidation of the position of Moscow and the growth of its political ambitions there developed a definite tendency to escape from the cumbersome control exercised by Byzantium. Vasili I of Moscow took exception to the interference of the emperor in Russian ecclesiastical affairs and prohibited mention of the emperor's name at church services on the ground that "we have a Church, but we have no tsar [emperor] and do not want to have one." The patriarch sent him in reply a severe rejoinder which clearly expressed the fundamental doctrine of the eastern Church on the relations between the Church and the state. "It is impossible for Christians to have a Church and not to have a tsar," the patriarch wrote in 1393, "because the Church and the state are in a close alliance and continuous interaction and it is impossible to separate one from the other. . . . The holy tsar occupies a high place in the Church. . . . Listen to Peter, the apostle, who said: 'Fear God, honor the tsar!' " The patriarch went on to explain that there was only one "tsar of the universe"—the Byzantine emperor—and that all the other claimants to the title were mere imposters. The admonition of the patriarch, as Miliukov points out, was not forgotten but became the basis of the claims of the Muscovite grand dukes and tsars after the downfall of Constantinople, when they proclaimed themselves successors of the Byzantine emperors.

The Greek Church had itself paved the way for the impending breach with its eastern dependency. Constantinople had studiously implanted in Russia a deep contempt and hatred for the western Church, an attitude that was to withstand the test of centuries. The Russian theologians of the eleventh and twelfth centuries went so far as to raise the question whether it was permissible for a churchman to use the plates that had been used by the adherents of the "Latin creed." Prejudice and hatred somehow take root easier than do brotherly love and forebearance. Unfortunately for Byzantium, the emperors and the patriarchs, upon the return in 1261 of the Emperor Michael Paleologue to Constantinople, after its protracted occupation by the crusaders, found it necessary under the pressure of external conditions to carry on almost continuous negotiations with the papacy for the reunion of the Churches. These maneuvers were watched in Russia with great suspicion. In 1436 Constantinople nominated Isidor, a Greek or a Bulgarian, as the Russian metropolitan, rejecting Jonah, the candidate of the Grand Duke Vasili II. Isidor, who reached Moscow in 1437 and was duly installed, left five months later for the Council of Ferrara-Florence, where he represented the Russian Church. In the stormy proceedings of the Ferrara-Florence Council (1438–1439), Isidor played a leading part as the protagonist of the reunion of the Churches on the conditions dictated by the pope, and for this he was rewarded by the title of cardinal and papal legate. It was in this new capacity that he returned to Moscow in March, 1441, where he celebrated a mass in the Uspensky Cathedral and officially proclaimed the reunion of the Churches. This announcement was represented by the Chronicle as a great surprise to the Grand Duke Vasili, the clergy, and the people of Moscow. In fact, however, Isidor on his way from Italy had spent several months in Lithuania, where the union of the Churches was well received, and Moscow, of course, could not have been totally ignorant of his activities. Three days after his arrival in Moscow he was arrested and incarcerated in a monastery. He was tried and condemned by a council of Russian bishops, but in spite of threats of being burned at the stake or buried alive he resisted all pressure to induce him to renounce his "heresy." In September, 1441, Isidor escaped abroad, presumably with the connivance of the Moscow authorities, who were anxious to get rid of him.

The Russian Church found itself in an anomalous and embarrassing position. It had definitely rejected the union, and the majority of the Greek clergy were also opposed to it. The patriarch, however, was a Uniat. Moscow hesitated for several years, but finally, in 1448, Jonah was elected metropolitan by a council of Russian bishops and higher clergy, whereupon the dependence of the Russian Church on Constantinople was, for all practical purposes, brought to an end. The political turmoil in Constantinople and the capture of the city by the Turks in 1453 prevented any effective attempt on the part of the patriarchate to restore its former supremacy over the Russian Church. The victory of the Turks over Byzantium was duly interpreted by the Russian theologians as a manifestation of divine wrath over Constantinople's betrayal of true Christianity.

In the fifteenth century the Byzantine tradition was too firmly rooted in Russia to disappear merely because of the severance of the official link between Constantinople and Moscow. The Russian Church had already rendered important services to Muscovite absolutism by proclaiming the divine origin of the secular power and by putting at the latter's disposal the ecclesiastical weapon of excommunications and interdicts, as Metropolitan Alexis and others had done. Its transformation into a national Church with the election of Jonah was soon to drive it to far more ambitious efforts along the same lines. The breach with Constantinople, moreover, had deprived the Church of whatever independence it had enjoyed in the past. As long as the metropolitans were nominated and consecrated in Constantinople, they were beyond the reach of the Russian grand dukes. After the election of Jonah by a council of the Russian clergy, this safeguard no longer existed, but it was some time before the Moscow grand dukes fully asserted their powers over the Church. The first metropolitan to be removed from office by order of the secular authority was Varlaam (1521); the same fate befell Metropolitan Daniel (1539) and Metropolitan Joasaph (1541). These arbitrary infringements of the prerogatives of the head of the Church were also in conformity with the practice, if not with the theory, of Byzantium.

LETTERS

The Church and the Byzantine influence it represented left a deep imprint on the cultural development of the Russian people. It is generally believed that until the conversion of the eastern Slavs to Christianity they had no written language. The Church-Slavonic alphabet, from which has evolved the present Russian alphabet, was borrowed from Bulgaria and was itself an adaptation of the Greek alphabet for the use of the southern Slavs. Literacy was introduced in Russia simultaneously with Christianity, primarily to serve the purposes of the Church. But although the eastern Slavs formerly had no written language, they presumably had an oral literary tradition reflecting the popular beliefs and customs of the pre-Christian era. This tradition survived the conversion of Russia and continued to exist for centuries side by side with the new Christian literature borrowed largely from Byzantium. The bitter though futile denunciations of pagan storytellers by the so-called *Stoglav* Council in the middle of the sixteenth century offers an eloquent proof of the robust vitality of the national folklore. The popular epos and Christian literature influenced each other to a certain extent, although their relationship remained antagonistic. The Church, looking upon the pagan tradition with hostility, did its best to eliminate it. Popular songs and legends were transmitted by word of mouth, and the inimical attitude of the Church, which largely controlled the preparation of the written records, effectively prevented the preservation for posterity of the national epos. The bulk of the available early literature—and only a few manuscripts have escaped destruction—thus represents merely the Christian literary tradition which was accessible to only a thin layer of the educated or, more precisely, the literate class. This reflected the aspirations and interests of an infinitesimal section of the people. No authentic record of the popular epos has been discovered and, presumably, it never existed. Old customs and beliefs have left but the slightest trace in the documents of the earlier period, and no systematic attempt to record the national epic was made until the middle of the nineteenth century. Moreover, it is generally admitted that the survival of folklore has suffered important modifications in the course of time. Under these conditions any attempt to present a comprehensive survey of Russian cultural developments previous to the seventeenth century meets with insurmountable obstacles and is necessarily incomplete and one-sided. The sources have preserved merely the Christian literature, while the bulk of the national epic has been irretrievably lost.

In the official Church literature Byzantine influence was supreme. Translations from the Greek formed by far the largest part of the early Russian libraries, and the principal channel for the expansion of Greek learning in Russia was the adaptation of translations available in the Balkan Slavic countries, especially in Bulgaria and, to a lesser degree, in Serbia. A somewhat smaller number of literary works were directly translated from the Greek. Most of these translations, which included the New Testament and the more important sections of the Old Testament, served the purposes of the Church. The Book of Psalms (Psalter), especially an annotated version directed against Judaism, and various collections containing prayers, hymns, and so on, seem to have enjoyed some popularity. Somewhat broader in their content were the translations of sermons, expositions of dogmas, and especially the records of the lives of saints. The Greek *Synaxarion,* or *Martyrologium,* a collection of the lives of saints, as well as a more detailed work of the same type known in Russian as *Chetia-Mineia,* brought to Russian readers some information regarding Church history. The purpose of such collections, however, was chiefly didactic: by extolling the achievements of the saints and martyrs they placed before the reader an instructive object lesson and a worthy example for imitation. The appeal of this type of literature was enhanced by elements of poetical description and fantasy (for instance, in dealing with miracles) which made more palatable the austere asceticism of Christian morals and were probably not altogether useless in counteracting the attraction exercised by the pagan epic. The curiosity of the Russian readers about history had to be content with a translation of Greek chronicles that interpreted world events strictly in conformity with the tradition of the eastern Church and offered a picturesque mixture of information drawn from the Bible and other sources, a largely fantastic story typical of the early Middle Ages. A somewhat more matter-of-fact knowledge of canon law and Byzantine legislation was gained from the *Kormchaia* and from the so-called *Nomokanon*. Science was represented by the translations of commentaries on the creation of the world in six days (*Shestodnev*) and especially by the *Physiolog*, an ambitious treatise on the legendary qualities of animals and minerals. In addition to these works of orthodox Greek theology, Russia inherited from Byzantium a body of apocryphal literature, that is, compositions rejected by the Church as contrary to official dogma. It is believed that the bulk of this type of literature reached Russia by way of Bulgaria and Serbia. There were also a few translated works that may be classified as quasi-history, such as the story of the downfall of Troy, or *Alexandria*, a highly imaginative account of the life of Alexander the Great.

The early literary efforts of native origin were hardly more than slavish imitations of the Byzantine patterns. They included eulogies of local saints, somewhat naïve and haphazard polemics against Catholicism, such as the treatise "On Faith, Christian and Latin" ascribed to Theodosius, one of the founders of the Monastery of the Caves (Kiev), sermons, and lives of the saints. Some of the Church orators studiously cultivated the elaborate rhetoric and rich imagery of their Greek masters. To this school belonged Metropolitan Ilarion (middle of the eleventh century), Climent Smoliatich, and Cyril, bishop of Turov (twelfth century). The writings of these literati were within the grasp of only a small élite. Other theologians, addressing themselves to a less select audience, discarded Byzantine rhetoric and endeavored to expound the fundamentals of Christian dogma and ethics in a language accessible to the average man. The outstanding representatives of this school were, in the eleventh century, Luke Zhidiata and Theodosius of the Monastery of the Caves, and in the twelfth, Elijah, bishop of Novgorod. Commendable as the intentions of these theologians undoubtedly were, their writings display much crudeness and a truly remarkable confusion of thought. Serapion, bishop of Vladimir, who lived in the second half of the thirteenth century, occupied an intermediary position between the two schools. Another Russian contribution to religious literature was the early thirteenth century collection of lives of saints known as *Pecherskii Paterik*, which eulogized the holy endeavors of the monks of the Monastery of the Caves and gave some account of the monastery's history. Mention should also be made of the record of the pilgrimages of Daniel to Jerusalem (1106–1107) and of Anthony to Constantinople (about 1200).

By far the most important sources for determining the history and the cultural level of Russia in the early centuries were the Russian chronicles, the character of which has already been discussed.[1] It is a matter of particular regret, therefore, that the most ancient available copies of the Chronicle go back merely to the last quarter of the fourteenth century, although one of the Novgorod chronicles has been preserved in a manuscript of the thirteenth century. This record is not, however, regarded as typical of such compilations. The situation is even worse when we turn to the early lay literature represented by the *Tale of the Host of Igor*, a poetical description of an unsuccessful campaign of Prince Igor against the Cumans in 1185. This celebrated work was discovered in 1795 in a manuscript which, it is believed, could not have antedated the sixteenth century. The first edition of the *Tale of the Host of Igor*, published in 1800, meritorious as it was for its time, unfortunately fails to meet the requirements of a more exacting age. The only manuscript of the great epic was destroyed in the conflagration that swept a large part of Moscow in 1812. The unique character of the work and the absence of any reference to it in the available manuscripts led to the suspicion that it was a forgery. In 1834, however, there was discovered in an authentic manuscript of the fourteenth century another epic dealing with the victory of Dimitry Donskoy over the Tartars in 1380, an account that was clearly a paraphrase of the *Tale of the Host of Igor*. The authenticity of the latter is thus considered established. Unhappily, the shortcomings of the first edition were such as to make the study of the *Tale of the Host of Igor* both extremely laborious and somewhat inconclusive. The editors themselves admitted that the text they published was difficult to decipher and that certain passages were unintelligible. The discovery in 1864 of a manuscript copy made for Empress Catherine from the original manuscript failed to produce any conclusive evidence. While much has been done by Russian scholars to restore the text of the *Tale of the Host of Igor*, the handicaps they have to overcome will appear from the fact that it still remains uncertain whether it was written in prose or in rhyme. It is nevertheless believed that the *Tale of the Host of Igor* was the work of a contemporary writer, that its author was not a cleric but probably a member of the

[1] See p. 13.

prince's military retinue, that it reflected the national pagan epic, and that it was not an isolated work but rather an outstanding example of military epic stories forming an important part of the lay literary tradition.

The Tartar domination further retarded the already slow process of Russia's cultural development, but it did not bring about any fundamental change. The stagnation of cultural life observed in Russia in the thirteenth to fifteenth centuries may be ascribed to other causes. The removal of the cultural center from Kiev to Vladimir and Moscow weakened the old ties with Byzantium, that fountain of Russia's spiritual inspiration. Moreover, in the tenth and eleventh centuries Byzantium, in spite of its political vicissitudes, was living through a period of cultural renaissance. But in the twelfth to fourteenth centuries, with the multiplication of political reverses and uncertainties, the cultural life of Byzantium entered an era of decline. "Rigid scholasticism, attachment to the letter and neglect of the contents, the beginnings of religious-national exclusiveness, growing hostility towards the Catholic west, a sharply negative attitude towards all other denominations, especially towards the Mohammedans, rejection of the inheritance of the ancient world, side by side with complacence"— all these elements, which left their imprint on Russia's early cultural development, became even more predominant with the political and spiritual decay of Constantinople (Speransky). The literary life of Russia under the Mongol rule was particularly barren of achievement. Although religious literature continued to develop along the lines of the Kievan period, it was even more than before kept in the shackles of Greek Orthodox scholasticism. A few more translations of works of medieval learning were added to the dust of the monastery libraries. The Mongol invasion was reflected in several tales which eventually were incorporated in the Chronicle. The monks continued to keep the records of current events, lives of the saints were written according to accepted formulas, sermons were composed and preached. The uninspiring character of this meager output merely emphasizes the cultural sterility of the period.

The chief reason for the barrenness of early Russian literature was probably the absence of a demand for reading material on the part of the public. Tatishchev, who wrote in the first half of the eighteenth century and used sources which have since disappeared, maintained that at the very beginning of the Christian era in Russia love for learning was prevalent, and he claimed that both Greek and Latin were taught in numerous schools. Yaroslav of Kiev (1019–1054) was represented by the Chronicle as a lover and collector of manuscripts. Vladimir Monomakh (1114–1125) was said to have been a man of good education, and his father, Vsevolod, was reported to have mastered five languages. One should not, however, give too much credence to the eulogistic remarks of the chroniclers, and Tatishchev's panegyric is in contradiction to the little we know about the period he discusses. Golubinsky was undoubtedly much nearer to the truth when he wrote that "literacy and not enlightenment (*prosviashchenie*)— these words sum up the whole of our history over the long period from Vladimir to Peter the Great." There must have been some schools and a few men who knew Greek, for otherwise the Greek metropolitans and bishops could hardly have performed their duties. It is doubtful, however, that these schools taught anything but the rudiments of reading and writing, and the number of their students could not have been large. What has been said about the educational standards of the clergy explains why no complete translation of the Bible was available until the very end of the fifteenth century, five hundred years after Russia's conversion to Christianity. It is believed that Vasili II (1425–1462), the founder of the Muscovite state, was illiterate. The truth of the matter would seem to be that men able to read and write were rare exceptions. No wonder, therefore, that literature made little progress. Until as late, perhaps, as the end of the fifteenth or the beginning of the sixteenth century, the works of Greek and native theologians merely gathered dust on the shelves of monastery libraries.

THE ARTS

Russian art, like her literature, developed under the strong influence of the Greek Orthodox Church. By the time Russia accepted Christianity, the "golden age" of Byzantine art (sixth and seventh centuries) was over and the work of Greek artists had to conform with the rigid requirements of the established ecclesiastical tradition. This, however, did not prevent Byzantium from experiencing two more important artistic revivals—one in the ninth and tenth centuries and another in the thirteenth and fourteenth centuries. The Greek art of this period continued nevertheless to be hedged within the narrow limits set by the inflexible tradition of the Greek Orthodox Church. The artistic trends of Constantinople were reflected in Russian works of art, and for centuries Russia was content with copying Byzantine models. Manifestations of the national creative genius only timidly and gradually infiltrated into the works of the Russian artists.

The most ambitious and imposing architectural monuments of Kievan Russia were the churches. Vladimir and Yaroslav erected large cathedrals and other places of worship in Kiev and in the various centers of southern Russia. The stone churches were the work of foreign architects and artisans who were, however, assisted by native craftsmen. These buildings and their internal and external decoration followed what had become the established patterns of Byzantine church architecture, although recent students have detected other foreign influences—Scandinavian, Armenian, Georgian. The churches of Novgorod and Pskov differed somewhat from those of the south and, it is believed, reflected the Romanesque style of western Europe and were, perhaps, influenced to some degree by native wooden church architecture, especially in the shape of their roofs. The monuments of the Vladimir-Suzdal period (twelfth and thirteenth centuries) were a step forward as compared with their Kievan predecessors. Their lines were more harmonious, their decoration more elaborate, sometimes even sumptuous. It is a matter of dispute among art experts whether the Vladimir-Suzdal type of architecture was the result of Asiatic or of Romanesque and Italian influences. The latter explanation seems the more probable, and it is also likely that Italian influence reached Russia by way of Byzantium, where in the meantime there had developed a somewhat novel form of architecture and ornamentation. Although the Vladimir-Suzdal architecture was not the manifestation of an original national style, it became the accepted model for Russian church building until the end of the fifteenth century. Ivan III (1462–1505) ordered Italian architects imported to Moscow to beautify the new capital and to reproduce faithfully the cathedrals of Vladimir-Suzdal. It was only towards the end of the fifteenth century that the national type of architecture, which had evolved in the building of wooden churches, began to receive official recognition. It found its full expression in the bizarre and magnificent cathedrals of Vasili Blazhenny erected in Moscow in the middle of the sixteenth century. Departure of the national architectural style from the Byzantine tradition provoked a strong reaction among churchmen and government officials, for departure from tradition was considered nothing short of heresy. Stern efforts were made in the seventeenth century to force church architecture back to the familiar forms of Vladimir-Suzdal. These efforts, combined with new and strong western influences, succeeded in stifling the development of a national architectural style. This does not mean, of course, that Russian architecture of the following period was purely imitative and barren of real achievement, but merely that it developed along cosmopolitan lines adapted somewhat to Russian conditions. Although native masters not infrequently succeeded in leaving the indelible imprint of their genius on the monuments they created, their art was rooted in a tradition borrowed from abroad.

The early Russian paintings, frescoes, and mosaics with rare exceptions dealt with religious subjects. Scholarly examination of these works of art is relatively recent and goes back merely to the beginning of this century. There has been considerable disagreement among the experts in attributing to artists the paintings of the eleventh to thirteenth centuries. Most of the known specimens were probably the work of Greek artists. Nevertheless, it has been affirmed by some recent students that even the frescoes of the eleventh and twelfth centuries, whose Greek origin is generally admitted, display certain characteristics foreign to Byzantine art, chiefly in the use of colors (A. J. Anisimov). In the thirteenth century the gradual emancipation of Russian iconography timidly asserted itself in a departure from the conventional manner in the painting of faces and figures. Something of the aristocratic refinement was gradually lost, but this was replaced by greater sincerity and spontaneity in the faces, by a certain inner warmth. The carefully arranged draperies and folds of the vestments in the Byzantine models gave place to straight lines which made the whole composition appear flat, two-dimensional. There was more movement in the figures, brighter colors were used. It is admitted that these characteristics of Russian church painting were not clearly expressed until the middle of the fourteenth century.

The nature of the influences that affected Russian painting in the fourteenth and fifteenth centuries is highly controversial. Some students are inclined to see in the icons of this period the influence of Italian masters; others maintain that the Russian artists drew their inspiration, as in the past, from Byzantium, which, it will be recalled, was then passing through a period of artistic revival. The growth of a definitely Russian school of icon painters was probably influenced by the increase in the number of wooden churches, where icons replaced the mosaics and frescoes of the more sumptuous stone churches of the eleventh to thirteenth centuries. There was, moreover, an ever in- creasing demand for icons on the part of the general public. The superstitious adoration of the icons typical of Russian Christianity led to a desire on the part of churchmen to have them in their houses and if possible not one but several, since each image of the Blessed Virgin or of a saint was believed to possess supernatural powers and to protect its owner in various emergencies. The reproduction of icons for commercial purposes must have contributed to that process of "simplification" of the Byzantine models which is characteristic of the period. The relative isolation of northern Russia during the Mongol domination was probably another factor that facilitated the process of emancipation in the field of art.

The fifteenth century is considered by some students as the high point in the development of Russian icon painting. Andrew Rublev, at the very beginning, and Dionysius of the Therapont Monastery at the very end of the century are representatives of a tradition that has produced works of great purity and beauty. The promising be- ginnings of the national Russian school of iconography were soon to encounter the same obstacles that obstructed the development of na- tional architecture: the Church, the government, and a large body of conservative churchmen opposed to the free inspiration of the artist a stern determination to prevent any change in official iconog- raphy. The evolution of icon painting could not, however, be com- pletely halted, in spite of the repressive measures enacted in the six- teenth and the seventeenth centuries. But just as in the case of architecture, the effect of this opposition, combined with new western influences, diverted the artistic genius of the nation into different channels and effectively checked a national tradition that seemed full of promise.

Another important branch of medieval artistic endeavor—illumi- nated manuscripts—fared better. Some of the fine examples preserved display an interesting combination of Byzantine, Bulgarian, and Serbian motifs with eastern designs and original Russian compositions that have been preserved in the embroideries still used on towels, aprons and shirts. On the other hand, sculpture was non-existent in Russia. It would seem that iconoclasm, in spite of its condemnation by the Seventh Ecumenical Council (787), survived in the hostile attitude of the eastern Church towards statues. In this respect, too,.

the Russian Church slavishly followed in the footsteps of its Byzantine masters. Among the articles of jewelry, silver, and gold plate and church vessels, the finer specimens are usually attributed to foreign craftsmen, and it is certain that some of the ornaments used by the wealthier classes show definite eastern influence.

Little need be said about music. The use of instrumental music at religious services was prohibited, and the hymns and chants borrowed from Byzantium and the southern Slavs were sung in unison. Information on the musical standards of the period is admittedly inadequate, but it would seem that they were primitive in the extreme and in keeping with the low educational level of the clergy. Popular songs, about which little is known, were discouraged and denounced together with all other manifestations of the pagan tradition.

THE CHURCH AND CULTURAL DEVELOPMENT

Taken as a whole, the cultural achievements of Russia in the second half of the fifteenth century were humble even when measured by the standards of the time. One must not forget that the unification of the country under the rule of Moscow took place almost 150 years after Dante wrote the *Divine Comedy*. The Mongol domination alone does not fully account for this unhappy state of affairs, although the generally disturbed conditions during this period hindered cultural progress. The chief educational agency was the Church. It was the Church that introduced literacy, created the early Russian literature, assumed the task of instructing the nation in the principles of Christianity, contributed to the advancement of arts and sciences. These commendable endeavors, unfortunately, were not only conducted on a modest scale, for which the Church was not alone to be blamed, but they were also accompanied by policies that could not but hamper cultural progress. Intransigence and hostility to every manifestation of national genius the moment it infringed upon the sacrosanct orthodox tradition exercised their deadening effect in every field of artistic or literary activity. The mass of the lower clergy and the vast majority of the leaders of the Church were hardly qualified for the task that confronted them. The consequence was that five hundred years after its conversion to Christianity Russia remained illiterate almost to a man and, at heart, largely pagan. Golubinsky speaks of Russia's "tiny and peculiar culture (*prosviashchenie*)" on the eve of the Mongol invasion. In the next two hundred years the situation was not improved.

PART TWO

THE FIRST
MOSCOW PERIOD

CHAPTER VII

THE CONSOLIDATION OF ABSOLUTISM

❋

POLITICAL UNIFICATION

Muscovite absolutism was still in its infancy in 1462, at the death of Vasili II. His son, Ivan III (1462–1505), and his grandson, Vasili III (1505–1533), completed the structure of the autocratic state. Ivan, who when a boy was his father's co-ruler with the title of grand duke, became the sole occupant of the Moscow throne at the age of twenty-two. Solovev has optimistically described Ivan as "the fortunate descendant of a long line of wise, hard-working, and parsimonious ancestors." Unfortunately, the rise of Moscow had little to do with wisdom, hard work, or parsimony. Yet Ivan proved to be a worthy successor to his father, pursuing the same policy of unification and employing methods similar to those used by Vasili II after his victory over Dimitry Shemiaka.

The most significant achievement of the reigns of Ivan III and Vasili III was the expansion of the area under the direct control of Moscow. This process of territorial aggrandizement brought far-reaching changes in the international status of Muscovy and remodeled its political and social institutions. Finding themselves in a much stronger position than Vasili II had been, Ivan and his son could often achieve their aims by mere pressure which, when necessary, was backed by a display of force. Like Vasili II, Ivan III and Vasili III did not openly break with the past and did not overtly abolish the political structure of medieval Russia with its multitude of quasi-sovereign rulers. Ancient formulas continued to be used in interprincely agreements and in the testaments of the princes and grand dukes. This attachment to a legalistic tradition could not detract from, or obscure the momentous nature of, the change that was taking place.

The efficacy of the Muscovite pressure was first demonstrated in the case of the principality of Vereia, held by one of Ivan's senior relatives, Prince Michael. For no obvious reasons, and without any compensation, Michael proceeded to transfer to Ivan one part of his domain after another. Vereia itself, which was confiscated by Ivan as a punishment for the desertion of Michael's son to Lithuania, was later returned to Michael as a grand-ducal grant, but only for his lifetime. After Michael's death in 1486, Ivan inherited what was left of the Vereia principality by virtue of a testament thoughtfully drawn for Michael in the Moscow chanceries. In the sixties all the princes of Yaroslavl, including the local grand duke, surrendered their sovereign rights to Ivan and entered the service of Moscow. The motives that induced them to take so drastic a step remain obscure, but the bitter comments of the Yaroslavl chronicler suggest that the action was taken under duress. In 1474 the Rostov princes followed suit, sold the remnants of their depleted "patrimony" to Moscow, and entered its service. The seventies and eighties brought the formal annexation of Novgorod, this time by force of arms and the abolition of its ancient liberties. Somewhat earlier, in 1472–1473, Perm, a former dependancy of Novgorod, fell under the rule of Moscow. The grand duchy of Tver, the most important political unit still in existence after the annexation of Novgorod, soon suffered a similar fate, although the position of Tver had seemed particularly strong. Ivan's first wife, Maria, was the daughter of the Tver grand duke. The independence of Tver had been specifically guaranteed by agreements entered into by Ivan, and the Tver troops participated in Moscow's campaign against Novgorod. Ivan, however, showed neither gratitude nor desire to live up to the obligations he had assumed, relations with Tver became strained, and Michael of Tver sought support against Moscow in Poland. In 1485, when Tver was besieged by Ivan, Michael escaped to Lithuania and the grand duchy of Tver was incorporated in the Muscovite state. A similar fate overtook Viatka in 1489.

The process of political unification continued in the reign of Vasili III. Pskov, which was actually under the control of Moscow in the reign of Ivan III, was formally annexed in 1510 and was, like Novgorod, deprived of its representative institutions. The grand duchy of Riazan, which still enjoyed a somewhat illusory political independence, was reduced to the position of a province in 1517 after its ruler, Fedor, was accused of maintaining treasonable relations with the Crimean Tartars and was imprisoned in Moscow.

The ambitions of the Muscovite grand dukes were no longer limited to the acquisition of lands held by the weaker Russian princes. Since the conquest of Constantinople by the Turks in 1453, Moscow was beginning to look upon itself as the successor of Byzantium and the head of the Greek Orthodox world. Ivan III reminded the Hungarian envoy, who visited him in 1501 on behalf of Alexander, grand duke of Lithuania and a brother of Vladislav of Hungary, that the Russian lands annexed by Lithuania in the fourteenth and early in the fifteenth century were once ruled by his ancestors and that he was entitled to them. These dynastic pretentions found a favorable soil in the dissensions that developed in Lithuania. The union between the western and eastern Churches proclaimed by the Ferrara-Florence Council of 1439 was officially accepted in Lithuania, and Metropolitan Gregory, who was appointed to the Lithuanian see in 1458, was a Uniat. This led to considerable discontent among the large Orthodox population of Lithuania and to a movement of protest among the many princes and magnates who belonged to the Greek Church. The matter was brought to a head by a decree of 1481 which prohibited the construction or even the renovation of Orthodox churches. A conspiracy to murder Casimir, king of Poland and grand duke of Lithuania, was organized by a group of Russo-Lithuanian nobles who also planned to secede from Lithuania and transfer their allegiance to Moscow. The plot was discovered and its leaders were executed. Some of the conspirators, however, managed to escape and put themselves under the protection of Ivan III. A number of the Russo-Lithuanian princes, following their example, went to Moscow and petitioned Ivan to admit them to his service together with their hereditary estates. According to the then prevailing custom, local princes enjoyed the privilege of changing their allegiance without forfeiting their rights to the principalities they had inherited from their ancestors. In the fifteenth century the Lithuanian grand dukes attempted to curtail this privilege by writing into the agreements with the local princes provisions binding the latter not to sever their principalities from Lithuania. Moscow and Riazan also had agreements with Lithuania stipulating that they should refrain from admitting to their service princes formerly under the Lithuanian rule "with their hereditary estates." Nevertheless, Ivan graciously accepted the Lithuanian fugitives and claimed sovereignty over their hereditary domains. Lithuania found itself under the necessity of yielding, and by the Treaty of 1494 Moscow acquired a con-

siderable territory along its western border. The agreement was consecrated by the marriage between Alexander of Lithuania (who in
1501 became also the king of Poland) and Ivan's daughter, Helen.
It was specifically provided that Helen should not be forced to abandon
the Greek Orthodox Church. The new dynastic ties, instead of improving the Moscow-Lithuanian relations, made them worse. Ivan,
maintaining that Helen was subjected to strong pressure to embrace Roman Catholicism, refused to believe his daughter's denial that
such pressure was being brought upon her. In the meantime Russo-
Lithuanian princes continued to drift to Moscow, where they received
a warm welcome. In the summer of 1500 Russian troops invaded
Lithuania, and after two years of hostilities the armistice of 1503
transferred to the rule of Moscow the territory along the upper Oka
and the land of Chernigov-Sever, with nineteen towns, including the
city of Chernigov. Armed conflict with Lithuania was soon resumed.
The two countries were in a state of warfare from 1512 to 1522.
Smolensk, which had been under Lithuanian rule since 1404, was occupied in 1514 by the Russians, who succeeded in retaining it in
spite of the defeat the Russian army suffered the same year on the
river Orsha. By the terms of a provisional agreement of 1522, Smolensk
was left to Moscow "until the conclusion of peace." The armistice was
to last for five years, but peace negotiations dragged indefinitely and
Smolensk remained in Russian hands. In 1523 the principality of
Sever, which still retained its local dynasty, was finally incorporated
in the Muscovite state as a province, and its last prince, who, it was
rumored, was carrying on treasonable negotiations with Poland, was
thrown into prison.

The territorial acquisitions of Ivan III and Vasili III were impressive. To some fifteen thousand square miles held, according to Kliuchevsky, by Vasili II at the time of his death his two immediate successors added at least forty thousand square miles. The policy of unification pursued by Ivan and Vasili was endorsed by the Muscovite
Church hierarchy. The Metropolitan Philip preached obedience to
the people of Novgorod, and his successor, Gerontius, sent two messages to Viatka urging submission. The fate of the boyars, well-to-do
landlords, and merchants in the territories annexed by Moscow was
not a happy one. It will be recalled that mass deportations followed
the abolition of the representative institutions of both Novgorod and
Pskov. Similar policies were used in Yaroslavl, Viatka, and Riazan. In

case of open or suspected opposition the leaders of these provinces were arrested, flogged, tortured, and put to death. Ivan III and Vasili III were, indeed, worthy successors of Vasili II.

The territorial unification under the rule of Moscow did not remove the possibility of a new partition, since the ancient rules governing the property of the patriarchal family were left intact by the testament of Vasili II. Ivan III had four brothers who viewed with little enthusiasm the growth of the power of the Moscow grand duke at the expense of the junior members of the dynasty. They considered the diminution of their own authority as a violation of the secular tradition. When Yuri, the eldest of the junior brothers, died without issue in 1472, Ivan appropriated the whole of his domain. The other brothers considered themselves entitled to a share, and for the time being Ivan settled the impending conflict by turning over certain provinces to his brothers Boris and Andrew Junior (*Menshoi*). The third brother, Andrew Senior (*Bolshoi*), however, got nothing from Ivan, but received some compensation from the domain of his mother. In 1473 Boris and Andrew Junior concluded with Ivan an agreement by which they recognized as their "senior brother" not only Ivan but also his son and heir and renounced all claims to the Moscow throne as well as to their share of Yuri's estate. These two princes also waived their rights to any accretion of the grand duchy of Moscow, which they promised to defend as the legitimate possession of Ivan and his issue. In violation of custom, no reciprocal obligation was assumed by Ivan. There seems to be little doubt that the agreement of 1473 was signed by Boris and Andrew under duress. Ivan's brothers were deeply hurt by his failure to share with them the proceeds of the conquest of Novgorod, in which they had taken an active part, and their discontent was soon translated into action. They took advantage of Ivan's impending conflict with the Golden Horde to revive their claims to Yuri's estate and to demand the resumption of the traditional relations between the grand duke and the junior princes. They sought the support of Casimir of Poland and Lithuania, to whom—it will be remembered—Vasili II in his testament entrusted his widow and family. They also intrigued against Ivan in Novgorod. Casimir, who was disturbed by the growing strength of Moscow, especially after the conquest of Novgorod, attempted to organize against Ivan a coalition in which the Golden Horde, the Teutonic Order, and Sweden were to take part. This project failed, but in the meantime something approaching a state of war had developed between Ivan and his brothers. In the course of this strife, which was reminiscent of those of the earlier period, the territory of Pskov suffered devastation. The advance of Khan Akhmad in 1480 forced Ivan to revise his position, at least for a time. He assured his brothers that he was willing to accept their conditions, with the result that the invading Tartar army was confronted by the united forces of the Muscovite princes. No sooner was the Tartar danger over, however, than Ivan forgot his promises. Only one of his brothers—this time Andrew Senior—received a share in Yuri's much-disputed estate, and that merely as a grand-ducal grant and not in recognition of his legitimate claim. The agreements concluded by Ivan with his brothers in the eighties further accentuated the subordinate position assigned to them in the agreement of 1473. The princes acknowledged the exclusive right of Ivan and his issue to the grand-ducal domain, which now included not only the grand duchy of Moscow-Vladimir, but also Novgorod, Tver, and Pskov. The agreements, moreover, recognized the grand duke of Moscow as the supreme leader of all military forces and acknowledged his right to control foreign relations to the exclusion of the junior members of the dynasty. Under these conditions the hereditary rights of the junior princes, which still existed in law, became in fact hardly more than those of the other landlords, and were coming to assume the character of mere grand-ducal grants which could be revoked at the sovereign's pleasure. The ephemeral nature of the hereditary rights enjoyed by Ivan's brothers was soon made clear. Andrew Junior died in 1481 and left practically the whole of his domain to Ivan, presumably in settlement of a debt he owed the latter. The domain of Boris passed on his death in 1494 to his two sons, but reverted to the grand duke when they died without issue, one in 1504 and the other in 1513. Andrew Senior was less fortunate than his brothers. He showed too much independence, was suspected of attempting to escape from his brother's perhaps not unduly affectionate guardianship, and in 1491 failed to send his troops to Ivan's support in a new struggle with the Tartars. Andrew was accused of treason, arrested, and three years later died in prison. His sons lived and died in exile. The methods employed by Ivan for consolidating political power in his hands and in those of his issue were not vastly different from those that brought other lands under the rule of Moscow.

There still remained the vexed question of Ivan's successor. The grand duke was married twice, first to Maria, princess of Tver, who died in 1467, and then in 1472 to Sophie Paleologue, a niece of the last Byzantine emperor. Ivan's son by his first wife died, but he left a son, Dimitry. There was some uncertainty and a great deal of intrigue among the boyars over the question whether Ivan should be succeeded by his grandson Dimitry or by Vasili, Ivan's elder son by his second wife. In 1498 Ivan decided in favor of Dimitry and crowned him his co-ruler and successor at a ceremony in the Uspensky Cathedral at which Ivan himself and the metropolitan officiated. Soon, however, the supporters of Sophie and her son had the upper hand. Dimitry was arrested and died in prison in 1509. The Moscow throne went to Vasili, but Ivan III made it clear that it was for him alone to decide who should rule the Muscovite state.

The testament of Ivan III followed traditional lines in dividing the country among his five sons. The share of Vasili, grand duke of Moscow, embraced the grand duchies of Moscow and Vladimir, Novgorod, Pskov, and Tver, and was therefore immeasurably larger than the territories given to his brothers. Moreover, the testament provided that the domains of the junior princes were to revert to the grand duke should the former die without male issue. The rights of coinage and of jurisdiction in the more serious criminal cases, which in the past had belonged to each member of the dynasty, were now made the prerogative of the grand duke. The junior brothers also recognized Vasili's leadership in an agreement prepared simultaneously with the testament. The traditional phraseology of the testament notwithstanding, it was an actual triumph of political absolutism. The junior princes were in all matters to take the orders of the grand duke of Moscow.

The little that is known about the relationship between Vasili III and his four brothers suggests that it was sadly lacking in harmony. Dictation from Moscow was still a novelty to which it took time to become reconciled. In 1511 Simeon, prince of Kaluga and one of Vasili's brothers, was accused of planning to escape to Lithuania. His official disgrace and punishment were prevented by the timely interference of the family and the Church dignitaries, and he died seven years later, presumably in peace. Another brother, Dimitry, was severely reprimanded by Vasili for disregarding his orders and for carrying on plundering expeditions. A third brother, Yuri, is known to have been under the continuous supervision of Vasili's agents, who reported his movements to the grand duke. Yuri, too, was accused of treasonable relations with Lithuania, but a reconciliation with Vasili followed. There is no record of any conflict between Vasili and his younger brother Andrew.

The succession question with which Ivan III had had to wrestle confronted his son in a somewhat different guise. Vasili III was married to Solomonia Saburov, who was childless. In 1525, over the opposition of an influential group of boyars and churchmen but with the approval of the Metropolitan Daniel, whose predecessor, Varlaam, had been deposed and incarcerated in a remote monastery, Vasili forced Solomonia to take the veil, and a few months later he married Helen Glinsky, descendant of a Russo-Lithuanian princely family. By his second wife he had two children, Ivan and George. In conformity with the ancient custom, the dying Vasili divided his realm between his two sons and made his brother Yuri sign an agreement recognizing Ivan as his "senior" and as heir to the Moscow throne. Vasili's testament, unfortunately, has not been preserved. The death of George without issue led to the consolidation of the entire territory of the Muscovite state in the hands of Ivan and, by removing an opportunity for political dismemberment, further contributed to the establishment of absolutism.

MUSCOVY'S INTERNATIONAL POSITION

Significant changes in the international position of Muscovy occurred during the reigns of Ivan III and Vasili III. The Mongol domination, already on the wane towards the end of the rule of Vasili II, was officially terminated in 1480. The Golden Horde itself was wiped out of existence by the Crimean Tartars in 1502. The Muscovite state regained its sovereignty, but the Tartars remained. The Tartar kingdoms of Kazan, the Crimea, and Astrakhan, as well as separate hordes leading a nomadic life in the southern and eastern steppes, continued for many years to be a source of danger and of preoccupation for the Moscow government. Intermittent warfare against the Crimean and the Kazan Tartars filled the reigns both of Ivan III and of Vasili III. Conflicts were followed by negotiations, negotiations and military action sometimes taking place simultaneously. The Russian grand dukes succeeded at times in imposing their candidates as rulers of the Kazan kingdom, but such arrangements never lasted long. Both Ivan and Vasili showed marks of great respect towards the Crimean Tartars and were subject to extortions by the rapacious khans. In spite of Moscow's conciliatory spirit, Tartar raids took place at frequent intervals. In 1521 the Mongol detachments advanced to the walls of the capital, from which Vasili had fled. The invaders retreated only after they had been given a written promise that the grand duke would resume the payment of tribute, a promise which, presumably, was not fulfilled, for military operations were soon resumed. Maintaining a guard for the defense of its southern and eastern frontiers remained one of Moscow's urgent tasks.

The relations of Moscow with its western neighbors and other European countries proceeded along different lines. The grand duchy of Moscow in the days of Vasili II was still practically encircled by Russian lands and had no common frontiers with western nations. The territorial unification of the Muscovite state altered this situation and brought the Moscow government face to face with new and broader problems. It has already been pointed out that Ivan and Vasili not only succeeded in winning over important territories from Lithuania but also proclaimed that they were no longer reconciled to the loss of Russian lands then under Lithuanian rule, thus formulating the national principle of Muscovy's future policy. The relations with the Teutonic Order followed an uneven course. The Germans had every reason to dislike the westward expansion of Muscovy, which presented a real danger to their political independence. In the reign of Ivan III the knights had a number of bloody encounters with the Russians and actively supported Lithuania in her wars with Moscow. In 1517, however, they concluded an alliance with Moscow against Sigismund I, of Poland and Lithuania, a move that led to the defeat of the Teutonic knights by Poland and showed a decline of their influence.

Moscow's international relations, however, were no longer limited to her immediate neighbors. In 1492 Ivan sent a message to the Turkish sultan, and five years later a Russian envoy visited Constantinople. The practical consequences of these *démarches* were nil. Relations with Hungary were established in 1482 and the first Hungarian ambassador arrived in Moscow in 1501. Pope Alexander VI attempted to persuade Ivan to join the Christian rulers in a crusade against the Turks, who were menacing Italy. In 1496 Ivan concluded an alliance with Denmark directed against Sweden. Solovev has observed that Muscovy was discovered by western Europe about the same time as the American continent. Poppel, an adventurous German knight, was greatly surprised to find that there was another Russian state northeast of the Russian territories governed by Lithuania and Poland. After reporting his discovery on his return to Germany, he was sent back to Moscow in 1489 as the ambassador of the German emperor. This first contact with the Holy Roman Empire was followed by several visits by Russian envoys whose chief object was to find a suitable husband for Ivan's daughter, an enterprise in which they failed. Ivan also maintained relations with Venice, which supplied the grand duke with the architects and artisans he needed for the beautification of his capital.

In the reign of Vasili III the participation of Muscovy in European diplomacy became more active. An alliance with Emperor Maximilian against Poland was concluded but proved of little practical value, and in 1518 Vasili sent the first official communication from Moscow to France, suggesting an alliance against Poland, a diplomatic move that brought no response. He was more successful in concluding in 1508 a sixty-year armistice with Sweden. Relations with the Hanseatic League, which had been practically discontinued under Ivan III, were resumed in 1517, and there was an exchange of envoys between Moscow and Pope Leo X which, however, proved fruitless. The grand duke was cool to the reunion of the Churches urged by the pope, nor did he commit himself to the anti-Turkish crusade advocated by Rome. Just as futile were the attempts of Moscow to obtain the support of the Turkish sultan against Lithuania and the Crimean Tartars.

The *début* of the Muscovite state on the diplomatic stage was thus modest. Yet the former isolation from Europe had been broken: Russia was no longer a *terra incognita*. Western Europe was gradually awakening to the fact that the European world did not end on the northeastern frontier of Lithuania and Poland.

"MOSCOW—THE THIRD ROME"

While western Europe was slow and, perhaps, reluctant to take cognizance of Muscovy's political ascendancy, the transformation that had brought about the birth of the autocratic state could not but impress the Russians themselves. The authority and prestige of the grand dukes of Moscow were greatly enhanced by the fate of its old mentor, Byzantium, and by that of its secular enemy, the Golden Horde. Since 1448, as a consequence of the Ferrara-Florence Council,

Russia had elected and consecrated its own metropolitans, thus achieving *de facto* independence from the patriarch of Constantinople. Five years later Byzantium was conquered by the Turks, and in 1480 Khan Akhmad's withdrawal from the banks of the Ugra River, with the subsequent collapse of the Golden Horde, raised Muscovy to the status of a sovereign state. These two events directly affected the position of the Russian Church, which was now left for the first time face to face with the formidable power of Muscovite absolutism, with neither Constantinople nor Sarai to defend its ancient privileges against possible encroachments by the grand dukes. The Church chose the road of submission and threw its influence to the support of the ambitions of the Moscow dynasty.

This attitude, if not entirely disinterested, was nevertheless in harmony with the tradition Russia had inherited from Byzantium. It will be recalled that the Russian Church had always favored unification and, in agreement with the Byzantine theory, had preached the doctrine of the divine origin of the secular power. The fall of Byzantium and of the other centers of Greek Orthodoxy in the Balkans under Turkish domination raised the question of leadership in the Greek Orthodox world. The unhappy fate of Constantinople was explained by the Moscow theologians as a punishment for accepting union with Rome. The successor of Byzantium, it was declared, was Muscovy, whose brilliant political progress at the very time when the ancient strongholds of Greek Orthodoxy were suffering desecration at the hands of the unfaithful was in itself striking evidence of divine grace and also of divine justice. The first Rome had fallen because it had betrayed true Christianity; Constantinople, the Second Rome, suffered a similar fate for a similar reason; Moscow, the Third Rome and the capital of the only truly Christian sovereign, was to continue forever. This curious doctrine, which was developed early in the sixteenth century in the writings of Filotheus, a monk in a Pskov monastery, was probably inspired by similar theories expounded a century earlier in the Slavic Balkan countries, especially in Bulgaria (Miliukov). The Russian theologian had merely to adapt the teaching of his Bulgarian predecessors to local conditions and to substitute Moscow for Tyrnov as the new capital of the Christian world. Although Ivan III and Vasili III appeared to their theologically-minded supporters as the logical successors of Emperor Constantine, some uneasiness about the absence of a definite historical and political link between Constantinople and Moscow was felt. The marriage of Ivan III with Sophie Paleologue, niece of the last emperor of Byzantium, who was killed by the Turks in Constantinople in 1453, provided some foundation for the dynastic and political claims of the Moscow grand dukes. These dynastic ties, however, were much too recent and unimpressive to satisfy the craving of Russian theologians for immemorial tradition. They soon devised a novel and imaginative historical and genealogical scheme which made the Moscow dynasty the direct descendants of "Pruss, brother of the Roman Caesar Augustus." The Kievan Prince Vladimir Monomakh (1113–1125) was said to have received from the Byzantine Emperor Constantine Monomakh (who died when Vladimir was two years old) the present of a crown and vestments which, according to the legend, have been preserved by his descendants. The imagination of the Russian theologians went even further: there came into existence a tale that Russia had received Christianity, not from Byzantium, but directly from Andrew, "brother of Peter the Apostle." The Moscow grand dukes thus became not merely the logical successors of the Byzantine emperors, but the direct descendants of the most ancient ruling house and the leaders of Greek Orthodoxy in their own right. Fantastic as were these pseudo-historical schemes, they gained general acceptance, were incorporated in the revised chronicles, and were later naïvely and ostentatiously displayed before puzzled foreign envoys by Ivan IV as facts of common knowledge. The newly born Muscovite autocracy longed for a suitable historical and genealogical justification; the Church eagerly supplied it.

The solicitude of the Church hierarchy for the strengthening of absolutism was not limited to ingenious excursions into history. The alliance between Church and state became the corner-stone of the teaching of an influential ultra-conservative theological school which derived its inspiration from the writings and untiring activities of Joseph Sanin, founder and abbot of the Volokolam Monastery and a contemporary of Ivan III. He was among the most outspoken champions of that rigid attachment to the letter of the dogma and to that external observance which is characteristic of Russian Christianity. Faith and blind obedience were declared to be the sole road to salvation; any attempt to reason regarding sacred matters was certain to lead to perdition. Quotations from the Scriptures, the more the better, were the only acceptable arguments, while any manifestation of independent thought was heresy and blasphemy. Joseph was just as

uncompromising in his defense and glorification of Muscovite absolutism. He maintained that "although the tsar was like other men
in his physical characteristics, in his power he was similar to God in
heaven." And he enjoined the members of the clergy, even the bishops,
never to argue with the monarch but merely, with his own permission,
to implore him and plead with him.

In spite of the subservient attitude of the Church hierarchy towards
the secular power, there was one question which was pregnant with
possibilities of conflict between the state and the Church: the question
of the estates owned by the monasteries. This type of landownership,
which, it will be remembered, increased substantially towards the end
of the fifteenth century, had in the past been respected by the Russian
princes and had enjoyed the protection of the Tartar khans. The traditional immunity of monastic estates received a rude shock when
Ivan III confiscated many of the lands owned by the Church institutions in Novgorod, a confiscation that followed the incorporation of
the "free city" into the Muscovite state. The Moscow government
needed land for distribution in service tenure. The ranks had been
steadily increased as a consequence of the rapid expansion of its territory and of the almost uninterrupted wars. The large ecclesiastical
estates were a coveted prize that did not escape the attention of the
grand dukes. Secularization, however, was a form of cooperation between the state and the Church that Joseph and his followers were
not prepared to accept. They were willing to serve Muscovite absolutism, and even invited the interference of the secular authorities
with the affairs of the Church, but they were also determined to preserve and, if possible, to increase the wealth the Church had succeeded
in accumulating in its hands. The services rendered to the autocracy by the higher ecclesiastical hierarchy were not unselfish, although,
according to Joseph's teaching, the wealth of the monasteries was to
be devoted exclusively to the relief of the poor. His own Volokolam
monastery was noted for the strictness of its regulations, which, unlike
those of the other monasteries, were rigidly enforced.

At the end of the fifteenth century and during the sixteenth, the
question of secularization was brought to the fore by a movement of
dissenters. The so-called heresy of the "Judaizers" was discovered in
Novgorod about 1470, at the time the "free city" was waging its last
and losing battle against Moscow. The teaching of the Judaizers is
known only from the writings of its opponents, among whom Joseph

of Volokolam was prominent. According to their detractors, the Judaizers denied the Holy Trinity, maintained that the Messiah had not
yet come, that Christ was a mere man, and that therefore Judaism,
and not Christianity, was the only true religion. These charges, however, must be treated with caution, since they were made in the heat
of polemics by the enemies of the new sect. If the charges were true,
the teaching of the Judaizers would constitute, not heresy, but a
repudiation of Christianity. Anti-Semitism was not unknown in the
Russian Church in the earlier centuries, and was probably fostered by
a similar attitude prevailing in Byzantium. The name of Judaizers was,
therefore, a useful weapon in combating the new religious movement,
which seems, as a matter of fact, to have been inspired by three Jews
—Skharia, Moses, and Samuel—who came to Novgorod in the seventies of the fifteenth century. It is believed that the teaching of the
Judaizers bore a resemblance to the earlier movement of the *strigolniki*.[1] The Judaizers denounced monasticism, rejected icons and prayers
for the dead, denied the necessity of churches and church services, condemned the Church hierarchy as based on simony, and, to make things
worse, proclaimed that "reason is supreme and is hampered by faith."
This heresy was in its essence a rationalistic movement influenced
probably by western-European learning which had reached Russia
through the instrumentality of Jewish authors. Its appearance in Novgorod may be explained by that city's old established western connections and also by the political crisis through which Novgorod was living at the time. The forcible removal in 1479 of Theophilus, last elected
archbishop of Novgorod, was followed by the appointment to the
Novgorod see of the two devout partisans of Moscow, Sergius and then
Gennadius (1484–1504), whose ruthless activities contributed to the
movement against the established Church.

The rationalistic attitude of the Judaizers was a thorn in the flesh
of the dominant group in the Church hierarchy led by Joseph of
Volokolam. To oppose reason to faith was in itself an unspeakable in-
sult to the tradition of the Russian Church, with its devotion to dogma
and external observance. By attacking monasticism and prayers for
the dead, the Judaizers undermined the foundation of the Church's
wealth and power. Joseph and his friends turned their thunder on the
heretics. Unfortunately for the official hierarchy, the Judaizers proved
to be better theologians than were their opponents. They drew freely

[1] See p. 134.

in their polemics on sources that were not accessible to their enemies since they were not available in a Russian translation. It was as a part of his campaign against the Judaizers that Gennadius arranged for the first complete translation of the Bible, a translation that contained some correction of the text previously in use. Ironically, in forging this weapon to combat western influences Gennadius had to depend largely on services of western scholars, since few Russians could be found to undertake the work of translating (Speransky). Gennadius, like Joseph, put faith in stronger methods than those of persuasion. He advanced the not very Christian view that one should not argue with the heretics, but "execute them, burn them at the stake, and hang them." He was eager to imitate the methods of the Spanish Inquisition, to which he referred with approval in his writings.

The Orthodox theologians themselves provided the Judaizers with an easy triumph which contributed to the spreading of the doctrine of the latter group. From the official point of view, 1492 was the seven thousandth year from the creation, and it was confidently expected that it would bring the second advent of Christ and the Last Judgment. These gloomy forecasts were supported by a variety of arguments drawn from the Scriptures, the Apocalypse of St. John, and the Apocrypha. The Judaizers took a skeptical view of the impending doom and, basing their prophecy on the Jewish calendar, maintained that the world still had some 1,747 years to go before it reached the fateful year 7,000. The Last Judgment having failed to materialize, the Judaizers did not refrain from pointing out that if the official Church had committed so gross an error in a matter of primary importance it might be wrong also on other disputed points. The argument was convincing, and after 1492, in spite of the persecution of the Judaizers, their movement appears to have gained in momentum. They had, indeed, adherents at the court of Ivan III, including his daughter-in-law Helen. The Metropolitan Zosima (1490–1494) is also frequently, and probably wrongly, represented as a Judaizer (Golubinsky), in spite of the fact that in 1490 he assembled a church council which condemned the heresy. He was relieved of his duties in 1494 on the ground that he was morally unfit for his office, but the actual reasons that led to his retirement are not clear.

The relatively lenient attitude of the Moscow government towards the Judaizers was influenced by the latter's advocacy of the secularization of ecclesiastical estates, a policy that commended itself to Ivan

III. Secularization was also urged, on high moral grounds, by the representatives of another dissenting movement, that of the so-called Volga hermits. The founder of this movement was one of the outstanding personalities of the fifteenth century, Nil Sorsky (1433–1508). Nil Sorsky has been represented by his chief opponent, Joseph of Volokolam, as a Judaizer, although it is difficult to see how his teaching could have been construed as heresy. His real and unforgivable sin against the official Church consisted in being a true Christian, a thing rare enough at any time in any country and all but unknown in the Muscovy of the fifteenth century. Nil Sorsky held that inner conviction, and not external observance, was the very essence of Christianity and that such conviction can only be achieved through a critical study of the Scriptures. In his opinion "to believe" was "to understand"—the opposite of the official view, which maintained that "to understand" was "to believe." Nil Sorsky, who had traveled widely in the Christian east, had spent some time at Mount Athos, and his experiences on the "Holy Mountain" affected his attitude towards monasticism. The conditions prevailing in Russian monasteries filled him with disgust. He severely condemned monasteries based on a communal organization, advocated the "hermitage" (*skit*) type of monasticism, and insisted on the necessity of the monks' divesting themselves of all earthly possessions and giving them to the poor. In his opinion wealth and monasticism were irreconcilable. The doctrine of Nil Sorsky, an outspoken opponent of the ownership of land by the monasteries, therefore, had an important bearing upon the relations between Church and state. He saw no reason why monks—the "living deads"—who have avowedly renounced all worldly interests should mix in politics or play any part at the grand-ducal court. He also insisted that the Church should retain its independence from the secular power. According to his view, the grand duke had no voice in ecclesiastical matters. While Joseph of Volokolam argued that it was quite immaterial whether "a sinner or a heretic was destroyed by brute force or by prayer," and Gennadius of Novgorod demanded the execution of the Judaizers, Nil Sorsky held that the Church should never use violence but must limit itself to spiritual weapons, such as persuasion and prayer. The teaching of Nil Sorsky, although heavily tinged with rationalism and asceticism, remained at the same time strictly within the doctrine of Greek Orthodoxy, and enjoyed for a time considerable popularity. After his return from Mount Athos he established between 1473 and 1489 a hermitage in the wild and inaccessible region east of the Volga, on the fringe of the Russian world. His example proved contagious, and the woods of northeastern Russia became dotted with hermitages. Thus the movement of the so-called *Zavolzhskie startsy*—literally "hermits beyond the Volga"—came into being. Incidentally, it played a part in fostering the colonization of the northeastern territories, since the hermitages became centers of attraction for many seeking to escape the oppression of the Muscovite state.

The rationalism of Nil Sorsky and his followers, and their attitude both towards monastic estates and towards the relationship between Church and state, singled them out for the attacks of the official hierarchy, led first by Joseph of Volokolam and later by the Metropolitan Daniel (1522–1539). Somewhat unexpectedly, the saintly hermits found support among an influential group of the boyars who, seeing in the secularization of monastic estates the only guaranty against the further encroachment of the state upon their own privileges, favored the independence of the Church from the state as a possible check on the arbitrariness of the grand-ducal rule. Both Ivan III and Vasili III hesitated for a time to take drastic action against the rationalists, and followed a somewhat vacillating policy. On the one hand, secularization advocated by the Judaizers and Nil Sorsky was tempting; on the other, the exaltation of the secular power by Joseph of Volokolam and his disciples was both useful and pleasing. The situation was further complicated by intrigues of rival parties at the Moscow court. These were the underlying causes of the ebb and flow in the persecution of the rationalists, with persecution gradually winning the upper hand. In Novgorod, Gennadius submitted the Judaizers to public indignities and clamored for their destruction. In 1490 the Metropolitan Zosima called a council which condemned the heresy but inflicted upon the culprits relatively mild punishments—excommunication and imprisonment. Four years later Zosima himself was removed from office as a sympathizer with the Judaizers, yet a number of Judaizer supporters continued to occupy important positions in the grand duke's immediate entourage. In 1499 the court party supporting Ivan's daughter-in-law Helen and her son Dimitry, whom Ivan III had made his co-ruler a few months earlier, suffered a shattering blow. Its leaders, Prince Riapolovsky and two Princes Patrikeev—father and son—were found guilty of treason and sentenced to die. Riapolovsky was executed, but the Patrikeevs were merely forced to take holy orders.

Helen and Dimitry were arrested in 1502, and Ivan appointed his son Vasili as his co-ruler and successor. The details of this unhappy affair remain obscure, but it was presumably rooted in the intrigues of the rival boyar parties supporting respectively Helen and Dimitry and Vasili and his mother, Sophie Paleologue. The change did not augur well for the rationalists, with whom Helen was known to be in sympathy, while the official Church hierarchy was on the side of Sophie and Vasili. The Church council of 1504 took up again the question of the Judaizers. This time Joseph of Volokolam and Gennadius received full satisfaction: the leaders of the heresy were burned at the stake, while their followers were either imprisoned or exiled to remote parts of the country.

A few months earlier Joseph had won another and even more important victory. At a Church council assembled in 1503 to discuss the not very exciting question of the status of widowed clerics, Nil Sorsky unexpectedly raised the vexed problem of monastic estates and denounced the practice on grounds with which we are familiar. His stand was supported by the grand duke himself. Joseph of Volokolam, who had left Moscow before the question of monastic estates came up for discussion, was hastily summoned to the capital. In the course of the debate its subject was broadened to include not only monastic but all ecclesiastical estates. Joseph, supporting his contention by innumerable texts and quotations, opposed secularization as contrary to the practice of the Church. He also advanced the celebrated argument that summed up his attitude towards the relation between Church and state: "If the monasteries are deprived of the villages they own, how will it be possible for an honorable and noble man to take orders? And if there are no honorable monks, where shall we find candidates for the metropolitanate, the archbishopric, the bishopric, and other honorable offices? And if there are no honorable and noble monks, then faith itself will be undermined." To Nil Sorsky a monastery was a place for prayer and meditation away from worldly ambitions and preoccupations; to Joseph it was primarily a training school of "honorable and noble" Church—and therefore state—officials. The position of Ivan in this controversy was somewhat puzzling. His sympathies, dictated by a pressing need for land to distribute in service tenure, and perhaps by a desire to increase the domain of the Crown, were on the side of Nil Sorsky. After the council rejected the latter's proposal, the grand duke requested from the council three more reports on the disputed issue. Yet he took no action except to impose restrictions limiting somewhat the rights of the monasteries to inherit estates, restrictions that were of little practical effect and seem to have been generally disregarded. Ivan also showed no resentment against Joseph and his friends who were opposed to secularization. The Church hierarchy, it is true, spared no effort to flatter and serve the new autocrat of All Russia. It was at this time that the legend of "Moscow—the Third Rome," was developed and entrenched. This was more than a mere travesty of history—it was also a program of political action, the subservience of the Church to the state. The question of secularization was indefinitely postponed, but the realization and fear that it might be reopened at any time hung like the sword of Damocles over the heads of the ecclesiastical dignitaries who espoused the view of Joseph of Volokolam on the true mission of the Church.

The controversies carried on in the first half of the sixteenth century by the disciples of Nil Sorsky were a reminder that the danger was not over. Nil Sorsky himself died in peace in 1508, but his tradition was continued in the writings of Vassian, the younger of the two Princes Patrikeev, who were forced by Ivan III to embrace monasticism. Vassian, a believer in the principles expounded by Nil Sorsky, left a number of works which show considerable courage, for they present an indictment of the conditions of his time. The rationalistic point of view was also expounded in the writings of another outstanding figure of this period, Maxim the Greek. A man of good education, Maxim before coming to Russia spent a number of years in Italy, where he learned to admire the work of Savonarola, who was, perhaps, his teacher. Savonarola's denunciation of the papacy for its absorption in worldly interests and his glorification of early Christianity left a deep imprint upon Maxim's mind. In 1518 he was sent to Russia at the request of Vasili III, who had decided to have certain religious books translated into Slavonic and also to correct some of the earlier translations. The polemics still continuing against the Judaizers were probably the reason behind Vasili's venture. The often quoted statement that Maxim came to Russia in order to translate some of the Greek and Latin books from the large grand-ducal library is based on a seventeenth century source and is questionable, since the very existence of such a library has been denied by competent students. The choice of

Maxim for the task was in a sense unfortunate because he did not know the Slavonic language. The work was carried on in two stages: Maxim translated the Greek texts into Latin, and then his assistants retranslated them into Slavonic. In spite of the inherent disadvantages of this method, Maxim's first translation won high praise. His second task included both translation and revision of texts already in use. The same cumbersome method of procedure was followed, and while Maxim succeeded in eliminating some of the old errors, new ones crept in. Tampering, even at the command of the grand duke, with ancient religious texts, however imperfect, was a dangerous enterprise in the Russia of the sixteenth and seventeenth centuries. Maxim, moreover, was a frank and vigorous critic of many of Russia's Church and state institutions, which had little in common with his exalted view of life. He was a close friend of Vassian Patrikeev, and shared the latter's aversion for monastic estates. Daniel, then metropolitan of Moscow, a devout disciple of Joseph of Volokolam, and one of the most sinister figures among the leaders of the Russian Church, dreaded the influence of Vassian and Maxim on Vasili III. He had personal reasons for hating the former, who, being related to the grand duke, was a powerful figure at the Moscow court (in spite of his earlier disgrace) and had opposed Daniel's candidacy for the metropolitanate. Using unsavory methods, Daniel struck first at Maxim and then at Vassian. In 1525 the unhappy Greek humanitarian and scholar was arrested and tried by a council of bishops over which the metropolitan presided. Maxim was accused of a miscellaneous assortment of crimes ranging from heresy and practice of black magic to treasonable intrigues with the Turkish sultan. His plea for permission to return to his native land was rejected and he was sentenced to excommunication and life imprisonment in the Volokolam monastery, that is, he was delivered into the hands of his worst enemies, for Volokolam was the stronghold of Joseph's tradition. Six years later Maxim was dragged out of prison and tried a second time. His opposition to monastic estates was among the accusations brought against him on this occasion. The object of this second trial remains obscure. Golubinsky ascribes it largely to Daniel's insatiable vindictiveness. The new trial changed nothing in Maxim's unhappy fate except that he was transferred to another monastery and continued to linger behind the bars of his ecclesiastical prison until 1551. He died five years later. It was during these long years of incarceration that he wrote some of his best works. The calvary of Savonarola, whom Maxim so deeply revered, was shorter if even more brutal: he was hanged and then burned at the stake by order of Pope Alexander IV.

Vassian shared the fate of his friend Maxim. An estrangement, the causes of which are not clear, took place between him and Vasili III. In 1531 Vassian was tried by a Church council on the charge of heresy, was found guilty, and imprisoned in the Volokolam monastery, where he died. There was no room in the Russian Church for dissenters, especially when they had the temerity to challenge ancient prejudices, to oppose reason to blind faith, and to attack the sacrosanct institution of ecclesiastical estates. The triumph of the school of Joseph of Volokolam was complete, but this meant that the Church had renounced all attempts to assert its independence from the secular power.

SOCIAL CHANGES

The landed nobility, like the Church, had contributed to the unification of the country and to the rise of absolutism. It was not long, however, before the Frankenstein monster devoured those who had brought it into existence. The political influence of the landed aristocracy rested, it will be recalled, on its ownership of hereditary estates and its ancient and jealously guarded right to accept service on its own terms under princes of its own choosing. The latter privilege, although frequently infringed, exercised a restraining influence upon the arbitrary policies of the earlier princes. Ivan III devised a novel and effective method for preventing the boyars from leaving the service of Moscow. He initiated a system of joint responsibility under which the relatives and friends of a boyar were made liable to heavy payments in the event of his escape. The first known instance of such an arrangement occurred in 1474, when eight boyars were induced to put up guaranties for the "non-departure" of Prince Daniel Kholmsky. The method was extensively used in the reigns of Vasili III and Ivan IV, with the result that the upper group of the nobility became entangled in a complex network of mutual guaranties. Although the right of the boyars to leave the service of Moscow was never formally abolished by either Ivan III or Vasili III, after the consolidation of political power in their hands the treasured privilege lost all practical significance. Towards the end of Vasili's reign there were left no independent Russian princes whose service the discontented Moscow boyars could enter. There still remained the possibility of abandoning

Moscow in favor of Lithuania and Poland. Such transfer of allegiance to a foreign ruler, however, was construed by the new national Russian state as treason, and the estates of the culprit were confiscated. There was only one master in Muscovy, and the boyars had to bow to his will.

The second pillar of the political influence of the landed aristocracy —its ancient right to own hereditary estates (*votchina*) unencumbered by any obligation to render services to the prince (except, of course, the payment of taxes)—was gradually but effectively destroyed by Ivan and Vasili. It was during this period that the practice of granting estates in service tenure (*pomestie*) received wide application. The Moscow government needed a large army to defend its ever expanding frontiers, especially in the south and in the east. Since the resources of the treasury were inadequate to meet the heavy military expenses, the granting of land in military tenure became the customary form of defraying the costs of army service. Although *de jure* the *votchina* and the *pomestie* were different forms of landholding, the former was gradually and without any specific legislation merged with the latter. This transformation had a certain logical connection with the disappearance of the boyars' right to take service under any prince while retaining possession of their estates wherever located. As the breach of allegiance to Moscow led to the confiscation of estates, conversely the enjoyment of an estate in Muscovy entailed the obligation to serve the grand duke. It would be unwise, however, to impute to the Russian statesmen of the fifteenth and sixteenth centuries any excessive attachment to formal logic. They were confronted with the concrete and urgent problem of enlisting all the resources of the country in the service of the state, eliminating any possibility of opposition. This they achieved by methods that were crude but effective, leaving the rationalization of the process to the future historians. The former sovereign princes whose domains were incorporated in the Muscovite state were the first to feel the effect of the policy of centralization. Many of them continued to live in their former principalities, enjoying a considerable degree of political independence. They exercised broad powers in local affairs and in taxation, administered justice, and maintained their own private armies. The danger inherent in this situation did not escape the vigilance of Moscow. Without the enactment of any general measure, little by little the traditional privileges of the former sovereign princes were curtailed. The former private armies were put under the command of military leaders appointed by Moscow. Both Ivan and Vasili, under various pretexts, deprived the princes of their hereditary domains, or at least of the capital cities of their former principalities, granting them instead estates somewhere else but without the power to administer justice and levy taxes. Under these conditions not much was left of the ancient privileges of the former sovereign princes except the high-sounding, if empty, princely title.

The hereditary rights of the boyars underwent a no less drastic transformation. The long-established practice of issuing both to ecclesiastical and to secular landlords letters patent conferring special privileges in administering justice and in collecting taxes [2] facilitated the erasure of the once clear distinction between *votchina* and *pomestie*. Although originally the letters patent had nothing to do with creating the right of ownership, they came gradually to be looked upon as the very source of proprietary rights, as the only reliable title to land. The Muscovite autocracy, by revising the former grants and by refusing to recognize the letters patent issued by any authority except "the grand dukes themselves," effectively established itself as the sole fountain of the right to own land. The enjoyment of estates was granted only in exchange for the obligation to serve the Crown. The change was ominous and, indeed, in a sense revolutionary, although it was introduced by piecemeal *ad hoc* decisions, and the principle of service as the basis of land tenure was not embodied in any legislative act. The legal practice governing land tenure in the reign of Vasili III was confused and lacking in uniformity. The majority of the landlords were enrolled in the military forces, but the exact character of their duties was not defined. Moreover, as late as the middle of the sixteenth century some of the holders of estates did not serve the state directly, but were attached to the establishments of the boyars, of government officials, and even of persons having no definite standing. Some still succeeded in escaping service altogether (Diakonov). In spite of these departures, the general tendency to make government service compulsory for all landlords was unmistakable. The harshest manifestations of this policy, as well as of Moscow's determination to break up the political influence of the boyars, were the mass deportations of landlords applied in Novgorod, Pskov, Yaroslavl, Viatka, and Riazan. The deportees were settled in remote parts of the country, where they received land in service tenure, their former estates being

[2] See p. 101.

distributed on a similar basis to men foreign to local tradition. The assumption by the grand dukes of unrestricted control over the entire land reserves reduced the once independent landlords to the position of servants of the state.

The diminution in influence in the position of the boyars was reflected in their relations with the Moscow grand dukes. As long as the landed aristocracy retained its economic independence and the right to withdraw allegiance to the sovereign, the Moscow rulers were anxious to have its support, especially since their interests had in the past often been identical. After the establishment of absolutism this support was no longer needed, and the interests of the boyars and of the Crown were at times in conflict. Many of the nobles, indeed, were looked upon with suspicion by the Moscow government, and the charges of treason brought against them were frequent. An outstanding example of the methods by which Ivan dealt with the boyar opposition is furnished by the execution of Prince Riapolovsky and the incarceration of the two Princes Patrikeev in monasteries. These methods were by no means novel, but the high standing of the accused men and the severity of the sentences could not have failed to produce the desired impression in boyar circles. Under Ivan, and especially under Vasili, the boyar duma, the somewhat informal but nevertheless authoritative council of higher government officials drawn from the boyar class, suffered an eclipse. It continued to exist and to function, but the intolerance displayed towards their advisers by Ivan and Vasili silenced all expression of adverse opinion. Bersen-Beklemishev was curtly ordered by Vasili to leave the duma for expressing his views too freely and was eventually decapitated for speaking disrespectfully of the grand duke. Vasili was in the habit of settling important questions of state within a small group of personal advisers, some of them of humble extraction. The political influence of the boyars, as a social class, was fading away.

Although there was a strong feeling of discontent and even of hostility among the landed nobility, it failed to express itself in any organized attempt to resist the march of absolutism. This puzzling state of affairs must be explained by the lack of unity and *esprit de corps* among the boyars themselves. The Moscow aristocracy of the fifteenth and sixteenth centuries was comprised of many varied elements, of people who had drifted into the new national capital under the pressure of changing political fortunes. Prominent among them

were the former Russian sovereign and quasi-sovereign princes, Lithuanian princes who entered the service of Moscow, and the boyars who
had formerly held office under these once independent rulers. These
foreign elements gradually merged with the old Moscow boyar families.
The struggle between the newcomers and the old servants of the
Moscow throne for lucrative offices and court influence led to the
creation, with the sanction of the Moscow grand dukes, of a peculiar
institution known as *mestnichestvo* (from *mesto* [place]). *Mestnichestvo* was the arrangement of the members of the aristocratic families
in a hierarchical order, their respective positions entitling them to
definite places at the grand-ducal table, at court functions, in the
boyar duma, and in government service. The chief elements that determined the respective position of each noble was the genealogical
standing of his family and the government offices held by his ancestors.
Official registers dealing with these matters were kept by special departments. The essence of the system consisted in an attempt to
stabilize the relative positions of the various families. According to
Kliuchevsky, *mestnichestvo*, unlike feudalism, did not create hereditary
rights to the tenure of definite offices, but established a hereditary relationship in the relative positions of the various families with reference
to the offices held by their members in the government service. What
really mattered was, not the office itself, but the respective positions
of the various officeholders. This system, which probably had its origin
in the customary arrangements preceding territorial unification, called
for extraordinarily complex computations and led to endless and bitter
conflicts among the leading boyar families. It worked in practice as a
check on freedom of appointment by the grand dukes and later by the
tsars, since the entire structure of the official hierarchy was controlled
by inflexible and almost hopelessly confused rules. That this cumbersome institution survived until the end of the seventeenth century was
due, at least in part, to the fact that after 1550 some of the higher
military offices were exempted from the application of what Kliuchevsky aptly described as the *"mestnichestvo* arithmetics." Much of the
energy of the boyars had been absorbed in the litigation to safeguard
the relative positions of their families. Instead of uniting to oppose the
encroachment of absolutism on their ancient privileges, the Moscow
nobles, in order to uphold the family honor, fought one another,
sometimes in bodily conflict and to the considerable detriment of
their venerable beards. According to the then prevailing view, death

itself was preferable to the unspeakable disgrace of either sitting at the grand-ducal table or serving in the army "below" a man whose ancestors' record did not entitle him to the higher position.

Another reason for the absence of an organized boyar opposition was the casual manner in which both Ivan III and Vasili III proceeded with the fundamental revision of the traditional privileges of the nobility. They never passed any general measure forbidding the boyars to serve under another ruler or making land tenure conditional on government service, nor did they abolish the boyar duma. They displayed much ruthlessness in dealing with individual nobles, but they never openly attacked the aristocracy as a class. This absence of definite government action, which might have served as a focal point for the crystallization of boyar opposition, has sometimes been cited as proof of the insight, shrewdness, and even political wisdom of Ivan and Vasili. It is more likely that they were acting without a definite plan, on the spur of the moment, and under the pressure of political exigencies, without clearly realizing the full import of the measures they were taking. The transformation that took place in the position of the upper classes was nevertheless of far-reaching importance to Russia's future.

The new status of the Moscow grand dukes was reflected in the appearance of their capital and in the changed tone of court life. Both Ivan and Vasili devoted much attention to the beautification of Moscow. Italian architects erected a number of cathedrals and churches, grand-ducal palaces built of stone replaced the old and less pretentious wooden structures, the Kremlin was surrounded by stone walls with towers. Court etiquette, probably not without the exercise of some influence by Sophie Paleologue, became much more stiff and elaborate. Ivan, who frequently used the title of "Sovereign (gosudar) of all Russia by the grace of God," was referred to, in some official documents, as "tsar and autocrat," and the two-headed eagle of Byzantium was adopted as the official emblem of unified Russia.

On the foundation laid by Vasili II, his son and grandson erected the imposing edifice of the autocratic state. This was, of course, purchased at a price. "The unification of northeastern Russia was achieved through the destruction of all local independent political forces, whose functions became absorbed in the authority of the grand-ducal throne," writes Presniakov. "These forces, however, doomed as they were by historical conditions, were the custodians of the Russian legal and social institutions based on immemorial custom. Their downfall undermined the stability of the traditional framework of the state. The new social structure was to be built up from the ruins of the past by the grand-ducal power, which sought not only unity but also unhampered freedom in disposing of the forces and resources of the realm. Political unification (*edinoderzhavie*) under Moscow led to Muscovite absolutism."

CHAPTER VIII

THE FIRST TSAR

Ivan the Dread

---- ✳ ----

THE RULE OF THE BOYARS

The long reign of Ivan IV (1533–1584) constitutes one of the most puzzling and disputed pages of Russia's history. The distressing variety of conflicting interpretations is due primarily to the cause that has been so frequently emphasized in this discussion—the inadequacy of available sources. "Materials for the history of Ivan the Dread are far from being complete," writes Professor Platonov, an outstanding student of Russia's sixteenth and seventeenth centuries, "and those who have no first-hand knowledge of the sources may be surprised to learn that there are whole years and even periods of years for which no information is available on Ivan's private life and affairs." No wonder, then, that, according to the same author, there remains "ample opportunity for guesswork and fanciful interpretations."

At the time of the death of his father, Vasili III, Ivan was an infant, three years old. His mother, Helen, governed the country in his name with the assistance of a group of boyars headed by Prince Ivan Ovchina-Telepnev-Obolensky, who, it was rumored, was something more than a friend to the grand duchess. The ancient feuds between the princely and boyar families, feuds that had been kept more or less under control during the stern rule of Vasili, broke out again with new force. Many of the representatives of the nobility were suspected, sometimes not without good reason, of treasonable relations with Lithuania and Turkey, or of conspiring against Ivan and his mother. Suspicion fell upon the two surviving brothers of Vasili, Yuri and Andrew. They were both arrested, Andrew together with his wife and son, Vladimir. Andrew died in prison. Helen's uncle, Prince

Michael Glinsky, Prince Ivan Vorotynsky, Prince Ivan Belsky, Michael Vorontsov, and many others found themselves behind bars, while a large number of their followers and friends met an even worse fate. Helen died suddenly in 1538. According to foreign reports (Herberstein) she was poisoned. Prince Ivan Obolensky was arrested seven days later and starved to death in prison. This change, however, had no real effect upon the political situation, and the strife between the boyar families continued for another ten years. The princes Shuisky, Belsky, and Glinsky played a leading part in the bloody conflict waged on the steps of the throne, a struggle carried on by vile intrigues accompanied by deportations, confiscations of estates, tortures, and executions. The contending parties displayed the scantiest respect for the feelings and person of their youthful sovereign, some of their acts of violence being perpetrated in the presence of Ivan. The Metropolitan Daniel was forced to relinquish his office in 1539. Two years later his successor, Joasaph, suffered a similar fate and was incarcerated in a remote monastery. Ivan's mentors did not hesitate to invade the privacy of his bedroom, where a political opponent was suspected of seeking safety. Ivan himself has drawn in his celebrated letters to Prince Kurbsky an impressive, if perhaps somewhat over-dramatized, picture of the indignities inflicted upon him by the leading boyars. It is believed that the unhealthful conditions under which the young monarch spent his boyhood had a great deal to do in determining his outlook and in framing his future methods and policies.

IVAN IV

Faulty and fragmentary as is the available information bearing on Ivan's character and private life, a brief recapitulation of at least the most important facts seems essential, for the young grand duke early asserted himself as his country's autocratic master. The savage cruelty, heavily tinged with sadism, that is one of the outstanding characteristics of Ivan's rule became apparent while he was still a boy. From the moment he mastered the manly art of riding, the future tsar, accompanied by a joyful band of boisterous and irrepressible youngsters, was frequently seen galloping in the streets of his capital and in the countryside, freely using his whip on the frightened townsmen and villagers. It was not long before this pastime began to alternate with excursions into the field of extreme sexual license. Ivan's character presented an inextricable maze of contradictions. His depravity in no way interfered with his deep piety, which was, however, of a distinctly Russian brand. Were the assertion not so insidious, one might be tempted to describe his conduct as an almost perfect specimen of the then prevailing attitude towards Christianity: rigid attachment to its dogmas and external observances and complete disregard for its inner meaning, for the principles of Christian morality which Nil Sorsky and the Volga hermits so rightly treasured. Endowed with an unusual memory and with no mean, albeit somewhat erratic, literary abilities, Ivan read much and assimilated an amazing number of biblical and historical texts, which he quoted, usually incorrectly, in his wordy speeches and messages. He surely qualifies as the most literate and articulate among the Russian sovereigns, except for Catherine II. It seems likely that the theological education of Ivan owed much to the influence of the Metropolitan Macarius (1542–1563), a man of considerable erudition, who succeeded in preserving until his death the friendship of his young sovereign. Macarius was a devout disciple of Joseph of Volokolam and a firm believer in the subordination of the Church to the state, provided that the Church retained its ancient privileges, especially its vast estates. Ivan, in spite of his profound piety, showed on many occasions flagrant disregard for elementary decency in his treatment of the Church and its dignitaries. The metropolitans who followed Macarius found it difficult to maintain themselves in office. His immediate successor, Anastasius, retired in 1566, officially for reasons of health. Herman, who came after him, was almost immediately removed from office. Philip, the next metropolitan, had the temerity to plead with the tsar for some of the men sentenced to die. He was roughly handled, sent to a remote monastery, and there strangled in 1569 by Maliuta-Skuratov, one of Ivan's lieutenants. The members of the clergy, both high and low, fared no better than did the head of the Russian Church. Pimon, archbishop of Novgorod, who had to bear the full impact of Ivan's fury during the punitive expedition against Novgorod in 1570, was removed from office after he had been forced to endure many indignities. There is some disagreement in the sources as to the fate of his successor, Leonid. According to one account he was sewn into a bear's skin and thrown to the dogs; according to another account he was strangled. It was a common occurrence for Ivan's victims to meet their doom in churches, and not infrequently during the mass. Church properties and the clergy were singled out for the special attention of the invaders during the Novgorod punitive expedition of 1570. Church buildings were desecrated, plundered, and burned; priests were publicly flogged, tortured, and murdered. And yet Ivan seldom missed a mass, and spent much of his time composing monastic rules or in such pious exercises as devising elaborate and dignified ceremonies for the consecration of the metropolitan.

Ivan was the first ruler of Russia openly to espouse the doctrine of political absolutism. In 1547, at the age of seventeen, he was solemnly crowned tsar of All the Russias, and thus officially assumed a title that had been loosely used by his ancestors for a century or more. The only coronation known in the earlier Russian history was that of Ivan III's ill fated grandson Dimitry, who never reigned. The Chronicle represents Ivan's coronation as the fulfillment of his personal wish. It seems more likely, however, as suggested by Golubinsky, that the desirability of the more resounding title was impressed upon the young prince by the Metropolitan Macarius, that champion of semi-theocratic absolutism and the unification of Russia. The anomalous position of the Russian Church and Ivan's own rigid dogmatism in ecclesiastical matters, as well as his changing moods, are illustrated by the fact that doubts had arisen concerning the validity of a coronation performed by the Russian metropolitan. Ten years after the ceremony, in 1557, Ivan requested the patriarch of Constantinople to confirm his new title. No answer was made from Constantinople until 1561, when the patriarch wrote to Ivan expressing his willingness to confer upon him the title of tsar, but declaring that a coronation performed by a mere metropolitan was invalid and demanding that the ceremony should be repeated by a representative of the patriarch. The Constantinople patriarchate, solely tried by the Turkish rule, was eager to reassert its supremacy over the Russian Church. Ivan in the meantime had overcome his former scruples, and no further action was taken in the matter. The new title added nothing to the actual powers of the occupant of the Moscow throne. It merely served to emphasize the already unchallengeable supremacy of the Moscow dynasty over the descendants of the other Russian rulers.

Ivan held a most exalted view of the nature of his high office. In his voluminous pronouncements, especially in his letters to Prince Kurbsky, he expounded a somewhat crude yet comprehensive theory of monarchical absolutism. To him the powers of the sovereign were of divine origin. He was God's own representative on earth. It was his duty to be the actual ruler of his country and not a mere figurehead. No human institution, such as the council of boyars, should exercise any control over the will of the sovereign. The Church, too, should occupy a strictly subordinate position. It was the interference of the Church with secular matters, according to Ivan, that brought about the downfall of Byzantium. The legitimacy of the Moscow dynasty was established by virtue of the principle of heredity, through the passing of the throne from father to son. The genealogy of the House of Riurik thus acquired special importance. In his anxiety to prove that he was not only Russia's monarch by the grace of God but also the offspring of the world's most ancient and illustrious princely house, Ivan espoused the grotesque and fanciful theory of "Moscow—the Third Rome" and raised the vagaries of obscure theologians to the dignity of an official state doctrine. In negotiations with foreign nations Ivan and his ambassadors continuously referred to "Pruss, brother of the Roman Caesar Augustus," as the Russian tsar's ancestor, and they treated with ostentatious contempt European rulers who, like the kings of Poland, owed their Crown to the whims of an electoral college and not to divine grace. None of the elements of Ivan's political outlook were original or novel. Nevertheless, the combination of the various elements and the method of presentation, with its bizarre assortment of distorted biblical texts and sometimes puzzling historical parallels drawn from miscellaneous sources, would seem to justify Professor Valdenberg's conclusion that Ivan deserves a place among the few authors who have made a real contribution to Russian medieval political theory.

In questions of practical policy, however, Ivan occasionally departed from the absolutist theories in which he sincerely believed. When, after the death of Sigismund Augustus, Ivan was regarded as a possible candidate for the Polish throne, he put aside his favorite doctrine of monarchy by the grace of God and his contempt for constitutional limitations, and was not only willing but indeed eager to accept election. He also solemnly promised the Polish nobles to preserve their ancient rights and privileges and "if conditions so require" to extend them. Still less reconcilable with Ivan's exalted view of monarchy was the installation in 1574, as the Russian tsar or grand duke, of Simeon Bekbulatovich, a Tartar prince who had embraced Christianity. The Chronicle reports that Simeon was actually crowned in the capital, while Ivan assumed the title of prince of Moscow and treated the new ruler with all outward marks of respect. Simeon never exercised any actual power, and his illusory reign lasted for only a brief period. He was removed from Moscow and sent to Tver. It seems impossible to supply a rational explanation for the strange episode of Simeon Bekbulatovich. Some historians are inclined to treat it as a practical joke. But what an extraordinary manner of enjoyment for a tsar who believed in the divine origin of monarchical rule.

Proud as Ivan was of his imaginary descent from "Caesar Augustus," he was nevertheless anxious to establish a dynastic link, through marriage, with one of the European ruling houses. Considerations of international politics were not foreign to this scheme. After the death of his first wife in 1560, Ivan sought the hand of Catherine, sister of Sigismund Augustus, king of Poland. The tsar's proposal was rejected and Catherine married John, duke of Finland, who was a brother of Eric, king of Sweden. John was an advocate of an alliance between Sweden and Poland against Moscow. A misanthrope, verging on lunacy, Eric arrested his brother and sister-in-law, exterminated a large number of their supporters, and concluded with Ivan an extraordinary agreement under the terms of which he undertook to surrender Catherine to the Muscovite tsar in exchange for Ivan's promise of the cession of Estonia and of an alliance against Poland. Ivan, who in the meantime had married a second time, presumably intended to make the unhappy duchess of Finland his mistress, although the official pretext was to hold her as a hostage to exercise pressure on Poland. Special Russian envoys spent a whole year in Sweden waiting for the handing over to them of Catherine, but Eric could not make up his mind to carry out his curious arrangement with Ivan. An uprising in 1568 against Eric, whose mental condition had completely deteriorated, resulted in his overthrow and the accession of John of Finland to the Swedish throne. The new monarch's ambassadors to Moscow were confronted with the surprising request that they deliver to Ivan their queen, Catherine, in accordance with the undertaking entered into by Eric. They refused, of course, and the matter was finally dropped. This strange episode and Ivan's maniacal persistence in trying to obtain the custody of an unfortunate woman whom he had never seen sheds considerable light on his mental state and ethical standards.

The failure of Ivan's Polish matrimonial venture did not discourage him. A great admirer of England, he conceived towards the end of his life the idea of an English bride. The political advantages of such an alliance were dazzling. Elizabeth, the Virgin Queen, being beyond his reach, Ivan was prepared to accept one of her relatives. Preliminary investigations were initiated in Moscow and, curiously, were entrusted to Bogdan Belsky and Athanasius Nagoï, brother of Ivan's bride of a few months. A special embassy was dispatched to England, and after long delays Mary Hastings, daughter of Lord Huntingdon and a relative of the queen, was suggested as a possible bride. There is nevertheless considerable doubt that the match between Mary Hastings and Ivan was ever seriously considered in London. Finally, and greatly to the tsar's disappointment, his offer was rejected. European sovereigns displayed no undue haste in allying themselves with the self-styled descendant of the Roman Caesar.

The subjects of the Russian autocrat were less fortunate. When Ivan decided to contract his first marriage, a decree directed the nobility, under threat of extreme penalties, to send their daughters to the provincial governors, who made a preliminary selection of eligible young women. The final choice was made in Moscow. The total number of Ivan's wives remains uncertain, and historians hesitate between five and seven. No one has ventured to estimate the number of his mistresses. Anastasia, his first wife, the only woman who for a time succeeded in keeping the tsar's affection, was believed by him to have been poisoned by his enemies. A similar fate, according to Ivan, befell two more of his wives, two were forced to take the veil, and one was drowned by Ivan's orders. Little wonder that Mary Hastings showed no excessive enthusiasm for the crown that was so gallantly offered to her. The *démarches* Ivan made in London indicate that he was determined to get rid of Maria Nagoï, his seventh wife (if seventh she was). She was saved by Mary Hastings' refusal to marry Ivan and by his death shortly thereafter.

There seems to be little doubt that Ivan suffered from the mania of persecution. His writings are full of bitter denunciations of his real and imaginary enemies. He saw treason everywhere around him, and he ruthlessly eliminated, one after another, practically all the men who at one time or another had the misfortune of being admitted to his council. Execution accompanied by most ingenious tortures was the fate of high and low, especially after 1560, when Ivan reached the conclusion that in his early days he had been merely a tool in the hands of his advisers. The tsar's wrath fell upon the members of his family, his cousin Prince Vladimir Andreevich, upon Church dignitaries, princes, boyars, and common people. His intimate counselors of the earlier period, Adashev and the priest Silvester, were sent into exile, and a large number of Adashev's relatives, including children, were put to death. Later came the turn of the executioners themselves, and some of Ivan's favorite henchmen—Prince Viazemsky, even Fedor Basmanov—perished after untold tortures. It is reported that Fedor Basmanov, on Ivan's order, first murdered his father, Alexis, who also had once enjoyed the favors of the tsar. The deportations and executions applied, as in the case of Adashev, not only to those immediately suspected but also to their families, relatives, and friends. Occasionally the lust for destruction appears to have been the reason for Ivan's savagery. Such, for instance, was the plundering of Novgorod in 1570 on the mere suspicion that the ancient city was planning to go over to Poland. In the midst of fantastic orgies of blood and murder Ivan never forgot what he understood to be his duty as a faithful son of the Russian Church. He kept lists of the men murdered and distributed money to the monasteries to pray for the eternal rest of his victims. These lists contained over four thousand names, but the actual number is believed to have been much larger. Obsessed by the dread of plots and impending political calamities, Ivan in 1569 wrote to Queen Elizabeth asking for asylum in England in the event that he should be forced to leave Russia. He wanted to make the arrangement reciprocal, a thoughtful attention which Elizabeth, however, declined. In 1581, in a moment of uncontrollable anger, Ivan with a blow of his staff murdered his son and heir, Tsarevich Ivan, supposedly because the latter had attempted to protect his wife, an expectant mother, from the tsar's brutality. This crime weighed heavily on Ivan's already overburdened conscience. He died in the spring of 1584, and on his deathbed, when already delirious, he took monastic vows. This symbolic act was, in a sense, the fitting end of a stormy, eventful, and unhappy life.

The known facts of Ivan's biography are such as to make it practically impossible to present them in a favorable light. Nevertheless, while no scholar has attempted the thankless task of condoning the crimes of the first tsar, a surprising number of the members of the craft, including some of its most eminent and righteous representatives, have displayed no small ingenuity and resourcefulness in devising economic and psychological interpretations and citing mitigating circumstances in partial apology for Ivan's behavior. The most popular and widely used of these arguments was developed at some length by Ivan himself, especially in his letters to Prince Kurbsky. The fundamental trait of Ivan's character, it is argued, was his deep distrust and suspicion of all with whom he came in contact. It was this state of mind that was largely responsible for most of his conduct. Ivan's suspicious disposition, again, resulted from his having been brought up as an orphan under the tutelage of a small group of selfish, grasping, unscrupulous, and ruthless boyars. The Shuisky and the Belsky had done much to encourage the evil inclinations of the young monarch, especially his tendency towards cruelty. His distrust was further stimulated by the events of 1553, when, during a severe illness that seemed likely to prove fatal, his closest advisers, who had replaced the old court camarilla, hesitated to take the oath to the tsar's infant son. Some of them favored Ivan's cousin, Vladimir Andreevich, as Russia's next ruler. His resulting disillusionment, it is held, had much to do with Ivan's subsequent policies. Following in the footsteps of Ivan, who had skillfully exploited the "betrayed righteous ruler" and the "poor orphan" motives, the historians have written much on these rather touching themes. It is, of course, self-evident that the conditions under which Ivan was brought up were not favorable to prepare him for his duties. These conditions and the subsequent conflicts with the boyars fail nevertheless to provide the key to much of the tsar's later activities, not to mention the general consideration that an affectionate family is not an unmixed blessing and that loving parents frequently do more harm to their children than the wickedest of guardians to their wards. Professor Platonov is substantially right when he says that the character of Ivan remains an enigma, but there is also truth in Professor Sergeevich's description of the tsar as a "mentally unbalanced philosopher on the throne." And it was the element of folly that only too often had the upper hand.

REFORMS

In dealing with the domestic policies of Ivan it is customary to divide his reign into two periods, one characterized by constructive measures and useful reforms, the other largely negative in results. This division appears artificial, and it may be argued that the change of policies that took place around 1560 was not as sharp as is often assumed. The Chronicle records an instance of the treatment meted out by the tsar to a delegation of the inhabitants of Pskov who complained to him about the injustice they had suffered at the hands of the *namestnik* (appointed governor). For reasons that remain obscure, Ivan was angered by the petition presented to him by some seventy distinguished citizens of the once free city. His displeasure expressed itself in a characteristic manner. He poured boiling wine on the unfortunate delegates, burned with a candle their long hair and venerable beards, and ordered them to lie naked on the floor. They were saved from a presumably even worse fate by the miraculous interference of divine Providence, which, causing a large church bell to fall down in Moscow, distracted the tsar's attention. In the excitement provoked by this ominous occurrence the tsar forgot, according to the Chronicle, to attend to the less urgent business of executing the delegates. The incident just described took place in the summer of 1547, that is, at the very beginning of the supposedly benevolent period of his reign, a few months after Ivan's coronation and his marriage to Anastasia, who is represented as having exercised a soothing influence upon her husband.

Shortly after the Pskov episode, Moscow was swept by a fire which destroyed much of the city, including parts of the Kremlin, and is reported to have caused the death of some seventeen hundred people. The fire was used by the Shuisky, Zakharin, and other boyar families as a pretext for getting rid of the tsar's relatives, the Princes Glinsky, whose influence had been strong at the court since the removal and execution of the leaders of the Shuisky group (1543). An angry mob, incited by the enemies of the Glinsky family, accused the latter of having been responsible for the fire. Prince Yuri Glinsky, dragged from the Uspensky Cathedral, where he had sought refuge, was murdered, and Prince Michael Glinsky, who attempted to flee to Lithuania, was seized. The political influence of the Glinsky thus came to an end, a change that proved of more than passing importance, since their successors in Ivan's favor were men drawn largely from a social group other than the landed aristocracy. For the next ten or twelve years Ivan is believed to have closely followed the advice of a selected council (*izbrannaia rada*) which was dominated by the priest Silvester and by Alexis Adashev, descendant of a family that had been in service under the Muscovite grand dukes but did not belong to the aristocracy. According to some historians the Metropolitan Macarius was prominent in this inner circle, and the imprint of his personality can be seen in certain policies of the regime. In his later years Ivan complained that he had long been a puppet in the hands of Silvester, Adashev, and their friends.

In the middle of the sixteenth century the Moscow government was confronted with a number of pressing problems. It will be recalled that the administration of the provinces was carried out through the distribution of *kormlenie*, that is, the appointment of governors who collected taxes, administered justice, and retained as their remuneration a part of the revenue that passed through their hands. These governors were appointed for brief periods, usually for a year, but some remained in office much longer. The drawbacks of this system, which lent itself to abuses, were not all due to the rapacious appetites of the appointees. The Code (*Sudebnik*) of 1497 contained but the scantiest provisions to ensure the equitable administration of justice. As long as the governor was in office, next to nothing could be done to prevent him from exceeding his powers. But when his appointment had expired he was liable for any damage he might have caused by abuse of power. This arrangement resulted in much vexatious litigation, which occasionally ended to the disadvantage of the former officials and led to their ruin. In the first half of the sixteenth century a number of measures were taken to define more precisely the relations between the population and the governors, and especially to limit the fiscal powers of the latter. A more important step in the same direction was the transfer of the police and some of the judicial functions from the governors to the elected officials. The chief purpose of this change was the prevention of banditry and other crimes which the governors failed to check. The privilege of an elected police and judiciary was originally granted by special charters (*gubnaia gramota*) issued at the request of the local communities. The earliest available charter of this type, which goes back to 1539, was granted when Ivan was nine years old. The police and judicial officers were elected by the free population of the administrative subdivision, or *uezd*. The head of the new administration for each *uezd* (*uezdnyi starosta*) was always drawn from the upper stratum of the freemen, that is, from among the men enrolled in government service. The elected police and judiciary, first granted to communities that petitioned for it, was gradually extended to other communities. From a right and a privilege the election of police and judges became an obligation and a duty. Kliuchevsky has aptly described the reform as the mobilization of local forces for the maintenance of public safety. Its compulsory character was revealed in the provision making the community jointly responsible for any damage that might result from the misconduct of its police and judicial officers even when the latter, as sometimes happened, were not elected but were appointed by the government. The community, moreover, having assumed—sometimes against its will—responsibility for the maintenance of public safety, was also made responsible for the good behavior of all its members. The community as a whole was liable to heavy fines if one of its members was found guilty of a crime.

A further move in the direction of local self-government was made around 1550–1552, when the financial administration of some of the *uezd* was transferred from the governors to elected officials headed by a *zemskii starosta* (elder). The introduction of this new form of self-government was optional. It was known as "zemstvo," and its officers were vested with police and judicial in addition to fiscal powers. A law passed in 1555 abolished the old *kormlenie*, but only in theory, for in practice they continued to exist. One of the principal functions of the zemstvo administration was the collection of taxes and dues which had been revised and consolidated. Malfeasance of zemstvo officers was punishable by death and confiscation of their property for the benefit both of their victims and of the informers. If the estate of a guilty officer was inadequate to meet the claims brought against him, the community as a whole was jointly responsible for the deficiency. These aspects of the reform are particularly noteworthy because the zemstvo have been traditionally considered as the strongholds of liberalism in the Russia of the nineteenth and twentieth centuries and as the standard-bearers of democratic ideals. There is therefore a tendency, to which many have yielded, to approach the zemstvo institutions of Ivan IV from the point of view of a different age. Kliuchevsky has rightly pointed out that the nature of institutions of local government is determined, not so much by the fact of their being either elected or appointed, but rather by the functions they perform and by the extent of their freedom from interference by the central authority. It is only fair to observe that the information available regarding the zemstvo institutions of the sixteenth century is grievously incomplete and that even the text of the law of 1555 was not preserved. It seems reasonably clear, nevertheless, that these institutions offered little opportunity for local initiative and were government agencies for the performance of onerous and irksome tasks. The joint responsibility of the communities appears to have been the mainspring of the system. The reform, therefore, was hardly a step towards real self-government. It was rather the creation of a machinery different from *kormlenie*, but perhaps just as crude and ruthless, for the exaction of revenue from a sorely tried population.

The financial and administrative reforms of Ivan IV called for the revision of the Code of 1497, which, as I have pointed out, was in part responsible for the mismanagement of the provincial administration. A new Code (*Sudebnik*) was prepared in 1550 and was submitted for approval to the *Stoglav* Church council that met the following year. Based largely on the body of law it was designed to replace, the Code of 1550 attempted to improve judicial procedure by introducing, for instance, responsibility of the governors (*namestnik*) for irregularities of members of their administration, and by limiting to one year the time when an action could be brought against the governor. The Code also contained several novel provisions relating to such matters as the relations between landlords and tenants. Nevertheless, it was primarily concerned with judicial procedure, and it attempted to eliminate the use in courts of immemorial customs. These were to be replaced by the provisions of the new statute. Concerning matters not dealt with in the Code, the puzzling and much discussed Article 98 provided for amendment after the issue had been submitted to the tsar (*doklad*) and in accordance with the decision (*prigovor*) of "all boyars." This provision, if interpreted literally, would have constituted a limitation on the absolute powers of the tsar by making legislation conditional on an affirmative decision by "all boyars" (Sergeevich). The apparent innovation has been ascribed to the influence of Silvester, Adashev, and their friends. No limitation of the tsar's legislative powers, however, can be detected in Ivan's subsequent constitutional practice. The wording of Article 98 was therefore merely the customary reference to the traditional consultation of the tsar with the boyar duma (Diakonov). The Russia of Ivan the Dread was as remote from a constitutional monarchy as she was from local self-government.

Of much greater practical value was the decree of 1556 regulating the rights and duties of men holding estates in service tenure (*pomestie*). It will be recalled that this type of landholding was steadily encroaching on the ancient form of landownership unfettered by any personal obligation towards the state (*votchina*). By the middle of the sixteenth century military service became obligatory for all landholders whether their estates were of the *votchina* or *pomestie* type. The decree of 1556 introduced a certain uniformity in the working of this complex system. The number of men to be provided for the army, as well as the nature of their equipment, was determined by the size of the entire holding, comprising both *votchina* and *pomestie*. The granting of land in military tenure was supplemented by the payment of a monetary wage, a practice that might have antedated the reign of Ivan IV. The landholders subject to the obligation of military service were known as *sluzhilye liudi, deti boyarskiia* or *dvoriane* (singular *dvorianin*), and they formed an important group from which later developed the Russian nobility (*dvorianstvo*). Both the holding of the estates and the obligation to serve in the army were made hereditary, and failure to perform the latter resulted in the loss of the former. The active service of a *dvorianin*, according to the decree of 1556, began at the age of fifteen and continued until his death or incapacitation. On his death the estate, together with obligations attached to it, passed to his sons, who were entitled to additional land grants if their respective shares fell below the prescribed norms. Provisions were also made for the maintenance of the widow of a *dvorianin* and for the support of his daughters until the age of fifteen, when they were supposed to marry. The decree of 1556, which consolidated, systematized, and expanded previous legislation, according to Kliuchevsky, created a comprehensive system that was not lacking in harmony. "All the children of a *dvorianin* are enrolled in government service," he writes; "the son who has reached the specified age on horseback defends the country; the daughter gets married and provides new reserves of soldiers." The Muscovite tsars were prepared to take care of their armed force, but they expected everyone to do his duty, beginning rather early, at the age of fifteen.

An important innovation during the reign of Ivan IV was the calling together of the first *zemskii sobor*, or assembly of representatives of various social groups. The origins of this institution and its early history have been the source of much confusion. It was long believed—and the opinion is still held by some historians—that Ivan IV called the first *zemskii sobor* in 1550. Professor Platonov, however, has established that the only available copy of what purported to be Ivan's opening address to the *zemskii sobor* of 1550 could not have been written before the end of the seventeenth century. No other direct information on the *zemskii sobor* of 1550 being available, the character and the very existence of such a gathering is highly problematical. The historian is on firmer ground in dealing with the *zemskii sobor* of 1566, when the government convoked representatives of various groups to discuss the conditions of peace with Lithuania. This assembly, which expressed itself in favor of continuing the war rather than renouncing Russia's sovereignty over Livonia, consisted of the higher clergy, members of the boyar duma, representatives of the *dvoriane*, and representatives of commerce and trade. It was the presence of this latter group that distinguished the assembly of 1566 from any consultation previously held. The *zemskii sobor* of 1566 acted in an advisory capacity, and its members were not elected but were appointed by the government. It was not, as Kliuchevsky has made clear, in any sense a national assembly, but a consultation of the government with its agents. The members of the *sobor* were not spokesmen for local interests; they were government officers familiar with the situation in the provinces, and they were called together to supply information, to answer questions, and to carry out decisions. Although this gathering is sometimes described as democratic in character, such was not the case. This was the only *zemskii sobor* convoked during the reign of Ivan IV. At the turn of the sixteenth century the membership of the *zemskii sobor* became more representative of local feelings, although the assembly continued to preserve its advisory character. The *zemskii sobor*, like so many other Russian institutions, originated through government fiat and was not an instrument for the formulation of a crystallized public opinion seeking self-expression, and even less was it an organ for the defense of public interest against the central authority.

Considerable activity was displayed by the government of Ivan IV in Church matters, on which he placed the unmistakable imprint of his own religious formalism and of the peculiar philosophy of his chief adviser in ecclesiastical matters, the Metropolitan Macarius. Macarius, as has already been pointed out, was a devout disciple of Joseph of Volokolam and a believer in the close cooperation of the Church with the state, subject to the preservation of the Church's privileges, especially the retention of its vast landholdings. To Macarius, Moscow was not only the "Third Rome" but also the "Second Jerusalem." It was his aim to invest the Russian Church with an imperishable glory that would eclipse that of the hated western Church, and to raise its moral and intellectual level in keeping with its newly acquired universal significance. According to his own standards Macarius succeeded in the first but not in the second of these enterprises. Two Church councils, called in 1547 and 1549, added to the calendar thirty-nine saints, more than had been admitted to the calendar in the five centuries of Russia's earlier history. Further canonizations took place in the following years. The new saints had in the past enjoyed local recognition. This mass canonization on a scale without parallel in the history of Christianity was, in a sense, the mobilization of spiritual forces for the glorification of the national Russian Church, that self-appointed leader of the eastern Christian world.

In 1551 the proposal for the eradication of the evils from which the Church was suffering was taken up by the Church council. This council is known as the *Stoglav* (literally "hundred chapters") because its proceedings and decisions have been preserved in a document divided into one hundred paragraphs. Curiously, the convocation of the council was not mentioned in contemporary chronicles. The council had to answer questions put to it in writing in the name of the tsar but presumably drafted by Macarius. The questions submitted to the council, as well as its decisions, present an indictment of the clergy and the monasteries, a picture of illiteracy, abuse of power, callous indifference to the sufferings of the poor, drunkenness, debauchery, neglect of ecclesiastical duties, ignorance of Church canons and services, indifference to, and encouragement of, pagan practices. The fact that the head of the Church collaborated or even took the initiative in exposing these conditions speaks in his favor and indicates his sincerity and determination to remedy the evils. The decisions of the council, however, did little to improve the situation. Questions of morality and Church reform were debated on the same footing with such trivial matters as the prohibition against the shaving of beards, the use of two or three fingers in making the sign of the cross, and other minor details of Church ritual. It was, indeed, the latter decisions that eventually assumed major importance in the history of the Church. The council condemned the abuses and irregularities brought to its attention; for instance, it specifically prohibited the practice of usury, which was indulged in on a large scale by the monasteries and the bishops; ordered the revision and correction of books, demanded the opening of hospices and homes for the poor and the establishment of schools and attempted to remedy some of the defects in the administration of the ecclesiastical courts. If most of these decisions remained pious wishes and were never put into effect, the Church itself was at least in part to blame. It turned a deaf ear to the tsar's suggestion that it should participate in financing the relief of the poor, nor is there any indication that the proposed new schools were ever opened. A characteristic instance of the council's attitude was presented by its handling of the question of raising funds for the redemption from captivity of Russian prisoners. The council proposed to levy a special tax to provide the money needed. The deposed Metropolitan Joasaph, to whom the decisions were communicated, urged the Church itself to assume the charge on the ground that the people were already overtaxed. This plea was ignored. The council also restored the practice, prohibited as uncanonical by the Council of 1503, of charging fees for the consecration of clerics. It is difficult not to see the influence of Macarius in these decisions. Professor Golubinsky, a warm admirer of Macarius, has been reluctantly led to the conclusion that the Council of 1551 left the Church in the same position as before. The decisions of the council were barren of practical results and remained a mere "historical document."

The Council of 1551, of course, considered the problem of ecclesiastical estates, although it made only the slightest contribution towards its solution. The watchful Macarius would have prevented any effective move in this direction. The Church, however, made one minor concession: in the future the preliminary consent of the tsar was to be obtained before an ecclesiastical institution could accept or purchase land. This restriction, however, failed to stem the growth of Church holdings. Further restrictions were enacted after the death of Macarius, in 1573 and again in 1580, when the Church was forbidden, under the threat of confiscation, to acquire land; but this drastic provision was not enforced, and the delegates to the *zemskii sobor* of 1648 pleaded in vain for the sequestration of land appropriated by Church institutions in contravention of the law of 1580.

Among the constructive measures of Ivan's reign one should mention his not uniformly successful efforts to import foreign artisans, craftsmen, and doctors, especially from Germany and from England, and also the establishment of the first Russian printing press.

OPRICHNINA

The earlier part of Ivan's reign was by no means free from friction and open conflict with the landed aristocracy or from outbursts of his uncontrollable temper directed not only against the boyars but also against men of more humble status. The tsar's displeasure aroused by the attitude of his advisers during his illness in 1553 and by their hesitation to take the oath of allegiance to his son is an illustration of the former, while the reception Ivan gave the Pskov delegation in 1547 is an instance of the latter. In 1557–1558 Ivan's counselors opposed the war for the possession of Livonia. Members of the noble families occasionally attempted to escape to Lithuania, as did the Princes Simeon and Nikita of Rostov in 1554. There was considerable opposition among the aristocracy to the influence exercised at the court by the Zakharin, kin of Anastasia, Ivan's first wife. This friction developed into an open breach around 1560, when Anastasia died and Ivan abruptly dismissed his advisers Silvester and Adashev. Silvester was incarcerated in the remote Solovetsky monastery, and Adashev died —it was rumored that he committed suicide by taking poison—while under arrest in Dorpat. The severity of Ivan's already stern rule greatly increased, and the families and friends of the former favorites perished at the hand of the executioner. Upon the slightest suspicion and on any pretext men of the highest standing were arrested, deported, or put to death. Their families and servants shared their fate, and their estates were confiscated. Those who were lucky escaped by merely confessing their crimes and treasonable intentions, sometimes perhaps imaginary, and by providing surety for future good behavior. How extensive was this system of interlocking guaranties will appear from the instance of Prince Ivan Mstislavsky, who admitted in 1571 conspiring with the Crimean khan. He was bound over to three boyars who put up a guaranty of twenty thousand rubles, a large sum for those days. The three guarantors themselves provided 285 sureties.

Much has been written about the reasons for Ivan's breach with Silvester and Adashev. Nevertheless, Solovev's observation that the sources provide no satisfactory explanation of either the rise or fall of the tsar's once all-powerful counselors still holds good. It seems reasonably clear that Ivan's disposition prevented him from trusting anyone for long. The estrangement between the tsar and the aristocracy was further widened when in 1564 Prince Andrew Kurbsky, a prominent member of the Silvester-Adashev group and a favorite of Ivan, abandoned his military command and went over to Lithuania, with which Moscow was at war. His flight proved to be of particular interest because it led to the celebrated correspondence between the tsar and Kurbsky, a correspondence which, although consisting of only four letters, was spread over a period of fifteen years (1564–1579) and remains one of the most revealing documents of this period.

Early in December, 1564, the good people of Moscow witnessed an unusual occurrence: the tsar, accompanied by his family and a numerous retinue carrying his jewels, treasury, and household belongings, left the capital and departed for an unknown destination. The royal caravan finally settled down at Aleksandrovskaia Sloboda, which became a kind of second capital for the rest of Ivan's reign. A month later, in January, 1565, two messages from the tsar were received in Moscow. One was a savage and sweeping indictment of the boyars as traitors, grafters, and embezzlers, and of the clergy, from the metropolitan down, as their accomplices and abettors. The tsar was so distressed by the prevailing conditions, the message said, that he had decided to give up his kingdom and let divine Providence choose his future abode. This certainly sounded like an abdication. The second message was addressed to the merchants, artisans, and common people, who were exonerated from any responsibility for the sovereign's displeasure. The combined effect of the two messages was to plunge Moscow into a state of desolation and distress the magnitude of which the Chronicle has probably exaggerated. A delegation sent to Aleksandrovskaia Sloboda had no difficulty in persuading Ivan to reconsider his decision. It may be surmised that the ultimate outcome of his peculiar maneuver was a foregone conclusion and that he never seriously intended to give up the throne. The tsar graciously consented to resume his royal duty, but only on his own terms, which were willingly conceded. Ivan demanded a free hand in dealing with the traitors, the creation of a special royal domain (*oprichnina*) exempt from the jurisdiction of the general administration and subject to the direct control of the tsar, and the payment of a huge indemnity of 100,000 rubles to meet the expenses of his flight from the capital. Ivan's return to Moscow was celebrated by the execution of a number of leading boyars.

The legislation dealing with the establishment of the *oprichnina* has not been preserved, and the reticence of the Chronicle and other sources accounts for the variety of interpretations of this curious institution. *Oprichnina* is an ancient term denoting an entailed domain, usually the estates settled on the widow of a sovereign prince. By creating the *oprichnina* Ivan split his realm into two parts: the so-called *zemshchina*, which continued to be administered in the old traditional way by the boyar duma and other organs and officers of the Muscovite administration, and the *oprichnina*, where a parallel hierarchy of administrative organs and officers was brought into existence. The *oprichnina*, to repeat, was the tsar's personal domain, and the primary duty of the *oprichniki* was to exterminate "treason" in the other half of the realm, the *zemshchina*. There is much truth in Kliuchevsky's definition of *oprichnina* as an all-powerful security police. The importance of this function was symbolized by the appearance of the *oprichniki*: dressed in black and mounted on black horses, they carried attached to their saddles a dog's head and a broom.

The *oprichnina*, however, had another and, in the long run, far more important function, which has been emphasized by Platonov: the responsibility for finally breaking down the political influence of the landed aristocracy. One may accept this proposition even without subscribing to Platonov's view that the policy in question was intentionally devised and consistently enforced by Ivan. The provinces, cities, and even certain Moscow streets included in the *oprichnina* were cleared of their boyars and landowners, who were moved to other parts of the country, while their estates were distributed among the *oprichniki*. Compulsory transfer of population was a familiar device often used by the Moscow rulers of the past. It will be recalled that Ivan III and Vasili III applied it to the annexed territories of Novgorod, Viatka, and Pskov. Ivan IV repeated the operation in Kazan after its conquest in 1552, and again in Pskov and Novgorod in 1569. In 1550 he settled one thousand picked men around Moscow after compulsory removal of the former owners. With the establishment of *oprichnina* a similar policy was followed on a much larger scale. According to Platonov, the provinces assigned to *oprichnina* eventually comprised nearly half of the entire territory of the state. They were so distributed as to embrace those sections where the former princely families still retained a footing. These families were now uprooted, the old ties uniting them to the local people were broken, and the former hereditary estates of the nobility passed into the hands of newcomers whose title to the land had no other source than the pleasure of the Muscovite autocrat. The segregation of the two parts of the realm, moreover, proved largely illusory. The *oprichnina* gradually assumed control of the chief domestic markets and of the principal trade routes. The result was that the *zemshchina*, with its flickering tradition of local independence, was brought under the sway of the *oprichnina* and forced to accept a complex hierarchy of officials and landholders unreservedly controlled by the state. The two most significant consequences of *oprichnina* were the final destruction of the political influence of the old landed aristocracy and the forcible transfer of land on a huge scale.

There were in the situation many elements that obscured the actual significance of the social evolution that had been set in motion, or, more exactly, greatly accelerated by *oprichnina*. Enrolled among the *oprichniki* were representatives of the noblest families in the land, for instance, the princes Shuisky, Skopin, Pronsky, Sitsky, Trubetskoy, Odoevsky. Nor did the wrath of the tsar strike only the princes and boyars of the *zemshchina*. Ivan's favorite *oprichniki*, the two Basmanov and Prince Viazemsky, were put to death in a manner that made even the Muscovites shudder. The attention of contemporary observers, both domestic and foreign, was naturally centered on the seemingly boundless resourcefulness Ivan and his *oprichniki* displayed in devising new tortures and on the fantastic and almost unbelievable ritual that was a part of their daily routine. The Aleksandrovskaia Sloboda was transformed into a kind of fortified monastery governed by strict quasi-monastic rules written by Ivan himself. In that stronghold the tsar and his favorites dressed in monastic garb and divided their time between lengthy Church services and prolonged and extravagant orgies broken by visits to the torture chamber. It would be idle to attempt to discover a rational economic, social, or psychological interpretation of this bloody nightmare, a tale that contained all the elements of an obscene penny novel. The Aleksandrovskaia Sloboda and all that it stood for was Ivan the Dread at his worst.

FOREIGN RELATIONS

The reign of Ivan IV, like those of his predecessors, was filled with foreign wars. Hardly a year passed that the Muscovite army was not fighting on one of Russia's interminable, loosely defined, and often arbitrarily established frontiers. The most significant and lasting achievement of Ivan's rule was the eastward expansion of the Russian state. The Tartar kingdoms of Kazan and Astrakhan on the Volga were long a source of friction. Ivan, taking advantage of internal dissension within the Tartar states, conquered and annexed Kazan in 1552 and Astrakhan in 1556. The final subjugation of the adjoining territories required a number of years and heavily taxed the resources of the Moscow government. From the national point of view the sacrifices may be considered to have been well worth while, since the entire basin of the Volga was brought under the control of Russia. The eastward movement of Muscovy, resumed towards the end of Ivan's reign, led to the annexation of western Siberia. This important venture was carried on by private initiative and was the result of the trading activities of the powerful Stroganov family, who held important concessions in the eastern part of the country. Since the middle of the sixteenth century the rulers of the nomad Siberian tribes had accepted a vague allegiance to the Moscow Crown, an allegiance that was honored in the breach rather than in the observance. The Stroganov maintained a private army recruited largely from the Cossacks and unruly Muscovite and Lithuanian fugitives who in loosely organized bands roamed the steppes of southern Russia. In 1581 a band of these mercenaries and soldiers of fortune under the leadership of Ermak Timofeevich was sent by the Stroganov beyond the Urals. This expedition resulted in the conquest of western Siberia by 1583. Ivan, who in the early stages of the expedition threatened the Stroganov with his displeasure for involving him in a conflict with the Siberian rulers and promised to send the Cossacks to the gallows, changed his mind when the venture proved a triumph. The emissaries of Ermak were acclaimed on their arrival in Moscow, and Ermak and his fellow Cossacks won for themselves a lasting place in the galaxy of Russia's national heroes.

Important as were Russian victories in the east, and the annexation of Kazan and Astrakhan, they did not remove the Mongol danger. The southern frontier continued to be subject to invasion by the Crimean Tartars, who occupied an impregnable position on the Black Sea peninsula. Raids by Crimean horsemen, which took place annually and sometimes two or three times a year, brought in their wake terrible devastation. What the Crimean raiders were after was not territorial conquest, but booty and especially prisoners of war. The slave markets of Europe, Asia, and Africa were glutted with human cargoes supplied by Mongol incursions into Muscovy, Lithuania, and Poland. The Crimean Tartars, moreover, were always ready to enter into alliances with Russia's western enemies. The conquest of the Crimea by the Turks in 1475, which added further to the awe inspired in Muscovy by its southern neighbors, diverted much of the energy of the Moscow government to the defense of its southern border. A complex network of fortifications, outposts, and military settlements was gradually built up, and in 1571 a comprehensive plan of defense was elaborated in Moscow by a commission under the leadership of Prince Vorotynsky. In spite of these precautions and the sacrifices involved, the raids nevertheless continued almost unchecked. In 1571 the Tartars besieged Moscow, burned down its suburbs, and carried away about 150,000 prisoners. In the following year a huge army of 120,000 again invaded Russia but was stopped by Prince Vorotynsky before it succeeded in reaching the capital. This ever present Tartar menace kept Muscovy in a state of continuous tension.

The relations between Ivan and the western nations proved disastrous. The intermittent conflicts with Poland, Lithuania, and Sweden resolved themselves into a contest over the possession of the domain of the Livonian Order of German knights, an institution that was living through a crisis. The century-long antagonism between the German feudal aristocracy and the local population was aggravated by the movement for secularization that spread to Livonia from Germany with the progress of the Reformation and by dissensions among the leaders of the order and those of the Church. In 1558 Ivan invaded Livonia. The early stage of the campaign was successful for Moscow. Livonia was overrun by Russian troops, but the knights, realizing that the independence of their order was doomed, sought to escape Muscovite domination by putting their territories under the protection of their other neighbors. Courland became a fief of Poland, Livonia proper accepted the suzerainty of Lithuania, Estonia that of Sweden, and the Island of Oesel went to Denmark. The Livonian war thus became a war with Lithuania, Poland, and Sweden. It lasted, with some interruptions, for twenty-five years.

The death of Sigismund Augustus of Poland in 1572 proved to be an important turning point. After the short reign of Henri de Valois of France, the Polish-Lithuanian throne was occupied by Stephen Batory, prince of Transylvania. Batory, an able military leader, supported by a well equipped professional army, inflicted a number of disastrous defeats upon the Russians, although he failed to take Pskov, which was besieged in 1581. In 1582, by a peace settlement between Ivan and Batory negotiated by Antonius Possevinus, a Jesuit and a papal envoy, Moscow was forced to give up all its acquisitions in Livonia. The peace settlement with Sweden made the following year was even more onerous. Sweden received, in addition to Estonia, the Russian territories on the shores of the Gulf of Finland, from Narva to Lake Ladoga. Russia's westward expansion suffered a severe blow. Moscow's huge reserves of man power, handicapped by an antiquated military organization, proved an uneven match for Batory's better disciplined and ably led army. The Polish king whom Ivan had so often treated with contempt as an upstart and adventurer paid the tsar in kind. "Even a miserable chicken, when her brood is menaced by a hawk or eagle, protects it with her wings," he wrote to Ivan, "and you, two-headed eagle (for such is the emblem of your seal), keep in hiding." It is more likely, however, that the principal reason for Russia's defeat was not the inadequacy of her military organization or the reluctance of the tsar to assume personal leadership of his troops, but the unsettled internal conditions in a country living under a regime of terror. Whatever may have been the cause, all the sacrifices of a protracted and costly campaign proved futile. The window to Europe remained shut as tightly as ever.

Although the ports of the Baltic Sea continued to remain inaccessible to Russia, a new maritime route to western Europe was unexpectedly discovered in 1553, when one of the three ships equipped by the Fellowship of English Merchants for Discovery of New Trades reached the White Sea. Richard Chancellor, the leader of the expedition, went to Moscow, where he was graciously received by Ivan. The tsar, who had a great fancy for the English and cherished the vain hope of an Anglo-Russian alliance, conferred upon the Muscovy Company organized in London valuable monopolistic trade privileges. This, however, did not prevent Ivan from arresting the English merchants and confiscating their goods when his repeated *démarches* to bring about an alliance met with no response. The merchants were soon released, and the privileges of the company, temporarily withdrawn, were restored. Ivan's disappointment with England's coolness towards the proposed alliance found its expression in a characteristic letter addressed to Queen Elizabeth and scoffing at the excessive interest taken by the English in commercial matters. In this epistle he

RUSSIA
FROM THE XIIIth TO THE END OF THE XVIth CENTURY

Kievan State in the XIIth Century

Boundary of Russian principalities, 1240

Principality of Moscow, 1300

Conquered by Lithuania, Teutonic Knights, Poland, and Turkey 1340-1430

Principality of Moscow, 1462

Territory of Novgorod, 1462

++++ Limit of Golden Horde conquests in the XIIIth and XIVth Centuries

Boundary of Territories reconquered by Russia by 1530

Semi-dependant areas, 1462-1533

Russian lands retaining partial independance at the end of the XVth Century

Territories annexed in 1533-1584

Conquered in the XVIth Century, annexed in the XVIIth Century

Boundary of the Russian State at the end of the XVIth Century

Scale of Miles
0   200   400

applied to the Virgin Queen the uncomplimentary epithet of *poshlaia devitsa*, which may be rendered, in the absence of an English equivalent, as "common wench."

Throughout Ivan's reign the relations between Moscow and the Holy See showed no signs of a *rapprochement*, and the tsar displayed no interest either in the reunion of the Churches or in the crusade against the Turks advocated by Rome. Nevertheless, when the Livonian war took an unfavorable turn, Ivan approached Pope Gregory XIII and obtained the mediation of the papal envoy, Possevinus, who took an active part in negotiating the peace settlement between Moscow and Batory. The service rendered to the tsar by the Holy See did not bring any nearer a cooperation between Moscow and Rome on the questions which the papacy considered vital.

AN APPRAISAL

Glancing back at the stormy and often puzzling events of Ivan's long reign, and making full allowance for the inadequacy of available information, it seems difficult not to agree with Kliuchevsky that the negative aspects of his rule are by far the more important. It would require a wide flight of imagination to detect constructive elements in his early reforms, while the horrors of the *oprichnina* constitute one of the darkest pages in Russia's history. The literary performance both of Ivan and of his most articulate antagonist, Prince Kurbsky, who knew foreign languages, made a number of translations, and wrote a history of Muscovy, indicates that at least the upper classes of Russia were no longer immune to cultural influences. These, however, were rare exceptions. Solovev quotes instances of high officials occupying most responsible positions in the administration who were unable to sign their names. The *Stoglav* painted a distressing picture of the conditions prevalent among the clergy and the monastics, leaders in the field of Russian education, but it did nothing to improve conditions except to pass pious resolutions. The two principal literary ventures of this period are highly characteristic of the general cultural levels. The so-called *Chetia-Mineia* was a huge collection of the Church books, including the lives of the saints, prepared under the supervision of the Metropolitan Macarius. The enterprise, which took about twenty years for completion, was an attempt to provide the Russian Church with a storehouse of religious knowledge in keeping with what Macarius imagined to be its world-wide significance. However, according to Golubinsky, an admirer of Macarius, the collection was devoid of any practical usefulness. The second literary offering was the *Domostroi*, a handbook of practical behavior, a volume frequently but without sufficient evidence ascribed to Silvester. The *Domostroi* is imbued with a spirit of rabid conservatism, and its endeavor to apply to domestic relations the rules drawn from the Scriptures presents one of the most striking examples of the formal attitude towards religion which so heavily colored Russia's earlier development. As Speransky has so well put it, the ideals of the author are all in the past, to him any innovation is damnable, any departure from tradition and custom a crime.

Ivan's reign was a triumph of political absolutism. The autocrat by the grace of God wielded immense powers unlimited by any form of control, and his authority was unchallenged over a huge territory that now extended beyond the Urals, to the heart of Asia. Nevertheless, the inner weakness of the political structure, supported merely by force made possible by the absence of organized opposition, did not escape the attention both of Russian and of foreign observers. Kurbsky foretold its approaching doom, and Ivan himself was not entirely blind to the realities of the situation. "The body is exhausted, the spirit is ailing, the spiritual and physical wounds are multiplying, and there is no doctor to cure me," he wrote, no doubt in all sincerity, in his testament in 1572. "I waited for someone to share my sorrows, but there is no one; I found nobody to console me, for good I was repaid by evil, for love by hatred." Strange as such words may appear from the pen of a man who destroyed all his friends, they give a fair picture of the vacuum that surrounded the Moscow throne. The unification of the realm, it will be recalled, was achieved by Ivan III and Vasili III at the price of the suppression of all local independent political forces and of ancient legal and social institutions. This process was brought to its completion in the reign of Ivan IV. Torn by irreconcilable social and economic antagonisms only temporarily kept in check rather by the lack of inner unity and cohesion than by the terroristic methods of Ivan the Dread, Russia was steadily moving towards a major political crisis.[1]

---

[1] Following the example of Sir Bernard Pares, who has a unique gift for discovering English equivalents for Russian terms, I have used "the Dread" instead of the customary "the Terrible" as a part of Ivan's name. "The Dread" seems to render more accurately the meaning of the Russian epithet *Gronzyi*.

CHAPTER IX

"THE TIME OF TROUBLES"

———————————— ✳ ————————————

THE SOCIAL AND ECONOMIC BACKGROUND

The severe crisis Muscovy lived through at the turn of the sixteenth century is known in Russian historiography as *Smutnoe vremia*, or The Time of Troubles. The beginning of this period, which was brought to a close with the election to the throne of Michael Romanov in 1613, is variously placed at the death either of Ivan the Dread or at that of his son Fedor in 1598. The extinction of the Muscovite dynasty with the death of Fedor offers a certain formal justification for accepting the latter date as the starting point of the great upheaval. A closer study, however, reveals that the actual causes of the crisis were much deeper than mere dynastic changes; they were rooted in the social and economic maladjustments that accumulated in the course of the sixteenth century and reached a breaking point towards its close.

The feeble-minded Fedor inherited from his father an empire seething with discontent. The brutal methods by which unification was achieved under Vasili II, Ivan III, and Vasili III imposed heavy sacrifices on every social group, from the former sovereign princes and the landed aristocracy down to the humble toilers of the soil. The rule of Ivan IV, with its regime of political terror, its drastic and ruthless remodeling of the social structure, and its endless and ruinous wars, not only exhausted the country's financial and economic resources but also created a state of inner disequilibrium and a multitude of social conflicts that made an explosion seemingly inevitable. At the end of the reign of Ivan the Dread every social class, nursing deep and real grievances, faced the future with fear and foreboding. The old aristocracy of birth had seen itself forcibly evicted from its ancestral estates, shorn of much of its political influence, and forcibly enrolled

209

in the service of the state. Not a few of its most illustrious representatives had met with ignominious death at the hands of the executioner, and much of its accumulated wealth was gone. Together with other landlords, the boyars and the descendants of former ruling princes were confronted with the menace of ruin as a result of the depopulation of their estates and, in common with the rest of the people, they had to carry the crushing burden of military expenditure.

The other classes did not fare much better. It might be supposed that the government could count on the support of the large and rapidly increasing group of *sluzhilye liudi* (also known as *deti boyarskiia* and *dvoriane*), that is, hereditary tenants holding land (*pomestie*) subject to the obligation of military service. The *dvoriane* of the sixteenth century, however, were a motley agglomeration of people drawn from every stratum of society, including the slaves (*kholopy*). It was only towards the very end of the century that the sons of priests and the slaves were debarred from holding *pomestie*, and this in the central provinces alone, for no such restriction was in force in the territories along the southern frontier. The economic position of the *dvoriane* differed as widely as their social status. The size of the *pomestie* varied from large estates held by highly placed officers to a modest plot with perhaps only one peasant household on it, and farmed sometimes by the labor of the *dvorianin* himself. Such very small *pomestie* were common in the south. A group composed of elements so far apart both economically and socially would hardly be expected to develop an *esprit de corps* or a common policy. Compulsory service in the army was the sole tangible link between the descendants of the former ruling princes and the slaves of yesterday, and this was certainly not enough to make them forget their century-old prejudices and antagonisms. The economic position of the rank and file of the *dvoriane*, moreover, was often precarious. The land reserve the government had at its disposal and used for distribution in military tenure proved inadequate to meet the demand of a rapidly growing military class. The actual size of the *pomestie*, therefore, was frequently below the prescribed norm. The *dvoriane* were settled primarily on the estates confiscated from former sovereign princes, boyars, and other owners. The vast territories acquired by Muscovy in the east were also eventually converted into *pomestie*. Much of the large area of Crown land (*zemli gosudarstvennyia, zemli dvortsovyia*) was used for the same purpose, to the considerable detriment of the free peasant-tenants living on such land. The farming population attempted to escape the new hardships the encroachment of the *pomestie* brought in its wake by moving elsewhere. The economic well-being of the *dvoriane* and their ability to perform their military duties depended on the conditions of their *pomestie*, which, again, could not be made profitable if they were deserted by the tenants. In the second half of the sixteenth century Muscovy, especially in its central and western territories, was experiencing a severe labor shortage, which led to keen competition among the landlords for the available reserves of man power. The depopulation of many parts of the country is a fully established fact, the explanation of which may be traced back to the general political conditions, the military defeat in the Livonian war, and frequent Tartar invasions, especially those of 1571 and 1572, the eastward expansion of Russia with its irresistible if illusory promise of land and freedom, and last but not least the spreading of the *pomestie* form of tenure. Whatever may have been the reasons, a truly amazing number of people seem to have given up their old places of settlement and taken to the road. A *pomestie* abandoned by its tenants was of no use to its holder, and the government had a double reason for putting a check on a process of migration which not only deprived the state of a large number of taxpayers, who no longer could be reached, but also undermined the economic foundation on which rested the organization of the military class. Moscow took a number of measures to protect the *dvoriane* from the danger threatening them both from above and from below.

The position of the rank and file of the *dvoriane* was menaced from above by the wealthy and powerful secular and ecclesiastical landlords who exploited for their own benefit the plight of their weaker neighbors. In theory all landlords, irrespective of their social standing, were subject to the payment of taxes and the performance of various services. In practice, however, the government often granted to the landlords special privileges exempting them, usually for a term of years, from the performance of some or all of the obligations assessed upon their land. Although such privileges were occasionally given to landlords of humble status, the chief beneficiaries were those who had access to high places, especially the Church. When the fiscal burden of a landlord was reduced, it promised lower taxation to his tenants and created a strong inducement for the peasant farmers living on an estate not in the privileged class to give up their tenancy and move to the land of a lord who could offer them better protection. Only too frequently the tenant's gain proved fictitious, the additional exactions of the landlord more than wiping out whatever benefit the tenant might have derived from his modest share of tax privileges. With the growth of peasant indebtedness the right of the tenants to move away became conditional on the liquidation of the debts they owed their landlord. As the farmers themselves were seldom in a position to meet this requirement, the actual transfer of a farmer depended in practice on the ability of the new lord who wanted his services to provide the necessary funds. Under these conditions the wealthy landlords in the fierce competition for agricultural labor had a decided advantage over those handicapped by lack of funds, and they made a most unscrupulous use of it. The *pomestie* which lost its peasant farmers was laid waste and frequently fell into the hands of the big landlords, chiefly the monasteries. The cycle of the small landholder's ruin was thus completed. Little wonder that the rank and file of the *dvoriane* were restless and clamored for relief. Several measures, with which we are already familiar, were taken in the reign of Ivan IV to check the steady flow of land into the hands of the monasteries. A most drastic restriction on the expansion of ecclesiastical estates, introduced by the Church councils of 1580 and 1584 under the strong pressure of the government, prohibited the further acquisition of land by ecclesiastical institutions and ordered the sequestration—with or without compensation—of Church estates formerly held by the *dvoriane*. The granting of exemption from taxation to ecclesiastical institutions was prohibited by the Code of 1550 and by the Church councils of 1580 and 1584. These legislative enactments, however, failed to put an end to a deeply rooted practice and, as I have already pointed out, the delegates to the *zemskii sobor* of 1648 demanded without success the confiscation of Church properties acquired in violation of the law.

The *dvoriane* and other landlords were far more successful in their struggle with the menace from below, the desertion of their peasant farmers. At the time of the unification of the country the majority of the free farming population were tenants working on land owned by the state or by private lords, either secular or ecclesiastical. The right of the tenants living on private estates to relinquish their tenancy was gradually curtailed, it will be remembered, by limiting the time when such transfers could take place to a brief period around St. George's

Day (November 26) and by the indebtedness of the tenants to their landlords. The St. George's Day rule, which in the past had had only local application, was made general by the Code of 1497 and the Code of 1550. No tenants were permitted to relinquish their tenancy except during the week preceding and the week following St. George's Day. The two Codes, which also determined the rent (*pozhiloe*) due from the tenants for the use of farm buildings, contained a few more provisions dealing with the minor obligations of a departing tenant. Neither of the two Codes made any reference to other limitations on the freedom of the tenants, restrictions known to have existed before 1497, such as the tenant's obligation to settle his debts to the landlord before leaving, not to mention outright prohibition of the tenant's moving away, instances of which have already been noted.[1] It would be unwise, however, to deduce from the silence of the Codes that the earlier restrictions not referred to therein were no longer operative. Legislative drafting in old Muscovy was notoriously defective. No penalty, for instance, was provided for the violation of the St. George's Day rule and other provisions dealing with the relinquishment of tenancy by a farmer. Nevertheless, infringement of these legal requirements was actionable, and the offending tenants were compelled to return to the landlord they had "unlawfully" abandoned. There are indications, unfortunately lacking in definiteness, that other restrictions on the freedom of the tenants existed in the sixteenth century. Diakonov has tentatively advanced the opinion that some landlords received, as a special privilege, the power to prevent their tenants from relinquishing their tenancy during a specified period of time known as *zapovednyia leta*. The evidence bearing on this question, however, is inconclusive, and there is no agreement among the authorities on the exact meaning of the term.

The most powerful cause militating against the free and orderly movement of the peasant tenants was the burden of their indebtedness. It was customary for a farmer to obtain a subsidy from his landlord, and we have seen that he was required to pay rent for the use of farm buildings. Interest at the rate of 20 per cent and more was charged on a loan. The tax burden was greatly increased as a consequence of frequent wars, and the tenant was caught in the inextricable mesh of arrears owed to the landlord, who usually was also the collecting agent for the government. There was nothing in the law itself to

[1] See pp. 105–107.

prevent a tenant from relinquishing his tenancy without settling his outstanding debt to the landlord. Although the tenant was free to abandon the landlord, the debtor was at the mercy of his creditor. The Code of 1497 confirmed the ancient rule according to which the delinquent debtor became the slave of the creditor. By subsequent legislation, life slavery was altered to slavery until the debt had been repaid, a change that was not of much practical significance. How desperate was the plight of many tenants appears from the provision of the Code of 1550 which relieved the tenant who sold himself into slavery (*polnoe kholopstvo*) from the obligation of complying with the usual regulations attached to the relinquishment of tenancy. The disease must have been severe indeed to make palatable such a remedy. Contemporary records, especially the writings of authors favoring secularization, give an illuminating and distressing picture of the gross exploitation of the rural community. For a tenant overburdened with debt the only legal method of starting anew was to accept financial assistance, to be "bought off" by another landlord who needed his services. The obvious drawback for the tenant in this procedure was that he merely changed masters and usually increased the volume of his obligations. Opportunities for such assistance, if assistance is the right term, were not lacking in the second half of the sixteenth century, when the flight of the population brought about keen competition for agricultural labor. The transfer of tenants, which was accompanied by extreme brutality, led to violent outbursts reaching a climax around the fateful date of November 26 (St. George's Day). The small landowners, with arms in hand, often met the recruiting agents of their wealthy competitors, plundered the establishments of their tenants who desired to leave, and kept the tenants in irons.

The scramble for human labor extended to the peasants living on state land, the so-called state peasants (*gosudarstevennye krestiane*). These farmers were organized into agricultural communities whose members were jointly responsible for the payment of taxes and the performance of various obligations towards the state. The state was directly concerned with preventing such communities from losing their members, since every desertion necessarily reduced the paying capacity of the community as a whole. The state peasants who maintained their tenancy for a more or less protracted period, the exact length of which cannot be determined, were known as *storozhiltsy* ("old-timers"), and came to be looked upon as permanently attached to their farms. The *storozhiltsy* who had been induced to leave or had wandered away and settled down on private estates were forcibly returned to the communities they had deserted. A similar disability was incurred by tenants living on private estates (*vladelcheskie krestiane*) if their tenancy extended over a protracted but, again, undeterminable period of time. They, too, were known as *storozhiltsy*, and were deprived of freedom of movement, although they were not attached to land and had been reduced to a status of personal dependence on their landlord. There was an important distinction between the two cases. The enforced attachment of the state peasants was motivated by fiscal and police considerations, by the desire of maintaining the paying capacity of a peasant community. The limitation imposed on the *storozhiltsy* living on private estates had a different source. It was the direct outgrowth of their indebtedness to the landlord, which prevented them from taking advantage of their right of moving away. Because of failure to exercise this right, although through no fault of their own, they were considered as having forfeited it altogether. It was a kind of *longi temporis praescriptio*. In the first case the restriction was imposed for the benefit of the state, in the second for the benefit of the landlord. No general legislation dealing with the *storozhiltsy* has been preserved, although the practice of denying them the right to relinquish their tenancy was in effect from the middle of the fifteenth century. Diakonov describes these tenants as the first Russian serfs.

It was from these two roots—the indebtedness of the peasant tenants to their landlords and the fiscal policy of the Muscovite state—that the institution of serfdom evolved gradually and in a piecemeal fashion. Its origins are lost in the darkness of the ages and it did not reach its full development until the middle of the seventeenth century. In the sixteenth century a combination of peculiar circumstances, with which we are already familiar, contributed to the acceleration of the process of enslavement of the once free tenants. The *oprichnina* of Ivan the Dread, with its reshuffling of landlords on a gigantic scale, could not but throw into confusion the masses of the farmers. This confusion was further aggravated by the spread of the *pomestie* form of landholding, accompanied, as it was, by the creation of a vast number of small estates with the resultant close personal dependence of the tenants on their landlords. The conversion of large tracts of state land into *pomestie* put the population of such estates for the first time under the control of a lord, a change which meant extra burdens and exactions, much closer supervision, and often the loss of those institutions of self-government—limited and imperfect though they were—that the state peasants had formerly enjoyed. Close-knit and seemingly inextricable as was the network of legal and quasi-legal restrictions woven by the cupidity and greed of secular and ecclesiastical landlords around the peasantry, it was unable to strangle altogether that desire for freedom and decent conditions that flickers in some obscure corner of the mind and heart of every human being however humble, inarticulate, and downtrodden. Since the ingenuity of the Moscow chanceries had tightly closed every loophole that would permit a peasant farmer to improve his position, he took the law into his own hands and fled from the oppressors. The expansion of the Russian frontier towards the east during the reign of Ivan IV added impetus to the process of migration. This reprieve, however, proved short-lived, for the government was not slow in distributing the newly acquired territories as *pomestie*, and the fugitives from advancing serfdom soon found themselves in conditions similar to those they had attempted to escape. For those who were longing for freedom and adventure, there was still another haven in the no man's land in the southern steppes which separated Muscovy from the Crimean Tartars. In the sixteenth century the territories north of the Black Sea were swarming with fugitives from Muscovy, Poland, and Lithuania. Known as the Cossacks, and loosely organized into semi-military groups under an elected leader, they made a precarious living chiefly by brigandage and by entering the military service of whoever cared to pay them. The inroads of Muscovy into the steppes were slow and cautious, although not a few of the Cossacks had enrolled in Russia's military force and settled along the southern frontier.

The flight of the population to the east and south spelled ruin to the landlords in the western and central provinces, and, as has already been noted, it was the small landlords who were the hardest hit. They clamored for protection and for stricter measures to prevent their tenants from leaving. Restrictions multiplied, spurring the peasants to renewed efforts to escape them. In the opinion of Professor Platonov, the spread of the *pomestie* form of tenure was one of the determining factors in the onward march of serfdom. The volume of litigation over fugitive tenants reached appalling dimensions. The much-discussed decree of November 24, 1597, attempted to stem the tide of judicial disputes and to mitigate the resulting confusion by providing that no action for the return of runaway peasants should be brought after five years. The administration of this decree and later legislation having the same object were facilitated by the records of censuses taken in a number of provinces (*pistsovyia knigi*). By "fugitive" peasants the decree of 1597 presumably meant the tenants who had left their landlords in contravention of the St. George's Day rule and other regulations, or without settling their outstanding debts. The decree, however, has been interpreted by a number of historians, including so eminent an authority as Professor Sergeevich, as a clear indication that a previous decree, the text of which has been lost, had definitely abolished the right of the tenants to move away and had specifically ordered their attachment to the land. This interpretation, however, is unwarranted. The right of the peasant tenants to relinquish their tenancy was never formally repealed, although it was unobtrusively yet effectively rendered inoperative by a judicial and administrative practice that deliberately sacrificed the personal freedom of the tenants to the economic interests of their landlords and of the state.

The profound and painful transformation that altered the face of agricultural Russia had reverberations in the urban settlements. The development of city life in Muscovy was slow, and many of the so-called cities in the sixteenth century were still largely military centers with little or no commerce and industry. The progress of commerce was handicapped, among other things, by the government's fiscal policy, which endeavored to centralize trade activities in a restricted number of localities in order to facilitate the collection of taxes levied on commercial transactions. In the second half of the sixteenth century a certain stratification developed among the burghers, or *possadskie liudi*, a term used to describe all those engaged in commerce and industry and living chiefly, although not exclusively, in urban settlements (*possad*). This process grew out of the practice of appointing wealthy merchants as government agents for the collection of taxes on commercial transactions and for representing the state in other matters relating to trade. The task was both exacting and onerous, and since it carried no direct remuneration the appointees were elevated to the dignity of *gost*, or member of a "hundred" (*gostinaia sotnia, sukonnaia sotnia*). The title was not merely honorary, since it exempted the recipients from the jurisdiction of the ordinary courts and relieved them of the payment of taxes. The merchants selected to act as agents of the government were drawn from the well-to-do stratum of the trading community because wealth was the chief guaranty for the conscientious performance of their duties. The granting of these privileges worked to the detriment of the other burghers, who under the then existing system of taxation had to assume the tax burden from which the privileged group was exempted. A struggle between the privileged and the non-privileged burghers ensued. The plight of the latter was aggravated by the influx into the cities, especially into those in the western and southern parts of the country, of military officials, the *dvoriane*, who were exempted from the taxes paid by the burghers, since they were not supposed to participate in business activities, but who in practice often took advantage of their privileged position to compete with the local traders. Wealthy and powerful landlords, especially the monasteries, frequently maintained on their estates adjoining the trading centers (*sloboda*) competing establishments run by their slaves (*kholopy*) or tenants. The latter also enjoyed taxation privileges which they used to the detriment of the other traders. The combined effect of these conditions was similar to the one we have observed in the agricultural districts: the population of the cities gradually abandoned them and wandered away, and the cities of Muscovy were, according to Platonov, dying a slow death. Since this migration, of course, meant a loss of revenue, the government embarked on a series of measures that had for their object the attachment of the burghers to their cities, to their shops and trades, just as it had attached the peasants to their villages and fields.

Such were the social and economic conditions towards the end of the sixteenth century. They did not, of course, affect uniformly every part of the country. The north, remote as it was from the theater of international conflicts, was not directly involved in the process of social transformation that reached its highest point in the central provinces of old Muscovy. In the conquered and colonized territories of the middle and lower Volga, the situation was complicated by the resistance of the local tribes (Cheremissy, Votiaki, Mordva, Bashkiry), who were not yet reconciled to the Russian domination and the rule of the landlords introduced by it. The southern frontier was thronged with the milling thousands of fugitives from the Muscovite yoke.

The consequences of this uprooting of large masses of the people, which was at the bottom of the impending crisis, were foreseen with almost uncanny accuracy in a book published in 1591 by an English observer, Giles Fletcher, the elder, who visited Russia in 1588–1589.[2] The Moscow government was less perspicacious. To the rising wave of popular discontent that manifested itself in every social group from the titled boyars to the fugitive peasants it had nothing to oppose except increased police restrictions amounting to complete regimentation and the ruthless elimination of every vestige of freedom the people might have enjoyed in the past. That this policy finally triumphed is one of the major tragedies of Russia's history. It would have been impossible for the country to have accepted it without at least a movement of revolt.

TSAR FEDOR AND BORIS GODUNOV

Tsar Fedor (1584–1598), who succeeded Ivan IV, enjoys the melancholy distinction of being the only occupant of the Moscow throne about whom there is complete agreement among the historians: the son of Ivan the Dread was a feeble-minded weakling whose sole passion was the ringing of church bells and whose fixed and sickly smile betrayed his mental condition even to the most casual observer. By irony of fate, on his stooped and helpless shoulders descended the mantle of that absolutism of which his father had been both the exponent and the living incarnation. In striking contrast with Ivan's sinister and dominating figure, Fedor slipped through the fourteen years of his reign like a shadow, effaced without leaving any imprint on the course of events. His only claim to recognition consists in his failure to provide the throne with an heir, thus bringing to an end the Moscow branch of the Riurik dynasty. I have pointed out that the significance of the reign of Ivan the Dread was largely negative; the statement holds true of his son's rule, although in an entirely different sense.

The palace intrigues and the struggle between the rival boyar groups, kept in check by Ivan's regime of terror, were resumed after his

[2] Fletcher's volume, *Of the Russe Common Wealth*, was an indictment of absolutism. It immediately attracted much attention and was confiscated by the English government at the request of the Russia Company. A Russian translation issued in 1845, 250 years later, suffered a similar fate at the hands of the government of Nicholas I, and its editor was deprived of the chair he held in the University of Moscow.

death. Although many aspects of this conflict cannot be definitely traced, it appears that there existed a cleavage between the nobility of ancient lineage—the princes Shuisky, Vorotynsky, Golitsin, Kurakin —on the one hand, and the less illustrious, although distinguished and well born families, which may be described as court nobility, on the other. Prominent among the latter were the Romanov, descendants of the Koshkin-Zakahrin-Yurev family, and the Godunov. Both the Romanov and the Godunov owed much to the favors of Ivan IV and to their family alliances with the dynasty. Anastasia Zakharin, Ivan IV's first wife and Fedor's mother, was a Romanov, while Tsar Fedor was married to Irina, sister of Boris Godunov. The distinction between the ancient and the court nobility should not be pushed too far, since it was gradually obliterated by frequent intermarriages and other ties which welded the ruling families into a homogeneous group. Nevertheless, the resentment of the old aristocracy against the relative newcomers to the higher state and court offices, newcomers who were regarded as usurpers, was a factor in the situation, but the attempt of the ancient families to regain their former position failed lamentably. From almost the first months of Fedor's rule, Boris Godunov, the tsar's brother-in-law, asserted himself as Russia's real master, and it was not long before his chief opponents disappeared from the political stage. The Golovin were the first to go into exile, then came the turn of the venerable Prince I. F. Mstislavsky, who was forced to retire to a monastery. In 1587 a movement of the Moscow populace against the Godunov led to the disgrace and exile of the Princes Shuisky and of a large number of their relatives and followers. The Metropolitan Dionysius was deposed and incarcerated in a monastery. It was rumored later that Mstislavsky and the elder Shuisky, who both died in exile, were murdered at Boris's instigation. The road was then clear for Godunov's triumphant progress.

The character and policies of Godunov have long been one of the storm centers of Russian historiography. The interpretations vary from outright condemnation of Russia's first elected tsar as an unscrupulous and ambitious villain, to warm defense of him as the only enlightened statesman Muscovy ever had, and as the victim of calumnies and of events beyond his control. Despite this maze of conflicting opinions, it is safe to maintain that the determination to wear the Crown and to found a new dynasty was the great moving power behind Boris's behavior, an ambition that did not necessarily make him either a scoundrel or a saint. A man of considerable ability and shrewd political sense, Godunov seems to have overcome to a remarkable degree the handicap of a lack of education. He is usually represented as having been illiterate, although Platonov has discovered contemporary documents bearing his signature. A favorite of Ivan the Dread, Boris received his political training in the poisoned atmosphere of Aleksandrovskaia Sloboda, although he was not listed as an *oprichnik*. He was married to the daughter of Maliuta-Skuratov, Ivan's most hated henchman. Godunov's political ascendancy under Fedor's nominal rule was amazing. Taking advantage of his sister's influence over the feeble-minded tsar, Boris, after eliminating his enemies, rapidly built for himself at the Moscow court a position that made him the actual ruler of the country. His name invariably appeared in official documents immediately after that of the tsar, and he was referred to by the English as "prince," "licutenant of the empire," and "lord protector of Russia." Foreign relations were conducted in the joint name of the tsar and Boris. Godunov surrounded himself with elaborate etiquette, which duplicated that of the Kremlin, and his son Fedor, probably as early as 1595, was significantly enough made a participant in his father's political activities. The position of the Godunov was further enhanced by their wealth, which was very large, even if the probably exaggerated accounts of foreign observers are discounted.

Boris Godunov, first as regent and later as tsar, had to wrestle with complex international problems. The disastrous war waged by Ivan IV for the possession of Livonia was ended in 1582 by a ten-year armistice. But the Polish danger was not over. Stephen Batory, with the approval of the Holy See, was planning an anti-Turkish crusade which was to lead him to Constantinople by way of Moscow, the Caucasus, Persia, and Asia Minor. This grandiose and fanciful scheme was put to rest by Batory's death in December, 1586. The thrones of Poland and Lithuania were then both vacant. The candidacy of Tsar Fedor was advanced but met with no success, and in spite of Moscow's opposition to the election of Sigismund III, of the Swedish royal house of Vasa, he became Batory's successor (1587). The much-dreaded union between Poland, Lithuania, and Sweden materialized in 1592, when Sigismund succeeded his father, John III, as the king of Sweden. However, Sigismund's ardent Catholicism and disregard for Swedish constitutional arrangements provoked such opposition in his native land that he was soon forced to withdraw to Poland. The death of the impetuous Batory and the subsequent estrangement between Sweden and Poland materially improved the international position from the point of view of Moscow. A fifteen-year armistice was concluded with Poland in 1587 and confirmed by Sigismund in 1591. In 1590 Moscow, in an attempt to recover the territories lost by Ivan IV to Sweden, succeeded in occupying Yam and Ivangorod, but failed to take the port of Narva. A peace settlement concluded in 1595 restored to Muscovy the territories lost in the preceding Russo-Swedish war, but Narva remained under Swedish control, and for another hundred years an outlet on the Baltic Sea was denied to Russia.

The relations between Moscow and the Tartars on her southern and eastern frontier continued along traditional lines. Mongol invasions became somewhat less frequent, and although the Crimean Tartars advanced to the walls of the capital in 1591 they were routed by the Russian troops. The Crimean khan took his revenge the following year, when his horsemen overran and plundered the territories of Tula and Riazan. Some progress was made with the gradual expansion of Russian influence in the Caucasus, a process that had started soon after the annexation of Astrakhan. Boris Godunov also carried on successfully the task of reconquering western Siberia, where the Cossack garrisons were wiped out and their leader, Ermak, was killed in the course of an uprising of the natives in 1584. The Russian troops occupied western Siberia in 1586 and consolidated their position by establishing a number of military and trading posts, including the future city of Tobolsk.

On the initiative, presumably of Boris Godunov, Moscow obtained by somewhat unsavory methods a final emancipation from the patriarchate of Constantinople. It will be recalled that the Russian Church had been *de facto* autocephalus since Isidor's unfortunate peregrination to the Ferrara-Florence Council. Yet it seemed fitting that the "Third Rome," which was also the "Second Jerusalem," should have its own patriarch. Preliminary steps in this direction, taken in 1586, had met with no response from the eastern patriarchs with whom rested the final decision. In 1588 Jeremiah, Patriarch of Constantinople, came to Moscow soliciting financial help. He was partly bribed, partly coerced, and partly tricked into approving the creation of a Russian patriarchate. The delicate negotiations were carried on exclusively through lay channels, chiefly by Godunov himself. When the question was settled, a Russian Church council was assembled and went through the motions of choosing three candidates from whom the tsar was to make the final selection. Job, Metropolitan of Moscow and Godunov's creature, became the first holder of the exalted office. The eastern patriarchs, confronted in 1590 with a *fait accompli*, peevishly gave their sanction to a decision they believed to be of questionable canonical validity. They rejected, however, Moscow's claim that the new patriarch should be given third place in the order of precedence among the eastern patriarchs and firmly relegated the patriarchate of the "Third Rome" to the fifth, that is, the last place. Moscow refused to accept the decision, which was again confirmed by the patriarchs in 1593, and a futile and academic controversy ensued. Since the Russian Church had been independent from Constantinople for nearly 150 years, the creation of the patriarchate made no real difference, nor did it help the Church to emancipate itself from its dependence on the secular power, as the fate of the Russian patriarchs was soon to make abundantly clear.

In dealing with the peasant question, Boris followed the policies of his predecessors. It will be recalled that his decree of 1597 provided a five-year limit for bringing actions for the recovery of fugitive peasants. The decrees of 1586 and 1597 attempted to introduce some order in the practice prevailing among the landlords of accepting "free" peasants as slaves, thus depriving the state of taxpayers. The decrees of 1601 and 1602 limited the right of peasants to move from one landlord to another to such tenants as resided on small estates. The latter measure is usually interpreted as directed to the defense of the rank and file of the *dvoriane* against raids on their man power by their wealthy neighbors. On the other hand, in contravention of the decisions of the Church councils of 1580 and 1584, Boris resumed the distribution both of land and of taxation privileges to the monasteries and the bishoprics. His policies favored the advancement of serfdom, contributed to the growth of discontent among the masses, and thus prepared his downfall.

While Boris Godunov failed to introduce any significant changes in the economic and social policies of the Muscovite government, he spared no effort to win popular favor by timely displays of beneficence, by broad if somewhat vague promises of better things in the future, and by the kindness of his personal behavior, which offered a pleasing contrast to the ways of Ivan the Dread. It is generally believed that during his regency Boris enjoyed considerable popularity, especially with the rank and file of the *dvoriane* and the populace of the capital. The death of Fedor early in 1598 raised the question of the succession to the throne. Fedor left no children, his only daughter having died in infancy. The Crown was handed by Fedor to his wife Irina, who refused to accept it and took the veil. The Patriarch Job then offered the throne to Boris Godunov in the name of the Church, the boyars, and the entire people. Boris, however, declined, and insisted on the calling of a *zemskii sobor*, or assembly of representatives of the various social groups. The *zemskii sobor* duly met and, under the leadership of the patriarch, unanimously elected Boris, who, after refusing the Crown, presumably as a matter of form, finally accepted it. Professor Kliuchevsky's illuminating analysis of the *zemskii sobor* of 1598 reveals that it was organized along the lines of its predecessor of 1566 and that nothing in its constitution offers a justification for the frequent accusation that it was a sham. It will be remembered, however, that the *zemskii sobor* was an appointed and not an elected assembly. Under these conditions opportunities for direct and indirect pressure were practically unlimited, especially for a man like Boris, who had been for fourteen years the undisputed master of the country. Information from Polish sources (the correspondence of Andrew Sapieha) discloses that the position of Godunov before his election was not quite so impregnable as would appear from Russian records. It was rumored that his claim to the throne was contested by at least three candidates, of whom the most formidable was Fedor Nikitich Romanov. That Boris did not feel quite secure appears from the extraordinary measures taken by the government immediately after Tsar Fedor's death, when all the frontiers were closed and relations with other countries were suspended. The opposition to Godunov was not disarmed by his triumph at the 1598 *zemskii sobor*. Palace intrigues and agitation among the populace continued. The pathetic figure of the elderly and blind Prince Simeon Bekbulatovich, once grand duke or tsar of Moscow through the whims of Ivan the Dread, was dragged from retirement and groomed as a candidate for the throne. Boris felt so uneasy about his position that he made the people take an oath of allegiance, presumably the second one, by which Simeon Bekbulatovich was specifically repudiated. It was not long before the new tsar turned to sterner measures. In 1600–1601 Bogdan Belsky and Fedor Romanov, both mentioned by Sapieha as Boris's competitors in the race for the Crown, were called to pay the penalty. Belsky was put through the torture chamber, flogged, and thrown into prison in a distant Volga town. The whole Romanov family and a large number of their kin were accused of using sorcery in order to win the Crown. The charge was based on a frame-up concocted by the chief of the police, Simeon Godunov. Fedor Romanov, the head of the family, was forced to take monastic vows under the name of Filaret and was incarcerated in a remote monastery. His wife, too, took the veil, while the other members of the family, including Fedor's son Michael, the future tsar, were exiled to distant parts of the country. Many of them died in captivity, and it was rumored that they were murdered by Boris's agents. Haunted by suspicion and fear, Godunov soon lost his former easygoing and amiable manner. Spying, especially by slaves on their masters, was made a civic virtue which received public recognition and reward. Deportations, confiscations of property, and executions were again of daily occurrence. As in the days of Ivan IV, the upper classes were living under the sword of Damocles. Fate itself seemed to have conspired against Boris. The great famine of 1601–1603 brought much suffering to the populace; and profiteering by merchants and landlords, both secular and ecclesiastical, increased the hardships and created much bitterness and indignation. Confiscation of estates was accompanied by the release of slaves who were not permitted to accept the patronage of another master. Other slaves were simply turned out by their owners, who found it difficult to provide for them. Banditry assumed alarming proportions. New rivulets of starving, uprooted, and desperate humanity were pouring into the mighty stream steadily fed by the flight of the peasants from the advance of serfdom. Boris's earnest efforts to provide relief for the hungry were necessarily inadequate, and his popularity was rapidly waning. The forces of discontent and social protest needed merely a banner and a leader around whom they might rally. In a melodramatic fashion this leader appeared in 1603 in Poland and took the name of Tsarevich Dimitry. The slogans written on his banner were lacking in precision, but this merely increased their appeal to the masses.

THE PSEUDO-DIMITRY

Tsarevich Dimitry was the son of Ivan IV by his last wife, Maria Nagoï. After Ivan's death, Dimitry, his mother, and her relatives were sent to Uglich, where they lived under the supervision of Moscow agents headed by Michael Bitiagovsky. In May, 1591, the boy Dimitry died under mysterious circumstances. A commission of investigation presided over by Prince Vasili Ivanovich Shuisky decided that he cut his throat by accident in an attack of epilepsy to which he was subject. Dimitry's mother and the Nagoï, as well as the people of Uglich, thought differently and ascribed the boy's death to murder by Boris's agents. Bitiagovsky and a number of the members of Dimitry's entourage were put to death by the excited populace. The government of Godunov retaliated. Maria Nagoï was forced to take the veil and exiled to the wilderness of Beloozero. Her relatives, too, were sent into exile, and so many of the inhabitants of Uglich were executed and deported that the town was said to have lost most of its population. According to tradition, even the church bell that rang the alarm at the time of Dimitry's death was removed. The responsibility of Boris for the events of 1591 was never definitely established, although his guilt was later officially proclaimed by Vasili Shuisky, who himself eight years earlier had exonerated Boris. Gossip that the life of the tsarevich was endangered by the ambitious aspirants to the throne was current in Moscow, and rumors reported by Fletcher in a book written while Dimitry was still alive pointed to Godunov as the logical perpetrator of the crime. It is questionable, however, to what extent Dimitry was a real obstacle in Boris's path to power. Muscovy had no definite law of succession, although custom made the son his father's heir. The position of Dimitry was nevertheless particularly vulnerable. He was Ivan's son by his seventh wife, and his legitimacy was open to serious doubts, since the Russian Church recognized the validity of no more than three marriages. Gossip involving Boris in the alleged murder did not seem to affect his popularity in the years immediately following the tragedy of Uglich, nor did they prevent his election to the throne in 1598. That the unhappy affair of 1591 was pretty well forgotten even in Uglich is indicated by the fact that the emissaries of Vasili Shuisky, sent there in 1606 to recover the body of the tsarevich, who was about to be added to the calendar of Russian saints, had difficulty in locating the grave. While it is reasonably certain that Dimitry actually perished in 1591, the question of Godunov's guilt or innocence in the absence of conclusive evidence necessarily remains a matter of opinion.

Rumors that Dimitry had miraculously escaped the knife of the assassins, which began to circulate in Moscow as early as 1600, took definite shape in 1603, when the Pretender, after some peregrinations among the Polish magnates, established his headquarters on the banks of the Dniester, at the castle of Sambor, the residence of George Mniszek, a Polish nobleman of adventurous disposition, whose lavish ways of living had led him into financial trouble. The identity of the Pretender is one of the insoluble mysteries of a period that produced many enigmas. The Moscow government officially announced that he was Gregory Otrepev, an unfrocked monk and former serf of the Romanov and of their kin, Prince Boris Cherkassky. The accuracy of this statement has often been questioned. Available information, however, indicates that the pseudo-Dimitry was a native Russian who knew Polish well and some Latin. A good horseman and swordsman, the Pretender moved with ease among the Polish nobility. He was recognized as the true Dimitry by the Polish government, in spite of Moscow's objections, and was permitted to use Polish territory as a base for his operations against Moscow, although he was not given official support. In the spring of 1604 the Pretender embraced Roman Catholicism, a decision that strengthened his ties with the clerical circles of Poland, where the idea of the union of the eastern and western Churches, and of the introduction of Catholicism to Russia, was very much alive. His infatuation for Marina Mniszek, his Sambor host's ambitious daughter, led to their engagement and eventually to their marriage, thus creating an additional link between the Pretender and Poland. Those who have seen Mussorgsky's opera *Boris Godunov* will remember the enchanting if historically inaccurate love scene between Dimitry and Marina. It would be a mistake to imagine that because of the Pretender's many Polish connections his venture was a machination of Poland, of the Jesuits, or of the Holy See. Platonov's careful analysis of available evidence makes it clear that the appearance of the pseudo-Dimitry was essentially a Russian phenomenon. The idea of using the Pretender as a weapon against Boris Godunov was probably evolved in boyar circles, and circumstantial evidence points to the Romanov. The persecution of the Romanov and other noble families after Boris's accession was a consequence of their anti-Godunov activities, which finally crystallized around the person of the Pretender. The connivance of Poland made it possible for the pseudo-Dimitry to organize his movement and to make a start, but the success of the enterprise was due to the weakness of the Moscow government, the benevolent neutrality of many representatives of the Russian upper classes, and the enthusiastic reception by all those who had lost faith in the existing order and who, in the phrase of the Communist Manifesto, had nothing to lose but their chains. With a small army of some 3,500 to 4,000 men, a motley group where Polish knights and soldiers of fortune rubbed shoulders with fugitive Russian peasants, the Pretender crossed the Dnieper in October, 1604, and began to advance towards the capital. The southern territories, with their unruly masses of Cossacks and disaffected small landholders, went over solidly to his side. The *dvoriane* and the burghers acclaimed the pseudo-Dimitry as their liberator from a tyrannical government. The small Polish nucleus of his army was rapidly submerged in the mass of his Russian supporters. In spite of some military defeats and the resistance of government troops, his progress towards Moscow assumed the character of a national movement. The sudden death of Boris Godunov in April, 1605, removed the last obstacle and opened the gates of the capital to the Pretender, while army units, one after another, proclaimed their allegiance to Dimitry, and the popular rancor and hatred of the Godunovs was given free vent. It is not surprising, therefore, that the reign of Fedor Godunov, who had succeeded his father, lasted for merely six weeks. The flower of nobility, headed by the Mstislavsky, the Golitsin, and the Shuisky, hastened to desert the young monarch. Vasili Shuisky, who had previously testified to Tsarevich Dimitry's death in Uglich, reversed himself, declared that the boy had escaped assassination, welcomed the Pretender, and administered the oath to him taken by the Moscow populace. Fedor Godunov was murdered with perverse cruelty, and his mother was strangled in the presence, it is believed, of Prince Vasili Golitsin. The life of Ksenia, Boris's reputedly beautiful daughter, was spared, and she became the mistress of the Pretender. Even Boris's body was removed from the Arkhangelsky Cathedral to an obscure monastery. The fall of the dynasty was accompanied by an orgy of mob rule directed not only against the supporters of Godunov, such as the Patriarch Job, who was deposed and exiled, but also against all those who because of their wealth or position were singled out for the hatred of the rabble. On June 20, 1605, the pseudo-Dimitry made a triumphal entry into Moscow.

His success proved just as ephemeral as the union of the many elements that constituted his following. As is so often the case, the men who gathered under the Pretender's banners were fighting, not for, but against something. They were temporarily united by a common hatred of the Godunov and of all for which they stood. But the aspirations and desires of those who cheered the Pretender in the streets of Moscow had little in common. The boyars were dreaming of the restoration of their ancient privileges and of a patriarchal government of which they would be the leaders. The rank and file of the *dvoriane* clamored for larger *pomestie*, higher wages, and a firmer hold on the peasants living on their estates. The masses of the peasantry, and especially the Cossacks, who contributed so largely to the success of the movement, cherished a vague ideal of land and freedom, of a new social order where serfdom would not be the sole reward of the tillers of the soil. The foreign mercenaries demanded their pound of flesh, while the Jesuits and the Polish clericals were scheming for the reunion of the Churches. To reconcile these conflicting claims was a superhuman task.

The Pretender failed to accomplish the miracle. Some of his measures, such as the demobilization of the army, which permitted the *dvoriane* to return to their estates, and the generous distribution of money among the members of this group, contributed to his popularity. On the other hand, there was much irritation among the boyars, who were often publicly humiliated, while complete *parvenus* and, still worse, foreigners, were raised to high positions in the councils of the new tsar. The Church was alarmed by the pressure of Catholicism, the Pretender's ill disguised indifference to Orthodox ritual, and his disturbing habit of exacting large sums from ecclesiastical institutions with occasional confiscation of Church properties. There was serious friction with Poland over trivial matters of title and etiquette. The boyar families exiled under Godunov were returned to Moscow. The Romanov were treated with special consideration, the monk Filaret being raised to the dignity of the Metropolitan of Rostov. The Shuisky, however, soon found themselves in serious difficulties, and Vasili Shuisky was even sentenced to death for some treasonable activities a few weeks after he had welcomed the pseudo-Dimitry to Moscow. The sentence was commuted at the last moment, and after four or five months of exile the Shuisky family was allowed to return to the capital. The Pretender's foreign entourage and his way of living, which departed from the rigid customs of the Kremlin, raised much apprehension in conservative circles, while his accessibility and the simplicity of his manner helped him to retain the affection of the humbler section of his followers in spite of his failure to interfere drastically in their behalf. Rumors of subversive activities reached the ears of the new tsar, who even took the precaution of forcing Prince Simeon Bekbulatovich to take the monastic vows (March, 1606). On March 8, 1606, the Pretender was married in Moscow to Marina Mniszek, who arrived with a large retinue of Polish noblemen and Bernardine and Franciscan friars. The moment, however, was considered ripe for getting rid of the Pretender. Popular disturbances instigated by the boyars broke out on May 12, and on May 17 the pseudo-Dimitry was murdered in the Kremlin. Hundreds of Poles and Lithuanians were slaughtered, but Marina and her father escaped unharmed, and were exiled to Yaroslavl. On May 19 Vasili Ivanovich Shuisky was proclaimed tsar of Russia.

THE TSAR VASILI IVANOVICH SHUISKY

The overthrow of the Pretender and the accession of Shuisky came about through a palace revolution in which the Moscow populace was merely a tool in the hands of boyar interests. Conservatism of the deepest hue was Shuisky's official creed. Although his proclamations made reference to his yielding to the prayers of the people, special emphasis was placed on Shuisky's right to the throne as the representative of the senior branch of the House of Riurik, and he promised to conduct the government according to the immutable tradition of his ancestors, the Muscovite tsars. The heritage of absolutism, contrary to the opinion of some historians, was fully upheld in the oath taken by the new tsar, and no constitutional limitation of his powers should be read into his vague promises to refrain from arbitrary persecutions. An appointee of the aristocracy, Shuisky was proclaimed tsar without any legal formalities, such as election by a *zemskii sobor.* Dynastic claims being the official foundation of Shuisky's rule, he displayed considerable ingenuity in eliminating any possible pretenders who might have a title to the throne. Even the aged Prince Simeon Bekbulatovich, although blind and seemingly innocuous in his monastery, was not overlooked, and was removed to the inaccessible Solovetsky Monastery on an island in the White Sea. Once more reversing his position on the death of Tsarevich Dimitry, Shuisky made him a national saint. The boy Dimitry, according to official announcements, had been murdered by order of Boris Godunov in 1591. His miracle-working remains, discovered in Uglich, not without difficulty, were solemnly transported to Moscow. Anyone who longer refused to believe in Dimitry's death was confronted with the unchallengeable authority of the Church.

These extraordinary measures, however, failed to produce the desired effect. Widely circulated rumors maintained that Dimitry was still alive and would soon be heard from again. There was no unity among Shuisky's supporters, and friction developed immediately within the very circle that brought him to power. The Romanov were rewarded for their part in the affair by the "nomination" of Filaret to the patriarchate as the successor of the deposed Ignatius, who had held the office under the Pretender. While Filaret was in Uglich arranging for the transfer of Dimitry's remains, his "nomination" was canceled, he was shifted back to the metropolitanate of Rostov, and the leadership of the Russian Church went to Hermogen. The ambitious head of the Romanov family found it difficult to become reconciled to his demotion, the reasons for which have remained obscure, and the powerful influence of his klan was thrown against Shuisky. The removal of many high officials and members of the aristocracy who were close to the Pretender inevitably created numerous enemies for the new regime. The Moscow populace, moreover, to whom Shuisky had appealed on more than one occasion and who carried through the *coup d'état* of May 17, continued to interfere sporadically in public affairs, exercising at times a disturbing pressure on the none too stable government.

The situation outside Moscow was still more serious. The radically inclined masses of the Cossacks and small landholders saw in the "boyar tsar"—as Shuisky was sometimes called—the triumph of a system they feared and hated. About half of the territory of the realm refused to submit to the new government, the opposition centering in the south and east, with many adherents in the western territories, while the north continued to support Moscow. The *dvoriane* were in dread of reprisals for the enthusiastic reception they had given the Pretender and feared that their advancement in the military hierarchy under Shuisky's oligarchial rule was in jeopardy, while the fugitive peasants and slaves who formed the main body of the Cossacks realized that the new government meant to them the knout and serfdom. Against these they were determined to fight. Prince Gregory Shakhovskoy, a nobleman with personal grudges against Shuisky, assumed direction of the movement, which soon developed a leader from among the Cossacks, Ivan Bolotnikov, an adventurous runaway slave. Under the guise of restoring Dimitry, Bolotnikov unfolded in his inflammatory proclamations a program of social revolution. He preached murder, incited the peasants and slaves against their masters, the poor against the rich, and promised to the exploited the land, wealth, wives, and daughters of their oppressors. His appeal had immense success among the peasant masses and the restless population of the border regions. Bolotnikov's revolutionary army found itself fighting against the Moscow government side by side with a detachment of the *dvoriane,* who as landowners and slaveowners could hardly be expected to be in sympathy with the Cossack demands. In October, 1606, the rebel forces were within sight of Moscow.

The revolutionary character of the Cossack movement was realized not only in the capital but also all over the country, and this made it possible for Shuisky to rally around his unsteady throne the proprietory and conservative groups. The detachments of the *dvoriane* who had been arrayed against the Moscow government quickly changed their mind and went over to Shuisky. The desertion of their allies sealed the fate of the Cossacks; the invading army was defeated by Shuisky in December, 1606, and was forced to retreat to Kaluga and Tula. The struggle continued through 1607, until government troops swept over the southern and eastern provinces and suppressed the uprising with an inhuman cruelty that fully matched that of the Cossacks. Tula was taken in October, 1607, and the leaders of the rebel forces, including Bolotnikov and Shakhovskoy, fell into Shuisky's hands. The victory of the government was apparently complete. Although the rebels had fought with desperate courage, the task of pacification proved even more formidable than the achievement of victory itself. Moscow was led to realize that dynastic considerations were secondary to the social aspect of the struggle. Indeed, pretenders were numerous in 1607–1608, when a score of insurgent leaders assumed the title of "tsarevich" coupled with such fanciful names as Peter, Fedor (a never born son of Tsar Fedor), Laurentius, Savely, Simeon, Vasili, Eroshka, Gavrilka, Martinka, a grotesque array of revenants whose connection with the Moscow dynasty would have taxed the resources of the most imaginative historian. These imposters were obviously a mere pretext for a continuation of the struggle against a hated regime.

Shuisky, emboldened by his victory, repeatedly refused the offer of assistance from King Charles IX of Sweden, and proceeded with a number of measures, primarily punitive and deterrent, designed to eliminate the causes of the uprising. The rebel provinces, which represented one-third of the realm, were submitted to a reign of legalized plunder, and thousands of prisoners were executed, many of them by slow drowning, a particularly inhuman form of torture. The fugitive peasants and slaves among the prisoners were returned to their former masters or were handed over to other landlords who agreed to provide for them. Some of the runaway state peasants were forcibly repatriated in the communities they had deserted, while, quite illogically, the mass of the prisoners of war was set free to trek back to the southern steppes, where it formed a vast reserve of starving and desperate humanity ready to join any subversive movement.

Beginning in the spring of 1607, the Moscow government issued several decrees that tightened police supervision over the relations between the landlords and the peasants, on the one hand, and the landlords and the state, on the other. The chief object of these edicts was to stop the flight of the population that was at the root of the social upheaval. Public authorities were made responsible for keeping everyone firmly attached wherever he was supposed to belong. This legislation, however, did nothing to remove the causes that had forced the peasants to give up their farms and to flee. Shuisky, according to Platonov, was not blind to the nature of the movement that nearly toppled him from his throne, but he was under the delusion that the situation could be cured by police measures. To the impetuous demand of the rebellious masses for land and freedom he replied by multiplying police restrictions. The Church made its contribution to the triumph of the boyar reaction by solemnly releasing the people from their oath of allegiance to the Pretender. At the unusual ceremony the deposed Patriarch Job officiated jointly with the new Patriarch Hermogen. The rebels had lost, and serfdom's hold over the peasant millions was firmer than ever.

The struggle, however, was not yet over. A second Pretender, whose identity is even less certain than that of his predecessor, made his appearance in June, 1607, and assumed the name of Tsarevich Dimitry. He, too, found asylum in Poland, where the ground was thoroughly prepared for a new adventure against Moscow. The massacre of May 17 and the indignities inflicted upon the Polish ambassador were keenly resented by King Sigismund, especially since they came at a time when Polish influence in Moscow seemed to be firmly entrenched. Poland, moreover, was herself emerging from a civil war which had left behind much bitterness and disaffection, as well as large detachments of armed men only too anxious to join any military enterprise that promised glory and booty. A campaign against Muscovy held out the promise of both. From the very beginning of his career the Second Pretender was largely dependent on Polish troops. His Polish-Lithuanian army comprised well disciplined and well equipped detachments under Polish magnates, like Jan Peter Sapieha and Prince Roman Rozynski, who, in the spring of 1608, assumed the command. The remnants of the scattered Bolotnikov army and the many discontented elements on the southern fringe of Muscovy were skillfully canvassed, organized, and armed by Alexander Lisowski, a Lithuanian leader who took refuge in Russia after the defeat of the uprising against Sigismund. Ivan Zarutsky and other Cossack chieftains were not slow in proclaiming their allegiance to the resuscitated Dimitry. Few, if any, of the Second Pretender's followers actually believed that he was the Dimitry who had escaped death in Moscow on May 17; he was merely a banner which everyone tried to use for his own purpose. During the winter of 1607–1608, while Shuisky was celebrating his victory over Bolotnikov and demobilizing his army, the forces of the Second Pretender vastly increased in number and achieved a certain cohesion.

War between the Second Pretender and Moscow began in the spring of 1608. The rebel troops advanced without meeting much resistance and established their headquarters at Tushino, a few miles from Moscow. Rozynski's attempt to take the capital by storm on June 25 was successfully resisted, although it threw the city into a state of panic. The insurgents organized an elaborate blockade of Moscow which was by no means ineffective although it was never complete. Shuisky, finding himself in a desperate plight, appealed for help not only to the Russian cities which continued to support his government but also to foreign powers. In June, 1608, he concluded an agreement with King Sigismund which provided, among other things, for the withdrawal of the Polish and Lithuanian troops serving with the insurgents. Through his relative, Prince Michael Skopin-Shuisky, he also opened negotiations with Sweden. In the meantime the insurgents invaded the northern provinces which had been spared in the earlier stage of the civil war and promised rich booty. The north was relatively free from the disaffected elements that teemed in the south, and although the people were not overenthusiastic about Shuisky, they found the invaders even less palatable. The northern urban and agricultural communities continued to enjoy a certain degree of self-government for which the Polish mercenaries and the Russian gentry and Cossacks gathered under the banners of the Second Pretender, who was usually referred to among his opponents as the "Vor (criminal, brigand) of Tushino," displayed but the scantiest consideration. Exasperated by the brutality and the exactions of the insurgents, the sturdy peasants of the north arrayed themselves solidly against them. After suffering severe defeats in guerrilla warfare, the people's militia succeeded, by the spring of 1609, in clearing the northern territories of the rebel troops and prepared to move farther south for the relief of Moscow. In February, 1609, Shuisky signed an agreement with Sweden, ceding to that country Russian territories on the shores of the Gulf of Finland in exchange for Swedish military assistance. Prince Michael Skopin-Shuisky, an able and popular military leader, rallied around Novgorod a large number of the supporters of the government and cautiously advanced towards Moscow at the head of an army that had been greatly reinforced by some fifteen thousand Swedish, French, English, and Scotch mercenaries. The hard-pressed Pretender, after a violent quarrel with Rozynski which cost him most of his Polish support, abandoned Tushino early in 1610 and fled to Kaluga. Thus the blockade of Moscow collapsed.

The relief experienced by the Moscow government was marred by other dark clouds that were gathering on the political horizon. The possibility of a union between Poland and Muscovy had long been in the air. It is reported that at the end of 1605 an emissary of Shuisky and other boyars had negotiated secretly with Sigismund and had offered the Russian throne to his son Wladyslav. The subsequent unfortunate experiences of the Poles in Moscow and the disturbed conditions of the country could not have left the Polish government indifferent. The alliance between Russia and Poland's enemy, Sweden, was considered as a sufficient reason for direct intervention, and in September, 1609, the Polish troops besieged Smolensk. Sigismund sent a delegation to Tushino and urged the Polish detachments to join the national colors. This offer was given a mixed reception since many of the Poles at Tushino had not so long before fought against Sigismund. Nevertheless it led to a final split between the Cossacks and the Poles and to that quarrel between Rozynski and the Pretender that precipitated the latter's flight to Kaluga. The Polish troops, too, left Tushino and withdrew to Volokolam. Early in April, 1610, following the sudden death of Rozynski, which contributed to the disintegration of the Pretender's Polish army, the majority of the military forces went over to Sigismund while the most intransigent elements turned to banditry.

Tushino, which for about two years had played the part of a second capital, was rapidly slipping back into oblivion. Its short-lived and sinister prominence was due to the extraordinary decadence of Muscovy's never too high standards of political decency. The hardships imposed on Moscow by the blockade, the lure of easy profits and advancement, the unpopularity of Shuisky's rule, and the uncertainty of the general outlook led to the creation of an amazingly large group known by the succinct name of *perelety* or "migratory birds." The *perelety* were those boyars, ecclesiastical dignitaries, *dvoriane*, government officials, merchants, and individuals among the common people who made it a practice to transfer their allegiance at more or less frequent intervals from Moscow to Tushino and from Tushino back to Moscow, trading as the price of their dubious repentance and questionable support the grants and advancements they had succeeded in wresting from Shuisky for still larger estates and higher offices distributed by the Pretender, and vice versa. The precarious position of both Tsar Vasili and the pseudo-Dimitry and their desperate need of assistance from whatever source and at any price made possible this revolting state of affairs. Many of the aristocratic families had their representatives at Tushino, where they shared with men of humble extraction the doubtful honor of membership in the boyar duma. The leading place among the Tushino notables was held by Filaret Romanov, who, since he fell into the hands of the Pretender, when he took Rostov in October, 1608, had been living in Tushino in the anomalous position of a "prisoner" who was also revered as their patriarch by the insurgents. Marina, too, came to Tushino as a "prisoner," accepted the Pretender as her husband, and followed him later to Kaluga. Filaret was more cautious and non-committal. That he was not too proud of his activities at Tushino is suggested by the fact that this unhappy episode was passed over in silence by his official biography prepared in 1619. When events took a clearly unfavorable turn for the Second Pretender, Filaret and the Tushino aristocracy turned to Poland. Early in February, 1610, they negotiated with

Sigismund an agreement that made his son Wladyslav tsar of Muscovy and at the same time provided for the inviolability both of the existing Russian state institutions and of the Orthodox Church. Specifically upholding the rights of the landlords over their peasants and slaves, the agreement was prompted by a spirit of rigid conservatism, although it safeguarded the right of the *dvoriane* to advancement and promotion on the basis of service and merit and not merely of ancestry: the family trees of many of the Tushino notables were not very impressive. With the conclusion of the agreement Tushino suffered a final eclipse. The Polish troops were gone. The Cossacks who had nothing to hope for from Sigismund joined the Pretender at Kaluga, while the Tushino "aristocracy" drifted to Sigismund's camp near Smolensk. Filaret followed the latter course but was intercepted en route by government troops and in May, 1610, was brought to Moscow amidst rejoicing that so distinguished a "prisoner" had finally been liberated from captivity. He continued to keep in touch with the Poles.

Once more the outlook for Shuisky was brighter. Sigismund met with unexpected resistance, and Smolensk defended itself with magnificent courage. The Pretender at Kaluga seemed to be at the end of his rope. On March 12 Prince Michael Skopin-Shuisky made a triumphant entry into Moscow, where he was received as a savior. Young, popular, and successful, he was considered by many as Tsar Vasili Shuisky's probable successor. Prince Michael's days, however, were numbered. Late in April he contracted a mysterious illness to which he succumbed, and it was widely rumored that he had been poisoned by his relatives, who resented his popularity. The place of Skopin-Shuisky at the head of the huge army which was to defeat Sigismund was taken by the tsar's brother, Prince Dimitry Shuisky, a man of mean disposition, mediocre ability, and uncertain courage. Under his undistinguished leadership the Russian troops, in spite of their vast numerical superiority, were routed at Klushino on June 24 by Hetman Stanislas Zolkiewski. Although their wages were often in arrears, Shuisky's foreign soldiers fought gallantly, but when they found themselves cut off from their base many of them went over to the Poles, while the Swedes withdrew to Novgorod. The Russian commander in chief fled, leaving behind his baton—insignia of his high office—his sword, his gold-embroidered standard, his carriage, and his treasury. The *dvoriane* scattered to their villages and towns, and turned a deaf ear to further calls to arms. Zolkiewski proceeded towards Moscow without meeting any opposition. Spurred to action by the disgrace of Shuisky, the Pretender left Kaluga and advanced to within a few miles of the capital. In the city itself two powerful groups were working for the overthrow of a regime whose ineptitude has been abundantly proved. Supported by Zakhary Liapunov, a Riazan *dvorianin*, who throughout his chequered career commanded a large following, Prince Vasili Golitsin was busily preparing his own candidacy. The Tushino group, headed by Filaret and his kin Ivan Saltykov, were agitating on behalf of Wladyslav. A movement of the Moscow populace, instigated by Liapunov and Saltykov, proclaimed on July 17 the deposition of Shuisky, disregarding Patriarch Hermogen's eloquent plea on his behalf. Two days later the former tsar was forced to take the monastic vows and was locked up in the Chudov Monastery, in the Kremlin. His wife was compelled to take the veil, while his brothers were arrested. According to Platonov's judicious observation, the dethronement of Shuisky removed the very symbol of a political order that had already ceased to function. Moscow was thenceforth to be ruled by a provisional government of the boyar duma headed by Prince Fedor Mstislavsky.

THE POLISH RULE

Although the new government never exercised any real control over the country, it found itself under the necessity of making a decision of the utmost importance. Both Zolkiewski and the Pretender were at the gates of Moscow. Confronted with the alternative of choosing between Polish rule and the revolutionary forces of the Cossacks supporting the pseudo-Dimitry, the Moscow aristocracy preferred the former. A hurriedly summoned assembly of uncertain composition acted as a *zemskii sobor* and elected Wladyslav to the Russian throne. The population took the oath to the new tsar, and Zolkiewski, after defeating the Pretender, who was forced to retreat to Kaluga, made his entry into the capital. The conditions proposed by the boyars and accepted in the name of Poland by the hetman were embodied in the agreement of August 17, 1610. It was largely a restatement of the earlier agreement reached in February between the Tushino leaders and Sigismund, except that it was even more conservative. The provision for the promotion of the *dvoriane* according to merit was dropped and replaced by one safeguarding the privileges of the ancient nobility. A

delegation comprising 1,246 members—a *zemskii sobor* in itself—
and headed by Prince Vasili Golitsin and Filaret left for the camp of
King Sigismund near Smolensk in order to arrange for the arrival
of the new tsar and to insist on certain additional safeguards such
as the conversion to Greek Orthodoxy of Wladyslav, who was still
under fifteen years of age. According to the picturesque expression of
the Chronicle, he "was to be reborn to a new life, like a blind man who
has recovered his eyesight." What the Muscovites had in mind was
a "personal" union with Poland with no interference by foreigners
in Russian affairs. Sigismund, however, had a different program. He
intended to rule Muscovy himself and if possible in his own name and
not in that of his son. Zolkiewski resigned his command and was replaced by Alexander Gosiewski, who soon established in Moscow a
military dictatorship. The boyars were not only deprived of actual
participation in the administration of public affairs but were superseded by former Tushino dignitaries and officials of humble extraction, among whom Fedka Andronov was particularly notable. The
huge Russian delegation at the Smolensk camp fared no better. The
negotiations proved sterile, Sigismund insisting on the return of the
Russian emissaries to Moscow in order to ensure his own election to
the throne. Some of the members of the embassy allowed themselves
to be bribed or persuaded, but the leaders, including Filaret and
Golitsin, demurred, were arrested, and deported to Poland. Moscow
was again in a state of turmoil, and the anti-Polish feeling was rising.
Gosiewski had to take extraordinary measures to provide for the
safety of his troops. When in December it became known that Sigismund was planning to mount the Russian throne, Patriarch Hermogen
in a solemn announcement forbade the people to take the oath of
allegiance to a Roman Catholic tsar. The patriarch's anti-Polish activities played an important part in subsequent events. He was soon
incarcerated by the Poles, and in January, 1612, died in his cell, where,
it is said, he was starved to death or strangled by his jailers.

The reaction against an oppressive foreign rule which, moreover,
was generally believed to endanger Greek Orthodoxy, considered by
the Russians as the sole true religion, manifested itself first in Riazan,
under the leadership of Prokopy Liapunov, and in Nizhni-Novgorod.
The murder of the Second Pretender in Kaluga in December, 1610,
removed one of the obstacles to unified national action against the
Poles, although agitation continued in favor of his son, Ivan, born

to Marina soon after. Encouraged by Patriarch Hermogen, who maintained secret relations with the insurgents even while under arrest, the movement spread to a number of cities and was supported by the remnants of the Tushino Cossack army led by Prince Dimitry Trubetskoy and Ivan Zarutsky, the protector and presumably the lover of Marina. When the joint forces of the militia (*opolchenie*) and the Cossacks approached Moscow in the spring of 1611, the small Polish garrison withdrew within the fortified enclosures of the Kremlin and Kitaigorod, the rest of the city having been destroyed by fire during the uprising of March 19.

The leaders of the Russian troops gathered around the capital made an attempt to reconstruct a national government. A crude administrative machine was built up and orders were issued in the name of "the whole land." But these efforts were doomed to failure. The heterogeneous elements brought together under Liapunov's banners by the common hatred of the Poles were too divided to make cooperation among them lasting and effective. Liapunov won the support of the Cossacks by promising them "personal freedom and government grants" (*volia i zhalovanie*) and by assuring the runaway peasants and slaves that they would not be discriminated against and had nothing to fear. The masses responded to the appeal and clamored impatiently for the fulfillment of the promise. The result was a conflict similar to the one that had wrecked the short-lived alliance between Bolotnikov and his *dvoriane* confederates in 1606. It was a clash between the forces of social revolution and those of agrarian conservatism. The social complexion of the leaders of the militia was reflected in a curious document known as the Decision (*prigovor*) of June 30, 1611. Although issued, as usual, in the name of "the whole land," it represented the views of the *dvoriane* group alone. The Decision established a provisional government consisting of Liapunov, Trubetskoy, and Zarutsky, whose powers were vaguely limited by a kind of military parliament. The administrative machine was consolidated and reorganized. The whole structure of land grants was revised, and excessive allocations, such as those so lavishly distributed both by Sigismund and by the Pretender, were to revert to the state. The existing relationship between the landlords and the peasants was preserved, and the fugitive peasants and slaves were to be returned to their masters. The mistrust of the Cossacks was disclosed in a provision which put them under the control of the *dvoriane*. The contrast between Liapunov's promises and the terms of the Decision of June 30 could not have been more striking, and it is difficult to find an explanation for his change of mind except that, grossly misjudging the situation, he was prepared to sacrifice the success of his anti-Polish crusade to the interests of the landlords and serfowners. It was not long before he paid the penalty: he was murdered by the Cossacks on July 22. The *dvoriane* forgot all about the salvation of the country from a foreign yoke and fled in disorder, leaving the Cossacks in control of the administrative machine created by the militia leaders— all that was left of the national Russian government. In the hands of desperate marauders this machine became an instrument of ruthless oppression.

Other calamities befell Moscow in the summer of 1611. In July, Novgorod severed its ties with Moscow and accepted the suzerainty of Sweden. A little earlier, on June 3, Smolensk had finally been taken by the troops of Sigismund. Europe, and especially Rome, paid homage to Poland's brilliant victories, and Sigismund yielded to the temptation to hold in Warsaw in October an elaborate celebration at which the former Tsar Vasili Shuisky and his brothers, now Polish prisoners, were ostentatiously displayed with little good taste as living examples of the vicissitudes of human fortune. The frivolous Polish monarch, like so many of the Russian rulers, failed to see the writing on the wall.

The disaster of the Liapunov venture was grave but not irreparable, and it taught the conservative elements the impossibility of reconciling the aspirations of the Cossacks with the interests of the landed proprietors. There were many among the *dvoriane* who felt, as did the Moscow boyars in electing Wladyslav, that social revolution at home was more to be feared than was a foreign tsar on the throne. Even Hermogen, that epic figure in Russia's struggle for national independence, urged the people of Nizhni-Novgorod in a message which reached them in August, 1611, to fight the claims of the *Vorenok* (little brigand, the Pretender's or *Vor's* son), who was supported by Zarutsky and the Cossacks, while the imprisoned patriarch made no reference either to Sigismund or to the Poles. Dionysius, prior of the Troitsky Monastery, advocated in his well known proclamations a very different policy. His monastery was situated near Moscow, and Dionysius was in contact with the Cossacks and their leaders. The prior, whose monastery owned large estates, was inclined to minimize, without ignoring them, the misdeeds of the Cossacks, and called the country to support them in their struggle against the Poles and the Russian traitors in Moscow. The Church was just as divided as the country itself. If Hermogen's program—the Cossacks first, the Poles afterwards—was finally followed, it was due to causes deeper than the moral authority of the patriarch.

After the collapse of Liapunov's militia in August, the Volga towns were among the first openly to defy the Cossack authorities. Early in October Kuzma Minin, a Nizhni-Novgorod butcher and one of Russia's national heroes, stirred by his eloquence an audience of local officials (zemstvo elders) to pass from recriminations, complaints, and prayers to constructive action for the reestablishment of order. Minin was a man of conviction and organizing ability. The ground had been prepared by past unfortunate experiences, and the movement gained momentum in a remarkably short time. A shrewd tradesman, Minin provided the new militia (*opolchenie*) with sound financial backing derived from voluntary donations and compulsory levies. He continued to hold the strings of the public purse while the leadership of the military force was entrusted to a local nobleman, Prince Dimitry Pozharsky, a soldier with a distinguished record. The Volga towns one after another joined the movement, which early in 1612 not only embraced the whole north and east of Russia but was receiving support from other parts of the country. The *dvoriane*, many of whom had been deprived of their estates, hastened to rally around Minin and Pozharsky. The program of the movement was essentially conservative. In a proclamation issued at the end of 1611 or early in 1612, the Cossacks were denounced, both Marina's infant son and the Polish king were repudiated, and the election of a new tsar was promised. The chief object was the restoration of order. The Cossacks in their camps near Moscow understood what this meant, and Zarutsky moved his forces to Yaroslavl in the hope of cutting the chief line of communication between Nizhni-Novgorod and the northern provinces with their vast resources of men, money, and supplies.

The civil war was resumed once more. Zarutsky's designs were frustrated, and Pozharsky not only established himself in Yaroslavl but also succeeded in freeing the northern provinces from the Cossack bands. Leaving the Cossacks to wrestle with the Poles besieged in Moscow, Pozharsky remained at Yaroslavl from March until August, building up and organizing his movement. A *zemskii sobor*, believed to be fairly representative in membership, was assisting the leaders of the government. The militia, equipped and trained, gained a distinct advantage over the Cossacks, although it never succeeded in making a creditable showing against the Poles. Plans had been made to proceed with the election of a new tsar in Yaroslavl without waiting for the liberation of Moscow when the Cossack leaders informed Pozharsky that the Polish hetman Jan Chodkiewicz was coming to the rescue of his countrymen who were besieged in the Russian capital. Pozharsky moved his militia towards Moscow, and the two Russian armies, which had not yet made peace among themselves, had to face the common enemy. The meeting with the militia proved fatal to the poorly disciplined and loosely organized Cossack force. The troops of Pozharsky, avoiding the mistake committed by Liapunov, kept aloof from the ally they did not trust. Dissensions aggravated by suspicions of betrayal developed within the Cossack camps. Their command broke down, and a portion of the men, led by Zarutsky, retired to Kolomna and later to Riazan and Astrakhan in vain pursuit of their dream of land and freedom. In their first encounter with the troops of Chodkiewicz, the Cossacks hesitated to help the militia and thus contributed to the success of the Polish general in getting supplies and men into the Kremlin. A little later, at the end of September or early in October, the Cossack leader, Prince Trubetskoy, concluded with Pozharsky an agreement that established a semblance of unity within the Russian forces but did not eliminate frequent discord and open clashes. Time, however, was working against the Poles, who gallantly defended themselves behind the walls of the besieged capital. With admirable fortitude they endured incredible privations, and although reduced to cannibalism they refused to lose faith in the promised rescue that was always postponed. On October 22 the Cossacks took by assault Kitaigorod, one of the two Polish strongholds. Four days later the Kremlin capitulated. It was again the Cossacks who in December defeated Sigismund in his belated attempt to recapture Moscow. The *dvoriane*, according to Kliuchevsky, had conclusively demonstrated during these troubled years their unfitness for the business of war, which was both their profession and their national duty. Included among the flower of the Russian aristocracy released from Moscow were Michael Romanov and his mother, who had to be protected from a hostile crowd.

THE NEW DYNASTY

The task that awaited the makeshift government of Pozharsky, Minin, and Trubetskoy in liberated Moscow, was a great deal more difficult than had been their victory over a handful of starving and exhausted Poles abandoned by their own king and diet. The *dvoriane* wanted to go home, and by December most of them had been demobilized and had left Moscow. The Cossacks were still unruly, and showed little respect for the central government and the local authorities. The most urgent business was the election of a new tsar. The repeated appeals sent from Moscow for the dispatch of delegates to a *zemskii sobor* had met, it appears, with a mixed reception. Nevertheless the delegates began to gather in the capital in January, 1613. Although information on the composition and proceedings of the *sobor* is incomplete, it is believed that it was the first truly representative gathering ever known to have assembled in the Russian capital. Candidates for the throne were many, including several foreign princes: Wladyslav, who had a following among the Moscow aristocracy, one of the sons of the king of Sweden with whom Pozharsky had negotiated, and some of the members of the Hapsburg dynasty. These, as well as the boy Ivan, son of Marina and the Second Pretender, were all ruled out by the *sobor*. Russia was to have a Russian tsar. There still remained a multitude of aspirants drawn from the nobility. There followed a bitter electoral campaign involving much mutual recrimination, direct and indirect pressure, outright intimidation, and bribery. Prince Pozharsky, for instance, is said to have spent considerable sums in promoting his own candidacy. From the struggle for the throne that unfolded itself at the meetings of the *sobor* and behind the scenes, Michael Romanov emerged the victor. He was elected on February 7 and after a hurried and secret canvass of opinion in the provinces, was proclaimed tsar on February 21, 1613. The choice was in the nature of a compromise between the conservative and the radical elements of the national assembly. An important factor in Michael's favor was the eminence of his family, which for over three hundred years had been closely associated with the Moscow court and its administration. On the one hand, the Romanov were related to the House of Riurik and Michael was a nephew of Tsar Fedor, a fact that made him acceptable to the conservative elements enmeshed in the dynastic tradition. On the other hand, Michael's father, Filaret, had been elevated to the metropolitanate of Rostov by the First Pretender and had acted as patriarch under the Second Pretender. This won the Romanov the support of the Cossacks when it became clear that Ivan, the infant son of the Pseudo-Dimitry and Marina, who was the Cossacks' first choice, was unacceptable to the majority. The Poles, indeed, scornfully referred to Michael as "the Cossack tsar." Filaret's imprisonment in Poland at the time when the *sobor* was held added an aura of martyrdom to the luster of the Romanov family, and their numerous influential relatives and satellites spared no effort in fostering Michael's candidacy. Last but not least, the utter insignificance of the young Romanov spoke strongly in his favor. A sickly boy of sixteen whose forceful father was behind Polish bars, Michael appeared to many as a convenient tool for achieving their own aims. After their unfortunate experience with Godunov and Shuisky, the Muscovite constituent assemblies displayed a notable predilection for children. Michael's predecessor on the throne had been Wladyslav, his junior by a year or two. What the leaders of the *zemskii sobor* really wanted, according to Kliuchevsky, was not the tsar best qualified for the task, but the one who would be the easiest to handle. The official version, of course, recorded no such base considerations, and the decision of the *zemskii sobor* solemnly proclaimed that the entire Orthodox people, including babies (*mladentsy*), unanimously implored Michael to accept the Crown. Who could have resisted so moving an appeal? The obscurity that surrounded the tsar-elect is suggested by the fact that his exact whereabouts were not known to the delegation sent by the *sobor* to offer him the Crown. He was discovered in a Kaluga monastery with his mother, known as Sister Martha after she had been forced to take the veil. Martha, conforming to tradition, refused for a while to give her consent and blessing, as Ivan IV and Boris Godunov had gone through the motions of refusing the Crown on somewhat similar occasions, one in 1564 and the other in 1598. It is probable, however, that there was more sincerity in Martha's reluctance and tears, the experiences of the last four tsars having been not exactly encouraging. On March 14, however, Michael accepted the Crown, and his coronation took place in Moscow on July 11. Although it has occasionally been advanced that the powers of the new tsar were made subject to definite constitutional limitations, this view is not supported by available evidence. The first Romanov ascended the steps of the throne of Ivan the Dread formally clothed with all the traditional and unlimited powers of Muscovite absolutism.

THE ABORTIVE REVOLUTION

The revolutionary storm that had ravaged Russia for fifteen years and had subsided with the election of Michael Romanov left surprisingly few traces on the political and social structure. The outburst, which originated in the awakening of the masses, could hardly have been more violent. It led the country to its first social revolution accompanied by frequent changes of dynasties, foreign occupation, desolation, hatred, impoverishment—all the usual manifestations of civil war. No country has ever lived through a more cruel ordeal. Yet the torn and bleeding Muscovy over whose reconstruction the Romanov were to preside was not vastly different from the realm that the feebleminded Fedor had inherited at the death of Ivan the Dread. Not a single constructive political idea had evolved through the many changes of political regimes. The energies of the Moscow leaders were centered on the restoration of the past and not on the demands of the present, and least of all on those of the future. Like a rocky island unbattered by an angry sea Muscovite absolutism emerged from the tempest as formidable as ever.

It has often been pointed out that this revolutionary turmoil completed the downfall of the old landed aristocracy. This is true, although the process of its decline, begun with the unification of the realm, had made progress under the regime of the *oprichnina*. The events of 1598–1613 merely expedited the final breakdown of the political influence enjoyed by ancient princely and boyar families. The significance of the change was further minimized by the fact that the successors to the nobility of birth were not the masses of the people, but a relatively small and select group of the *dvoriane* who owed their wealth and influence to the sovereign's pleasure. The formation of this social class was already well advanced in the sixteenth century. The new aristocracy, deriving its power from state and court offices and government grants, displayed, moreover, an uncommon aptitude in following the example of its predecessor, the nobility of ancient lineage. Even the institution of *mestnichestvo*,[3] seemingly incompatible with a regime dominated by new blood, not only survived until the end of

[3] See p. 179.

the seventeenth century but was developed and strengthened. The new upper class was anxious itself to forget and to make others forget its too recent origin. It was therefore a change of personalities rather than a remodeling of the social structure. The Church, too, retained through the vicissitudes of the civil war and foreign occupation both its vast estates and its ancient privileges. The institution of serfdom, although not at the time known by that name, came out of the tribulations of the revolutionary years not only without having lost anything of its hold on the masses of the peasants, but rejuvenated, officially accepted and stronger than before, and remained the very foundation of the Muscovite state. The contact with foreigners who came as conquerors or as hired mercenaries had left no discernible imprint on Russian life, except that it probably stimulated that xenophobia from which no country is ever free, thus contributing to the narrow and chauvinistic exclusiveness and the fear and hatred of any departure from tradition so apparent in the Russia of the seventeenth century.

The Cossacks and the masses of the peasants and slaves gained nothing by the revolutionary upheaval of which they were the moving force, and their movement collapsed miserably. Even those intransigent elements who followed Zarutsky and Marina in their flight to Astrakhan soon deserted their leader. The fugitives were captured in the summer of 1614 and brought to Moscow, where Zarutsky was executed and Marina's infant son hanged. The unhappy Polish adventuress either died or was murdered under conditions that remain obscure. Some of the Cossacks, it is true, received concessions through being allowed to organize into semi-autonomous military communities on Russia's southern border. They, however, represented a small minority. With the exception of those who succeeded in escaping beyond the frontier where the long arm of the state could not reach them, the masses of the peasants and slaves were returned to their masters. It is difficult to suggest an adequate explanation of the dissolution of a movement that for a time had seemed to have in its hands the destinies of the nation. To dismiss it as merely anti-social does not help much, especially since the methods of its opponents were in no way better than those of the Cossacks. Nor is it obvious that even when judged by the standards of the early seventeenth century the ideal of land and freedom was necessarily inferior to that of "order" based on serfdom and enshrined in autocracy. The failure of the revolutionary forces to achieve at least some of their objectives—for if Michael was actually elected by the Cossacks he was a "Cossack tsar" only in name—may, perhaps, be ascribed to the anarchistic character of the movement, the inability of its leaders to keep it under control, their lack of vision, and, above all, that deeply-rooted tradition of passive submission which, while not incompatible with sporadic violent outbreaks, invariably forces the rebellious slaves to resume the hated yoke. The powerful torrent of the revolt, having spent its energies, was forced back underground, but the mighty streams feeding it had not been brought under control, and new devastating floods were in the making.

CHAPTER X

THE FIRST ROMANOV

---※---

THE TSARS MICHAEL, ALEXIS, AND FEDOR

The election of Michael Romanov, founder of a dynasty destined to reign for three hundred years, removed an element of political uncertainty that had played its part in the events of the Time of Troubles. There remained, however, other factors both international and domestic which were more directly responsible for the crisis than was the extinction of the Moscow branch of the House of Riurik. The situation confronting the young tsar was fraught with danger. Wladyslav tried to cling to the Muscovite Crown, which had slipped from his hands before he had had an opportunity to wear it, the Swedish troops were in Novgorod, the state treasury was empty, the land was exhausted and largely in ruin after years of civil war and foreign invasion, the Cossack bands had not yet been reduced to obedience, and most important of all, the profound feeling of discontent that had provoked the revolutionary movement, by no means dead, at times threatened to sweep away in a tidal wave of popular anger the new dynasty and the social order which it represented.

A striking feature of Russia's history in the seventeenth century was the distressing mediocrity of the men on whose shoulders rested the burden of national reconstruction. If, as seems likely, one of the chief reasons for the election of Michael Romanov was his utter insignificance, those who manipulated the election might well have congratulated themselves: not only Michael, but also his son and grandson were singularly free from any pretensions to actual leadership in the affairs of the nation. In a country that found itself on the rim of the abyss as a result of the gross inadequacy of its political and social structure, the first three Romanov—Michael, Alexis, and Fedor—invariably turned to the past for inspiration and guidance.

The gradual infusion of new ideas and new institutions that paved the way for the reforms of the eighteenth century took place largely under the pressure of inexorable circumstances which helped to break down the superstitious attachment to tradition characteristic of Peter I's predecessors.

There is some uncertainty about the constitutional arrangements during Michael's long reign (1613–1645). As I have pointed out, the theory frequently advanced that his constitutional powers were limited by an agreement—sometimes held to have been a secret agreement imposed upon the tsar-elect by the leading boyars—is not supported by contemporary evidence. In 1613 the position of the old boyar aristocracy, heavily compromised by its cooperation with the Poles, was such as to make an attempt on its part to limit the powers of the Crown highly improbable. The precaution, moreover, would have been both superfluous and of dubious efficacy. An ailing, self-effacing and docile young man, Michael was only too anxious to let others govern in his name. The youthful tsar was a weakling brought up under the tutelage of a domineering mother, who after she was forced to take the veil became Sister Martha. He had had hardly any schooling and had lived through the hardships of exile and of the blockade of Moscow. The leading figures in the first six years of Michael's reign were his mother, an embittered and rapacious woman, and her numerous relatives, among whom the Saltykov particularly distinguished themselves by their intrigues, extortions, and abuse of power. In 1619 Filaret, Michael's father, was finally released from Polish captivity, and on his return to Moscow was elevated to the patriarchate which had remained vacant since Hermogen's death in 1612. A reluctant prisoner in the frock he had been compelled to take by Boris Godunov, Filaret, formerly Moscow's foremost dandy, had in the course of his long incarceration, in his subsequent peregrinations to the court of the Tushino Pretender and in his Polish captivity lost the amiable disposition that once had made him so popular. Devoid of theological education, the new head of the Russian Church was disillusioned, ruthless, brutal, and immensely ambitious. His position as the father of a young and insignificant tsar opened to him magnificent vistas. The place he occupied at the Moscow court was somewhat similar to that held by Boris Godunov at the court of Tsar Fedor, but Filaret went a great deal further. He assumed the title of *velikii gosudar,* equivalent to "Majesty," and while officially recognized as Michael's co-ruler he became the actual master of the country. The tsar, full of filial devotion and well justified humility, willingly accepted the tutelage of his authoritative parent. The resulting diarchy, in which the leading member was the head of the Church, made the Russian government appear to be a kind of theocracy. It lasted until Filaret's death in 1633 and left no trace on the constitutional structure. An attempt by Patriarch Nikon to revive this form of government a few years later led to his undoing. Stripped of its ecclesiastical trappings, the rule of Filaret is reduced to a phenomenon familiar in Russia's history before and after Michael: government by a favorite. In the case of Filaret, by a historical accident, the favorite happened to be both the patriarch and the father of the tsar. Like all favorites Filaret hastened to get rid of his predecessors. The Saltykov, accused of an unsavory intrigue directed against the tsar's bride-to-be, Maria Khlopov, an intrigue that led to a breach of the engagement, were promptly exiled. Martha, too, was relegated to a monastic cell. Prince Boris Repnin, a friend of Filaret, acquired for a time considerable influence at the court; but immediately after Filaret's death the Saltykov were recalled, while the theocratic diarchy disappeared as suddenly as it had come. Patriarch Joasaph, who succeeded Filaret, was the latter's nominee, schooled in perfect obedience. The Chronicle reports with satisfaction that he never contradicted his master.

Michael died in 1645, and his wife followed him within a few weeks. The Moscow throne was again occupied by a boy of sixteen, Alexis (1645–1676), Michael's only son, who, unlike his father, had received a careful education according to the standards of the time. At the age of ten, when his scholastic career came to an end, he could read and write; he sang prayers and hymns, and was fully conservant with Church services. Alexis's literary legacy comprises letters, descriptions of dreams, notes for speeches, and even attempts of a higher order which the author presumably believed to be verses. His rigid conservatism, his profound belief in the divine origin of his powers, and his sense of piety verging on bigotry were tempered by inborn kindness and broad human understanding, qualities all too seldom found within the precincts of the Kremlin. Brought up in the barbarous atmosphere of the Russian court, Alexis combined to a surprising degree the crudeness of manner prevailing in his milieu with an occasional revelation of delicacy of feeling that would do honor to a more enlightened age. He was at his best when dealing with friends tried by misfortune. His intellectual equipment, however, was limited, and he took the same passionate interest in trivial questions of etiquette and in the minor wrongdoings of obscure officials as in vital problems of state. The tsar's truly admirable spirit of forbearance expressed itself at times in a surprising fashion. Commenting, for instance, on the defeat suffered by his troops in an encounter with the Germans in 1657, he wrote to a cousin: "We have lost fifty-one men killed and thirty-five wounded of all ranks. I am thankful to God that from an army of three thousand only this number has suffered; all the other men are well because they had fled; they themselves cry that such a misfortune [*grekh:* literally "sin"] should have befallen them. . . . And the Germans against whom our troops fought were only two thousand strong; we were more numerous, yet the misfortune [*grekh*] came upon us!" The supreme chief of the Muscovite army was not lacking in a broad comprehension of human fallibility.

Following tradition as well as his personal inclinations, Alexis maintained at the palace a throng of beggars and feeble-minded creatures, sometimes vulgar impostors, known as *iurodivyi,* for whom the pious Russians had a deep veneration. The tsar provided them with generous meals and found no small recreation in their not very enlightening chatter. At the same time under the influence of his favorites, who had been contaminated by western ideas, Alexis allowed himself to adopt certain innovations; he introduced foreign furniture in the palace, established an orchestra, eased the regime of seclusion that was formerly the fate of the tsarina, witnessed with his family and court theatrical performances, and provided his children with a fairly liberal education. This was, however, as far as he went. In his jovial manner he accepted the novelties which added to his comfort and enjoyment, but he was not the man to undertake the rejuvenation of the archaic machinery of the state. Kliuchevsky, who calls Alexis the kindest of Russians, is forced to admit that in spite of his inborn good qualities and his sincere efforts to do the right thing he never succeeded in rising even an inch above the level of the most uncouth of his subjects. Platonov, not an unfriendly historian, is led to the conclusion that Alexis's energies were absorbed by the performance of the complex Church and palace ritual that was the daily routine of the Kremlin. The conduct of public affairs was left to officials under the supervision of favorites who succeeded one another in the good graces of the monarch. The tsar's tutor, Boris Morozov, came first, and was followed by Prince Nikita Odocvsky, Patriarch Nikon, Athanasy Ordin-Nashchokin, Artamon Matveev. The favorites usually ended in disgrace, and their position was rendered all the more precarious by the intrigues of the tsar's numerous relatives, who enjoyed a traditional quasi-immunity.

Tsar Alexis, who was married twice, first to Maria Miloslavsky and after her death to Nathalie Naryshkin, a ward of the tsar's favorite, Matveev, had three sons and several daughters. Of the three sons, Fedor and Ivan were by his first wife, the youngest, Peter, the future emperor, by the second. When Alexis died unexpectedly at the age of forty-seven, he was succeeded by his eldest son, Fedor (1676–1682). A boy of fourteen, the new monarch had little control over the political situation at the Kremlin, or over the complications caused by family strife. Fedor was of delicate health, and his brother Ivan was mentally deficient, a situation that was of evil augury for the Miloslavsky and their kin. The death of Alexis was followed by the usual struggle for power and influence, the rival boyar families grouping themselves around either the Miloslavsky or the Naryshkin and the Matveev. Probably for the first time in Russia's history, women—the late tsar's daughters, sisters, and aunts, forerunners of the array of feminine rulers who mounted the throne in the eighteenth century—openly took an active part in the war of calumny and intrigue. Fedor, who received a good education under the guidance of Simeon Polotsky, one of the literary luminaries of the period, knew both Polish and Latin and tried his hand at writing poetry. Confined to the sickroom, the young tsar, like his immediate predecessors, left the administration of public affairs in the hands of favorites, Ivan Yazikov and Alexis Likhachev. Prince Vasili Golitsin, an outstanding supporter of western ideas, also enjoyed the confidence of the tsar. Fedor left no personal imprint on the course of Russia's history. After his death the seemingly barren tree of the Romanov dynasty suddenly gave proofs of unsuspected vigor. Whatever may have been the faults of the next two rulers—Tsarevna Sophie and Peter—neither was a figurehead or a protective screen for palace intrigues.

FOREIGN RELATIONS

The foreign policies of the first Romanov were determined largely by the unhappy inheritance of the Time of Troubles. It has been computed that of the seventy years that elapsed between the accession of Michael and the death of Fedor about thirty were filled with wars, at times waged simultaneously on several fronts. The liberation of Russia from foreign intervention was the immediate task superimposed upon the secular struggle against Sweden, Poland, and the Crimean Tartars, who were now backed by the resources of Turkey. Hostilities against Sweden, which was holding Novgorod, were after protracted negotiations terminated by the peace of Stolbovo, in 1617. Russia paid an indemnity and ceded to Sweden the territories on the southern shore of the Gulf of Finland reconquered by Boris Godunov. She, however, recovered Novgorod and the other provinces that had been occupied by the Swedes, and the claim to the Russian throne of Philip of Sweden, brother of Gustavus Adolphus, was formally dropped. War against Sweden was resumed in 1656 over the question of the control of Poland and Lithuania, coveted by both Tsar Alexis and King Charles X of Sweden. In 1661 Russia was forced, by the onerous terms of the Peace of Cardis, to renounce the Livonian territories held by her troops.

Russian relations with Poland-Lithuania were more complex, the struggle more protracted and costly, even though it led to a considerable expansion of the Russian state. In 1613 Wladyslav, reduced to inaction by the unyielding opposition of the Polish diet, had not yet abandoned his claims to the Moscow Crown. The uncertainty of the Russians themselves regarding their new dynasty appears from the curious fact that an embassy sent to Poland in March, 1613, to arrange for an exchange of prisoners was specifically instructed to refrain from making any reference to Michael and to deny his election in case the issue was raised by the Poles. Military operations between Poland and Russia were resumed in 1618, but the forces at the disposal of Wladyslav were inadequate; although he succeeded in advancing towards Moscow he was unable to take the Russian capital. By the terms of an armistice for fourteen and a half years, concluded at Duelino at the end of 1618, Poland retained the provinces of Smolensk and Seversk, while Wladyslav refused even to renounce his claim to the Russian throne. Although the *début* of Michael on the international stage was modest, the termination of hostilities with both Sweden and Poland offered Muscovy a much-needed breathing space. The expiration of the term of the armistice in 1632 coincided with an interregnum in Poland caused by the death of Sigismund III. Moscow deemed the moment propitious for settling its old accounts with

Poland, and the Russians began by besieging Smolensk in a campaign that proved a fiasco. The newly elected Polish king, Wladyslav IV, supported by a large force of Cossacks from Polish Ukraine, cut off the Russian army commanded by Michael Shein, hero of the defense of Smolensk in 1609, and forced it to surrender. The unhappy Russian commander in chief was eventually executed in Moscow, while Poland and Russia in 1634 concluded an "eternal peace" under the terms of which Wladyslav collected an indemnity and retained Smolensk and the Seversk provinces but finally renounced his claim to the Moscow Crown. This was all that the first Romanov succeeded in wresting from his old enemy.

"Eternal peace" with Poland lasted for barely two decades. It was brought to an end by the interference of a new political factor that had gradually come into being in the steppes of the Black Sea and had played an important part in the revolutionary events of the Time of Troubles. This factor was represented by the Cossacks who had settled in the western part of the frontier region known as Ukraine, extending along the shores of the Black Sea from the foot of the Carpathian Mountains to the Urals. In the narrow meaning of the term, Ukraine was used in the middle of the sixteenth century to denote the southern possessions of Poland-Lithuania, a vast territory whose uncertain boundaries comprised the basins of the Bug and the Dnieper extending east to form a watershed with the Donets, that is, roughly the region immediately north of the steppes bordering on the Black Sea and the Sea of Azov. These lands, once a component of the Kievan empire, are also known as Little Russia (*Malorossiia*). The southern part of Ukraine, formerly a highway of the Asiatic invaders, remained throughout the earlier centuries of the history of eastern Europe a no man's land inhabited by a mixed population which consisted of fugitives from Muscovy, Lithuania, and Poland with a probably large admixture of descendants of the nomadic tribes, a roving mass of humanity not yet crystallized in any definite social formation and making a precarious living chiefly by brigandage, but also by fishing, hunting, beekeeping, cattle raising, and occasional cultivation of land. The main settlements of the Cossacks were on the principal rivers of the southern steppes—the Dnieper, the Don, and the Volga. The steady pressure of the Muscovite and the Polish-Lithuanian colonization, bringing in its wake the economic and social conditions the Cossacks were endeavoring to escape, forced them farther south. Rooted in the nomadic tradition of the steppes and fed by the uninterrupted stream of disaffected elements fleeing Polish and Muscovite oppression, the Cossacks were slow in settling down in organized communities. Gradually, however, there came into being a peculiar form of semi-military organization based, at least in principle, on equality and autonomy. The earlier communities of this type first appeared, probably, on the Don, where they functioned in the middle of the sixteenth century. A similar community on the lower Dnieper received the name of *Zaporozhskaia Sich* or *Zaporozhie*. Both Muscovy and the Polish-Lithuanian state were anxious to harness these unruly frontiersmen and enroll them in the service of their respective governments. Military expeditions against the Crimean Tartars and Turkey, whose shores they reached, like the Varangians of old, in their light but sturdy boats, were a prominent feature of the Cossack activities and an important source of their revenue. The geographical position of the Cossack settlements identify them as the outposts of Poland and Russia against the Moslem world. Yet it was only gradually that the Cossacks were drawn within the direct sphere of influence of Muscovy and Poland. Until the end of the sixteenth century the Don Cossacks were practically independent, and it was not until 1570 that they assumed a vague obligation to serve Ivan the Dread. Poland, too, exercised a somewhat uncertain jurisdiction over the Dnieper Cossacks. In the sixteenth century Polish control took the form of enrollment of the Cossacks in the service of Polish and Lithuanian magnates who had acquired large domains in the fertile southern provinces. The practice was later made general by the creation of a state frontier guard. The Cossacks serving in this force were known as "registered" (*reestrovye*) Cossacks, received important privileges, and were paid a wage. In Polish Ukraine, "registered" Cossacks, who increased in number from a few hundred in 1570 to six thousand in 1625, formed a privileged group among the population of the steppes. It was the policy of the Polish as well as the Muscovite government to reduce the masses of the Cossacks not on the rolls to their condition before they fled south, that is, serfdom or slavery. This led to a cleavage among the Cossacks themselves by fostering the military organization of the privileged group of the "registered" Cossacks and by fomenting discontent among the Cossack masses, who found themselves once more facing the doom of serfdom.

The stronghold of Cossack liberties was the *Zaporozhskaia Sich*.

Although there is no definite information as to its origin, some authorities believe it may date from the end of the fifteenth century. Located on the inaccessible islands near the Dnieper rapids and protected from the intrusion of Polish officials and punitive expeditions by the wilderness of the forests, the *Sich* became the refuge of the most militant elements among the Cossacks. Early in the seventeenth century it appeared in the guise of a military order or brotherhood headed by an elected hetman and organized along military lines. A general assembly of the members elected the officials and decided all important questions. The *Sich* itself was a military camp from which women were excluded. The married Cossacks lived outside, and many of them were engaged in agriculture. Until the end of the sixteenth century the population of the *Sich* was highly fluid, seething with feverish activity in the summer months, especially at times when popular unrest brought fresh waves of recruits. In winter it was largely deserted except for small detachments in charge of military stores and other property, while the bulk of the Cossacks drifted into the cities and villages to reassemble again at their military headquarters early in the spring. Although the Cossacks belonging to the *Sich* liked to refer to themselves as "knights" (*rytsari*), the organization had little in common with the knightly orders of western Europe. Chivalry was incompatible with the crude, primitive instincts of the starving outlaws that formed the body of the brotherhood. The Cossacks, at their best, were mercenaries and soldiers of fortune; at their worst they were brigands to whom nothing was sacred and who were capable of the greatest atrocities.

The very nature of the Cossack army singularly disqualified it for the role of the champion of Greek Orthodoxy and of national unification under Moscow, a role forced upon it by the course of events. Although nominally members of the Orthodox Church, the majority of the Cossacks displayed a marked indifference in religious matters. No church existed in the *Sich* in the seventeenth century, and ministers of religion were excluded from the capital of *Zaporozhie*. In their plundering expeditions the Cossacks made no distinction in the treatment they meted out to the churches and clergy, whether Catholic or Orthodox. While more closely related to Muscovy than to Poland by linguistic and ethnographical ties, the Cossacks were free from chauvinism or nationalistic exclusiveness. The ranks of the brotherhood were open to non-Russians, and the leader of the

Cossack uprising of 1591–1592 was a Polish nobleman and adventurer, Christopher Kosinski. The uprising itself was directed largely against Prince Constantine Ostrozhsky, a pillar of Russian influence and Orthodoxy in Ukraine.

The estrangement between the Cossacks and Poland was the result of a long chain of events beginning with the Act of Liublin (1569) which merged Lithuania and Poland in a single state. The consequence of this change was the strengthening of Polish influence in Lithuania, including its Russian provinces. Polish administration was substituted for the former Russian officials and the once free expanses of the steppes were colonized by Polish noblemen—*szlachta* —who instituted serfdom and imposed much heavier obligations on the people. The inevitable unfavorable reaction was strengthened by the practice of Polish landowners, admitted by Polish historians, of administering their estates through Jewish intermediaries, who thus acquired extensive powers over the property and even the lives of the tenants. Churches, too, were occasionally leased to the Jews, a state of affairs which led to abuses and stimulated anti-Semitism. These conditions would seem designed to awaken the religious sentiment of the Orthodox population. Fuel was added to the religious controversy by the excessive zeal of the Jesuits, who, disturbed by the spread of Protestantism in eastern Europe, appeared in large numbers after 1570 in Lithuania and Poland. They soon concentrated their attack on Greek Orthodoxy and, taking advantage of the social and political ascendancy of Poland, converted to Catholicism a number of Russo-Lithuanian magnates and landowners. This often meant the forcible conversion to Catholicism of the Russian population living on the estates of nobles and the taking over of Church buildings and properties by the Catholics. The aggressive policies of the Roman Church were facilitated by the extraordinary decadence of the Orthodox hierarchy in the Ukraine. According to Kliuchevsky, the only social group in the Polish-Lithuanian state at the end of the sixteenth century that could compete with the Cossacks in absence of social and ethical standards and in moral "savagery" (*odichanie*) was the higher Orthodox clergy. To make things worse, a group of Russian ecclesiastical dignitaries in Lithuania, led by the bishops Terletski and Pociej, negotiated in 1595 the union between the Western-Russian Church and Rome. This move provoked strong opposition, and the meeting of the Church council, which assembled at Brest in

1596 resulted in a cleavage within the Western-Russian Church, the supporters and the opponents of the union mutually excommunicating one another. The Polish government and the Holy See, however, regarded the union as an accomplished fact and treated the recalcitrant followers of Orthodoxy as heretics and rebels. The supporters of the union, encouraged by the Catholics, displayed extreme intolerance. The non-Uniat Orthodox communities were deprived of their clergy and their churches, while the Uniat archbishop of Polotsk, Joasaphat Kuntsevich, went to such extremes as sanctioning the desecration of the graves of the non-Uniats, a shocking procedure made necessary, according to his apologists, by mysterious visions which demanded the "purification" of the ground surrounding the confiscated non-Uniat churches. Kuntsevich, murdered in 1623 during a popular uprising, was eventually canonized by the Church of Rome. These policies had their inevitable consequences: the dormant issue of Orthodoxy versus Catholicism became one of the burning problems of the day.

The Cossacks, however, had more immediate reasons for discontent with the Polish rule. The policy of the Polish government towards the Cossack army was contradictory and inconsistent. Poland, needing the services of the Cossacks, encouraged their military organization, but, unable to control it, often found itself in conflict with the knights of *Zaporozhie*. The raids against Turkey and the Crimean Tartars, which the Cossacks considered their legitimate occupation, led to protests accompanied by threats of reprisals from the sultan and the khan. In 1584 some thirty Cossacks were tortured to death at Lemberg in the presence of a Turkish emissary to appease the wrath of the Sublime Porte. In time of political stress the Polish government accepted the services of any Cossack, but often their wages were not paid, and when the emergency was over the government tried to reduce the strength of the "registered" Cossacks to the number prescribed, thus forcing the others under the yoke of serfdom. Various vexatious and largely unenforceable restrictions were devised from time to time by the Polish government in a futile attempt to break down the spirit of the *Zaporozhie* knights. The cumulative effect of these conditions, of which the rapid disappearance of the relative freedom once enjoyed by the frontiersmen was probably the most important, paved the way for the breach between Poland and Ukraine.

The inconsistencies of the Polish attitude towards the Cossacks had justification in the behavior of the Cossacks themselves. Allegiance to the Polish Crown meant little to them, they never hesitated to sell their services to the highest bidder, were equally eager to fight the Turks under the banners of the German emperor, or Moscow and the Crimean Tartars under those of Poland, or to join arms with Moscow or the Tartars against Poland. Numerous Cossack uprisings took place at the end of the sixteenth century and during the first half of the seventeenth. Originating in the confused social conditions prevailing in Ukraine, these revolts were generally free from any national or religious motives. As the persecution of the Orthodox Church increased, the Cossacks at times espoused the cause of Orthodoxy. In 1620, under the protection of the troops of Hetman Sahaidachny (Peter Konashevich), Theophan, patriarch of Constantinople, by consecrating in Kiev an Orthodox metropolitan and six bishops, reestablished the Orthodox hierarchy of western Russia, which had been inoperative since the union of 1595. Metropolitan Job Boretsky and his successor, Peter Mogila, founder of the Kievan Academy, which played so important a part in the intellectual life of Russia, assumed the leadership in the struggle against Catholicism, a struggle in which the Cossacks continued to display a sporadic interest. A series of new Cossack uprisings, which all ended in defeat, led in 1638 to the practical abolition of the autonomy of *Zaporozhie*. The elected hetman and other officers were replaced by Polish noblemen appointed by the Crown. The "registered" Cossacks, many of whom had acquired land, were deprived of their farms, while those not on the rolls had no choice left except rebellion or serfdom. A decree of Wladyslav IV, king of Poland, legalizing the Orthodox hierarchy established in 1620, did little to appease the resentment of the masses of the Cossacks. It required ten years, however, before the movement of revolt crystallized under the leadership of the Bogdan Khmelnitsky. In 1648 Ukraine arose against Poland, and the Cossacks of Khmelnitsky, supported by the peasantry and in alliance with the Crimean Tartars, inflicted a crashing defeat upon the army of the king. Jan Casimir, successor to Wladyslav IV, who had died in the meantime, concluded with Khmelnitsky the Peace of Zborov (1649), which restored Cossack self-government and increased the number of "registered" Cossacks to forty thousand, but did nothing to improve the position of the masses. Neither side was satisfied, and hostilities were resumed in 1650. Betrayed by their Tartar allies, Khmelnitsky, who had proclaimed himself hetman of *Zaporozhie,* was forced to accept the peace treaty of Belaia Tserkov, which reduced the number of "registered" Cossacks to twenty thousand. This was even less acceptable than the Zborov treaty. Realizing his inability to win alone a victory over Poland, Khmelnitsky appealed in 1651 to the Tsar Alexis, asking him to take Ukraine under his protection. Moscow, remembering its recent defeats at the hands of Poland, hesitated for three years. In the meantime war in the Ukraine continued, and the Cossacks met with severe reverses. The country, overrun by enemy troops, suffered terrible devastation. The government of the tsar still shrank from making a decision, not only because it feared war with Poland but also because it had little sympathy with the plans of Khmelnitsky, who dreamed of making Ukraine an autonomous duchy under the suzerainty of Moscow. Khmelnitsky had to repeat his offer, to threaten that he would make peace with Poland and turn against Muscovy or that he would accept the suzerainty of the sultan or the Crimean khan before the cautious politicians in the Russian capital made up their minds and, after obtaining the approval of a *zemskii sobor,* finally agreed to the incorporation of Ukraine in the Russian state. In January, 1654, the Cossacks took the oath of allegiance to the tsar. Under the terms of the agreement concluded between Khmelnitsky and Moscow, the number of "registered" Cossacks was increased to sixty thousand, the existing legal and social institutions—including serfdom—were retained, and the right of the Cossacks to self-government was solemnly confirmed. The hetman was given the power to carry on diplomatic relations, except with Poland and Turkey.

War with Poland was the immediate result of the incorporation of Ukraine in the Muscovite state. On this occasion the Russian troops, supported by the Cossacks, did uncommonly well. In 1654–1656 they not only took Smolensk but also occupied a large part of Lithuania, including the cities of Vilna, Kovno, and Grodno. Russian victories were facilitated by the invasion of Poland from the north by Charles X of Sweden, who captured Warsaw and Cracow and proclaimed himself king of Poland. The days of Jan Casimir's rule appeared to be numbered, but the independence of Poland was saved by the conflicting ambitions of her two enemies: Tsar Alexis coveted the Polish Crown, while King Charles wanted Lithuania, which was occupied by the Russian troops. Moscow, suspending hostilities against Poland, turned against Sweden in a futile attempt to establish itself on the shores of the Baltic Sea. An inconclusive Russo-Swedish war was brought to an end in December, 1658, by an armistice which led to the Peace of Cardis (1661), by which Russia abandoned the territories held by her armies. Poland profited by the much-needed breathing space to recover from the blows she had suffered.

Faithful to the Cossack tradition, Khmelnitsky paid no more attention to his new allegiance to Moscow than to his more ancient obligations towards Poland. At a time when his new suzerain, Tsar Alexis, was waging war against Sweden, the Cossack hetman carried on surreptitious negotiations with Charles X and Prince George Rakoczy of Transilvania, negotiations which aimed at the division of the Polish-Lithuanian state and the creation of an autonomous duchy of Ukraine under the suzerainty of the Swedish-Polish king. Khmelnitsky died in 1657, and it may be questioned whether he deserved the imposing equestrian statue erected to him in Kiev and the aura of national hero, defender of Orthodoxy, and empire builder that surrounds his name in the writings of patriotically-minded Russian historians. A true Cossack, he lived and died an adventurer and soldier of fortune, distinguishing himself from the other leaders of *Zaporozhie* chiefly by his vast ambition, tireless energy, and a certain quality of romantic imagination often stimulated by an excessive use of alcohol. In this respect, too, he was a true Cossack.

The death of Khmelnitsky was followed by a period of social unrest in Ukraine verging on civil war. There was a bitter antagonism of long standing between the "registered" Cossacks, who in the seventeenth century were largely landowners, and the masses of the Cossacks not on the rolls, destitute, and the easy prey of rapacious landlords. This group was known by the apt name of *golota*: "have nothing." There was no unity among the "registered" Cossacks themselves, and in spite of their theoretical equality there developed among them a local aristocracy, *starshina* (elders), whose members filled important offices and owned large estates and whose chief ambition was to be merged either with the Polish *szlachta* or with the Russian *dvoriane*. The burghers were concerned over the threat that the annexation to Moscow might present to the privileges they enjoyed under the Polish-Lithuanian rule. The clergy, too, feared the loss of its estates, while the religious issue was complicated by the conflict between Catholicism, Orthodoxy, and the Uniats. The instability of domestic conditions was reflected in sudden and frequent changes of Ukrainian foreign policy. The successor of Bogdan Khmelnitsky, Hetman Ivan Vygovsky, went over to Poland, and in 1659, with the assistance of the Crimean Tartars, inflicted a defeat on the Russian troops at Konotop. He was overthrown by the Cossacks, and the next hetman, Yuri Khmelnitsky, son of Bogdan, went over to the side of Moscow but almost immediately repudiated his allegiance when the tsar became involved in a new war with Poland. The unity of Ukraine was broken: the "Right Bank Ukraine," west of the Dnieper, under the leadership of Khmelnitsky remained faithful to Poland; the "Left Bank Ukraine," east of the Dnieper, elected Ivan Briukhovetsky to be its hetman and returned to the fold of Moscow. Briukhovetsky was rewarded with the title of boyar and, although of humble origin, married a Princess Dolgoruky. The *starshina* of the Left Bank Cossacks was elevated to the dignity of *dvorianstvo*, received estates from the Crown and, abandoning one of the Cossacks' cherished traditions, became an owner of serfs. The Russo-Polish war was terminated in 1667, with both countries exhausted by the protracted struggle which had been aggravated in Poland by a civil war. Under the terms of the armistice of Andrusovo, concluded for thirteen and a half years, Russia retained the provinces of Seversk and the Left Bank Ukraine, as well as the city of Kiev on the right bank, which, however, was to be evacuated by the Russians after two years, a provision that was never fulfilled. Other territories held by the Russian troops were returned to Poland.

The partition of Ukraine and the nature of the agreement entered into by Briukhovetsky and Moscow could not but add to the political confusion. This confusion was further increased by Moscow's policy of centralization and exactions and by the rivalry between Briukhovetsky and Peter Doroshenko, hetman of the Right Bank Cossacks since 1665. Briukhovetsky paid dearly for his boyar title and his betrayal of Cossack liberties. His hasty repudiation in January, 1668, of the pact with Moscow and his appeal for the protection of the sultan did not save him from the wrath of his countrymen. He was murdered while Ukraine was reunited under the leadership of Doroshenko, who attempted to cut the Gordian knot of political entanglements by breaking off with both Moscow and Poland and accepting the suzerainty of the Turkish sultan. The revival of the persecution of the Orthodox Church that followed the abdication of Jan Casimir and the election of Michael Wisniowiecki to the Polish throne made more palatable Doroshenko's new political orientation. The process of the inner disintegration of Ukraine, however, was too advanced to allow a lasting truce. In the spring of 1669 the Left Bank Cossacks, under the pressure of Moscow, elected their own hetman, Demian Mnogogreshny, who hastened to pledge allegiance to the tsar. In spite of this service he was soon suspected of high treason and in 1672 was exiled to Siberia. He was succeeded by Ivan Samoilovich. In the late summer of the same year the huge army of the Turkish sultan, Mohammed IV, invaded Ukraine. There followed a protracted war that involved Poland and eventually Russia. Poland suffered a defeat, and by the Peace of Zurawno (1676) ceded to Turkey a large portion of the Right Bank Ukraine. In 1676 Doroshenko submitted to Moscow and disappeared from the political stage. By the Russo-Turkish armistice of Bakhchisarai (1681) Russia retained the territory east of the Dnieper and the city of Kiev on the western bank of the river. Moscow, however, failed to obtain the control of *Zaporozhie* and had to resume the payment of an annual tribute to the Crimean khan, a vassal of the Sublime Porte. In the meantime Ukraine had become a shambles. This period of her history is known as "the ruin" (*ruina*).

The hold of Moscow over the Left Bank Ukraine and Kiev remained precarious as long as it was based on the armistice of Andrusovo and, in the case of Kiev, on its violation. The final annexation of these territories took place against the background of European *Grosse Politik*. King Jan Sobieski of Poland (1674–1696), who had long been urging a crusade against the Turks, concluded an alliance with Austria and in 1683 defeated the Turks near Vienna. The holy alliance against Islam was joined next year by Venice and had Pope Innocent XI for its patron. The participation of *Serenissimos Moschorum Czaros*, that is, Ivan and Peter, who after the death of Tsar Fedor jointly occupied the Russian throne under the regency of their sister Sophie, was considered by the allies essential for the success of the crusade. Protracted negotiations with the Moscow government followed. It was not until the spring of 1686 that Sobieski reluctantly agreed to the *conditio sine qua non* of Moscow's assistance. The signature of an "eternal peace" between Poland and Russia provided for the final cession of the territories Moscow held under the terms of the Andrusovo armistice, including the city of Kiev. Events proved that Sobieski had made a poor bargain. The campaign against the Crimean Tartars led in 1687 by Prince Vasili Golitsin, Sophie's principal adviser and lover, ended in a retreat of the Russian troops. Hetman Samoilovich, who had opposed war with Turkey and the Polish alliance, was held responsible for the disaster, deprived of his office, and exiled to Siberia. At the insistence of Golitsin, Ivan Mazepa, who later acquired so unhappy a notoriety, became Samoilovich's successor. Golitsin's second campaign against the Crimea in 1689 was no more successful than the first, a fact which could not be concealed by the efforts of Sophie to represent Russian defeats as victories and her lover as a hero. The net result of wars over the possession of Ukraine, conflicts that lasted with interruptions from 1654 to 1689, was the annexation by Russia of the Right Bank Ukraine and of the city of Kiev. The cost in human lives, suffering, and wealth was out of proportion to the results achieved, especially since the southern frontier remained at the mercy of the Crimean Tartars.

Russia's eastward expansion in Asia in the seventeenth century met with less resistance, although her path there, too, was by no means uniformly easy. Immense territories extending to the North Pacific and the Arctic Ocean gradually came under the control of the tsars, and in the middle of the century Russian detachments reached the Amur and the Chinese frontier. A Muscovite embassy visited Peking in 1565. Intermittent hostilities between the Russians and the Chinese led to the peace treaty of 1689, which excluded Russia from the Amur basin. In spite of this setback Moscow obtained a firm hold over the Siberian empire which still remains one of her great potential assets.

Of more immediate consequence than the acquisition of distant possessions which for centuries were to remain unexplored was the establishment of closer diplomatic relations between Moscow and the European countries. Muscovite ambassadors made their first and not always gracious bows at a number of European courts. England, France, Holland, Austria, Venice, Rome, and the Porte showed marked interest in the political and economic possibilities offered by the distant eastern state. The eagerness displayed not only by Sobieski, but also by the papacy, Vienna, and Venice in seeking Russia's cooperation in the anti-Turkish crusade was indicative of the changed attitude of Europe towards Moscow, even though the results of the venture were not encouraging. Kliuchevsky rightly observes that while the Muscovy of Michael and Alexis was weaker than that of Ivan IV and his son, it was far less lonely in Europe. Of still greater significance, perhaps, was the infiltration, on however modest a scale, of new ideas and of some knowledge of the world which resulted from the increased contact with foreigners both in Russia and abroad. There gradually came into existence in the Russian capital a small group of people who had become aware that the customary Muscovite way of living was not the only one, nor necessarily the best.

CENTRAL AND LOCAL GOVERNMENT

It took a long time before western ideas began to show their influence upon the structure of the Muscovite state. The revolutionary crisis Russia lived through at the turn of the seventeenth century, as I have already pointed out, was barren of constructive results. There was, however, one institution that came into prominence during the first four decades of the Romanov rule and which, had it been permitted to grow and develop, might have led the country along a different path from the one it was fated to follow. This institution was the *zemskii sobor*, or assembly of representatives of various social groups, an advisory body that made its appearance in the middle of the sixteenth century. It will be recalled that the *zemskii sobor* in the reign of Ivan the Dread consisted of government agents and was in no sense an elective or representative assembly. Its function was to carry out the decisions of the government rather than to tender advice. During the Time of Troubles, when the frequent changes of dynasties and the revolt of whole sections of the country against Moscow weakened the central authority, local communities and their self-governments were forced not only to assume control of local affairs but also to enter the field of national politics. The representatives of the cities and provinces were often in consultation during the troubled years; they combined their resources in organizing resistance to the Poles and the Cossacks, and Michael Romanov, as we know, ascended the throne on the invitation of a *zemskii sobor*, which was not only an elective but also, it is believed, a representative national assembly.

The new tsar was at first too helpless and too harassed by international complications and domestic difficulties to do without the body to whom he owed his position. The *zemskii sobor* of 1613 continued in session until 1615, when newly elected deputies were invited to assemble in the capital, but from 1613 to 1622 the *zemskii sobor* functioned as a permanent institution. Then came an interval of ten years during which no information is available regarding the *zemskii sobor*.

In 1632 it was once more convoked in connection with the impending war with Poland. The *zemskii sobor* is known to have assembled on two other occasions during the reign of Michael: in 1637–1638 and in 1642, when relations with Turkey became strained. In the reign of Alexis the *zemskii sobor* met four times: in 1645, to confirm the accession of the tsar; in 1648–1649, to discuss the new Code (*ulozhenie*); in 1650, to deal with the rebellion in Pskov; and in 1651–1653, to pass on the annexation of Ukraine. No *zemskii sobor* was summoned during the balance of Alexis's reign and in that of Fedor, although the government did confer on several occasions with representatives of selected groups immediately affected by the business in hand. The last two instances of the convocation of a *zemskii sobor* are alleged to have taken place in April and May, 1682, when Tsarevich Peter and then Tsarevich Ivan were elected to the throne.

This enumeration of the assemblies of the *zemskii sobor* is only approximate since there is no agreement among the authorities, even as to their exact number. The terms "the whole land," "the whole people," "the whole state," used somewhat euphemistically to describe the *zemskii sobor*, were avowedly abused, and one must be cautious not to interpret too literally such references in the sources. Even with this reservation, the above list gives a fair picture of the rise and fall of the institution of *zemskii sobor* and would seem to suggest that it was hardly more than an accident in the constitutional development of the country. It functioned regularly only during the first nine years of Michael's reign, when the authority of the Crown was notoriously weak, was later assembled in emergencies at long intervals, and finally slipped into oblivion. Although information on the organization and work of the *zemskii sobor* is incomplete, it is probably no exaggeration to say that it never was an institution in the accepted meaning of the term. We know of no definite rule concerning the composition of a *zemskii sobor* nor is it clear in what manner and by whom the delegates were elected. While it is believed that a *zemskii sobor* should consist of the higher clergy, the boyar duma, and the elected representatives of the *dvoriane* and of the merchants and tradesmen, in practice this requirement was not observed. Each *zemskii sobor* differed considerably in its composition from those that preceded and those that followed it. The *dvoriane* predominated in the assembly, and Moscow sent the largest delegation. There are known instances of deputies having been appointed by local gov-

ernors (*voevoda*) instead of being elected, although such procedure
was discouraged by the Moscow chanceries. On the other hand, the
government itself at times effectively prevented real representation
by denying the delegates the opportunity of getting together. For instance, in 1642 only five days elapsed between the order for the convocation of the assembly and the actual meeting of that body. The
peasantry, which constituted 90 or 95 per cent of the population,
was of course not represented except, it is believed, at the *zemskii
sobor* of 1613, the one elected under revolutionary conditions. The
zemskii sobor had no legislative power, and its decisions were not
binding unless they were sanctioned by the tsar.

Although the delegates to the *zemskii sobor* were to be chosen from
among the most deserving members of the respective groups, the general level of the assembly could not have been high. At the *zemskii
sobor* of 1648, which discussed the new Code, about half of the delegates are known to have been illiterate. The assembly, moreover, was
called together, with few exceptions, to meet pressing emergencies
which involved financial and other sacrifices. The delegates who had
failed to secure the benefits demanded by their constituencies and
brought home instead the unwelcome news of increased taxes occasionally insisted on special protection against the wrath of the
electors. Participation in the *zemskii sobor* thus became a burdensome
duty hardly of a nature to encourage the development of representative institutions. The *zemskii sobor*, needless to say, never attempted
to limit the powers of the Crown. Kliuchevsky has observed that the
tendering of advice when ordered to do so is not the exercise of a
political right, especially when the advice is usually followed by a
compulsory contribution to the state treasury. In spite of these limitations the *zemskii sobor* played a role in the political life of the country,
chiefly by voicing the general dissatisfaction with the conduct of
public affairs, exactions, and various abuses. Some of this criticism was
sharp enough, and it was probably responsible for abandonment of
the practice, however imperfect, of consulting elected delegates.

The government of Alexis, in spite of the many difficulties it had
to face, was much stronger than that of his predecessor. The tsar, high
government officials, and ecclesiastical dignitaries felt that they could
govern the country without the cumbersome machinery of an elective
body which sadly failed to appreciate the benefits of an absolutism it
never openly challenged. The bureaucracy that had firmly entrenched

itself in the strongholds of the Moscow chanceries had no use for an institution that questioned its wisdom. The *dvorianstvo*, which had become the leading class, was still too divided to make effective use of the elective assembly it dominated. It was to the Crown that the nobles looked for the extension of their privileges and especially for the consolidation of serfdom, which was their chief interest. The short-lived experiment in *zemskii sobor* came practically to an end in 1653. The idea, however, survived for a while but not among the ruling class. In 1662, for instance, when the government consulted the Moscow merchants in connection with the social unrest caused by debasement of the currency and the high cost of living, the Moscow burghers petitioned the tsar to call together the representatives of all social groups to discuss the emergency. The plea met with no response. Representative institutions were incompatible with the police state that was in the making, and the modest growths of democracy, which might have developed into something better in a different climate, died in their infancy on the parched Russian soil.

The whole trend of Russian life in the seventeenth century was in the direction of centralization and ever expanding government regimentation. There was no comprehensive program of reforms conceived in the light of a definite political philosophy: both reforms and philosophy were equally alien to the first Romanov and their advisers. Muscovite immemorial tradition was their inspiration and their guide. But they were confronted with pressing problems which they had to solve as well as they could. Of the momentous consequences of their activities, the tsars and their bureaucratic entourage (*diaki*) were blessedly unconscious.

The central administration was carried on through government departments inherited from the sixteenth century and known as *prikazy*. The number of the *prikazy* was large, something like fifty during the reign of Michael, and subject to frequent changes. Their jurisdiction was capricious and uncertain, they were established in a haphazard fashion, without any definite plan and often continued to function by the force of inertia, no one exactly knew why. The resulting machinery of the central government was cumbersome and unmanageable in the extreme. Under the pressure of necessity attempts were made in the course of the seventeenth century to bring some cohesion into the system of government which was characterized by centralization without coordination. Some of the *prikazy* were grouped together under the control of one official while others were merged in a single department. It would be easy to overrate the resulting improvement, especially since new *prikazy* continued to make their appearance. Nevertheless the changes introduced by Michael and Alexis facilitated the central administration reform undertaken by Peter I.

The tendency towards centralization was more apparent in provincial administration, where the provinces and cities were put under the rule of an appointed governor, *voevoda*, who was the chief representative of the Crown and for all practical purposes the master of the territory under his jurisdiction. His powers, which included the administration of justice in civil cases, were as broad as they were ill defined. In theory the *voevoda* differed from his predecessors, the holders of *kormlenie* in the fifteenth and sixteenth centuries, in not being authorized to exact tribute from the population he governed. Theory and practice, however, found themselves at variance. Opportunities for exactions and abuse of power were practically unlimited, and the temptation was too great to be resisted. Solovev has drawn a vivid picture of the frame of mind of a prospective *voevoda*, his family, and retinue. "The *dvorianin* is happy as he prepares to leave the city where he is to assume the duties of governor—the office is honorable and lucrative (*korm sytnyi*). His wife is happy—she, too, will get presents; happy are his children and nephews—the zemstvo elder after visiting on a holiday father and mother, uncle and aunt, will not fail to pay them his respects; the entire household is happy—housekeepers and servants—they anticipate abundant food; the little children jump up in the air—they will not be forgotten; the voevoda's fool (*iurodivyi*), in his elation, talks more nonsense than ever—he will pick up a few scraps. They all are getting ready to move, knowing that the prey will not escape them." The local people did not share this jubilant mood, although they obediently provided the governor and his kin with what they considered to be their legitimate due. In 1621 the government specifically enjoined the governors not to accept bribes and to refrain from other abuses. This well intentioned order, which was repeated in the latter part of the century, failed to eliminate a practice sanctioned by tradition and inherent in the nature of things. At the *zemskii sobor* of 1642 the representatives of the provinces made clear what they thought of their administrators when they sullenly declared that "Your Majesty's governors have reduced the people of all stations to beggary and have stripped them to the bone." The practice of summoning *zemskii sobor* was soon discontinued, but the *voevoda* remained. Towards the middle of the reign of Michael they were to be found everywhere in Russia except in the northern provinces, where local self-government was retained.

The zemstvo or institutions of local self-government established in the reign of Ivan the Dread, continued to function, but they assumed even more than before the character of government agencies and not that of representatives of local interests. The attitude of the local communities towards the *gubnoi starosta*, an elective police and judicial officer, is somewhat uncertain. Instances are on record of cities petitioning the government and actually obtaining the privilege of electing a *gubnoi starosta*, who performed the duties of a governor, only to revise their position within a few years and demand the substitution of a *voevoda* for the elected official. Men capable of performing administrative duties in the Russian cities of the seventeenth century were rare, and the joint responsibility of the community for the behavior of their elective officers made experimentation in self-government perilous. Its ultimate consequence might prove even more disastrous than the exactions of the governors one accepted as an inevitable evil. Usually the zemstvo institutions functioned side by side with the *voevoda* and under his close control and supervision. In the seventeenth century the sphere of their activities, never too comprehensive, was further restricted. In addition to such minor functions as the election of the local priest and parish officials, the zemstvo officers were left in charge of the distasteful and burdensome task of collecting taxes. The duties of local self-government were thus reduced to the obligation of providing the central authority with a body of officials for the collection of revenue, officers who received no remuneration from the treasury and whose good behavior was guaranteed not only by the threat of penalties but also by the joint responsibility of the communities who were ordered to elect them.

A further step towards administrative centralization was the consolidation of the districts (*uezd*) into larger administrative units (*razriad*), a move which had for its object the better organization of national defense. This administrative adjustment, inaugurated by Michael and continued by Alexis, laid the foundation for the administrative reforms of Peter I.

CHAPTER XI

SOCIAL, RELIGIOUS, AND CULTURAL DEVELOPMENTS IN THE SEVEN-TEENTH CENTURY

※

CHANGES IN THE SOCIAL STRUCTURE

It was the social structure of Muscovy that showed the full effect of the policy of centralization and restrictive control characteristic of the first Romanov. This policy was the product of the exigencies of the situation solved in the light of the Muscovite tradition. The election of Michael Romanov in 1613 removed the dynastic element but did nothing to remedy the deeper causes of the crisis. The Time of Troubles left the country prostrated and bleeding. The restless masses uprooted by the revolutionary storm had not yet settled down. The treasury was empty. The economic collapse was nearly complete. Villages and towns abandoned by their inhabitants became the rule. Fields were rapidly being converted into wooded wildernesses, and the once prosperous trading and industrial communities were shambles.

The new government had not only to repair the ravages of the past but also to provide for the imperative requirements of an uncertain present and a dark future. We have seen that both Michael and Alexis engaged in protracted wars that would have taxed the resources of a rich state, which Muscovy was not. Wars demand men and money. To raise funds and recruit troops in the Russia of the seventeenth century presented immense difficulties. The two problems, moreover, were closely interrelated.

The Muscovite armed force comprised two distinct elements: the *dvoriane* militia, which was called together only during military emergencies, and the standing army which originated in the middle of the fifteenth century. The earliest regiments of the standing army were the *streltsy* and the "registered" Cossacks. The deplorable showing made by the militia in the wars with Poland and Sweden demonstrated the inferiority of untrained Muscovite troops. This experience, coupled with the appearance in Russia at the beginning of the seventeenth century of large bodies of foreign mercenaries, led to the expansion of the standing army and the formation of regiments known by names borrowed from foreign languages—*draguny, reitary, soldaty.* The enlisted men, who were quartered in military agricultural settlements, like the *dvoriane,* received grants of land which, however, they farmed themselves, while the *pomestie* of the *dvoriane* were cultivated by the labor of the tenants and, later, of the serfs (Sergeevich). The regiments of the standing army, although composed, like the militia, of farmer soldiers who in time of peace engaged in agriculture, differed from the militia in the greater permanency of their organization. The professional soldiers had to undergo a regular training in the art of warfare. They were captained either by Russians who had mastered the rudiments of the military science or by foreigners—Germans, Swedes, Scotsmen, Poles, Lithuanians, even Greeks and Serbians. The God-fearing Moscow government, however, refrained from engaging the services of the French lest they contaminate the men under their command with the "heresy" of Roman Catholicism. The Russians somehow never learned to hate Protestantism quite so much as they did the Church of Rome. It will be recalled that the *dvoriane* in addition to the enjoyment of their *pomestie* were entitled to a monetary wage which was not, however, a regular source of revenue but was rather in the nature of a special grant to meet the cost of equipment and to defray expenditure during the time of actual service with the colors. The amount of the wage paid to the *dvoriane* was lacking in uniformity and depended on the state of the treasury and the pleasure of the tsar. Men serving in the standing army also received a wage which in certain cases, for instance, that of the *streltsy,* was a definite annual sum. It is, however, questionable whether all the regiments of the standing army were on a fixed wage basis (Sergeevich). In time of war both the militia and the standing army received monetary payments from the treasury. Although service in the standing army tended to become hereditary and passed from father to son, there was no hard and fast line between the *dvoriane* and the professional soldiers, and there are instances on record of the same men serving, at different times, with the militia and with the standing army (Sergeevich).

Military service, moreover, was compulsory for all social classes, from the *dvoriane* to the burghers and peasants. Slaves, too, were occasionally drafted for the military forces. The burden of the military service, however, was unequally distributed among the various social groups. In the case of the *dvoriane* it was a personal duty, justified by the fact that they derived their living from the *pomestie* granted to them by the state and cultivated by the servile population. The burghers and peasants who depended for their livelihood on their own labor were under no such personal obligation. They were merely required to provide a specified number of soldiers for each urban or village community. The actual burden of the military service for these groups thus depended on the ability of their respective communities to maintain their population at a certain level, that is, to check the tendency of their members to wander away. The seventeenth century saw a great expansion in the size of the armed force and an even greater increase in the expenditure for its maintenance.

The complex financial structure of the Muscovite state was characterized by a feature that played an important part in the social evolution of the country. A number of taxes were of the "apportioned" type, that is, a definite amount was apportioned by the central government among the administrative subdivisions. The determination of the amount (*oklad*) to be raised by each subdivision was computed according to the number of *sokha* it contained. *Sokha* was a territorial unit comprising either a specified area of farm land or a definite number of households. The size of the *sokha* varied greatly according to what was presumed to be the productivity of the land and the taxpaying capacity of the inhabitants. Cadastral surveys (*soshnoe pismo*) were made from time to time and served as the basis for the apportionment among the subdivisions; the quotas were then reassessed locally upon the taxpaying population. The communities were jointly responsible for the fulfillment of the quotas as well as for the efficiency and integrity of the tax officials they elected. In the seventeenth century the Moscow government was most of the time in desperate need of funds, and the tax burden was steadily and rapidly increased. In the search for greater revenue the fiscal system was subjected to important modifications. The household (*dvor*) was gradually substituted for the *sokha* as the basis of apportionment, and after the census of 1678–1679 became the usual fiscal unit. The practical consequence of the new method was that labor power rather than land and property was made the basis for the computation of the levies. The traditional method of assessing taxes, however, was preserved. The territorial subdivisions continued to receive from Moscow quotas which were then reapportioned among the taxpayers. A certain consolidation of the taxes and a unification of the fiscal administration took place, and this may be considered to have been an improvement. Other financial measures were less successful, for instance, the great increase introduced in 1646 and ignominiously abandoned two years later, in the rate of the salt tax, an increase that resulted in the decline of revenue and caused much popular unrest. An extravagant excise on tobacco proved just as disastrous and unworkable. Even less defensible was the ill advised experiment with the substitution of copper coins for silver embarked upon in 1656. This debasement of the currency, which brought about a sharp rise in the cost of living, much hardship for the masses, and large profits for unscrupulous speculators, led to a popular rebellion. In 1663 the government was forced to redeem in silver the copper coins at a mere fraction of their face value.

For the smooth working of the Muscovite military and financial machine there was needed a firmly settled population rooted in its villages and towns, dutifully cultivating the land of the *dvoriane*, providing recruits for the army, and above all paying taxes. These characteristics were exactly what the population of Muscovy lacked. The truly amazing flight of the masses that we noted at the beginning of the Time of Troubles was, if anything, intensified by the revolutionary upheaval, and continued unabated in the seventeenth century. This is not surprising, since the conditions that forced peasants and burghers to flee were all preserved under the rule of the first Romanov. From many points of view the situation, indeed, was probably worse than it had ever been before. The government was continuously calling new men to the colors, and the burden of taxation had reached a breaking point. The collection of tributes was accompanied by extreme brutality. Although the *zemskii sobor* of 1613 decreed the return to the Crown of large tracts of land presented to their followers by Russia's shadowy rulers during the Time of Troubles, the practice of such distributions was almost immediately resumed on a large scale by Tsar Michael. This meant heavier burdens and near serfdom for the peasants living on the former Crown land. The logical escape from an unbearable situation was to wander away from one's legal domicile and to try to start anew somewhere else, for as long as the fugitive was not caught in the net of the census officials at his new place of settlement he enjoyed freedom from both military service and taxation. Opportunities for such escape were not lacking in a country where labor was at a premium. Evasion of obligations towards the state was further facilitated by the remarkable development during the first half of the seventeenth century of the ancient institution of "voluntary" slavery, which could be either temporary (*zakladnichestvo*) or for the natural life of the person who entered the contract (*kabalnoe kholopstvo*). In either case the official consideration on which slavery was based was a loan, although it is believed that in many cases the loan was fictitious. There were certain technical differences between *zakladnichestvo* and *kabalnoe kholopstvo*, and some authorities maintain that the former was not really slavery. Nevertheless those who accepted this status shared with the slaves, it would seem in breach of the law, the by no means unimportant privilege of being exempted from taxation and from the performance of other state obligations. It was this consideration that induced an ever increasing number of people to trade their precarious personal freedom for the tangible benefit of tax exemption coupled with the protection of a powerful lord. The monasteries and ecclesiastical dignitaries, who were among the most privileged landlords, particularly benefited by the services of "voluntary" slaves. Among those who sought this drastic method of escape from their difficulties were people drawn from every stratum of society, especially the burghers and also the *dvoriane*.

The interplay of these complex cross-currents created a situation that threatened to become intolerable. The mass desertion of the taxpayers, on the one hand, undermined the resources of the treasury and dried up the reservoir of man power that fed the army; on the other, it greatly increased the burden of the remaining section of the population and encouraged evasion. The *dvoriane* whose estates had been abandoned by the tenants were no longer capable of performing their military obligations, the merchants and tradesmen were confronted with the competition of men who no longer paid taxes and, under the protection of their powerful lords, had invaded the field of commerce and industry. To make things even less palatable, the taxpayers who remained had to make good the deficiency of those who had left. *Dvoriane* and burghers clamored for relief. They demanded the protection of their interests against the deserters from their own ranks, against the Church and the powerful lords, and above all against the peasants. The government was only too eager to meet their wishes but, of course, not by attempting to remedy the conditions that had brought about so disastrous a state of affairs. Stricter police supervision and more rigid regimentation was the method that suggested itself to minds trained in the seclusion of the Muscovite chanceries. The police state that came into being, while containing important elements of novelty, was fundamentally in harmony with the tradition of absolutism, just as the conditions that had precipitated the crisis were the logical development of past history. The two social groups to which Michael and Alexis were still willing to listen—the *dvoriane* and the burghers—themselves helped to build the dungeon in which Russia was to linger for more than two hundred years, until its shattered remnants were swept away in the revolutionary storm of 1917.

The foundation for the future evolution of the Russian state was laid by the Code (*ulozhenie*) of 1649, which was prepared with the participation of a very informal *zemskii sobor* dominated by the *dvoriane*. The *zemskii sobor* met following a particularly violent popular uprising whose echoes had not yet completely died away. The Code of 1649 was an improvement on its two predecessors, the Codes of 1497 and 1550, which were hardly more than collections of rules of procedure (*sudebnik*). The new Code, the first Russian attempt at codification in the broad meaning of the term, was vastly inferior to the model it followed closely, the Lithuanian Statute (*Litovskii Statut*) of 1588. The fact that the Code of 1649 remained in operation until 1833 should not be interpreted as a proof of its merits but rather, as Kliuchevsky has suggested, as an indication that Russia could do without a decent collection of laws. The amazing volume of legislation issued in Moscow in the second half of the seventeenth century, legislation that in part superseded the Code, indicates that the Code failed to achieve its main objective. In spite of these shortcomings the influence of the Code was by no means negligible. Imbued with the spirit of rigid conservatism, the framers of the Code had embodied the idea of the complete subordination of the interests of the individual to those of the state. To assure the army its quota of recruits and the treasury an uninterrupted flow of revenue was the chief concern of the legislators. To attain this purpose the population of Russia was divided into hereditary classes or "estates" (*soslove*) whose members were firmly attached to their habitat and status and assigned definite duties.

The first attempt to restrict the freedom of movement of the burghers in order to check tax evasion goes back to the Code of 1550. Further measures for the repatriation of the fleeing townsmen were enacted in the second half of the sixteenth century but met with indifferent success. The *zemskii sobor* of 1619 took notice of the depopulation of the towns, called for a search for the runaway burghers, including those who had sold themselves into "voluntary" slavery, and ordered their repatriation. This distasteful operation was repeated in 1638. The Code of 1649 consolidated and generalized earlier legislation by providing that the burghers must continue to reside wherever they were living at the time the Code was issued. They were even forbidden to move from one town to another. No taxpayer thereafter was to be permitted to become a "voluntary" slave, and those who had already done so were to be forcibly returned to their former status and place of residence. The knout and Siberia were the penalty for disobeying the law. In spite of the severity of the punishment violations must have been frequent, since a decree of 1658 provided capital punishment for burghers who moved to another town and even for those who married outside their own town. This measure likewise failed to immobilize the townsmen, and a decree issued in 1682 permitted those of them who had illegally changed their place of residence to remain where they were but repeated the prohibition of further transfers of domicile under the threat of forcible repatriation.

The capacity of the burghers to pay taxes was impaired not only by the desertion of their fellow townsmen but also by competition on the part of a miscellaneous group of people, from the *dvoriane* to the slaves, who established themselves in settlements (*sloboda*) adjoining the towns and engaged in business under the protection of their powerful secular and ecclesiastical lords. The Code ordered the confiscation of all *sloboda* and prohibited the building of new ones, a decision which deprived the Church, especially the monasteries, of an important source of revenue. Peasants and others not paying the taxes assessed on the burghers were forbidden to own commercial and industrial enterprises. The townsmen thus acquired a monopoly in industrial and commercial pursuits. They also succeeded, after a number of futile attempts, in curbing the competition of foreigners. Taxes paid by the latter were raised and their privileges were curtailed. The

New Statute of Commerce (*Novotorgovyi Ustav*) of 1667 excluded foreign merchants from participation in retail trade, which was reserved exclusively for native burghers.

The *dvoriane*, like the burghers, emerged in the middle of the seventeenth century as a distinct social group, hedged off from the rest of the population and having definite rights and duties. A number of legislative enactments, beginning with the Code of 1550, tried unsuccessfully to enjoin the impoverished *dvoriane* and their kin from selling themselves into slavery. The prohibition was made definite and comprehensive by a law of 1642 which also ordered those who had become slaves to be restored to their former status. The Code of 1649 confirmed this rule. There was no longer any escape from the obligation of service in the army, which was the *dvoriane's* chief duty and which thus became hereditary. There also developed a tendency to impart to the *dvoriane* a caste character. In the sixteenth and early seventeenth centuries the *dvoriane* frequently petitioned the government not to add to their ranks through the enrollment of men drawn from the other classes. These requests were motivated by a realization of the inadequacy of the land reserve from which the *pomestie* of the *dvoriane* were carved, a shortage that was intensified by the influx of outsiders. The voice of the *dvoriane* was finally heard, and in the seventeenth century the government issued repeated orders that only sons or kin of the *dvoriane* should be admitted to their ranks. The law of 1642 and the Code of 1649 deprived all social groups other than the *dvoriane* of the right to own estates farmed by servile labor, thus conferring upon the future nobility a valuable privilege. The *dvoriane*, moreover, won an important victory over the Church. The Code of 1649 prohibited the further expansion of ecclesiastical estates, to which the *dvoriane* had long objected, although it did not sequester the estates already in the possession of the Church. The judicial privileges enjoyed by the Church were curtailed, and the clergy was made subject to the jurisdiction of a new lay department, *Monastyrskii prikaz*. A further step in the organization of Russia's new ruling class was made in 1682 when the archaic institution of *mestnichestvo*, that is, the complex system of rules which determined the relative position of each member of the official hierarchy according to precedent, was abolished. It was obviously out of place in a society dominated by new blood. With its disappearance the tsar was free in the appointment to high offices of men of his own choice, although

mestnichestvo had never succeeded in effectively limiting this prerogative of the Crown.

Strange as it may appear, the prohibition of selling oneself into
slavery or near slavery was resented in seventeenth century Muscovy.
When this provision of the Code of 1649 became known, the large
fraternity of "voluntary" slaves protested and denounced the tsar
and his legislation in no uncertain terms. Their attitude will appear
less puzzling if we remember that there was no room for personal freedom in our sense of the term in the vast empire over which the Kremlin
cast its dark and sinister shadow. When confronted with the choice
between the status of a freeman, with its inescapable and crushing
burdens, and dependence on a lord whose rule, which might or might
not be unbearable, could be terminated under certain conditions, the
second alternative was at least worth considering. The Moscow government was interested in the soldier and the taxpayer, and knew and
cared nothing about personal rights. Thus, as Kliuchevsky tersely put
it, did personal freedom become an obligation enforced by the knout.

The knout, that guardian of the personal freedom of the relatively
small group of *dvoriane* and burghers, was put to a very different use
when dealing with the peasantry who formed the vast majority of the
population. It was to the accompaniment of its monotonous and
unceasing whistling that the peasants were driven into a state of serfdom that differed but little from slavery. It will be recalled that the
process of enslavement, which was well advanced by the end of the
sixteenth century, grew out of the fiscal policy of the government and
the indebtedness of the peasant tenants to their landlords. The same
forces continued in operation during the reigns of Michael and Alexis.
The right of the tenants to relinquish their tenancy died away, as I
have said, without any legislative enactment, and there are no signs
of its existence after the Time of Troubles. Other factors contributed
to the growth of serfdom. It should be noted that many aspects of
this process are highly controversial and that there is no agreement
among the authorities. Nevertheless the general trend is reasonably
clear. Among the contributing factors was the drastic restriction on
the formerly permitted practice of entering the service of a lord (a
practice which must be distinguished from tenancy, since it did not
involve the use of land) without losing one's personal independence.
The first known restriction on this type of service was introduced in
1597. The Code of 1649 decreed that a freeman who served a lord

for merely three months must give his master a *kabala*, that is, renounce his status as a freeman. It also became customary in the second quarter of the seventeenth century for the tenants to give their landlord a written undertaking that they would continue to live on the allotments assigned to them until their death, an undertaking which amounted to the specific renunciation of their former right to relinquish their tenancy. The dependence of the tenants on their lord, based in the past on the fact of their indebtedness, thus received a contractual character. The resulting relationship was known as *krestianskaia krepost* from which serfdom—*krepostnoe pravo*—probably derived its name. These novel departures were the outcome of the government's determination to pin down the elusive taxpayer to a definite community where he could be reached. For the peasants, it will be remembered, were paying taxes, and continued to do so after they became serfs. The *zemskii sobor* of 1619 ordered a search for the runaway peasants and their forcible return to the communities they had deserted. The census of 1627–1628 was used as conclusive evidence of a peasant's legal residence, that is, he and his descendants were to stay where the census found them. In spite of all prohibitions, however, the flight of the peasants continued, and the landlords and the government redoubled their efforts to put an end to it. An important issue repeatedly raised by the *dvoriane* was the repeal of the time limit (*urochnyia leta*) beyond which legal action could not be taken for the return of the runaway peasants. The time limit, which was five years according to the decree of 1597, was increased to fifteen in 1607, reduced to five by a decree of Tsar Michael, and increased once more to ten in 1640–1641. The Code of 1649 abolished the time limit, making it possible for the landlords to recover their fugitive peasants whenever they succeeded in finding them. This decision forged a new and even stronger bond between peasant and landlord. The former contractual relation became a hereditary obligation sanctioned by the law. The Code also imposed severe penalties for harboring runaway peasants and devised elaborate rules, including registration with a special department, *Pomestnyi prikaz*, to prevent the practice. It nevertheless continued, as is made clear by innumerable complaints and frequent litigation and by the necessity in which the government found itself to repeat the interdict and to increase the severity of the punishments.

The Code of 1649 and other legislation failed to define clearly the relations between the lord and his servile population. The peasant was treated sometimes as a taxpayer, sometimes as a bondsman or a mere chattel at the mercy of the lord. The Code did not succeed in reconciling the conflicting interests of the state and those of the landlords, and the resulting legal situation was confused and contradictory. The landlords were prohibited from converting their peasants into slaves, for this would mean that the latter would be no longer taxable. The servile population could not be transferred from a *pomestie*, a Crown estate held by the *dvorianin* in service tenure, to a *votchina*, a privately owned estate, because such a transfer would diminish the value of state property. Other provisions, however, were interpreted as giving the landlord the right to exchange his peasants, to sell them without land, to mortgage them, to give them away. The Code provided that if a landlord or his kin or servant had murdered a peasant belonging to another landlord, "the best peasant" of the guilty party, together with the peasant's wife, children, and property, were to be given as compensation to the landlord who had suffered the loss. This provision, which was incorporated in the Code, was based on a decree issued in 1625. The servile population, therefore, was not merely attached to land, as it is sometimes held, but was actually turned over in bondage to the landlords. The question of the kind of services to which the lord was entitled was left entirely in the dark, nor was there any provision defining the property rights of the bondsmen. If such rights existed at all, it is difficult to see how they could have been enforced. For the judicial and police powers the landlords had accumulated in the course of earlier centuries were consolidated and extended. The *dvoriane* were the fiscal officers of the Crown responsible for the performance by the servile population living on their estates of its obligations towards the state. The Code contained some vague provisions designed to protect the person of the bondsmen from abuses on the part of their masters. In the general setup of Russian serfdom these provisions were, at best, benevolent platitudes and pious wishes. From the middle of the seventeenth century the once clear dividing line between the former peasant tenants, now bondsmen or serfs, and the slaves tended to disappear, although certain technical differences survived until the decree of January 19, 1723, which finally wiped out the distinctions by making the entire servile population subject to the poll tax.

POPULAR UNREST

The totalitarian state which the bureaucratic entourage of Michael and Alexis built up had an influence upon the destinies of Russia it would be difficult to overrate, even though the effects were different from those intended. The crude and naive scheme of pinning down human beings to their estates, workshops, and peasant cottages, as children arrange dried butterflies in glass-topped cases, could not and did not work. The picture of economic decay and profound uneasiness was eloquently revealed in the sullen statements aired by the representatives of the *dvoriane* and of the burghers at the *zemskii sobor* and on every other occasion when their advice was sought in an emergency. And they spoke for the relatively privileged groups who, nevertheless, revolted when they lost the "right" to exchange "freedom" for slavery. The largely futile wars waged by Alexis were a further drain on the resources of the nation and contributed to the spread of discontent. Police measures alone and the copious use of the knout were not sufficient to bring about that perfect regimentation the Moscow chanceries were striving to achieve. The uninterrupted stream of government decrees both repetitious and contradictory could not and did not check the appalling state of turmoil which prevailed in the land. The *dvoriane* hid themselves by the thousand to escape service with the colors, the burghers and the serfs persisted in their disorderly and largely aimless peregrinations, and the southern steppes, that haven of the disaffected elements, continued to receive a seemingly endless flow of destitute and desperate humanity.

If the police state failed to achieve its immediate objectives, it introduced into Russian life an element that poisoned it for centuries. Serfdom, like a cancer, undermined the forces of the nation, crippled its growth, hindered its economic and social development. For generations the energies of the *dvoriane* were centered on mutual recriminations and sordid squabbles over fugitive serfs, preventing the new ruling class still in the process of formation from reaching inner cohesion and from developing an *esprit de corps* that might have been a check on autocracy. Deriving their privileges exclusively from the pleasure of the sovereign, the *dvoriane* were the last to aspire to any limitation on the powers of the Crown. The Church, disturbed by the restrictions imposed upon it by the Code of 1649, was more than ever subservient to the wishes of the Kremlin. It was living, moreover, through a severe inner crisis. In the man hunt for fugitive serfs, which was one of the distressing characteristics of this period, ecclesiastical dignitaries and the monasteries vied with the lay landlords both in savagery and in resourcefulness. The peasants, of course, paid the oppressors in kind. They not only fled but also seldom missed an opportunity to square accounts with their masters. Landlords were murdered, manor houses were set afire, and the fugitives displayed particular cunning in destroying the documentary evidence on which rested the hated yoke of serfdom. The deeply rooted and widespread discontent was bound to express itself in mass action. The reign of Michael, and especially that of Alexis, when serfdom was finally enshrined, was a period of recurring popular uprisings.

The first years of Michael's rule were from many points of view a continuation of the Time of Troubles. The defeat of the Cossack movement led by Zarutsky and the execution of the leader in 1614, events which I have already related, did not put an end to the activities of the Cossack bands. They still roved about the country and gave no little trouble to the Moscow government, which tried by a combination of persuasion, bribery, and ruthless suppression to put an end to the rule of terror. The Cossacks, who were not the organized Cossack army but a cross section of the disaffected elements, were supported by the half-conquered tribes from the fringe of the Muscovite state, such as the Tartars and the Cheremissy, and they made many recruits among the local people. A clear sign of the general unsettled conditions was the reappearance of pretenders claiming descent from Vasili Shuisky or the Pseudo-Dimitry. Such were Ivan Luba, Alexander Nashchokin, Ivashka Vergunenok, Timoshka Akundinov, crude impostors who sought the protection of Poland, of the Crimean khan, of Turkey. The still tottering Moscow autocracy, always on the alert for fresh revolutionary outbursts, negotiated with the governments involved, demanded and succeeded in obtaining the suppression of these impostors. Insignificant in themselves, these pretenders kept alive the tradition of the Time of Troubles.

The social character of the uprisings became clear during the reign of Alexis. A revolt broke out in Moscow in the summer of 1648. Ostensibly directed against Boris Morozov, who was married to a sister of Alexis's first wife (Maria Miloslavsky), and two outstanding personalities of the bureaucratic Olympus, Leonid Pleshcheev and Peter Trakhaniotov, both of them kin of the tsarina, the movement had deeper roots. The salt tax and the inequities of the favorites' rule were among the grievances of the populace, which besieged the tsar in the Kremlin. Alexis's tearful personal appeal to the rebellious mob proved of no avail, and he was forced to surrender Pleshcheev and Trakhaniotov, who were put to death. Morozov's life was saved, but he was exiled to a remote monastery. The revolt of 1648 had wide reverberations throughout the country, even in distant Siberia. Next year came the near rebellion of the disgruntled "voluntary" slaves who were forcibly restored by the Code of 1649 to the former legal status, a movement that was suppressed in its initial stage. In 1650 Pskov and then Novgorod, exasperated by exactions, arose against Moscow and also against their own boyars. The government in its dismay summoned a *zemskii sobor* which persuaded Pskov to lay down arms, an act of submission that did not save the once "free city" from the customary punitive expedition. The economic crisis precipitated by the substitution of copper coins for silver in 1656 opened a new era of nation-wide unrest and led to a severe outburst in Moscow in 1662. Thousands of people were tortured, executed, or deported to Siberia.

In the sixties the revolutionary elements which played so important a part in the history of Ukraine found their leader in the person of Stenka Razin, who gained wide popularity by daring exploits along the shores of the Caspian Sea. In 1669 he returned to the Don covered with glory and carrying large booty. In the summer of 1670 Razin started against Moscow a campaign which, however, was directed, not against the tsar, but against the boyars and the landlords. The movement at the beginning met with extraordinary success. The peasants hastened to murder their masters and went over en masse to the side of the Cossack leader. He was soon in control of the Volga from the mouth of the river to Simbirsk. The native tribes received him as their liberator, for Razin's triumphant progress was accompanied by an extermination of the landlords. His good fortune did not last long, however. He suffered a defeat near Simbirsk at the hands of Prince Bariatinsky, who was in command of some of the modernized regiments of the Muscovite army. Razin fled south and attempted to raise the Don Cossacks, but was arrested by the more conservative Cossack elements, was surrendered to the Moscow government, and executed in 1671. His venture was typical of the Russian revolutionary movement in the seventeenth century. Spontaneous, violent, anarchistic and savage, it never succeeded in exploiting its initial success, and in spite of the support of the masses invariably collapsed when confronted with organized resistance. Brief as was the career of Stenka Razin, he became the central figure of a popular epic, and his exploits, largely imaginary, are celebrated in songs still heard in Russia. His memory is kept alive by many landmarks named after him along the Volga. This persistence of popular tradition is an indication that the bloody and futile adventure of an obscure, illiterate, and drunken Cossack was representative of a lasting mood of the Russian people. According to the legend Razin miraculously escaped death and a hundred years later reappeared on the Volga, the scene of his many exploits, under the name of Emilian Pugachev. This naive popular fancy, as Walizsewski has observed, contains an element of inner truth. The struggle for the overthrow of serfdom associated with the name of Razin has been in the background of Russia's history ever since.

The Moscow autocrats were not unaware of the state of the public mind. The experiences of Alexis with the Moscow populace in 1648 were as revealing as they were unpleasant, and damaging to the authority of the Crown. Beneath the Pharisaic pretense of quasi-paternal rule, and behind the pomp and circumstance of the Muscovite court, it was not difficult to discern the dread and suspicion of the masses. When the news of the defeat of the Russian troops by a combined force of Poles, Tartars, and Cossacks at Chudnov (1660) reached Moscow, the tsar made hasty preparations to abandon the capital because he suspected and feared the probable reaction of his "faithful" subjects. It was a paradoxical situation: while even the most revolutionary elements, such as the Razin bands, proclaimed their fealty to the Crown, the occupant of the throne lived in perpetual dread of the people he ruled. These fears were not without justification. For if the populace of Moscow manifested no intention of overthrowing the tsar, it was in the habit of treating his august person with a complete lack of respect.

PATRIARCH NIKON AND THE CLEAVAGE IN THE CHURCH

The state of fermentation prevailing in seventeenth century Russia was aggravated during the reign of Alexis by a movement of dissenters which led to a cleavage in the Church. The immediate causes of the breach were so trivial that it is difficult to comprehend how they could

have created so much bitterness and could have provoked an estrangement which has lasted to this day. No question of dogma was involved
in the dispute which centered on changes in the phrasing of certain
religious texts retranslated from the Greek, the spelling of the name
of Jesus, and minor points of ritual, such as the use of three instead
of two fingers in making the sign of the cross, the repetition of the
exclamation *alliluia* thrice instead of twice during Church services,
or the direction to be followed by religious processions: according to
the movement of the sun or against it. To explain why disagreement
about matters so petty and non-essential has grown into a major
cleavage, it must be remembered that attachment to external observances has always been an outstanding characteristic of Russian
Christianity. Religious practices were reduced to the superstitious
repetition of traditional formulas whose magic power was believed to
be the greater the less one understood what they meant. The departure
from custom in such matters appeared to many Russians as heresy and
blasphemy. There were other reasons why the opposition to the reforms embarked upon by Nikon and Alexis was stiffened. Having
borrowed Christianity from Byzantium, Moscow had long bowed to
the authority of the Greek Church in questions of faith. This confidence was shaken when at the Ferrara-Florence Council the Greek
Church accepted union with Rome, which Moscow so self-righteously
hated. It will be recalled that the *de facto* independence of the Russian
Church from Constantinople, which followed the Ferrara-Florence
Council, received its legal recognition with the creation of the Russian patriarchate and that this was accompanied by the official acceptance of the doctrine of "Moscow—the Third Rome," which proclaimed that the Russian Church was the only repository of true
Christianity. Although the Byzantine Church had repudiated the
Ferrara-Florence union, its unhappy status under the Turkish rule was
interpreted as an indication of divine wrath, nor was it deemed likely
that the Greek hierarchy could have maintained the purity of the
ancient faith under conditions so adverse. The Moscow government
had itself fostered an attitude of contemptuous superiority towards
the former Greek teachers of the Russian Church. The very low educational and intellectual level of the Russian clergy, moreover, made
them suspicious of any innovation, and they looked askance at the
invasion of the sacred field of religious practices by men of learning,
especially when they were tinged with Latinism. The fact that the

reforms undertaken by Nikon were based on the superior authority of the Greek Church and that they were carried into practice with the assistance of theologians who were conversant with western science and who even—*horribile dictu*—knew Latin was bound greatly to strengthen the opposition that they would have encountered under even the most favorable conditions.

The distressing state of affairs prevailing in the Russian Church in the middle of the sixteenth century and so eloquently described in the decisions of the *Stoglav* council of 1551 was in no way improved in the course of the next hundred years. The standards of the clergy continued to remain almost unbelievably low. There developed among other practices that of cutting down the rather unbearable length of Church services by having different parts of the service recited and sung simultaneously, with the distressing effect one may well imagine. The Greek hierarchs who visited Russia repeatedly drew the attention of the leaders of the Russian Church to the regrettable departures from Byzantine customs, criticisms which failed to produce immediate result since the Orthodoxy of the Greeks themselves was under suspicion. Sporadic attempts to correct the Russian religious texts begun in the first half of the sixteenth century, when the learned Greek Maxim paid dearly for his zeal, were continued in the seventeenth, but since they were usually entrusted to men who did not know the Greek language they merely led to a multiplication of errors. An important factor paving the way for the reforms of Nikon was the establishment in Kiev during the second quarter of the seventeenth century by the Kievan metropolitan Peter Mogila of a theological academy which was modeled on the Jesuit colleges. Here Orthodox clerics were taught Greek and Latin. Some of the former pupils of this academy found employment at the printing office in Moscow where religious books were published. By comparing the Russian texts with the Greek originals, they discovered a number of grievous errors. The idea began to gain ground within a restricted circle that the Russian texts were not necessarily infallible and that perhaps not all the Greek texts were untrustworthy. In 1649 Tsar Alexis invited to Moscow two of the luminaries of the Kievan school, Arseny Satanovsky and Epiphany Slavenitsky, who later took a leading part in the correction of the religious texts. Fedor Rtishchev, an intimate of the tsar who held a high office at the Kremlin, extended his powerful protection to the representatives of Kievan learning.

There also came to the fore a small but influential group of church-men who shared the prevailing suspicion of the Greeks and the disciples of the Kievan Academy but who were nevertheless anxious to reform the Russian Church services, to make them more accessible to the masses by removing their excessive and boring formalism. In this atti-tude one may detect a kinship with the ideas of the Reformation. Headed by Stephen Vonifatev, confessor of the tsar, the group in-cluded among others a popular preacher, Ivan Neronov, the priest Avvakum, future leader of the dissenters, and Nikon, who was soon to be elevated to the patriarchate.

Nikon, born of a peasant family, received no formal education but somehow learned to read and write. Endowed with considerable elo-quence, indefatigable energy, and seemingly insatiable ambition, Nikon took the monastic vows at an early age since the frock was an essential requirement for elevation to the higher ecclesiastical offices. On one of his visits to Moscow, Nikon was presented to Tsar Alexis, who was always accessible to the servants of the Church, even to those of hum-ble standing. The pious and impressionable Alexis immediately fell under the spell of Nikon's forceful and dominating personality and developed for him an affectionate admiration which made him for a time a tool in the hands of his new spiritual adviser. The opportune death of Patriarch Joseph, whom, it was rumored, Alexis planned to remove, cleared for Nikon the path to the highest office in the Rus-sian Church. In 1652 a Church council, obedient as usual to the will of the tsar, elected Nikon to the patriarchal see. Following tradi-tion, the latter at first refused and made himself besought. The tsar, prostrating himself on the floor of the Uspensky Cathedral, implored the patriarch-elect to yield to the supplications of the crowds, which dutifully imitated the example of the monarch. Nikon demanded complete obedience and full power to reestablish order in the Church. Both were gladly promised to him.

Breaking definitely with his former nationalistically-minded friends, Nikon proclaimed his determination to restore harmony between the Russian and the Greek Churches by eliminating the irregular prac-tices which the former had erroneously adopted. There is no reason to doubt the sincerity of Nikon's desire to free the Church from its state of disorder and decadence. His ambition, however, went further. He was convinced of the supremacy of the ecclesiastical power over the secular, and he resented the limitations imposed by the Code of

1649 on the traditional privileges of the Church in matters of jurisdiction and landownership. Although his signature was appended to
the Code of 1649, Nikon denounced it as an "accursed book, the
devil's law." He was determined, and succeeded for a time, in restoring the theocratic diarchy which had existed in the days of Patriarch
Filaret. Like Filaret, Nikon assumed the title of "Majesty" (velikii
gosudar), surrounded himself with regal pomp, and his name invariably appeared next to that of the tsar in official documents. A shrewd
and scheming politician, the new patriarch was aware that his plans
had but the slightest foundation in the Russian tradition. Byzantine
theory, which emphasized the supremacy of the Church over the
state, furnished him with a useful potential weapon, if the former respect for Byzantium could be restored. These considerations were
not entirely overlooked in Nikon's conversion to Hellenism. Appearing
later before his judges, Nikon went so far as to declare, in referring
to the secular power of the Roman see, that the pope should be
honored for the good he had done, a statement that must have sounded
like the worst heresy to the devout Russians.

Basing his position on the charter of 1593 establishing the Russian
patriarchate, a document that made it a duty of the Moscow patriarch
to exterminate all innovations as endangering the unity of the eastern
Church, and also on the denunciation of many Russian religious
practices by several Greek hierarchs who visited Moscow in 1651 and
1652, Nikon with characteristic ruthlessness initiated his policy of
unification. The provocative and brutal character of his methods invited opposition, which was not slow in manifesting itself. On his own
authority, and without the sanction of a Church council, Nikon in
1653 ordered the number of genuflections (zemnoi poklon) performed
during the reading of a certain prayer reduced from the customary
twelve to four and prescribed the use of three instead of two fingers
in making the sign of the cross. He then launched a crusade against
icons that departed from the Byzantine pattern and showed Italian
influence. Houses were searched for the offending images and they
were publicly destroyed, sometimes by the patriarch himself. The
conservative and traditionally-minded clerics and laymen were horrified, and some of them protested. They were summarily chastised and
exiled to remote parts of the country. In 1654 began the correction of
religious books which was carried on by the learned Kievan monks
and Greek clerics. Some five hundred Greek texts were brought to

Moscow, a miscellaneous collection which comprised the works of Homer, Sophocles, Demosthenes, and only about seven manuscripts dealing with the questions of Church ritual. The revised Manual of Church Services (*Sluzhebnik*) issued in 1655 was based on a Greek volume published in Venice in 1602. The slim basis of this reform was known in Moscow and added to the apprehensions of the conservative element, whose fears were not allayed by the fact that the correction of the books was ordered by a Church council and the first revised volume approved by another Church council in which Greek and Serbian hierarchs took part. Other Church councils followed, discarding one after another the probably irregular although innocuous customary practices of the Russian Church. A rapidly increasing number of churchmen who refused to accept the changes paid dearly for their attachment to the old ritual. Avvakum was exiled to Siberia. Neronov and his friends were anathematized. Yet no general measures were taken against the recalcitrant adherents of the condemned practices. The Tsarina Maria was known to be among the objectors, as were her relatives Theodocia Morozov and Princess Eudoxie Urussov. The government and the patriarch himself displayed puzzling inconsistencies in their attitude towards the dissenters. While some of the dissenters were severely dealt with, the prohibited practices were tolerated even in Moscow and in the palace of the tsar.

In 1658 came a breach between Alexis and Nikon. The overbearing manner and impetuous disposition of the patriarch had created for him innumerable enemies at the court, among the aristocracy, in the Church, and in the country at large. In spite of his zeal in promoting Church reforms, he did nothing to improve the position of the clergy, and treated his subordinates with the utmost lack of consideration. Alexis, who was reaching maturity, became tired of Nikon's tutelage and resented his despotic interference in the affairs of state while excluding the tsar from participation in those of the Church. The immediate cause of the estrangement was as trivial as all the separate incidents of this bizarre and dramatic story. Nikon, incensed by an alleged offense against one of the members of his retinue at a court reception, left the capital for the Voskresensky Monastery and announced that he was no longer to be considered the Moscow patriarch. He presumably expected that he would be urged to return. The theocratic diarchy so dear to his heart had, however, no root in the Russian tradition, and the tsar's affection for him, which was the sole foundation of his power, was gone. Nikon was not asked to return, and there followed a long period of uncertainty as to the actual position of the head of the Church. Alexis, undecided and torn by conflicting emotions, appealed to the Russian and Greek clergy to bring some order to a situation which was further complicated by Nikon's reversal of his position and his declaration that he was still the Russian patriarch even if he declined to be patriarch "in Moscow." The conflict lasted for eight years, during which Nikon made several dramatic but futile appearances in the capital, still hoping to recover his former influence over the tsar. Finally a Church council to try Nikon was summoned in 1666 and was attended by the patriarchs of Alexandria and Antioch, who also represented the absent heads of the church of Jerusalem and that of Constantinople. The tsar himself acted as the prosecutor, displaying an amazing lack of self-control and dignity, while Nikon, who knew that he was doomed, was arrogant, composed, and vindictive. The council deprived him not only of the patriarchal see but also of the rank of bishop, and ordered his incarceration in the remote Therapontov Monastery. He accepted the verdict with defiance and bade farewell to the Greek Church, whose cause he had championed, by describing the Greek patriarchs as "vagabonds" in quest of alms. The impoverished titular heads of eastern Christendom were far too dependent on Moscow's bounty to recall the proud Byzantine tradition of the primacy of the ecclesiastical power over the secular. They obligingly, if somewhat ambiguously, announced the doctrine that it was the duty of the Russian patriarch to "obey the tsar in all political questions." The majority of the council endorsed this view, and to those Russian clerics who opposed it (curiously, they were among those who had fought against Nikon) were meted out appropriate Church punishments. The Russian Church was rewarded for its devotion to the principles of autocracy by the restoration of its jurisdiction in civil and in some criminal cases. The *Monastirskii prikaz*, which since 1649 had tried the clerics in civil cases, was abolished in 1677.

While the controversy over Nikon dragged on, the correction of books continued and the resistance to the reform became stronger and spread to the most distant parts of the realm. The government itself showed signs of hesitation and uncertainty, an attitude that could not but encourage the dissenters. A purely Russian Church council was assembled in the spring of 1666 and was asked to determine whether the Greek patriarchs were truly Orthodox, whether the Greek books were to be trusted, and whether the decision of the council of 1654 which ordered the correction of the Russian texts was valid. The answers to all the questions were in the affirmative. Then came the council with the participation of the Greek hierarchs, an assembly that met in the autumn of 1666 and extended its work into 1667. While, as we have seen, it condemned Nikon, it upheld his work. The council also anathematized all those who refused to accept the revised ritual and use the corrected books. What was essentially a disagreement about trivialities became a schism, the *raskol*. The dissenters (*raskolniki*), who usually call themselves old-believers (*starovery*) or old-ritualists (*straoobriadtsy*), were expelled from the Church as heretics. Intolerance and refusal to make the slightest concession were equally characteristic of each side and pushed both the Church and the dissenters to the worst excesses. With the anathema of 1667 the conflict between the official Church and its opponents entered upon an acute stage.

The government proceeded to exterminate "heresy" by the same methods by which Christianity had been introduced to Russia, that is, by fire and sword. There is nothing like persecution to incite religious fanaticism. The brisk reversal of the attitude of the official Church towards its historical tradition and its somewhat unexpected discovery of the infallibility of the Greeks was a severe blow to the nationalistically-minded Russian theologians. The formalism of Muscovite piety saw in the changes in ritual and in religious texts the abandonment of Christianity itself. Propaganda against the reform fell on fertile soil. The masses of the peasantry, the burghers, and not a few of the *dvoriane* felt that the state was about to deprive them of their last treasured possession, the hope of eternal salvation. The Solovestsky Monastery on the White Sea refused to accept the corrected books, and after the excommunication, ordered by the council of 1667, revolted. There followed a siege by the government troops which did not succeed until 1676 in breaking the resistance. Ardent defenders of the old faith appeared in large numbers and were eagerly listened to. The most famous among them was the priest (*protopop*) Avvakum, whose fanatical zeal brought on him untold sufferings and won him the crown of martyrdom: he was burnt at the stake in 1681 by order of the young Tsar Fedor. Avvakum and his disciples saw in the reform of Nikon nothing short of the advent of the antichrist. This belief was strengthened by the expectation of the end of the world, which was to come in 1666 or 1669, and when the dreaded event failed to materialize new computations indicated that 1698 was to be the fateful date. There was some confusion as to who was the antichrist. Although Nikon fitted well in the part, he was soon eliminated. The tsars Alexis, Fedor, and Peter succeeded him in the imagination of the old-believers as the embodiment of evil. As long as the end was approaching and inevitable, the important thing was not to be contaminated by the heresy into which the official Church and the state standing behind it had fallen. The census and, later, the poll tax were particularly feared as the seal of the Apocalyptical Beast. To escape the abomination no sacrifice was too great. In the northern and eastern provinces, where many of the old-believers had taken refuge, there developed an epidemic of mass suicide by burning. Between 1672 and 1691, when the movement subsided, thirty-seven human holocausts are known to have taken place. The total number of victims is estimated at over twenty thousand. The violence of the resistance of the old-believers increased with the zeal of the persecutors. Mass suicide by fire reached its highest point in the regency of Sophie, who decreed in 1684 that unrepentant old-believers should be burned at the stake. Religious fanaticism was stimulated not only by exalted prophets but also by a plethora of morbid adventurers who exploited mass psychosis for petty personal gains. With the termination of the regency of Sophie and the closure of the most violent period of persecution, the practice of mass suicide died away.

The movement of dissenters, however, remained. Its stronghold was in the inaccessible wooded wilderness of the north and the northeast, and it spread to Siberia, and along the Volga to the regions of the Don and the Dnieper, where it found many adherents among the Cossacks. Among the unruly elements of Ukraine the religious controversy received a social and revolutionary tinge. The schism was equally harmful to the state and to the Church. It provided a banner and a point of reliance for many of those who could not become reconciled to the existing conditions. It deprived the Church of some of its most devout members and, since those who remained within the fold of official Orthodoxy did so not because they approved of the reforms of Nikon but rather because they were indifferent to questions of faith and dreaded persecution, the Church found itself even more than before dependent on the state, on the police, and on the army.

The unfortunately conceived and ruthlessly executed reforms of Alexis and Nikon greatly accelerated that process of the subjugation of the Church to the state which culminated in the reforms of Peter I. The policies of the government towards the dissenters changed more than once in the course of the next two and a half centuries, but the existence of schisms remained an element of weakness which worked to the detriment of both the state and the Church.

WESTERN INFLUENCES

It has been rightly observed by Kostomarov and later by Miliukov that in spite of its reactionary character, its fanaticism, the crudeness of many of its doctrines, and the often revolting practices of some of its sects, the movement of the old-believers was a healthy indication that the masses were awakening from their "secular religious indifference." It was the first time that the Russian peasants and burghers had been carried away by a religious emotion colored by an element of social protest, an emotion for which they were willing to fight and to die. This startling development, which was a shock to the Muscovite bureaucracy, was typical of the deep inner crisis through which the country was living. Both the government and the masses sought nothing but the preservation of the past. Yet new forces and new ideas were irresistibly breaking through the seemingly immutable barriers and were preparing the way for the different if not necessarily better Russia of the eighteenth century.

In spite of its conservatism the government of the first Romanov found itself compelled to turn to western Europe for the solution of its urgent problems. It has already been noted that the poor showing of the Muscovite militia necessitated the employment of large bodies of foreign troops and, later, the reorganization of the Russian army according to western standards and the enrollment of a considerable number of foreign soldiers of fortune within its ranks. The modernization of the army created a demand for new weapons, rifles, artillery, munitions. Purchases abroad being both costly and unsatisfactory, the government took the initial timid steps towards the development of Russia's natural resources by importing foreign engineers and by granting concessions to foreign capitalists. In 1632 the Dutch merchant Andrew Vinius established the Tula armament works which were later taken over by the government. Other concessions were granted to foreigners in various parts of the country where deposits of iron ore were discovered. Glass and potash works were also established, and the government imported a large number of skilled craftsmen—weavers, watchmakers, masons, smelters, ironmasters, painters. Even doctors and astrologers were not overlooked, strange as this may appear in a country that looked askance at western science. It was the duty of foreign craftsmen to train the Russians in their respective trades. From the middle of the seventeenth century Moscow toyed with the idea of building a Russian merchant fleet, leasing ports on the Baltic since the attempts to obtain them by force of arms had proved a failure. The first vessel of the Russian mercantile marine was built by the Dutch and was launched on the Caspian Sea in 1669. A year later it was burned by Stenka Razin.

The practical results of these uncoordinated and sporadic efforts were modest. Yet they brought the Russians into a closer contact with Europe than they had ever experienced before. A special suburb where the foreigners resided had existed in Moscow from the days of Ivan the Dread. It was known as the "German Settlement" (*Nemetskaia Sloboda*), since to the Russian masses all foreigners were Germans. The settlement was abolished during the Time of Troubles, but the large influx of foreigners in the following years led to friction between them and the natives, and in 1652 the scattered foreign population of the capital was confined within a new German Settlement. The fear of contamination by foreign ways and "heresies," never absent from the mind of Tsar Alexis and his government, inspired this attempted segregation. The foreigners had their churches and a school and built up a small European community in the heart of medieval Muscovy. Their ways of living had a certain effect upon those of Russia's upper classes, a development that was further stimulated by the reports of Russian missions which visited European countries. Among the intimates of Tsar Alexis there were a number of men who were eager to imitate western Europe without, however, abandoning the sacrosanct Muscovite tradition. To this group belonged Boris Morozov, Fedor Rtishchev, Athansy Ordin-Nashchekin, Artamon Matveev, and Prince Vasili Golitsin. Few of them went further than the adoption of certain western customs, the decoration of their houses by European craftsmen, the use of more elegant carriages. Tsar Alexis, it will be recalled, developed a liking for theatrical performances and for the ballet. A ballet and theatrical school was established under the direction of a German pastor, Johann-Gottfried Gregory, in 1673, that is, at a time when even elementary schools were still practically non-existent. After the marriage of Alexis to his second wife, Nathalie Naryshkin, the regime of seclusion, which had been the fate of the tsarina in the past, was liberalized.

These modest concessions to western influences went hand in hand with the most rigorous measures for the maintenance of what was believed to be true Orthodoxy. Decrees made it compulsory to attend Church during the frequent lents, fasting and holy communion were made a duty (1659), and work on Sundays and holidays was prohibited. It became a criminal offense to look at the new moon, to play chess, and to use popular musical instruments, although the tsar maintained a German orchestra. The infringement of these rules was punishable by the knout. Nothing, however, was done to discourage drunkenness, for the government derived important revenues from the sale of liquor. According to contemporary evidence drunkenness was prevalent, which may be explained, at least in part, by the fact that it was the only form of recreation on which the authorities looked with lenience. Reports of foreigners who visited Russia at that time present a dreary picture of the conditions prevailing in every class of society. These are corroborated by the writings of the Russians themselves—Prince J. A. Khvorostinin, Patriarch Nikon, Grigory Kotoshikhin. Even if allowance is made for exaggerations in the denunciations of men who had good personal reasons for disliking the Muscovite government, the uniformity of their opinions remains impressive. Illiteracy, coarseness of manner, untidiness of the most revolting nature, lack of refinement, were common even among the aristocracy and in court circles. The very pious Tsar Alexis was in the habit of talking at the top of his voice during Church services and never hesitated to interrupt the proceedings by the rudest remarks if the officiating cleric, in his opinion, committed an error. He used his fists freely on the highest state dignitaries, and the knout was generously applied to both high and low. The moral standards were, if possible, even more debased. Marriages were uniformly arranged by the parents, and it was common practice to trick the young men into matrimony by substituting at the last moment the unprepossessing daughter for the more attractive one. Wives were at the mercy of their husbands, and the most shocking kind of promiscuity was prevalent among the lower classes, where large families were usually crowded into a single room. According to Solovev, trustworthy evidence indicates that no other country, either in the east or in the west, displayed the same indulgence as did Muscovy towards sexual perversion. It was the favorite subject of ribald jesters and had many adherents who took little trouble to conceal their inclinations.

Education made but little progress in the course of the seventeenth century. The Church council of 1551 revealed an appalling picture of the ignorance of the clergy and ordered the establishment of schools. The Church council of 1666–1667, which deposed Nikon and anathematized the old-believers, had to repeat the decree of the council of 1551 whose decisions in other fields it so severely condemned. The new program was less ambitious. It merely directed the priests to teach their children to read and write, since priesthood had become largely hereditary. But even this modest wish was not fulfilled, and more than a hundred years later, in the last quarter of the eighteenth century, a large number of the clerics were still illiterate. Nevertheless the seventeenth century brought some recognition of western science. The chief propagandists of ideas of enlightenment were the former pupils of the Kievan Academy who began to appear in Moscow and played the leading part in the reforms of Nikon. The proposal for the creation in Moscow of a school patterned after the Kievan Academy had been under discussion since the forties of the seventeenth century. It, however, met with strong opposition, not only because learning as such was looked upon with suspicion but also because the Kievan Acadamy was under Latin influence, and Latinism suggested to the leaders of the Russian Church Roman Catholicism and the road to perdition. In spite of these difficulties a school where Kievan monks taught was organized in 1648–1649 near Moscow by Fedor Rtishchev at the Andreevsky Monastery, which he had built and endowed. The number of students in this first theological institution of the capital was restricted, but its influence was considerable. A strong impetus to the advancement of higher theological education was given by the schism. The old-believers damned western science; the official Church excommunicated the old-believers. It was only logical for the official Church to show a greater tolerance towards learning. Paisius Ligarid, metropolitan of Gaza, expressed the view of the Greek hierarchs when he declared that the fundamental cause of the schism was the absence of schools and libraries. Simeon Polotsky, an eminent representative of the Kievan school and tutor of Alexis's children, became in 1666 the head of a new theological school which provided the usual course of medieval colleges with special emphasis on grammar and Latin. The school, which had only four students, all nominated by the government, appears to have been discontinued in 1668. The venture nevertheless was important as the first official recognition of the necessity of higher education. There followed a long controversy as to whether a future academy should be under Greek or Latin influence. Medvedev, a disciple of Simeon Polotsky, and a supporter of Latinism, in 1682 became the head of a Moscow school modeled on the Kievan Academy. Simultaneously the defenders of Hellenism opened a printing press and a school devoted to the study of Greek. The two antagonistic movements were both opposed to the Reformation, which had begun to make converts in Moscow. In 1687 the two schools were merged in the newly established Slavono-Greek-Latin Academy, which became not only the center of higher learning but also the all-powerful arbiter in educational and religious matters. The charter of the academy conferred upon it the monopolistic right of teaching foreign languages and "liberal sciences." Under the threat of confiscation of property, no one was permitted to have teachers of Latin, Greek, or other languages without the permission of the academy. Only its graduates were allowed to own books in foreign languages, or to discuss, even privately, questions of religion and faith. Foreign scholars, admitted to Russia only with the academy's permission, were subject to its supervision. Expression of doubt regarding Greek Orthodoxy was punishable by deportation to Siberia, and conversion to another faith, derogatory references to the official creed, icons, or holy relics led the culprit to the stake. Supervision of all these matters was entrusted to the academy, which thus became, in the expression of Solovev, "a terrifying inquisition." The members of the faculty took an oath to uphold Greek Orthodoxy and were threatened with the stake if their teaching in any way reflected on the official creed or suggested that other denominations might be comparable with the True Faith. It proved impossible to carry out these requirements in practice since the stale Byzantinism of the seventeenth century had nothing to offer. The very names of the subjects taught at the academy—philosophy, physics, Latin—were a provocation to the ultra-conservative elements who had inspired the charter. The brothers Likhud, learned Greek monks who headed the academy, showed no little zeal in detecting Latin heresies and a marked devotion to the Byzantine tradition. In spite of their efforts to live up to the rules imposed upon them by the charter, they were denounced in 1693 as playing the role of Judas by the patriarch of Constantinople, who himself had suggested their appointment. They were removed the next year, and the academy went through a period of decadence from which it was rescued by the triumphant return of Latinism. "The condition into which the building of the Moscow Academy had fallen at the beginning of the eighteenth century," writes Professor Miliukov, "with its caving-in ceilings, its dilapidated fireplaces, its students unable to obtain instruction—presented an accurate picture of the general state of Russian education at the time of the reforms of Peter the Great." It was not really a question of reform, but rather one of laying the foundation of the Russian school system.

If next to nothing was done under the first Romanov for the advancement of education, the period was nevertheless not completely sterile. A small number of the members of the upper class came to realize that there was much Russia could learn from western Europe. Simeon Polotsky was the tutor of Alexis's children, who mastered Latin and Polish. Ordin-Nashchekin, who was for a time the tsar's minister of foreign affairs, and Prince Vasili Golitsin, who held the same office in the regency of Sophie, were both conversant with foreign languages. Western learning came to Muscovy chiefly by way of Poland, through the disciples of the Kievan Academy, and it left an imprint on Russian literature. The spreading of the art of book printing tended to increase the output of reading matter, but the various branches of knowledge did not fare equally well. Mathematics made no progress at all. Handicapped by the use of Slavonic characters instead of Arabic figures, which did not gain general acceptance in Russia until the eighteenth century, few Muscovites were reckless enough to venture beyond addition and subtraction. The only textbook on arithmetic used in the seventeenth century was an adaptation of an antiquated text probably more than a hundred years old. The first printed textbook on arithmetic appeared in 1703 and was in lineal descent from this earlier uninspiring production. Some interest was shown in geometry, which, however, had nothing to do with Euclid, who was rediscovered by western Europe in the twelfth century. Geometry was literally understood as the art of measuring land surfaces, and the rules of the mysterious science as stated in Russian treatises were as fanciful and unintelligible as they were erroneous. The *Elements* of Euclid was not made available to the Russians until

1719, and the first textbooks on algebra and trigonometry were published in 1730. Astronomy and astrology were represented by erudite discussions based on medieval European science, and there was nothing regarding the epoch-making theories of Copernicus, Kepler, Galileo, and Newton. The notions of medicine and natural history continued to be drawn from the scholastic manuals of the thirteenth and fourteenth centuries. The humanities, while still enmeshed in medieval scholasticism, showed a stronger tendency towards emancipation. The old historical manuals were revised, and events of Russian history were rearranged according to a definite pragmatic scheme which had for its object the representation of Russia as a national state. This process, however, really dated from the fifteenth century. A welcome departure from tradition was the appearance of memoirs and artless descriptions of current events, but the customary approach of representing historical events as the eternal conflict between good and evil continued to permeate the more pretentious works. More encouraging was the increasing output and circulation of elementary textbooks, especially grammars, since if progress was to be made it was obviously necessary to begin by learning to read and write. Rhetoric, dialectics, and philosophy were practically unknown except to the few students of Simeon Polotsky and other Kievan monks. The intellectual treasures of seventeenth century Russia were hardly more than a pale reflection of European scholasticism of the twelfth and thirteenth centuries.

A tendency towards emancipation from dogmatic Christian morals typical of the earlier Russian literature may be observed in popular collections such as *Velikoe Zertsalo* and *Rimskiia Deianiia*, borrowed from western Europe. Although they were dominated by the traditional moralizing attitude, these collections provided their readers with lay reading matter, tales of adventure, and love stories intended to amuse rather than to educate. Such literature, both translated and original, made a place for itself and found an ever increasing number of readers. This novel departure had a marked influence upon the evolution of the literary language, an evolution whose beginnings go back to an earlier period. There gradually developed two literary styles: one used by the religious and one by lay authors. The cleavage between the two did not occur until the eighteenth century, but the strengthening of lay literary tendencies towards the end of the seventeenth prepared for the parting of the ways.

Russia's other cultural achievements were not impressive. Torn between superstitious attachment to tradition and the requirements of a changing world, the Moscow government, while favoring immutable customs, was forced to make concessions to western ideas. Incompetent, timorous, and ruthless, the first Romanov had little to offer for the solution of the difficulties facing the country—some of which were of their own making—except an ever increasing police supervision and the knout. These all-powerful remedies were applied alike to social, economic, religious, moral, and educational problems. The number of hours to be spent in church, personal views on sacraments and religion, what one should read and how to spend hours of leisure, one's place of residence and occupation—all these and many other questions were "solved" by government fiat. Although such measures failed to achieve their purpose, they fostered a general state of discontent which among the masses found expression in popular uprisings. Among the thinking elements of the upper class the feeling of dissatisfaction took the form of a realization that the existing state of affairs could not continue indefinitely and that far from being the chosen country Muscovy was a very sad place indeed. The eccentric Prince Khvorostin (who died in 1625) had nothing but contempt for Russia and the Russians and called the tsar the "Russian despot." Khotoshikhin, a disgruntled government official who escaped to Sweden in 1664, gave vent to similar feelings in a book written abroad. George Krizanic, a Croat enthusiast who came to Russia in 1659 full of hopes and intense faith in the triumph of panslavism under the leadership of the Russian tsar, experienced much disillusionment and, finding himself in exile in Siberia, traced in his writings the most unflattering picture of the country of his dreams, a country in which he, however, continued to believe. These men, so unlike one another, felt that only education and the acceptance of western civilization could lead Russia out of the blind alley in which she found herself. Ordin-Nashchekin was a convinced "westerner" and, according to Kliuchevsky, his political program, which was never put into effect, had many points in common with that of Peter I. Prince Vasili Golitsin, who continued the tradition of Ordin-Nashchekin, is credited with a comprehensive plan of political and social reconstruction which included the abolition of serfdom. In the conditions of the seventeenth century such a scheme, if it actually existed, had no chance of being adopted.

The deeply rooted discontent which incited the masses to revolt and made the few liberal-minded men at the top cast envious glances over Russia's western frontier was, probably, among the factors that paved the way for the reforms of Peter I. It focused attention on the ineptitude of the Muscovite autocracy, imperatively called for change, and pointed out that this time light was expected to come from the west.

PART THREE

THE
ST. PETERSBURG
PERIOD

The stifling effect of lack of freedom is felt through the entire course of our modern history and is reflected in the abnormal repression of the intellectual and moral life of the nation and of its educated classes.

—A. N. PYPIN, *Istoriia russkoi literatury* (History of Russian Literature) (4th ed., St. Petersburg, 1911), III, 362.

CHAPTER XII

RUSSIA BECOMES A EUROPEAN POWER

The Regency and the Tsar-Reformer

———————————— ✳ ————————————

SOPHIE'S ROAD TO POWER

The reign of Peter I, which is an important landmark in Russian history, opened in a manner that gave no indication of the changes to come. Indeed, the conditions prevailing in the Kremlin and in the capital in the years immediately following the death of Tsar Fedor were in keeping with the worst tradition of old Muscovy. Fedor died childless, and in the absence of a definite law of succession there was uncertainty and confusion as to the next occupant of the throne. Immemorial custom pointed to Fedor's next of kin. The family situation at the tsar's death, however, was lacking in clarity. Fedor was survived by a brother, Ivan, six sisters (all of them children of Tsar Alexis by his first wife, Maria Miloslavsky), and by a half-brother, Peter, Alexis's son by his second wife, Nathalie Naryshkin. At the time of the death of Fedor, Ivan, who was half blind and mentally deficient, was an adolescent of fifteen. Peter, a boy of ten, showed on the contrary robust vitality and physical strength surprising in off-spring of the Romanov family. The situation lent itself to a war of intrigues between the rival klans of the Miloslavsky and the Naryshkin supporting, respectively, the candidacies of Ivan and Peter. A novel element in the struggle was the appearance on the political stage of Tsarevna Sophie, one of Alexis's many daughters, an unprepossessing but intelligent, well educated, and ambitious woman of twenty-five. Immediately after the death of Fedor (April 27, 1682), the supporters of the Naryshkin succeeded, with the connivance of Patriarch Joakhim, in nominating Peter as Fedor's successor, and their choice was confirmed by a gathering of the Moscow populace sometimes represented

307

as a *zemskii sobor*. Ivan was left out of the picture, and this was a bad omen for the Miloslavsky and their kin since the relations between Alexis's relatives by his first and second marriage were highly strained. The Miloslavsky, however, were not prepared to abdicate their privileged position without a struggle. They found their leader in Sophie, who was on the worst possible terms with her stepmother, Tsarina Nathalie Naryshkin. The *streltsy* provided the instrument which made it possible for Sophie and her confederates to achieve their purposes.

The *streltsy* were a peculiar semi-military formation of seventeenth century Muscovy. They were organized in regiments, lived in special settlements (*sloboda*) in the capital and, in addition to their military duties, were engaged in various trades. Armed, rebellious, and poorly disciplined, the *streltsy* were a permanent menace to the government of the Kremlin. Many of them were in sympathy with the old-believers and resented the persecution of the dissenters. Considerable unrest among the *streltsy* manifested itself towards the end of the reign of Fedor. The praetorian guards of Muscovy nursed some probably well founded grievances against their commanding officers and suspected Fedor's favorites Yazikov and Likhachev of being partial to the *streltsy* chiefs whom the soldiers accused of corruption and misappropriation of regimental funds. Some of the *streltsy* regiments refused at first to take an oath of allegiance to Peter when his election was announced. Although they were later prevailed upon to take the oath, they immediately pressed the new government for the redress of their grievances and the Kremlin meekly submitted to their demands. The accused commanding officers were ordered to pay the regiments large indemnities, and some of them were handed over to the *streltsy* and flogged in front of their men, a procedure that could hardly have been conducive to the restoration of discipline. Several high officials who had incurred the displeasure of the *streltsy* were summarily dismissed. This exhibition of the government's weakness added fuel to the kindling flame of rebellion.

Sophie and the Miloslavsky saw their opportunity. They conducted among the *streltsy* a skillful propaganda campaign directed against the Naryshkin and their friends. Prince Ivan Khovansky, a popular military commander under Alexis and a confirmed old-believer, and Ivan Miloslavsky were particularly active in the underhand campaign on Sophie's behalf and succeeded in winning over the *streltsy* by promising them increased pay and various privileges should the regime of the Naryshkin be superseded by the rule of Alexis's manly daughter. On May 15 and the two following days the *streltsy* repeatedly invaded the Kremlin and in full view of Peter, Ivan, and Tsarina Nathalie put to death a number of their relatives and supporters, including two of Nathalie's brothers and Artamon Matveev, whose ward she was. The palace guards and officials, trembling for their lives, themselves handed over to the infuriated mob Ivan Naryshkin, a brother of the tsarina, who had succeeded in hiding himself for two days in a cupboard in his sister's bedroom. The rebellious populace and the *streltsy* swept throughout the city and pillaged the houses of many of the boyars and the well-to-do, ignominiously killing the owners. The *streltsy* issued an appeal to the enslaved population (*kholopy*) calling on them to arise against their masters, and destroyed the documents bearing on serfdom in the archives of the *Kholopii prikaz*. The events of May 15 and 17 were in the full sense of the term a revolutionary movement characteristic of Russia's seventeenth century. Bloody, cruel, and anarchic like its numerous predecessors, it failed to achieve any broad purpose.

But the triumph of Sophie and the Miloslavsky appeared to have been complete. The Naryshkin family was practically wiped out and its political influence seemingly destroyed. Even the elderly Cyril Naryshkin, Peter's grandfather, who escaped the massacre, was compelled on May 18 to take monastic vows and was locked up in a distant monastery. On the same day the government rewarded the *streltsy* by granting them an increase in pay and a large lump-sum indemnity for more or less imaginary arrears. Since the treasury was empty, the money was provided by converting into coins silverware collected throughout the country. A large number of high officials against whom the *streltsy* had grievances were deported. Sophie conferred upon the rebellious regiments the honorary title of "court infantry" (*nadvornaia pekhota*) and appointed Prince Khovansky to be their commander. She thus fulfilled her part of the bargain. There still remained the chore of giving a semblance of legality to the accomplished *coup d'état*. At the request of the *streltsy* a *zemskii sobor* of the most questionable complexion was hastily summoned, and after an erudite, if brief, discussion of the appropriate precedents in Byzantine and even Egyptian history the members of this assembly became somewhat unexpectedly converted to the idea of political diarchy. On May 26 Ivan was proclaimed *the first* and Peter *the second* tsar, a novel arrangement due, according

to Sophie, to divine inspiration. The *streltsy*, who were daily entertained at the Kremlin by Sophie, demanded that she accept the regency
during the minority of her brothers. Faithful to tradition she went
through the usual comedy of refusing the offer, but finally accepted it
on May 29. The diarchy became a trinity headed by a seemingly in-
domitable maiden, Russia's first female ruler since the legendary days
of Princess Olga in the tenth century.

The *coup d'état* was inspired not only by the desire of Sophie
to escape incarceration in a convent, which would have been her fate
under a Naryshkin regime, but also by her vast ambition stimulated
by a romantic reason. Alexis's heavy-set and shapeless daughter, whose
ugly face was covered with a growth of hair, was madly in love with
the "westerner" Prince Vasili Golitsin, one of her father's influential
advisers. Her letters leave no doubt as to the intensity of her passion.
Sophie was intelligent enough to realize that probably the only way
to retain Golitsin's flickering affection was to confer upon him the
supreme honor of sharing with her the throne of the tsars, although
the execution of this scheme would require the eventual elimination
of her brothers. In the meantime Golitsin, who had taken no immediate part in the uprising of the *streltsy*, assumed the direction of
Russia's foreign affairs and became Sophie's most trusted counselor.

THE RULE AND FALL OF SOPHIE

The rule of the regent, resting on the shifting foundation of a military *coup d'état*, was anything but secure. The *streltsy* were not prepared to return to their unexciting routine and continued to interfere
in the conduct of affairs of state. Many of them, as has already been
pointed out, were in sympathy with the old-believers and considered
the reforms of Nikon heresy. Their new chief, Prince Khovansky, who
was an ardent supporter of the old faith, would seem also to have
nursed the ambition of mounting the throne, either as Sophie's consort or after her overthrow. The religious issue came again to the fore,
and a discussion of the respective merits of the old and the new faiths
was held on July 5 in the Kremlin at the request of the *streltsy*. The
theological debate, as was not uncommon in Muscovy, soon degenerated into a brawl, and the regent, who was present, was insulted by the very men to whom she owed her exalted position. Indeed, she was told that she was by no means indispensable and might

do well to retire to a convent. In the following weeks the *streltsy* became even more unmanageable. They claimed that all the boyars should be handed over to them as enemies of the two tsars and of the people. Khovansky, whose popularity with his men was great, was the leader of the subversive movement. Persistent rumors of an impending uprising forced Sophie, her brothers, and the court to flee the capital under the pretext of a pilgrimage. The *dvoriane* and other troops on whom the government could rely were hastily mobilized in preparation for the coming struggle. Sophie succeeded in luring Khovansky to the village Vosdvizhenskoe, where a celebration in honor of her patron saint was to be held. The commander of the *streltsy* and his elder son were arrested and executed on September 17. The *streltsy* answered Sophie's stern measure by open rebellion, occupied the Kremlin, and prepared for a siege by government troops, while the regent and the court withdrew behind the walls of the fortified Troitsko-Sergievsky Monastery. After protracted negotiations the *streltsy* were finally prevailed upon to lay down arms and to take a new oath of allegiance to Sophie, who promised them forgiveness on condition that in the future they would obey the government and refrain from undue interference with their commanding officers. On October 8 the agreement was formally accepted, but it was not until a month later that Sophie and the court mastered enough courage to return to the capital. Fedor Shaklovity, a man of humble origin, was put in charge of the *streltsy*.

The uprising had wide repercussions in the south, especially among the Cossacks. Its character disclosed the deep-rooted social antagonism that was undermining the structure of old Muscovy, although the real nature of the unrest was obscured by palace intrigues. The two elementary forces behind the bloody events of the summer of 1682 were the protest of the old-believers against the reforms of Nikon and the even more powerful protest of the masses against the yoke of serfdom. The agreement between Sophie and the *streltsy* specifically provided that the ranks of the latter should be purged of all extraneous elements, especially of runaway slaves, who were to be returned to their former masters. The ukase of February 13, 1683, went further. It stated that bondsmen taking advantage of the prevailing unrest had forced their lords to release them from their obligations. All such arrangements were declared null and void, the bondsmen so released were to be seized, "mercilessly flogged," and either turned over to their former lords or deported to Siberia "for all time to come." By this trustworthy method Moscow hoped to restore public order.

The rule of Sophie was as brief as it was eventful. The provisional character of her power—which was to last until the majority of her brothers—hung like the sword of Damocles over the regent. Ivan was not considered dangerous because of his physical and mental deficiencies and because he belonged, like Sophie, to the Miloslavsky klan. The case of Peter, however, was different. That precocious adolescent reached maturity at a surprisingly early age, and the relations between Sophie, on the one hand, and the Tsarina Nathalie and the surviving members of the Naryshkin family, on the other, continued to be highly strained after the events of 1682. The foreign and domestic policies of the regency both contributed to the downfall of Sophie. Whatever prestige the regime might have gained by the conclusion of "eternal peace" with Poland in 1686 was destroyed by the disastrous campaigns of Prince Golitsin against the Crimean Tartars in 1687 and 1689.[1] The enlightened views ascribed to Prince Golitsin [2] had little effect upon the conduct of domestic affairs. The persecution of the old believers was resumed with great violence, alienating much of the not too dependable support of the *streltsy*. Sophie and Golitsin, moreover, were suspected of being in sympathy with certain allegedly Roman-Catholic doctrines expounded in the writings of Simeon Polotsky and in those of Silvester Medvedev, a learned monk who was close to Shaklovity and the court circles. To make things worse, Golitsin was on friendly terms with the Jesuits, thus giving rise to rumors that the regency was leaning towards the Church of Rome. Nothing could have been more distasteful to the pious Russians. Shaklovity, who enjoyed considerable influence with Sophie, especially during Golitsin's absences from the capital, was a ruthless intriguer and made innumerable enemies for the regime. Contemporary evidence provides a distressing picture of the conditions prevailing in every class of society. Ecclesiastical and lay dignitaries vied in savagery and corruption. The free use of the knout, the torture chamber, confiscations of property, and deportations were powerless to bring any improvement but inevitably increased the number of those who hoped for a political change.

[1] See pp. 264–265.
[2] See p. 302.

It was natural that the disaffected elements should gravitate towards Peter and the Naryshkin. After Tsar Fedor's death the boy Peter was left much to himself and spent most of his time away from the capital, in the village of Preobrazhenskoe, where he gathered a large group of young men, chiefly of lowly descent, with whom he indulged in his favorite pastime, military drilling. He thus built the nucleus of a military force from which eventually developed the regiments of the imperial guards. The *poteshnye,* as Peter's playmates were originally called, proved very useful when it came to the final contest between the youthful tsar and his sister. Peter was still too young and inexperienced to assume the personal leadership of his supporters, whose number was rapidly growing, but he was ably seconded by Lev Naryshkin, Tsarina Nathalie's brother, and especially by Prince Boris Golitsin, his tutor and a cousin of Vasili Golitsin.

The activities in Preobrazhenskoe could not but deeply disturb Sophie. As early as 1687 she attempted, with the assistance of Shalkovity, to change her title from "regent" (*pravitelnitsa*) to that of "autocrat" (*samoderzhitsa*), but the plan met with opposition even among the *streltsy* and had to be abandoned. Friction and conflict between Sophie and Peter's supporters became more and more frequent. The final clash occurred in August, 1689, when Peter refused to grant an audience to the "heroes" of the disastrous Crimean campaign who came to thank him for favors granted to them in the tsars' name and in the face of Peter's opposition. Sophie, seemingly determined to get rid of her brothers and to proclaim herself the sole ruler of Russia, assembled on August 7 a large force of the *streltsy* in the Kremlin. Peter, informed of her purported intentions, took refuge in the Troitsko-Sergievsky Monastery, where he was joined by his *poteshnye* and other loyal troops. The tide that carried Sophie to power seven years earlier was now against her. Patriarch Joakhim, sent by the regent to negotiate with Peter, went over to his side. The Moscow populace and the *streltsy* showed little enthusiasm for Sophie's plans, and when she attempted to visit her brother she was intercepted on her way and ordered to return to Moscow. A final appeal to the *streltsy* was a failure, and the regent was compelled to surrender Shaklovity to Peter. Vasili Golitsin, accepting the inevitable, hastened to present himself at the Troitsko-Sergievsky Monastery, was deprived of his office, and deported. Shaklovity and some of the *streltsy* leaders were put through the torture chamber and then executed. Silvester

Medvedev suffered a similar fate, although his execution did not take place until 1691. Sophie was locked up in a convent. The unhappy woman was thus deprived by the same stroke of her lover and of the supreme power to which she had so desperately clung. Nine years later, in 1698, she was accused of instigating a new uprising of the *streltsy* and was compelled to take the veil. She died in 1704.

With the elimination of the regent in 1689, the diarchy was formally restored, but Ivan had no active part in the government and was retained as a mere ungainly accessory and displayed at public ceremonies. With his death in 1696 the Byzantine and Egyptian precedents that had so much impressed the pseudo-*zemskii sobor* of 1682 were shelved and Peter became both in fact and in law the sole occupant of the Russian throne.

PETER'S YOUTH

Peter was born in the Kremlin on May 30, 1672. He was Tsar Alexis's fourteenth child and the first-born of his father's second wife, Nathalie Naryshkin, offspring of a family in modest circumstances. Unlike Fedor and Sophie, who were conversant with foreign languages and were the pupils of the renowned author Simeon Polotsky, Peter received practically no formal schooling. This neglect is probably explained by the fact that at the time of Alexis's death Peter was merely three years old. When the infant reached the age of five, he was entrusted to the care of Nikita Zotov, whose intellectual horizon was limited. Although selected for his task on the ground not only of familiarity with the Scriptures but also of exemplary behavior, Zotov was an inveterate drunkard, and his extraordinary capacity for consuming liquor was an important element in the somewhat unorthodox career the future had in store for him. Zotov was an earnest teacher, and dutifully imparted to his august pupil the rudiments of reading and writing and made him commit to memory much of the theological verbiage that formed the essence of Muscovy's seventeenth century learning. Peter was a bright boy, but he displayed greater capacity for memorizing Church services and prayers than for mastering the mysteries of orthography. Until the end of his days his spelling and his grammar remained as fantastic as they were diverting. The events of 1682 brought even Zotov's meager schooling to an abrupt end. Tsarina Nathalie and her son were no longer welcome in the Kremlin and spent most of their time in the village of Preobrazhenskoe, one of

Alexis's favorite residences in the neighborhood of Moscow. Nathalie understood little about learning and cared even less. She had lived through a terrible personal experience and was absorbed in painful memories and in intrigues against the hated Sophie. The financial resources of the tsarina, moreover, were scarce. Peter, liberated from the rigid etiquette of the Kremlin, was allowed his freedom and, within the limitations imposed by the general political setup with which we are familiar, became at the age of ten practically the master of his destiny. No other royal prince ever had a better claim to call himself a self-made man.

It was probably sheer boredom and a healthy craving for active out-door life that led Peter to make his escape from the tearful atmosphere of his mother's chambers into the broad sunshine of the streets, meadows, and woods of Preobrazhenskoe. Unusually tall and physically developed for his age, the young tsar, like so many boys, had a marked predilection for military exercises. The formation of his *poteshnye* regiment is believed to date from 1683, when Peter was merely eleven. He threw himself into the organization of the *poteshnye* with characteristic energy and gradually succeeded in building up, with the assistance of his elders, a military force that played a by no means unimportant part in the events of 1689. The majority of the men came from families in humble circumstances and were usually referred to as the *poteshnye* "stableboys," but some of the aristocratic families were also represented. The government of Sophie complacently supplied Peter's private army with money, arms, artillery, and uniforms. A miniature fortress, Presburg, which was built on the Yausa River, became the center of maneuvers. The young tsar served in the ranks, and it was at this time that he developed an unfortunate liking for playing the drum, a form of recreation in which he indulged with his customary verve until the end of his life, to the great discomfort of those court officials who had an ear for music. The casual discovery in a barn in the village of Izmailovo of a dilapidated English sailboat, whose presence in this remote place is not easy to explain, became the starting point of Peter's devotion to things nautical, an interest that eventually led to creation of the Russian fleet. He experimented with the boat first on the Yausa, then on a pond near Moscow, but in 1688 transferred his activities to Lake Pereiaslavl, where he proceeded to build boats with the assistance of Dutch sailors. Peter's keen, if erratic, interest in technical matters of which the Russians were ignorant brought him in contact with the motley group of foreign expatriates who populated Moscow's German Settlement. Among his early foreign friends was the Dutchman Franz Timmermann, who courageously undertook to teach Peter arithmetic, geometry, artillery, and fortification. There is no question about the enthusiasm of the student, but the qualifications of the instructor are more doubtful, for even his most elementary computations were not infrequently wrong. Such minor setbacks in no way dampened Peter's ardor. To this young, eager, and robust barbarian, Timmermann and his like represented the distant, mysterious, and omnipotent western culture. European civilization was first introduced to Peter in the guise of a Dutch sailor, and he never freed himself from the spell of this to him enchanting vision. In his early days Peter liked to call himself a bombardier, but after the visits he paid in 1693 and 1694 to Archangel, where for the first time he saw the sea, he sealed his alliance with nature's most unconquerable element by assuming the humble but to him most desirable rank, that of skipper. Throughout his life he emulated with considerable success in his dress, speech, manners, and way of living the example of the Dutch seamen. The army, the navy, and western Europe as represented by the German Settlement were the three great influences that dominated Peter's reign. They all came into his life when he was still under twenty. It was also during this early period that he contracted the restless habit of moving continuously from place to place, a habit that was in itself a revolutionary departure from the ritualistic immobility and poise traditionally maintained by his august ancestors.

On January 27, 1689, when only sixteen, Peter married Eudoxie Lopukhin, daughter of a palace functionary. The matrimonial venture was not a success, and two months later Peter had deserted his wife and was again on Lake Pereislavl in the more congenial company of the Dutch sailors and his *poteshnye*. The overthrow of Sophie produced no immediate change in his way of living. Peter still showed little interest in affairs of state, and the business of government was left in the hands of his uncle, Lev Naryshkin, and other relatives, whose ranks were swollen by twoscore or threescore of the Lopukhin, kin of Tsarina Eudoxie. The usual squabble for a share of the spoils appears to have been the chief interest of the Naryshkin, Streshnev, Lopukhin, and other supporters of Nathalie and Peter who invaded the Kremlin after the fall of Sophie. "It would be idle to look in court circles for a division into parties favoring the old and the new, into conservative and liberals," writes Kliuchevsky. "The struggle was between instincts and manners equally crude, not between ideas and schools of thought." Peter in the meantime continued to amuse himself by building on Lake Pereiaslavl boats that were never used and eventually rotted away and by organizing large-scale maneuvers often accompanied by heavy casualties and occasional loss of life. He appeared at the Kremlin but rarely, and even when he was in Moscow preferred to spend his time in the company of his friends in the German Settlement.

COMPANIONS AND PLEASURES

The companions for whom Peter abandoned his young wife and the stuffy, uncongenial atmosphere of the palace were an ill assorted group of men bound together by no common program or higher ideals. Most influential among them in the early years of Peter's reign were two foreigners, Patrick Gordon and Francis Lefort. Gordon, a typical soldier of fortune, was a Scotchman born near Aberdeen about 1635. Offspring of a family of small lairds, he received a meager education in a village school in his native Scotland but acquired some practical experience by serving, in turn, the German emperor, the Swedes, and the Poles. He was employed on diplomatic missions by Tsar Alexis in 1665 and by Sophie in 1685, took part in Prince Vasili Golitsin's ill fated Crimean campaign and was promoted to the rank of general. Affable and a man of the world, Gordon enjoyed considerable popularity in the German Settlement and, in spite of the marked difference in age, became one of the young tsar's intimate friends. Even more influential in Peter's inner circle was the Swiss Francis Lefort, son of a Geneva pharmacist, who came to Russia in 1675 at the age of twenty-two. An adventurer who went through many shady experiences, Lefort had hardly any schooling, although he mastered several foreign languages. Completely emancipated from the puritanic inhibitions of his Geneva childhood, Lefort was an indefatigable dancer and good company, with a fabulous capacity for consuming alcohol. Peter had for him a seemingly unbounded affection which Lefort retained until his death in 1699. Although neither Gordon nor Lefort knew anything about the navy, Peter made both his friends admirals at a time when the Russian fleet itself was still in an embryonic stage.

Peter's Russian companions were drawn from every class of society.

Ivan Buturlin, Prince Michael Golitsin, Prince Fedor Romodanovsky, and Boris Sheremetev came from old and well established families of the Muscovite aristocracy. Others, however, were men of modest origin. The outstanding representative of new blood was Alexander Menshikov, son of a "stableboy" who, according to tradition, had started in life as a street peddler. Illiterate, unscrupulous, ambitious, and very handsome, Menshikov had a dazzling career. Created a prince of the Holy Empire in 1706, when he was thirty-three, he held high offices in the civilian administration, in the army and in the navy, and accumulated an immense fortune a large part of which was acquired by dishonest means. His influence with Peter was even greater than that of Lefort. The tsar's affection for Aleksashka, as the favorite was affectionately called, at times bordered on real passion, and in letters written in his peculiar vernacular Peter addressed Menshikov as *"min Herzenskind," "min bester Frint," "min Bruder."* Although some estrangement took place between the two men towards the end of the reign, Menshikov was one of the few public figures of the period who succeeded in maintaining himself in power until the tsar's death.

Peter's time and energy were not entirely absorbed by military maneuvers and shipbuilding activities on Lake Pereiaslavl and later at Archangel. Not a little of both was spent on the preparation of elaborate fireworks, a hobby which was introduced to Peter by Gordon and which remained one of his favorite recreations. Even more engrossing, however, were the truly monstrous festivities frequently arranged for Peter in the German Settlement, especially in the spacious mansion of Lefort. Complete informality prevailed at these gatherings, where Peter met foreign belles whose venal charms made him forget the disappointments of his married life. Drinking, however, was the chief object of the convivial assemblies, and compulsory and intemperate use of liquor was seemingly the only real link that held together the heterogeneous company of men of whom Russia's future reformer was the center.

Drunken orgies, needless to say, are not peculiar to any time or country and are, indeed, a part of the life story of many world figures from remote antiquity to our own day. It was the elaborate and fantastic ritual with which Peter surrounded his debauchery and the maniacal persistence, so unlike the haphazard and casual nature of most of his activities, with which he adhered to it throughout his life that gave his drunken bouts their real significance and shed much light on the character of the first emperor and the conditions of his time. The conclave of Peter's friends known as "The Most Drunken *Sobor* of Fools and Jesters" came into existence around 1690. Its two titular heads were Nikita Zotov, Peter's former tutor, and Prince Fedor Romodanovsky, chief of the security police (*Preobrazhenskii prikaz*), high master of the torture chamber. Zotov received the mock title of "Pope" (*Kniaz papa*) or "Patriarch," while Romodanovsky was elevated to the "dignity" of "Prince-Caesar," "King of Presburg." The *sobor* was dedicated to the worship of Venus and Bacchus, usually designated by the fanciful Russian names of "Eremka" and "Ivashka." The quasi-ecclesiastical hierarchy in which the members of the *sobor* were organized and its elaborate ceremonial were a gross and indecent parody on the institutions and ritual both of the Orthodox and of the Catholic Churches. In the hierarchy of drunkards Peter occupied the humble rank of deacon, and he never failed to display towards his "superiors," especially the "Patriarch" and the "Prince-Caesar," the utmost respect. The latter two dignitaries had their own courts and enjoyed all the outward manifestations of power. Voluminous instructions written in Peter's own hand and dealing with the organization and functions of the *sobor* bear witness to the delight he took in inventing bizarre, lewd, and grotesque ceremonies. Participation in public functions in which the *sobor* played a leading part was compulsory under the threat of heavy penalties.[3] Public processions and masquerades lasting usually for several days were attended by the royal family, court and state officials, the diplomatic corps—all in fancy dress and playing strange musical instruments, with Peter in a Dutch sailor's suit vigorously beating the drum. Such obligatory celebrations became more and more frequent towards the end of the reign. Among the high-lights in the activities of the Most Drunken *Sobor* were the weddings of the tsar's jesters Turgenev in 1694 and Shansky in 1702; the wedding of the "Patriarch" Nikita Zotov, a septuagenarian, in 1715; the election of Peter Buturlin as Zotov's successor after the latter's death in 1717; Buturlin's wedding to Zotov's aged widow in 1720; the celebration of the Peace of Nystadt in 1722. For these occasions Peter himself devised elaborate ceremonials which were as ribald as they were imaginative. Preparations for the Zotov

---

[3] Mathew Golovin, who refused to play the part of a demon assigned to him on the occasion of the wedding of Zotov in 1715, was stripped on the ice of the Neva and covered with soot. He contracted pneumonia and died soon after.

wedding kept government and court circles busy for four months, and the tsar in person supervised all arrangements. Even greater attention was paid to the election of the new "Patriarch" in 1717, and this at the very time when Peter was engaged in the tragic conflict with his son Alexis, a conflict that led to the execution of the tsarevich a few months later. In the midst of the momentous war with Sweden, Peter always found time to answer the silly and clumsy letters of his drunken friends, messages filled with repetitious, obscene, and vulgar jests.

Ingenious theories have been advanced to read into the extravaganza of the Most Drunken *Sobor* high political and social motives such as salutary warnings to the masses against the unhealthy reactionary tendency of the Russian Church and the dangers of Catholicism. All such explanations must be discarded. The Most Drunken *Sobor* of Fools and Jesters had no ulterior motives and under the enthusiastic leadership of the tsar-reformer merely endeavored to live up to its name.

FIRST ENCOUNTER WITH EUROPE

Noisy military games and experimentation with shipbuilding, fireworks, and drunken orgies could not indefinitely satisfy Peter's craving for action and his keen, if primitive, curiosity regarding technical matters. The rather formidable boy of Preobrazhenskoe had grown to manhood, and with the death of his mother, Tsarina Nathalie, in 1694, he became more than ever master of his destiny. In 1695 Peter undertook a campaign against the Turks and besieged the port of Azov but suffered defeat. He returned to the charge the next year, and this time Azov capitulated. In the triumphant march of the Russian troops in Moscow, Peter in the uniform of a captain followed afoot the gilded chariots of Admiral Lefort and Generalissimo Shein. Russia's victory over the Turks, which came as a surprise to western Europe, was followed by another surprise of a different kind. Peter had resumed the practice of Boris Godunov of sending young Russians to study abroad. He now decided to find out for himself what western Europe was really like. Lefort was probably instrumental in persuading his friend to break with tradition and establish a precedent: Peter was the first Russian sovereign since the visit of Princess Olga to Constantinople in the tenth century to cross the frontiers of his realm on a peaceful mission.

The tsar traveled incognito under the name of Peter Mikhailov, non-commissioned officer of the Preobrazhensky regiment. He was on the staff of an embassy headed by Lefort and Fedor Golovin which left Moscow in March, 1697, with the official purpose of paving the way for a holy alliance of the Christian states against the Turks. The unofficial mission of the embassy was to hire abroad shipbuilders, sea captains, and artisans skilled in naval and military matters. What Peter was seeking in Europe, as Kliuchevsky observes, was "western technique, not western civilization." The embassy traveled by way of Riga and Libau, giving Peter his first opportunity to see the Baltic Sea. The tsar then went to Mittau, Königsberg, and Berlin, spent four months in Holland, and early in 1698 crossed to England. In April he was back in Holland and proceeded by slow stages to Vienna, intending to go from there to Italy. The news of a new *streltsy* uprising forced him to change his plans and to hurry back to Moscow. He reached the capital at the end of August, after an absence of fifteen months.

Peter's incognito was loosely observed, and in the course of his travels he was entertained in a manner befitting his rank by the sovereigns and dignitaries of the countries he visited. In Königsberg he met Friedrich III, elector of Brandenburg, and dined at Koppenbrügge with the electress of Brandenburg, Sophie Charlotte, who was reputed to be one of the most beautiful and brilliant women of her time, and with her mother, Sophie, electress of Hanover. In England Peter was cordially received by King William III, whom he had already met at Utrecht, and in Vienna by Emperor Leopold. On his way to Moscow he had an interview with King Augustus II of Poland, elector of Saxony. The impression the tsar left at the European courts was anything but favorable. The strangeness of his appearance and behavior, his fits of uncontrollable temper, his revolting untidiness, his ignorance of the elementary rules of decent conduct, and his aversion to the use of knives and forks made him a most embarrassing guest at court functions. Europe was more disgusted and shocked than amused. The romantic German princess Sophie Charlotte, however, found the Russian giant not lacking either in charm or in intelligence in spite of the coarseness of his manners.

To shine in polite society was not one of Peter's ambitions. The real object of his journey was to master at least the rudiments of shipbuilding, navigation, and the military arts. At Königsberg he took what must have been a very short course in artillery and was duly awarded a diploma. In Holland he worked in shipbuilding yards first at Zaandam and then at Amsterdam. Although the visit to Zaandam lasted only a few days, the legend of the "royal carpenter of Zaandam" has been kept alive, and the tourists who go to the sleepy Dutch town are still shown the humble shack where Peter is supposed to have lived and worked. The tsar's restless disposition and his irrepressible desire to see and know everything make it somewhat questionable whether he actually spent much time in the Amsterdam shipyards. During the four months Peter stayed in Holland he traveled about the country and inspected factories, mills, shipyards, museums, hospitals, and public buildings. He studied architecture, engineering, fortification, book printing, anatomy, natural history, drawing, engraving, and even dentistry. As if these pursuits were not varied enough, Peter is reported to have built with his own hands a boat, a bed, and a Russian steam bath for his personal use, and to have cooked many of his meals. It might be doubted whether studies or practical training carried on under such conditions had much real value, especially since Peter did not neglect to pay calls on the families of his Dutch cronies from Moscow's German Settlement and since the tradition of the Most Drunken *Sobor* was duly maintained in the hospitable taverns patronized by seamen and longshoremen.

Peter, however, took his work seriously, and according to his statement it was the desire to acquire a better knowledge of the theory of shipbuilding that led him to cross to England, since the information on the subject that he had gathered in Holland appeared to him inadequate. The same indefatigable and restless activity he had displayed in Holland characterized his stay in England. About six weeks were spent at Deptford, but he also went to London, Oxford, Woolwich, and Portsmouth. He visited shipyards, factories, workshops, the observatory, the mint, the Tower of London, and the theaters; he witnessed the maneuvers of the English fleet, attended a meeting of the Royal Society, and received a delegation of English bishops. As in Holland, the lighter side of life was not forgotten, and recreations took the habitual form. When Peter left Deptford, the comfortable house of Admiral John Evelyn, which had been put at his disposal, was a shambles: everything breakable was destroyed and even the garden presented a picture of desolation. In this instance, at least, the Muscovites had definitely the upper hand in their encounter with western culture.

The practical political results of Peter's first visit to western Europe were slight except that Russia was officially introduced to the western world. The voyage was costly, but the tsar had satisfied some of his curiosity and he brought with him to Moscow hundreds of foreign artisans and technicians. The changing fortunes of the Northern War and the precarious condition of Peter's health, undermined by an incurable disease contracted at an early age, made him a frequent visitor to other European states. In a life replete with dramatic developments none was more striking than the contrast between Peter's first test of European life and the gruesome task that awaited him on his return to old Muscovy.

REBELLION OF THE STRELTSY

The uprising of the *streltsy* in 1698 was in large part another outburst of the public unrest which had been the basic cause of the stormy events of 1682 and 1689 and which continued to manifest itself after the fall of Sophie. While the tsar was busily engaged in his novel hobbies, incomprehensible to most of his subjects, the country was ruled by Moscow officialdom, which was not better and in certain respects might have been even worse than its predecessors. Peter's unorthodox behavior, and especially his intimacy with foreigners, bred suspicion and disaffection. Shortly before the tsar left for western Europe in March, 1697, a plot against his life was discovered by the security police. The conspiracy, which had supporters among the *streltsy* and the Cossacks, aimed at the reestablishment of the regency of Sophie with Peter's infant son, Alexis, on the throne. The leaders of the movement—among them a commanding officer of the *streltsy* and several men of distinguished lineage—were put through the torture chamber and executed. A ghoulish feature of the sinister proceedings was the exhumation of the body of Ivan Miloslavsky, Sophie's uncle. His remains were brought to the place of execution in a carriage drawn by pigs and were so placed that the blood of the victim ran over the coffin. This was one of the first major public demonstrations of Peter's resourceful and revengeful cruelty.

The discontent among the *streltsy* was fostered by recognition of the fact that they were losing their political influence and had been rapidly superseded by new regiments created by Peter. In the campaigns against Azov in 1695 and 1696, the *streltsy* had suffered heavy losses, their pay was often in arrears, and they resented their enforced absence from Moscow, where they had left their families and the various industrial and commercial enterprises in which they freely engaged. The rebellious mood of the *streltsy* reached a breaking point when it became known that they were not to return to the capital: their regiments were assigned quarters in Azov and along the southwestern frontier. Peter and his foreign friends, especially Lefort, who became extremely unpopular with the *streltsy* during the Azov campaigns, were accused of deliberately plotting the ruin of Muscovy's ancient force. A rebellion of the *streltsy* broke out in the early summer of 1698, and several regiments marched towards Moscow with the avowed purpose of getting rid of foreigners and, presumably, of restoring the rule of Sophie. The insurgents, however, were defeated by the troops of General Gordon, who carried out mass executions of prisoners. An investigation into the ramifications of the conspiracy was started by Romodanovsky, head of the dreaded police, but on his unexpected return to Moscow Peter took matters in his own hands and instituted a reign of terror unparalleled in Russian annals since the bloody orgies of Ivan the Dread. Fourteen torture chambers in Preobrazhenskoe were kept busy day and night, and the refined cruelty of the torments surpassed anything Russia had known in the past. The number of the accused men and women on whom Peter and his henchmen exercised their sinister art exceeded 1,700. The chief purpose of the investigation was to link Sophie and her sisters with the conspiracy. Their flesh torn by the knout, their bones broken on the wheel, some of the accused could not withstand repeated grilling on slow fire and admitted that they had approached the former regent, but her complicity nevertheless was not formally established. Tortures were followed by waves of mass executions, gallows and execution blocks being erected in the Red Square, around the convent where Sophie was incarcerated, in Preobrazhenskoe. On September 30, 201 men went to their death; on October 11, 144; on October 12, 205; on October 13, 144; on October 17, 109; on October 18, 63; on October 19, 106; on October 20, 2. Hanged in the vicinity of Sophie's convent were 197 victims, three of them in front of her window, holding in their dead hands copies of letters the *streltsy* were alleged to have written to the unfortunate princess. Peter himself acted as the chief executioner, and his favorites did their best to emulate the example of their master: Menshikov and Romodanovsky displayed considerable skill in chopping off heads, but Prince Boris Golitsin was less adroit and his clumsiness in swinging the ax prolonged the agony of his victims. The priests accused of connivance with the insurgents shared the fate of the *streltsy*. The corpses of the murdered men were not removed for five months. The bloody bath was temporarily interrupted by Peter's absence from the capital but was resumed with undiminished violence in January, 1699. A few days before the new wave of executions Peter and the Most Drunken *Sobor* held a noisy celebration, which comprised a particularly obscene masquerade, to inaugurate the new luxurious mansion built for Lefort at the expense of the treasury. Having recovered from the effects of the homage they had paid to Venus and Bacchus, the members of the convivial assembly hastened to the torture chambers of Preobrazhenskoe, the execution blocks and gallows. The number of mutilated bodies removed from Moscow at the end of February exceeded one thousand. The horrible scenes in Moscow were reenacted at Azov and Torzhok, where several regiments of the *streltsy* were stationed. The Moscow and Azov regiments of the *streltsy* were disbanded, the men were debarred from serving in the army, and their families were expelled from Moscow. The political influence of the *streltsy* was thus definitely broken, although the provincial regiments, while deprived of their ancient privileges, continued to exist until 1705, when they were finally done away with after a new uprising at Astrakhan.

Peter himself carried on the examination of his sisters Sophie and Martha. He did not, however, put them through the torture chamber as he did his son and heir, Tsarevich Alexis, twenty years later. Evidence against Sophie must have been slight, since she was merely forced to take the veil and continued to be kept under strict supervision in a Moscow convent where she had been a prisoner since 1689. Martha was also compelled to take the veil and was incarcerated in a remote convent.

With the exception of minor repercussions among the restless population of the Don region, the country accepted the bloody events of 1698 with characteristic indifference. Not a few of the Muscovites probably derived a morbid pleasure from the grandiose spectacle in which the tsar was the central figure, since the sight of human suffering and executions has always had a strange fascination for the masses, irrespective of time and place. By one of those ironical coincidences of which the reign of Peter is full, the revival on an unprecedented scale of Muscovy's worst tradition of barbarism was accompanied by the first spectacular attempt at "westernizing" at least the outward appearance of the upper classes. On the day after his return from his European travels, Peter was not only seen in public in western dress but, armed with a pair of shears, he proceeded to cut off the venerable beards of the court dignitaries. To the pious Muscovites a beard was a matter of utmost importance, since, according to the teaching of the Russian Church expounded at length by Patriarch Joakhim (who died in 1690) and by his successor Adrian, it was essential to the preservation of the "image of God" in which man is made. Its loss, it was argued, reduced human beings to the level of cats and dogs and inevitably led to eternal damnation. From the Orthodox Muscovite point of view the tsar-barber was a far more dangerous revolutionary than the tsar-executioner. It is typical of Peter's general method that in cutting beards he was assisted by the court jester Turgenev.

A CHARACTERIZATION

It would be, of course, unfair and unreasonable to form a judgment of Peter's character on the basis of his earlier experiences alone, even though at the turn of the century he was nearing the end of his third decade. The nature of his subsequent activities and of his reforms was determined largely by the course of the Russo-Swedish war which began in 1700 and lasted until almost the end of his reign. It will appear from the following pages that the passage of years and the burden of responsibilities had left a surprisingly slight imprint on the outlook and methods of the tsar-reformer. Throughout his extraordinary career he remained the restless and impetuous man whose uncontrollable temper, unorthodox behavior, and complete contempt for ordinary decency had shocked and bewildered both old Muscovy and western Europe in the earlier years of his rule. An indefatigable worker, he wrote and rewrote in his own hand not only practically all legislative acts, which came in rapid succession, but also most of the diplomatic communications that were given out under the signature of his ministers. He had an almost unbelievable capacity for dealing with innumerable questions in the course of a day. Peter retained until his death an unfaltering belief in the magical power of western technique and an unswerving devotion to the army, and especially to the navy. No obstacle was formidable enough to make him give up a decision he had really at heart, and no sacrifice in wealth and human lives was considered too great. Human life, indeed, meant nothing to him. The ambition to make Russia a naval power, an ambition difficult to comprehend in a man brought up in the midst of the Russian plain far from the sea, led Peter to transfer the capital to the newly conquered territories on the Gulf of Bothnia so that he could be in daily contact with his beloved fleet. In disregard of all strategic, political, and economic factors, not to mention ordinary common sense, St. Petersburg, eventually one of the most enchanting capitals of Europe, arose from the bleakness of the northern marshes, a gigantic enterprise purchased at the price of hundreds of thousands of human lives and untold sacrifice of wealth.

Throughout his life Peter remained accessible to people of humble condition and retained his predilection for modest surroundings which were strangely in contrast with the elaborate pageantry of official celebrations and the luxury of some of the palaces erected around the new capital. He reveled in playing the part of one of the rank and file, and it was only after the victory of Poltava in 1709 that he assumed the rank of general and rear admiral. The victorious termination of the war with Sweden in 1721 brought him a new promotion: he became admiral of the fleet. His personal courage was somewhat uncertain. In 1689, when the news of Sophie's alleged conspiracy reached him in Preobrazhenskoe, he abandoned his mother and pregnant wife and, dressed merely in a nightshirt, galloped to the Troitsky-Sergievo Monastery. There is little doubt that he lost his nerve at the battle of Narva in 1700 and fled, leaving his troops to their unhappy fate, yet he fought gallantly nine years later at Poltava and in a number of other instances displayed great personal courage. Peter's highly nervous and moody temperament probably accounts for the seemingly irreconcilable contradictions in his conduct. He suffered from an early age from a nervous tic which distorted his otherwise pleasant features. This affliction is ascribed by his apologists to the shock of the events of 1682, when many of his relatives and supporters were murdered by the *streltsy* in his presence. It is more probable, however, that it was the result of his intemperate drinking and, perhaps, of the disease from which he eventually died.

Peter's relations with his immediate collaborators remained until the very end a peculiar mixture of jovial friendliness and extreme brutality, at times not untinged with sadism. He never learned to control his temper, and fist blows and strokes of his heavy stick (*dubina*) were freely distributed, even to his closest friends, such as Lefort and

Menshikov, and the knout was impartially administered to high and low. Peter was both harsh and sentimental. Anne Mons, one of his early mistresses, was thrown into prison when he discovered that she had another lover. She was, however, eventually released and married the Prussian envoy Keyserling. Marie Hamilton, believed to be the offspring of a Russified branch of the great Scotch family, was less fortunate. She had a short liaison with Peter, who was succeeded in her affections by Ivan Orlov, one of the tsar's *denshchik*—an office which combined the duties of an orderly with those of an aide-de-camp. A member of the household of Tsarina Catherine, Peter's second wife, Marie Hamilton was guilty of the serious crime of infanticide, having killed a newborn child she had by Orlov. In spite of the intervention of Catherine and Tsarina Praskovia, widow of Tsar Ivan, who both pleaded on behalf of the young woman, Peter sentenced her to death, and was himself present at her execution, which took place in March, 1719, only a few months after the tsar's son, Tsarevich Alexis, expired in the torture chamber of the fortress of Peter and Paul. The greatest tolerance, however, was displayed by Peter towards Menshikov, and there were subjects on which he was distinctly sentimental. The old Izmailovo boat, affectionately surnamed "the grandfather of the Russian fleet," became the center of an elaborate cult for which the tsar himself devised detailed and fanciful rules, just as he did for his drunken orgies. The boat, indeed, had a prominent place in the festivities held in 1722 and 1723 to celebrate the termination of the Swedish war.

SECOND MARRIAGE

Peter's family affairs were highly unorthodox. His marriage with Eudoxie Lopukhin, as already pointed out, was not a success, and he soon deserted his wife for the easygoing belles of the German Settlement. While in London, early in 1698, Peter decided to get rid of his consort, and on his return to Moscow had her incarcerated in a convent in Suzdal. Several months later, in June, 1699, the unhappy Eudoxie was compelled to take the veil. Thus at the very time when Peter was taking the first steps towards the "westernization" of Russian manners, he disposed of his unwanted spouse according to the trustworthy method of old Muscovy.

The tsar's first liaison of some duration was with Anne Mons, daughter of a German wine merchant or jeweler, and a former mistress of Lefort. This rather commonplace romance came to an end in 1703, and it was about this time that Catherine, the future empress, made her humble appearance on the historical stage. Her origin is somewhat uncertain. She was probably born in 1683 in a peasant Polish or Latvian family of Skovorotski or Skovorotchenko in Swedish Livonia. Her parents having died when she was still a child, she was brought up in Marienburg by the Lutheran pastor Glück in whose household she worked as a servant. The capture of Marienburg by the Russian troops in 1702 started Catherine on her extraordinary career. It is believed that the young woman passed through several hands before joining the household of Menshikov, whose mistress she became, and that it was at the house of the favorite that Peter first met her, around 1703. By October, 1705, she had given birth to two children whom Peter recognized as his own. Catherine became the great feminine influence in Peter's life, but it was not until 1712 that he decided to make the Livonian peasant girl his legitimate consort. Catherine could barely sign her name and, according to contemporary evidence, possessed neither beauty nor distinction. But she was robust, unpretentious, gay, and capable of thoroughly enjoying the salty practical jokes of which Peter was so uncommonly fond. She bore her lover who was later her husband eleven children, most of whom died in infancy, and as Peter's almost inseparable companion she shared with him the fatigues of innumerable campaigns. Catherine was in the full sense of the term a trooper's wife, whose influence upon her husband was remarkably soothing, especially during the nervous fits to which he was subject. The correspondence between Catherine and Peter [4] breathes real, deep, and simple affection, and the letters, although at times so coarse as to forbid publication, are not untouched by gentle humor. The patronage of Catherine was naturally sought by those who had to deal with the tsar, and it was probably her powerful protection that saved Menshikov, in spite of his misdeeds, from the worst manifestations of Peter's wrath. It would also appear that the interference of Catherine was not always disinterested and that it could be obtained in exchange for suitable presents. The tsarina, mindful perhaps of the fate of Eudoxie, Mons, Hamilton, and others, considered it prudent to make provisions for the evil day when Peter's affection might fail her. This is what very nearly happened towards the end of her husband's reign.

[4] The letters of Catherine were dictated to a secretary because she was illiterate.

THE FATHER AND THE SON

The relations of Peter with his son and heir, Tsarevich Alexis, form the darkest chapter of the tsar's life story, which contains only too many pages that cannot be condoned or passed over in silence. Tsarevich Alexis was born early in 1690 and was Peter's first child by Eudoxie. The tsar paid little attention to the boy, who lived with his mother until her incarceration in the Suzdal convent in 1698. Later he was entrusted to the care of foreign tutors, Martin Neugebauer and Baron Heinrich Hissen, under whose guidance he acquired a good command of German and French. He was not averse to western ideas, although he disapproved of many of his father's activities. The tsarevich was deeply religious and displayed little aptitude for the military and naval warfare in which Peter took such a passionate interest. He nevertheless served as a private in the campaign of 1703, participated in the capture of Narva in 1704, and for ten more years fulfilled various military missions. In 1709 Alexis was sent abroad, where he continued his education and, obedient to his parent's will, married in 1711 a German princess, Charlotte Wolfenbüttel, whose sister, Elizabeth, was the wife of the future German emperor, Charles VI. The union was not a happy one, and the difficulties of the young couple were aggravated by a chronic shortage of money and by the tsarevich's dissolute habits. In striking contrast with his father, Alexis was of delicate health but, like Peter, he was given to heavy drinking. The relations between the tsarevich and the all-powerful Menshikov, who openly insulted the heir to the throne and his wife, were strained, and this added to the tension that had always existed between Peter and his son by a hated wife. It was probably inevitable that the young man should be looked upon as the leader of the potential opposition by all those who resented Peter's policies, the ruthlessness of his methods, the intolerable burden of wars, the extravagance of his private life and behavior. And it was also inevitable that Alexis should express at times, especially when he was under the influence of liquor, sentiments that showed little evidence of filial piety.

In October, 1715, Charlotte died in giving birth to a son, Peter. A few days later Alexis received from his father a letter which the tsar described as "a last warning." Alexis, the message said, had proved his incapacity and had neglected his duties, and unless he took immediate steps to mend his ways he would be disinherited. The next

day Catherine, who since 1712 had been Peter's legitimate consort,
gave birth to a boy, who was also named Peter. The dynastic aspect of
the situation was thus fundamentally changed: Alexis was no longer
the only potential male heir—his baby son and his half-brother were
both in line for succession to the throne. After consulting his friends
the tsarevich, who feared the worst, humbly admitted his failings and
renounced his right of succession, asking merely for permission to
live quietly on his estates. This solution, however, was considered far
too mild and was also deemed to be potentially dangerous. The tsar
replied in January, 1716, demanding that Alexis take monastic vows
and threatening, in case of refusal, to treat him as a criminal. Alexis
again agreed, but Peter hesitated to take the irrevocable step and
let the matter drag until August, 1716, when he wrote to his son from
Copenhagen urging him either to report at once at the Russian army
headquarters abroad or to make immediate arrangements for entering
a monastery. Alexis, who even in his wife's lifetime had developed a
passionate attachment for a Finnish peasant girl, Euphrosine Fedorov,
a serf of Prince Nikita Viazemsky, saw in Peter's offer a last chance
of salvation. He expressed a desire to go abroad and at the end of
September left St. Petersburg accompanied by Euphrosine. Instead
of joining Peter, however, Alexis made his way to Vienna. Arriving in
November, he threw himself on the mercy of his brother-in-law, Emperor Charles VI. The court of Vienna was much embarrassed by the
appearance of the unwanted visitor but nevertheless decided to hide
him first in the castle of Ehernberg, in the Tyrol, and later in
Naples. The fugitive was followed by Russian emissaries, Peter Tolstoy
and Captain Rumiantsev, who had instructions to obtain his surrender either by peaceful negotiations or by the use of force, includ-
'ing threats of war. The presence in Poland of numerous Russian
troops, which might easily invade Silesia and Bohemia, gave point to
the forcible representations of the tsar, especially since Vienna was
still at war with Turkey and war with Spain was just beginning.
Charles had little desire to become involved in a serious conflict with
Russia over an issue as trivial as Alexis's family troubles. Tolstoy and
Rumiantsev followed the tsarevich to Naples and with the assistance
of Austrian officials persuaded him to return to Russia. The tsar
solemnly promised him his "best love" and, more specifically, complete forgiveness, freedom to reside wherever he pleased, and permission to marry Euphrosine.

These promises, however, were not honored. Alexis reached Moscow on January 31, 1718, and three days later was confronted by Peter before a large assembly of the higher clergy and civilian dignitaries. Forgiveness, he was now told, was to be purchased at a price: Alexis was to name all those who had helped him to flee abroad and he was to renounce his right to the throne in favor of his half-brother, Catherine's infant son. The tsarevich dutifully complied and talked freely. Every name he mentioned meant the torture chamber, the knout, executions, deportations to Siberia. In his fury of vengeance Peter endeavored to link with the alleged conspiracy Eudoxie, Alexis's mother. Nuns, mercilessly flogged by a captain of the guards, failed to establish a connection between the former tsarina and the imaginary plot, but it transpired that Eudoxie had had a miserable love affair with an army officer, Glebov. He was impaled, his friend Dosipheus, bishop of Rostov, who under torture admitted having prophesied the death of Peter and the accession of Alexis, was broken on the wheel, and Eudoxie was exiled to a convent in the bleakness of northern Russia. St. Petersburg was submerged in a new wave of terror. "Innumerable accusations have given a sinister aspect to this capital," wrote the French diplomat La Vie in January, 1718; "it is as if the place was visited by a plague; everyone is either an accuser or an accused."

The suffering and blood of the innocent victims failed to save the tsarevich from his doom. Euphrosine, who had been detained abroad by advanced pregnancy, arrived in St. Petersburg in April and was subjected to an investigation. She proved a willing and talkative witness and volubly reported the unflattering remarks about his father that Alexis had made to her and to his friends. Her evidence was seized as a pretext for reopening the whole matter. On June 14, Alexis, who until then had escaped incarceration, was thrown into a dungeon of the fortress of Peter and Paul. The day before a council of ecclesiastical and state dignitaries had been called together and ordered by the tsar to decide whether his son by his behavior had nullified the promise of forgiveness which brought him from Naples to St. Petersburg. The clergy, with whom rested the decision of the moral issue, made a non-committal answer quoting examples from the Old and the New Testament in support of both clemency and just punishment. The ecclesiastical dignitaries, who, perhaps, had in mind the fate of the bishop of Rostov, closed their historical excursion into the Scriptures with the sanctimonious but vague statement that "the heart of the tsar is in God's hands." Alexis made one more appearance before the august assembly of his judges, and after that events moved swiftly to the inevitable *dénouement.* On June 19 the tsarevich was put through the torture chamber and received twenty-five strokes of the knout. The operation was repeated, and on June 24 Alexis was sentenced to death by a court of 127 high state officials on the charge of having plotted the overthrow of his father with the assistance of Austrian troops. A new session in the torture chamber of the fortress of Peter and Paul was held in the presence of Peter, Menshikov, and other dignitaries on the morning of June 26. Later it was officially announced that Alexis had died at six o'clock in the afternoon of the same day. He was buried in the cathedral of the fortress of Peter and Paul on June 30 in the presence of Peter and Catherine. The journal of Menshikov notes that on June 29 there was a brilliant court function to celebrate the anniversary of His Majesty's patron saint and the launching of a new unit of the fleet, the *Lesna.* The function, the journal observes, was particularly gay.

The apologists of Peter have produced elaborate arguments to prove that Alexis's unhappy fate was determined by high considerations of state and that the tsar had done violence to the most elementary principles of humanity in order to safeguard his lifework from destruction. All such theories contain a large element of wishful thinking. The confessions extracted from Alexis and his alleged accomplices were merely admissions of intentions obtained by the copious use of the knout, and they failed to provide a shred of evidence that a conspiracy actually existed. It is, moreover, self-evident that Alexis could not possibly have overthrown his father with the help of Austrian troops since the government of Vienna had never considered giving him any assistance. The fate of Euphrosine is noteworthy. Not only did she escape the terrible destiny of all the others who were even remotely connected with Alexis, but she received a share of his inheritance and, according to some reports, was treated with great kindness by Peter and Catherine, married an army officer, and lived quietly and comfortably in St. Petersburg for some thirty years.

THE EPILOGUE

The closing years of Peter's reign were saddened by other family tragedies. His infant son and heir Peter died in 1719. The successful termination of the war with Sweden, it is true, brought the tsar to the pinnacle of his glory. He assumed the title of "Father of the Country, Emperor, and Great," and in December, 1721, the two highest bodies of the realm, the Senate and the Holy Synod, conferred the title of empress upon Catherine. On May 7, 1724, the solemn coronation of the former Livonian servant girl took place in a magnificent ceremony without precedent in the annals of Russia, except for the coronation of the ill fated Maria Mniszek, consort of the Pseudo-Dimitry. A few months later, in November, Peter made the painful discovery that his wife had a lover, the young and handsome chamberlain, William Mons, brother of the tsar's former mistress.[5] Peter himself conducted the investigation, Mons was accused of embezzlement, sentenced to death, and decapitated. The fate of Catherine seemed to hang on a thread, and her downfall was generally anticipated. Her protégé and Peter's lifelong friend, Menshikov, was also under a cloud and was deprived of some of his high offices. New sensational developments, however, were cut short by Peter's illness and death. His herculean constitution had been undermined by various excesses and the ravages of an incurable ailment. The tsar's condition was aggravated by an acute cold he had contracted while attempting to save some soldiers whose boat had capsized near Kronstadt. He died on January 28, 1725. The detailed report sent to his government by the French ambassador, Camperdon, on February 10, 1725, leaves no doubt that Peter's death was due to complications caused by a chronic venereal disease.

[5] It seems likely that the liaison between Catherine and Mons had lasted for several years before it was discovered.

CHAPTER XIII

RUSSIA BECOMES A EUROPEAN POWER

War, Diplomacy, and Finance

---※---

THE NATURE OF PETRINE WARS

Peter's predilection for military ventures both on land and on the seas largely determined the character of his reign. Professor Kliuchevsky has computed that of the thirty-five years of his rule, from the overthrow of Sophie to his death, only the closing year, 1724, was free from war, and that during the preceding thirty-four years Russia was at peace for no more than thirteen months. The incredibly costly wars of Peter are often represented as the more or less inevitable and in the end beneficial stages of the inexorable historical process which eventually led to the creation of a unified empire with outlets on the Baltic and on the Black Seas. The determination of what is a nation's historical destiny is necessarily a hazardous and arbitrary undertaking, and the immediate motives behind Peter's reckless military enterprises, so far as they can be discerned at all, are not easily reconcilable with the heroic and noble vision of his apologists. A closer examination of the facts which resulted in the bloody conflicts between Russia, on the one hand, and Turkey, Sweden, and Persia, on the other, leads to the highly unsatisfactory conclusion that the wars that filled the reign of Peter were largely of his own making, that they were embarked upon without any realization of what they actually meant, and without any definite and clear object in view. Fighting on the southern, eastern, and northeastern frontiers was, no doubt, in the tradition of old Muscovy, but so was the struggle against Poland, which became Peter's not always helpful ally in the war against Sweden. It thus follows that if the tsar carried on the military tradition of his predecessors in certain respects, he violated it in others, even though military cooperation with Poland had not been unknown in earlier times. The exigencies of wars, however, were the moving power behind practically all Petrine reforms from which the westernized Russia of the eighteenth century slowly and painfully emerged.

FROM AZOV TO POLTAVA

The military career of Peter began with two campaigns against the port of Azov, then a possession of Turkey. There is no information on the reasons for Russia's attack on Turkey, but popular rumors fixed the responsibility on the tsar's favorite, Lefort, who, in spite of his ignorance of military matters, was in his capacity of general and admiral among the leaders of both expeditions. The Azov campaigns may be considered as the continuation on a vast scale of the military games of Preobrazhenskoe and Lake Pereiaslavl. The attempt to take Azov in 1695 proved a failure, but the following year, with the assistance of a fleet built at Voronezh, the Turkish fortress was forced to capitulate and after protracted negotiations was ceded to Russia by a treaty signed in July, 1700. Peter took part in both campaigns, in the first with the rank of bombardier, in the second with that of a captain of the navy. The tsar was overjoyed at Russia's first victory over Turkey, but some of the foreign observers took a more cautious view, which proved to be justified by subsequent events.

The Azov campaigns, however, were a mere prologue to the military struggle with Sweden which lasted from 1700 to 1721. It seems likely that the idea of the Swedish campaign originated in Peter's mind in Vienna in 1698, when it became clear that Emperor Leopold and other European rulers had no desire to participate in the anti-Turkish crusade sponsored by the tsar. The plans took a more definite shape in the course of an interview between Peter and King Augustus II of Poland at Rawa, where the tsar for a while broke his return journey to Moscow. Augustus, elector of Saxony, tall, handsome, athletic, and one of the most unscrupulous scoundrels ever to ascend the ill fated throne of Poland, at once captured the imagination of the tsar and they became intimate friends. Augustus was bound by his *pacta conventa* with Poland to recover certain former Polish territories that had passed under the sovereignty of Sweden. The real moving power behind the Swedish campaign, however, was a romantic and passionate Livonian nobleman, Reinhold Patkul, who for personal and patriotic reasons dreamed of wresting Livonia from the Swedish Crown and transferring it to the rule of Poland or to that of Augustus and his issue, should he cease to occupy the Polish throne. A secret coalition against Sweden was formed in the autumn of 1699 by Russia, Poland, and Denmark, the latter country nursing a grudge against Holstein-Gottorp, whose Duke Frederick enjoyed the support of his brother-in-law and friend, Charles XII of Sweden. Military operations against Sweden were started by Poland and Denmark early in 1700. Peter, according to the terms of the alliance, was not to enter the fray until after the conclusion of peace with Turkey. On August 8, 1700, Moscow finally received the welcome news that the protracted negotiations with Turkey had been brought to a satisfactory conclusion. On the same date Denmark, which had suffered a heavy defeat at the hands of Charles XII, hastened to make peace, and on the following day, August 9, the Russian troops invaded Livonia. Peter announced in his manifesto that the reason for the war was his desire to avenge the insults suffered by his ambassadors at the hand of Swedish officials during their passage through Riga in 1697.

Born in 1682, Charles XII, king of Sweden, was the last representative of that formidable breed of adventurers and soldiers of fortune whose bloody exploits filled the history of central Europe in the sixteenth and seventeenth centuries. His complete contempt for danger, reckless courage, and reputed military genius inspired his small, but well trained, well equipped and well disciplined army to perform military deeds that threatened for a time the established order in Europe. Peter had the candor and common sense to admit in the program for the celebration of the Peace of Nystadt, drafted on August 16, 1724, that Russia had entered the war blindly, without any realization either of the strength of the enemy or of her own unpreparedness.

This severe verdict was only too well justified. The war started in a most disastrous fashion. The defection of Denmark and the failure of Augustus to take Riga by siege were followed by the crushing defeat of the Russian army in the battle of Narva, a Swedish fortress on the Gulf of Finland (November 20, 1700). For two months some 40,000 Russians had been making feeble and ineffective attempts to capture Narva when the unexpected news came that Charles was approaching with an army of some 8,000. Peter fled, abandoning the command of his troops to the newly arrived French general, Prince Charles Eugène de Croy, who proved unable to check the irresistible desire of the

Russian warriors to emulate the example of the tsar. The triumph of Charles could not have been greater: the flower of the Russian army was no more. The eighteen-year-old Swedish adventurer had captured a number of Russian generals, large army stores, and the whole Russian artillery, which, however, was of doubtful practical usefulness. The victor of Azov became overnight the laughingstock of Europe. Peter was in despair, cried like a child, and for a time could think of nothing but peace at any price. He soon recovered, however, and proceeded with truly amazing energy to reorganize his army, create a new artillery, and build a fleet.

Charles, who himself helped his adversary by granting him a much-needed reprieve, paid little attention to the Russians but spent several years pursuing Augustus through Poland and later through Saxony. In 1704 the Polish diet, acting under the strong pressure of Sweden, deprived Augustus of the Polish throne and elected Stanislas Leszcynski to be his successor. Going from defeat to defeat, Augustus was forced in September, 1706, at Altranstädt, to sign a secret agreement with Sweden. This document terminated his alliance with Russia and recognized Leszcynski as Poland's legitimate king.[1] Peter was not very happy in the choice of his allies. In the meantime Russia, taking advantage of the fact that the main forces of Charles were engaged elsewhere, succeeded in conquering Ingria, where Peter, in May, 1703, founded the city of St. Petersburg, and also Livonia. These Russian victories in no way disturbed Charles, who confidently expected in due time to make a clean sweep of the Muscovites. Finding himself without allies and face to face with his dreaded enemy, Peter attempted in 1707 to make peace with Sweden through England as an intermediary, but nothing came of it because the tsar insisted on retaining St. Petersburg and the adjoining territories, a proposal which Charles refused to entertain.

At the end of 1707 Charles threw his main forces against Peter. He again occupied Grodno, which had previously been surrendered to his troops early in 1706 by a rapidly retreating Russian army. Grodno was considered as a strategical key position from which the Swedes could move either into the Baltic provinces, wiping out Peter's seemingly ephemeral conquests, or to Moscow, the very heart of Russia. Charles decided to carry his campaign into Russian territory, crossed

---

[1] The agreement also provided for the surrender of the unfortunate Patkul, who was handed over to the Swedes and broken on the wheel.

the river Berezina, and reached Mogilev, while Moscow was hastily preparing for a siege. The Swedish king paused for a while, awaiting the arrival from Livonia of General Löwenhaupt, who was to bring him supplies, munitions, and fresh troops. At the end of September 1708, however, Löwenhaupt suffered a defeat at the hands of the Russians near the village of Lesnaia, and the shattered remnants of his corps, which eventually rejoined the main Swedish army, had neither artillery nor military stores. Confronted with a very serious situation, Charles turned south and marched into Ukraine, where he expected to find ample supplies for his hungry soldiers and where he had a secret ally, the Ukrainian hetman Ivan Mazepa.

Mazepa, a native of Ukraine, had been brought up by the Jesuits, received a title of nobility from the Polish King Jan Casimir, and, it will be recalled, became hetman of Ukraine with the strong support of Prince Vasili Golitsin, Princess Sophie's ill fated favorite.[2] The inherent difficulty of Mazepa's position, resulting from the complexities of the social and political antagonisms that beset Ukraine and led into serious trouble every hetman since the days of Bogdan Khmelnitsky,[3] was aggravated in the reign of Peter by pressing demands for the participation of the Cossacks in the wars of Russia's restless autocrat. The majority of the population of Ukraine, it will be remembered, consisted of people who had fled from the oppressive rule of both Muscovy and the Polish-Lithuanian state. The union of Ukraine with Russia was anything but a love match, and there were many among the Cossack and non-Cossack population of the southern steppes who shared the dislike of the Russians themselves for the policies of Peter and suspected, with very good reason, that Moscow was planning new and drastic inroads on their cherished liberties, which had already suffered grievous curtailment.[4] Mazepa, a traitor

[2] See p. 265.
[3] See pp. 260–262.
[4] These apprehensions were only too well justified. Early in 1710 a Muscovite official was attached to the hetman, whose powers were to be exercised in the future with the consent of the tsar's representative. The instructions specifically assigned to the joint jurisdiction of the hetman and the appointed official the following functions: maintenance of peace and prevention of treasonable activities; supervision of foreign relations; appointment and confirmation in office of higher officials; imposition of sentences involving capital punishment; granting of estates and the cancellation of such grants. An additional secret instruction directed the Muscovite official to keep a close watch over all the activities of the hetman and other higher Cossack officers and to prevent them from carrying on treasonable relations with Turkey, the Tartars, Poland, Sweden, and the disaffected Cossacks

and a villain, according to the official Russian historiography, was motivated by the legitimate and honorable desire to safeguard the autonomy of his country and to save it from destruction by siding with the probable winner, although his methods were those of the most unscrupulous politician. Like so many European statesmen Mazepa overestimated the ineptitude of Russia and the military genius and good fortune of Sweden's dashing king, and he was unfortunate enough to embrace the cause of Charles XII at the very moment when the lucky star of the latter was about to suffer an eclipse. The hetman was engaged for some time in underhand negotiations with Stanislas Leszcynski, king of Poland, and in the spring of 1708 entered into direct relations with Charles, to whom he promised his support. Peter was warned of the plot both by Colonel Iskra and a high Cossack official, Vasili Kochubey, who felt outraged by

who followed Mazepa. Muscovite troops were to be used to suppress any subversive movement. In September, 1710, the number of the tsar's representatives attached to the hetman was increased to two. These measures, which were in violation of the agreement of 1654 (see p. 261), were received with consternation by the freedom-loving people of the steppes. The Moscow government endeavored to counteract the inevitable hostile reaction by posing as the defender of the lower classes against the Cossack upper stratum (*starshina*) and by undermining the authority of the hetman. "It is essential for our security in Ukraine to foster hostility between the hetman and the officers commanding Cossack regiments," wrote Prince Dimitry Golitsin, military governor (*voevoda*) of Kiev in 1710, and he argued that by refusing the granting of favors to the supporters of the hetman Moscow would weaken its prestige and encourage the common people of Ukraine to send in secret denunciations of the allegedly illegal activities of local notables. These predatory policies and inroads on Ukrainian autonomy were pursued by Peter in spite of the fact that Mazepa's successor, Hetman Ivan Skoropadsky, was the tsar's own creature. In 1717 Peter ordered Skoropadsky to marry his only daughter to a Russian nobleman, Count Peter Tolstoy, and rewarded him for his willing compliance with imperial command by the granting of an estate. But the powerful support of his Russian relatives did not save Skoropadsky and Ukraine from further humiliations. An imperial manifesto of May, 1722, established the Ukrainian college (*Malorossiiskaia kollegiia*), consisting of Russian army officers under the presidency of the Brigadier (later General) Veliaminov and vested with wide powers in all administrative, judicial, financial, and police matters. Early in 1723 the Cossack regiments were put under the command of Russian colonels and in October of the same year a secret instruction was sent by the Senate to Veliaminov directing him to bring pressure on the Cossacks to petition St. Petersburg for the abolition of local courts. In the meantime Skoropadsky died (June, 1722), and Paul Polubotok, colonel of the Chernigov Cossack regiment, was appointed hetman pro tem pending new elections. Polubotok took a courageous stand against the illegal interference of the Ukrainian college with local affairs and, together with the other Cossack leaders, repeatedly petitioned the government to hold the promised election of a hetman. These activities proved his undoing. In a decree of June, 1723, Peter declared that "from the first Hetman the liaison of his young daughter with the elderly Mazepa, but the tsar disregarded their charges and, after a trial, the two men were handed over to the hetman and executed, in July, 1708. At the end of October, Mazepa was forced to bring his double game to an end and went openly into the Swedish camp. He was followed, however, by only about two thousand men, while the mass of the Cossacks remained aloof. Baturin, the hetman's capital and stronghold, was captured, pillaged, and burnt to the ground by Menshikov, and a few days later a new hetman, Ivan Skoropadsky, was elected and installed in office in the presence of Peter. The Church, always eager to support the state, hastened to excommunicate Mazepa and his followers.

The campaign of 1709 opened for Charles under the worst possible

---

Bogdan Khmelnitsky, and even to Skoropadsky, all hetmans were traitors," and intimated that the new incumbent of the office would be, not elected, but appointed after careful scrutiny. Polubotok and several Ukrainian notables who came to St. Petersburg with a new petition were arrested in November, 1723, on the charge of miscellaneous crimes, from forging the signatures on the petition to murder and treasonable relations with Turkey. The intercession of Empress Catherine, who was allegedly bribed, on behalf of the Ukrainian leaders produced no immediate results (it will be remembered that at the end of 1724 the position of Catherine herself was compromised by the discovery of her liaison with Mons), and Polubotok died in prison. The other accused were more fortunate. Their case was decided in February, 1725, after Peter's death, and although the Ukrainian notables received heavy sentences these were immediately commuted to compulsory residence in St. Petersburg. Most of the convicted men were permitted to return to Ukraine a year later. The knout, however, was administered to those among the accused who were of lowly descent and they were deported to Siberia. In the meantime Veliaminov and his Russian colleagues continued to rule Ukraine, without succeeding, of course, in pacifying the country. The restoration of the office of hetman was decided on in principle early in 1726, in the reign of Catherine I, and was carried into effect in 1727 under her successor, Peter II. The chief reason for the change was the desire to enlist the support of the Cossacks against Turkey. The Ukrainian college was abolished, self-government restored, at least in principle, and the taxes and levies imposed by Veliaminov repealed. Fedor Naumov, who was appointed to represent the St. Petersburg government at the hetman's court, was sent to Ukraine with instructions to assure the election of the Russian candidate, Daniel Apostol. These instructions he carried out to the letter, and on Oct. 1, 1727, Apostol was elected and confirmed in office by the tsar. After Apostol's death in January, 1734, the government of Empress Anne decided not to proceed with the election of a new hetman but to return to an administrative regime similar to that inaugurated by Peter in 1722. In 1747 Empress Elizabeth, acting under the influence of her lover, Alexis Razumovsky, a native of Ukraine, ordered the restoration of the office of hetman, and three years later Cyril Razumovsky, a brother of the favorite, was "elected" by the Cossacks in accordance with instructions received from St. Petersburg. The final abolition of Ukrainian autonomy came in the reign of Catherine II. See p. 555.

auspices. The hardships of his rapidly dwindling army, cut away from its base and suffering from an acute shortage of foodstuffs and military supplies, were aggravated by the rigors of an exceptionally severe winter. Mortality among the Swedish troops was high, and the stoic Norse warriors remarked with grim humor that they had three doctors to fight epidemics: vodka, garlic, and death. On June 27, 1709, after a few inconclusive encounters in the earlier part of the year, came the battle of Poltava, in which the Swedish army was overwhelmingly defeated. Charles, suffering from a wound received earlier, had to watch the rout of his soldiers from a stretcher while the Swedish commanding general, Field Marshal Rehnsköld, the Chancellor Count Piper, many officers, and some two thousand men were made prisoners by the Russians. Four days later the remnants of the retreating Swedish army under General Löwenhaupt, having reached the Dnieper, which they were unable to cross, surrendered to Menshikov. King Charles and Mazepa, however, managing to get to the other bank of the river, took refuge in Turkey, where Mazepa died in September, 1709.

In spite of the numerical insignificance of the opposing armies—the total effectives at the disposal of Charles in Russia in 1709 did not exceed 20,000—Poltava was in the full sense of the term the vindication of Narva. The defeat and flight of Sweden's reputedly invincible king not only filled Peter and his collaborators with legitimate pride, enthusiasm, and boundless exuberance but also produced a deep impression in Europe and definitely brought Russia into the broad arena of European politics. The Poltava victory, however, failed to achieve the one result for which the whole of Russia was longing —to put an end to the war that was bleeding the country white. The European Powers, which had only shortly before refused to be bribed into an alliance against Sweden by Peter's repeatedly proffered generous offers of subsidies and men, now hastened to align themselves with the conqueror of Charles XII. Leszcynski, whose hold on Poland had always been precarious, fled to Pomerania in the late summer of 1709 and Augustus was reinstated as Polish king. Released by the pope from the obligations imposed upon him by the agreement of Altranstädt, Augustus met Peter at Thorn and on October 9, 1709, the two monarchs concluded a new alliance against Sweden. A secret amendment to the treaty signed a few days later provided that Livonia should become the hereditary property of Augustus as elector of Saxony. A military alliance against Sweden was concluded between Russia and Denmark on October 11. A little later Peter met King Frederick I of Prussia at Marienwerder and negotiated an alliance which, however, was purely defensive. In the meantime hostilities continued along the Baltic and in Finland, and in the course of 1710 Russian troops occupied Viborg, Riga, Reval, and other cities.

THE CAMPAIGN OF THE PRUTH

The triumphant progress of the new arbiter of eastern Europe suffered almost immediately a severe check which barely missed developing into a major catastrophe. Disturbed by the activities of Charles XII, who with the support of France was agitating against Russia, Peter demanded the surrender of his adversary by Turkey. The Sublime Porte had not forgotten its defeat at Azov and had resisted all attempts by Russia to keep a fleet in the Black Sea, traditionally considered by Constantinople a *mare clausum*. It was with extreme reluctance that Turkey in 1701 accepted Peter Tolstoy as the first permanent Russian resident at the sultan's court. The anti-Russian arguments of Charles thus fell on willing ears and appeared all the more convincing since they were reenforced by a generous flow of gold supplied by the friends of the Swedish king, while the financial resources at the disposal of Tolstoy were relatively slight. Overconfident and exasperated by the intrigues and exactions of Turkish notables, Peter, in October, 1710, issued an ultimatum demanding the removal of Charles from Turkey and threatening war in case of non-compliance. Much to his dismay the divan took him at his word and on November 20, 1710, declared that a state of war existed between the two countries, while the unfortunate Tolstoy was locked up by the Turks in the Seven Towers Castle, where he remained for seventeen months. Counting on the support of the Orthodox Slavs living under Turkish rule and on the secret alliances he had concluded with the hospodars of Wallachia and Moldavia, Peter at the head of an army of over 40,000 men invaded Turkey in the early summer of 1711. This first Russian crusade for the liberation of the Balkan Slavs failed to bring the expected response. The anticipated help did not materialize, and early in July the Russian army found itself on the river Pruth without supplies of any kind and surrounded by a Turkish and Tartar army of vastly superior strength. To escape certain defeat and probable captivity, Peter, whose entourage included Catherine—

not yet his legitimate wife—and a large number of ladies of his court, demanded the cessation of hostilities on Turkey's own terms. By the treaty of July 12, 1711, Russia agreed to return Azov to Turkey, to raze a number of adjoining fortified cities, to refrain from interfering with Poland and the Cossacks, and to grant free passage through her territory to Charles XII. The vice chancellor and future baron, Peter Shafirov, and the son of the Russian commander in chief, Field Marshal Sheremetev, were retained by Turkey as hostages until the conditions laid down in the treaty had been fulfilled. The terms of the treaty appeared to Peter as almost incredibly lenient, since his instruction to the Russian delegate, Shafirov, had provided for much greater sacrifices, including the abandonment of Livonia—except for Ingria and his beloved St. Petersburg—and even Pskov and other Russian provinces, the reinstatement of Leszcynski on the Polish throne, and generous presents to the sultan. Fortunately for Russia the Turks were not interested in continuing the war and were satisfied with considerably less than what Peter was prepared to give. The tsar and his army escaped captivity, but the sacrifices involved in the conquest, fortification, and settlement of Azov and the seacoast had all been made in vain. The humiliating and largely unnecessary defeat on the Pruth came as a sad anti-climax to the victory of Poltava.[5]

DYNASTIC ALLIANCES

The second phase of the Northern War, as the conflict with Sweden is usually known, was as much a war of diplomacy, intrigue, and shifting alliances resulting from conflicting national interests and dynastic ambitions as it was a struggle on the battlefields and on the high seas. In the years following the disaster of the Pruth, the Russian army and the young Russian navy did, on the whole, uncommonly well. In 1713–1714 the tsar's troops conquered Finland, a brilliant naval victory was won by the Russian fleet over the Swedes near Hangöudd

---

[5] Considerable friction developed in connection with the execution of the Russian-Turkish treaty. Peter at first refused to withdraw his troops from the ceded territories until Charles had left Turkey. The matter, however, was settled when Azov was surrendered by the Russians in February, 1712. The Swedes, actively supported by the French ambassador, continued to agitate for resumption of the Turkish-Russian war and bribed a number of high Ottoman officials. It was held by the Sublime Porte that the presence of Russian troops in Poland and Russia's interference with the Cossacks was a violation of the treaty of 1711. In October, 1712, Tolstoy, Shafirov, and Sheremetev were locked up in the Seven Towers Castle, and at the end of November the sultan declared war on Russia.

(Hangö) on June 25, 1714, and the occupation of the Aland Islands brought the Muscovites within fifteen miles of Stockholm. The campaign in Sweden's German provinces also met with success, and heavy contributions were collected from Hamburg and Lübeck by the victorious Russian generals.

The diplomatic side of the picture was less satisfactory. The impending eclipse of Sweden as a great Power and the dramatic appearance of the Muscovites on the shores of the Baltic Sea upset the political balance to which Europe had grown accustomed and created a feeling of deep uneasiness not only in Vienna, Copenhagen and Amsterdam but also in Paris and London. The city of London was particularly disturbed by the unwelcome possibility that the profitable Russian trade, carried in the past almost exclusively in English and Dutch bottoms, might pass into the hands of Russian traders upon the creation of a Russian merchant marine. The behavior and manners of the tsar and the conduct of his generals and troops in the invaded territories were not of a nature to inspire respect or restore confidence. Russia's ally, Poland, torn by internal dissensions, overrun and devastated by successive waves of foreign invaders, was drifting towards an inglorious end, and as early as 1703 her partition was suggested by Frederick I of Prussia and by Vienna in 1710. The termination of the War of the Spanish Succession put an end to the hostilities between England, Austria, and Holland, on one side, and France, on the other, and paved the way for the more active intervention of these states in central and northern Europe. Dynastic changes contributed their part to the transformation of the European order. After the death of Queen Anne in 1714, the elector of Hanover mounted the English throne and became King George I. In the following year the death of Louis XIV of France led to the establishment of the regency under the duke of Chartres, who governed during the infancy of Louis XV.

Fortunately for Peter, however, Charles quarreled with his Turkish friends, who had finally reached the conclusion, not perhaps uninfluenced by the presents distributed by the Russian representatives, that the Swedish king should cut short his stay in Turkey. The issue came to an open clash, and in an encounter with the Turks in the early spring of 1713 Charles fought with his usual courage, but lost not only a part of his ear, the tip of his nose, and four fingers but also his liberty, and found himself behind the bars of a Turkish prison. Peace between Russia and Turkey was restored in June, 1713, by the "preliminary" treaty of Adrianopol, which was made "permanent" in 1720. Charles was eventually released by the Turks and appeared at Stralsund late in 1714.

Peter's untiring and partly successful efforts to establish dynastic alliances with foreign ruling houses were viewed with the greatest suspicion in the Germanic world, where they were interpreted as moves towards direct annexations and the expansion of Russian influence. The marriage of Tsarevich Alexis with Princess Charlotte Wolfenbüttel in 1711, it is true, had no important political consequences except that the ineffective protection temporarily extended to Alexis during his flight by his brother-in-law, Emperor Charles VI, contributed to the estrangement between St. Petersburg and Vienna. Other dynastic alliances arranged by the tsar proved more important. In 1710 Anne, daughter of Peter's brother and former co-ruler, Ivan, was married to Frederick Wilhelm, duke of Courland. She later became empress of Russia. In 1716 Anne's sister, Catherine, was married to Charles Leopold, duke of Mecklenburg. Charles Frederick, duke of Holstein-Gottorp, a nephew of King Charles XII of Sweden and therefore in line of succession to the Swedish throne, was favorably looked upon by Peter as a suitable husband for either of his two elder daughters, Anne and Elizabeth. The duke, who candidly claimed that he loved and admired equally both sisters (Nathalie, the tsar's youngest daughter born in 1718 was presumably too young to inspire passion even in the lovesick pretender to the Swedish Crown), came to St. Petersburg in 1721, became engaged to Anne in November, 1724, and married her in May, 1725, that is, after Peter's death.

Nothing may appear less worthy of attention than the record of alliances between ungainly Russian princesses and obscure German princelets. These alliances, however, enmeshed Peter and Russia in a network of dynastic jealousies and intrigues, made the tsar the ardent champion of some of Europe's most unworthy princes in their petty quarrels, complicated the international situation, delayed for probably several years the termination of the Northern War, and introduced into the political life of Russia a nefarious element whose pernicious effects will appear from the following chapters. Peter's political and dynastic ambitions were not satisfied by matrimonial alliances with third-rate German princely houses. What he dreamed of was a *rapprochement* with France sealed by close family ties. In 1716 the Russian representative in Paris raised the question of a marriage between Tsarevich Alexis, whose wife, it will be remembered, had died, and the daughter of the duke of Orléans. The tsar soon conceived the more ambitious project of marrying his daughter Elizabeth to King

Louis XV, and the advancement of this unsuccessful scheme was one of the reasons for his visit to Paris in 1717, when Louis was merely seven. Other French bridegrooms—the son of the duke of Bourbon and the son of the duke of Chartres—were suggested in Paris, but negotiations were eventually broken off.[6]

SECOND STAGE OF THE NORTHERN WAR

The imbroglio of European diplomacy in the first quarter of the eighteenth century, especially after Peter's "most glorious victory" (*preslavnaia viktoriia*), as the Russians invariably referred to the defeat of the hungry and exhausted Swedish army at Poltava, is of a nature to make any brief presentation not only incomplete but also necessarily misleading. It is, broadly, correct to say that Sweden had the sympathy and indirect support of Turkey, England, Holland, and France, while Poland, Denmark, Prussia, Hanover, and Saxony (Augustus occupying simultaneously the Polish and the Saxon thrones) were most of the time on the side of Russia, with the German emperor maintaining an uneasy neutrality tinged with strong hostility to the growth of Russian influence in Germany and Poland. The German states, eager as they were to wrest with Russian assistance the German provinces held by Sweden, were no less anxious to free themselves from the tsar, his generals, and troops, and were deeply disturbed by Peter's unceremonious interference with the affairs of Courland, Mecklenburg, and Holstein. The German political pamphleteers, whose writings were widely read, ascribed to Peter the most sinister designs and extravagant plans of annexation. Denmark, having abandoned under pressure her wider territorial claims, succeeded in retaining Schleswig, formerly under the rule of Holstein, and viewed with concern the somewhat unexpected political *rapprochement*, cemented

---

[6] In 1723 there were discussions of a possible match between the Infant Ferdinand of Spain and the tsar's youngest daughter, Nathalie, aged five. She died two years later.

A few words may be added about the fate of Peter's new German relatives. The duke of Courland, husband of the tsar's niece Anne, died in January, 1711, a few months after his wedding, it is believed from the consequences of immoderate drinking. The duke of Mecklenburg, husband of Peter's second niece, Catherine, was a libertine, a drunkard, and a scoundrel. His uncontrollable temper and contempt for the rights of his subjects led him into infinite troubles with the German emperor and the people of the duchy. He was deposed in 1736 and died in prison in 1747. The duke of Holstein, Peter's son-in-law, however, won the affection and confidence of Empress Catherine I and played a part in Russian affairs during her reign.

by dynastic ties, between Holstein and Russia. The Polish magnates, exasperated by the predatory policies of Augustus and the depredations of the Saxon troops quartered in the country, formed in 1715 a "confederation" with the nobles of Lithuania and arose against their king. Although Peter, with reason to doubt the good faith of Augustus, accused him of treasonable relations with Sweden and of anti-Russian intrigues in Turkey and France, he came gallantly to the rescue of his unworthy friend. The confederates, while negotiating with the tsar, waited in vain for assistance from Sweden and the German emperor and, after their desperate appeal to the Sublime Porte remained unanswered, were forced by Peter to make peace with Augustus (October, 1716). The German troops, as provided by the agreement between the confederates and the king, left the country but, in violation of the tsar's promises, were immediately replaced by a Russian army corps, a change by which Poland had little to gain. Having saved Augustus's Polish Crown, Peter opposed the attempts of the former to make it hereditary, insisting on the perpetuation of the institution of elective kingship that had been, in part, responsible for the anarchic conditions prevailing in Poland.

In the meantime military operations against Sweden continued, and her German possessions passed one after another into the hands of the allies (1712–1716). The fruit of these victories, however, fell largely to Prussia, who not only took no part in the fighting but even refused to supply the allies with artillery during the siege of Stettin on the ground that this would involve her in hostilities with Sweden and that the operation was too costly. The ingenious plan by which Prussia benefited was born in the fertile mind of Baron Görtz, minister of Christian Augustus, prince-bishop of Lübeck, who administered the duchy of Holstein during the infancy of his nephew, Charles Frederick. Görtz had previously won over Menshikov to the idea of a marriage between Charles Frederick and the tsar's daughter Anne and then developed a new scheme according to which the conquered German provinces were to be "sequestered" and put under the joint administration of Prussia and Holstein. Prussia was to pay for this bounty by supporting the claim of the young duke of Holstein to the Swedish throne, while from the Russian point of view the arrangement had the advantage of ranging Prussia on the side of the allies in the struggle against Sweden. Peter approved the plan (1713), and Prussia, without firing a shot, found herself in control not only of Stettin but eventually also of Rügen, Stralsund, Wismar, indeed, of the whole of Pomerania. The king of Denmark was greatly shocked, since he, too, had designs on the conquered provinces, but he had to bow to the decision of the allies, and the relations between Denmark, on the one side, and Russia, Prussia, and Holstein, on the other, were further strained.

In 1715 the scope of the anti-Swedish alliance was broadened. After protracted and tortuous negotiation Denmark was prevailed upon to cede Bremen and Verden to Hanover, and in February, 1715, King George I of England declared war on Sweden, but only in his capacity of elector of Hanover. In May of the same year the alliance was joined after much hesitation and bickering by Frederick William I of Prussia. An attack on the Prussians in Pomerania by King Charles XII, who had returned from Turkey at the end of 1714, forced the hand of the cautious Prussian monarch. In December, 1715, Stralsund, which was defended by Charles himself, capitulated to a joint Danish and Prussian force, but the Swedish king succeeded in escaping. Peter was much distressed that the Russian troops had had no part in the operation. The impending marriage of the tsar's niece to the duke of Mecklenburg in April, 1716, and the appearance of a considerable Russian force in that duchy became the source of new frictions between Peter and the allies. The tsar had promised the duke of Mecklenburg as part of Catherine's dowry the city of Wismar still to be conquered from the Swedes. Denmark, Prussia, and Hanover, however, frustrated his plan by occupying Wismar themselves and by refusing the Russian general Repnin and his troops even admittance to the city (April, 1716). It was Peter's turn to bow to the decision of the allies in order to prevent an open breach. The tsar had for some time been convinced that the best method to achieve a speedy termination of the war would be by landing an expeditionary force on the southern shore of Sweden, a venture in which he needed the cooperation of Denmark. The other allies, however, showed little enthusiasm for the project, and although a large fleet consisting not only of Russian and Danish but also of English and Dutch vessels assembled in Copenhagen in 1716 under the leadership of Peter, the practical results of this demonstration, although flattering to the tsar's nautical ambitions, were nil, and the expedition to Sweden had to be postponed. Little success was achieved elsewhere. King George of England refused to take an active part in any joint military action until the Russian troops were withdrawn from Mecklenburg. The visit paid by Peter to Paris in 1717 failed to produce tangible results, and the war dragged on amidst petty quarrels, mutual suspicions and recriminations, and abortive peace moves. The brief and dramatic reappearance in the center of the political stage of the resourceful Baron Görtz very nearly succeeded in completely changing the course of events.

Görtz, generally considered as one of the most unscrupulous and sinister figures in an era when standards of political behavior were almost incredibly low, was introduced to Charles immediately after his return from Turkey, at once won the confidence of Sweden's knight errant, and became his minister and trusted adviser. Ruthless, corrupt, and ambitious, the Holstein diplomat was a man of keen intelligence, imagination, and vision. He conceived the idea of restoring the greatness of the Swedish Crown, which he expected to pass after Charles's death to the young duke of Holstein, by accepting the inevitable consequences of defeat and by rebuilding Sweden's continental possessions with the assistance of a new powerful ally, the Russian tsar. The proposed marriage between Princess Anne of Russia and the duke of Holstein was a part of the general plan, which was not lacking in a certain grandeur. Görtz worked for it with remarkable perseverance and skill. Charles, burning with desire for revenge and possessed with a maniacal lust for more fighting, and Peter, anxious to end the war with Sweden and to repay in kind the intrigues and underhand dealings of his allies, both willingly adopted Görtz's scheme. After protracted preliminary negotiation and many delays, the representatives of the two nations met on the Aland Islands in May, 1718. The chief Swedish representative was Görtz, while the Russian delegation was headed by Andrew Ostermann and General Jacob Bruce. It was the essence of Görtz's plan that Sweden should cede to Russia most of the territories the latter had conquered, receiving in return the full cooperation of the tsar in obtaining suitable territorial compensation at the expense of the other members of the anti-Swedish alliance. The intention expressed by Peter in the early stage of the negotiations to protect the essential interests of his allies was soon forgotten, and he agreed that Russian troops should be used to enforce the territorial claims of Charles "wherever he chooses" (*gde emu nuzhno*), but more specifically in Hanover and Denmark. In spite of the agreement between the tsar and the king on the basic points, the negotiations proved difficult, and their outcome was still uncertain when Charles was killed in action at Fredrikshald in December, 1718. He was succeeded on the throne by his younger sister, Ulrica Eleonora. The Swedish supporters of the duke of Holstein lost all influence, the duke himself fled the country, and Görtz, who was generally hated in Sweden and was publicly denounced as a hireling of the tsar, was arrested and executed. The situation was thus fundamentally changed, but the negotiations on the Aland Islands went on, both parties playing for time. In July, 1719, a large Russian expeditionary force landed in Sweden, devastated the coast, and the advance Cossack detachment reached points within less than two miles of Stockholm. In September the Aland negotiations were finally broken off by Sweden.[7]

The death of Charles XII had other important repercussions. Sweden, exhausted by the long war and ruled by a constitutional queen, was obviously no longer a danger to the other European nations. King George of England, anxious to restore a semblance of the old balance of power and to check Russian expansion, led the way towards reconciliation by concluding with Sweden in the summer of 1719 a treaty of peace by which Hanover received Bremen and Verden. Augustus, as elector of Saxony, negotiated a preliminary peace agreement with the new Swedish government. Prussia followed suit early in 1720 and received Stettin, and in the summer of the same year Denmark brought the long war to an end by a treaty which granted her Schleswig but made her return to Sweden all other territories held by Danish troops. The efforts of London, seconded by Paris and Vienna, to isolate Russia were thus largely successful and the "Northern Alliance" was no more. King George went so far as to send to the Baltic the English fleet under Admiral Norris with orders to cooperate with the Swedish navy as part of England's program of forcing the tsar to accept her mediation of the Swedish-Russian conflict. Peter retaliated by announcing the breaking off of diplomatic relations with London, a decision which was specifically declared not to affect in any way

---

[7] The nature of the Aland Islands negotiations could not be kept secret, and their progress was followed with keen interest in the diplomatic circles of Europe. In August, 1718, Spain made Peter the offer of a Russo-Swedish-Spanish alliance directed against Vienna and London. The plan provided for the landing in Scotland of Russian and Swedish troops, which were to overthrow King George and restore the Stuarts. Peter was much interested in this fanciful scheme, which was abandoned upon the death of Charles XII, and he continued to follow closely the agitation for the restoration of the Stuarts.

Anglo-Russian trade. The naval action of England, however, was lacking in vigor, and fresh landings of Russian raiding parties in Sweden in 1720 and 1721 strongly suggested that Peter was determined to carry on. Sweden was no longer in a position to continue the struggle. Frederick, prince of Hesse-Cassel and husband of Ulrica Eleonora, was elected king of Sweden in 1720 and with the assistance of the French ambassador to St. Petersburg, Camperdon, who had previously represented France in Stockholm, peace negotiations between Russia and Sweden were resumed at Nystadt in April, 1721. The peace treaty, signed on August 30, 1721, transferred to Russia "for all time to come" the provinces of Livonia, Estonia, Ingria, a part of Karelia with the city and district of Viborg, and the islands of Oesel and Dagoe. The expression "for all time to come" was an ingenious subterfuge to meet the Swedish condition that none of the ceded territories should fall into the hands of the duke of Holstein,[8] although the provision was not without advantage from the Russian point of view since it lent a semblance of legality to the annexation of Livonia, which, under earlier agreements, with Augustus, constituted his share of the spoils. Russia returned to Sweden the whole of Finland, except for the portion of Karelia assigned to her by the treaty, paid a compensation of two million Dutch taler, and agreed to refrain from interfering with the internal affairs of Sweden, including the succession to the throne.[9] The inhabitants of the ceded territories were to retain the property and other rights they had enjoyed under Swedish rule.

The Treaty of Nystadt, although by no means a dictated peace, was a magnificent victory for Russia. Old Muscovy, the *terra incognita* of a century ago, had established herself on the shores of the Baltic Sea, and she retained her Baltic provinces (to which Courland was added

[8] During the Nystadt negotiations Peter diligently defended the interests of his future son-in-law whom he had not yet met. One of the reasons for delay in concluding the treaty was the tsar's insistence that the duke of Holstein should be declared heir to the Swedish throne. This demand was eventually dropped.

[9] The latter condition was not observed by Peter, who never ceased intriguing for the promotion of the candidacy of the duke of Holstein for the Swedish throne. He even offered the friends of the duke in Sweden the support of the Russian fleet. Although the Swedish government was aware of these activities, it deemed it wise to conclude with Russia in February, 1724, a defensive alliance providing for mutual support in case of aggression against either country by a *Christian* state. A secret clause requested the two governments to take concerted action for the restoration of Schleswig to Holstein. Another secret clause, directed against King Augustus's attempts to make the Polish throne hereditary, imposed upon the contracting parties the obligation of maintaining the existing constitution of Poland.

in 1795) until 1918, when Latvia, Estonia, and Lithuania regained an ephemeral independence only to be swallowed two decades later (1939–1940) by a communist Russia. No less significant was the spectacular increase in the direct and indirect participation of Russia in European affairs. Peter's frequent visits to western capitals and watering places and the truly remarkable activity displayed by his ambassadors and representatives were in themselves clear indications that Muscovy's comparative isolation had come to an end. The Russian troops had crossed the western frontier of their old familiar battlefield, Poland, and had besieged, pillaged, and burned the cities and villages of Germany, Denmark, and Sweden. The Russian navy was no longer a dream or a nightmare but a reality. If the tsar's foreign envoys were not always welcome, their views and demands could no longer be brushed aside with impunity. An uninterrupted flow of gold, precious stones, furs, and other presents exacted from a starving country streamed from the Russian embassies into the coffers of rapacious and venal European statesmen, diplomats, and adventurers of various hues. Others received decorations, titles, and landed estates.[10] Russian troops and generous subsidies from a chronically empty treasury were offered to all and sundry, and although promises were not always honored both men and money were freely used for the advancement of nebulous political schemes and conflicting dynastic and other ambitions of Poland, Denmark, Saxony, Prussia, Hanover, Courland, Mecklenburg, Holstein, and the Balkan Slavs. The nature of the welcome given by other European Powers to their new partner is suggested by the delays and bargaining that accompanied the recognition of the imperial title assumed by Peter in 1721. Prussia and Holland granted recognition at once; Sweden in 1723; Saxony in 1733; Turkey in 1741; Austria and England in 1742, and France and Spain in 1745. Poland, however, did not grant recognition until 1764. From time to time, moreover, recognition was ungraciously withdrawn; for instance, by Sweden in 1741 and by France in 1768. These petty setbacks, vexatious as they were to the court of St. Petersburg, could not obscure the basic fact that by the end of the reign of Peter, Russia, both geographically and diplomatically, had become a part of the European system.

[10] The Duke of Marlborough, for instance, was offered in 1707 the choice of the principalities of Kiev, Vladimir, and Siberia (whatever that may mean), an enormous ruby, the grand cross of the order of St. Andrew, and a large sum of money.

SIBERIA AND PERSIA

Until the end of the Swedish war the eastern countries played a minor part in Russian foreign policy. Two embassies sent to China, one in 1692 and one in 1719, to establish diplomatic and commercial relations came back empty-handed. An attempt was made in 1714 to build a military and trade outpost on Lake Yamish, in Siberia, but mass desertion of the troops necessitated its abandonment two years later. A small military force which fought its way to the Asiatic principality of Khiva in 1717 not only failed to persuade the local ruler to accept a Russian protectorate but was eventually wiped out and its leader executed. Russia had better luck in Persia. A cavalry officer, Artemi Volynsky, was sent in 1715 to the shah's court as a permanent representative of the tsar. His instructions provided, among other things, for a study of possible water routes between the Caspian Sea and India. Although Volynsky was not permitted to remain in the Persian capital, he succeeded in concluding a commercial treaty with the government of the shah. He was then appointed governor of Astrakhan, and it is believed that his reports urging the necessity of strong Russian military action in the Caucasus and Persia were largely responsible for the Persian campaign of 1722. The chaotic political and economic conditions in Persia, which interfered with the interests of Russian traders, and the fear of Turkish expansion towards the Caspian Sea were probably the reasons that determined Peter to embark on a new war at a time when the country was more than ever longing for peace. Accompanied by Catherine, the tsar left Moscow in May, 1722, and assumed command of an army which, including the Cossacks and Kalmyks, exceeded 100,000 men. Peter and some of his troops embarked at Astrakhan, while the body of the army followed by land the shores of the Caspian Sea. The invaders met with little resistance, and on August 23 Derbent surrendered without a struggle, but the shortage of foodstuffs and fodder, caused by the disorganization of supplies and aggravated by the unwieldy and seemingly unwarranted size of the army, forced Peter to return to Astrakhan, where he arrived in October. The war continued, and Baku was taken by the Russians in the summer of 1723. By virtue of a peace treaty signed at St. Petersburg on September 12, 1723, Russia obtained the southwestern and southern shores of the Caspian Sea with Baku and Derbent, while the tsar promised the shah the use of the Russian troops for the maintenance of order in Persia. The Persian government, however, delayed the ratification of the treaty, and in the meantime friction developed between Russia and Turkey, the latter country, at the instigation of England, challenging Russian conquests on the Caspian shores. Threats of war were made by the Turkish government, but in 1724 the matter was peacefully settled through the mediation of the French ambassador, Marquis de Bonac, and by the Treaty of Constantinople, which traced the somewhat illusory frontiers between Russian and Turkish possessions in the region of the Caspian Sea. The settlement of the thorny question was immediately endangered by an appeal for protection addressed to the tsar by the Armenians. Peter felt that he should not remain indifferent to the fate of his coreligionists suffering under the rule of the unfaithful. His death, however, prevented him from adding the Armenians, Georgians, and other Christian peoples of the Caucasus to the already long list of those whose cause had been championed and fought for in various parts of the continent by the tsar and his army. Russia's hold on the new provinces proved as ephemeral as their acquisition had been costly; some ten years after the signing of the Treaty of Constantinople the Russian government, which was about to declare war on Turkey, returned the conquered territories to Persia in order to secure the latter country's cooperation in the impending struggle against the Sublime Porte.

THE ARMY AND THE NAVY

Men, ships, military equipment, and money are the essential prerequisites of war. The pursuance of the Northern War to a successful conclusion was the central interest of Peter's reign, and it is the examination of the activities immediately connected with the creation and maintenance of the military establishment that offers the key to his reforms.

Attempts at the modernization of Russia's armed force were made in the seventeenth century when the militia of the *dvoriane* was supplemented by a standing army organized more or less along the lines of the armies of western Europe.[11] It would seem, however, that the experiment had been permitted to deteriorate by the end of the century, and the bulk of the troops that participated in the first Azov campaign of 1695 consisted of the old militia. The Preobrazhensky

[11] See pp. 272–274.

and the Semenovsky regiments of the guards, Peter's first military innovation, evolved gradually from the ranks of the tsar's playmates in youthful games and reached the status of full-fledged military units about 1690–1691. Numerically insignificant (the number of men serving in the guards was 3,700 in 1700 and only 2,600 towards the end of the reign), the guards, as it will appear from subsequent discussion, eventually became an extremely important factor in Russian political and social life, but the inferiority of their number prevented them from playing a decisive role on the battlefields, although they usually made a better showing than the other troops. The army with which Peter began the war against Sweden was 35,000 to 40,000 strong, and the early contingents were supplied largely by the enrollment of volunteers, a group that comprised men of all conditions, including slaves, who were granted the privilege (revoked in 1727) of joining the army irrespective of the consent of their masters. The low quality of this human material and the inadequacy of their training were convincingly proved by the catastrophe of Narva. In the following years recruiting was put on a more definite basis, the government requiring a specified number of households to provide one recruit, although both the size of the levies and the number of households responsible for the recruits varied within a very wide range. According to the authoritative computations of Professor Miliukov, the total number of men called for service in 1700–1709 was 200,000, although the total military force during this period never exceeded 100,000.[12] The balance represented the losses suffered not so much on the battlefields as from mass desertions and from the extraordinarily high mortality among the soldiers due to hunger, cold, and incredible living conditions. Under the system then in force it was the duty of the communities to supply a new recruit for every soldier who dropped from the ranks for whatever reason, the soldiers thus being "immortal." The concentration of the recruits in depots where they received some training before joining their regiments, and especially the protracted character of the war which for years kept men with the colors, led to the transformation of the militia into a regular army. The new Army Regulations (*Voinskii ustav*) were not issued until 1716, that is, when the Northern War was nearly over. By the end of Peter's reign the

---

[12] Kliuchevsky estimates that during the first ten years of the war the number of men called was about 300,000, while the entire population was approximately 14,000,000.

effectives of the regular army exceeded 200,000; to this number must be added some 100,000 Cossacks and a large but undetermined force of native troops, such as the Kalmyks and other eastern peoples.

The Russian navy is properly considered as Peter's own creation, although the vision of a Muscovite fleet sailing the high seas had appealed to some of the earlier tsars. Starting with early experimentations on the Yauza, Lake Pereiaslavl, and at Archangel, naval construction was carried on in earnest for the first time at Preobrazhenskoe and at Voronezh in preparation for the second campaign of Azov (1696). The heavy sacrifices made in the following years to build a fleet for the Black Sea proved futile when Azov itself had to be abandoned to the Turks after the Russian defeat on the Pruth in 1711. The Russian man-of-war that proudly brought the Muscovite ambassador, Ukraintsev, to Constantinople in 1699 was not fated to be followed by other Russian vessels for many decades to come. Just as unrewarding were the tsar's shipbuilding activities at Archangel in the summer of 1702. With the conquest of Ingria and the founding of St. Petersburg (1703), Peter established navy yards on the Svir River, and the next year Russian men-of-war made their appearance in the Baltic Sea. By the end of his reign the Baltic fleet comprised some 800 vessels of various types, not a few of them built abroad, manned by 28,000 sailors. The young Russian navy had an important part in the final victory over Sweden, yet it would be an error to believe that with the conquest of the Baltic shores Russia became a maritime Power in the accepted sense of the term. The apprehensions of the English government and of the English and Dutch merchants that the acquisition of the Baltic provinces would lead to the creation of a strong Russian navy and mercantile marine proved, like so many seemingly well founded generalizations about future trends, at variance with the actual course of events. According to Veselago, the historian of the Russian navy, nine years after Peter's death the number of seaworthy armed vessels had been reduced to fifteen, with no officers to command them. Peter's dream of Russian naval greatness, indeed, was never fulfilled, and the bulk of her sea-borne trade continued to be carried in foreign bottoms.

WAR EXPENDITURE AND PUBLIC FINANCE

"Money is the artery of war" Peter wrote in his quaint language to the newly established Senate in 1711, and, indeed, the financing of the rapidly expanding military and naval establishment remained one of his chief preoccupations. War expenditure increased from 2.3 million rubles in 1701 to 3.2 million rubles in 1710. The cost of the maintenance of the army alone in 1724 was estimated at over 4 million rubles, while appropriations for the navy, which were 80,000 rubles in 1701 increased to 444,000 rubles in 1710, to 600,000 rubles in 1720, to 1.2 million rubles in 1724, and to 1.4 million rubles in 1725. The meaning of these figures, which it is not claimed are either comprehensive or exact,[13] is made clearer by comparing them with the total state revenue. Total receipts, which in 1680 were 1.4 million rubles, rose in 1701 to 3.0 million rubles, in 1710 to 3.3 million rubles, in 1720 to 7.5 million rubles, and in 1724 to 8.5 million rubles. From 1701 to 1708 military expenditure consumed about 80 per cent of the total revenue, and in the 1725 budget, the first to show the full effect of the last and most important financial reform introduced by Peter, three-quarters of the receipts were allocated to the maintenance of a peacetime military force. To meet the rising tide of expenditure and prevent the unbalancing of the budget, the government found itself forced to evolve a novel financial policy, one that largely determined the nature of other reforms.

Financial reforms, like all the reforms of Peter, came piecemeal, under the pressure of necessity, without plan or proper coordination, the various measures, indeed, frequently working at cross-purposes. The important thing was to raise the funds so desperately needed for the prosecution of the war; the rest did not matter, although Peter repeatedly emphasized that taxes should be levied without "unduly burdening the people," a pious wish which the financial experts of a more enlightened age have not yet discovered how to put into effect. One of the first expedients used by the Moscow government was the debasement of currency by reducing the amount of silver in the monetary units in circulation. The fictitious gains thus realized by the treasury provided an important source of "revenue" during the early years of the war, and a considerable portion of the "profits" derived from this monetary operation, which was repeated several times, was

[13] The above figures are taken from a detailed study of Russia's financial policy in the first quarter of the eighteenth century by Prof. P. N. Miliukov, first published in Russia in 1892. A useful summary of the findings is available in French in Paul Milioukov, Ch. Seignobos, and L. Eisenmann, *Histoire de Russie* (Paris, 1932), Vol. I. The figures quoted by Kliuchevsky differ somewhat from those given by Miliukov, but the discrepancy in no way affects the conclusions.

spent in subsidies to King Augustus of Poland. This spurious method of financing inevitably led to the depreciation of the currency. The purchasing power of the ruble declined something like 50 per cent during Peter's reign, a consideration that must be kept in mind when comparing the figures of revenue and expenditure given above. The debasement of currency went hand in hand with the broadening of the basis of taxation. Suggestions for new taxes were eagerly listened to, irrespective of the position of their authors, a practice that led to the creation of a special service of *pribylshchiki*, literally "profit-makers," whose duties consisted in devising new sources of revenue and usually also in administering the new taxes they had invented. The originator of this rather unpopular branch of public administration was Alexis Kurbatov, a former slave and butler of Prince Kurakin. Kurbatov, traveling with his master abroad, conceived the idea of a stamp duty which he submitted to Peter in 1699. The stamp duty was immediately put into effect, and Kurbatov, rewarded by a generous grant of estates, became in 1705 the head of the newly established central financial department (*Ratusha*) and one of Peter's most influential advisers. He was appointed vice governor of Archangel in 1711, but later quarreled with Menshikov and died in 1721 while on trial on charges of embezzlement. His career was successfully emulated by a number of men of humble origin, and it is noteworthy that former slaves and serfs were well represented in the fraternity of *pribylshchiki*. Their ingenuity, stimulated by substantial personal inducements, resulted in a real orgy of taxes which were of greater credit to the resourcefulness of their authors than to the wisdom of the government. Tributes were collected on fisheries, mills, harnesses, hats, boots, hides, and leather, beehives, rents (including rents paid for "corners," when several people shared the same room), storage of ice for the summer, cellars, smokestacks, and the sale of such articles of food as watermelons, cucumbers, nuts, "and others." Carriers had to contribute to the treasury one-tenth of their fares, innkeepers one-quarter of their receipts. Private bathhouses (*bania*), most primitive establishments commonly found even in the shacks of peasants as the only means of maintaining some semblance of cleanliness, were taxed according to the social standing of the owners. A still more elaborate gradation was introduced in the tax on mustaches and beards, to which the Russians were so devoutly attached, the rate varying from one hundred rubles a year for wealthy merchants to thirty rubles for Church attendants and the Moscow populace. The beards of the peasants were tax-free so long as their owners remained in their villages, but one copeck was levied every time a bearded muzhik entered or left a city. The Tartars and other non-Christian peoples were liable to a marriage tax appropriately collected by the "Honey (*medovaia*) Chancery," which also took care of the tax on beehives. Kliuchevsky has aptly observed that funerals would seem to be the only potential source of revenue overlooked by Peter's bright young men, an omission the Church did its best to remedy by exacting from the families of the deceased whatever the traffic would bear.

Trade monopolies, which did not escape the attention of the treasury officials, were considerably increased in number. The salt monopoly, established in 1705, resold salt at a profit of 100 per cent. In the same year the government took over the sale of tobacco, which, since 1698, had been in the hands of an English firm. Tar, chalk, fats, fish oil, potash, caviar, bristle, and several other articles became government monopolies the number of which reached a peak in 1714. All oak coffins were collected by the government from the makers and resold in the monasteries at four times their original price. The profits of some of these commercial ventures proved illusory or insignificant, and strong opposition on the part of Russian and foreign merchants, combined with the spreading of mercantilist ideas towards the end of Peter's reign, brought about a revision of policy. A decree of 1719 provided that trading in all commodities, except potash and tar, might be freely carried on by merchants after payment of certain duties. Yet the state tobacco monopoly, which had never been profitable, was not given up until 1723, and the levies on salt in the form of either royalties or excise were retained until almost the end of the nineteenth century. Many of the new taxes, moreover, did not produce the expected yield, and receipts from this source were usually below the estimates, while the vexatious character of the imposts made them extremely unpopular.

The prospect of a substantial deficit in the budget for 1710 made the government reconsider the question of direct taxation. The yield of the chief direct tax, the "household (*podvornaia*) tax," was computed by multiplying the rate of the tax by the number of taxable households.[14] In the early years of the reign of Peter, the number of such households was determined by the census of 1678, which was

[14] See p. 274.

out-of-date. A new census was taken in 1710 for the purpose, it is believed, of ascertaining the increase in the number of taxpayers. Instead of the anticipated gain in population, the returns of the census, imperfect as they undoubtedly were, unfolded a most distressing picture of the depopulation of the country. The average decrease in the number of households for Russia as a whole was 20 per cent, rising to 40 per cent in the northern provinces and reaching in some of the smaller territorial subdivisions 52, 56, and 57 per cent. An increase in the number of households was registered only on the Volga, in the province of Kazan (17 per cent); and in the province of Siberia (48 per cent), that is, in the areas of relatively recent colonization. In the Asiatic portion of the province of Siberia the increase in the number of households was considerably greater, 169 per cent; but the total population of that vast region remained insignificant, rising from 10,000 households in 1678 to 28,000 in 1710. It must be emphasized that the data of the census of 1710 were highly imperfect, not only because the methods of census taking were of the crudest but also because the census dealt, not with individuals, but with "households," a vague and uncertain unit that was never properly defined or clearly understood. Nevertheless it is believed that the general picture emerging from the dreary figures of the census probably reflected fairly accurately the plight of the country after ten years of the Northern War. Official records supply interesting information on the causes of the disappearance of some 19,000 households of the total number of 154,000 that had vanished between 1678 and 1710: householders driven away, presumably, by the exactions of the government and the landlords, 37.2 per cent; "direct government action," that is, conscription for military and other purposes (building of St. Petersburg, work in shipyards, construction of canals, and so on), 20.4 per cent; brigandage and mendicity, 0.9 per cent; with "natural causes" accounting for the balance of the cases about which information is available. The results of the census could not have been more unsatisfactory from the point of view of the treasury: instead of increasing, the number of households had fallen off from 791,000 in 1678 to 637,000 in 1710. After some hesitation the government took the drastic step of ignoring the census of 1710 except where the new figures, like those for the province of Kazan, favored the treasury. The assessment of the household tax continued to be computed on the basis of the larger number of households which the census of 1710 had proved to be fictitious. This meant, of course, that in practice the surviving households had to pay the share of those that had vanished as a consequence of the government's "direct" and "indirect" action or from "natural causes."

THE POLL TAX

The mere manipulation of statistical data, however ingenious, could not provide a solution of Russia's financial difficulties. Further debasement of the currency and the piling up of indirect taxes were tried again and proved increasingly ineffective. The old and trusted method of levying direct taxes for specific purposes displayed a similar tendency: the special assessment of half a ruble per household imposed in 1713 to defray the expenses of the Turkish war yielded one-third of the amount anticipated. Peter's economic advisers, including amateur economists, were inclined to blame the spread of vagrancy and the flight of taxpayers for the financial predicament. A new household census taken in 1716–1717 disclosed a further decline in the number of households and brought out the significant fact that the process of apparent depopulation had extended to southeastern Russia, that is, to the very areas where one would have expected to find an influx of runaway peasants from the other provinces. The decline of the number of households in some areas was considerably in excess of its increase in others, and the discrepancy suggested that the flight of the peasants to new places of settlement might not be quite so important as had been thought. It was at least possible that the merging of two or more households into one in order to avoid taxation, as well as the laxity of the census takers, might have had something to do with the recorded fall in the number of households. It was argued that while the number of households was shrinking, the households themselves were becoming larger.

The logical thing to do, therefore, was to change the basis of assessment and to substitute a poll tax for the tax on households. The desirability of introducing the poll tax had been discussed in Russia since the end of the seventeenth century, and the adoption of this form of taxation was urged upon Peter by some of his unofficial advisers, especially in 1717. He accepted the suggestion, as he had so many others, without any realization of its real implications, for his interest in public finance, as Kliuchevsky has so well put it, was centered on two factors that were to him cardinal points: the soldier who was to be provided for, and the peasant who was to foot the bill. The method mattered little if the object was achieved. The broader the base of the tax, the better. The poll tax therefore was to be levied on male "souls" —a peculiar terminology that shocked even some of Peter's contemporary admirers, such as the peasant author Pososhkov. A decree issued by the Senate on November 26, 1718, ordered a census of the entire male population, "not omitting old men and the latest babies," an order that did not apply to the privileged classes who were exempted from the poll tax. The census, which began in January, 1719, proved a cumbersome affair, new complications arising from wholesale frauds and evasions and from the government's repeatedly expanding the scope of the census by including within the taxable class various ill defined groups of people not formerly liable to the household tax. The incomplete preliminary figure of some three million taxpayers available in 1721 was deemed unsatisfactory. A verification, or supplementary census (*reviziia*, literally "revision," a term retained in subsequent practice), was ordered in the middle of 1721 and was carried out, first by local authorities, and in 1722 and 1723 by the military officers quartered in the provinces. As a result of these stringent measures (evasion was severely punishable) the total number of taxpayers in 1724 rose to 5,570,000, of whom 169,000 were living in cities. The revenue from the poll tax was earmarked to defray military expenditure, and the rate "per soul" was arrived at by dividing the estimated amount of such expenditure by the number of taxpayers.

The financial results of the reform were highly satisfactory. The yield of all earlier direct taxes was 1.8 million rubles; the revenue from the poll tax which replaced them was estimated at 4.6 million rubles, that is, the government benefited to the extent of 2.8 million rubles. This higher revenue was welcome, since the position of the treasury was desperate. In October, 1722, Menshikov informed the Senate that soldiers in many regiments had not received their pay and had deserted en masse. In February, 1723, the government ordered that the salaries of civilian employees should be paid, not with money but in state-produced goods. In April of the same year all state salaries and wages had been temporarily cut by one-fourth, and the distribution of grain allowances (a customary and important addition to monetary wages) was suspended. With the introduction of the poll tax the budget was balanced, at least in theory, but the practical difficulties remained. According to an official statement in 1726, the receipts of the poll tax in 1724 were 18 per cent short of the estimates. There is no question, however, that revenue had greatly increased. Professor Miliukov has computed that, taking into account the depreciation of currency, state revenue in 1724 was three times as great as that of 1680 and twice as much as that of 1701. The gain of the treasury was inevitably the loss of the taxpayers, and the poll tax worked particularly to the detriment of the mass of landlords' serfs. The inequitable basis of the poll tax is self-evident. A peasant household was taxable according to the number of its male members, so a large number of the latter, if it represented old men and children, was a liability and not an asset. A decree issued two years after Peter's death, on January 9, 1727, referred to the burden of the poll tax as one of the causes of the ruin and flight of the "poor Russian peasants." The decree of January 9, 1723, which made the entire servile population liable to the poll tax, eliminated all remaining distinctions between the serfs and other classes of bondsmen, thus bringing to its conclusion a process that was well advanced in the seventeenth century. *Krepostnoe pravo*, or serfdom, which was to last for almost 140 years, was more firmly entrenched than ever before.

CHAPTER XIV

RUSSIA BECOMES A EUROPEAN POWER

Administrative Reforms, Industry, and Trade

---❊---

EARLY ATTEMPTS AT ADMINISTRATIVE CENTRALIZATION

The administrative reforms of Peter, by-products of military exigencies, admit of concise and accurate treatment even less than does the military and diplomatic history of this period. Although the first of these reforms, that of 1699, is often represented as a step towards local self-government it was actually hardly more than an effort to enlist the services of the well-to-do burghers in collecting public revenue. It will be recalled that in the seventeenth century local administration was carried on by appointed military governors (*voevoda*) and elected officials.[1] The most important duty of the latter was the collection of taxes, the community being jointly responsible for the good behavior and efficiency of the officers it elected. Since the bulk of the indirect and some of the important direct taxes were levied in urban settlements, the government in 1679–1681 passed several measures designed to identify with the collection of revenue the social group that offered the greatest guarantee of the adequate performance of the burdensome duty—the wealthy Moscow merchants. The two outstanding features of the reforms of 1679–1681 were the further limitation of the powers of the *voevoda* in fiscal matters and the attempted concentration of revenue in central government departments, or, as Professor Miliukov put it, the differentiation of financial administration and the consolidation of receipts. The reform of 1699 followed similar lines.

The decree of January 30, 1699, partly restated and amended earlier

[1] See pp. 270–271.

legislation by providing that in view of the hardships suffered at the hands of the *voevoda* by the burghers, the latter should be permitted to elect their own officials. These officers were to be known by the Dutch name of *burgmester*, and were to administer the collection of taxes and to try civil and commercial cases. A similar privilege was extended to the peasants living on land owned by the state and by the Crown. The extension of local self-government, while optional, was also conditional, for the decree provided for the doubling of the tax assessment of the communities that chose to free themselves from the "offenses, imposts, exactions, and bribes" of their *voevoda*. This characteristic piece of legislation, which indicates what the Moscow government thought of its administrators, failed to provoke an enthusiastic response. Of the seventy cities about which information is available, eleven accepted the reform, thirty-five rejected it, while twenty-six duly elected the new officers but said nothing about the doubling of the assessments. As the price asked by the government for the curtailment of the powers of the *voevoda* was obviously excessively high, the requirement of double assessment was dropped and the election of the *burgmester* was made compulsory, with the result that the office of *voevoda* disappeared in northern Russia although it was retained in other parts of the country where military governors continued to exercise wide powers over the peasants living on the estates of private landlords, a group that was not to be found in the north. A decree of 1702 abolished the office of *gubnoi starosta*, an elective fiscal and judicial officer chosen by the local nobility, and substituted for him a board of from two to four members, also elected by the *dvoriane*. The administration of local affairs was to be carried on jointly by the *voevoda* and the elected officials whose special task was to prevent any abuse of power on the part of the former. The provincial *dvoriane*, whose ranks had been badly depleted by repeated calls to the colors, displayed complete indifference towards the right conferred upon them by the decree of 1702, and the institution it created proved stillborn. Instead of being elected, the representatives of the *dvoriane* were frequently appointed after being nominated by the very *voevoda* whose activities it was their duty to supervise. After a few years of uncertain existence the abortive attempt at establishing a minimum of public control over administrative officers died away without, it would seem, having been formally abolished.

Of greater practical importance was the Moscow Office of the

Burgmester (Burgmesterskaia palata) created by the decree of January 30, 1699. This institution, which soon received the name of *Ratusha* (from the German *Rathaus*), consisted of elected representatives of wealthy Moscow merchants and had under its jurisdiction the local *burgmester* offices. The revenue collected by these offices was forwarded to the *Ratusha*, which thus assumed the character of a ministry of finance and, under the energetic administration of Kurbatov, for a time played an important part in the financial administration. The government, continuously pressed for money, hoped to find a solution of its difficulties in the consolidation of receipts, an object which, however, was never fully achieved in spite of the transfer to the *Ratusha* of a number of revenues formerly collected by various *prikazy* (central departments). The war requirements that inspired the partial consolidation of financial administration in the hands of the *Ratusha* were responsible for the appearance of several new *prikazy* in charge of the army, navy, and military supplies. Each *prikaz* was assigned specific sources of revenue, some of them by no means inconsiderable, which were collected independently of the *Ratusha*. Even more fatal to the unification of financial administration was the inability to meet the steadily growing war expenditure. Fiscal centralization having fallen short of expectations, Peter decided to try decentralization once more. He wrote to Kurbatov, who had made heroic but futile efforts to save the fiscal system of which he was the leading spirit, that "nothing could be worse than the existing order."

DIVISION OF RUSSIA INTO PROVINCES

The division of Russia into provinces under appointed governors (*gubernator*) was the next stage of the reform from which evolved the administrative structure of provincial government that survived until the Bolshevik revolution. Although designed primarily as a method for forging a direct and permanent link between specific army units and the groups of taxpayers providing for their maintenance, the new provinces furnished the territorial framework for the organization of all governmental activities. The basic ideas of the reform were not novel. Army districts enjoying a certain degree of fiscal autonomy, that is, levying themselves the taxes necessary for the maintenance of the local military force, came into being under the pressure of military emergencies in the frontier regions of Russia in the seventeenth century and were known as *razriad*.[2] Muscovite bureaucracy was both slow and notoriously corrupt. The elimination of the costly and cumbersome *prikazy* (central departments) as the intermediate link between the tax collector and the disbursing officer appeared imperative when the vital interests of national defense were at stake. Following precedents, Peter established in the early years of his reign several army districts endowed with financial autonomy in the sense indicated above. The localization of the administrative machinery was due in every case to some pressing need. It was applied in Voronezh, which after 1695 became a center of shipbuilding, an enterprise that demanded large expenditure; in Azov, whose annexation involved Russia in a vast scheme of settlement and fortification such as the building of the port of Taganrog; in the newly acquired Ingria, Karelia, and Estonia, a territory comprising the future capital St. Petersburg, whose military commander and chief administrator, Menshikov, used officially in 1705 the title of *gubernator generalis*; in Smolensk and Kiev, which held key positions in Russia's defense in the early stages of the Northern War; in Astrakhan after the suppression of the bloody uprising of 1705. Some of the other important territories—Siberia, Ukraine, Kazan—were governed from Moscow by special *prikazy*, an arrangement that further facilitated transition to administrative decentralization.

Administrative and financial decentralization appeared to present several advantages over the system that it superseded. The new governors were to reside in their respective provinces and, being men of the tsar's own choice, they were expected to display greater efficiency than the numerous officials of the distant Moscow chanceries. Peter also felt that the concentration of funds in the hands of the governors offered a guarantee that the money would not be diverted to purposes other than that which he considered particularly important, that is, the prosecution of the war. Administrative centralization, such as that traditionally maintained in old Muscovy, moreover, had lost much of its *raison d'être*, since Peter spent in his capital merely a few days each year. As a matter of fact, by 1708, when the administrative reform was inaugurated, Russia was in the peculiar position of a country that had no real capital: Moscow was rapidly losing its control over the vast realm while St. Petersburg had not yet stepped in to take its place.

[2] See p. 271.

The reform began with the decree of December, 1707, ordering the division of the country into eight provinces.[3] Their boundaries followed, by and large, those of the territorial subdivisions already in existence, although there were important modifications dictated partly by considerations of expediency and partly, perhaps, by the maneuvers of the ambitious governors-to-be, who used their influence to expand the limits of the territories they were to rule. Peter being absent from the capital most of the time during the next two years, the reorganization of local administration made little progress. It was not until March, 1711, that all the heads of the provinces received the title of "governor" (*gubernator*) and were ordered to transfer their headquarters from Moscow to the principal city of their respective provinces.

The original structure of provincial administration, as outlined for the province of Ingermanland in 1707, that is, before the general plan of reorganization was put into operation, consisted of the governor, who was the chief executive of the province, and of appointed officials in charge of finance (*oberkommissar*), grain collection (*oberproviant*), local troops (*oberkommendant*), and administration of justice (*landrikhter*). The provinces were subdivided into districts (*uezd*), and each district was ruled, under the general supervision of the governor, by an appointed *kommendant* who, like the *voevoda* of the earlier days, was vested with military, fiscal, police, and judicial powers. The framework of the provincial government suffered important modifications in the following years. A seemingly novel principle was introduced by the decree of April 24, 1713, which provided that the governor should be merely the chairman of a board consisting of *landraty* (their number varied from eight to twelve) and that the highest authority in the province was to rest not with the governor but with this board. This institution, like the title of its members, was borrowed from the Baltic provinces, and Peter played for a while with the idea of having the *landraty* elected by the local nobility, but nothing came of it and the *landraty* were actually appointed by the newly created Senate from lists of candidates submitted by the governors. In 1715, moreover, the *landraty* were put in charge of new territorial subdivisions of the provinces, the *dolia* (literally "fraction"), with functions similar to those of the *kommendant* or

[3] The eight original provinces were those of Ingermanland (later St. Petersburg), Moscow, Kiev, Smolensk, Archangel, Kazan, Azov, and Siberia. The number of provinces was increased to nine in 1711 and to twelve in 1719.

voevoda, and in this capacity they were rather the governor's subordinates than his colleagues and advisers.

DISINTEGRATION OF CENTRAL ADMINISTRATION

The remodeling of the provincial government that took place in 1715 was closely tied up with the reform of the army that had for its object, as has already been pointed out, the direct financing of army units from the proceeds of the taxes collected by the governors independently of the Moscow *prikazy.* To achieve this purpose the army was reorganized on a territorial basis,[4] an arrangement suggested, according to Professor Miliukov, by the practice of old Muscovy, by the pressure of circumstances, and probably to some extent by the example of Sweden. Between 1708 and 1711 the governors-to-be and the Moscow officials carried out the complex task of allocating the regiments among the provinces in accordance with what was supposed to be the taxable capacity of the latter. The division of the provinces into *dolia* in 1715 was designed as a measure for the more equitable distribution of the financial burden. A *dolia* consisted, in theory, of 5,536 taxable households, and the regiments were reallocated according to the number of *dolia* comprised in each province. In practice, however, it proved impossible to create territorial subdivisions containing 5,536 households, or even approximately that number, and the figure itself was the result of computations as crude as they were fanciful. It would seem that the idea of reorganizing the army on a territorial basis received a strong impetus after Peter's "most glorious victory" at Poltava in 1709, when the tsar over-confidently expected the speedy termination of the war. Whatever might have been the advantage of local financing of army units in time of peace, it proved unworkable under wartime conditions, and the conflict with Sweden dragged on for another decade. The concentration of troops in the frontier regions or abroad made it difficult or even impossible for the regiments to obtain money and supplies from the distant localities that were supposed to provide for them. The appointment in 1711 of special commissars from the provinces to serve as liaison officers between the governors and the army units failed to remedy the situation. Hungry men who received no pay turned into bands of marauders, and the fleet was unable to put out to sea for lack of supplies. The

[4] There is no evidence that the reform provided for local recruiting; it merely introduced a different method of financing army expenditure.

confusion was aggravated by the fact that while the governors were chiefly responsible for the maintenance of the troops, the Moscow *prikazy* in charge of the army and navy were retained, and there was no clear delimitation between the functions of the local and central authorities. The resulting situation has been properly described as chaotic. Far from working the miracle expected from it, fiscal and administrative decentralization endangered the very fruits of Peter's hard-won victories.

The reform of 1708–1711 merely completed the disintegration of central government, a process that was already well advanced. The boyar duma, once a numerous assembly of the highest state officers, which had ceased to function by the end of the seventeenth century without being formally abolished, was succeeded by the tsar's "private chancery" (*blizhniaia kantseliariia*) and the "council (*konsiliia*) of ministers," institutions of uncertain complexion and indefinite jurisdiction. With the organization of the new provincial government, some of the *prikazy* were abolished, while others were deprived of their most important functions. The tsar, the very fountain of power, made but brief appearances in his capital, and in the absence of the customary direction from the center the administrative machine appeared to be on the verge of a breakdown.

THE SENATE

The reconstruction of the organs of central authority began casually with the appointment on the eve of Peter's departure for the ill fated campaign of the Pruth in 1711 of the "Governing Senate," originally a provisional institution which was to exercise supreme authority during the tsar's absence. The Senate, however, like the provinces, was fated to last until the Bolshevik revolution. It became the chief administrative organ, the highest judicial authority, and at times it also exercised something approaching legislative functions, especially in formulating and interpreting the cryptic and often obscure decrees of Peter. The supremacy of the Senate, however, was largely theoretical, even in its dealing with administrative matters. The new body not only did not impose any limitation on the absolute powers of the tsar but also occupied a subordinate position in relation to some of the higher officials enjoying the confidence of the sovereign, the so-called "supreme lords" (*verkhovnye gospoda*), who were granted the privilege of addressing the Senate "by order of His

Majesty." Of the nine senators appointed in 1711, none belonged to Peter's intimate circle. The Senate, nevertheless, played a by no means unimportant part in centralizing governmental activities, its liaison with the provincial administration being maintained through special commissars appointed by the governors. A beginning of the restoration of fiscal unification was achieved through the imposition upon the governors of the duty of submitting their budgets to the Senate, with the provision that the provincial commissars attached to the latter should be subject to corporal punishment once a week in case the provinces they represented failed in the fulfillment of their fiscal obligations. This stringent measure is explained by the basic preoccupation of Peter, which was behind most of his reforms: the Senate, according to an instruction of 1711, was primarily designed to ensure the collection of funds for the conduct of the war, "since money is the artery of war." The function of the Senate as an organ of control, especially of financial control, was emphasized by the decree of March 5, 1711, which directed the high assembly to appoint an "intelligent and good man, whatever his social standing," to fill the newly established office of *oberfiscal*. The duties of this official consisted "in supervising secretly the administration of public affairs, in collecting information concerning inequitable judicial decisions, misappropriation of public funds, and other matters." The alleged offenders, even those of the highest rank, were brought before the Senate sitting as a court, and in case of conviction the *oberfiscal* was entitled to one-half of the fines imposed. There was, however, no redress if the charges were dismissed, while the decree prescribed "cruel punishment" and confiscation of property for those victims of the *oberfiscal* who "held resentment" (*dosadovali*) against him for indictments the Senate had refused to sustain. Spying was elaborated into a comprehensive and complex system, secret agents (*fiscaly*) being appointed in every branch of the central and provincial administration. The immunity enjoyed by the *oberfiscal* and the members of his extensive staff led to gross abuses, and since the senators themselves were among the favorite targets of denunciations relations between them and the secret agents nominally under their control were anything but harmonious. A decree of March 17, 1714, defined more precisely the duties and responsibilities of the secret service and imposed some restraint on its activities by providing that if a charge was proved to be made maliciously or from selfish motives the accuser was to suffer the punishment which, in case of conviction, would have been meted out to his prospective victim.

The authority and prestige of the Senate, moreover, were attacked not only from below but, what was more important, also from above. Peter had the unfortunate habit of addressing the high assembly in most abusive and offensive terms, accusing its members, sometimes with good reason, of corruption, inefficiency, and stupidity. The procedure of the Senate and its decisions were made subject to minute and vexatious supervision. A decree of November, 1715, attached to the Senate an "inspector general" (*generalnyi revizor*), or "supervisor of decrees." Vasili Zotov, an army officer and son of Peter's lifelong companion Nikita Zotov, was appointed to the new office, whose duties comprised the speeding up of the work of the Senate and the enforcement of its decrees. Zotov, who was assigned a desk in the hall where the assembly met, maintained a register of all decisions. He bitterly criticized the laxity of the senators and complained that while the keeping of the minutes of proceedings in all governmental institutions had been made obligatory by a decree of 1714, the records of the Senate disclosed that only one case had been decided before Zotov's appointment and three more cases during the three years of his tenure of office. In 1721 officers of the guards were appointed in rotation for the term of one month to watch over the procedure of the Senate and to make sure that it followed official instructions. Alleged irregularities brought reprimands to the guilty senators, and after three warnings were ignored a report was sent to the tsar. The use of abusive language or breach of the peace—a not uncommon occurrence—made it mandatory for the guardsman on duty to lock up the offender in the fortress. It is noteworthy that in 1721 the Senate counted among its members some of the highest officers of state—Field Marshal Prince Menshikov, the Chancellor Count Golovkin, the Vice Chancellor Baron Shafirov, Admiral Count Fedor Apraksin. In the spring of 1722, with the creation of the office of the procurator-general responsible to the tsar alone, the Senate became even more stringently controlled. The procurator-general represented the person of the sovereign at the meetings of the Senate, no decree of that body was valid without his approval, and he was responsible for the enforcement of the law. The procurator-general was the chief of the Senate chancery, heading both the secret service of the *fiscaly* and the newly established body of public prosecutors. The first holder of the office, Paul Yaguzhinsky, a former orderly of Peter and successor to Menshikov in the tsar's affection, was considered by his contemporaries as the most powerful man in Russia, next to the tsar himself, and the undisputed master of the Senate.

ADMINISTRATIVE COLLEGES

The Senate obviously could not perform all the functions of the former central administration, whose disintegration had been hastened by the reform of 1708–1711. The gradual emergence of St. Petersburg from the Finnish swamps as the new capital was probably an element contributing to the reconstruction of the institutions of central government. Although the transfer of the Senate from Moscow to St. Petersburg was ordered in 1712, it was not actually effected until 1714. In the meantime the unhappy senators spent many dreary weeks negotiating the nearly impassable roads between the old capital and Peter's "paradise" to which they were frequently summoned by the tsar.

The reform of central government, unlike the other reforms of Peter, was preceded by lengthy deliberations. Central departments embodying the collegial principle had long appealed to the tsar, not only because they were held to operate successfully in Sweden and Prussia but also, perhaps, because they seemed to offer a method of getting rid of the personal rule prevalent in the Muscovite *prikazy*. The earliest known plan for remodeling Russia's central government along collegial lines appeared in a memorandum submitted to Peter at his own request by the "pious and learned Francis Lee, M.D.," during the tsar's stay in England in 1698. The idea was first tried in practice in February, 1712, when an order was issued for the formation of a "college of commerce," a measure inspired presumably by another project of foreign origin. The actual organization of the new institution, however, met with difficulties, and three years later it was still in an embryonic stage. Lack of clear understanding of the problems involved and of men possessing the necessary practical training was deemed to be among the chief obstacles. Both could be remedied, in Peter's opinion, by learning from western Europe. In 1715 he enrolled in the Russian service Heinrich Fick, a former Holstein civil servant and a proponent of the collegial form of government. Fick was sent to Sweden, with which Russia was still at war, and spent there a year making an extensive first-hand study of the Swedish administration, reputed to be one of the best in Europe. In 1717 Peter added to his retinue of foreign advisers Baron Luberas, a native of Silesia and another authority on collegial government. The two learned and industrious Germans produced a mass of documents, reports, and memoranda bearing on the proposed Russian institutions, which were to follow closely the Swedish model. Luberas, who went on a recruiting mission to various German states and to Bohemia, brought with him to Russia 148 foreign "experts" to be employed in the future colleges. This number being deemed insufficient, the ranks of the new administrative services were filled with Baltic Germans from the newly acquired provinces and with Swedish prisoners of war.[5] The formation of nine colleges was announced in December, 1717, and their presidents were duly appointed, but another two or three years passed before the new institutions began to function. The nine colleges were as follows: foreign relations; state revenue (*kammer kollegiia*); justice; state control (*revizion kollegiia*); army; admiralty; commerce; extractive industry and manufactures (*berg i manufaktur kollegiia*); and state expenditure (*shtats-kontora*). The colleges, whose number was somewhat altered by subsequent legislation, introduced certain important modifications in the administrative practice of old Muscovy. The new central departments exercised their respective powers over the entire territory of the country, while the former *prikazy* were often organized on a territorial basis, that is, they fulfilled all governmental functions within specific geographical areas. Each college was governed, in theory, by a board of eleven members comprising a president, a vice president, and a foreign adviser. The decisions were to be reached by a majority vote. The first presidents of the colleges were named from among the highest Russian officials and were assisted by foreign vice presidents. The colleges, which were originally independent from the Senate, were subordinated to that body in July, 1721. After this reform their presidents, who were also members of the Senate, found themselves in a highly anomalous position: in their capacity of senator they were their own superiors as heads of colleges—one of those paradoxes produced by bureaucratic ingenuity which Gilbert and Sullivan put to such excellent use. With his customary frankness Peter admitted that the awkward situation was due to a lack of foresight, and in Janu-

---

[5] Not all prisoners of war, however, were so fortunate. In 1706 the patriarch of Jerusalem wrote to Peter urging him to prohibit the then prevalent practice of selling Swedish prisoners into slavery to the Turks.

ary, 1722, he appointed new college presidents who were not members of the Senate and occupied in the bureaucratic hierarchy a more modest standing than did their predecessors. However, the presidents of three colleges—those of foreign relations, army, and admiralty—were retained and continued to hold their senatorial seats much to the detriment of the symmetry of the administrative structure.

LOCAL GOVERNMENT

Peter's erudite and doctrinaire German counselors were not satisfied with the mere duplication of Swedish administrative colleges which in Sweden formed an integral part of what appeared to them to be a harmonious governmental system. Fick's enthusiastic advocacy of the adoption by Russia of the institutions of Swedish local government on which he and his colleagues had assembled voluminous documentation was all the more eagerly listened to since the provincial reform of 1708–1711 was anything but successful. In his unfaltering belief in the miracle-working power of governmental fiat, the tsar paid but scant attention to the fundamental differences between Russia and Sweden. He failed to realize that the administrative machinery gradually evolved by a small and relatively wealthy country such as Sweden, with her closely knit and firmly established social organization resting on the keen sense of solidarity and responsibility of every group of her population, could not be duplicated on the immense expanses of his sparsely populated empire, which possessed neither the financial resources nor the political tradition and sturdy social virtues of its northern neighbors. Peter naively imagined that the administrative system built up in Sweden by the patient efforts of generations could be erected from the ruins of Muscovite bureaucracy by merely translating, or mistranslating, Swedish statutes and regulations and making them compulsory by decrees enforced by the police and the knout.

After a brief discussion in which Fick played a leading part, the Senate issued a decree (November 26, 1718) providing for the introduction of local government based on the Swedish model, which, however, was to be adapted to Russian conditions by introducing various simplifications that sacrificed some of the essentials of the Swedish system.[6] The new administrative regime, which was to be

[6] For a useful summary of the chief differences between the Swedish and the Russian systems, cf. Paul Miliukov and others, *Histoire de Russie*, I, 378–387.

put into operation in 1720, retained the division of Russia into provinces (*guberniia*) but increased the number to twelve. Within the provinces there were formed new territorial-administrative subdivisions: the counties (*provintsiia*), which replaced the *dolia* of 1715, with each county embracing several districts (*distrikt* or *uezd*). The powers of the provincial governor were limited to military and judicial matters, and the newly created counties were designed to become the basic units of local administration. A county was headed by a *voevoda* (a title of rather unsavory association and only recently abolished) assisted by several officials whose functions and even titles bore a close resemblance to those of the corresponding Swedish officials. A district was administered by a land commissar (*zemskii kommissar*) who had a variety of duties but was primarily the tax collector. The Russian reform, however, omitted altogether the lower and basic unit of the Swedish administrative structure: the parish (*socken, kirchspiel*). Commenting on this all-important feature of the project submitted by Fick, the Senate, in its decision of November 7, 1718, made the melancholy observation that "not only has the parish no place in Russian administrative practice" but also that "there are no intelligent men among the peasants" to fill public offices. Peasants living on state land therefore retained their ancient primitive form of self-government under the close supervision of police officials, while peasants living on the estates of private landlords remained, as in the past, at the mercy of their masters.

The reform of 1718, a characteristic attempt to superimpose upon native institutions those of foreign origin, led to much confusion aggravated by the new territorial distribution of the army, which became fully effective with the termination of the Northern War and the moving of the troops to their newly assigned quarters in rural districts. It will be remembered that the cost of the military establishment was to be defrayed from the proceeds of the poll tax levied locally, that is, the taxpayers were to provide for the maintenance of the troops quartered in their midst. This arrangement led to the formation of a new territorial-administrative unit, the regimental district (*polkovoi distrikt*), which cut across all other administrative subdivisions. The collection of the poll tax was removed from the jurisdiction of fiscal officials and was entrusted to special commissars elected by the local nobility and working in close cooperation with the military (1723). The latter, moreover, received broad police powers and displayed but the slightest respect for the civil administration. According to Kliuchevsky, the resulting situation actually amounted to an invasion of the countryside by the soldiery, a situation unparalleled in Russia's annals since the early days of the Mongol rule. This vicious system was fundamentally altered shortly after Peter's death. An unusually eloquent decree of January 9, 1727, unfolded a distressing picture of the ravages that had been wrought, and subsequent legislation subordinated the commissars to the *voevoda* and prohibited army officers from participating in the collection of the poll tax. Although these measures failed to eliminate the interference of the military with fiscal matters, the rural population derived no small relief from the transfer of the troops to new quarters in the cities and towns.

FATE OF THE ADMINISTRATIVE REFORM

Other administrative reforms suffered a like fate. An attempt to establish provincial and local courts based on the Swedish model and independent from administrative officers was made in 1719 but was given up three years later. The new cumbersome, costly, and inefficient bureaucracy provoked bitter complaints. A German official of the college of state revenue, Kochius, author of a report which was an indictment of the reform, wrote in 1723 that "where there was formerly one official to lord it over the peasants now there are ten . . . and some of them are no shepherds, but rather wolves who prey on the flock." Peter's successors shared this view. In 1726 and 1727 the provincial office-holders with high-sounding German and Swedish titles were one after another eliminated as superfluous. The instruction (*nakaz*) of September 12, 1728, a document imbued with a spirit of rigid conservatism, summed up previous legislation and remained for almost fifty years the charter of local government. Under its provisions the governor of the province, the *voevoda* of the county, and the *voevoda* of the cities and towns were clothed with plenary administrative and judicial powers within their respective jurisdictions. The administration of the cities was made subject to the close supervision of that of the county, and the latter to the provincial governor. The instruction of 1728, therefore, while retaining the general framework of the territorial-administrative structure of local government introduced by Peter, marked a return to the administrative practice of the seventeenth century.

A somewhat similar process is discernible in the sphere of central government. The college of manufactures was abolished in 1727 on the ground that its members were merely drawing salaries but did no useful work. Even earlier, in 1726, the membership of the boards of colleges was cut down by half because, according to the Senate, the larger membership rendered the reaching of decisions more difficult. Since the presidents of the colleges had far greater influence than did the members of their respective boards, the deliberations of these assemblies mattered little in practice and the collegial element remained a dead letter: the personal rule of the presidents was in no way different from that of their predecessors, the heads of the *prikazy* in old Muscovy.

MUNICIPAL GOVERNMENT

The administrative reforms of Peter ended as they began, with an attempt at the reorganization of municipal institutions, although, strictly speaking, the *Ratusha* and *burgmesters* of 1699 were fiscal agencies and had little to do with local self-government. The backwardness and poverty of Russian urban settlements, the majority of which differed but slightly from villages, did not escape the attention of Peter's advisers, and the projects of Fick, who was something of a perfectionist, contained far-reaching plans for the remodeling of the social and administrative structure of Russian urban communities to conform with that of the Swedish and German cities. In 1718 the tsar issued a laconic decree ordering the introduction of municipal institutions patterned after those of Riga and Reval, the two ancient Germanic trading centers of the newly conquered Baltic provinces. By virtue of a decree of February, 1720, the first model *magistrat* (city council) was set up in St. Petersburg; a year later it was reorganized as an organ of central government under the name of *glavnyi* (chief) *magistrat*. Embodying in its structure the familiar collegial principle and subordinated directly to the Senate, the *glavnyi magistrat*, which was intended to play the part of a ministry of municipal affairs, was vested with broad judicial and administrative powers and was directed to proceed at once with the reorganization of municipal government. The charter of municipal institutions, which in spite of Peter's repeated threats of drastic punishments for delay was not enacted until the end of 1724, divided the urban population into three groups: (1) wealthy merchants, doctors, druggists, jewelers, captains of merchant ships, and painters, who constituted the "first guild"; (2) small merchants, traders and artisans, who formed the "second guild"; (3) the balance of the urban population, wage-earners and laborers, who were described as the "common people" (*podlye liudi*). The conduct of city affairs was in the hands of a *magistrat* (municipal council) consisting of a president and several members. These officials were elected by the two "guilds," but only those belonging to the "first guild," that is, a small minority, were eligible for office. The "common people," who according to Professor Kizevetter constituted in the middle of the eighteenth century from 50 to 90 per cent of the urban population, were not entitled to vote. The law of 1724 explained the reasons for the limited nature of municipal franchise. City officials continued to be responsible, as in the past, for the collection of taxes and the performance of other obligations imposed by the state; and although the principle of joint responsibility of the community for its elected officers was retained it was deemed expedient to restrict the choice of officeholders to the well-to-do class. The functions of the municipal councils, however, were not limited to tax collection, but extended to administrative, police, and judicial matters. It was their duty to provide for the advancement of local trade and industry, the promotion of social welfare, and the minute regulation of the life of the citizens, but in practice these activities amounted to very little. A novel feature of the municipal setup was the election of officials for an indefinite term, thus conferring upon them a *de facto* permanency of tenure. This arrangement, coupled with the wealth of the social group that had the monopoly of municipal offices, put the municipal government under the control of a small oligarchy of wealthy merchants, and it was with full justification that the legislation of 1724 described the members of a *magistrat* as the "chiefs of the city." [7]

The reform of 1724 made an unsuccessful attempt to organize the urban population on a corporate basis. Each of the two guilds and the common people had their elected elders, who, however, played a subordinate part in the conduct of public affairs. The endeavor to create professional associations (*tsekh*, from the German *Zeche*) of artisans along the lines of western European corporations or guilds (in the usual meaning of the term) met with little success. The nearest

---

[7] The Russian term *nachalnik* used in the instruction of 1724 means literally "superior," or "chief," and connotes the idea of an officer of the Crown whose orders it is wise to obey.

approach to self-government was the town meeting (*possadskii mirskoi skhod*) consisting of all male taxpayers. Although in law this assembly had the authority to levy rates, administer social welfare, and elect lower police and other officials, the municipal councils and the *voevoda* for the most part prevented the exercise of these powers. The chief activity of the town meetings was the drafting of innumerable petitions describing the plight of the burghers, eloquent and moving documents that found their resting place in the files of local chanceries. Any vestige of self-government was repugnant to the Muscovite bureaucratic tradition firmly entrenched behind the imposing façade of the Petrine reforms. The municipal councils themselves, although a mere travesty of municipal government, were soon judged to be too independent. Two years after Peter's death, in February, 1727, they were made subject to the control of the local governor and *voevoda*, and six months later the *glavnyi magistrat* (ministry of municipal affairs) was abolished, thus completing the integration of municipal institutions in the bureaucratic structure of local administration.

THE REFORM AND ADMINISTRATIVE PRACTICE

The above outline of Peter's administrative reforms is necessarily somewhat confused and lacking in sharpness. Confusion, however, was an essential feature of the reform, and the intentional or unintentional elimination of this factor would tend to distort the picture and produce a misleading impression. An appraisal of the reform as a whole discloses that while it failed to establish a well balanced governmental system, it nevertheless marked some progress over the conditions prevailing in the seventeenth century. By the end of Peter's reign the structure of central government headed by the Senate had achieved a certain coherence. The jurisdiction of the colleges, unlike that of the old *prikazy*, was comprehensive and delimited according to the functions performed. There was a greater uniformity in the territorial structure of local government and less overlapping in the activities of central and provincial authorities. The coordination of the various parts of the governmental machine, however, was not consistently carried through. As has already been pointed out, not all the colleges were subordinated to the Senate, and many remnants of the former bureaucratic agencies which survived were but loosely integrated with the new institutions.

It would be an error, moreover, to attach much importance to the remodeling of the administrative framework. The wishes of the tsar's favorites were often far more potent factors in determining policies than were the decrees of the Senate. The "supreme lords" (*verkhovniki*)—Menshikov, Apraksin, Golovkin, Yaguzhinsky—were for all practical purposes above the law. As the years passed Peter leaned more and more heavily on the regiments of the guards as an administrative agency. Officers and sometimes non-commissioned officers and even privates of the guards were entrusted, in increasing numbers, with responsible tasks in the sphere of both domestic and foreign policy. It will be recalled that in 1721 officers of the guards were appointed to watch over the proceedings of the Senate. Other guardsmen acted as members of special courts in particularly important cases, superseded governors and ambassadors, and, in their capacity as personal representatives of the tsar, enjoyed at times unlimited powers.

The extra-legal activities of Peter's special emissaries had some justification in the appallingly low standards of personal behavior and honesty prevailing in governmental circles. Unfortunately, the cure was often worse than the disease: the arbitrary rule of irresponsible and ambitious army officers was not of a nature to increase the practically non-existent respect for law, and it introduced a new and by no means negligible source of confusion in the working of the administrative machine. Relations between the various institutions and the holders of high offices created by Peter were only too often lacking in harmony. Contemporary records are full of bitter mutual denunciations and recriminations coming from the Senate, the colleges, governors, the procurator-general, and the *oberfiscal*. Inefficiency and inability to adhere to orderly rules of procedure already noted in the Senate continued to remain outstanding features of the operation of administrative institutions. Towards the very end of Peter's reign, in January, 1724, a decree recapitulating the provisions of earlier legislation prescribed an elaborate scale of punishments, from fines to confiscation of property and "political death," for officials who in the performance of their duties used abusive language or were guilty of disorderly conduct. The decree specifically mentioned the Senate, the Holy Synod, the colleges, and the law courts. Vulgar brawls were common occurrences, with senators and princes rolling on the floor in a free-for-all fight. Fines and more rigorous punishments were liberally meted out to the highest functionaries without success in improving the situation. In 1715 two senators were punished by having their tongues branded, while Korsakov, vice governor of St. Petersburg and Menshikov's close associate, was publicly flogged. In 1719 at least five senators were fined for being subject to improper influences. The indiscriminate use of the torture chamber and the knout as a consequence of charges unsupported by adequate evidence led to the publication in 1722 of a curious official ruling which provided that tortures and corporal punishment, if followed by exoneration, should not be considered a reflection on the victim's honor.

Spoliation and corruption, firmly rooted in Muscovite administrative tradition, continued to flourish under Peter's regime. The tsar, although apparently resigned to the practice of the officials in accepting bribes as a customary addition to their meager salaries, at times took unsparing measures against the functionaries guilty of misappropriation of government funds. The reports of the zealous Kurbatov and of Alexis Nesterov, who as *oberfiscal* had the duty of supervising the conduct of officials and protecting the interests of the treasury, are filled with charges of illegal practices perpetrated by the highest functionaries. Both Kurbatov and Nesterov, however, were themselves not beyond reproach: the former, as already noted, died under indictment for embezzlement, while the latter, convicted of a similar crime, was executed. Prince Mathew Gagarin, governor of Siberia and a notorious grafter, ended his days on the gallows, and Peter Shafirov, a man of humble Jewish extraction, after becoming a baron, vice chancellor, and senator received a death sentence. This at the last moment was commuted to exile, from which, however, he was recalled in the reign of Empress Anne to resume his seat in the Senate.[8]

Stern and ruthless as at times was Peter's justice, it did not strike at some of the most notable lawbreakers, spoliators, and grafters. None enjoyed greater immunity than Prince Menshikov, whose misdeeds were innumerable, flagrant, and freely acknowledged. But there were moments when even his lucky star went under a cloud. He received

[8] The career of Shafirov is all the more noteworthy since Peter, for all his liking of foreigners, was violently anti-Semitic. "I would much rather have Mohammedans or heathens than Jews," the tsar declared according to Solovev. "The Jews are scoundrels and rascals. . . . They will find in Russia neither homes nor trade, however hard they try to bribe those around me." Menshikov, who was largely instrumental in bringing about the downfall of Shafirov, shared his master's attitude towards the Jews. Two years after Peter's death, in 1727, he issued an order that "no Jews shall be admitted to Russia for any reason."

from Peter repeated warnings, was chastised by the tsar's own hand, and was ordered in 1717–1718 to pay huge fines that ran into hundreds of thousands of rubles. Yet his official position remained unimpaired, although his immediate collaborators were publicly flogged and sent into exile. The real source of Menshikov's strength would seem to have been the unfaltering support of Empress Catherine, his former mistress, and also that intimate link which united the once very handsome guardsman and his imperial master, a link to which some historians have given a sinister interpretation. Menshikov, moreover, was not the only one to enjoy quasi-immunity. Yaguzhinsky's well known remark to the tsar, quoted by Solovev, "We all steal, the sole difference is that some do it on a bigger scale and in a more conspicuous manner than others," was the candid admission of a fact of general knowledge. The cynicism of the procurator-general of the Senate, the highest judicial officer, is said to have greatly amused Peter. The tsar's seemingly boundless leniency towards his favorites, whom he placed and maintained at the top of the official hierarchy, a leniency amounting to connivance, was of course an open secret and could not but weaken the deterrent effects of the punishments so lavishly distributed to other officials.

PROMOTION OF INDUSTRY

The measures taken by Peter for the promotion of industry and trade constitute probably the least revolutionary although by no means the least disputed of his reforms. The creation of a huge modernized army equipped according to the standards of western Europe, the building of the navy, and far-reaching changes in the practices of the court and of the upper classes brought forth a new demand which the primitive industries of old Muscovy were unable to meet. The urgent nature of this demand, especially for military and naval supplies, coupled with the difficulties of importing the needed articles because of the unsatisfactory state of international communications and the perennial shortage of funds from which the Russian treasury was suffering, suggested the fostering of domestic industries and the establishment of new ones with the assistance of craftsmen imported from abroad. Similar policies, it will be recalled, had not been uncommon in seventeenth century Russia and even earlier.[9] Considerations of expediency were blended with arguments supplied by the mercantilist

[9] See pp. 295–296.

doctrine, which was then the accepted economic creed in Europe, a doctrine that had made converts in Russia in the reign of Tsar Alexis. The influence of mercantilist ideas, as Professor Pokrovsky rightly observes, might be traced in the "New Statute of Commerce" (*Novotorgovyi Ustav*) of 1667. The peasant author Pososhkov, a contemporary of Peter, was a militant advocate of mercantilism in its crudest form. In the reports submitted to him by two of his influential advisers, Fedor Saltykov in 1714 and Baron Luberas some three years later, the tsar was urged to embrace mercantilist policies. Moreover, Peter had ample opportunities to familiarize himself with current trends of European economic thought and legislation during his frequent stays abroad, especially on his visit to France, that stronghold of Colbertism, in 1716–1717. It is in the economic measures of the closing years of his reign that the influence of mercantilist doctrines is particularly noticeable.

In the course of the seventeenth century, Muscovite extractive and metallurgical industries had made some progress, and there were also a few manufactures producing woolens, paper, glass, and a restricted number of other articles. Foreign craftsmen were usually closely associated with industrial enterprises, the larger of which were owned by the Crown or by the state, although there were instances of manufacturing establishments owned privately and protected by special concessions and privileges. The early policies of Peter followed the traditional methods of his predecessors. It will be recalled that during his first voyage abroad he engaged for the Russian service a large number of skilled foreign craftsmen. He continued this practice in later years and also sent young Russians abroad to be trained in the various trades. Extensive explorations of Russia's national resources resulted in the discovery of important deposits of ores and other industrial minerals, and with the outbreak of the Swedish war there came into existence a great many foundries and armament works as well as enterprises manufacturing articles of military equipment, such as army cloth and canvas for sails. Most of such enterprises were organized by the government but were eventually transferred to private companies, which were also usually established for the manufacturing of articles of general consumption. Since the Russians displayed a reluctance to embark on industrial ventures, the government offered the manufacturers the inducement of generous subsidies; exemption from taxation; freedom from government service for the owners, their children, and skilled workers; free importation of machinery and raw materials; free supply of labor; high tariff protection or outright exclusion of competing foreign articles; and, in some cases, a monopoly of the domestic market.

The bounties conferred upon the manufacturers carried with them heavy obligations towards the state, which exercised far-reaching supervision over the enterprises. A decree of 1712 ordering the transfer of government-owned linen works to the merchant Andrew Turka and associates provided that the new owners should be rewarded by the Crown for good management and the resulting increase in revenue; if, however, inefficient management led to a decline in revenue Turka and his associates were liable to fines of one thousand rubles each. In a number of instances slow-moving Russian manufacturers-to-be were summarily ordered by the government to organize companies for the promotion of various branches of industry. The statute (*reglament*) of the college of manufactures issued in 1723 directed that "the state-owned factories already in operation or to be established be transferred to private individuals," thus generalizing a policy followed during the preceding years. A company headed by Baron Shafirov, Count Tolstoy, and Count Apraksin received in 1717 the monopolistic right to manufacture silks, brocades, and velvets, while the importation of these commodities was prohibited. In 1718 the prohibition was extended to the import of hosiery and certain types of woolens (kersey). The tariff of 1724 introduced high customs duties ranging from 50 per cent to 75 per cent ad valorem on napkins, tablecloths, linen, sailcloth, silks, needles, iron. Paper, leather goods, hosiery, and certain varieties of woolens paid the relatively moderate duty of 25 per cent ad valorem.

These measures were designed to promote the establishment of large industrial enterprises by removing the obstacles which had prevented their development in the past. Under Peter's predecessors the progress of industries employing primitive technical methods and manufacturing crude and cheap articles (for instance, nails and other inexpensive iron goods) was effectively checked by the competition of small artisans (cottage industry). The successful operation of large industrial establishments producing higher-grade merchandise, such as fine cloth, silks, and brocades, was hindered by lack of technical knowledge and skilled labor, by the competition of cheaper and better goods imported from abroad and admitted on the payment of a moderate duty, and also, it would seem (although this is a much disputed point), by lack of capital. It was expected that these difficulties would be overcome by the policies outlined above. Peter's ultimate object, inspired by the mercantilist doctrines, was to make Russia independent of the import of manufactured articles from abroad. A decree of 1712 providing for the establishment of mills and manufacturing army cloth expressed the hope that five years later it would be no longer necessary to purchase "beyond the seas" material for uniforms.

The majority of Russia's new manufacturers were drawn, as Professor Tugan-Baranovsky has made clear, from among the merchants. Foreigners in Russia were relatively few, and the size of the enterprises they owned was, with one or two exceptions, smaller than that of the industrial establishments belonging to Russian entrepreneurs. The *dvoriane*, too, had a minor part in industrial activities. Menshikov and Shafirov were identified with several industrial ventures which, however, were not uniformly successful. The factory manufacturing silk, brocades, and velvets organized by Shafirov, Tolstoy, and Apraksin soon found itself in difficulties, in spite of its monopolistic position. In 1721 eight merchants were admitted to the partnership, and in 1724 they took over the enterprise after repaying the founders the capital they had invested. The preponderance of merchants among the early Russian industrialists has led Tugan-Baranovsky to the conclusion, warmly defended by his numerous followers (Pokrovsky, Liashchenko, and other Russian Marxists), that by the end of the seventeenth century Russia had reached a stage of "commercial capitalism" and that the accumulation of capital in the hands of the merchant class had provided the necessary economic basis for the industrial policies of Peter. According to this school of thought, government subsidies played a minor part in the promotion of industry, which was financed primarily by commercial capital. Other students have pointed out that while the number of merchants in seventeenth century Muscovy was considerable, their operations were usually conducted on a humble scale and that available information strongly suggests not an excessive accumulation but a perennial shortage of commercial capital. "The majority of the shares subscribed by the partners in industrial enterprises," writes Lappo-Danilvesky in his authoritative discussion of the situation in the first quarter of the eighteenth century, "were not large even when converted into rubles of present value. Moreover, the number of such capitalists was relatively small and they felt a pressing need for government subsidies." Kulisher, who shares this view, emphasizes the fact, supported by a mass of contemporary evidence, that a shortage of capital was one of the great difficulties hindering Russia's economic development throughout the eighteenth century. It was the accepted rule of the college of manufacture to make loans to the promoters of industrial enterprises, and with the sanction of the Senate such loans might be interest-free for a specified number of years.

INDUSTRIAL LABOR

Many of the industrial enterprises established in the reign of Peter were quite large. The Moscow mills manufacturing sailcloth employed 1,162 workers, the Shchegolin textile mill 730, the Mikliaev textile mill 742, the Sestroretsk ironworks 683. Some 25,000 serfs were "attached" to the nine smelting works and ironworks in Prem, and 508 peasant households to the armament works in Tula, for early Russian industry depended almost exclusively on servile labor. The imposing number of workers employed did not, however, indicate a concentration of the productive processes and the establishment of factories in the modern meaning of the term. The work was usually carried on in a number of small buildings or sheds and not infrequently in the workers' own cottages. In 1712 Peter ordered the building of large shops in the ancient Tula armament works "in order to improve supervision and to speed up production." In 1718 the new shops were ready, but the concentration of production failed to materialize and in 1733 several of the workshops were ordered to be pulled down since the manufacturing of arms continued, as in the past, to be handled by the traditional method of cottage industry. Under these conditions technical progress was practically nil.

The problem of industrial labor presented seemingly insurmountable obstacles to the development of new industries. The Code of 1649 [10] had herded the entire population into closely segregated social groups, each assigned its definite duties, watertight compartments from which there was no legal escape except by the sovereign's pleasure. Although this scheme was never fully enforced, it hampered the growth of a class of free industrial labor, a development for which the Code of 1649 made no provision. The labor force for the new in-

[10] See pp. 277 *et seq.*

dustrial enterprises could be supplied from two sources: the undeterminable but undoubtedly large group of human derelicts who had
somehow evaded the restrictions of Muscovite legislation and were
making a precarious living on the fringes of organized society, and
that never failing reservoir of man power, the servile population.
Peter made liberal use of both. Beggars, prostitutes, and criminals
were rounded up and sent to factories and workshops. Illegitimate
children brought up in orphanages shared a similar fate. The owner
of the needle factory, Tomilin, was officially directed in 1717 to recruit
his workers among "the youths who beg in the streets." A decree of
1721 laid down the rule that women "who were to be punished for
their faults" should be sent to factories either for a term of years
or for life. In his zeal for the promotion of Russia's economic development Peter even violated the sacred right of the landlords to recover
their runaway serfs: the decree of July 18, 1722, prohibited the return
of fugitives that had found employment in industrial enterprises. The
provisions of this decree, however, were not a move in the direction
of personal freedom, since the runaway serfs merely exchanged one
master for another. Whatever doubt might have existed as to the
position of "free" labor was removed by a decree, issued in 1736,
during the reign of Empress Anne, ordering the attachment to the
factory "for all time to come" of those workers (and their families)
who had learned their trade in the establishment, a measure promoted
by the fierce competition for skilled labor among the manufacturers.
The stubborn protest of the enslaved workers, although it led to several
bloody rebellions and brought upon them punitive expeditions, failed
to improve their position. It has been often and rightly said that the
industrial enterprises created by Peter were not very different from
penal institutions.

The chief sources of industrial labor, however, were not the human
dregs netted by the Muscovite police, but the servile population.
It was customary to endow new factories not only with capital,
land, buildings, and machines, but also with workers. The decree
of January 18, 1721, infringed another prerogative of the *dvoriane*
by granting the "merchants" who owned industrial enterprises the
right of purchasing serfs on two conditions: (1) that the servile
population and the enterprise were to be considered as an entity
and (2) that they were not to be disposed of separately. The serfs
were thus attached to the industrial establishment in which they

were to work, and the rights of the owners were subject to important limitations. The "possessionary" (*possessionnyia*) works, as enterprises of this kind came to be officially known, were under the meticulous supervision of the government, which regulated the volume and quality of production, the conditions of employment, and the remuneration of labor. This control was much resented by the owners and proved a real obstacle to the introduction of better methods of production while not improving the lot of the working people. Possessionary works thus created a new and particularly harsh form of serfdom which survived until the emancipation of 1861, having long outlived whatever justification or usefulness it might have had in the early eighteenth century. The exploitation of servile labor by the owners of possessionary establishments and the futile struggle of the workers against their masters present one of the most tragic and pathetic pages in the entire unhappy tale of Russian serfdom. From the point of view of labor, the industrialization of Russia by Peter was, indeed, purchased at an exorbitant price.

FAILURE OF INDUSTRIAL POLICIES

The result of the great and costly effort for the promotion of industry was not altogether satisfactory. The number of large industrial enterprises operating at the end of the reign of Peter is estimated at about two hundred. Stimulated by army orders, the smelting and iron industries did uncommonly well, especially in the Ural region, and Russia's output of cast iron ranked among the largest in Europe. Incidentally, one of the country's greatest industrial fortunes, that of the Demidov family, had its origin in the iron and armament works of that period. The textile, leather, paper, glass, tobacco, and sugar industries all made some progress, and there were establishments manufacturing hats, hosiery, and other articles. Peter maintained with his customary exuberance that Russian unbleached cloth was "almost equal to that of Holland," and there is evidence that some foreign observers had a high opinion of Russian textiles. Yet the fate of the textile mills does not support this optimistic view. Although operating on a modest scale, several of them failed to find a market for their goods and were forced to cut down production. In 1727 Russian merchants complained that the quality of Russian goods was deplorably low, while they cost twice as much as similar articles imported from abroad. Among the commodities mentioned in this connection

were needles, hosiery, woolens, linen, silks, and brocades. The good
faith of the complainants may be suspected since the merchants were
agitating for downward revision of the tariff of 1724.[11] In 1740, however, the government itself admitted in a decree that army cloth of
Russian manufacture was of "very inferior quality and had no resistance to wear." The army, therefore, had reason to look back with
regret to the days when its uniforms were made of imported cloth.
Moreover, it was discovered in 1730, according to Miliukov, that a
number of industrial establishments existed merely on paper; in 1744
forty-four enterprises were closed by order of the government because
of inefficiency and because of the low quality of their produce, while
quite a number had themselves suspended operations which had
proved unprofitable.

That lack of coordination and disregard for Russian conditions
which has been noted in other fields of Peter's tireless activity manifested itself in his economic policies. A decree of 1715, for instance,
directed that in the future unbleached cloth should be of greater
width than had been usual in Russia, a measure which had for its
object the substitution of the domestic product for the wider imported cloth. The carrying out of this order would have required the
reequipment of a large number of artisans with new looms, and was
impracticable since there was no room for the bigger looms in the
small, crowded peasant cottages. It is held that the attempts to enforce the decree of 1715 worked serious hardships on the weavers and
greatly harmed an important and well established branch of cottage
(or domestic) industry essential to the successful operation of the
large textile enterprises.

New industries required raw materials, and the government enacted
numerous measures designed to promote, by a characteristic combination of mercantilist arguments and threats of severe punishments, the
development of mineral resources and the cultivation of hemp, flax,
jute, sugar beets, tobacco, and grapes which were used for making
vinegar. Much attention was paid to horse and sheep breeding, since
both horses and wool were essential for the army. Timber being

---

[11] The tariff was actually revised in 1731, when the duties were scaled down to
the uniform level of 20 per cent ad valorem on articles competing with those
produced in Russia and considered particularly important, and to 10 per cent
on all others. One of the reasons for the abandonment of Peter's aggressive pro-
tectionism was the extraordinary development of contraband, with its inevitable
adverse effect upon customs receipts.

needed for the fleet, Peter issued detailed orders for the protection of forests, including minute regulations which specified the size of coffins and the type of wood from which they were to be made. There is no evidence that these all-embracing bureaucratic schemes wrought any real change in the condition of agriculture and rural industries, but the record discloses that some of them, for instance, the fanciful attempt at fostering silkworm breeding, collapsed miserably.

DOMESTIC AND FOREIGN TRADE

The commercial policies of Peter were largely influenced by mercantilist doctrines and by his determination to transfer the headquarters of Russia's foreign trade from Archangel to St. Petersburg. The provisions of the Code of 1649, which attempted to make domestic commerce the exclusive privilege of the burghers (*possadskie liudi*), were never fully enforced and the bulk of domestic trade continued to be carried on by traders or other social groups, especially by the peasants, who used various subterfuges to get around the law. The stringent rules laid down by the Code of 1649 were eased in 1699 and 1700, and in 1711 was issued the comprehensive order permitting "people of all social groups (except men serving with the colors) to engage freely in commerce anywhere" provided they paid the taxes to which all merchants were liable. According to Kulisher, this measure was inspired by fiscal motives since in the past evasion of taxation by traders not belonging to the merchant class had been made possible by nominal and illicit partnership or other arrangements with the members of the latter group. Further opportunities for private initiative in the field of domestic commerce were provided by the abolition, about 1719, of state trading monopolies on which Peter had leaned so heavily in the earlier years of his reign.[12] In conflict with the policy of allowing domestic commerce greater freedom was the official encouragement of private trading companies which were granted monopolistic privileges. A company organized by Menshikov and Shafirov received the exclusive right to sell the produce of the northern fisheries, and although it was discontinued in 1721 the principle of private monopolistic trading was retained and was extensively used in the first half of the eighteenth century, especially under Empress Elizabeth.

Mercantilism found its fullest expression in the approach to problems of foreign trade. Peter inherited from his predecessors a discrimi-

[12] See p. 360.

natory system of customs charges under which the amount of the duty to be levied was determined, not by the nature of the imported article, but by the nationality of the importer. Goods consigned to foreigners were subject to much heavier imposts than were those consigned to native merchants. This method, which was retained by Peter until 1724, led foreign importers either to assume fictitious Russian nationality or to use the services of Russian agents who posed as independent importers but were actually representatives of foreign firms. In 1724, as has already been pointed out, Peter introduced a stiff protective tariff with the result that the former legitimate trade was diverted into contraband channels, much to the advantage of smugglers and police and customs officials but at a considerable loss to the treasury. Other measures for the promotion of foreign trade included the establishment of Russian commercial delegations in a number of European commercial centers and in China, but their efforts brought little practical result. The tsar's ardent desire to make Russia into a country exporting manufactured goods in Russian bottoms was never realized, and until the fall of the empire some two hundred years later she continued to export chiefly agricultural produce, raw materials, and semi-manufactured goods. The great trading companies of the Hanseatic cities, England, the Netherlands, and France, which Peter wished to emulate, had no counterpart in Russia, and her foreign commerce remained largely in foreign hands. Technical backwardness, lack of capital, absence of credit and banking facilities, and the inborn aversion of an essentially continental people to the sea defeated all governmental efforts for the promotion of a merchant marine. Discriminatory taxation of goods imported or exported in foreign bottoms, practiced by Peter and his successors in the eighteenth century, merely brought about more evasion of the law, and this was facilitated by the provision that vessels carrying a definite proportion of Russian seamen were considered as being under the Russian flag. The land-bound nation, and especially its trading classes, never understood or shared its first emperor's enthusiasm for the sea.

ARCHANGEL AND THE BALTIC PORTS

Peter was far more successful in diverting foreign trade to the ports of the Baltic Sea, especially to St. Petersburg. The economic progress of the new capital, however, was hindered by the deplorable state of the roads and by the high cost of transportation, a result of its remoteness from the old Russian trading centers. Archangel on the White Sea was St. Petersburg's chief competitor partly because it was accessible by the cheap water route of the Dvina, while lower freight charges gave the older port a distinct advantage over its recent rival. Moreover, merchants, both Russian and foreign, displayed extreme reluctance to exchange the familiar trading ground of Archangel for the discomforts and uncertainties of St. Petersburg, where the cost of living was very high. Peter, who had always been keenly interested in water transportation, planned to remedy the disadvantages of the new capital's geographical position by building a comprehensive network of canals that would link together the principal Russian rivers. The first attempts in this direction were made in connection with the annexation of Azov, when a permanent outlet to the Black Sea became for a time one of the principal objects of Moscow's foreign policy. With the loss of Azov to Turkey in 1711, the costly work of canalizing the rivers of southern Russia, an enterprise in which thousands of men are said to have died, was abandoned, but the plan of linking the Neva with the Volga was relentlessly pursued. After many disappointments and setbacks the water system uniting the Baltic and the Caspian seas was roughly completed in 1732, that is, seven years after Peter's death.

Trusted and speedier methods were used to convert St. Petersburg into the center of the empire's foreign trade. A number of wealthy merchants were summarily ordered to build houses in Peter's "paradise" and to reside there permanently. Ships loaded in St. Petersburg paid lower charges than those loaded in Archangel (3 per cent and 5 per cent of the value of cargoes, respectively). A decree of 1713 ordered that hemp, hides, caviar, tar, and potash must be exported exclusively by way of the new capital. This restriction was eased in 1715, when the compulsory share of St. Petersburg was reduced to one-half of the total exports of each commodity, but it was increased to two-thirds in 1718. In the same year the government prohibited the export of grain from Archangel and the importation through that port of silks and brocades. These measures achieved their object in a surprisingly short time. While only one ship entered the St. Petersburg harbor in 1713, the number of such vessels increased to 75 in 1720, and to 180 in 1724. The decline of Archangel was even more spectacular. The average annual number of ships visiting that port was 126 in

1701–1705, 154 in 1711–1715, 142 in 1716–1720; it dropped to 50 in 1721–1725, and to 34 in 1726–1730. All direct restrictions on the trade of Archangel were removed in 1727 and the discriminatory charges in 1762, but it never recovered anything like its former position in Russia's foreign commerce.

Peter's efforts for the promotion of the Baltic trade were not limited to St. Petersburg but extended also to the ancient trading city of Riga, the most important of the newly acquired Russian ports on the Baltic Sea. The number of vessels entering Riga declined from 359 in 1704 to 15 in 1710, after the Russian conquest, but rose to 388 in 1725. The recovery of Riga was due not so much to the measures taken by the Russian government as to its well established position as an important outlet for the foreign trade of Poland. Other Russian Baltic ports, especially Revel and Narva, fared less well and lost most of their trade to St. Petersburg. The geographical advantages of the Baltic ports over remote Archangel would undoubtedly have resulted in the eventual shift of trade from the White Sea to the Baltic even if the Russian government had not used methods of coercion. The ruthless interference of Peter with the delicate mechanism of foreign commerce disrupted many old-established trade connections and worked much hardship both on Russian and on foreign merchants, but the object in view was probably attained in a shorter time than would have been the case without government intervention: by the end of the eighteenth century half of Russia's foreign commerce passed through St. Petersburg.

APPRAISAL OF ECONOMIC POLICIES

The heated controversy among Russian authors as to whether Peter's economic measures diverted the country from the "normal" course of her development and were "artificial" or whether they were a "necessary" stage in her historical evolution would seem to be largely futile and beside the point. Some of the measures, for instance, the promotion of industries engaged in work for the army, or the shifting of foreign trade from the White to the Baltic Sea, were dictated by the exigencies of the situation and, in that sense, may be considered as "inevitable" if not necessarily beneficial. Others, such as the fostering of domestic production by monopolistic privileges and tariff barriers, or the creation of large industrial enterprises employing servile labor, cannot be defended on any reasonable ground, and their subsequent history strongly suggests that these ventures were ill advised. Moreover, many of the tsar's plans remained paper schemes, and the methods he used were such as to destroy much of the usefulness his policies might otherwise have possessed.

CHAPTER XV

RUSSIA BECOMES A EUROPEAN POWER

Social Conditions, the Schools, and the Church

———————————— ✳ ————————————

SOCIAL POLICIES

The changes wrought by Peter not only in the ways of living but also in the appearance of his subjects were probably the most spectacular manifestation of that process of "westernization" through which the country was passing. The garb of many Muscovites, especially that of the boyars, with its high bonnets and long vestments with flowing sleeves, was cumbersome and ungainly. Beards, traditionally regarded as an indispensable and, indeed, sacred attribute of every male from the tsar down to the last muzhik, did not improve the looks of the Russians, even though fashions must be judged by the standards of their own time. Having discovered in the Dutch sailors the living embodiment of western culture, Peter was not satisfied with his own faithful adoption of their dress and manners, but proceeded with his usual impetuosity to force European enlightenment upon his countrymen by making them look like western Europeans. As has already been pointed out, his first move on returning to Russia in 1698 was to trim the beards of palace officials in Moscow with his own hands. It soon appeared that this unprecedented act was not merely one of the pranks of which the tsar was uncommonly fond. A decree of January, 1700, directed the boyars, the *dvoriane*, and the entire urban population to adopt "Hungarian" dress. A more explicit edict of 1701 provided that all men and women, except the clergy and the peasants, were to wear "German, Saxon, or French" clothes, and under the threat of fines and "cruel punishments" prohibited the manufacture and sale of old-fashioned Russian garments. The order was repeated several times, and the severity of punishments for disobedience increased with the result that by 1705 western dress was in general use at least among the upper classes.[1] A compromise solution was found for the vexed question of beards by making them subject to a special tax, graduated according to the social standing of their owners.[2] The use of tobacco, condemned by the Russian Church as an "accursed herb," was not only promoted through its free sale by an English firm and later by a state monopoly but was also encouraged by the example of the tsar, who seldom parted with his pipe.

The transfer of the capital from Moscow to St. Petersburg facilitated the breaking up of old social habits and prejudices. Peter hastened the evolution by making compulsory the type of social intercourse he had found so enjoyable and profitable on his visits to the German Settlement and during his stays abroad. A decree of 1718 laid down detailed rules for informal social gatherings (*assamblei*) held in private houses and freely attended not only by army officers and the *dvoriane* but also by merchants and artisans. The tsar was a frequent visitor at these gatherings where guests, sometimes uninvited, danced, played games, smoked, and drank. Women were not only permitted but, indeed, ordered to attend, thus marking a breach with the traditional seclusion that was still largely their fate at the turn of the century. An even more drastic move towards the emancipation of women was embodied in an earlier decree (1702) which prohibited marriages without the consent of both bride and bridegroom. This legislative enactment was liberal for its time, even though it failed to modify a deep-rooted custom which survived in certain circles up to the time of the revolution of 1917 and perhaps even later.

A long series of often repetitious and sometimes contradictory decrees dealt with problems of municipal betterment and social welfare in the broadest meaning of the term. In 1700 Moscow was endowed with eight pharmacies, and in 1706 there was established a hospital under the direction of a Dutch doctor who also became the director of a medical school. In 1704 the Muscovites were commanded to build stone houses as a safeguard against frequent and devastating fires, and five years later all government and court officials received an order to build stone houses in St. Petersburg, which Peter described,

---

[1] It would seem, however, that even the aristocracy for many years retained its predilection for Russian dress. An inventory of the wardrobe carried into exile in 1730 by the Princes Dolgoruky, a family particularly close to the throne, discloses, according to Korsakov, "a surprisingly large number of 'pre-reform' garments."

[2] See pp. 359–360.

somewhat euphemistically, as the "holy land." The ambitious and impracticable scheme, inaugurated in 1704, of having the streets of Moscow paved with stones eventually had to be abandoned, and in 1709 the more modest plan calling for the repair of existing wooden pavements and sidewalks by the houseowners was made enforceable by heavy fines and the knout. Although homes for the destitute were maintained by some of the monasteries at the beginning of Peter's reign, mendicity, encouraged by the traditional Russian attitude towards charity, was widely prevalent and brought forth a number of stern measures. Begging in the streets of Moscow was prohibited in 1705, beggars were arrested and punished, whatever money they happened to have was confiscated, and the givers of alms were made liable to fines. Half of such fines were turned over to the police officers who apprehended the lawbreakers. In 1718 Moscow had ninety homes with some 4,000 destitute, but mendicity was as common as ever, and new, severe measures against the beggars were enacted in 1717 and again in 1723. The police received strict orders to arrest prostitutes, who, together with the beggars, were drafted to supply labor for newly established industrial enterprises. Quite illogically, the government itself destroyed with one hand what it attempted to accomplish with the other. No provision was made for the maintenance of the thousands of people who lingered for years in Russia's prisons awaiting a trial that might never come. Unless fortunate enough to be cared for by relatives or friends, the prisoners were dependent on public charity, and it was customary to send them, chained together, to beg for alms in the streets. During the reign of Peter, when the report of alleged subversive activities was made a duty and was encouraged by no inconsiderable rewards, the number of people arrested on the flimsiest charges increased beyond anything Russia had known in the past. Pososhkov, an enthusiastic admirer of Peter, maintained that many burghers preferred begging to any other occupation, that they sent their children in the streets to solicit alms, and even posed as prisoners in order to carry on their peculiar pursuit unmolested. "It is a shameful state of affairs," he wrote, "that the streets are made practically impassable by crowds of beggars and prisoners in quest of alms"—in spite of the Draconian measures taken by the government.

Another humanitarian venture, the care of illegitimate children and destitute orphans, proved disastrous to those whom it was intended to benefit. Decrees issued in 1712, 1714, 1715, and 1720 dealt with the establishment of homes to provide for infants of this group. Originally attached to churches, orphanages, which were at first maintained at the expense of the state, were in 1724 transferred to the monasteries. The ultimate fate of the inmates of orphanages was not a happy one. A decree of 1723 directed that orphans should be assigned and "attached forever" to those who assumed responsibility for their education. Twenty years later the Senate confirmed this measure by providing in the decree of July 11, 1744, that orphans and children of destitute parents should be handed over to landlords and owners of industrial enterprises who were willing to pay their poll tax and whose serfs they became. The relief provided for illegitimate children and orphans thus became the road to serfdom. The Senate was motivated in its decision by the argument that there were no state-supported orphanages and that the only alternative to serfdom for destitute children was starvation, mendicity, and brigandage. This measure remained in force until 1761.

More pressing, and of greater immediate importance, was the question of public safety. The sale of long knives was prohibited in 1700 because they were frequently used for the settlement of quarrels, and two years later dueling was made a criminal offense punishable by death. But the chief menace to the life and property of the citizens came from brigands who infested the countryside and invaded the cities. This danger was increased by the distressing conditions of the roads, which made traveling both perilous and slow. In 1722 it took the Netherlands ambassador five weeks to negotiate the distance between Moscow and St. Petersburg, along the main highway of the empire. The majority of the brigands were serfs fleeing the yoke of serfdom, and army deserters escaping the even more intolerable burden of military service in which men only too often received neither pay nor maintenance. One of the first measures of the newly created Senate in 1711 was to establish along the Moscow-Smolensk road military patrols with orders to hang brigands on the spot. The records of the college of justice disclose that in 1719 bands of highwaymen, several hundred strong, organized along military lines, practically ruled the region of Novgorod and captured by assault the town of Meshchovsk, releasing their imprisoned comrades. "There is nothing pleasant to report about Moscow," wrote Field Marshal Sheremev to Peter's secretary in 1718. "Moscow is a hotbed of brigandage, everything is devastated, the number of lawbreakers is multiplying, and executions never stop." Twenty-four brigands were put to death in one day at St. Petersburg in 1722. The government, unable to stop an evil rooted in social conditions, relied on measures of repression. In 1723 the citizens of Moscow were ordered to organize night patrols of local residents armed with guns or, if they had none, with clubs; the streets were closed at night by movable barricades, and the houses were protected by high fences.

LITERATURE

It is with a feeling of relief that one turns from the dreary picture of lawlessness and brutality to the more congenial realm of cultural and educational policies. One of the minor but irritating obstacles to Russia's intercourse with western Europe was the old Muscovite calendar, which reckoned time from the creation of the world and began the year on September 1. The practice to which the Church and a large section of the population, especially the old-believers, were superstitiously attached was abandoned in 1699 when the Julian calendar was officially adopted. In 1703 appeared the first Russian newspaper which published miscellaneous information on domestic and foreign developments. Arrangements were made in 1700 with an Amsterdam firm for the publication of maps and books in the Slavonic language, but the results of this enterprise were disappointing and publishing activities were transferred to Russia. In 1708 the old Slavonic alphabet was simplified and the new style was followed in all lay publications, the ancient Slavonic form being retained only in books for the use of the Church. This reform, beneficial in itself, contributed to that estrangement between the Church and the other educated groups which is one of the characteristics of subsequent intellectual history. It was no mere accident that the first volume printed according to the new orthography was a textbook on geometry, since Peter had a conviction that geometry, which is essential to navigation, was the real key to all knowledge.

There is a general agreement among the students of Russian literature (including Pekarsky, Tikhonravov, Pypin) that while the literary activities of the first quarter of the eighteenth century failed to make any contribution to belles-lettres, they nevertheless marked an important step away from the stifling tradition of the past with its distressing intellectual barrenness. Tikhonravov has rightly observed that the literary activities, or more precisely the publishing activities, of this period bear the unmistakable imprint of Peter. The interests of the tsar were primarily utilitarian, hence the steady stream of dictionaries and translations of textbooks on arithmetic, geometry, fortification, architecture, geography, engineering, navigation, shipbuilding. The lighter side of the social evolution was reflected in *Iunosti chestnoe zertsalo* (The Honorable Mirror of Youth), the translation of a German manual on how to behave in polite society, a rather clumsy production which, however, enjoyed great popularity. The tsar's voluminous correspondence dealing with books published or to be published discloses not only that he personally supervised the choice of volumes and himself often edited the translations, but also that his intellectual horizon was broader than might be legitimately inferred from his background and general behavior. It appears that Peter was genuinely interested in Russian history as well as in the history of foreign countries. He undertook the publication of a collection of Russian chronicles and ordered the preparation of a history of Russia from Vasili II to his own day. The intrinsic value of these works was not high, and some of them, for instance, a dissertation by Baron Shafirov (1717) on the causes of the war with Sweden, were crude apologies or even shameless glorifications of the tsar's policies. Yet, according to Pekarsky, the translation of Pufendorf's *Introduction to the History of Europe* (1718) retained, in compliance with Peter's orders, a most unflattering reference to Russia and the Russians which the translator thought it wise to omit. The translation of the first part of Pufendorf's *De officiis humanis et civis* was ordered by Peter in 1721 but was not published until after his death.

The in many ways revealing diaries of their European travels left by Peter's contemporaries, Peter Tolstoy, Boris Sheremetev, Prince Boris Kurakin, and Count Andrew Matveev were not published until much later. The remarkable books of Ivan Pososhkov, to which several references have been made, suffered a similar fate, but they have preserved an illuminating picture of a shrewd and inquiring mind which combined a deep attachment to conservative tradition with a burning protest against social injustice. The literary activities of the Church were, of course, continued side by side with the new lay literature, and some of these religious writings will be noted later in this chapter. Humble and uninspiring as were the offerings of the Moscow printing press, they brought Russia into closer contact with European thought than had ever before been attempted and made a weak yet not ineffective attempt to pierce the veil of oriental seclusion in which old Muscovy had so long and so obstinately shrouded herself.

THE THEATER AND THE FIRST MUSEUM

The popular theater was unknown in Russia before the eighteenth century. Although plays had been produced in the Kremlin under Tsar Alexis and were part of the scholastic routine in the theological academies of Kiev and Moscow, the theater had never reached wider audiences. Peter therefore broke new ground when, after witnessing several plays during his first visit to Europe, he hired a company of German actors to appear on the Russian stage and to train young Muscovites in dramatic art. A special building was erected in the Red Square in Moscow where plays were given in 1702–1703 in both Russian and German. The repertory consisted of some fifteen tragedies and comedies, chiefly translations of current German offerings dealing with the romantic and involved adventures of personages drawn from mythology and from ancient history (Scipio Africanus and Sophonisba, Alexander the Great, Julius Caesar) and with the romantic tribulations of gallant and noble German knights. Molière's *Le Médecin malgré lui* was also included in the repertory. Russian audiences, needless to say, could not understand German, and the translations prepared by the officials of the *Posolskii prikaz* (department of foreign affairs) were such as to be of little help to the spectators. According to the historian of the Russian theater, Morozov, the text of the Russian version of Molière's *Les Précieuses ridicules* scheduled for production in 1708 was unintelligible. The incongruities of the Russian text were due not so much to the translators' inadequate knowledge of foreign languages as to their hopeless inability to comprehend the situations around which the German and French plays were built and the lack in contemporary Russian of terms that would adequately render the meaning of foreign authors. The Red Square theater closed its doors after a few performances, but plays continued to be given for more select audiences, especially under the patronage of Princess Nathalie, Peter's sister. Allegorical pageants extolling the tsar's victories and linking him to mythological heroes were duly written and staged on ceremonial occasions, but it is safe to assume that their elaborate imagery remained beyond the grasp of the vast majority of the spectators.

Peter's inborn curiosity, stimulated by visits to the museums of

Europe, led him to purchase pictures, statues, books, manuscripts, maps, medals, coins, miniatures, and mathematical and physical instruments. Many of these objects were acquired by him personally in the course of his travels, while others were obtained through his ambassadors in Amsterdam, Paris, Rome, Venice, and other places. A decree of February, 1718, directed everyone who had discovered some unusual or ancient object to turn it over to the government. Peter, however, was primarily interested in curios and not in works of art, and following a morbid predilection for freaks of nature he assembled a vast assortment of "monsters" preserved in alcohol. These not very pleasant exhibits formed the nucleus of the first Russian museum (*kunstkamera*), which was incorporated in the newly established Academy of Science and was open to the public free of charge. The bulk of the tsar's and other private libraries (for instance, those of Tsarevich Alexis and Baron Shafirov, and the books confiscated in the Baltic provinces and elsewhere during the Russian military occupation) was eventually transferred to the library of the Academy of Science, and in 1728 the facilities of the library were made available to the general public.

SCHOOLS

At the end of the seventeenth century Muscovy had no educational institutions except the two theological academies of Kiev and Moscow and a few scattered church schools which, like the Moscow Academy, had a mere handful of students and led a precarious existence. The modernization of the army and of the administrative services, the creation of a navy and of novel industrial enterprises clamored for men possessed of a technical knowledge that Russia was unable to supply. The practice of sending young Russians to study abroad and of enrolling foreign "experts" was followed throughout Peter's reign, but these methods were costly and the results obtained often disappointing. The solution of Russia's educational problem depended on her ability to build up an adequate school system; this she approached in that casual manner and narrow utilitarian spirit which characterized most of Peter's reforms. The Sukharev Tower in Moscow became in 1701 the home of the newly founded "school of mathematics and navigation" and was directed by Farwharson, a former professor from Aberdeen. Although as indicated by its official designation, Russia's first lay educational institution was primarily designed to train officers for the navy, its graduates actually occupied positions in every branch of government service. In 1715 the school was moved to St. Petersburg and became the Russian Naval Academy. The number of students was fixed at 300 in 1715, but by 1724 the actual enrollment had reached 394; in April, 1725, after Peter's death, it declined sharply to 180 and in 1745 it dropped still further to 102. In spite of the stringent measures taken by the government, the sea apparently had no appeal for young Russians.

The needs of the army were cared for by a school of army engineers and an artillery school, both established in Moscow in 1712 but soon transferred to St. Petersburg. The number of cadets in these institutions was insignificant: a limit of 60 at the school of engineering in 1724, and 30 at the artillery school in 1721.[3] Actual enrollment, however, was at times below these modest figures.

The so-called "Glück Gymnasium," named after its founder although it was a state-sponsored institution, was established in Moscow in 1705, the first, and short-lived, experiment in providing a school not tinged with narrow professionalism. Ernst Glück was the Marienburg Lutheran pastor in whose house the future Empress Catherine I once worked as a servant. Glück came to Moscow as a prisoner of war, but he soon won the confidence of the tsar and became the founder of the gymnasium which offered its students a breath-taking curriculum, including French, German, Swedish, Greek, Latin, Hebrew, oriental languages, literature, rhetoric, ethics, philosophy, riding, dancing, and even courses in good manners ("compliments according to the German and the French rites," as the announcement put it). The teachers were all foreigners, and the number of students was fixed in 1706 at 100. Attendance at the gymnasium was at first voluntary, that is, no definite contingent of students was assigned to it by the government; but the number of students in 1715, according to Vladimirovsky-Budanov, was only five, and the school closed its doors. Glück did not live to see disaster; he died in May, 1705, a few weeks after the founding of the gymnasium.

An unsuccessful attempt to introduce compulsory elementary education was made in 1714, when the government decreed the establishment in each province (*guberniia*) of two "mathematical" (*tsifernyia*) schools, also known as "navigation" schools. The subjects taught included arithmetic, geometry and trigonometry, and, presumably,

[3] The number was increased to 90 in 1735.

reading and writing. The surprising character of the curriculum and the fact that the "mathematical" schools were in the jurisdiction of the Admiralty suggest, according to Vladimirovsky-Budanov, that their object was to train men for the navy. The teachers were drawn chiefly from the graduates of the Naval Academy, while the prescribed quota of students, whose ages varied from ten to fifteen, was to be recruited by local authorities among the children of local residents, irrespective of their social standing (decrees of February 29, 1714, and December 28, 1715). A decree of 1714 provided that young men who failed to complete the course should not be permitted to marry. In spite of this threat and the ruthless measures taken by the officials to fill the quota of students, the "mathematical" schools made little progress. Of the 47 teachers sent from Moscow to the provinces, 18 came back because there was no one to teach, and of the total number of 1,389 students enrolled in these schools during the first ten years of their operation only 93 completed the course, the balance having deserted (Vladimirovsky-Budanov). The ill fated experiment ended in 1744, when the last eight "mathematical" schools still in existence were merged with the "garrison" schools founded in 1732 and maintained with regimental funds. Instruction in "garrison" schools was conducted by army officers and non-commissioned officers, and the students were trained for a military career.

One of the reasons for the vicissitudes of the "mathematical" schools arose from their competition for students with the parochial schools (*eparkhialnyia*) established by the Church Statute (*Dukhovnyi reglament*) of 1721. In 1727 there were 46 parochial schools with some 3,000 students.[4] Although originally admission to schools of every type was open to all children irrespective of the social standing of their parents, this rule was soon found to be in conflict with the general policy of the state to keep the members of the various "estates" (*soslove*) attached to their original legal and social status. Since government service and other occupations were largely hereditary, it was not unreasonable to request that the young people should be trained for the particular function they were predestined to fulfill. Schools therefore tended to acquire an occupational character and to restrict admission to members of the appropriate social group. Thus it was provided in 1715 that children of the *dvoriane* alone might be ad-

---

[4] In 1737 the number of students in these schools increased to 5,000 and in 1783 to 11,000.

mitted to the St. Petersburg Naval Academy, while the Moscow school of navigation in the Sukharev Tower, which continued to function until 1752, admitted only low-born students, who received a more elementary education than that given cadets of the Naval Academy. The school of military engineers and the artillery schools were also primarily designed to train young *dvoriane,* although class distinctions in these branches of the service were not so clear-cut as they were in the navy. The decree of January 16, 1716, excluded the *dvoriane* from "mathematical" schools, which were thenceforward to be reserved for children belonging to the lower "estates." The parochial schools drew their students largely from the children of the clergy, a group that, according to Miliukov, accounted for 45 per cent of the total student body of the "mathematical" schools during the first ten years of their existence. Thus the establishment of parochial schools, which trained their pupils for the priesthood and had a prior claim on the descendants of clerics, dealt the "mathematical" schools a blow from which they never recovered.

One should not, however, overstress class distinctions among the obstacles to the progress of education in the first half of the eighteenth century. The class principle was not consistently applied, and certain schools, for instance, the "garrison" schools, admitted children of army privates and even those of vagrants side by side with the offspring of noble families. Moreover, the selection of the student body on the basis of class origin as laid down by the law was frequently disregarded in practice, and it must be borne in mind that the *dvorianstvo* was not a closed caste. The development of the school system was hindered by other and more powerful causes, such as the lack of textbooks and properly trained teachers, the fanciful character of the curricula, with their grotesque overemphasis on mathematics, the forcible recruiting of the student body, the almost incredible harshness of school discipline, and last but not least, the reluctance of the parents to allow their children to follow a scholastic career. Evidence was not lacking that the possession of an academic diploma and a hard-won mastery of trigonometry bore no direct relation to the position a youth might aspire to occupy in government service and that there were many less onerous ways of achieving one's ambitions. Hence the difficulties in filling the quota of students and the mass desertion of students from their unwanted alma mater.

The church schools displayed greater vitality than did other educational institutions, perhaps because they had behind them a certain tradition which the lay schools lacked. Under the leadership of the more enlightened clerics some of the parochial schools enlarged their programs and reached the status of theological seminaries with a course of studies extending over nine years. The legal status of these institutions was determined by a law of 1737. In 1738 there were 17 seminaries with 2,600 students, and although progress was retarded in the following years [5] they played an important part in providing the academic cadres for both lay and ecclesiastical institutions.

THE ACADEMY OF SCIENCE

Another potential center of intellectual activity was the Academy of Science. It is believed that the idea of endowing Russia with an institution bearing so high-sounding a title was suggested to Peter by the illustrious German philosopher Leibnitz, whom he met in Torgau in 1711 and again in Karlsbad in 1712. The ambitious German thinker, who was largely responsible for the founding of the Prussian Academy in Berlin (1700), liked to imagine himself in the part of a "Russian Solon" and outlined for Peter the plan of a Russian academy. He was rewarded with an honorary title and a pension but died in 1716, before the new institution took shape. Leibnitz's celebrated disciple, Christian Wolff, who carried on a correspondence with Peter, was somewhat more reserved but not unfavorable to the project of his master. Peter's visit to the French Academy in Paris in 1717 probably contributed to his decision to emulate the example of the more enlightened European countries. All arrangements for the Russian Academy of Science were completed in January, 1724, but it did not begin to function until December, 1725, after Peter's death. The charter of the academy, which followed the general lines of the plan prepared by Leibnitz, provided for an institution of higher learning that should combine the advancement of science with educational activities. Seventeen fellows, some of them men of distinction, were imported from Germany. Their duties included, in addition to the promotion of knowledge, the teaching in a university and in a gymnasium (secondary school) attached to the academy. Since no Russians qualified to attend university courses were available, eight students were imported from Germany, a number inadequate for the seventeen professors who, in order to meet the requirements of the charter, had oc-

[5] In 1764 there were 26 seminaries with 6,000 students.

casionally to attend each other's lectures. The gymnasium at first fared better, but soon ran short of students, who had to be recruited wherever they could be found. The scholarly achievements of the first fellows, however, were not inconsiderable, and their very presence in St. Petersburg introduced a novel and beneficial strain in the life of the capital. Yet the resulting situation was incongruous: an illiterate country, which had neither elementary nor secondary schools worth mentioning, found herself in possession of an institution for the advancement of learning where imported scholars discussed in a foreign tongue Liebnitz's principle of *identitatis indiscernibilium* and kindred subjects. It was not, perhaps, inappropriate that the Russian Academy of Science should have been inaugurated by Empress Catherine I, a former Lithuanian peasant girl, who never mastered the mysteries of reading and writing.

THE CHURCH

The appearance of lay literature and secular schools was a sign that the Church was losing its former monopoly of cultural activities, a monopoly that was in part responsible for Russia's illiteracy and intellectual stagnation. The long-drawn-out process of the subjugation of the spiritual power by the state reached its culmination during the reign of Peter. The superstitious attachment to tradition and to the letter of external observances characteristic of Russian Christianity was rudely shaken by the tsar's militant iconoclasm; the resulting feeling of indignation and bewilderment among the clergy and the believers was aggravated by the methods employed, which were such as to overtax the broadest tolerance and understanding, qualities in which the Russian Church hierarchy was wanting. Peter's contempt for court etiquette, his predilection for foreigners, his travels abroad, and the forcible westernization of the dress and manners of his subjects scandalized all conservative elements; in their dismay they turned to the Church for protection and leadership. Patriarch Joachim, who died in 1690, hated the German Settlement and outlandish ways as much as Peter liked them. Adrian, the next patriarch, was appointed over the tsar's objections at the insistence of Tsarina Nathalie, and although he was much too cautious openly to criticize the young ruler, he was opposed to such unheard-of innovations as the use of tobacco and the shaving of beards. After Adrian's death in 1700, Peter, remembering perhaps the recent conflict between Tsar Alexis and Patriarch Nikon, left the vacancy unfilled and appointed Stephen Yavorsky "keeper and administrator of the patriarchal see," an office he held until the abolition of the patriarchate and the creation of the Holy Synod in 1721.

This initial step was followed by others directed against the authority and independence of the Church. In 1701 it lost control over its vast ecclesiastical and monastic estates, which were transferred to the administration of the *Monastirskii prikaz*,[6] an institution abolished in 1667 but revived under the leadership of an energetic lay officer, Ivan Musin-Pushkin. Although no secularization of Church properties was ordered, ecclesiastical dignitaries and monasteries were permitted to enjoy merely a portion of their former revenue, the balance being used to defray other expenses, especially the cost of the army. Appropriations for the maintenance of the monasteries, for which Peter had a strong dislike, were parsimoniously measured out and were further revised downward in 1705. The jurisdiction of ecclesiastical courts was curtailed and that of the lay judges of the *Monastirskii prikaz* was once more extended both to clerics and to the residents of Church estates. Musin-Pushkin, moreover, interfered with Church administration, and Stephen Yavorsky repeatedly, although unsuccessfully, petitioned the tsar for permission to retire. In 1711 the newly created Senate ruled that thenceforth bishops might be consecrated only after the preliminary approval of the candidates by that body.

The elevation of Yavorsky to the highest office in the Church was itself a revolutionary departure from tradition. Stephen Yavorsky (1658–1722) was brought up in the theological academy of Kiev but later became converted to Roman Catholicism and studied in Jesuit schools at Lemberg, Vilna, and Posnan. On his return to Russia he was readmitted to the fold of the Orthodox Church, took holy orders, and taught at the Kievan Academy, where he made a great reputation for learning and eloquence. First introduced to Peter in February, 1700, Yavorsky was created metropolitan of Riazan in March and "keeper and administrator of the patriarchal see" in October of the same year, shortly after the death of Patriarch Adrian. The breathtaking rise of the former pupil of the Jesuits, who had once repudiated Greek Orthodoxy for Catholicism, would have been unthinkable in the old Muscovy and required all of Peter's determination and dis-

[6] See pp. 279, 292.

regard of conventions. Yavorsky, who had a good command of Latin and was familiar with western theology, spared no effort in glorifying the tsar's earlier policies in pompous sermons crowded with flattering allegories and composed according to the rules of medieval scholasticism. Peter saw in him a useful tool for combating the reactionary tendencies of the Russian clergy. It soon became clear, however, that Yavorsky, in spite of his renunciation of Catholicism, had retained intact his belief in the supremacy of the spiritual power and that, while he gladly supported Peter in his struggle against the stale Byzantinism of the Russian Church, he cherished the ambition of becoming himself the pontiff of eastern Christianity with the title of patriarch. It is likely that in 1700 Peter had no definite plan for abolishing the patriarchate; but as years went by, and the interference of the state with the Church became more pronounced, Yavorsky lost his former enthusiasm for the tsar-reformer. He wrote a number of sermons containing veiled attacks on the tsar, most of them never delivered but preserved in his papers with the annotation "*non dictum.*" In 1712, however, he publicly castigated the regime of police spying and made transparent allusions to the irregularities of Peter's private life. The Senate took offense, prohibited Yavorsky from preaching, and forwarded the incriminating sermon to Peter, who, however, showed unusual leniency and accepted the half-hearted apologies and disingenuous explanations of the "keeper and administrator of the patriarchal see." But the authority of Yavorsky was shaken, and his influence was further weakened by his unsuccessful intervention on behalf of Tsarevich Alexis. By a curious turn of fortune, the erstwhile Catholic and admirer of reforms drifted into the position of the leader of those who, while remaining within the fold of the official Church, resented the innovations and pleaded the cause of old Muscovy. Yavorsky's voluminous treatise *Kamen very* (The Stone of Faith), an elaborate attack on Protestantism, and largely a compilation of arguments borrowed from Catholic theologians, was published in 1728, six years after the author's death. Although Yavorsky succeeded in maintaining himself at the head of the hierarchy until the end of his days, he left no personal imprint on the reform of Church administration by which the fate of the Russian Church was determined for the succeeding two hundred years.

Peter found a much more willing collaborator and the Church a far more influential leader in the person of Theophan Prokopovich

(1681–1736), whose early life story bears traits of similarity with that of Stephen Yavorsky. Son of a small tradesman, Prokopovich graduated from the Kievan theological academy, went to Poland, where he became a Uniat and took holy orders in a Uniat monastery, and then spent three years in Rome as a student in the College of St. Athanasius. He returned to Russia in 1702, repudiated his recent conversion, once more took orders—this time as a member of the Greek Orthodox Church—and received a chair in the Kievan Academy. Prokopovich, a man of erudition, an able theologian, and an eloquent preacher, was also an ambitious and ruthless and intriguing politician who resorted to any means to achieve his personal aims and destroy his enemies. His unfaltering adulation of Peter, unhampered by any such dogmatic scruples as eventually dampened Yavorsky's early zeal, did not prevent him, after the emperor's death, from seeking and winning the protection of Ostermann and Biron, the all-powerful favorites of Empress Anne, whose regime had nothing in common with the enlightenment that Prokopovich had championed under the tsar-reformer. Prokopovich's first acquaintance with Peter went back to 1706, but his real influence began in 1709, when he delivered, in the presence of the tsar, an eloquent panegyric upon the Poltava victory. Peter was frankly delighted, and the scheming cleric hastened to consolidate his position by delivering an equally laudatory discourse extolling the genius and virtues of the then omnipotent favorite, Prince Menshikov. In 1711 he was invited to join the tsar during the Turkish campaign and was then appointed rector of the Kievan Academy. In 1716 he came to St. Petersburg and was made in 1718 bishop of Pskov and in 1724 archbishop of Novgorod, an office he retained until his death.

Probably the best educated Russian of his time, Prokopovich assembled a library of some 30,000 volumes, was a patron of the arts and sciences, and kept an open house, the earliest Russian approximation of a literary salon. He was the first among the Russian theologians to accept the views of Copernicus and Galileo, who were anathema not only to his contemporaries, for instance, Yavorsky, but also to writers of later generations. Prokopovich's writings dealing with dogmatic questions are said to constitute an important and lasting contribution to Russian theology. But he was also a dramatist, a poet, and above all a publicist. A severe critic of scholasticism, Prokopovich endeavored to free himself from the scholastic tradition, and his sermons, although by no means a model of simplicity, dealt with the burning questions of the day and were a marked improvement on the involved and obscure imagery of Yavorsky. In his eagerness to combat the forces of reaction and to provide an apology for every measure adopted by the government, including the trial and execution of Tsarevich Alexis, the zealous preacher often forgot the restraint imposed by his sacred office and descended to the level of a political pamphleteer, giving free vent to his mordant and merciless irony. Although base considerations of self-interest were not foreign to Prokopovich's endorsement of Peter's policies, his cooperation with the tsar would seem to have had an ideological basis. The former student of the College of St. Athanasius had grown to be one of the most uncompromising opponents of the Church of Rome. In his theological writing he showed predilection for Protestant authorities and was unsuccessfully denounced by Yavorsky as a Calvinist. Papacy, according to Prokopovich, was the worst of all evils, and he elaborated an ingenious and comprehensive theory of monarchical absolutism which specifically denied the supremacy of the spiritual power. He branded as "papalism" the claim of the clergy and monasteries to a privileged position in the state, and maintained that the acceptance of such doctrines was incompatible not only with the rights of a sovereign "by the grace of God" but also with his duties, for, in Prokopovich's opinion, the monarch must closely regulate the activities of his subjects in every field and provide for their welfare and happiness. No theory of the state could have been more pleasing to Peter than this dogma of the divinely guided police state,[7] and the resourceful theologian was given the opportunity to embody some of his ideas in legislation. The Church Statute of 1721, which reads in part rather like a political satire than like the constitutional charter of a Christian Church, was largely his work. This truly remarkable document provided for the reorganization of Church administration and outlined a comprehensive program of educational activities. The patriarchate was abolished

---

[7] The Petrine ideal of the police state found its most eloquent expression in the Statute of the *Glavnyi magistrat* (1721) which provided an exhaustive list of the duties of the police. Police officers were expected not only "to force everyone to work and to follow an honorable trade" and "to prohibit excessive domestic expenditure," but also "to bring satisfaction of all human needs" and "to educate the young according to the Commandments of Our Lord in moral purity and to train them in honorable sciences." The police, the Statute triumphantly proclaimed, is "the very soul of citizenship" (*dusha grazhdanstva*).

and replaced by a collegial body, the Holy Synod. "From an administrative organ embodying the collegial principle," the Statute explained with utmost frankness, "there is no reason to fear rebellions and confusion that grow out of the control of the Church by an individual." The common people, it argued, were incapable of understanding the proper functions of the head of the Church and were often led to believe that he was superior to the tsar. The clergy and the patriarch himself have at times used their powers to promote disaffection, and the masses were only too often willing to follow them because they believed that God, too, was on the side of the Church. "When the people learn that Church administration is established by decrees of the monarch and decisions of the Senate, it will remain docile and will lose all hope that the clergy will support rebellious movements."

The Holy Synod was organized along the same lines as the other administrative colleges, except that its members were drawn from the rank of the clergy, including the "black" clergy, or monks. A decree of March 11, 1722, put the Holy Synod under the supervision of a chief procurator, whose duties were somewhat similar to those of the procurator-general of the Senate. It also directed that the new official should be selected among the "good and courageous" army officers. The chief procurator, always a layman, became the actual head of Church administration, his powers were steadily expanded, and he was eventually raised to the rank of minister of the Crown. The Holy Synod, whose members were appointed by the tsar and enjoyed no permanency of tenure, found itself in the position of merely another government department subordinated to the Senate, with which it was often in conflict. The importance of the changes in Church administration cannot be overestimated. Although the Russian Church, as has been indicated in the previous discussion, never succeeded in living up to the proud tradition of the supreme spiritual power that it had inherited from Byzantium, it had, until 1721, its autonomous administration, headed by ecclesiastical dignitaries (first the metropolitans of All the Russias, then the patriarchs, and finally the "keeper and administrator of the patriarchal see") who recognized no secular authority except that of the Crown. The Muscovite tsars often interfered with ecclesiastical affairs, yet there was some truth in Prokopovich's charges that the Church continued to remain "a state within the state." But this situation had been brought to an end. Although the Statute of 1721 definitely provided that in purely religious matters the Holy Synod was to exercise "the full rights and powers of the patriarch," in questions of Church administration it became a bureaucratic department at the mercy of a lay chief procurator and of a special service of "inquisitors" headed by a "chief inquisitor" whose duty it was to detect heresies and to spy on the clergy. The creation of the Holy Synod, which survived until the revolution of 1917, destroyed whatever political influence the Church had enjoyed. Although the validity of the reform, from the point of view of canon law, was open to doubts, the patriarchs of Antioch and Jerusalem, more than ever dependent on Russia's bounties, hastened (September, 1723) to recognize the Holy Synod as their "brother." Ironically, both Yavorsky, a bitter opponent of the reform, and Prokopovich, its chief protagonist and author, were appointed members of the Synod and were forced to cooperate in carrying out measures that completed the incorporation of the Church within the framework of the bureaucratic state.[8]

Peter, who regularly attended divine service, displayed a notable lack of respect for his spiritual leaders. The Most Drunken *Sobor* of Fools and Jesters was a particularly striking manifestation of that attitude of irreverence which found even more authoritative expression in the character and language of many legislative measures. An order was issued in 1722 that no new churches should be built without permission from the Synod, and clerics and monks were classed, together with vagrants and beggars, among the people who were prohibited from entering St. Petersburg. The tsar was particularly critical of the monasteries, which appeared to him as hotbeds of debauchery and centers of subversive activities. A decree of 1723 attempted to stabilize the population of the monasteries by providing that thenceforth no one should be permitted to take holy orders and that vacancies created by the death of monks were to be filled by appointment of former soldiers. A year later, in January, 1724, came another decree which contained an indictment of Russian monasticism and defined its object as the relief of the sick, aged, destitute, and orphans, and the training of the higher officers of the Church hierarchy. Monasticism was thus approached from the utilitarian standpoint, although there were signs that the government was not indifferent to the spiritual

---

[8] The *Monastirskii prikaz*, which went through several transformations in 1720–1725, was closed in the latter year and its functions were transferred to a collegiate organ subordinated to the Holy Synod.

well-being of the believers. Auricular confessions were made compulsory in 1716 under the threat of fines, an order which was repeated in 1718 and amplified by the provision that made obligatory church attendance on Sundays and holidays. The real reason for the latter measure was disclosed in 1719, when it was officially explained that government decrees were read in churches and that non-attendance, therefore, was an indication of indifference towards the reforms. The absentees were rounded up and punished. Talk during the mass was prohibited, and fines of one ruble were collected from offenders before they were permitted to leave the church building. According to Semevsky, who made a special study of the archives of the security police, the information obtained by the confessors was sometimes used against the accused in the torture chambers of the *Preobrazhenskii prikaz*. Religion was, indeed, pressed into the service of the police state.

Peter's indifference to matters of dogma led to a somewhat greater tolerance in religious questions than had been customary in the past.[9] In 1707 Prince Boris Kurakin offered the Holy See various privileges for the Catholic Church in exchange for the non-recognition of Stanislaw Leszcynski as king of Poland, but in 1719 the persecution of the Jesuits, inaugurated by Patriarch Joakhim after the fall of Sophie, was resumed with much violence. Protestants, who had a powerful defender in Theophan Prokopovich, fared better, in spite of attacks on them by Stephen Yavorsky. The most liberal measure of the regime was probably the decision of the Holy Synod (1721) legalizing marriages between the members of the Orthodox Church and those of other Christian denominations. In the early years of his reign Peter held the view that no coercive measures should be used against the old-believers, but his attitude changed when it appeared that the dissenters were in opposition to the reforms. The doubling of the tax assessment of the old-believers in 1716, which led to resistance and bloody repressions, was followed by the introduction of compulsory special dress for the adherents of the "old faith" (1722). The dissenters once more sought refuge in the wooded wilderness of northern and eastern Russia, and some of them, when tracked down by punitive expeditions, preferred death by self-burning to surrender. The persecutions of this period, however, were basically different from

---

[9] This indifference at times assumed the character of violation of Church canons, for instance, when Peter decreed the divorce of his favorite Yaguzhinsky.

those of the seventeenth century: they were not so much crusades for the elimination of heresy as a drive to crush political opposition.

THE DVORIANE IN HARNESS

The military and administrative reforms of Peter had a far-reaching effect upon the social structure, especially on the position of the *dvoriane*, although the legal framework erected by the Code of 1649 was largely retained. The chief duty of the *dvoriane* in the seventeenth century was military service, and their chief privilege (shared, however, by the Church) was the ownership of landed estates farmed by servile labor. The basic elements determining the position of the *dvoriane* were left undisturbed, but the burden of service was increased and the hold of the landlords over the serfs was tightened. The old Muscovite militia was organized on a territorial basis and was called together only in emergencies, allowing its members considerable time for administering their estates. The regiments of the westernized army, unlike those of the militia, were comprised of men drawn from every part of the country, and the protracted character of the Northern War made service with the colors permanent. The demand for man power following the creation of the navy and the increase in the size of the army was met by recruiting men from every social group, and in the new regiments the *dvoriane* found themselves serving side by side with their serfs. Moreover, the mushroom growth of the civilian administration and various novel industrial and building activities called for large contingents of employees and supervisors to direct the work of hordes of conscripted laborers. The *dvoriane*, the most privileged social group in the realm, were expected to provide officers for the army and to fill the ranks of civil servants. The easygoing days when they were permitted to vegetate on their estates, making more or less casual and unwilling appearances in the militia (an obligation they frequently dodged), were now over. Peter liked to describe himself as a servant of the state, and he never understood or admitted that others might not share this ambition. It was not his habit, moreover, to pay attention to the wishes of his subjects: whether they liked it or not, all able-bodied members of the privileged class were to be assigned to jobs and were to be taught how to do their duty.

The carrying out of this program presented difficulties, since the *dvoriane* particularly hated the navy and showed none of the tsar's enthusiasm for the army or government service. Severe measures were taken, therefore, to eradicate the prevalent practice of evasion. In 1711 the newly established Senate was entrusted with the function (formerly exercised by one of the *prikazy*) of preparing a register of all *dvoriane*, of assigning them to various positions, and of keeping up-to-date records of their professional career. Registration was supplemented by reviews held at irregular intervals and attended by *dvoriane*, from boys in their teens to gray-haired veterans. The case of each was examined by officials, senators, and the tsar himself, and only those found unfit for service were permitted to retire to their estates. A decree of March 2, 1711, provided that an informer who had denounced an eluding *dvorianin* was to be given as a reward the property of the would-be slacker. In the following years punitive measures for evasion of government service came in rapid succession and increased in severity, reaching their culmination in a decree of January 11, 1722, which inflicted upon the evading *dvoriane* the supreme penalty of "public disgrace" (*shelmovanie*) and put them outside the law, that is, they might be robbed, wounded, and murdered with impunity, while the whole of their property was sequestered, and attached to gallows in public squares were special announcements bearing their names—"like those of traitors."

On January 12, 1722, the day after the publication of the Draconian law just quoted, the administration of all matters relating to the *dvoriane* and their service was transferred to the office of the *Heraldmeister*, a newly appointed officer attached to the Senate. According to an instruction of February 5, 1722, the principal duties of this official consisted in keeping a register of the *dvoriane*, including a separate list of their male children; in maintaining a school with a "brief" course of instruction in "economics and civics for the offspring of illustrious families and of families of modest condition"; and in preventing more than one-third of the members of each family from entering civil service, so as to avoid a shortage of naval and military officers. The *Heraldmeister* exercised important functions in keeping the *dvoriane* in check and in determining their career, since he proposed candidates for vacancies in civil service, although he had little influence over army appointments. As to the school, with its inviting curriculum of "economics and civics," it was never opened, and the scheme was pigeonholed together with many others of Peter's projects.

Under Peter government service covered more of the life span of those engaged in it than had previously been the case. The registration of the children of the *dvoriane* and the appearance at the reviews of boys of ten to fifteen years led to the first stage of the young men's official career. Some of them were sent abroad to study, while others were trained for the army or civil service by employment of the scant facilities at home. A decree of January 20, 1714, threatened those students in the "mathematical" schools who failed to master arithmetic and geometry with the penalty of celibacy. According to contemporary reports, the *dvoriane* hated geometry as much as they hated the sea; moreover, the few existing schools could accommodate only a fraction of the total number of eligible young men. Pososhkov relates that some of the more imaginative noblemen eluded government service by pretending to be feeble-minded. Peter attempted to discourage this fraudulent practice by ordering, in 1723, that those *dvoriane* whose mental condition prevented them from going to school or serving their country should not be permitted to marry and inherit landed estates.

Since schools were nearly non-existent, the normal beginning of a young *dvorianin's* career was apprenticeship, usually in the army and less frequently in some government office. But military service was tolerable only for those who had reached the rank of officer, a privilege reserved largely for the former privates of the guards. A decree of February, 1714, laid down the rule that only guardsmen were to be eligible to receive commissions, and a similar provision was contained in the Army Regulations of 1716. Peter liked to imagine that he had prepared himself for his exalted office by swinging the ax in Dutch shipyards; and he felt certain that a method which had succeeded so well with the tsar could not fail with his subjects—in accordance with the rule that the best way of learning a trade is by starting at the bottom. The three regiments of the guards—the Semenovsky and Preobrazhensky regiments, founded about 1690, and the "leib-regiment" of dragoons (later Horse Guards), established in 1719—took the place of colleges and universities as training schools where the youth of the upper class prepared for their professional career. The offspring of princely and other noble families served by the hundreds in the ranks of the guards, shared barracks with men of humble extraction, and dutifully performed the chores of army routine, receiving their share of corporal punishment. But later they got their reward in the form of a commission in the army, or—if their wealth and connections warranted—by being allowed to continue their service as officers in the guards, a happy status that opened the doors to the highest official positions. This peculiar complexion of the regiments of the guards explains the importance they assumed in the administration during the second half of Peter's reign [10] and the even more decisive political role they played in subsequent regimes.

Since government service was the hereditary duty of the *dvorianstvo*, it was both logical and fitting that men of humble origin who succeeded in making their way up the ladder of the official hierarchy should be admitted to membership in the highest "estate" of the realm. The granting of *anoblissement* was in keeping with Peter's own conception of the aristocracy as servants of the state, nor was it really at variance with Russia's historical tradition, for Muscovite nobility never acquired the character of an exclusive or close caste. Moreover, the growing demand for army officers and government officials could probably not have been met from the ranks of the existing *dvorianstvo*. The decree of January 16, 1721, which provided that every army officer, irrespective of his origin, was to be elevated to the dignity of hereditary *dvorianstvo*, was followed by a much more comprehensive legislative act, the so-called "Table of Ranks" (*Tabel o rangakh*) of January 24, 1722. The Table of Ranks was the result of a long and detailed study by the tsar, his advisers, and the Senate. It drew for the first time a clear line of demarcation between the civilian and the army service. All offices in each of these two branches were rearranged in hierarchical order in fourteen classes, and every army officer or civil servant was to start his career in the lowest class, proceeding gradually from grade to grade up the official ladder. The Table of Ranks reproduced the provisions of the decree of January 16, 1721, which conferred the dignity of hereditary *dvorianstvo* on every soldier who reached the lowest officer's rank, and extended the same privilege to civil servants who had attained Rank 8 in the official hierarchy. Government service thus became the principal source of the coveted distinction of *dvorianstvo* and opened the door leading to *anoblissement* for every one who had earned his officer's epaulets by drilling soldiers or who had diligently bent his back over official papers long enough to reach the specified grade in the civilian hierarchy.

The Table of Ranks remained in force with but minor changes until the revolution of 1917, and therefore has a claim to being one of

[10] See p. 382.

Peter's most lasting reforms. While it facilitated the influx of new blood in Russia's highest "estate," its democratic character has often been exaggerated. The principle of equality suggested by the requirement that all army officers and civilian employees must begin their career in the lowest grade of the official hierarchy was never fully applied in practice, and until the end of the empire young men who had the backing of wealth and powerful connections had no difficulty in rising to high offices, positions that, with rare exceptions, remained outside the reach of the less fortunate *dvoriane*. The path that led to hereditary *dvorianstvo* continued to be obstructed by many obstacles of an unofficial nature, by deep-rooted prejudices, and by the reluctance of the old families to accept newcomers in their midst. The aristocracy of ancient lineage looked askance at the newcomers, and some fifty years later, in the reign of Catherine II, persistently although unsuccessfully petitioned the Crown to remove the distasteful legislative provision for the *anoblissement* of army officers and civilian employees. The real and lasting effect of the Table of Ranks was not so much the democratization of the *dvorianstvo*, although this aspect of the reform should not be disregarded, as the recognition of the priority of official rank over nobility of birth. A bureaucracy that owes its position to the pleasure of the sovereign and is at his mercy is a more obedient tool in the hands of an autocratic government than an aristocracy that has a claim to social leadership in its own right. The Table of Ranks provided the bureaucratic state that was evolving in old Muscovy with a sharply outlined and durable framework and created a tradition of glorified government service that survived not only the removal of shackles, in which the *dvorianstvo* labored until 1762, but even, perhaps, the fall of the empire in 1917.

An entirely different fate befell Peter's abortive attempt to put an end to the practice, common among the *dvoriane*, of disposing of their landed estates and especially of dividing them among their children. By the beginning of the eighteenth century the once clear-cut distinction between hereditary estates unencumbered by any obligation of military service (*votchina*) and estates held in service tenure (*pomestie*) had disappeared, and the custom of providing every child with an equal share in the inheritance sometimes led to the breaking up of landed estates into very small holdings. The resulting impoverishment of the *dvoriane* and their inability to perform properly their military duties attracted the attention of the government, and Peter for years collected information on the law governing primogeniture and entail in western Europe. The outcome of this labor was the decree of March 23, 1714, which prohibited the sale or mortgage of any landed property and laid down rules regulating the transfer of such property after the owner's death. In case of testamentary succession an estate could be transferred to any of the sons of the testator at his choice, but it could not be divided. A similar rule was observed in case of intestacy, where the law determined the order of the heirs. Movable property, however, was not made subject to such restriction. According to the letter of the act, the prohibition against selling land applied not only to estates held by the *dvoriane* but also to landed properties in cities, such as the dwelling houses and shops owned by the burghers. The elaborate preamble to the decree, however, made it clear that Peter was primarily concerned with the position of the *dvoriane*. The official reasons for restrictive legislation of a type unprecedented in Russia's annals were manifold: to strengthen the financial position of the landowning class and thus protect the treasury from loss of revenue and the servile population from excessive exploitation; to enhance the social standing of the landed aristocracy; and to encourage disinherited sons to seek government employment or to engage in commerce or industry. The wording of the decree was obscure and in part contradictory, and the unsuccessful attempts at enforcement led to much confusion and discontent. The experiment was abandoned in 1730, in the reign of Empress Anne. In repealing the act the Senate was motivated by the following considerations: entail was regarded as contrary to the principle of divine justice which ordains that children should share equally in their father's estate; the economic effects of the law had proved disastrous, since loving parents desirous of providing for all of their descendants ruined estates by turning over agricultural implements, domestic animals, stocks of grain, and so on, to heirs other than the one who inherited the land; sales of land, far from being halted, had been increased, with depressing effect on land prices; members of noble families had become involved in litigation and murderous feuds; and, finally, the disinherited sons could not possibly engage in useful commercial and industrial pursuits for the reason that they continued to be drafted for service in the army and navy. Entail, basically an aristocratic principle, had no root in the Russian tradition, was ill adapted to the needs of the bureaucratic state, and was discarded after a few years' trial.

The aversion displayed by the *dvoriane* towards the policies followed by Peter did not prevent these measures from working important changes in the social texture and outlook of the upper class. Lifelong service, usually far away from home, and daily association with men coming from other parts of the country tended to weaken local allegiances and to build up a novel *esprit de corps* based on a certain identity of professional interests. Paying but brief and casual visits to their distant estates, the *dvoriane* lost contact with local needs and local people, and became primarily guardsmen, army officers, and government employees, giving little thought to family seats, except as a source of revenue. Their powdered wigs, clean-shaven faces, and western dress set them apart from the common people and contributed to the welding of the military-bureaucratic class of landowners into a homogeneous group that soon began to exercise a decisive influence upon the destinies of the country. Individually each *dvorianin* was at the mercy of the monarch, but as a class whose members filled every important office in the army and in the civilian administration the *dvorianstvo* was growing into a force which the Crown could not ignore much longer. Still lacking a corporate organization and electing but a few minor officials, it was not yet an "estate" (*état*) of the type familiar in western Europe, but was tending rather to become a kind of military-bureaucratic oligarchy powerfully represented at the court by the *generalitet*, a small group of highly placed office-holders, and by the "supreme lords" (*verkhovniki*), an even smaller clique of the tsar's confidential advisers.

GENERAL RESULTS OF THE REFORM

If the heavy burden imposed upon the unwilling *dvoriane* was not without its compensations, since it placed them in control of the army and of the administration and preserved their rights to the landed estates farmed by serfs, the unprivileged groups, especially the peasantry, had no reason to be grateful to the tsar-reformer. Endless and seemingly purposeless wars had drained the economic resources and reserves of man power. Russian soldiers, poorly clad, poorly armed, and poorly trained, went often without supplies or pay and died by the thousands on the battlefields of the Baltic provinces, Finland,

Poland, central Europe, Turkey, and Persia. In working on gigantic public enterprises, such as the construction of the Azov and the Baltic fleets and internal waterways, the fortification of the Azov littoral, and the building of Peter's "paradise" in the Finnish swamps, thousands of conscripted laborers perished from hunger, cold, and disease. In a number of instances their sacrifices were futile and the projects (for example, the entire Azov venture) were simply abandoned; in others hardships were aggravated by the tsar's capricious moods. He altered several times his plans for St. Petersburg, necessitating the removal of public buildings and private houses from one part of the Neva estuary to another. The introduction of the poll tax not only increased the financial burden of the servile population but also extended the yoke of serfdom to various groups that had previously enjoyed a semblance of personal freedom. Nothing was done to improve the position of the serfs. In April, 1721, it is true, came the much-quoted decree denouncing the custom of selling serfs "separately, like cattle, a practice which is not tolerated anywhere else in the world," but no remedy was provided except the benevolent suggestion that serfs should be sold in the future as entire families, and not as individuals. The usual heavy penalties, a characteristic attribute of Petrine legislation, were in this case conspicuously absent.

The discontent of the peasantry caused by the yoke of serfdom, military and labor conscription, and fiscal exactions was further fostered by disturbing and extravagant yet not unfounded rumors concerning the tsar's entourage and his personal behavior. The agitation of the old-believers, especially after the resumption of punitive measures against them, added to the general feeling of uncertainty and disaffection. Driven to desperation, the serfs employed against the tyrannical government the familiar weapons they had so often and so unsuccessfully used in the past: they fled and, when the opportunity presented itself, they rebelled. Authoritative contemporary documents bear melancholy evidence of the mass flight of army recruits and farmers who made their way to the southern steppes and the wooded wilderness of the northeast where one could still hope to escape the landlords, the recruiting officers, and the tax collectors. Restrictive measures, penalties, and punitive expeditions proved unable to check the peculiar process of internal migration which continued throughout Peter's reign.

Rebellions flared up here and there. The uprising of the *streltsy* in

Moscow in 1698 was followed by an even more extensive one in Astrakhan in 1705. In the same year the Bashkirs, a people of Mongol descent who lived along the Volga, exasperated by the exactions of a Russian governor, opened negotiations with the Crimean Tartars. A rebellion that broke out on the Volga in 1707 found a ready response among the Don Cossacks led by Kondraty Bulavin. These movements, which assumed threatening dimensions, were suppressed by Russian troops. Bulavin committed suicide, but Ukraine continued to seethe with discontent. Less extensive but violent and bloody uprisings of peasants and native tribes took place sporadically in various parts of the country, especially in the south and along the Volga, only to bring against the participants the customary punitive expeditions.

Just as indicative of the temper of the masses and quite as disturbing to the government was the sullen opposition which found expression in whispering campaigns carried on behind closed doors in taverns, monasteries, and private homes. The autocratic master of Russia would seem to have been possessed with an insatiable curiosity to know what was thought and said about him by the humblest of his subjects. As if the activities of the security police, which received so elaborate an organization in the reign of Peter, were not sufficient, the government spared neither threats of punishment nor promises of reward to induce private individuals to turn informers.[11] The magic formula "The word and the deed" ("*Slovo i delo*"), that is, a word and a deed directed against the sovereign, opened to informers the doors of police headquarters, and the wheels of medieval inquisition were set in motion. The archives of the dreaded *Preobrazhenskii prikaz* (security police) have preserved a remarkable collection of human documents which reveal how the common people felt about their tsar. From the confessions extorted in the torture chamber it appears that to a surprisingly large number of those caught in the network of the police, Peter was the living embodiment of the Apocalyptical Beast, an opinion widely shared by the old-believers. The

---

[11] According to Semevsky, detailed instructions designed to encourage private informers were contained in the following decrees: November, 1705; March 2, 1711; Aug. 25, 1713; Oct. 25, 1713; Jan. 25, 1714; Jan. 25, 1715; Sept. 26, 1715; Dec. 24, 1715; April 16, 1717; April 19, 1717; Jan. 19, 1718; April 16, 1719; Feb. 9, 1720; July 22, 1720; Feb. 19, 1721; Jan. 11, 1722, and "in many other decrees." M. I. Semevsky, *Tsaritsa Praskovia* (Tsarina Praskovia) (2nd ed., Moscow, 1883), p. 127.

thoroughness with which the authorities went into the details and possible implications of casual remarks dropped by a tavern keeper or a peasant woman sometimes years before the investigation was opened is truly amazing. The matter is of more than passing interest because spying and action by security police, which Peter did so much to implant, have remained ever since one of the pillars of Russia's government.

The price the contemporaries of Peter paid for the privilege of seeing Russia promoted to the dignity of a European Power was high. There is evidence that at least some of the influential representatives of the regime looked to the future with dark foreboding. In December, 1716, Admiral Count Fedor Apraksin, one of Peter's closest collaborators, wrote: "Truly, we move about in all affairs as if we were blind and did not know what to do; there is a terrible state of confusion everywhere, and who will help us out, and what shall we do next?" This cry of despair, which appears in a private letter addressed to the tsar's secretary, Makarov, is probably a fair statement of the feeling of those around the throne at the time, and Peter himself, for all his care-free boldness, was finally driven to realize that both Russia and the dynasty had reached a tragic impasse. In an autocracy the person of the monarch is of paramount importance. While the theory of monarchy "by the grace of God" was inherited by Russia from Byzantium and was expounded by Ivan the Dread in his writings, Peter was the first to give legislative recognition to a doctrine that had long received acceptance in practice. The Army Regulations of 1716 proclaimed that "His Majesty is an absolute monarch who is not responsible to anyone in the world for his deeds; but he has the right and the power to govern his realm and his lands, as a Christian sovereign, according to his will and wisdom." The Church Statute of 1721 restated the same principle in a formula which was retained with but minor modifications until 1917: "The power of monarchs is autocratic, and to obey it conscientiously is ordained by God himself." This exalted conception of monarchical absolutism was extended by Peter to the all-important question of succession to the throne. Old Muscovy had no law of succession, and although the Crown, according to tradition, passed to the eldest son, the rule was not always observed. Peter, however, had no direct male descendants except his grandson, the future Emperor Peter II, son of Tsarevich Alexis, whose unhappy fate has already been described. Determined to remove the boy Peter from the line of succession, the tsar promulgated on February 5, 1722, a decree which, after a bitter indictment of the late Tsarevich Alexis, proclaimed the emperor's right to appoint his own successor so that he might eliminate any member of the dynasty he considered unfit for the office. Theophan Prokopovich hastened with more zeal than good judgment to prepare an elaborate apology for this new act of the monarch's unfailing wisdom, but how Peter intended to exercise his newly acquired power remains an enigma. It is likely that he found himself in a state of perplexity similar to that so naively but eloquently expressed by Count Apraksin in 1716 and that his bewilderment was increased by the intimate tragedy that clouded the closing year of his reign. He died without appointing his successor, and after having devoted his life to the service of autocracy left the country without a master.

PETER AT THE BAR OF HISTORY

Peter the Great is the outstanding epic figure of Russian historiography. The keynote for the dithyrambic tributes of later poets, publicists, and historians was sounded by his lifelong apologist, Theophan Prokopovich, in a pompous funeral oration where the name of the tsar-reformer was linked with those of Samson, Japheth, Moses, Solomon, David, and Constantine. It early became customary to attribute to Peter superhuman powers and even divine origin, either unreservedly (Sumarokov) or with some qualifications (Lomonsov). With the spread of French influence in the second half of the eighteenth century, educated Russians began to modify their attitude towards the country's national hero, probably under the influence of criticisms of his despotic rule expressed in French literature, especially by Montesquieu. Karamzin (1776–1826), the first Russian historian of some importance, saw in the late emperor a genius and a great reformer, but he criticized the tsar's methods and felt that in many respects he went too far when he violated Russia's national tradition, her *Volksgeist*. In the first half of the nineteenth century this point of view received further support and became the center of a heated controversy between the so-called "slavophiles" and the "westerners." The former school of thought (Aksakov, Khomiakov, Samarin) believed in the inherent virtues of Russian institutions and deplored the destruction of the national tradition by the imposition of a foreign civilization. The slavophiles, nevertheless, admired the man whose work they hated, and they paid tribute to Peter's singleness of purpose, integrity, and energy. The westerners, on the contrary, preached the gospel of the universality of human culture, which in their opinion had found its highest expression in Germany, and they particularly praised Peter for breaking with the past and forcing Russia into the only road that would lead to progress and enlightenment. According to Belinsky, an eloquent exponent of this view, Peter was "the most extraordinary phenomenon not only in our history, but in the history of mankind; he is a deity who has called us into being and who has breathed the breath of life into the body of ancient Russia, colossal but prostrate in deadly slumber." Both slavophiles and westerners agreed not only in extolling the personality of Peter but also in considering his reign as a turning point in the history of the country, as a clear breach with the past.

In the middle of the nineteenth century Russian scholars became acquainted with the ideas and methods of the German historical school. S. M. Solovev and his colleagues and disciples understood history as a process of organic development, one which they endeavored to describe and explain. To them the reforms of Peter were not an extraordinary phenomenon of divine origin but the inevitable and logical consequence of conditions prevailing in the seventeenth century; and if in their interpretation the personality of the tsar lost its superman glamour, his activities no longer needed justification by appeals to the universality of human culture, for they were represented as manifestations of the inexorable process of historical development. This historical school rendered invaluable service to Russian historiography and at the same time it permitted nationalistic-minded historians to combine illuminating factual studies with the glorification of traditional heroes. The most striking example of this type of interpretation is offered by the writings of Kliuchevsky, whose name has been so often mentioned in these pages. His chapters on Peter the Great, written with that insight and literary skill of which he remains the unsurpassed master, trace a most unflattering picture both of the tsar and of his work. Yet he concludes what often reads like an indictment with the statement that "while the reform, as carried out by Peter, was his *personal* enterprise, an enterprise of *unexampled ruthlessness*, it was *not arbitrary* and was, indeed, *necessary*." This brief appraisal reveals the usual approach of Russian historiography

in dealing with Peter, an approach that has been elaborated with innumerable variations by the members of the craft.

Few historians thus far have succeeded in freeing themselves from
the spell of a deep-rooted tradition that goes back to Theophan
Prokopovich. There have been, of course, dissenting voices, for instance, that of Semevsky, who never expressed any admiration for
Peter; but Semevsky was concerned with separate and particularly
unpalatable aspects of the reign, such as the activities of the police
department, conditions prevailing in court circles, and the unhappy
romance between Catherine and Mons. The only two historians of
note who refused to do homage to "the founder of modern Russia"
were Miliukov and Pokrovsky. Miliukov, however, in a volume published in French in 1932, had somewhat modified his earlier views, and
Pokrovsky, who until his death in 1932 was the dean of Soviet historians, has since been repudiated by the Moscow scholars always obedient
to the wishes of the government. This ungracious act was not altogether unconnected with Pokrovsky's attitude towards Peter the Great.

While history has dealt kindly with the tsar-reformer, popular tradition has shown less restraint and, perhaps, sounder judgment. The
illiterate masses at times expressed their opinions through cheap popular lithographs, a medium within their reach. One of the most illuminating examples of this humble art is a picture representing the burial
of a cat by mice, a bitter and witty satire on Peter, his entourage, his
reforms, and the hypocritical and ostentatious display of official grief
that followed his demise. This lithograph, as well as several popular
tales in which Peter is assigned the part of antichrist, is attributed to
the old-believers, but the records of the security police and other
evidence leave no doubt that the dislike of the tsar and everything he
stood for was widely shared by people of every social group, irrespective
of their religious affiliation.

It seems strange that the almost unanimous judgment of history
should differ so widely from that of a large section of contemporary
opinion, nor is it obvious that the well established and generally known
facts about Peter, his policies, his character, his life, his reforms and
their consequences warrant the leniency displayed towards him by
Russian historians. An important reason for the glorification of the
tsar-reformer is probably the contagious effect of a historical and officially inspired tradition. Censorship and the inadequacy of docu-

mentary evidence made possible the spread and survival of the Petrine legend, a legend that received powerful support from Russia's greatest poet, Pushkin (1799–1837), who wrote at a time when Russian historiography was still in its infancy. Pushkin possessed an unmatched mastery of the Russian language, and the magic of his verse has a compelling power which is all but irresistible to those who speak the Russian language. Some of his most enchanting and best known poems eulogize Peter the Great; they have been learned by heart by generations of boys and girls, and they exercise an influence from which even the trained historian finds it difficult to free himself.

The most potent factor in the persistence of the Petrine tradition, however, is the cult of national heroes common to every national and nationalistic state. Russian historiography, like the historiography of other countries, is frequently inspired by vague and mystical notions such as national interest, historical destiny, and preordained tasks which a country must fulfill in order to achieve self-expression. In the fourteenth and fifteenth centuries the "historical destinies" of Russia were said to have clamored for the unification of the country, hence the justification of Muscovite absolutism. In the eighteenth century inexorable forces are represented as having imperatively demanded an outlet on the Baltic Sea and the westernization of institutions and even dress. Herein is found an apologia for everything that Peter did. Many Russian historians move with remarkable ease in the midst of these abstract and elusive notions, with the result that a scholar as eminent as Kliuchevsky asserts in the same sentence that the reforms of Peter were "personal" and "ruthless," "necessary" and "not arbitrary." From the point of view of the mystical philosophy borrowed from Germany, which underlies all such generalizations, the statement is practically self-evident, since Peter is regarded as an instrument in the hands of the omnipotent goddess of history.

Merely to disregard such preconceived and romantic theories suffices to reveal their fallacy. The majestic mirage disappears the moment one descends from the celestial regions inhabited by the framers of historical destinies. Viewed from the vantage point of lower altitudes, territorial expansion no longer appears the unmixed blessing it is held to be by nationalistic-minded statesmen and historians; such expansion, when accompanied—as was the case in the Petrine wars— with the devastation of once prosperous provinces and the piling up of crushing burdens on the people at home, assumes the character of a calamity. A country exhausted by decades of uninterrupted military struggle, ruthlessly regimented by a crude and corrupt bureaucracy, and seething with discontent is hardly in a mood to enjoy the fruits of a foreign civilization, even though her monarch carried on a correspondence with Leibnitz and issued decrees ordering the establishment of schools—without teachers, students, or books. Russia, moreover, was not hedged in by a Chinese Wall, and the infiltration of western ideas had begun long before Peter ascended the throne. Even if we assume that closer contact with Europe was eminently desirable, as it probably was, there is little evidence that the spectacular reforms of Peter really contributed much to the acceleration of this process. The moment the goddess of history, with whom the historians so freely commune, is excluded from participation in human affairs, the flimsy and fanciful temple of Petrine greatness crumbles into dust.

The communist leaders of Russia have recently joined the ranks of those upholding the Petrine tradition. The Soviet film *Emperor Peter I* presents a highly roseate picture of the tsar-carpenter struggling against overwhelming odds to lift barbaric Muscovy to the level of European culture, to build a new and better Russia. The parallel with the present endeavor of the Soviet government is unmistakable and the didactic purpose of the film almost too obvious. It is unquestionably true that there are striking similarities between the methods of Peter and those of Stalin, but they are not exactly of the kind the Moscow producers and historians care to emphasize.

CHAPTER XVI

THE ERA OF PALACE REVOLUTIONS

The Successors of Peter I, 1725–1761

---❊---

THE AFTERMATH OF THE GREAT REIGN

The thirty-seven years following the death of Peter, especially the period preceding the accession to the throne of his daughter Elizabeth, are often represented as a sad anticlimax to the achievements of the great reign, a temporary abandonment by unworthy heirs of the inspiring heritage handed down to them by the tsar-reformer. From 1725 to 1762 the imperial Crown changed hands seven times. To the grotesque and fantastic procession of monarchs who mounted the throne in the interval between the reign of Peter I and that of Catherine II must be added the even more numerous and bewildering array of their favorites, the actual masters of the country. The exotic courts of these rulers and the bizarre and sinister *cortège* of ignorant, licentious women, half-witted German princes, and mere children on whose shoulders in turn descended the imperial purple present a morbidly fascinating picture suggestive of the imaginative and unreal world created by some medieval craftsman and preserved in ancient Italian embroideries and in stained-glass windows. The immediate causes that started Russia on this devious course were the decree of 1722 conferring upon the sovereign the power to nominate his successor (a right Peter failed to exercise) and the dynastic alliances he had so eagerly contracted with various German princely houses. The real force behind eighteenth century Russia's palace revolutions and quasi-revolutions, however, was the regiments of the guards which Peter had founded and which he had raised to the position of one of the most influential government organs. It was they, in the last resort, who decided the fate of the throne. The vicissitudes suffered

ORDER OF SUCCESSION TO THE THRONE, 1645–1762

Order of succession after the death of Peter I is indicated by Roman numerals

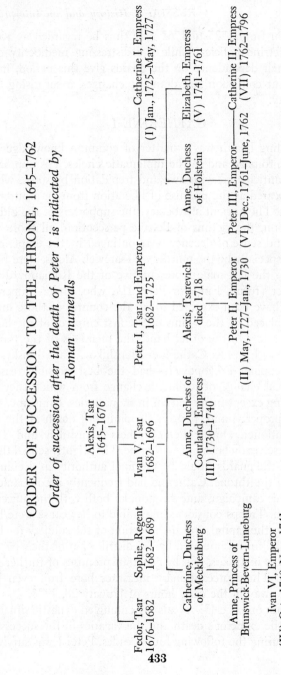

by the Crown from 1725 to 1762 may thus be regarded as a consequence of Petrine policies, while the distressing mediocrity of the rulers and their dependence on the guards give this period, in spite of its apparent confusion and dramatic changes, a surprising degree of inner unity.

CATHERINE I

Peter's failing health was a matter of common knowledge in his immediate entourage and in the diplomatic circles. His approaching demise was anticipated with awe and trepidation by some, while to others it appeared as the promise of liberation from an arbitrary and despotic rule. The ancient aristocracy, the supporters of the old Muscovite tradition, the victims of Petrine persecution, all those whose conscience and sense of decency were outraged by the emperor's behavior and especially by the murder of Tsarevich Alexis, were turning with hope to the last male representative of the Romanov dynasty, the boy Peter (future Emperor Peter II), who, under proper guidance, might have been expected to rid the country of those lowborn adventurers placed by the whims of the first emperor at the helm of the ship of state. On the other hand, the members of the tsar's immediate circle—Empress Catherine, Menshikov, Yaguzhinsky, Peter Tolstoy, Theophan Prokopovich—had the best possible reason to dread a radical change of regime, a change from which they could expect nothing except incarceration in monasteries, banishment, confiscation of property, and, perhaps, ignominious death at the hands of the executioner. During Peter's illness Menshikov and Tolstoy exerted themselves on behalf of Catherine. They rightly sensed that the regiments of the guards would be the final authority in deciding the succession to the throne. Catherine had frequently accompanied her husband in his campaigns and was popular both with the officers and with the men. Troops considered favorable to her cause were hastily summoned to the capital, and the affection of the soldiery for Peter's spouse was skillfully stimulated by the distribution of their pay, then sixteen months in arrears, and by generous promises of further monetary rewards. These precautionary measures bore fruit even before Peter passed away in the early hours of January 28, 1725.

The diagram on page 433 reveals the entangled dynastic situation at the time of the emperor's death and the vagaries in the succession to the throne during the following four decades. Peter I was survived by his grandson Peter, son of Tsarevich Alexis; by two daughters, Anne and Elizabeth, born to the future Empress Catherine before she was lawfully married; by three nieces—Catherine, Anne, and Praskovie [1] —daughters of his elder brother and former co-ruler, Tsar Ivan V; by his second wife, Empress Catherine; and by his first wife, the former Tsarina Eudoxie, whom he had forced to take the veil. The decree of February 5, 1722, did away with the traditional order of succession, which pointed to the boy Peter, then nine years old, and when it became clear that the emperor was likely to die without appointing an heir, government dignitaries assembled at the palace on the night of January 27 to decide who should succeed him. Prince Dimitry Golitsin, a representative of the old aristocracy who had spent many years abroad and was one of the best educated men of his time, proposed a compromise solution: the boy Peter to be emperor and the country to be provisionally ruled by a regency consisting of Empress Catherine and the Senate. Peter Tolstoy, who had been instrumental in persuading Tsarevich Alexis to return to Russia from Italy, objected to the Golitsin proposal and demanded that Catherine should be recognized as Russia's autocratic ruler. In the meantime the officers of the guards had drifted into the council chamber and noisily proclaimed their allegiance to the empress; any potential opposition was nipped in the bud by the even more vociferous demonstrations of fealty to Catherine by the two regiments of the guards which had been summoned to the palace. The elder statesmen bowed to the inevitable, and all those present at the conference signed an act making Catherine empress of Russia in her own right even before Peter I had rendered his last breath. A manifesto issued the same day in the name of the Holy Synod, the Senate, and the *generalitet* (holders of offices of the four higher classes according to the Table of Ranks), announced the accession of the empress and justified the unprecedented action on the ground that Catherine had been crowned in 1724 by her imperial husband. The change of political regime took place without any serious disturbance, and the few old-fashioned people who questioned the propriety of taking an oath of allegiance to a female ruler who was, moreover, a former Lithuanian peasant girl, the mother of Peter's illegitimate children, and the mistress of

---

[1] Princess Praskovie played no political part and does not appear in the diagram. It is believed that she was secretly married to General I. I. Dmitriev-Mamonov. She died childless in 1731.

Menshikov and Mons were soon brought by the security police to re-
cant their error. The seemingly trivial episode of Catherine's election
was of more than passing interest since it established the pattern for
the palace revolution throughout the eighteenth century: the selection of the monarch by a casual group of higher officials supported by
the regiments of the guards.

Catherine filled only too well the part assigned to her by her supporters. A coarse, illiterate, and licentious woman with neither the
ability nor the desire to conduct the affairs of state, she left the
government in the hands of Menshikov. Yet the position of the "overbearing Goliath," as Menshikov was frequently called by his enemies,
was once more fraught with danger. Catherine, freed from the restraint imposed on her by fear of her formidable husband, endeavored
to forget the loss of William Mons in the company of noble and
handsome international adventurers, the Baltic German Reinhold
Löwenwolde and Peter Sapieha, scion of the great Polish family. Debauchery and intemperate drinking were undermining her once robust
constitution, and it soon became apparent that her reign would be a
short one. Moreover, Charles Frederick, duke of Holstein, who in
May, 1725, married the Tsarevna Anne, won the confidence of Catherine, and together with his scheming minister Bassevitz, claiming full
credit for having engineered her accession to the throne, interfered in
Russian affairs. Rumors of an impending *coup d'état* in favor of the
boy Peter, backed by the Ukrainian army under Prince Michael Golitsin, were circulated in the capital early in 1726.

Menshikov had innumerable enemies, and his arrogant attitude
towards the Senate made cooperation between them extremely difficult. His desire to secure for his rule a more solid foundation than
that afforded by the personal favors of Catherine and his efforts to
enlist support of leading personalities among the old and the new
aristocracy were probably instrumental in bringing about the creation
of a new central organ, the Supreme Privy Council (*Verkhovnyi Tainyi
Soviet*). This Council, organized by virtue of a decree of February 8,
1726, consisted of six members—Field Marshal Prince Menshikov,
president of the army college; Admiral Count F. M. Apraksin, president of the admiralty college; Count G. I. Golovkin, the chancellor;
Baron A. I. Ostermann, the vice chancellor; Count P. Tolstoy and
Prince D. M. Golitsin, who had both held various high offices. Of this
group Golitsin alone was a member of the old Muscovite nobility. The

Council, which was to advise the empress on all important measures, had the power to issue decrees. It was somewhat reminiscent of the old irregular and informal gatherings of higher officials under Peter I, with the all-important difference, however, that unlike her predecessor Catherine took no active part in the conduct of the affairs of state and the Supreme Privy Council became in fact, if not in law, the actual ruler of the country. The Senate, which had the temerity sometimes to disagree with Menshikov, was deprived by a decree of March 11, 1726, of its title of "Governing" Senate and became the "High" Senate; it ceased to be the central administrative institution and was reduced to the status of a mere college. The office of the chief procurator of the Senate was not formally abolished, but with the transfer of the once all-powerful Yaguzhinsky to the less exalted position of Her Majesty's chief equerry the vacancy remained unfilled. The triumph of Menshikov over the Senate and his old antagonist Yaguzhinsky was somewhat offset by an imperial order of February 17, 1726, appointing the duke of Holstein to the Supreme Privy Council in spite of the favorite's strenuous opposition. Menshikov, however, had many ingenious schemes for ensuring his own future. In the summer of 1726 he persuaded the empress to lend the support of the Russian troops to the promotion of his candidacy to the throne of Courland, a fanciful plan that had to be abandoned because of the opposition of Poland, which exercised a vague feudal jurisdiction over the duchy.

The failing health of Catherine and the ascendency of the duke of Holstein in Russian affairs called for a solution of the vexed question of the empress's successor. The boy Peter, son of Tsarevich Alexis, was clearly in line of succession as the only surviving male member of the dynasty, and his tender age suggested seemingly unlimited possibilities for using him as a tool in the hands of a properly constituted regency. Too many of Catherine's intimate advisers, however, had been involved in the unhappy affair of Tsarevich Alexis not to feel some apprehension about the accession of the murdered man's son. The ever resourceful Ostermann conceived the promising plan of bridging over old family feuds by marrying Peter to his seductive aunt, Tsarevna Elizabeth, who was his senior by some six years and to whose charms the precocious boy was by no means indifferent. However, nothing came of this proposal, partly because of the opposition of the Russian clergy and partly because Menshikov had discovered another solution which, from his point of view, offered most dazzling prospects: a marriage between his daughter Maria and young Peter. With the assistance of the Austrian ambassador, Count Rabutin,[2] the consent of the empress to the proposed union was obtained in March, 1727. A few weeks later, on May 6, Catherine died after a painful illness. The next day the Supreme Privy Council, the Senate, the Synod, and the higher officials met at the palace and took cognizance of a testament allegedly signed by the late empress. This document provided for a novel and arbitrary order of succession. The imperial Crown was to pass to Peter and his descendants or, in case of the extinction of his line, to Catherine's two daughters: first to Anne of Holstein and her descendants, and then to Tsarevna Elizabeth and her descendants. The daughters of Ivan V, who represented the senior branch of the dynasty, were not even mentioned. During the minority of Peter the empire was to be governed by the Supreme Privy Council, which was to be composed of nine members, including Tsarevna Elizabeth and the duke and duchess of Holstein. The testament, which is believed to have been a forgery, having been approved by the high assembly, the regiments of the guards, assembled in front of the palace, cheered the accession of the new emperor, Peter II.

PETER II

Menshikov appeared to be at the pinnacle of his power. Peter, then eleven years old, came to live in the home of his prospective father-in-law, and his engagement to Maria Menshikov was celebrated on May 25. Elevated to the dignity of generalissimo, Menshikov was more than ever the country's absolute ruler, since the other members of the Supreme Privy Council deemed it wise to follow his wishes. Far from sharing in the councils of the regency, the duke and duchess of Holstein found their position in St. Petersburg untenable, and at the end of July, 1727, they left for Kiel, where the duchess died in May, 1728, soon after giving birth to a son, the future Emperor Peter III. Tsarevna Elizabeth, absorbed in amorous adventures, had neither the

---

[2] Count Rabutin enjoyed particular influence at the Russian court after the conclusion of the Russo-Austrian alliance on Aug. 6, 1726. It will be remembered that young Peter was a nephew of the wife of Emperor Charles VI (see p. 330). Both the Austrian and the Danish courts were anxious to eliminate the duke of Holstein from participation in Russian affairs since his claims to the Swedish throne and to Schleswig threatened the international situation. It is believed that the idea of a marriage between Maria Menshikov and Peter was suggested to Menshikov by officials in Austrian and Danish circles.

ability nor the desire to play a political role. Young Peter, whose education was entrusted by Menshikov to Ostermann, displayed little aptitude for study and spent his time in the joyous company of his sister Nathalie, one year his senior, and in that of his captivating aunt, Elizabeth. An influential member of Peter's entourage was the nineteen-year-old Prince Ivan Dolgoruky, offspring of an ancient aristocratic family which Menshikov had endeavored to win over to his side. The boy-emperor, unusually tall and physically developed beyond his age, with his band of youthful friends spent his time in festivities, hunting expeditions, and other less innocent recreations.

Except for a certain coolness in the attitude of Peter towards his bride, nothing suggested the impending downfall of Menshikov. The "overbearing Goliath," however, succeeded in antagonizing almost everyone, and the boy-emperor, irritated by his mentor's curt manners, lent a willing ear to the insinuations of friends who reminded him of the sinister part played by Menshikov in the tragic end of Tsarevich Alexis. A powerful cabal led by the Dolgoruky and, probably, by Ostermann, was preparing the blow directed at the man who had put Peter II on the throne. Menshikov suffered an attack of illness, and his temporary inactivity favored the conspiracy. The regiments of the guards, in the ranks of which Menshikov had begun his career, were prevailed upon not to intervene on behalf of the generalissimo. On September 7, 1727, Peter took up his residence in one of the imperial palaces, and the following day Menshikov was put under arrest. Not a single voice was raised to defend the man who only yesterday had seemed all-powerful. He was deprived of his offices and decorations and deported, with his family, first to his estate in Oranienburg (later Ranenburg, province of Riazan) and then to Berezov, in the bleakness of Siberia. He was accused of treasonable relations with Sweden and of other crimes, his fortune was confiscated, and he died in 1729 in exile. Peter's bride, Maria, followed her father to the grave a few weeks later.

The fall of Menshikov marked a return to the tradition of old Muscovy. In January, 1728, the court moved to the ancient capital for the coronation of the young emperor, and in the summer of the same year a number of central government departments were transferred to Moscow. The "paradise" of Peter the Great and all it stood for, many foreign observers believed, was doomed. The boy-emperor became the play-thing of the Dolgoruky. In February, 1728, Prince

Alexis and Prince V. L. Dolgoruky were appointed to the Supreme Privy Council, and Prince Ivan received the title of ober-chamberlain, an especial mark of imperial favor. The death in 1728 of Peter's sister Nathalie and the estrangement between the emperor and his aunt Elizabeth aided the Dolgoruky in keeping the youthful monarch under their own influence. On November 13, 1729, announcement was made of the engagement of Peter to the seventeen-year-old Catherine Dolgoruky, daughter of Prince Alexis, a move of which some of the more prudent members of the Dolgoruky family, mindful of the fate of Menshikov, did not approve. Their apprehensions were well founded, although the *dénouement* came in a manner no one could have foreseen. Early in January, 1730, when Peter was fourteen years and three months old, he was taken ill with smallpox and died at the Moscow Lefort Palace on January 19, the day fixed for his wedding. Upon his death the male branch of the Romanov dynasty became extinct.

EMPRESS ANNE

For the third time in five years the throne was vacant, and the dynastic situation was as obscure as ever. Immediately after the death of the boy-emperor, which occurred at 1:00 A.M., the members of the Supreme Privy Council met in a secret session at the Lefort Palace. In addition to the five regular members of the Council, the conclave included Prince M. V. Dolgoruky, Field Marshal Prince V. V. Dolgoruky, and Field Marshal Prince M. M. Golitsin, that is, the assembly consisted of the Chancellor Count Golovkin, the Vice Chancellor Baron Ostermann, four Dolgoruky and two Golitsin. Prince Alexis Dolgoruky made a meek and ineffective attempt to claim the throne for his daughter, the bride of Peter II: the scheming courtier had gone to the trouble of drafting a testament in which Peter II named Catherine Dolgoruky his successor and which her brother, Prince Ivan, signed with the emperor's name. According to Prince Alexis's plan, Field Marshal Dolgoruky and Prince Ivan, respectively lieutenant colonel and major in the guards, were to win over their regiments to the cause of the imperial bride, a scheme the field marshal had declared impracticable and in which he had refused to participate. The plea of Prince Alexis on behalf of his daughter was rejected by the conference, as was the proposal to follow the order of succession established in the "testament" of Catherine I. According to Prince

D. M. Golitsin, Catherine had no legal right to the Crown, her "testament" was worthless, and since her daughters had been born out of wedlock neither Tsarevna Elizabeth nor the young duke of Holstein, son of the late Tsarevna Anne, was in line for the throne. The candidacy of the first wife of Peter I, the former Tsarina Eudoxie (who was forced to take the veil in 1699 and who was imprisoned in the Schlüsselburg fortress by Catherine I and released after the accession of Peter II) was also examined and rejected. The choice was thus narrowed down to the senior branch of the Romanov—the daughters of the feeble-minded Tsar Ivan V. The eldest of the three sisters, Catherine, duchess of Mecklenburg, was eliminated because of her husband, who was rightly regarded as one of the most worthless German princelets and a potential source of infinite trouble, while the youngest sister, Praskovie, does not seem even to have been mentioned. Ivan's second daughter, Anne, duchess of Courland, commended herself to the conference chiefly because she appeared to have been schooled in perfect humility and obedience. To those members of the conference who dreamed of curtailing the arbitrary powers of the Crown, Anne might well have appeared as a most acceptable choice. An agreement was reached to offer her the imperial throne, but the invitation was qualified by important limitations on the powers of the future empress set forth in a separate document known as the "Conditions" (*konditsii*). Anne was requested to promise that she would not marry or appoint an heir and that she would continue "the now-existing Supreme Privy Council of eight members." It was further stipulated that without the consent of that body the empress should not declare war or make peace; impose taxes; confer army or civil ranks above that of colonel; deprive the *dvoriane* of their estates without a trial; grant estates; confer court titles on either Russians or foreigners or make court appointments; dispose of state revenue. The "Conditions" also stated that "the guards and other regiments" were to be under the direct control of the Supreme Privy Council. The document ended with the solemn declaration that by violating any of the above provisions the empress should forfeit her right to the Crown. The wording of the "Conditions" would seem to suggest that the self-appointed constituent assembly of eight members was planning to put Russia under an oligarchic regime, although what the chief proponent of the proposed limitations of autocracy, D. M. Golitsin, actually had in mind was an aristocratic form of government on the

Swedish model. The course taken by the Supreme Privy Council was presumably inspired by the events which, after the death of Charles XII of Sweden, led to the election of Ulrica Eleonora in 1719.

On the morning of January 19 the Senate, the Synod, and the higher ecclesiastical, military, and civilian officials assembled in the Kremlin and formally approved the election of the duchess of Courland, announced to them on behalf of the Supreme Privy Council by D. M. Golitsin. Nothing, however, was said about the "Conditions," although some of the members of the assembly had been previously informed of the proposed move. The secrecy which shrouded the action of the Supreme Privy Council added to the excitement, not unmixed with consternation, with which rumors of the proposed limitation of autocracy had been received in many influential circles. The Golitsin and, especially, the Dolgoruky had numerous enemies with excellent reasons to dread their advent to power. An oligarchy, many believed, was even more to be feared than an autocracy. The feeling of dismay was particularly strong among those who, like Yaguzhinsky and Theophan Prokopovich, were responsible for the accession of Catherine.

On the evening of January 19 a delegation headed by Prince V. L. Dolgoruky left for Mittau, Courland, to advise Anne of her election and to assure her that the "Conditions" represented the will and wishes of the entire people of Russia. In spite of the precautions taken by the government to cut off all communications between Moscow and Courland, emissaries of Yaguzhinsky, Prokopovich, and Reinhold Gustavus Löwenwolde (whose brother, Carl Gustavus, was believed to be intimate with Anne) [3] succeeded in reaching Mittau and urged the duchess to reject the "Conditions." Anne, nevertheless, appended on January 28 her signature to the document, which deprived her of all real power, and also to a letter of acceptance, drafted by Prince V. L. Dolgoruky, which made the concessions exacted by the Supreme Privy Council appear as a gracious gift of the new empress to her beloved people. The sanctimonious statement of the letter was incompatible with the stern wording of the "Conditions." Little wonder, therefore, that when both documents were officially communicated to the assembled Supreme Privy Council, Senate, Synod, and higher

[3] There is disagreement among the authorities as to which of the two brothers Löwenwolde was in Moscow at the time, and the sources are not clear on this point. Reinhold and Carl Löwenwolde, as well as a third brother, Frederick Casimir, enjoyed great influence at the Russian Court in Anne's reign.

officials on February 2 they were received with a conspicuous lack of enthusiasm. In an attempt to stem the rising wave of criticism, the Supreme Privy Council directed the *dvoriane* to submit in writing their own wishes concerning necessary reforms. Although the arrest of Yaguzhinsky, which was ordered simultaneously, was not conducive to the free expression of views at variance with those of the Council, the veil of secrecy was now lifted and the higher "estate" of the realm was offered an opportunity to voice its aspirations.

The throngs of the *dvoriane* gathered in Moscow in January, 1730, for the marriage of Peter II were thrown into great confusion by the circumstances of Anne's election. Foreign diplomats accredited to the Russian court [4] were inclined to interpret the heated discussions that took place everywhere as the manifestation of a strong political movement directed towards the establishment of a form of constitutional government on the English, Swedish or Polish model, or even of a republic. The texts of the twelve projects, most of them hastily written, submitted by the *dvoriane* in response to the request of the Supreme Privy Council, and preserved for posterity, do not support this conclusion. Professor Korsakov, author of the most important study of the events of January, 1730, rightly observes that "it would be idle to look for any clearly understood political ideals" in these petitions bearing 1,218 signatures, although they shed much light on the aspirations of the *dvoriane*. The projects disclosed a resentment of arbitrary rule, especially by favorites, and made proposals to curb the resulting abuses by providing for the participation in government of representatives of the *dvoriane* and by making the higher offices elective. Concrete proposals were advanced to prevent the oligarchical rule of individual families (the limitation on the number of members of the same family permitted to belong to the proposed governing body). The chief and most popular proposals for reform, however, voiced the professional grievances of the *dvoriane* and clamored for the shortening of compulsory service to twenty years; permission to enter the army and navy as officers, and not as privates and seamen; better pay for army men; the repeal of the extremely unpopular law of March 23, 1714, on entail. The widespread opposition to oligarchic rule, which continued to remain the basis of the revised project of reform elaborated by Prince D. M. Golitsin, and lack of any real un-

---

[4] The Saxon minister J. L. Lefort, a nephew of Peter I's favorite, Francis Lefort; the Spanish ambassador Duke de Liria; the French resident Magnan.

derstanding of the principles of representative government, and the devious methods used by the instigators of the *coup d'état* paved the way for the restoration of autocracy. The astute Ostermann, who was instrumental in drafting the "Conditions" but who after January 19 took no further part in the activities of the Supreme Privy Council on the pretext of illness, dreaded, as a German, the rule of the Dolgoruky and Golitsin. His new and simple plan consisted in persuading Anne that she was entitled to the Crown in her own right and that her election was therefore superfluous, and in convincing the *dvoriane* that the redress of their grievances was to come from the new sovereign, and not from an oligarchy. The higher clergy, led by Theophan Prokopovich, and many officers of the guards rallied to the support of this proposal.

On February 15 Anne made her entrance into the ancient capital of Russia. Four days earlier she had received in a suburb a delegation of the guards and, in violation of the "Conditions," proclaimed herself colonel of the Preobrazhensky regiment and captain of the Horse Guards. In the meantime the movement for the restoration of autocracy was gaining ground, and the Supreme Privy Council, which was informed of the actions of its opponents, decided on February 25 to arrest the leaders of the opposition, including two of the Council's own members, Golovkin and Ostermann. This decision, however, was never carried out. On the morning of February 25 the imperial palace was surrounded by troops led by officers favoring the restoration of autocracy, and a delegation presented to the empress a petition with eighty-seven signatures, demanding the convocation of a representative assembly of the *dvoriane* to draft proposals for the reorganization of the government. The content of this petition was not what Anne had been led to expect, but the officers of the guards who filled the chamber hastened to make their wishes known by clamoring for the restoration of the absolutism. With the consent of the empress the motley gathering withdrew to an adjoining hall, and a few hours later they presented Anne with a new petition, with 166 signatures, requesting her to restore autocracy, to abolish the Supreme Privy Council, and to issue a constitutional act determining the character of administrative institutions. The petition also expressed the wish that the Senate should resume its functions as the central organ of the regime and that the higher offices should be filled by election. Anne graciously agreed to accept the autocratic power "offered to me by my people" and dramatically tore up the "Conditions" in front of the assembled dignitaries and army officers. The short-lived experiment in an aristocratic-oligarchic monarchy thus came to an end. Aristocracy as an organized social group did not exist in early eighteenth century Russia, and the whole venture was alien to the country's historical tradition. Both the attempt at the limitation of absolute rule and the movement for its restoration were a palace affair and had no popular support.

At the time of her accession to the Russian throne Anne was thirty-seven. Married at the age of seventeen to Frederick Wilhelm, duke of Courland, who died in January, 1711, a few weeks after the wedding, the young widow had spent nineteen years in Mittau, in the abnormal position of a ruling duchess without a duchy. Courland, which from the middle of the sixteenth century had been a fief of Poland, became after the establishment of Russia on the shores of the Baltic a bone of contention between the two Powers. Frederick Wilhelm was succeeded by his childless uncle Ferdinand, who resided most of the time in Danzig and took little part in the government of Courland, which was left in the hands of Peter Bestuzhev-Riumin, Russian agent at the ducal court and the duchess's lover. Anne had had hardly any education, although she eventually acquired a fluent command of the German language. Ignorant, superstitious, bigoted, and sensual, she found her position in Mittau all the more difficult because the perennial shortage of funds made her entirely dependent on the parsimonious subsidies of the Russian court. Her letters, written with complete disregard for spelling and grammar and addressed to her imperial relatives and to the favorites of the day—Menshikov, Ostermann—and members of their families, were models of humbleness and self-effacement. Anne, indeed, appeared to be properly trained for the part D. M. Golitsin and his colleagues had in mind when they offered her the Russian Crown.

In 1726 Anne implored the consent of Catherine to her marriage with the brilliant international adventurer, Count Maurice of Saxe, who had succeeded in getting himself elected duke of Courland by the local diet.[5] Her request was rejected, and she soon found solace

[5] Maurice of Saxe was an illegitimate son of King Augustus II of Poland. His election to the throne of Courland provoked much criticism among the Polish nobility and met with the uncompromising resistance of Russia. Forced by the Russian troops to withdraw from Mittau, Maurice became eventually one of the outstanding generals in the French army of Louis XV.

in a liaison with Ernst Johann Biron (or Bühren), a minor court official of German extraction who once had studied at the University of Königsberg and who was an expert horseman. It was decided by the Supreme Privy Council that Biron should not accompany the newly elected empress to Moscow, but this unofficial condition was no more observed than were the others, and upon the arrival of Biron in Russia he became the chief power behind the throne.

The rule of Anne was extravagant and harsh and revealed evidence of a crude and strangely distorted mind. Freed at last of her Mittau surroundings, the new empress reveled in the luxury of the imperial court and became the central figure in an uninterrupted succession of palace and Church functions of great splendor. An excellent horsewoman and a good shot, Anne dreaded solitude and shared the predilection of Peter I for freaks of nature. The imperial residences were filled not only with animals and birds, especially those trained in the performance of tricks, but also with giants and dwarfs, hunchbacks and cripples, beggars and fools, while a large retinue of women, especially selected for their ability to chatter, spent hours spinning stories for the empress's entertainment. Endowed with a quaint sense of humor, Anne had inherited Peter I's fondness for practical jokes and mock ceremonies. In 1734, for instance, she celebrated the marriage between two of her court jesters—Prince N. F. Volkonsky and Prince A. M. Golitsin, offspring of two of Russia's most illustrious families. The same Golitsin figured again in 1740 as the bridegroom, this time of a Kalmyk woman of outstanding ugliness, at an elaborate wedding performed in a mansion built of ice.

Like so many of her successors, Anne repeatedly proclaimed her intention to govern "in the spirit of Peter the Great." Symbolic of this determination was the return of the court and government to St. Petersburg at the end of 1731. The manifesto of March 4, 1730, dissolved the Supreme Privy Council and reinstated the Senate, with a membership of twenty-one, in its former position as the highest administrative organ. In October, 1730, Yaguzhinsky was reappointed chief procurator of the Senate, an office that had remained vacant since 1726. It soon became clear, however, that these seemingly basic alterations of the administrative structure were of small practical importance. A decree of November 10, 1731, recognized the existence of a new central administrative institution, "the Cabinet of Her Imperial Majesty," which had been unofficially functioning for several months.

A creature of Ostermann, who dominated it, the cabinet consisted of three ministers appointed by the empress. It enjoyed comprehensive and ill defined powers which made it the successor of the Supreme Privy Council in all but name.[6] The resulting eclipse of the Senate was emphasized by the appointment of Yaguzhinsky to the Berlin embassy at the end of 1731, the post of chief procurator remaining vacant for nearly ten years.

Mindful of the part played by the guards in the restoration of autocracy, Anne endeavored to strengthen her position by organizing the Izmailovsky regiment. Count Carl Gustavus Löwenwolde, a trusted and intimate friend of Anne in the days when she was duchess of Courland, became colonel of the new regiment, whose officers were to be drawn from among the Baltic nobility. Crushing blows were dealt to those involved in the movement for the limitation of autocracy. One by one the Dolgoruky, the Golitsin, and their friends were deprived of their offices, deported to remote parts of the country, imprisoned, tried, and executed. The dreaded *Preobrazhenskii prikaz* (security police), abolished in the reign of Peter II (April 4, 1729), was revived in March, 1731, and became the Privy Chancery (*Kantseliariia Tainykh Rozysknykh Del*). Under the expert guidance of General A. J. Ushakov, who had won his spurs in the secret service of Peter I, it instituted a real reign of terror. There was no safety for anyone, and mere suspicion of an unfavorable attitude towards the regime was sufficient for the arrest of men and women, irrespective of social status. Thousands of people went through the torture chamber and disappeared in the fastness of Siberia, many of them never to be heard of again.

Anne's reign has gone down in history as *Bironovshchina*, or the rule of Biron. The favorite, however, had no official position in Russia. He held the court office of ober-chamberlain, his influence resting on his intimacy with the empress. In 1730 he was created count of the Holy Roman Empire and in 1773 was elected duke of Courland

---

[6] The original members of the cabinet were Golovkin, Ostermann, and Prince A. M. Cherkassky. After the death of Golovkin in 1734, the vacancy was filled by the appointment of Yaguzhinsky, an old enemy of Ostermann, introduced into the cabinet at the request of Biron. Yaguzhinsky died in April, 1736, and for two years the cabinet consisted of two members. In April, 1738, A. P. Volynsky was raised to the dignity of cabinet minister, but his conflict with Biron and Ostermann proved his undoing and he was executed in June, 1740. He was succeeded by A. P. Bestuzhev-Riumin, another enemy of Ostermann. After the death of Golovkin, Ostermann was usually referred to as "the first cabinet minister."

by a submissive Mittau diet acting under Russian pressure, the election being duly ratified by King Augustus III of Poland. Biron, however, continued to reside in St. Petersburg, where his authority was not unchallenged. He was on the worst possible terms with the two other powerful German personalities of the reign: Ostermann, who directed Russia's foreign policy, and Field Marshal Burkhard Christoph Münnich, commander of the Russian armies. It is also believed that Biron had to share Anne's intimate favors with Count Carl Gustavus Löwenwolde until the latter's death in 1735. The sphere of Biron's influence, therefore, great as it was, was in fact less comprehensive than is often imagined.

Anne was ailing and childless, and the question of her successor naturally occupied palace circles. The empress and her advisers were determined that the Crown should be retained in the hands of the descendants of Ivan V, to the exclusion of the issue of Peter I. The only offspring of the senior branch of the Romanov family was Princess Anne of Mecklenburg, or Anna Leopoldovna, daughter of the empress's sister Catherine. Biron's plan for a marriage between the princess and his son Peter was defeated by the opposition of Ostermann and of the young woman herself, who chose, as the lesser evil, to marry Prince Anthony Urlic of Brunswick-Bevern-Luneburg, a man for whom she, however, had little affection. A boy born of this union in August, 1740, provided a temporary solution of the dynastic riddle. The empress was taken ill early in October, 1740, and died on October 17. On her deathbed she appointed the infant prince of Brunswick to be her heir, while Biron was to exercise the regency until the baby emperor, who was given the name of Ivan VI, had reached the age of seventeen. This arrangement was devised by a handful of high officials at the instigation of Biron.[7] On this occasion the Senate, the Synod, and the higher dignitaries were not even consulted, nor were the guards taken into the confidence of the conspirators.

[7] The testamentary dispositions of Anne which were announced on October 18 introduced a novel order of succession. It provided that if Ivan VI died without issue the throne was to pass, in order of seniority, to the other male children of Princess Anne and Anthony Urlic. Solovev has rightly observed that since no provision was made for the order of succession of any children Princess Anne might have by another husband (in case of Anthony Urlic's death or of a divorce), the act of October 18 actually established the right of the descendants of Anthony Urlic to the Russian Crown, the House of Brunswick thus superseding the Romanov dynasty.

IVAN VI AND EMPRESS ELIZABETH

Strong as was the German influence at the court of Empress Anne (Biron, Ostermann, Münnich, the Löwenwolde, the Brunswick family, and many others), it was further intensified during the thirteen months following her death, a period when the empire became the play-thing of a small clique of German adventurers guided by selfish motives. Biron, autocratic master of the country by the grace of his mistress and of a few conspirators, was a subject of the Polish Crown and had never taken the trouble to learn the Russian tongue. Although his assumption of office occurred without serious friction, he became the focal point of general hostility. Not only was he made to bear full responsibility for the ignominy of the preceding reign but—and this was of greater immediate consequence—he was cordially hated by Münnich, Ostermann, and the prince and princess of Brunswick, the latter considering themselves entitled to the regency. Mistrusting the guards, Biron ordered the transfer to the capital of other army units and incautiously toyed with the idea of an army reform that would amount to the disbandment of the existing regiments of the guards by filling their ranks with men drawn from the unprivileged classes. The inability to win over the support of the guards was fatal to the rule of Biron, which lasted for merely twenty-two days. In the early hours of November 9, 1740, he was arrested by a small group of guardsmen led by Münnich, while Princess Anne proclaimed herself regent in a manifesto issued in the name of the Senate, the Synod, and the higher officials. Biron received a death sentence, but this was set aside and he was deported with his family to Pelym, Siberia.[8]

The new regent was a muddle-headed, bizarre woman dreaming of the imperial Crown but incapable of any clear-cut decision or vigorous action. For days she remained locked in her bedroom in the company of her lady-in-waiting Julie Mengden, for whom she had an abnormal passion, and she refused to see anyone else except her lover, Count Lynar, Saxon minister at St. Petersburg. Oddly, Anne was planning to marry Julie Mengden to Lynar. After the *coup d'état* of November 9, 1740, Münnich had become "first minister," but he was forced out

---

[8] In 1742, with the accession of Empress Elizabeth, Biron was permitted to reside in Yaroslavl, on the Volga. In 1762 he was recalled to St. Petersburg by Emperor Peter III and a year later was restored to the throne of Courland by Catherine II. In 1769 he abdicated in favor of his son Peter, the last ruling duke of Courland.

of office early in March, 1741, by Ostermann, who once more assumed the direction of Russia's affairs, while Prince Anthony Urlic, the consort of the regent, intrigued against everyone else in unsuccessful attempts to push himself, with the assistance of Ostermann, to the forefront of the political stage. The grotesque and sinister comedy of Germans fighting one another over the control of Russia was terminated by the palace revolution of November 25, 1741, the arrest of the Brunswick family, the deposition of Ivan VI, and the accession of Elizabeth.

Born in 1709, Elizabeth had lingered in relative obscurity until 1741. She received no formal education but acquired a fluent knowledge of German and French and was an expert dancer, accomplishments considered necessary for the part Peter I intended his daughter to play at Versailles. All efforts at providing the tsarevna with a French husband having failed, she became engaged to Charles Augustus of Holstein, bishop of Lübeck, who died in 1727 before the wedding ceremony. It would have been difficult to imagine for Elizabeth a less suitable part than that of the wife of a Lutheran bishop. According to contemporary accounts she was endowed with great beauty and personal charm which made her all but irresistible to men; and, being free from intellectual or moral scruples, she unreservedly abandoned herself to the *joie de vivre*. Her devout piety was not permitted to interfere with the demands of an impetuous temperament; according to the Spanish ambassador, Duke de Liria, the tsarevna "shamelessly indulged in practices which would have made blush even the least modest person." The social milieu Elizabeth chose for her recreations and amorous adventures proved to be an important link in the chain of events that brought her to the throne. The daughter of Peter I and Catherine I had inherited her parents' predilection for people of humble extraction, and she felt particularly at ease in the company of muscular guardsmen who were susceptible to the spell of her radiant and provocative beauty. One of her early love affairs was with Alexis Shubin, a subaltern in the Semenovsky regiment, and she had a protracted liaison with Alexis Razumovsky, an illiterate, powerfully built, and handsome Cossack lad who once sang in the palace chapel choir and lived to be count of the Holy Empire and field marshal of the Russian army. It seems extremely likely that it was Elizabeth's personal inclinations rather than any carefully thought-out political plans that led her to frequent the congenial atmosphere of the barracks, even though her smiling disposition and easy-going ways built for her a strong and faithful following among the guardsmen, who had grown accustomed to look upon themselves as the ultimate arbiters of the fate of the throne.

During most of the reign of Empress Anne, Elizabeth lived in retirement, taking no part in political activities and doing her best to keep on good terms with her imperial cousin, who might have decided at any moment to lock her up in some convent. The decadence of the government under the nominal rule of the baby emperor Ivan VI and the offer of assistance proffered to the tsarevna by France and Sweden gave new hope to the small band of men who were dreaming of getting rid of the Brunswick family and its supporters. Ostermann was the author of the Austro-Russian alliance of 1726 which had led to many complications between Russia and France and which after the invasion of Austrian Silesia by Frederick II of Prussia at the end of 1740 appeared particularly dangerous to Paris. The simplest way to remove the objectionable statesman and the policy he represented would be a *coup d'état* which would put Elizabeth on the throne. Marquis de La Chétardie, French ambassador to St. Petersburg, effectively employed himself in urging the tsarevna to overcome her fears and hesitations and supplied her with funds to stimulate the devotion of the guardsmen. Sweden went further, and on July 27, 1741, declared war on Russia with the avowed object of freeing that unhappy country from the inequitable rule of "foreign ministers," but really in order to recover some of the territories lost to Russia by the Peace of Nystadt. In her negotiations with De La Chétardie and Nolcken, the Swedish minister, Elizabeth had assumed various far-reaching obligations towards both France and Sweden, but she had refused to give her consent to any restitution of the provinces annexed by Peter I.

Although the negotiations were carried on in great secrecy, and chiefly through the instrumentality of Elizabeth's physician and factotum, the Frenchman Armand Lestocq, rumors about the conspirators' plans had reached Ostermann and the regent herself. On November 23 the regent had a frank discussion with Elizabeth which left no doubt that she was informed of the proposed *coup d'état* and had decided to arrest Lestocq. On November 24 came the order for the regiments of the guards to hold themselves in readiness for immediate departure for the Swedish front. These ominous moves triumphed over Elizabeth's indolence and indecision, for she must have fully realized that the failure of the conspiracy would mean for her, at best, incarceration in a convent, and she would have undoubtedly agreed with the English minister Finch that there was "not one bit of nun's flesh about her." The guardsmen's reluctance to leave their warm barracks for the bleakness of the Finnish winter and the hazards of war contributed to their zeal on behalf of the daughter of Peter I and to their dislike of the German rule. At midnight on November 24, Elizabeth, wearing a cuirass and holding a cross, left her residence in a sled accompanied by Lestocq, her old music teacher Schwartz, and a member of her household, Michael Vorontsov. She drove to the barracks of the guards, where the soldiery gave the picturesque *cortège* a rousing reception. At the head of a small body of troops Elizabeth then proceeded to the Winter Palace and arrested the regent, her consort, and the baby emperor while detachments of guardsmen rounded up and took into custody Ostermann, Münnich, and the other personalities of the fallen regime. None offered any resistance. A manifesto justified the *coup d'état* by referring to the order of succession established in the "testament" of Catherine I [9] and by stressing the theory that Elizabeth had accepted the Crown at the request of "all our faithful subjects," and especially of the regiments of the guards. One of the first official acts of the new empress was to proclaim herself colonel of these regiments, to whom, indeed, she owed much. Generous money rewards were distributed to the troops participating in the events of November 25, the grenadier company of the Preobrazhensky regiment being singled out for special honors. It was renamed "Her Majesty's Own Company" (*Leibkompaniia*) with the empress as its captain. Its officers and men received important advances in rank. They were raised to hereditary *dvorianstvo* and were granted estates from confiscated properties. For instance, Grünstein, son of a converted Jew from Saxony and a sergeant in the Preobrazhensky regiment, who had been particularly active in winning over the troops to the cause of Elizabeth, was rewarded with an estate inhabited by 927 male serfs. These details throw much light on the real character of the palace revolution of November 25, which has been so often represented as a national movement against the German rule. Chief

[9] Leaving aside the question of the authenticity of the "testament," the interpretation advanced in the manifesto was hardly convincing since in the order of succession established by Catherine I Elizabeth was preceded by the young duke of Holstein, son of Catherine's elder daughter, provided he had joined the Orthodox Church.

among the leaders of the revolution which restored to the throne "the blood of Peter the Great" were the French ambassador, Lestocq, Grünstein, and the German Prince Ludwig Hesse-Homburg, whom Elizabeth appointed commander of the St. Petersburg garrison and second in command of "Her Majesty's Own Company."

The change of regime was accompanied by the usual amnesty for the exiles of former reigns and by new trials, confiscations, and deportations. Although the manifesto of November 28 guaranteed the former regent, her husband, and children safe conduct to Germany and a substantial pension, this generous decision was soon revised and the Brunswick family was imprisoned, first in the fortress of Dünamunde, then in Ranenburg (province of Riazan), and finally in Kholmogory near Archangel. Ostermann, Münnich, the former vice chancellor Count M. G. Golovkin, and several other former dignitaries were sentenced to death but were given a reprieve at the last moment and deported to Siberia. Elizabeth was opposed to capital punishment, although it was not formally abolished,[10] and nothing was done to curtail the powers of the Privy Chancery (security police), which continued its sinister activities under the direction of Ushakov and, later, of Alexander Shuvalov. In 1743 the security police, instigated by Lestocq, who hated Austria, alleged that they had discovered a plot for the restoration of Ivan VI, a conspiracy involving the Austrian ambassador Marquis Botta. Although the torture chamber failed to produce any convincing evidence of guilt, several highly placed personalities, including two of St. Petersburg's foremost beauties, Nathalie Lopukhin and Countess Anne Bestuzhev-Riumin, wife of the well known diplomat and sister-in-law of the vice chancellor, were publicly flogged and had their tongues branded.

In spite of occasional relapses into Muscovite barbarism, there was an unmistakable improvement in the general tone of the court. The cripples, beggars, and buffoons so dear to Empress Anne were gone, and if the guardsmen, members of "Her Majesty's Own Company" who had free entry to palace functions, were not exactly accomplished courtiers at least they were not an eyesore. Balls, masquerades, the-

---

[10] The empress toyed with the idea of replacing capital punishment with "civic death," a notion which was never properly defined. An imperial order given to Field Marshal Lacy in 1743 prescribed, as a substitute for the death penalty, the cutting off of the right arm, slitting of nostrils, and hard labor for life. This composite punishment, which well illustrates Elizabeth's idea of clemency, proved impracticable since the mutilated convicts were no longer fit for hard labor.

atrical performances, and hunting expeditions followed one another and came much nearer to the coveted European model than anything Russia had ever known in the past. The precarious condition of the state treasury was not permitted to interfere with the extravagant luxury of palace entertainment, and although the empress had repeatedly decreed simplicity and economy in dress she left at her death a wardrobe consisting of some 15,000 gowns and many articles of masculine attire, which she was very fond of wearing. Distinctly, she did not teach by example. The strenuous routine of court life was interrupted by frequent pilgrimages to monasteries and visits to Moscow and other cities. On these trips Elizabeth was at times accompanied not only by the court but also by administrative bodies, with the result that thousands of horses and carts had to be requisitioned to provide transportation for officials, their servants, and luggage, as well as for furniture and domestic utensils, since even in Moscow imperial residences were lacking in necessary equipment.

Elizabeth proclaimed at the time of her accession, and she often reiterated in later years, her intention of returning to the tradition and methods of her father, Peter the Great. For a while she contemplated the repeal of all legislation adopted after 1725, a measure which for obvious reasons could not be put into effect. The decree of December 12, 1741, which became a kind of constitutional charter of the regime, attempted to restore the administrative order that existed at the death of Peter I. The Senate, under the personal guidance of the empress, was to resume its former position as the central governmental organ and was to exercise, through the office of the procurator-general, direct supervision over the administrative machinery. The conduct of foreign affairs was entrusted to the chancellor, Prince A. M. Cherkassky, and to the vice chancellor, A. P. Bestuzhev-Riumin. The cabinet was abolished as the highest governmental agency, but there was formed Her Majesty's private chancery, which was known as the "cabinet" and was headed by the empress's private secretary, I. A. Cherkasov. There were, of course, the usual changes in personnel, although some of the high officials, for instance, Prince Nikita Trubetskoy, procurator-general since 1740, were retained.

The new administrative organization, designed to make the Crown the active leader of the government, imposed upon Elizabeth a heavy personal burden, since the mass of routine business formerly dealt with by the cabinet ministers would now require her personal attention. The empress's time, however, was fully occupied by the exacting pageantry of court functions, amorous adventures, the meticulous care she gave to her declining beauty, and the very feminine interest she took in the most trivial happenings in the imperial household, while her frequent and protracted absences from the capital further interfered with her direct participation in government. Elizabeth made seven personal appearances before the Senate in 1742 and four in each of the years 1743 and 1744; but in the subsequent seventeen years of her reign she attended the meetings of that body only three times: once in 1753 and twice in 1754. Moreover, not unlike her father, she at times treated the Senate with great harshness, blaming it for the inefficiency and corruption of the administration. On November 29, 1761, for instance, the empress, through her private secretary, accused the senators of neglect of duty and of inability or unwillingness to deal with the affairs of state. If these reproaches were not undeserved, the failings of the Senate were due in no small degree to the inherent weakness of its position. Foreign affairs, the army and the navy, the police and the security police, as well as several other departments, were exempt from senatorial jurisdiction. Having no military or police force at its disposal, the Senate found it difficult to assure public order and security. The absence of a unified system of public finance and the growth of expenditure confronted the Senate with frequent and urgent requests to provide funds for large outlays not included in the estimates. On the other hand, the Senate was burdened with a mass of trivial details, such as the purchase of "good sable furs" or the hiring of cab drivers, activities which hardly belonged to the province of the highest administrative organ.

The smiling and seemingly care-free empress was most of the time inaccessible to her official advisers. State papers, diplomatic reports, and international treaties for months awaited imperial signature, and many of them went by default. The chief preoccupation of Russian statesmen and foreign diplomats was to find an "opportune moment" when the elusive monarch could be cornered and prevailed upon to issue an imperial order. Under these conditions Her Majesty's private chancery, which had no official standing among state institutions, acquired paramount importance, since the private secretary Baron (since 1742) Cherkasov and his successor, A. V. Olsufev, had a better chance than responsible officials to catch the empress in a receptive mood. Hidden influence flourished under this capricious personal regime, and the timely intervention of those close to Elizabeth was the surest method of obtaining a coveted decision. The reports of the Senate or the advices of the chancellor counted for little unless endorsed by Lestocq, Michael Vorontsov, Alexis Razumovsky, the brothers Alexander and Peter Shuvalov. In 1749 the young Ivan Shuvalov, a cousin of Alexander and Peter, became the official favorite, although he did not fully displace Razumovsky and had to share the affection of Elizabeth with several other men. Nevertheless his influence with the empress was great. Another important center of intrigues and underhand machinations was the so-called "young court" of Charles Peter Urlic, duke of Holstein, Elizabeth's nephew, who was brought to St. Petersburg. After his conversion to Greek-Orthodoxy he assumed the name of Grand Duke Peter, and on November 7, 1742, was proclaimed heir to the throne. On August 21, 1745, he married Princess Sophia Augusta Frederica of Anhalt-Zerbst, the future Empress Catherine II.

The deplorable chaos in administration and the impending entry of Russia in the Seven Years' War led A. Bestuzhev, one of the ablest statesmen of the Elizabethan era, to propose the creation of a new organ of government modeled on the Supreme Privy Council. Although this proposal was not fully accepted, a decree of March 14, 1756, established a Conference of ten members composed of the Grand Duke Peter and the higher state officers. The relationship between the Conference and other administrative institutions was never clearly defined, but for all practical purposes it became the highest organ of the realm, similar in its omnipotence to the Supreme Privy Council of Catherine I and to the cabinet of Empress Anne. The character of the administrative methods, however, remained unchanged, and in the words of the historian of the Senate (Presniakov) the Conference was largely "the instrument of intrigues, personal interests, and the influence of favorites." Count N. I. Panin has rightly observed that in the reign of Elizabeth Russia was governed not by "the authority of state institutions" but by "the power of persons."

CHAPTER XVII

THE ERA OF PALACE REVOLUTIONS

Foreign Relations

---※---

RUSSIA AS A GREAT POWER

Russia's newly acquired position as a great European Power, with the exacting obligations and uncertain advantages inherent in this impressive status, came to play an increasingly important part in the international policies of the empire. The Northern War, followed by the establishment of Russia on the shores of the Baltic, had made her a full-fledged member of the quarrelsome family of European nations. The political horizon of the court of St. Petersburg was no longer limited to the parochial disputes with Muscovy's next-door neighbors —Turkey, Poland, and Sweden—it embraced the whole of western Europe. Russian statesmen gradually became accustomed to interpret the elusive concept of "national interest" in terms of European politics and of the maintenance of the balance of power. The participation of Russia in European affairs, however, was influenced by a number of peculiar factors which determined the character of each international move. Particularly important were the dynastic ties between the Russian court and the houses of Holstein and Mecklenburg, the political predilections of Ostermann and Alexis Bestuzhev-Riumin, who largely controlled Russian foreign affairs during this period, the sympathies of the occupants of the throne and of their favorites and unofficial advisers, the persuasive power of foreign gold lavishly distributed—according to the custom of the time—to statesmen and courtiers by foreign envoys accredited to St. Petersburg, and, last but not least, the incessant war of intrigues waged around the throne. The interplay of these forces did not facilitate the charting of the course of the Russian ship of state in the midst of an international situation replete with dramatic changes.

FOREIGN POLICY UNDER CATHERINE I AND PETER II

From 1725 to 1740 the broad lines of Russia's foreign policy were determined by Andrew Ostermann, who was appointed vice chancellor after the accession of Catherine I and assumed the style of "first cabinet minister" upon the death of Chancellor Golovkin in 1734.[1] The cornerstone of Ostermann's diplomatic "system," to use a term in vogue in the eighteenth century, was a close alliance with Austria and an irreconcilable hostility to France because of her opposition to Russian interests in Sweden, Poland, and Turkey. Ostermann's policy was based on a not unreasonable interpretation of the European situation. The *rapprochement* between Austria and Spain, and the conclusion between those states of the Treaty of Vienna (April 30, 1725, N.S.), threatened to upset the balance of power established by the Peace of Utrecht (1713) at the end of the War of Spanish Succession. The Treaty of Vienna announced the acceptance by Spain of the Pragmatic Sanction guaranteeing the bestowal of all Austrian possessions upon Maria Theresa, the daughter of Emperor Charles VI; it was supplemented by secret clauses providing for the cooperation of Austria in restoring Gibraltar and Minorca to Spain (they were yielded to England by the Treaty of Utrecht); the partition—in case of the defeat of France—of French territories between the Spanish Bourbons and the Hapsburgs; and the strengthening of the ties between the Austrian and the Spanish dynasties through the marriage of two Austrian archduchesses and two Spanish infantes. England and France retaliated by concluding the so-called Hanoverian Alliance (Treaty of Herrenhausen, September 3, 1725, N.S.), which was professedly defensive but was actually designed to maintain the existing balance of power. Both hostile combinations of states were anxious to win the support of Russia. Ostermann's predilection for an Austrian

---

[1] Ostermann was born in Westphalia in 1686. He came to Russia in 1704 and filled various diplomatic positions during the reign of Peter I. An excellent linguist, Ostermann had a command of German, Dutch, Latin, French, Italian, and Russian. He took a prominent part in the negotiations of the Peace of Nystadt, was rewarded with the title of baron, and in 1730 was made a count on the occasion of the coronation of Empress Anne. Ostermann was arrested during the *coup d'état* resulting in the accession of Elizabeth, was tried and sentenced to death, but his sentence was commuted into one of exile to Berezov, Siberia, where he died in 1747.

alliance was favored by the appearance at the Baltic port of Reval, in May, 1726, of the English fleet, an unfriendly move inspired by the rumors of Russia's impending military and naval action against Denmark in support of the duke of Holstein's claims to Schleswig. Although the immediate consequences of this incident were limited to an exchange of sharply worded letters between King George I of England and Catherine, it did have a part in influencing St. Petersburg to sign, on August 6, 1726, a treaty of military alliance with Austria by which Russia became a member of the Austro-Spanish League. The contracting parties agreed to guarantee each other's possessions, to render military assistance in case of war, and to conclude no separate peace if war should come. A secret amendment to the treaty stipulated that Austria should aid in restoring Schleswig to the duke of Holstein and provided for Austrian assistance in case of a Russo-Turkish War. Europe became divided into two hostile camps. The Hanoverian Alliance was joined by Sweden in spite of Russia's opposition accompanied by threats and lavish bribes, by Denmark, and by a number of the smaller German states, while Prussia, who acceded to the alliance when it was first formed, withdrew about a year later and made an agreement with the German emperor (October 12, 1726, N.S.).

Catherine I's unfortunate devotion to her Holstein relatives, and especially her efforts either to restore Schleswig to her son-in-law, Duke Charles Frederick, or to provide adequate compensation for the loss of that province, resulted in much friction with Denmark, with the latter country's allies England and France, as well as with Sweden and Poland. The abortive attempt in 1726 to impose Menshikov as duke of Courland, the subsequent ejection by the Russian troops (August, 1727) of Count Maurice of Saxe, who had been elected to the throne of Courland by the local diet, and the forcing upon the duchy in 1737, at the point of Russian bayonets, of Anne's favorite Biron, tended to give the Russian policies in the Baltic the character of a political adventure. The death of Catherine I and the disgrace of Menshikov removed for a time the pernicious Holstein influence Ostermann had always opposed. The Russian vice chancellor favored a *rapprochement* with Denmark and Prussia while adhering to the Austrian alliance that he considered essential in view of the menacing attitude of Turkey and of the Russo-Persian War, which had been resumed in spite of the Treaty of St. Petersburg (1723). This policy was dictated largely by the exigencies of the international situation and a regrouping of the European Powers. By the Treaty of Seville (November 9, 1729, N.S.) Spain agreed to recognize the English possession of Gibraltar and the commercial interests of England and France as defined by the Treaty of Utrecht, while England and France promised their assistance in the introduction of Spanish garrisons into Tuscany and Parma. This arrangement was ratified by Vienna (March 16, 1731, N.S.) in exchange for the British guarantee of the Pragmatic Sanction. The Treaty of Seville, according to H. W. V. Temperley, was a turning point in the history of diplomacy which marked not only the collapse of the Austro-Spanish alliance but also the beginning of the disintegration of the Franco-British cooperation and of a gradual reversion "to the European system at the beginning of the eighteenth century—that of a union between France and Spain, opposed by the combination of England, Holland, and the emperor." Ostermann endeavored to bring his own policies in line with the general and welcome tendency towards appeasement that had manifested itself in Europe.

THE WAR OF POLISH SUCCESSION

The conciliatory attitude of the Russian vice chancellor began to produce results after the accession of Empress Anne. In March, 1732, Russia concluded a treaty of friendship with Austria and Denmark. The latter country agreed to pay a monetary compensation to the duke of Holstein for the loss of Schleswig and to accept the Pragmatic Sanction in return for a guarantee of her frontiers by Russia and Austria. A year later Russia and Denmark signed a treaty providing for mutual assistance in case of war. The death of King George I of England (1727), followed by an Austro-British *rapprochement*, paved the way for the resumption at the end of 1731 of diplomatic relations between St. Petersburg and London. The Russo-Persian War, which had dragged for several years and had proved costly both in men and in money, was ended by the treaties of 1732 and 1735 which restored to Persia the provinces ceded to Russia in 1723. Ostermann, who had opposed the Persian venture, had reason to be gratified, in spite of the unconditional abandonment of Peter I's onerous eastern conquests.

New troubles, however, were brewing on Russia's western border, the conflicting policies of St. Petersburg and Paris leading to a clash over Poland. The attempt made by France in 1725 to negotiate a Russian alliance failed both because of France's friendship for Turkey and because of her refusal to agree to the evacuation of the troops of the Hanoverian Alliance from Mecklenburg and to intervene on behalf of the duke of Holstein in the Schleswig question, the possession of that province by Denmark having been guaranteed by France and England. France's growing estrangement from England and the shelving by Russia of the Schleswig question with the accession of Empress Anne led Paris again to seek a better understanding with St. Petersburg. In 1732 Magnan, the French resident in the Russian capital, opened negotiations with Field Marshal Münnich [2] offering cooperation with Russia with the object of breaking up the Austro-Russian alliance. In spite of the powerful support of Münnich and Biron, who had been won over by generous presents, the French plan was wrecked by Ostermann's opposition and the irreconcilable policies of France and Russia in the question of Polish succession.

For several years before the death of King Augustus II of Poland early in 1733, the fate of the Polish throne had kept European courts and statesmen busy. The French candidate was the former king Stanislas Leszczynski, whose daughter was married to King Louis XV (1725). Russia and Austria, after some hesitation, agreed on the candidacy of Frederick Augustus, elector of Saxony and son of Augustus II. When the Polish throne finally became vacant, opinion in Poland appeared to be divided, although there was feeling against any foreign candidate. In spite of the threatening attitude of Russia and Austria, the energetic leadership of the Polish primate and interrex, Theodore Potocki, backed by the ambassadors of France and Sweden, resulted in the election of Leszczynski (September 12, 1733). This was regarded in St. Petersburg as a challenge to Russian interests not only in Poland but also in Turkey and Sweden, where French influence was strong. Russian troops under General Count Peter Lacy crossed the Polish frontier and on September 20 appeared on the right bank of the Vistula. King Stanislas and his principal supporters fled to Danzig. A "confederation" of Polish nobles obedient to the wishes of St. Peters-

---

[2] Burkhard Christoph von Münnich, born in Oldenburg in 1683, was the son of an officer of the Danish army. He served with the armed forces of France, Hesse, and Poland before entering the Russian service in 1721, when he was entrusted by Peter I with the supervision of the construction of the Ladoga Canal. Münnich was created count in 1728 and in 1732 was made field marshal, president of the war college, and governor of St. Petersburg. He was arrested during the palace revolution of 1741, was tried, and sentenced to death, but was reprieved and exiled to Pelym, Siberia. After the accession of Peter III Münnich was recalled to St. Petersburg.

burg and Vienna hastened to elect Frederick Augustus, who assumed the name of Augustus III (September 24). There followed a protracted siege of Danzig by Russian troops under the leadership of Lacy and, later (March, 1734), of Münnich. The city finally capitulated at the end of June, and Leszczynski escaped disguised as a peasant. In the early stage of the struggle France gave active assistance to her protégé and in May sent her fleet and a small expeditionary force to Danzig; this policy, however, was soon reversed and the unsuccessful candidate for the Polish throne was abandoned to his fate. Sporadic resistance by the Poles to Augustus was crushed with the help of Russian and Saxon troops. Leszczynski abdicated in January, 1736, and in June of the same year a new Polish diet made its peace with Augustus, who promised an amnesty and the speedy withdrawal of the Russian and Saxon armies. Throughout the War of Polish Succession Prussia maintained an uneasy neutrality. Although Austria refrained from a direct military intervention in Poland, France and her allies, Spain and Sardinia, declared war on the emperor. The Austrian army having suffered a number of defeats, Vienna appealed for Russian military assistance, in accordance with the provisions of the Austro-Russian treaty. In June, 1735, some 20,000 Russian troops under Lacy marched from Poland into Saxony and in August effected a junction with the Austrian army on the banks of the Neckar, near Heidelberg. A further advance of the Russian corps towards the Rhine was checked by the Austro-French armistice, and in November Lacy and his soldiers, who had taken no active part in the fighting, were hastily recalled to Russia, where their presence was made imperative by the outbreak of the Turkish War.

THE RUSSO-TURKISH WAR, 1735–1739

The ground for the Russo-Turkish conflict had been prepared by the long-standing controversy over the possession of certain ill defined frontier regions (the Kabardine district and the territory of the Kuban Tartars) and by frequent invasions of Russian border provinces by Tartar raiding parties. The Sublime Porte, moreover, took exception to the interference of St. Petersburg in Polish affairs, an interference interpreted in Constantinople as a menace to Turkish interests. Evoking the pleasing memories of the defeat of Peter I on the Pruth, Turkish statesmen made no secret of their low opinion of the Russian army and were inclined to discount the importance of the Austro-Russian alliance. Although the French ambassador to Turkey, Marquis de Villeneuve, aided and abetted by his English colleague, spared neither effort nor money to stimulate anti-Russian feelings, the war with Persia tied up the hands of the Sublime Porte, and the initiative in declaring war came from Russia. Ivan Nepliuev, Russian ambassador to Constantinople (recalled in September, 1735), and his associate and successor Veshniakov urged their government to attack Turkey, tracing in their reports an enticing picture of the decay of the Ottoman empire and of the enthusiastic support Russian troops were certain to receive from the Christian subjects of the sultan. The settlement in 1735 of the Russo-Persian conflict and the success of St. Petersburg and Vienna in forcing a reluctant Poland to accept Augustus III as her king strengthened the hand of the bellicose elements in the Russian capital. A small but influential group of Empress Anne's advisers, headed by Münnich in quest of laurels, successfully argued that the internal weakness and external difficulties of Turkey offered a golden opportunity for inflicting upon the hereditary enemy what might well prove to be a final blow. The war party having succeeded in convincing the empress, Ostermann sent the grand vizier a message in which he expounded the not very convincing theory that Russia was taking up arms with the sole object of putting the relations between the two countries on a solid and peaceful foundation. In spite of the fact that Russian troops under Münnich had crossed the Don in August, 1735, St. Petersburg strove for a year to maintain the pretense that Russia was fighting merely the Tartars, and not Turkey, and it was not until October, 1736, that the Russian representative, Veshniakov, left Constantinople.

The hopes entertained at St. Petersburg for a short and decisive campaign were soon dashed to the ground. Quarrels among Russian commanding officers—Münnich, Lacy, Prince Hesse-Homburg, and others—and the inadequacy of the supply and medical services disclosed the amazing ineptness of Russian army organization and nullified the effects of some remarkable feat of arms. In May, 1736, Münnich broke through the reputedly impregnable defenses of Perikop, the isthmus joining the Crimea to the mainland, and a month later he occupied and plundered the Crimean capital, Bakhchisarai, only to withdraw immediately with his army to the Russian Ukraine. In June, 1736, Russian troops under General Leontev took the fortress of Kinburn on the Dnieper while Marshal Lacy occupied Azov, which had been besieged for several weeks. But by the end of the summer the army of Lacy, too, had returned to Ukraine. These inconclusive results, unexpected after the initial success, alarmed the government of St. Petersburg, especially since Austria had been slow in fulfilling her obligations of military assistance, according to the terms of her alliance with Russia, while Persia had become involved in a war with the Great Mogul, which meant the suspension of Persian hostilities against Turkey. In dismay Empress Anne instructed Ostermann to explore the possibilities for the conclusion of an immediate peace. St. Petersburg, however, was cheered by the campaign of 1737, which culminated in the capture by the Russians of the fortress of Ochakov situated at the confluence of the Dnieper and the Bug (July 2). It is a moot question, however, whether this victory was achieved by the skill of the Russian commanders and the heroism of their troops, as claimed by Münnich, or whether, as alleged by several of his critics, it was a fortunate accident caused by an explosion of powder magazines in the fortress at the very moment when the Russian commander in chief had abandoned all hope of success. Whatever may be the correct version, capital was made of the Ochakov victory. The position of Russia was further strengthened by the military intervention of Austria, which finally took place in June, 1737, and by the initial success of the Austrian troops. One of the consequences of these developments was the breaking up in October, 1737, of the peace congress held in the frontier town of Nemirov, the exorbitant demands of both Russia and Austria having been unacceptable to Turkey. The Russian campaign of 1738, however, brought nothing but disappointments. Ochakov and Kinburn were evacuated by the Russians, and the attempt made by Lacy to invade the Crimea proved a costly failure. In May, 1738, Ostermann found himself forced to request the French ambassador at Constantinople, Villeneuve, to begin negotiations for a preliminary peace with Turkey, but since the Porte showed little inclination to respond to the overture of the allies there was no alternative to the continuation of the war. In July, 1739, Münnich, at the head of a large Russian army, invaded Moldavia, took the fortress of Khotin (Chocim) in August, crossed the Pruth, and early in September entered Jassy, where a delegation of local notables offered Anne the Crown of Moldavia. These military successes, however, came too late. Austria, which had embarked reluctantly upon the Turkish War and was experiencing financial difficulties and military reverses, concluded a separate preliminary peace with Turkey at the very time when the victorious Russian troops were occupying Moldavia. Exhausted by a long struggle, Russia followed suit and the Russo-Turkish War was ended by the Treaty of Belgrade (September 18, 1739, N.S.), which was negotiated through the mediation of France. By this treaty and supplementary protocols Russia retained Azov and the adjoining territory but the fortress itself was dismantled. Taganrog could not be fortified, and Russia agreed to maintain no vessels on the Black Sea and to carry on her trade in those waters exclusively in Turkish bottoms. These meager and in the main negative results of a war in which Russia had sacrificed some 100,000 men and huge sums of money were not rendered more palatable by the elaborate festivities held in St. Petersburg on the occasion of the ratification of the Treaty of Belgrade.

BESTUZHEV AND THE WAR WITH SWEDEN, 1741–1742

Seventeen hundred and forty was an eventful year in the annals of Europe. The death of Frederick William I of Prussia in May and the almost simultaneous demise in October of Empress Anne and of Emperor Charles VI led to the invasion of Silesia in December by the new Prussian king, Frederick II. This action precipitated the War of Austrian Succession, which occupied Europe for the next eight years and resulted in regrouping of European Powers. During the earlier part of the War of Austrian Succession, however, the attention of the Russian government was engaged elsewhere. The French mediation in the Russo-Turkish War produced a semblance of diplomatic *rapprochement* between Paris and St. Petersburg, and the adventurous Marquis de La Chétardie, made his appearance at the Russian court as ambassador of France. The chief purpose of his mission was to bring about a breach between Russia and Austria, but as there was little chance of achieving this object so long as Ostermann, a staunch supporter of the Austrian alliance, was in power, La Chétardie aided in preparing the overthrow of the baby emperor Ivan VI and of the regency of Princess Anne, although he probably claimed more than his legitimate share of credit for the success of the *coup d'état*. At the same time France was working at cross-purposes with Russia in Turkey, Poland, and especially in Sweden. Sweden had not yet resigned herself to the position of a second-rate Power, was not reconciled to the loss of the provinces ceded to Russia by the Peace of Nystadt, and resented the interference of St. Petersburg in her domestic affairs. A defensive alliance between Sweden and Turkey was concluded in 1739 with the object of a joint action against Russia, while anti-Russian feeling was stimulated by bribes distributed by the French ambassador to Stockholm. In the summer of 1739 the Swedish capital was shocked by the news that Baron Malcolm Sinclair, a member of the Swedish diet, and bearer of important dispatches addressed to the Porte, had been robbed and murdered by the emissaries of Münnich. It was an open secret that the crime had been instigated by the Russian ambassador to Sweden, Michael Bestuzhev. The disclosure produced a tremendous impression in Sweden, but it was not until July, 1741, when Swedish anti-Russian circles became convinced that St. Petersburg was in the midst of a political crisis, that the diet declared war on Russia. The first and only important military encounter in the campaign of 1741 took place at the end of August, when some 3,000 Swedes were routed by a Russian army of three times that number at Vilmanstrand, Finland. Three months later Elizabeth, whose cause Sweden officially pretended to champion, had mounted the Russian throne.

The foreign policies of Elizabeth, especially during the earlier years of her reign, followed a devious and uncertain course. Although the palace revolutions of 1740–1741 had as their consequence the banishment not only of the Brunswick family but also of the chief personalities of the two preceding regimes—Biron, Ostermann, Münnich—a certain continuity of foreign policy was assured by the appointment of A. P. Bestuzhev-Riumin to the office of vice chancellor (December 12, 1741). This made him the director of Russia's foreign relations, even before the death of the insignificant chancellor Prince Cherkassky (1742), whom he succeeded in 1744.[3] An enemy of Ostermann,

---

[3] Alexis Bestuzhev-Riumin was the son of Peter Bestuzhev-Riumin, political mentor and lover of the future Empress Anne in the days when she was duchess of Courland. Alexis Bestuzhev studied in Denmark and in Berlin (1708–1712), was present at the Congress of Utrecht, and in 1713 entered the service of George Ludwig, elector of Hanover. With the accession of the latter to the throne of England in 1714, Bestuzhev was sent to Russia as a special ambassador of George I, but soon returned to London, where he remained until 1717. He then entered the Russian service, filled various posts abroad, won the confidence of Biron, and with his support became "cabinet minister" in September, 1740. The overthrow of Biron some two months later led to the arrest and trial of Bestuzhev. He was sentenced to death, but his sentence was commuted to banishment and in October, 1741, he received full pardon and returned to the capital. He took no direct part in the palace revolution of November 25, although he was

Bestuzhev nevertheless carried on the political tradition of his predecessor and was a believer in the necessity of an alliance with Austria and of opposition to France. Departing from this basic premise, he expanded Ostermann's political "system" by advocating resistance to the expansionist tendencies of France's ally, Prussia, and cooperation with Saxony and especially with England.

The carrying out of the program was made difficult by the predilections of the empress and by the hidden influences to which she was subject. Elizabeth had ascended the throne with the assistance of two Frenchmen, Lestocq and La Chétardie, and was by no means immune to the charms of the gallant and amiable French ambassador. Botta, Finch, and Lynar—envoys, respectively, of Austria, England, and Saxony—on the other hand, had in the past maintained an attitude unfriendly to the daughter of Peter I, and Lynar, as already noted, was a lover of the deposed regent. Little wonder, therefore, that the accession of Elizabeth was regarded as a triumph for France and that the influence of La Chétardie appeared to be supreme.

Another obstacle Bestuzhev had to face was the reappearance of the pernicious Holstein influence, against which he fought as assiduously as had his predecessor, Ostermann. The empress's nephew, the duke of Holstein, who as Grand Duke Peter became in November, 1742, heir to the Russian throne, was a devout Holstein patriot and an admirer of King Frederick of Prussia. The Franco-Prussian influence which predominated in the entourage of the grand duke was further strengthened by his marriage with the young princess of Anhalt-Zerbst, the future Empress Catherine II. Catherine's mother was a princess of the House of Holstein, and her father was a Prussian general. The union was concluded against the advice of Bestuzhev, who wished Peter to marry a Saxon princess, but it had the approval of the Prussian king, Lestocq, La Chétardie, and Brümmer, the grand duke's

---

the author of the manifesto announcing the accession of Elizabeth. At the coronation of the new empress Peter Bestuzhev was created count, a title to which, according to the Russian law, his children were entitled even in their father's lifetime. Although Bestuzhev is known to have solicited private loans from the British government, he is considered as a man of integrity, only too rare in an age when the acceptance of pensions and bribes from foreign governments was common practice among statesmen all over Europe. One of Russia's most distinguished diplomats, Bestuzhev was a chemist of no mean ability and the inventor of the popular *tinctura toniconervina Bestuscheff*, known also as *élixir d'or* or *élixir de Lamotte*.

tireless and scheming Holstein minister. The "young court" became
the center of intrigues directed against Bestuzhev, and Holstein interests were pushed to the forefront of Russian policies.

The Holstein influence affected the issue of the Swedish war. With
the accession of Elizabeth, military operations in Finland came temporarily to a standstill, La Chétardie endeavoring to negotiate a peace
settlement. The empress and her ministers, however, refused to agree
to the Franco-Swedish demand for a restoration of some of the territories lost to Peter I or to a suitable compensation elsewhere, and
futile negotiations dragged on throughout 1742. In the meantime hostilities were resumed in March and proved a somewhat one-sided affair.
Meeting with little resistance, the Cossacks overran and plundered
Finland; Helsingfors capitulated on August 26, and Abo, the Finnish
capital, was occupied soon after. A peace conference met in Abo in
January, 1743, and after much wrangling produced a peace treaty
which was signed by Elizabeth on August 19. Under the terms of this
agreement Russia received a small slice of Finland with the fortified
towns of Vilmanstrand and Frederikshamn, a fraction of the Russian-
held territory the annexation of which St. Petersburg had originally
claimed. Russia's somewhat unexpected generosity, however, was purchased at a price. The Swedish throne was soon to become vacant,
the aged King Frederick (who had succeeded his wife Ulrica Eleonora
after her abdication in 1720) being childless and the queen having died
in November, 1741. The government of Stockholm seized the opportunity to trade the recovery of most of the conquered Finnish territory
for the acceptance of Elizabeth's candidate for the Crown of Sweden.
This candidate was Adolphus Frederick of Holstein, bishop of Lübeck,
and administrator of the duchy of Holstein during the infancy of his
nephew, the Grand Duke Peter. The settlement, which was opposed
by Bestuzhev, was the work of Lestocq and the Holstein ministers
Buchwald and Brümmer. This, the first open manifestation of
Bestuzhev's anti-French policy, resulted in a breach between the vice
chancellor, on the one hand, and Lestocq and his friends, on the other.
In view of the hostility of an important body of public opinion in
Sweden, especially the peasantry, to a crown prince imposed by Elizabeth and in view of the threatening attitude of Denmark, alarmed by
the probable repercussions of this move on the Schleswig question,
it was deemed necessary to provide Adolphus Frederick with a Russian expeditionary force. This ill advised venture proved unrewarding.

Adolphus Frederick soon learned that he could not expect to maintain himself in Sweden by relying openly on Russian support. In 1744, moreover, he married—much to the disappointment of the Russian court—a sister of Frederick II of Prussia, a brilliant and domineering woman who had little difficulty in winning over her husband to the French cause. A by-product of the Swedish war was the recall of La Chétardie. His overoptimistic reports about the probable outcome of the Russo-Swedish negotiations had caused embarrassment to the French government, and in the summer of 1742 the ambassador left St. Petersburg, parting with Elizabeth on friendly terms.

THE WAR OF AUSTRIAN SUCCESSION

The War of Austrian Succession put Russia's foreign policy to a severe test. The invasion of Silesia, in December, 1740, by Frederick II of Prussia was followed with a declaration of war on Austria by Bavaria and France. Maria Theresa, now queen of Hungary and Bohemia, appealed at once to her Russian ally for military assistance. But the St. Petersburg government, which was still in the hands of Princess Anne, Ostermann, and Münnich, displayed coolness towards the demands of Vienna and without repudiating the obligations imposed by the alliance endeavored to avoid them by arguing that Russia must await the action of Austria's other allies, that Russia had legitimate grievances against Austria for the latter country's conduct during the recent war with Turkey, and that the impending war with Sweden prevented effective help. Ostermann urged Maria Theresa to reach an amicable settlement with Frederick II by making reasonable concessions in order to strengthen her position in the struggle with France, Spain, and Charles Albert of Bavaria, who a year later was to be elected to the imperial throne (January, 1742). Russia, moreover, found herself enmeshed in a network of mutually incompatible international commitments. By bribing Münnich and Julie Mengden, Frederick II had succeeded in inducing the regent to sign a defensive alliance with Prussia early in 1741. Although the agreement was concluded after the news of the Prussian invasion of Silesia had reached St. Petersburg, the Russian government attempted to deny this and shielded itself behind the contention that the Prussian treaty had no effect upon obligations previously contracted with other Powers. The matter, which resulted in much ill feeling in St. Petersburg, especially between Münnich and Ostermann, was, according to the Prussian ambassador

Mardefeld, responsible for Münnich's retirement from the position of "first minister" (March, 1741). The declaration of war by Sweden in July and the uncertainties of the domestic political situation prevented Ostermann, a believer in the necessity of preserving the unity of Austrian possessions, from sending military assistance to Maria Theresa. Frederick in the meantime courteously but firmly declined a Russian request to intervene in the war with Sweden on the ground that Prussia was engaged in an armed conflict elsewhere.

The accession of Elizabeth brought no immediate change in the situation. The new empress, suspicious of the close ties between the House of Austria and the Brunswick family she had overthrown and sent into exile, lent a willing ear to the counsel of her pro-French and pro-Prussian entourage. But Bestuzhev was convinced that the interests of Russia would be best served by the advancement of the Austrian and the English cause. There followed a tug of war between the vice chancellor and his supporters, on the one hand, and Lestocq, the "young court" and their friends, on the other, with Bestuzhev gradually winning. Lestocq, an unscrupulous scoundrel simultaneously on the pay roll of England, France, and Prussia and created count of the Holy Empire by Charles VII (1744), engineered in the summer of 1743 the discovery of a bogus conspiracy for the restoration of Ivan VI. The alleged plot conveniently involved the Austrian ambassador, Marquis Botta, and several men and women prominent at the court of St. Petersburg, including Countess Anne Bestuzhev, sister-in-law of the vice chancellor. The unhappy Russian victims of Lestocq, as has already been mentioned, paid a terrible penalty, while the spirited defense by Maria Theresa of her ambassador, whom she knew to be innocent, strained the relations between St. Petersburg and Vienna nearly to the breaking point. Yet the "Botta conspiracy" failed to achieve its main object, since the empress's confidence in Bestuzhev remained unimpaired. The ranks of the pro-French party were reinforced in November, 1743, by the arrival in St. Petersburg of La Chétardie, although not in an official capacity, since the French government had refused to recognize Elizabeth's imperial title. The empress herself had solicited his return, and she gave her old admirer an affectionate reception. La Chétardie, faithful to his instructions, worked assiduously to bring Russia into the camp of France and Prussia.

Bestuzhev, however, more than held his ground. His agents, among them fellows of the Academy of Science, deciphered the secret codes used by foreign envoys to St. Petersburg, tampered with diplomatic mail, and provided the vice chancellor with copies of the confidential reports sent abroad. Special attention was paid to the correspondence of La Chétardie, the French minister D'Allion, the Prussian ambassador Mardefeld, and the elder Princess Anhalt-Zerbst, whose devotion to Prussian interests was well known. Bestuzhev withheld from his colleagues the revealing information that thus came into his possession but submitted to the empress carefully selected and annotated excerpts. La Chétardie was the first victim of this sinister procedure. His dispatches not only proved to be compromising politically but also contained unflattering and indiscreet personal observations about the empress. This was more than Elizabeth could bear: on June 6, 1744, the dreaded Ushakov, head of the security police, called on La Chétardie and ordered him to leave the capital within twenty-four hours. The elder princess of Anhalt-Zerbst, after being sharply reprimanded for interfering in political matters, was made to understand that her presence was no longer wanted, and she left Russia in September, 1745. The heir to the throne and his German wife, both of them admirers of Frederick II, were made subject to vexatious supervision, while Brümmer and Bergholtz, patriotic Holstein ministers of the Grand Duke Peter, were requested to leave Russia in 1746. The position of Lestocq was compromised by the La Chétardie disclosures, but his disgrace was postponed until 1748, when he was accused of carrying on relations with the enemies of the state and was exiled to Uglich. Bestuzhev had every reason to be satisfied: he was rewarded for his part in the fall of La Chétardie by the office of chancellor (1744), while Count Michael Vorontsov, a favorite of Elizabeth and then still a supporter of Bestuzhev, became the vice chancellor.

The trend of European affairs favored the policies of Bestuzhev. Russian and French interests continued to clash in Sweden, Poland, and Turkey, and the predatory aggressive moves of Frederick II lent color to the chancellor's theory that Prussia was to be dreaded even more than France. England, anxious to safeguard her Russian trade and to maintain the balance of power threatened by the Franco-Prussian combination, not only repeatedly urged St. Petersburg to send military assistance to Maria Theresa but also entered the road to closer cooperation with the government of Elizabeth, whose accession had at first been deplored by the British ambassador, Finch. Although

England had refused to send her fleet to the Baltic, as requested by St. Petersburg at the beginning of the war with Sweden, an Anglo-Russian agreement, limited in scope and aimed at the preservation of the *status quo* in central and eastern Europe, was concluded in Moscow on December 11, 1742. Maria Theresa was hard pressed by Frederick II, who, unappeased by the annexation of Lower Silesia ceded to him by the secret convention of Klein-Schnellendorf (October, 1741) and by the Treaty of Berlin (July, 1743), invaded Bohemia in August, 1744. Sacrificing the unfortunate Marquis Botta on the altar of expediency, Maria Theresa had him arrested and asked Elizabeth herself to decide what punishment should be meted out to the former ambassador whose hideous crime, the queen of Hungary now declared, she deeply regretted. The vexatious Botta incident out of the way, the road was open for a *rapprochement* between Vienna and St. Petersburg. Frederick II, having suffered military reverses in Bohemia, appealed at the end of 1744 for Russian assistance according to the terms of the Russo-Prussian alliance, or at least for the mediation of the empress, but he met with a curt refusal. The invasion of Saxony by Prussian troops produced a strong impression in St. Petersburg, and in October, 1745, the garrison of Courland was reinforced as a precautionary measure against Prussia. Bestuzhev, in spite of the opposition of Vorontsov, who did not favor participation by Russia in the hostilities, opened negotiations with the Maritime Powers for a subsidy to finance an expeditionary force against Frederick; but England, having already reached an agreement with Prussia (convention of Hanover, August, 1745), vetoed the proposal and the Treaty of Dresden (December, 1745) ended the war between Austria, Saxony, and Prussia by the cession of Silesia to Frederick.

Undaunted by this setback, Bestuzhev continued his anti-Prussian policy. In January, 1746, the Prussian ambassador Mardefeld, notified by the chancellor that he was *persona non grata*, was ordered to leave St. Petersburg. A defensive alliance with Austria, which, however, was to apply only to future wars, was concluded on May 22, 1746. This agreement provided, among other things, for an Austrian guarantee of the duke of Holstein's German possessions. Negotiations with England, which continued in spite of the rejection of the original Russian offer, culminated in the conclusion of two treaties, one in June and one in December, 1747. By these arrangements Russia, for an annual British subsidy, undertook to place at the disposal of Great Britain an army 30,000 strong in Courland, and to send another army of 30,000 to the Rhine, provided that £300,000 a year was paid four months in advance by England and Holland. The victories in the Netherlands by the French army under Maurice of Saxe were primarily responsible for the Maritime Powers' somewhat reluctant decision to hire Russian mercenaries. The slow progress of a Russian corps under General Repnin, which started for the distant Rhine at the end of January, 1748, was severely criticized by Austria, England, and Holland, while Poland violently protested against the devastation wrought by the Russian troops in transit through her territory. The Repnin force, however, never saw any fighting. The preliminary convention of Aix-la-Chapelle (April, 1748) brought to an end the war between France and the Maritime Powers, and the War of Austrian Succession was soon terminated by the Peace of Aix-la-Chapelle (October, 1748). Francis, duke of Lorraine and husband of Maria Theresa, was recognized as German emperor (Charles VII having conveniently died in 1745), and the annexation of Silesia by Prussia—the only significant territorial change resulting from the war—was guaranteed by the signatory Powers.

There is probably some truth in the assertion that the dispatch of the Repnin corps, by inducing France to moderate her demands, was instrumental in expediting the conclusion of peace. It should be noted, however, that in June, 1748, the allies, without consulting the St. Petersburg government, ordered Repnin to withdraw. Russia, moreover, was not admitted to the Congress of Aix-la-Chapelle, in spite of England's promise that she should have a voice in the peace negotiations. The sending of the Russian troops to the Rhine led to the recall of D'Allion, the French minister to St. Petersburg, and of Gross, the Russian minister to Paris. There was justification for the contemptuous remark of Marquis de Puysieux, French minister of foreign affairs, that it would have been more fitting for a great Power, such as Russia, to declare war on France than to sell her soldiers to a foreign government, even though the practice was by no means unknown in the eighteenth century. In 1748 and the years immediately following, the breach between Russia and France appeared to be complete; actually, however, it proved to be the forerunner of a closer cooperation inspired by the mutual distrust of Prussia, the only state to profit by the War of Austrian Succession.

THE SEVEN YEARS' WAR

During the seven years following the Peace of Aix-la-Chapelle, Bestuzhev, at the pinnacle of his power, pursued his program of isolating Prussia and of forging stronger bonds with England. Early in 1750 a Russian manifesto prohibited the service of Baltic nobles in foreign armies, a measure avowedly directed against Prussia. Frederick, irritated by this restriction and by the opposition of Russia to his Swedish policies, displayed towards Gross, the Russian minister at Berlin, a notable lack of courtesy, with the result that in October, 1750, Gross was recalled and diplomatic relations between the two courts were broken, the Prussian minister, Baron Goltz, having left St. Petersburg six months earlier. Not everything, however, went according to the chancellor's wishes. Relations with Austria were at times made difficult by the interference of Russia on behalf of the allegedly persecuted Orthodox subjects of Vienna, while the vexed question of Courland continued to be a source of friction with Poland and Saxony (Augustus III of Poland was also elector of Saxony), the Polish diet having repeatedly requested the release of Biron. St. Petersburg's dissatisfaction with the trend of affairs in Sweden led to threats of a Russian expeditionary force to defend Swedish "liberties" (1749–1750), but because of the protests of England, Austria, and Denmark no action was taken. At home the position of the chancellor was endangered by new hostile influences. In 1749 the young Ivan Shuvalov became the official favorite, thus strengthening the hold over public affairs of his cousins Peter and Alexander Shuvalov, who had often intrigued against Bestuzhev. There was also a growing estrangement between the chancellor and the vice chancellor, Vorontsov lending his support to the pro-Prussian and, later, to the pro-French party. Bestuzhev, however, succeeded in undermining Elizabeth's confidence in Vorontsov, and up to 1755 the vice chancellor had little influence in shaping Russia's foreign policy. In 1754 the chancellor unexpectedly found a new ally in the Grand Duchess Catherine, who was driven by the animosity of Vorontsov and the Shuvalov to seek his support.

Negotiations for an English alliance, which was the cornerstone of Bestuzhev's "system," proved laborious and dragged on for several years, the British government considering the Russian demand for a subsidy exorbitant. It was only after the arrival in St. Petersburg of the new British ambassador, Sir Charles Hanbury-Williams (June, 1755), that real progress was made and an Anglo-Russian convention was signed on September 19, 1755. In return for an annual English subsidy of £100,000, Russia undertook to maintain on the frontiers of Livonia and Lithuania an army corps of 55,000 men; in case of an attack on the possessions of the king of England or of those of his allies, these troops were to be available for service abroad in consideration of an annual English payment of £500,000. The ratification of the convention by the empress, delayed until February 1, 1756, was extorted by the chancellor by threat of resignations. The British ambassador, moreover, was notified that Russian troops could be used only in case of an attack by Prussia, a reservation that basically changed the nature of the agreement. The triumph of Bestuzhev was thus far from complete; in fact, the Anglo-Russian convention contributed to his undoing.

The event that revolutionized the international situation and swept away the fragile diplomatic structure built up by the Russian chancellor was the Anglo-Prussian alliance sanctioned by the convention of Westminster (January 16, 1756, N.S.). After the Peace of Aix-la-Chapelle, European capitals gradually awakened to the fact that the existing alignment of Powers, of which the antagonistic Anglo-Austrian and Franco-Prussian alliances were the center, no longer represented the interests of the respective countries. Vienna was not reconciled to the loss of Silesia; Kaunitz, who became Austrian chancellor in August, 1755, had since 1749 advocated the necessity of an alliance with France, and this was another source of friction between St. Petersburg and Vienna, because of Bestuzhev's opposition to a *rapprochement* with the court of Versailles. The breach in July, 1755, between England and France over the question of colonial policies and the control of the seas, even though there was no immediate outbreak of hostilities, led London and Paris to seek new alliances. George II of England, anxious to protect his Hanoverian possessions in the event of attack by France, turned for assistance not only to Russia but also to that country's prospective antagonist, Prussia. Frederick II was concerned primarily with the preservation of his recent conquests, an object he believed would be best served by the maintenance of European peace, but in the light of previous experience both Austria and Russia put little faith in his professedly peaceful intentions. With Russia hostile to Prussia, and France heavily engaged overseas and seemingly no longer in a position to uphold the European balance of power, Frederick after some hesitation became converted to the idea of an Anglo-Prussian alliance, especially after England had made a treaty of alliance with Russia. Hence the convention of Westminster, designed chiefly for the maintenance of the neutrality of the German states, bound the contracting parties to prevent their respective allies from hostile action against the European territories of either of the contracting parties. In case of an invasion of German territories, Prussia and England agreed to fight together for the restoration of peace. The governments of London and Berlin, believing that the new alliance was in no way incompatible with the international obligations they had previously assumed, were painfully surprised by the hostility with which the announcement of the convention of Westminster was received in Vienna, Paris, and St. Petersburg. The secrecy shrouding the Anglo-Prussian negotiations was in part responsible for the violence of this reaction and for the fact that the Anglo-Prussian convention, designed to uphold the *status quo*, actually precipitated a war. The immediate consequence was a defensive Franco-Austrian alliance (Treaty of Versailles, May 1, 1756, N.S.) supplemented by an agreement of June, 1756, providing for the restoration of Silesia to Austria and binding France not to make a separate peace with England. Russia, Saxony, and Sweden were invited to accede to the treaty. The newly established Russian ministerial Conference (March 14, 1756) adopted, over the objection of the Grand Duke Peter, a militant anti-Prussian policy and urged Vienna to take drastic action against Frederick. The king of Prussia, who had long clung to the illusion that St. Petersburg would remain neutral, finally realized his mistake and in August, 1756, invaded Saxony without even giving Augustus time to comply with his request to allow the passage of the Prussian army into Bohemia.[4] On December 31 Russia adhered to the Treaty of Versailles, agreeing in a secret article to assist France should England attack her in Europe. Under the terms of the secret provisions of the Austro-Russian Treaty of January 22, 1757, each of the contracting parties undertook to provide at least 80,000 troops against Prussia, not to conclude a separate peace, and to carry on the struggle until the restoration of Silesia to Austria and the liberation and indemnification

---

[4] It must be noted, however, that the sincerity of Frederick's desire for peace has often been challenged in historical literature.

of Saxony. Austria also agreed to pay Russia an annual subsidy of one million rubles.

While Frederick was battling the armies of Augustus and Maria Theresa in Saxony and Bohemia, the slow-moving Russian military machine was set into motion. In May, 1757, Russian troops under their commander in chief, Field Marshal Count Stephen Apraksin, crossed from Courland into Lithuania, and in June Memel capitulated to General Count William Fermor. In July the main body of the Russian army poured over the frontier of East Prussia, and on August 19 (August 30, N.S.) Apraksin won a major victory over the Prussians at Gross-Jägerndorf. Instead of being able to exploit his initial success, however, he found himself compelled to withdraw his troops east of the Nieman, to Poland, where he took up his winter quarters. An army council held at headquarters (September 28) approved the decision of the commander in chief on the ground of the inadequacy of transportation facilities, the disorganization of the services of supply, and heavy losses in men because of illness and desertion. The unexpected retreat nevertheless caused disappointment not only in St. Petersburg but also in Paris and Vienna, the ambassadors of the two Powers clamoring for energetic military action. On October 16, 1757, Apraksin was relieved of his command and was replaced by Fermor, in spite of the fact that the latter had endorsed the strategy of his predecessor.

The military campaign of 1757 had important repercussions on the domestic situation. The position of the chancellor was shaken by the Anglo-Prussian alliance, while the influence of the pro-French party headed by Vorontsov and the Shuvalov was strengthened by the arrival in St. Petersburg in the summer of 1757 of the French ambassador, Marquis de l'Hôpital. Apraksin was Bestuzhev's friend and appointee, and it was rumored that his cautious strategy was in part determined by the pro-Prussian and anti-war attitude of the "young court." Elizabeth had suffered an attack of severe illness in September, 1757, and the widely held belief that her reign was approaching its end made Russian statesmen and generals increasingly anxious to keep on good terms with the heir to the throne and with his consort. The eagerness displayed by Bestuzhev in denouncing Apraksin's retreat failed to save him from the worst suspicions. On February 14, 1758, the chancellor was arrested and deprived of his offices, dignities, and titles. Early in 1759, after a protracted investigation in which his alleged efforts to win the favor of the "young court" (and especially of Catherine) were among the principal charges, he was declared guilty of miscellaneous crimes deserving of capital punishment, but was actually exiled to one of his estates. In 1758 Vorontsov was appointed chancellor.

In the meantime military operations on the Russian front continued their eventful course. In January, 1758, Russian troops invaded East Prussia, Königsberg capitulated, and Fermor was made governor of the conquered provinces. This success was followed by a futile attempt to besiege the fortress of Cüstrin and by the battle of Zorndorf (August 14), which St. Petersburg chose to regard as a great Russian victory, although the commander in chief described it with more accuracy as a "most unfortunate incident," a statement justified by the poor showing of the Russian army and by its heavy losses. Fermor, like Apraksin a year earlier, found it necessary to withdraw first to Pomerania and then to the Vistula, where he took up his winter quarters much to the disappointment of St. Petersburg and to the distress of the Poles. The campaign of 1759 did not begin until April, and it was only in June that the main Russian army reached Posen. The slow progress of Fermor brought upon him the wrath of the government: Count Peter Saltykov was appointed commander in chief (May 8), and he took up his duties on June 19. This elderly soldier, whose undistinguished record inspired slight confidence, at first did uncommonly well. The Prussians suffered a defeat at Kay, on the Oder (July 12), and were routed by a joint Austro-Russian force at Kunersdorf, near Frankfort, on August 1 (August 12, N.S.). Saltykov received a field marshal's baton, and the victorious Russian army crossed the Oder, but the practical results of the campaign were again slight. There developed friction between the Russian and the Austrian commanders, and Saltykov was blamed by his government for his lack of initiative, insufficient cooperation with the Austrian ally, and for the poor discipline of his troops. His cautious campaign plan for 1760 was overridden in St. Petersburg, the government insisting on more effective cooperation with Austria. On August 22, 1760, Saltykov was officially informed that never since the outbreak of the war had Russia's position been less satisfactory, and on September 18 he was relieved of his command. His successor, Field Marshal Count Alexander Buturlin, whose chief qualification for office was his intimacy with the empress, fared no better than his predecessor. In September and

October of 1760 defenseless Berlin, occupied for a few days by Russian and Austrian forces, paid heavy indemnities, and in December the Russian troops, after repeated unsuccessful attempts, entered the east Prussian port of Kolberg, which had capitulated. By August, 1761, however, as a result of the inconclusive campaign in Silesia and Pomerania, Buturlin had lost his popularity with the St. Petersburg court. His impending disgrace was prevented by the death of Elizabeth on December 25, 1761 (January 5, 1762, N.S.), an event that brought to an end Russia's participation in the Seven Years' War.

So far as Russia is concerned, the most striking aspect of this great international struggle was probably the determination of Elizabeth to see it through and to eliminate Prussia as a factor in European politics. The empress had, indeed, for a time played with the idea of assuming in person the command of the army. Towards the end of the war Elizabeth demanded, as a part of her anti-Prussian program, the annexation of East Prussia. The coalition of Russia, Austria, France, Saxony, and the other Germanic states, only loosely held together, often appeared on the verge of a collapse. France, the first to lose interest in the European war, was devoting her energies to an unsuccessful attempt to defend her overseas empire, which was about to pass into the hands of England. Austria, Saxony, and Sweden showed increasing signs of fatigue and exhaustion and a growing desire for peace. Frederick, when he invaded Saxony in August, 1756, did not anticipate the uncompromising attitude of Russia, and he soon regretted his rash action. In the course of the war he was often on the brink of despair, and death by a stray bullet or by suicide appeared to him the only way out. The position of Prussia was, indeed, lamentable. Waves of foreign troops, especially the Russian irregulars—the Cossacks and the Kalmyks—wrought terrible devastation in the king's hereditary domain. The death of George II of England (October 25, 1760, N.S.), followed by the resignation of William Pitt (October 5, 1761, N.S.), had deprived Frederick of his principal ally, for Pitt had consistently translated into practical policy his assertion that "America has been conquered in Germany." George III, born and bred in England, took relatively little interest in his Hanoverian patrimony, which he had never visited; Pitt's retirement from office, therefore, was one of the hardest blows to befall the king of Prussia.

The death of Elizabeth altered the European situation. Her successor, Emperor Peter III, an admirer of Frederick, issued orders for an armistice, which was concluded on March 5. This was followed by the peace treaty of April 24 (May 5, N.S.), 1762. Drafted by Frederick himself at the request of Peter, the treaty, which restored to Prussia all the territories occupied by the Russian troops, was supplemented by a Russo-Prussian military alliance (June 16, N.S.) directed against Austria. Within a few weeks a Russian corps was on its way to fight side by side with the Prussians against Russia's erstwhile allies. Such was the result of the major military venture in which the daughter of Peter the Great had sacrificed innumerable lives and much of the national wealth. Dynastic alliances with German princelets and the tsar's arbitrary power to appoint his successor—both traceable to the political regime of Peter I—were at least in part responsible for the tragic and disgraceful *dénouement* of Russia's participation in the Seven Years' War.

CHAPTER XVIII

===

THE ERA OF PALACE REVOLUTIONS

Domestic Policies

————————————————— ✳ —————————————————

CHANGES IN THE SOCIAL STRUCTURE

The gradual realization by the *dvorianstvo* of its political power, which found expression in the part played by the regiments of the guards in the palace revolutions of the eighteenth century, not only contributed to the welding of this once heterogeneous group into a social class conscious of its interests but encouraged the nobility to use this newly acquired influence for the betterment of its social and economic status. In the interval between the death of Peter I and the accession of Peter III, the efforts of the *dvoriane* were directed towards two main objects: the easing of the burden of obligatory service and the strengthening of their hold over the servile population on their estates. These two policies were discernible in 1725–1761, although they did not reach their full development until the second half of the eighteenth century. The aspirations of the *dvoriane* were favored by the state of peace Russia enjoyed from 1725 to 1733 and from 1743 to 1757. The wholesale drafting of the *dvoriane* into lifelong service, especially in the army and navy, was dictated by the exigencies of the Northern War. With the return to peacetime conditions the demand for man power became less urgent, while the perennial shortage of funds experienced by the treasury suggested the desirability of releasing at least some of the noble landlords from government service so that they might devote themselves to the administration of their estates, taxation of servile labor being the chief source of state revenue.

The wishes of the *dvoriane* were expressed in the petitions they presented at the request of the Supreme Privy Council in February,

1730.[1] Empress Anne had promised the guardsmen, who had freed her from the restrictions imposed by the "Conditions," that they could count on the Crown for the redress of their grievances, and she had the best possible reasons for giving at least some semblance of satisfaction to the social group that had made her Russia's autocratic ruler. The unpopular entail law of March 23, 1714, was repealed in December, 1730.[2] A military academy (*kadetskii korpus*) for boys of noble descent aged thirteen to eighteen was established in St. Petersburg by a decree of June 29, 1731. The cadets received army commissions on graduation, being thus exempted from beginning their career in the ranks, an obligation the *dvoriane* had particularly resented. The number of students the academy could accept, however, was originally 200, and of this total fifty vacancies were set aside for the children of Baltic nobles. In spite of the increase in the size of the student body to 360 in 1732, when the academy began to function, the enrollment remained far below the number of young men eligible for admission. Notwithstanding its name, the military academy, which provided a comprehensive curriculum, was designed to train its pupils not only for the army but also for the civil service. Another demand of the *dvoriane* was partly fulfilled in 1732, when the pay of the Russian officers was raised to the level of that of foreigners serving with the Russian army, a measure which failed, however, to prevent mass evasion of obligatory service. An imperial manifesto of December 31, 1736, made a contribution towards granting the principal wish of the *dvoriane:* the term of compulsory service, both military and civil, was limited to twenty-five years; one male member of each family comprising two or more males was exempted altogether on the condition that he would attend to the administration of the family estates. The reasons given officially for this enactment, which was not made effective until the end of the Turkish war, was the shocking condition of the estates of absentee landlords, the accumulation of arrears in the poll tax, and the lawlessness of the servile population, which, under the loose and corrupt supervision of bailiffs, had neglected its fields and turned to brigandage. It was expected that the release of some of the *dvoriane* from government service would relieve the treasury from the necessity of providing for superfluous officers, would facilitate the collection of the poll tax, and would simplify the

[1] See p. 443.
[2] See p. 422.

problem of maintaining peace and order in rural districts. A supplementary decree issued early in 1737 laid down meticulous rules for the young *dvoriane's* scholastic training, as provided by the manifesto of December 31, 1736. They were requested to register with the proper authority at the age of seven and to present themselves for examination in required subjects at the age of twelve, at sixteen, and again at twenty. Those who failed to pass the tests were enrolled as common seamen in the navy, a deterrent deemed powerful enough to stimulate the young men's zeal for arithmetic and geometry, still an important part of the curricula.

The chief ambition of the *dvoriane*, however, was to escape army barracks and government offices. When at the end of the Turkish war in 1739 the manifesto of December 31, 1736, was finally put into operation, requests for dismissal from service were so numerous that the government found it necessary to give to the law an interpretation that amounted to partial repeal. Each application was carefully examined, and permission to retire was granted only to those whose military record and economic status were deemed such as to justify dismissal. Those civil servants who had had no service with the colors were not allowed to retire until they reached the age of fifty-five. It was indicative of the prevailing mood of the *dvoriane* that a considerable number of applicants for retirement were men in their early thirties whose names, according to custom, had been put on the lists of regiments when they were mere boys and who reckoned their term of service from that date, instead of from the age of twenty prescribed by the law.

While the practical consequences of the manifesto of December 31, 1736, fell short of the expectations of the *dvoriane*, and although their emancipation from the yoke of compulsory service was postponed until 1762, the noble landlords were more successful in their second major endeavor—the strengthening of their hold over the servile population on their estates. The serfs were deprived one by one of the few rights they had enjoyed in the past. The landlords were made responsible for the payment from 1722 of the poll tax assessed on their estates, and in 1731 they became government agents for the actual collection of this tax.[3] The identification of the interests of

---

[3] The poll tax was originally collected by special commissars elected by the local nobles; these officials carried on their duties in cooperation, first, with the military commanders and, after 1727, with the civil authorities (see pp. 377–378). In

the serfowners with those of the treasury, which delegated to them
the tax-collection function, contributed to the growth of serfdom.
The repeal, in 1727, of the decree issued by Peter I granting the
serfs the right to join the armed forces without the consent of their
masters, blocked one of the last ways of escape from the state of
bondage, since enlistment freed the soldier and his immediate family
from all obligations towards the landlord. The owners had long exercised unrestricted right to sell their serfs with or without land, as entire
families or as individuals. The half-hearted attempt of Peter I to discourage this practice in 1721 was in contradiction with his earlier
unrepealed decrees (those of December 17, 1717, and October 29,
1720) which legalized the sale and purchase of young men as army
recruits, a right specifically confirmed in 1747. Although the law contained no provision respecting the power of owners either to force
their serfs to marry or to influence their choice in marriage, in practice
such personal matters were frequently decided by the owner of the
estate: children born from the union of his serfs were an important
accretion to his wealth and added to the number of prospective taxpayers. If the bride and the bridegroom belonged to different lords,
the owner of the former was entitled to a monetary compensation
and the young woman became a serf of her husband's owner. In the
first half of the eighteenth century, apparently, the permission of the
owner of the bride was not required and the matter was settled by
the customary payment. A decree of 1724 stated that the owner of
the bride could not prevent her marrying an enlisted man if he had
paid the ransom. A decree of May 13, 1754, however, made the law
more drastic by providing that the marriage of a female serf to an
outsider (that is, a man who was not a serf of her lord) without written permission from her master constituted desertion.

The economic activities of the serfs were subjected to increasingly
rigid control. According to a law of 1724, a bondsman was forbidden
to engage in a trade that necessitated his residence beyond a specified
distance from his lord's estate unless he had his master's written permit endorsed by a public official. After 1744 bondsmen were required
to obtain in addition printed passports issued by the local governor
upon receipt of their owners' consent. A decree of August 1, 1737,

---

1730 the commissars were once more put under the control of the military, but
in 1731 the office of commissars was abolished and the collection of the poll tax
was entrusted to the landlords and their bailiffs.

deprived the serf of the right to purchase land, except in the name of his lord and with his permission, and a similar rule was applied to any industrial or commercial enterprise in which a serf might wish to engage. The general deterioration of the legal status of the peasantry was emphasized by the fact that, contrary to precedent, the servile population was not called upon to take the oath of allegiance to Empress Elizabeth on her accession in 1741.

The curtailment of the legal rights of the bondsmen had its counterpart in the extension both of the rights and of the duties of their owners. As has been pointed out, the landlords were made liable for the assessment of the poll tax on their estates and for its collection. The famine of 1733–1734 moved the government to impose upon the landlords the obligation of providing maintenance for their serfs and of supplying them with seeds (April, 1734). This regulation was repeated in 1750 and in 1761, but its practical effect appears to have been negligible, the landlords having had neither the desire nor the ability to give relief to their serfs. The latter were generally ignorant of their right to maintenance, a right which, moreover, they were unable to enforce. Of greater import was the expansion of the already broad and ill defined judicial and police powers of the landlords. By a decree of December 13, 1760, they were given the right to deport their delinquent serfs to Siberia, the male deportees being credited towards the landlord's quota of army recruits. This provision led to abuse, although the object of the law was commendable: to increase the population of Russia's vast Asiatic empire. The discretion enjoyed by the landlords in judicial matters is well illustrated by the decree of May 6, 1736, by which it was left to them to decide what punishment should be meted out to fugitive serfs, even to application of the knout, a chastisement that occasionally resulted in the death of the victim. As if the police powers of the landlords were not comprehensive enough, a decree of May 2, 1758, made it their duty to keep a close watch over the conduct of their serfs, while a decree of June 5, 1761, conferred upon the *dvoriane* the right to elect from their own midst the local *voevoda*, an official vested with broad executive and judicial powers. To complete the picture, it may be added that the section of the Code of 1649 prohibiting bondsmen from bringing complaints against their lord, except in case of alleged treasonable activities or misconduct with a female serf, was never repealed. This provision, however, was not strictly enforced, and although there were instances when serfs successfully petitioned the government for redress of their grievances, the uncertainty of their legal right to bring complaints made such proceedings hazardous and sometimes disastrous for the petitioners.

The right to own serfs tended to become not only more comprehensive but also more exclusive; that is, it was coming to acquire the character of a class privilege. Although in the first half of the eighteenth century the majority of serfowners were *dvoriane*, some of the estates cultivated by servile labor belonged to members of other ill defined social groups whose legal title to such estates would seem to have constituted a violation of the Code of 1649. By laws passed in 1730, 1743, 1746, and 1758 the titles of the non-*dvoriane* to own serfs were revoked. Particularly drastic were a decree of 1746, which prohibited the purchase of serfs by anyone who did not belong to the *dvorianstvo*, and a law of 1758 (*mezhevaia instruktsiia*), which ordered that all estates cultivated by bondsmen and owned by non-*dvoriane* should be taken over by the Crown. Thus by the end of the reign of Elizabeth the nobles had succeeded in establishing their right to the ownership of land farmed by servile labor, to the exclusion of all other private owners. The *dvoriane* continued to share this privilege with the imperial family, the Crown, and the Church. The economic position of the nobility was further strengthened by the creation of the State Nobility Bank (Decree of May 7, 1753). This institution, which opened its doors in 1754 and was endowed with a capital of 750,000 rubles, obtained from the proceeds of the liquor monopoly, provided mortgage credit for the noble landlords at 6 per cent interest, that is, at a figure below the prevailing market rate.

The economic advantages secured by the *dvoriane* were offset in no small degree by the impoverishment of the peasantry by whom the brunt of the cost of Peter I's imperial expansion had been borne. Early in 1725 Yaguzhinsky wrote to Empress Catherine I that a large number of farmers had disposed of their horses, cattle, and stocks of grain and were faced with starvation. Count Matveev, in a report based on a personal investigation of conditions in the province of Moscow, probably the most prosperous section of the country, traced a distressing picture of the general decay of the rural community (August, 1726). Thousands of farmers, he pointed out, had run away, and those who had stayed were reduced to a state of destitution. The onward march of serfdom under the rule of Peter I's successors contributed to the unhappy plight of the servile population. Driven to despair, the bondsmen had, as in the past, abandoned their farms and fled to the relatively inaccessible regions of the Urals and Siberia, to the southern steppes and the Caucasus, to the Baltic provinces and to Poland. In a letter to Empress Catherine, January 7, 1727, Yaguzhinsky maintained that practically every Polish landlord was harboring Russian fugitive serfs. Twenty-seven years later the situation had not improved; the Russian minister to Warsaw, Gross, reported on June 15, 1754, that on the estates of the Polish magnate Prince Czartoryski several thousand fugitive Russian serfs had settled. The inevitable and familiar consequence of this undesired migration was the depopulation of the countryside and a bitter scramble among the landlords for fugitive serfs. It was officially stated in 1735 that in certain localities the rural population had declined by more than half and that the position of the farmers who had remained was desperate because they were liable for the poll tax of those who had vanished. In an order forbidding beggars access to the capital (1741), the Senate made the melancholy admission that vagrants were drawn chiefly from among runaway serfs.

The government attempted to fight the evil of mass desertion by reducing the rate of the poll tax, an enlightened policy which was vitiated by a simultaneous increase in the exorbitant taxes on salt and spirits, both administered through state monopolies, and especially by the absence of any restriction on what the landlords were entitled to exact from their serfs. A flow of repetitious and largely futile legislation imposed drastic penalties both on runaway peasants and on the landlords who harbored them. Endless litigation between serfowners who endeavored to establish their title to a serf on the basis of records sometimes more than a hundred years old promoted the publication of the decree of May 13, 1754, making the census (*reviziia*) of 1719 the limit beyond which owners were forbidden to go in proving their claims. The decree also laid down rules as to how the fugitives and those who accepted them were to be handled, with heavy punishments for the former and equally heavy fines for the latter. In 1743 and 1744 special commissions were created in the Baltic provinces to bring about the repatriation of fugitive serfs, but they achieved little and were discontinued in 1753. Forgiveness and grants of land were promised in 1759 and 1761 to the serfs who had fled abroad if they would return, but this gesture of clemency failed to bring a response.

Flight, however, was only one of two traditional methods the peasantry had used in its struggle against the oppressors. The second method was rebellion, and it is not surprising to find that the reigns of Peter I's successors, especially that of Empress Elizabeth, were filled with peasant uprisings. These were particularly frequent and violent on the estates owned by the monasteries and among the serfs attached to industrial enterprises, where conditions were even more intolerable than on privately owned agricultural estates. Contemporary records provide numerous accounts of large bands of peasants, sometimes several thousand strong and armed with field guns, giving regular battle to the punitive expeditions sent against them. There were instances when private soldiers whose term of service lasted for life and whose fate was hardly more enviable than that of the serfs joined hands with the rebels only to be defeated by fresh contingents of government troops. These uprisings were invariably crushed, and their leaders either suffered the customary martyrdom on the wheel, the gallows, or at the whipping post, or else disappeared in the bleakness of Siberia. But the rebellious spirit generated by the conditions that the government and the ruling class had created and relentlessly enforced refused to die and led to new revolts.

FINANCIAL AND ECONOMIC POLICIES

Little need be said here about the economic policies of the immediate successors of Peter I. It soon became evident that the financial reforms of the first quarter of the eighteenth century had failed to bridge the gap between revenue and expenditure, and recurrent budget deficits, especially in time of war, remained the outstanding feature of Russia's public finance in 1725–1762. The poll-tax arrears alone were estimated in 1725 at about 1,000,000 rubles, and by the end of Elizabeth's reign the situation had not improved: the central department of state expenditure (*shtats-kontora*) disclosed in August, 1761, that its immediate liabilities were 2,565,000 rubles and its assets 121,000 rubles. This state of financial disorder was aggravated by the chaotic condition of public accounting and the prevalence of corruption. Various expedients were tried to balance the budget. In 1725 the size of the military establishment was cut and in 1736 and 1747 the wages of government officials and the bills for army supplies were paid in goods instead of in money. A levy on the wages of military, civil, court, and ecclesiastical officials was imposed in 1742. Officials responsible for the collection of taxes were made liable to fines or even to confiscation of property if they failed to produce the revenue assessed for the districts under their jurisdiction (1736, 1742). Sporadic attempts were made to cut down expenditure, and both Empress Anne and Empress Elizabeth issued decrees against the use of costly silks and lace, although the luxury of court entertainments tended to encourage extravagance among the upper classes. The practical results of these uncoordinated half-measures were nil; the treasury remained empty, and in 1747–1750 the wages of even Her Majesty's Own Company, that mainstay of the throne, were hopelessly in arrears.

Since the loss of public revenue had been caused at least in part by the flight of the taxpayers and by evasion of direct taxes, it was not illogical to shift some of the fiscal burden from direct to indirect taxation. The rates of the poll tax were reduced in 1725, 1742, and again in 1750–1758, while the prices of salt and alcohol, the sale of which was administered by state monopolies, were substantially increased. This tax-reform plan originated in the fertile mind of Count Peter Shuvalov, who submitted his program to the Senate in 1745 and had it adopted in 1750. He claimed, seven years later, that the financial measures he had initiated had yielded the treasury a revenue of some 15,000,000 rubles. The outbreak of the Seven Years' War called for large military expenditure and the Senate, at the suggestion of Shuvalov, proceeded with the devaluation of copper coins. These were withdrawn from circulation and reissued at twice their former nominal value, an operation only too familiar in Russia's financial history and one that proved no more successful in 1757 than it had in the past. Both Empress Anne and Empress Elizabeth contributed to the financial chaos by extravagant court expenditure and by lavish grants to their favorites. During the Seven Years' War Elizabeth spoke of selling her jewels and dresses to finance the struggle against Frederick, yet the building of the Winter Palace, on which some 1,500,000 rubles was spent between 1755 and 1759, was not interrupted.

Few important developments can be singled out in the field of commerce and industry. The central department of municipal affairs (*glavnyi magistrat*), created in 1721 and abolished seven years later, was revived in 1737 without, however, bringing any improvement either in municipal government or in the position of the merchants who formed the upper stratum of the urban population. City life continued to make little progress: in the middle of the century the burghers accounted for merely 3 per cent of the total population. Commerce derived some benefit not only from the introduction in 1729 of bills of exchange, the use of which, however, was restricted to merchants by the law of 1729 (*vekselnyi ustav*) and by subsequent legislation, but also from the establishment in 1754 in St. Petersburg of the Commercial Bank, although its operations remained negligible. Far more important was the abolition in 1753, at the suggestion of Count Peter Shuvalov, of internal customs (*octroi*) and the simultaneous removal of miscellaneous charges on the internal movement of merchandise. The resulting loss of revenue was made good by the imposition of heavy import and export duties consolidated in the tariff law of 1757, legislation marking a return to the protective policies of 1724, some of the duties reaching 80 per cent ad valorem or even higher rates. Trade monopolies fostered by Peter I in the early part of his reign and abandoned by him later were revived on a large scale, especially during the reign of Elizabeth, and became a source of gross abuse, since they were usually administered by outstanding officials of the regime (Count Peter and Count Alexander Shuvalov, Count Michael Vorontsov, Count S. P. Yaguzhinsky, and others) who were also responsible for the framing of the country's economic policies. A curious and characteristic measure "for the promotion of trade" was a decree of December 2, 1742, which prohibited the Jews from residing in Russia and ordered their deportation unless they chose to embrace the Greek Orthodox faith. There is no evidence, however, that the government actually attempted to enforce this Draconian law. A leading figure in the economic legislation and activities of the Elizabethan era was senator Peter Shuvalov, whose verbose and obscure projects occupied much of the Senate's time. A shrewd, unscrupulous, and ruthless businessman, and the inventor of a field gun of most questionable value, Shuvalov accumulated a vast fortune, but there is nothing to indicate that his far-reaching projects contributed anything to Russia's economic advancement.

SCHOOLS, LITERATURE, AND ART

While Peter Shuvalov concerned himself with economic, military and administrative matters, and his brother Alexander, head of the security police, watched over the safety of the throne, their youthful and handsome cousin, Ivan Shuvalov, endeavored to lend some dignity to his equivocal position as favorite of the aging Empress

Elizabeth by his generous patronage of science and art. Schools had made little progress in the second quarter of the eighteenth century,[4] and Empress Anne's military academy provided only limited facilities for the professional training of the young *dvoriane*. Empress Catherine II notes in her *Memoirs* that at the court of Elizabeth "one never spoke of art and science because everyone was so ignorant; it is very likely that half of the company could barely read and I am not certain that one-third could write." In 1754 Ivan Shuvalov, who had traveled abroad and was an admirer of France, submitted to the Senate a project for the establishment in Moscow of a university and two secondary schools: one for the *dvoriane* and one for boys drawn from other social groups in which the serfs, however, were not included. The project was approved on January 12, 1755, and in April of the same year the university began to function with Ivan Shuvalov as its curator. It consisted of three principal subdivisions or faculties: law, medicine, and philosophy; the lectures were to be delivered in Latin and in Russian. Although a decree of May 17, 1756, encouraged attendance by conferring on the graduates privileges both in military and in civil service, the response at first was not encouraging: in 1765, for instance, there was only one student in the faculty of law, and in 1768 the same situation arose in the faculty of medicine. The Moscow secondary schools fared somewhat better, and similar schools were established in Kazan in 1758. Shuvalov's more ambitious project (1760) for the founding of secondary schools in the principal cities and of elementary schools in the larger towns was indefinitely shelved. The University of Moscow, handicapped by the lack of qualified teachers and students, remained for decades a pitiful travesty of an institution of higher education, and it was not until the nineteenth century that it became one of the foremost centers of Russian learning.

No less significant was the emergence of the "new" Russian literature, that is, the appearance of literary works written in conformity with the literary tradition of western Europe, a development traced by Pypin, the eminent historian of Russian letters, to the decade of 1730–1740 and associated with the names of Kantemir, Trediakovsky, Sumarokov, and Lomonosov. These authors, who had lived and studied abroad, were under the influence of the pseudo-classical literature then prevalent in western Europe. Although these representatives

[4] See pp. 404 *et seq.*

of Russia's new literary movement followed slavishly the outward forms of the great classic and pseudo-classic works, they did endeavor to deal with Russian subjects and they made important contributions to the evolution of Russian literary language and, especially, to the elucidation of the rules of Russian versification. Prince Antiokh Kantemir (1708–1744), minister to London and later ambassador to Paris, was something of a dilettante and was best known for his satires, which have not yet lost their interest. Trediakovsky, Sumarokov, and Lomonosov, on the other hand, were Russia's first professional men of letters. Vasili Trediakovsky (1703–1769), son of a priest, was an indefatigable translator, author of numerous works, and professor of eloquence in the Academy of Science. His treatises on philology and grammar have won high praise from the greatest master of the Russian language, Pushkin, but his original poems could hardly have been clumsier or more ridiculous. Alexander Sumarokov (1718–1777), offspring of a noble family, is remembered chiefly as a playwright and the director of St. Petersburg's first Russian theater, which was opened in 1756. Although Sumarokov had the unfortunate habit of referring to himself as Russia's Racine or Voltaire, his writings, which enjoyed great popularity with his contemporaries, had nothing of the distinction of his great French models and were much nearer to the humble level of Trediakovsky's poetical offerings. Michael Lomonosov (1711–1765), son of a peasant fisherman from distant Kholmogory, province of Archangel, was professor of chemistry in the Academy of Science and a scientist as well as philologist, a poet and a historian. His poetical talent and the ease with which at short notice he composed high-sounding odes celebrating the virtues not only of Peter I, whom he admired, but also of the late tsar's less worthy successors—Anne, Elizabeth, Peter III, and Catherine II—saved him more than once from the unhappy consequences of an impetuous temperament stimulated at times by an excessive use of alcohol. His devotion to the cause of public enlightenment, however, was admirable, and although his patriotism was excessive and the originality of his contributions to science debatable, he is rightly regarded as one of the outstanding figures in the intellectual history of Russia.

History, like literature, showed the effect of the infiltration of western ideas. In his *Istoriia Rossiiskaia* (Russian History) Vasili Tatishchev (1686–1750), who had once served under Peter I in the campaigns of Narva, Poltava, and the Pruth, not only assembled a mass of information of a historical, geographical, and ethnographical nature, but also submitted the chronicles to a critical examination and challenged the still widely held theory of the beneficial influence of the Russian Church. Important contributions came from the German scholars. Among the German professors called to St. Petersburg, a place of honor belongs to Gerhard Frederick Miller (1705–1783), who, beginning his Russian career in 1725, carried out a detailed first-hand study of Siberia and wrote extensively on Russian history.

Pypin draws attention to the fact that in the first half of the eighteenth century literary works continued to circulate in handwritten copies and that some of the outstanding works of that period did not appear in print until many years later. The satires of Kantemir, for instance, were first published in Russian in 1762, eighteen years after their author's death; the first three volumes of the history of Tatishchev, who died in 1750, were brought out by Miller in 1768–1774, the fourth volume in 1784, and the fifth as late as 1848. It was only gradually that the printed word won its legitimate place. In 1755 appeared the first scientific and literary periodical, *Ezhemesiachnyia sochineniia* (Monthly Essays), published by the Academy of Science and edited by Miller. In 1759 Sumarokov founded the magazine *Trudoliubivaia pchela* (Busy Bee), the first private venture of the kind. Lack of funds and difficulties with the censor forced him to suspend publication a year later, but his initiative was not forgotten and he found many imitators in the latter part of the eighteenth century.

The advancement of national painting, sculpture, and architecture was encouraged by the founding in 1757 of an Academy of Arts, another creation of Ivan Shuvalov. But native talent in these fields, as well as in that of music, was not yet available. An Italian opera company made its appearance at the imperial court in 1736, and it was to the Italian architect, Count Bartholomew Rastrelli, that St. Petersburg owes some of its finest eighteenth century buildings, including the Winter Palace and the Smolny Convent, where Lenin made his headquarters during the Bolshevik revolution of 1917.

THE RULE OF FEAR

The chief impression that emerges from a survey of Russia's history in 1725–1761 is that of a country dominated by fear and pursuing an uncertain course under casual leadership and without the benefit of a constitutional charter, of an intelligible code of laws, or of a crystallized social structure. The revision of the antiquated Code of 1649 was ordered by Peter I in 1700 and again in 1718. His successors vainly wrestled with the same problem, but the successive legislative commissions were unable to fulfill their task and the futile discussion dragged on from decade to decade. In a much-quoted decree of August 16, 1760, Elizabeth unfolded a graphic picture of the state of lawlessness prevailing in the empire. She complained that laws were not enforced and that their violation went on unchecked. For this state of affairs she blamed "the domestic enemies who put their lawless selfish interests above their oath, duty and honor." Corruption and spoliation, according to the empress, were the rule in the courts and in every branch of administration, and she saw the roots of the evil in the indifference and inaction of the Senate and in the low moral level of the judiciary and of the civil service. It would seem, however, that the real causes of Russia's predicament were much deeper than those which suggested themselves to Elizabeth's superficial mind. The arbitrariness of the regime she had inherited from her predecessors and over which she had so complacently presided for twenty years had produced a general feeling of insecurity. The corruption of government organs and individual officials was the by-product of a political system that was the antithesis of the rule of law. The occupants of the throne, owing their Crown to the passing whims of a few palace functionaries and a handful of guardsmen, never knew what the morrow had in store for them. Even though by the end of the Elizabethan era the *dvorianstvo* was entrenched as a class, the personal security of its individual members was no greater than that of the lowest serfs. The ephemeral character of the wealth and power derived from tenure of high offices was well illustrated by the fate of Menshikov, the Dolgoruky, the Golitsin, Biron, Ostermann, Volynsky, and Bestuzhev. The vicissitudes of their fortunes were duplicated in a less spectacular manner among the rank and file of the *dvoriane* and of the burghers, while the destinies of the peasantry, that is, of the immense majority of the people, were in the hands of the landlords and of petty government officials. Insecurity and the dread of the future permeated the whole of Russia's social structure, from the occupant of the throne and the great landowners down to the humblest subjects of the Crown. Hence there was, on the one hand, a domestic policy that combined ruthless repression and the indiscriminate powers of the police with concessions to the social class seemingly best placed to protect the regime; and, on the other, general disaffection, which manifested itself in conspiracies against the rulers, evasion of service by the *dvoriane*, flight of the taxpayers, and peasant uprisings. On the eve of the accession of Catherine II, the Russian empire was governed by the arbitrary and capricious decisions of rulers conscious of the weakness of their position and concerned chiefly with maintaining themselves in power.

CHAPTER XIX

ENLIGHTENED ABSOLUTISM

Peter III and Catherine II

---- ✳ ----

THE REIGN OF PETER III

The brief reign of Peter III, one of the few monarchs in eighteenth century Russia to take the throne legally and without the support of a palace clique, proved a mere prelude to the long rule of his consort, Catherine II. Born in Kiel in February, 1728, Peter lost his mother, the former Tsarevna Anne, when he was a few weeks old, and his father, Charles Frederick, duke of Holstein, in 1739. He was brought to Russia after the accession of his aunt, the Empress Elizabeth, and in November, 1742, was received into the Greek Orthodox Church and proclaimed heir to the Russian throne. His marriage in 1745 with the princess of Anhalt-Zerbst was followed by the birth in 1754 of a son, the future Emperor Paul I.

Russian historiography has shown little leniency towards Peter III. He is usually represented as a libertine, a halfwit, and a drunkard whose contempt for ordinary decency and for the country over which he was called to rule made imperative his removal. The writings of Catherine II, especially her well known *Memoirs*, and those of Princess Dashkov and others among her satellites, have provided damaging accounts of Peter's character and mental condition. Although it has been often emphasized that this partisan evidence should not be accepted without close scrutiny, the testimony emanating from those immediately involved in the overthrow of Peter has been given somewhat greater credence than it would seem to deserve. Contemporary reports from less biased Russian and foreign sources, however, bring out Peter's many shortcomings and contain abundant references to the extravagances in which he freely indulged. To appraise the importance of these personal failings in shaping his tragic fate, they must be judged in the light of our general knowledge of the conditions then prevailing at the Russian court. Superficial and inadequate as was the education and training of Peter, both in Kiel and after his arrival in Russia, it was not inferior to that of his predecessors on the Russian throne. He owned a sizable library in which he took great personal interest. He spoke excellent German, very good French, and fairly good Russian, although his spelling in all three languages was poor. A passionate lover of music, Peter played the violin with perhaps more enthusiasm than skill. His predilection for the company of people of lowly descent, his liking for English beer, his delight in crude practical jokes were no striking departure from the routine of the Russian court since the days of Peter I. The union of the grand duke with Catherine was not a happy one, and he made no secret of his liaison with Elizabeth Vorontsov, niece of the chancellor. He is reputed to have had other mistresses, but this was in accordance with tradition, and Catherine, who had had at least three lovers while still a grand duchess, was no paragon of conventional virtue. The eccentricities of Peter's conduct, especially his lack of respect for the Orthodox Church and ritual, a disrespect that at times assumed most offensive forms, his admiration for Frederick of Prussia, with whom Russia was at war, and his absorption with the affairs of the duchy of Holstein led to friction between the heir-apparent and Empress Elizabeth, who is said to have considered his removal. Nothing, however, was done about it, and the accession of Peter took place in a decorous manner.

The domestic policies of Peter were surprisingly liberal, and might have been expected to win the hearts of his subjects. Many of the exiles of former reigns, among them Biron, Münnich, and Lestocq, were freed and appeared again in the capital and at the court. Far more unusual was the absence of new persecutions; the favorites of Elizabeth were permitted to continue unmolested, although Alexis Razumovsky was removed from the active list. On January 17, 1762, the emperor announced to the Senate his intention of freeing the *dvoriane* from the obligation of compulsory service, and on February 18 he issued a manifesto which put the service of the nobles on a voluntary basis, gave them the right except in time of war to resign from the army and civil administration, and granted them permission to travel freely abroad and to enter the service of foreign Powers. The joy with which the *dvoriane* received the manifesto was marred by the omission of any reference to the two other cardinal wishes of the nobility: freedom from corporal punishment and immunity of hereditary estates from confiscation. A cause for wider rejoicing was a decree of February 21 which abolished the security police, discouraged private informers, and directed that no one should be arrested on political charges or considered a suspect until the case had been investigated by the Senate. A similar liberal tendency inspired a decree of January 29 providing for the repatriation of the old-believers who had escaped abroad from Elizabethan persecutions and granting them freedom of worship. Measures were also taken to liberalize trade and to encourage foreign commerce by scaling down export duties. In this rather sweeping program of reforms the common people were not forgotten. On January 17 Peter ordered a reduction of the price of salt and expressed a wish to do away with the salt monopoly. The purchase by the manufacturers of serfs for employment in industrial enterprises— a particularly harsh form of serfdom which led to frequent peasant uprisings—was prohibited. The vexed question of Church estates was given a drastic solution by the establishment of a college of economy (*kollegiia ekonomii*) which, under the supervision of the Senate, was to take over the administration of ecclesiastical estates; monasteries and Church dignitaries were to receive annual sums according to approved schedules (decrees of February 16 and March 21). This secularization naturally provoked a protest from the clergy, whose members hastened to take their place in the ranks of the new regime's opponents. Peter also abolished on January 29 the Conference of ten members which since 1756 had been the chief administrative organ of the realm. The nature of these reforms offers no clue to the emperor's growing unpopularity, a development that played its part in his downfall. If, as it is often alleged, the measures listed above were suggested to Peter by his advisers and did not originate with him, this would merely prove that the emperor was willing to listen to advice that was not unenlightened.

Undue importance should not be attached to the disappointment caused in St. Petersburg by the sudden termination of Russia's participation in the Seven Years' War, by the abandonment of the Austrian alliance, and the substitution for it of one with Prussia. The war, which had never been popular in Russia, had already dragged on for several years; the country was weary and the treasury empty. Frederick had many admirers in Russia and elsewhere, and although Peter went too far in describing the Prussian king as "one of the greatest heroes in the world" and in parading his enthusiasm for Elizabeth's mortal enemy, there was little in his attitude towards Frederick to shock the susceptibilities of the army and of the court. It was Peter's refusal to follow the advice of Frederick, rather than his subservient attitude towards the king of Prussia, that contributed to the emperor's undoing. A fanatical Holstein patriot, Peter was determined to recover Schleswig from Denmark, and he exacted from a reluctant Frederick the promise to cooperate with Russia in a war against that Power (treaty of April 24). Frederick strove in vain to postpone the Russo-Danish conflict, partly because he was reluctant to divert any of his depleted forces for this new military venture, in which Prussia had little to gain, and partly because he feared the probable political repercussions of Peter's absence from his capital, since the emperor was determined to lead his troops in person. On May 21 General Rumiantsev, in command of the Russian army in Pomerania, was informed by Peter that war with Denmark was not only inevitable but must be considered as having already begun, a decision that was withheld from the Prussian ambassador to St. Petersburg, Baron von Goltz (who otherwise enjoyed the boundless confidence of the tsar), although Russia had previously agreed that the Schleswig question should be mediated in Berlin by the Prussian king. A war with Denmark for the benefit of Holstein would not be popular in Russia, especially with the army, as Frederick and von Goltz realized.

No less fatal to Peter's position was his attempt to reform the army. A strict disciplinarian and an expert drill-master, he viewed with disapproval the laxity that prevailed in Russia's military establishment under the rule of Elizabeth. On his accession Peter ordered a revision of the army organization and a redrafting of army regulations along Prussian lines; he dressed guardsmen in brand-new Prussian uniforms, and supervised in person the drilling of the St. Petersburg garrison. The emperor made no secret of his aversion for the Russian guards, to whom he referred as Janissaries and whose privileges he threatened to revoke while organizing new units of Holstein guards. These policies invited disaster by alienating from Peter the elements that had become the mainstay of the throne. His insistence that, contrary to custom, soldiers of high military rank should participate in drills offended many higher officials whose connection with the army had formerly been purely honorary. In the light of the experience of preceding reigns, it would seem that the principal reason for Peter's overthrow was not his lack of respect for the Church, his alleged intemperance, the irregularities of his private life, his unconventional behavior, or his avowed contempt for things Russian, but the disaffection of the guards and of their leaders. All other causes for discontent with the tsar merely contributed to the easy success of another palace revolution of which the guardsmen, as in the past, were the driving force. It was an unwritten law in eighteenth century Russia that a monarch who acceded to the throne legally and without the support of a cabal could not maintain himself in power.

THE REVOLUTION OF JUNE 28, 1762

While Peter wasted his opportunities by making dangerous enemies, Catherine spared no effort to win over the circles whose support was essential to the success of a palace revolution. Immense ambition was the outstanding characteristic of this extraordinary woman. She writes in her *Memoirs* that she foresaw little chance of happiness in her marriage with Peter and that on the eve of her wedding "ambition alone supported me; I had at the bottom of my heart I know not what that prevented me from doubting for even a moment that sooner or later I should become empress of Russia in my own right." Catherine, however, did not leave it to Providence alone to take care of her future, nor was she satisfied with building up a following by assiduously dissociating herself from the unpopular policies of her husband and by displaying respect for native Russian customs and for the Church. Her correspondence with Sir Charles Hanbury-Williams, English ambassador at St. Petersburg, reveals that in 1757 Catherine participated in a conspiracy which had for its object to maintain the right to the throne of her son Paul, even if Elizabeth, whose death at the time was considered imminent, should disinherit the Grand Duke Peter. "That Catherine shall reign—was considered as settled between her and Williams," writes Professor Chechulin, although the grand duchess was then still willing to share power, at least provisionally, with her husband. In pursuance of the plan, Catherine solicited and obtained through Williams subsidies from the English government, with which Russia was on the verge of war. With the accession of Peter, relations between him and his wife appear to have deteriorated, and he is reported to have contemplated a divorce or her imprisonment, in spite of the fact that in the earlier years he had been a lenient and tolerant husband and, indeed, had given all possible encouragement to a liaison between Catherine and Count Stanislas Poniatowski, the future king of Poland. In 1762 the overthrow of Peter became the only way for Catherine to achieve her ultimate object.

The proposed departure of Peter to lead his troops against Denmark seemed to offer the opportunity for which Catherine had been waiting. She had taken into her confidence several of the outstanding personalities of the regime, among them Nikita Panin, the well known diplomat and tutor of the Grand Duke Paul; Count Cyril Razumovsky, hetman of Ukraine; Field Marshal Villebois; Baron Nicholas Korff, director of the police. The all-important support of the guards was assured, largely through the efforts of Gregory Orlov, Catherine's lover since 1760 or 1761, and of his four brothers, who were popular with officers and men. The nineteen-year-old Princess Dashkov, wife of an officer in the guards and an enthusiastic admirer of Catherine, claimed a lion's share of credit for the success of the conspiracy, but she seems to have exaggerated the importance of the part she actually played. The reluctance of the guardsmen to leave their quarters at St. Petersburg for the hazards of the Danish campaign provided excellent ground for propaganda against the emperor. The chance arrest on June 27 of Passek, an officer of the Preobrazhensky regiment involved in the conspiracy, precipitated the *dénouement* by creating a threat that the plot might be discovered. In the early hours of June 28 Catherine, who was then living at Peterhof, was aroused from sleep by Alexis Orlov, and at once left with him and Vasili Bibikov for St. Petersburg. They were met en route by Gregory Orlov and Prince Fedor Bariatinsky, who took Catherine to the barracks of the Izmailovsky regiment, where the soldiers gave her an enthusiastic reception; the Semenovsky regiment, visited next, was just as eager in acclaiming the new empress. The clergy and higher officials hastened to emulate the example of the soldiery. After being solemnly proclaimed autocratic ruler of Russia in the Kazan Cathedral, Catherine, accompanied by a delirious and ever increasing crowd which included all the troops of the metropolitan garrison, proceeded to the Winter Palace, where the members of the Holy Synod and of the Senate were awaiting her. A hastily drafted manifesto announced the dethronement of Peter and the accession of Catherine. While the glad news was circulated to the military and civil authorities outside the capital, an unruly mob, in which soldiers predominated, ransacked wine cellars, and the bloodless revolution of June 28 was happily crowned with a great drunken orgy for which the government eventually paid the bill.

Peter, who was staying with his mistress and the court at his country residence in Oranienbaum, was unaware of the events unfolding in the capital. On the morning of June 28, accompanied by a large suite, he went to Peterhof to visit his wife, only to discover that she had mysteriously disappeared. When information about what had taken place in St. Petersburg reached the emperor, he sailed, after some hesitation, for Kronstadt. There he was refused permission to land, and returned to Oranienbaum, having previously rejected Münnich's more manly plan of proceeding to Reval and then joining Rumiantzev's army in Pomerania.

On the evening of June 28 Catherine, at the head of a large body of troops, started for Peterhof and Oranienbaum. Wearing the uniform of the Preobrazhensky regiment, her long locks fluttering in the breeze, the empress rode a gray stallion, with Princess Dashkov similarly attired prancing at her side. Peter offered no resistance, and after some abortive attempts at negotiations abdicated on June 29. According to Frederick II, the tsar "allowed himself to be overthrown as a child is sent to bed." The former emperor was put under arrest at the country estate of Ropsha, where on July 6 he was assassinated by his guards, headed by Alexis Orlov. The details of the murder were never fully revealed, and the part played in it by Catherine remains uncertain. The impunity of Orlov and the other men involved suggests that the assassination, if not directly instigated by Catherine, had her approval. The empress charged in her *Memoirs*, and intimated in a manifesto of July 6, 1762, that Count Alexander Shuvalov and Prince Nikita Trubetskoy were sent by Peter on June 28 to murder her. This accusation is disingenuous, since the two elderly courtiers, on their arrival in St. Petersburg, at once took the oath of allegiance to the empress and upon their retirement in 1763 were the recipients of valuable marks of Catherine's favor.

It is unnecessary to dwell here on the alleged "national" character of the movement that led to the fall of Peter III. The revolution of June 28 conformed to the familiar pattern and put on the Russian throne a German princess about whom at the time almost nothing was known outside narrow palace circles.

SEMIRAMIS OF THE NORTH

Princess Sophia Augusta Frederica of Anhalt-Zerbst was born in Stettin on May 2, 1729, N.S. Her early education was undistinguished, and when she was unexpectedly summoned to Moscow, where she was married in August, 1745, to her distant Holstein relative, the Grand Duke Peter, her only noteworthy accomplishment consisted of a fluent command of French, which she owed largely to her governess, Mademoiselle Cardel. The seventeen years following Catherine's marriage were probably the most trying period in her life. There was little affection in the grand-ducal household, although the estrangement between Catherine and her husband could hardly have been as complete as is often alleged, since Peter entrusted her with the management of his beloved duchy of Holstein. According to Catherine's *Memoirs*, she actually ruled the duchy until the fall of Bestuzhev in 1758.[1] It will be remembered that Empress Elizabeth showed much irritation with the "young court" and subjected it to a vexatious supervision. With the arrest of Bestuzhev the situation reached a point at which Catherine deemed it wise to ask Elizabeth to be sent back to Germany, although, as she complacently states in her *Memoirs*, this was a tactical and successful move in the war of palace intrigues. Throughout these difficult and perilous years Catherine, sustained by her ambition, occupied her time with political maneuvers, with extensive if somewhat haphazard reading, and with amorous adventures. While contemporary gossips and a malevolent tradition have exaggerated the number of her lovers, it is well established that a young and handsome courtier, Serge Saltykov, was admitted to intimacy with her from 1752 to 1754; he was followed in 1755–1758 by the seductive Pole, Count Stanislas Poniatowski, and in 1760 or 1761 by

[1] After Peter's abdication Catherine displayed a truly admirable magnanimity towards her former rival, Elizabeth Vorontsov, who was a sister of Princess Dashkov. The erstwhile mistress of Peter was ordered to reside at Moscow, where she was provided with a suitable establishment, and after her marriage in 1765 to Alexander Poliansky she was permitted to return to St. Petersburg. The empress acted as godmother to a boy born to the Poliansky and in 1782 she appointed their daughter her lady-in-waiting. These marks of imperial favor suggest that the services once rendered by Elizabeth Vorontsov in facilitating Catherine's liaison with Poniatowski were not forgotten and also, perhaps, that the alleged threats of divorce and imprisonment that Catherine had advanced in partial justification of the *coup d'état* of June 28 were not as real as it was officially claimed.

the robust Gregory Orlov, one of the leaders of the revolution of June 28 and first on the list of Catherine's official favorites.

The facile success of the palace revolution which put Catherine on the throne might have disguised but it could not alter the fact that her seizure of power had no legal justification and that she had little popular following. The lingering feeling of insecurity experienced by every Russian monarch since Peter I continued to make itself felt behind the pomp and circumstance of Catherine's reign. In the years immediately following her accession, it was generally believed both in Russia and abroad that her rule would be a short one. Although the murder of Peter III removed a center of potential opposition, rumors that the former emperor had miraculously escaped assassination received wide credence and brought forth a crop of impostors who, in turn, assumed the name of Peter III. The most formidable among them was Emilian Pugachev, leader of the peasant rebellion of 1773–1774. Other threatening clouds loomed large on the political horizon. The deposed Emperor Ivan VI and the Grand Duke Paul were considered by many as having a much stronger claim to the Russian throne than that of the former princess of Anhalt-Zerbst. In spite of the untiring efforts of Empress Elizabeth to obliterate the memory of Ivan, who since 1741 had been kept in confinement, first at Kholmogory and after 1756 at Schlüsselburg, he continued to enjoy a certain popularity in Russia and was not forgotten in the European capitals. Frederick II saw in him a formidable opponent to Peter III, and in September, 1762, Voltaire voiced the apprehension that "Ivan may overthrow our benefactress." Catherine was urged to strengthen her dynastic position by marrying Ivan, and immediately after her accession she had an interview with the prisoner of Schlüsselburg. She was confronted with a human derelict reduced to idiocy by long years of incarceration, and the only consequence of this meeting was orders to put Ivan to death in case of an attempt at his liberation. These orders were carried out to the letter when in 1764, a disgruntled army officer, Vasili Mirovich, made a desperate and futile effort to free Ivan from his jail.

The case of the Grand Duke Paul lent itself to no such simple and drastic solution. There were many in Catherine's entourage and in the country at large who shared the opinion of Nikita Panin, a participant in the revolution of June 28 and one of the empress's closest advisers, that she should exercise the office of regent during the infancy of her son and hand him the Crown on his coming of age. Catherine, however, was much too fond of power to give it up. Relations between the mother and the son, moreover, were lacking in warmth, and grew increasingly hostile as years went by. Paul, who knew the fate of his father, had to endure insolent treatment at the hands of Catherine's favorites, and he was excluded from participation in public affairs. The estrangement between the tsarina and her son was so patent that, in order to avoid invidious comparison, it was deemed wise to cancel the scheduled performance of *Hamlet* in Vienna during Paul's visit to that city in 1781. Permission to produce the same play in St. Petersburg was hastily withdrawn after the authorities became acquainted with the text, a decision which by arousing curiosity contributed to the popularity of Shakespeare with the Russian reading public. Although Paul was never involved in a conspiracy to overthrow his mother, many of those who disliked her rule looked to the grand duke as their leader. The empress was kept informed of the underground agitation on behalf of her son, which found its expression in several minor sporadic plots, and she remained on the alert and ready to defend herself and her Crown.

Frederick II, a good judge of men, remarked to Kaunitz in 1770 that "the empress of Russia is very proud, very ambitious, and very vain." This characterization is essentially correct and is corroborated by the nature of the relations between Catherine and her intellectual friends abroad, especially Voltaire, Diderot, and D'Alembert. Voltaire, in quest of honors and sinecures, had realized the possibilities offered by Russia long before the events of 1762. He had himself elected honorary fellow of the Russian Academy of Science in 1746, corresponded with Ivan Shuvalov, and through him obtained the commission to write a history of Peter the Great, the first volume of which appeared in 1759. The eagerness of Catherine to establish friendly relations with the sage of Ferney and other French philosophers was dictated not only by her admiration—not untinged, perhaps, with intellectual snobbery—for their work and ideas but also by less lofty considerations: she realized that the leaders of European thought would prove invaluable allies in building up her reputation abroad and in creating that atmosphere of praise and adulation she had always longed for, her frequent statements to the contrary notwithstanding. How sensitive Catherine was to European opinion appears from her request to Poniatowski to explain to Voltaire that he had been led by "the lowest and basest of men," Ivan Shuvalov, to believe that Princess Dashkov and not Catherine herself was the actual leader of the *coup d'état* of June 28. This message was sent on August 2, 1762, less than four weeks after the murder of Peter. Voltaire proved receptive to imperial advances, graciously accepted the bounties showered upon him from St. Petersburg and, although he declined persistent invitations to visit Russia, lent to the empress the authority of his moral support. He endorsed and perhaps even inspired the Russian campaign for the conquest of Constantinople and the liberation of Greece, welcomed the first partition of Poland as a victory of "tolerance" over "fanaticism," and heaped upon the Semiramis of the North fulsome praise which his French colleagues and their Russian followers deemed it advantageous to emulate. Catherine returned the compliment by proclaiming herself Voltaire's disciple.

Nine days after Catherine's accession, Diderot was invited to transfer to Russia the publication of the *Encyclopédie*, which had been suspended in France, and in 1765 the empress purchased his library; he, however, retained possession of his books and was granted a pension of one thousand livres per annum in the capacity of Her Majesty's librarian. These acts of imperial munificence received resounding publicity and provided a foundation for Catherine's reputation as a patron of Enlightenment. In 1773 Diderot visited Russia, and on his return to Paris eulogized the empress as an extraordinary human being who combined "the soul of Brutus with the charms of Cleopatra." D'Alembert was offered charge of the education of the Grand Duke Paul in 1762, and when he refused, on the pretext that he could not give up his work, he was urged by Catherine to bring with him to St. Petersburg "all his friends" and was promised "all comforts and pleasures" within her power and "greater freedom than he had ever known in France." D'Alembert, however, resisted the temptation and, after joining the choir of literati who sang the glory of Semiramis, he gradually lost his admiration for her and was one of the severest critics of the annexation of the Crimea in 1783.

Catherine's concern with what Europe thought of her and her desire to influence western opinion are revealed in her voluminous correspondence. Among the personalities with whom she corresponded regularly were Frederick II, Joseph II, Marie Geoffrin, Frau Bielke, Prince de Ligne, Falconet, Voltaire, Diderot, D'Alembert, the German littérateur Johann Georg von Zimmermann, and her many Russian collaborators. Highly revealing from the personal point of view are her remarkable letters to Baron Melchior von Grimm, a German publicist with extensive French connections and after 1774 the confidential agent of the tsarina in Paris. Madame Geoffrin, who presided over a political and literary salon in Paris, and Frau Bielke, her German counterpart in Hamburg, were particularly well situated to serve as the mouthpiece of the empress. In her letters, usually written in a light vein, Catherine endeavored to minimize the reverses suffered by the Russian armies and to exaggerate their victories; she discounted the importance of domestic disturbances such as the Pugachev rebellion and the disastrous flood in St. Petersburg in 1777. With scant respect for truth, she informed Voltaire in July, 1769, that owing to the low rate of taxation "there was not a single peasant in Russia who could not eat chicken whenever he pleased, although he had recently preferred turkeys to chickens." A few months later Catherine assured Voltaire that wars had been invariably beneficial to Russia's economic condition; the war with Turkey then in progress was no exception: "There are no shortages of any kind; people spend their time in singing thanksgiving masses, dancing and rejoicing." Not all of Catherine's correspondents accepted such statements with the apparent blind faith of the sage of Ferney; yet, couched as they were in informal and friendly language, these confidential communications from the throne could not fail to flatter those to whom they were addressed. They were widely discussed in influential circles and produced, at least in a measure, the effect intended.

Favoritism, which had long flourished at the Russian court, was elevated under Catherine to the dignity of a quasi-official institution. During the thirty-four years of her reign she had ten official favorites: Gregory Orlov, until 1772; Alexander Vasilchikov, 1772–1774; Gregory Potemkin, 1774–1776; Peter Zavadovsky, 1776–1777; Simon Zorich, 1777–1778; Ivan Rimsky-Korsakov, 1778–1780; Alexander Lanskoï, 1780–1784; Alexander Ermolov, 1785–1786; Alexander Dmitriev-Mamonov, 1786–1789; Platon Zubov, 1789–1796. Installed, in turn, at the palace in apartments adjoining those of the empress, the favorites were treated with regal generosity: titles, honorary offices, and gifts of estates, plate, jewels, and money valued at millions of rubles were tangible tokens of Catherine's affection. For she passionately loved most of these men, and her more intimate letters, especially those to Grimm and Potemkin, are filled with dithyrambic accounts of the beauty, charm, intelligence, and accomplishments of the elect of the moment. This capacity for sentimental attachment was coupled with an absence of vindictiveness towards those of her lovers with whom she was forced to part under conditions most women would have resented; the dismissal of a favorite, however unworthy, was never permitted to degenerate into persecution. As Catherine grew older, her favorites were chosen from among the younger men; Zubov, the last in line, was twenty-two in 1789, while the empress had just entered her seventh decade. The frequent changes in favorites after 1772, the resulting emotional storms which lasted occasionally for weeks or even months (for instance, in 1784 after the death of Lanskoï), and the intrigues produced by this peculiar situation seriously interfered at times with the smooth working of the administrative machine. Three of Catherine's lovers—Orlov, Potemkin, and Zubov—exercised great influence both upon domestic and upon foreign policies. In the first ten years of her reign Orlov was all-powerful, and he was the guiding spirit behind Russia's naval expedition to Greece and Turkey in 1769–1770. The discovery by Catherine of his many infidelities ended his political career, although she continued to treat him as a close and revered friend. Unlike Orlov, Potemkin retained his hold over the empress until his death, that is, his influence long outlived their liaison, which he himself had brought to an end. The secret of his power is traceable, at least in part, to his uncanny ability to control the choice of the favorites who succeeded him: with the exception of Zavadovsky and Zubov, whom he hated, they were all his nominees and his creatures. "The magnificent Prince of Taurida," as Potemkin was known in the latter part of his life, was practically omnipotent in the inner council of the tsarina, and he was closely identified with the ambitious plan for the expulsion of the Turks from Europe and for the creation of the "Kingdom of Dacia," which he intended to rule. Zubov, an impecunious, ignorant, ambitious, and arrogant youth, appeared to Catherine as the most talented and promising of her "pupils"—to use a term by which she liked to designate her favorites—and she groomed him to fill the place made vacant by Potemkin's death in 1791. High-sounding titles and honorary army and court offices were considered insufficient for achieving this purpose, so Zubov was appointed the actual head of the departments (colleges) of foreign affairs and of war. He mingled in European politics, devised fanciful schemes for the redrafting of the

map of Europe and Asia, played a part in the second and third partitions of Poland, and launched the so-called "Oriental project" for
Russian expansion in Persia and the Caucasus. Towards the end of
Catherine's reign he was as powerful as he was generally hated. The
death of the empress freed Russia from the arbitrary rule of the handsome guardsman whose manly charms had cast their spell over the
aged disciple of Voltaire.

The irregularities of Catherine's private life were not permitted to
interfere, except at periods of acute crisis, with the rigid routine of
a well ordered existence. She arose usually at six in the morning and
daily devoted long hours to the affairs of state and to reading and
writing. Although unprepared by her early education for any kind of
intellectual activity, she acquired the reading habit during the long
years of relative seclusion and idleness which had been her fate under
the rule of Elizabeth. According to her *Memoirs*, she first became
interested in novels, then turned to the letters of Madame de Sévigné
and to Voltaire, and still later to such books as *Histoire d'Allemagne*
by Father Barre and the works of Baronius, Plato, and Tacitus. She
claimed to have read from cover to cover the several volumes of
Pierre Bayle's *Dictionnaire historique et critique*—hardly suitable
fare for a young woman—and she became thoroughly acquainted with
the works of Montesquieu and of the Encyclopedists. To the end of
her days Catherine followed intellectual and literary movements
abroad, and her extensive library contained many important contemporary books which she not only read but carefully annotated.

Catherine began her literary career with the publication in 1767 of
the celebrated *Nakaz* (Instruction) to the Legislative Commission
which met that year. In 1768 appeared her translation (prepared in
cooperation with the members of her immediate entourage) of *Béli-
saire* by Jean Marmontel, a book condemned by the Sorbonne. In
1769–1770 the tsarina became the chief contributor and the *de facto*
editor of a satirical journal, *Vsiakaia vsiachina* (This and That), officially edited by one of her secretaries, G. V. Kozitsky. Her later writing comprised several comedies in Russian and in French, two historical tragedies inspired by Shakespeare, polemical works directed
against the detractors of Russia, librettos for musical comedies, peda-
gogical treatises and allegorical tales for the use of her grandsons, and
Notes on Russian History, an extensive survey in six parts covering
the period from the beginning of the Russian state to the second

half of the thirteenth century. In addition to these works, which were published anonymously in her lifetime, she left a mass of manuscripts that did not appear in print until much later. Particularly important among them are her *Memoirs*, which are preserved in several versions in French and in Russian. The collected works of Catherine, published with admirable care by the Russian Academy of Science in 1901–1907, fill twelve bulky volumes. This publication, however, comprises merely a fraction of her vast correspondence and does not include the *Instruction*. According to A. N. Pypin, who edited the works of Catherine for the Academy, the question of the literary merits of her writings does not arise. Although the tsarina had eventually acquired a fairly good command of spoken Russian, she had only a vague notion of grammar and spelling. The latter was entirely phonetic: Kliuchevsky quotes an instance where she succeeded in making four errors in the spelling of a very common Russian word of merely three letters. Catherine had a better knowledge of French, although it is believed that her writings in that language, too, underwent thorough editing before they were released, as was admittedly the case with her Russian works. It is not an easy matter, therefore, to determine the exact share of Catherine's authorship both of her literary productions and of her letters. The object of her writings was primarily didactic. Her satires and comedies slavishly followed foreign models, and her castigation of social evils conformed to the motto inscribed by her order on the curtain of the Ermitage theater: *Ridendo castigat mores*. The moralistic element was unmistakable, but her attempts at humor were not uniformly successful. *Notes on Russian History*, said to have been written with the assistance of two professors of the University of Moscow (Barsov and Chebotarev), had for their purpose to prove that Russian historical development compared not unfavorably with the developments of other countries, and to demonstrate the virtues of monarchical absolutism. The resulting clumsy compilation, according to Pypin, is significant merely as a presentation of Catherine's political program stated in terms of past history.

The views of Catherine on political and social questions received their fullest expression in the *Instruction* of 1767. The character of this treatise and its subsequent fate throw much light on her methods of work and on the sincerity of her attachment to the ideas of the Enlightenment. In a memorandum dated about 1780, Catherine stated that it had taken her over two years to write the *Instruction* and that she had worked on it in great secrecy. With commendable modesty, she informed Frederick II in a letter of October 14, 1767, that the statement of her political faith was borrowed from Montesquieu's *L'Esprit des lois* and from Beccaria's study on crime and punishment, and that her own contribution was merely "a line here and a word there," amounting altogether "to no more than two or three pages." "I have acted," she explained coyly, "like the crow of the fable who made itself a garment of peacock's feathers." The manuscript was submitted to the empress's advisers and she meekly accepted their revisions, which, as she admitted, resulted in the deletion of more than half of the original text, especially of the sections deemed inimical to serfdom. It was in this expurgated form that the *Instruction* was published on July 30, 1767.[2] These concessions, however, proved insufficient to allay the apprehensions of the powerful conservative elements. In September, 1767, the Senate issued a decree which provided that the copies of the *Instruction* distributed to government agencies should be made available only to the higher officials and that office employees and outsiders should not be permitted to consult them. In later years Catherine expressed conflicting views about her political credo. In a letter to Grimm of November 29, 1775, she described the *Instruction* as mere "verbiage" (*bavardage*) but on September 1, 1776, she wrote to the same correspondent that it was "not only good, but even excellent." In the meantime her outlook underwent radical changes. Her liberalism, never too vigorous, was undermined by the lamentable failure of the Legislative Commission in 1768 and by the Pugachev rebellion. The declaration of independence by the American colonies filled her with disgust and horror, and with the outbreak of the French Revolution she espoused the cause of reaction. Yet she never deliberately repudiated her former views, and a reference to her "republican soul" (*âme republicaine*), an expression of which she was fond, occurred in a letter to Zimmermann as late as January, 1789. It was in vain that the French royalist *émigrés* who had been received with open arms at the court of St. Petersburg agitated for the removal of La Harpe, the Swiss tutor of Catherine's grandsons and an admirer of the French Revolution. The empress jokingly addressed him as "*Monsieur le jacobin*," but left the education of the young grand dukes in his hands.

The lofty maxims Catherine so diligently copied from the "prayer

[2] For a discussion of the contents of the *Instruction*, see p. 546.

book of monarchs," as she described L'*Esprit des lois* in a letter to Madame Geoffrin, and from other sources were not in her case the expression of deep convictions to be translated into terms of practical policies. The airing of these theories in her writings was partly the manifestation of a naïve belief in the miracle-working power of liberal and radical formulas, and partly and chiefly a convenient means of obtaining easy applause and international publicity, a motive ever present behind her activities. Catherine had enjoyed the mild sensation created by the publication of the *Instruction*, which was banned in France. The same insatiable desire to be the center of attention and admiration, not unmixed with awe, played a part in the launching of far-fetched international schemes such as the "Greek project," the "Oriental project," and Armed Neutrality; in the spectacular meetings with foreign rulers; in the unsurpassed luxury of the imperial court; in the ostentatious patronage of art, of science, and of radical thinkers. Foreign and domestic artists and writers, eager to celebrate the imperishable glory of Semiramis, could count on generous subsidies from the Russian treasury. The glittering generalities of Montesquieu and Beccaria, however, were brushed aside the moment the prestige of the empress was deemed to be threatened. Although Catherine confirmed the decree of Peter III abolishing the Privy Chancery (security police), this sinister institution was revived without any legislative enactment at the beginning of her reign under the name of Secret Expedition (*Tainaia ekspeditsiia*). It was headed by S. I. Sheshkovsky, who had learned his trade in the Privy Chancery and who proved a worthy successor of his former chief, Alexander Shuvalov. Sheshkovsky, the most dreaded man in Russia, enjoyed the confidence of the empress. Among his many duties was that of investigating all cases, however trivial, of lese-majesty. Catherine had professed her detestation of tortures and corporal punishment, yet two of her ladies-in-waiting, Countess E. P. Elmp and Countess A. A. Buturlin, were flogged by Sheshkovsky's agents on the charge of having been responsible for the appearance of some cartoons which Catherine considered offensive. Even more significant was the savage and arbitrary persecution of N. I. Novikov, founder and head of the only educational and publishing enterprise of any importance in eighteenth century Russia.[3] The imprisonment in 1792, without a trial, of this devout champion of progress and the destruction of his work is ascribed by

[3] See pp. 600–602.

competent authorities (among them, Pypin) to the fact that he had had the temerity to enter successfully the field of cultural activities which Catherine regarded as her special preserve and where she would tolerate no competition.

CHAPTER XX

ENLIGHTENED ABSOLUTISM

Diplomacy and War

------------------------------- ✳ -------------------------------

DIPLOMACY AND WAR, 1762–1774

"Peace is essential to this vast empire," Catherine wrote towards the end of Elizabeth's reign; "what we need is a larger population, not devastation. . . . Peace will bring us greater esteem than the always ruinous uncertainties of war." The pressure of events, combined with her own longing for a dominating position in Europe and for military glory, made Catherine forget these dreams of her youth. She took a keen interest in international affairs and left a stronger personal imprint on Russia's foreign policy than that of any of her predecessors since Peter I. Under her rule Russia had no chancellor; the insignificant Michael Vorontsov, who had filled that office since 1758, went abroad on a protracted leave of absence in 1763 and retired two years later. Prince Alexander Golitsin, vice chancellor from 1762 to 1775, and Count Ivan Ostermann, his successor during the balance of the reign, were figureheads and exercised no real influence on the course of foreign relations. From 1763 to 1780 Nikita Panin was the actual head of the department of foreign affairs and Her Majesty's chief diplomatic adviser. Panin, a man of culture, and for over a decade Russian ambassador to Sweden, was not lacking in character and ability, and had a program of both domestic and foreign policy. His views, however, were often at odds with those of the court camarilla. He was opposed by Gregory Orlov and, later, by Potemkin, with the result that his influence was diminished long before his official retirement. Alexander Bezborodko, who succeeded Panin in 1780, was a tool in the hands of Potemkin and was relegated to an even more subordinate position with the ascendancy of Platon Zubov. Russia's foreign policy under Catherine was thus determined (with the exception, perhaps, of the early years of her reign, when the authority of Panin was strong), not by the titular head of the department of foreign affairs, but by the empress herself, subject to those influences to which she was so susceptible.

The first and most popular diplomatic move of Catherine was to call off the war with Denmark. There was a moment of hesitation as to the policy to be followed towards Prussia: a manifesto of June 28 denounced Peter for concluding peace with Frederick, Russia's "worst enemy," yet Field Marshal Saltykov was ordered to withdraw his troops from Prussia, which he had reoccupied after the news of the overthrow of Peter had reached him. Catherine, moreover, hastened to confirm the peace treaty of April 24, 1762, with Prussia. Contrary to Peter's engagements,[1] the Russian army took no further part in the Seven Years' War, and the empress assured Frederick of her desire to maintain friendly relations with Berlin. The Prussian king could once more breathe freely. He lost no time in responding to the advances of the new government of St. Petersburg, and his professed admiration for Catherine contributed to the establishment of that cooperation between the two countries which was soon to prove pregnant with grave consequences for the future of Europe. Frederick proceeded cautiously, however, and for once found himself in agreement with Vienna in declining Russia's proffered mediation of the Austro-Prussian conflict. Much to the disappointment of Catherine, the St. Petersburg government had no part in negotiating the Treaty of Hubertusburg (February, 1763) which terminated the Seven Years' War.

The *rapprochement* with Prussia was facilitated by Panin's advocacy of the so-called "Northern Accord." This scheme, which originated with the Russian minister to Copenhagen, Baron Nicholas Korff, sought to maintain the balance of power by opposing to the southern European states—France, Austria, and Spain—an alliance comprising Russia, Prussia, Sweden, England, Denmark, Saxony, and Poland. The real significance of this proposal, which was never adopted, consisted in the abandonment of Russia's alliance with Austria in favor of one with Prussia. The actual course of events, however, was determined by the desire in Berlin and St. Petersburg for territorial aggrandizement at the expense of Poland, and not by

[1] See pp. 479–480.

Panin's doctrinaire plan designed for the maintenance of the *status quo* and the preservation of peace in Europe.

The first manifestation of Catherine's aggressive designs against Poland was the revival of the high-handed policy of Peter I and Empress Anne in Courland, a duchy which, it will be remembered, was a fief of the Polish Crown. Since the fall of Biron in 1740 and his exile to eastern Russia this policy had been in abeyance, and in 1758 Prince Charles of Saxony, son of Augustus III of Poland, became duke of Courland with the consent of Empress Elizabeth. Peter III, however, decided to replace Charles by George of Holstein (in whose favor Biron obediently abdicated on April 16, 1762), but the events of June 28 prevented him from making his decision effective. After her accession Catherine requested the deposition of Charles and the reinstatement of Biron; threats and intimidation were used against Poland, Courland was occupied by Russian troops, and early in 1763 Biron was installed in Mittau, even before Charles had withdrawn from his former capital. Although Courland remained for another thirty years under the nominal suzerainty of Poland, she had become for all practical purposes a Russian protectorate, and was treated as such.

On the death of Augustus III in October, 1763, decision as to the succession to the Polish throne offered the eagerly awaited opportunity for Russian intervention in the affairs of Poland. Frederick and Catherine, who since early in 1763 had been carrying on an assiduous private correspondence, were prepared for the event and had agreed that the next king must be a native Pole and that the most suitable candidate would be Count Stanislas Poniatowski, the empress's former lover and a member of the powerful Czartoryski family. On April 11, 1764, N.S., was signed the Russo-Prussian treaty of alliance which provided for mutual military and financial assistance in case of war. The secret articles of the treaty bound the two governments to pursue a common policy in Sweden and to oppose constitutional changes in that country; to prevent any changes in the constitution of Poland and, if necessary, to defend by force of arms the existing political regime; to intercede with the Polish government on behalf of the "dissidents" (or "dissenters"), that is, the members of the Protestant and Greek Orthodox Churches living in Poland, and to seek the removal of the legal disabilities to which they were subject. The program laid down in the treaty was soon to prove Poland's undoing. In the meantime

Russian troops occupied Poland with the approval of the pro-Russian party led by the Czartoryski, and the Russian envoy, Prince Nicholas Repnin, by using bribes and intimidation, had no difficulty in securing the election of Poniatowski by the Polish diet (September 7, 1764, N.S.). According to Catherine, "Russia had adopted him [Poniatowski] as her candidate for the Polish throne because he had less right than any other candidate and therefore should be all the more grateful to Russia."

At the time of the election of Poniatowski, Poland was one of the largest states in Europe, with a population of some 11,000,000 or 12,000,000 and an area of about 280,000 square miles. Her political strength, however, had been sapped by an archaic constitution crowned by the institution of elective kingship, a system that deprived the head of the state of all real power. The outstanding feature of this system was the *liberum veto*, that is, the right of any member of the diet to interpose a veto. This had the effect not only of defeating the particular proposition under discussion but also of dissolving the diet and of nullifying its previous decisions. The device employed to overcome the resulting deadlock was the privilege of forming "confederations" or voluntary armed associations empowered to impose their will by force. Participation in the diet and in other political activities constituted (with rare exceptions) the privilege of the *szlachta* (nobility), representing about 8 per cent of the population. The vast majority of the members of this group, moreover, were clients of a few wealthy feudal families, and they voted and fought as ordered by their patrons. It was this form of government, which has been aptly described as anarchy tempered by civil war, that Catherine and Frederick, following the precedent set by Peter I,[2] undertook to perpetuate, if necessary, by military intervention.

The "dissidents," or non-Catholic Christian population of Poland, formed a heterogeneous group which had been subject in the seventeenth and the early eighteenth centuries to persecution by the Catholic majority and had been gradually deprived of political and civil rights. The ranks of the "dissidents" were swollen by fugitive Russian peasants who preferred the yoke of Polish serfdom and religious discrimination to what their own country had to offer them.[3]

---

[2] See p. 352 n. 9.

[3] Peter Panin (1763) ascribed the mass flight of the Russian peasants to Poland to the excessive exactions of Russian landowners, the sale of serfs apart from the

The Orthodox clergy of Poland, however, agitated in St. Petersburg for Russian intervention on behalf of the Orthodox communities in the republic, their freedom of worship having been stipulated in several Russo-Polish treaties, especially in the treaty of 1686.

The defense of Polish "liberties" and religious freedom offered a convenient pretext for carrying out the aggressive designs of Catherine and Frederick. The empress attached the greatest importance to Russian domination over Poland. It was essential, according to views expressed by Panin at the beginning of the reign, to Russia's strength and security and to her effective participation in European affairs. The election of Poniatowski was the first major step in this direction: the new king of Poland—intelligent and well educated, but pleasure-loving and weak—had received his Crown from the hands of Catherine's envoy, and the pressure of his creditors made him dependent throughout his life on the generosity of his former mistress. Yet even this puppet ruler and the pro-Russian party led by the Czartoryski could not submit without a struggle to Russia's importunate demands. Poniatowski, the Czartoryski, and their political friends wanted constitutional reform, hereditary kingship, and the limitation of *liberum veto*, measures to which not only Frederick and Catherine but also the rank and file of the *szlachta* were opposed. The question of the "dissidents" proved even more thorny. Catherine's championship of the cause of her co-religionists was not inspired by her devotion to religious tolerance, which she imperfectly practiced at home. Panin stated with utmost frankness (in an instruction to Repnin dated August 14, 1767) that the emancipation of the "dissidents" had for its object "the acquisition [by Russia] once and forever, through our co-religionists and the Protestants, of a firm and reliable party legally entitled to participate in the affairs of Poland." Russia intended "to appropriate (*prisvoit*) the right to protect the 'dissidents' for all time to come." Panin argued that the excessive strengthening of the Protestants was undesirable because it might promote Poland's cultural progress and the formation of a government capable of successfully resisting the wishes of St. Petersburg; the undue strengthening of the Orthodox communities, Panin maintained, was also dangerous in view of the mass flight of the Russian serfs to Poland, a flight which would be given added stimulus by the establishment of

land, the persecution of the old-believers, the harshness of army service, and the rise in the prices of salt and alcohol.

"freedom of worship combined with the advantages of a free people."
Both groups of "dissidents," therefore, were to be kept under Russia's control. At the same time Panin denied any intention of "waging a war for the propagation of religious creeds."

The Russian drive for the emancipation of the "dissidents" met with fanatical resistance on the part of the Catholic majority, which, however, was divided on the issue of constitutional reform. Poniatowski's offer of freedom of worship was not deemed acceptable in St. Petersburg because it made no provision for the granting to the "dissidents" of full political rights, Russian agents flooded Poland and carried on among the *szlachta* a campaign in which they promised Russia's protection of Polish "liberties"—and, if necessary, the dethronement of Poniatowski—on condition that the legal disabilities of the "dissidents" were removed. In the spring of 1767 numerous "confederations" sponsored by Russia were organized in various parts of Poland, and in June there was formed at Radom a "general confederation" which moved to the capital and summoned a diet. In the meantime Russian troops overran Poland, and in September occupied Warsaw, where Repnin, whom Catherine suspected of excessive leniency, had been reinforced by the empress's special envoy, the astute and ruthless Holstein diplomat, Caspar von Saldern. Repnin and Saldern behaved like conquerors in a subjugated country; by threats, arrests, and deportations of the leaders of the Catholic opposition, as well as by bribes, they wrested from a reluctant diet the acceptance of the terms decreed at St. Petersburg. Some minor concessions were made to the reform party led by the king: the use of *liberum veto* was limited to "state issues," while purely "domestic issues" (a vague and confused terminology) were to be decided by a majority vote. A Russo-Polish treaty of February 24, 1768, N.S., placed the Polish constitution under the guarantee of Russia "for all time to come," while a separate act proclaimed freedom of worship and conferred upon the "dissidents" full civil and political rights.

Catherine, Panin, and Repnin were congratulating themselves on their bloodless victory over Poland, but the real troubles were just beginning. Europe, especially Austria, Turkey, France, and Sweden, were alarmed by the display of Russian aggression. Even Frederick secretly disapproved of Russian policies in the matter of the "dissidents," although this did not prevent him from concluding, in April, 1767, a new military alliance with Russia designed to prevent

an armed Austrian intervention in Poland. The surrender of the Warsaw diet provoked a strong movement of revolt among the *szlachta*.
In March, 1768, a "confederation" under the banner of "liberty and
faith" was formed at Bar, in Ukraine, and the insurgent movement
spread to Galicia and to other parts of the country. Anti-Russian and
anti-royalist, the insurrection threatened to sweep away the tottering
government of Poniatowski, and the Polish senate in its plight demanded the protection of Russian troops, which would have been
forthcoming in any event. The struggle between Russia and the confederates, who were backed by Austria and received some assistance
in men and money from France, went on for four years and wrought
devastation in Poland. A consequence of this conflict was the outbreak of war between Russia and Turkey.

Turkey had watched with deep suspicion the progress of Russian
penetration in Poland. The sultan had refused to recognize the election of Poniatowski on the ground that it had been forced at the point
of Muscovite bayonets. The subsequent activities of Repnin were of
a nature to increase the apprehensions of the Porte. The anti-Russian
feeling at Constantinople, which was fostered by France, reached a
high pitch in the summer of 1768, when bands of Cossack irregulars
who had been perpetrating untold atrocities on Catholics, Uniats,
and Jews alike, invaded Turkish territory and burned and pillaged
several villages. The Porte, which had demanded the withdrawal of
Russian troops, first from the frontier regions and later from Poland,
after some fruitless negotiations arrested the Russian envoy to Constantinople, Alexis Obrezkov (September 25). The resulting war, for
which Russia was unprepared both militarily and economically, was
welcomed in St. Petersburg with the usual manifestations of optimism.
Some of Catherine's advisers felt, indeed, that the moment was opportune for the final solution of the "eastern question" in a manner
that would cover the empress with imperishable glory. Agents of the
brothers Orlov had been for some time in touch with the Christian
subjects of the sultan, and it was intended to use them for the advancement of Russia's designs, just as the "dissidents" had been used in
Poland. The plan sponsored by Gregory Orlov provided for an uprising
of the Balkan Slavs and the Greeks (officially described as the "Spartan
people"), the creation of the independent states of the Crimea, Moldavia, and Wallachia, and—as the ultimate object—the eviction of
the Turks from Europe. Catherine was also contemplating the possi-

bility of annexing the Caucasus.[4] The death blow to Turkey was to be dealt by a Russian naval expedition which was to reach the Turkish shores by way of the Mediterranean, occupy the islands of the Archipelago, defeat the Turkish fleet, and raise the banner of revolt among the Christian populations of the Balkans while the land forces of Russia were moving on Constantinople from the east and from the north. Four years earlier, in 1765, Catherine had voiced the opinion that "we have too many ships and men, but we have neither a navy nor sailors." Orlov's plan for a naval expedition, however, proved irresistible, and in July, 1769, a Russian fleet under Admiral Spiridov sailed from Kronstadt, followed in the autumn by a squadron commanded by Admiral Elphinston.

The low quality of the ships, the inadequate training of the officers and men, and their poor discipline inspired forebodings among Russian diplomats who had had an opportunity to inspect the vessels en route to the Mediterranean. Count Ivan Chernyshev, Russian ambassador to London, for instance, dolefully remarked in a letter to Panin: "Since 1700 the navy has cost Russia over one million rubles; and what have we got? Very little, indeed, next to nothing." Alexis Orlov, who for reasons of health was residing in Italy, was appointed commander in chief of the expedition. He wrote to the empress after a review of his force at Livorno that his hair stood on end and his heart bled. In the early spring of 1770 the Russian squadron reached the Turkish shores, but the anticipated insurrection of the Christian populations proved a failure for which the lack of organized support on the part of the Russian instigators of the movement was at least in part responsible. On June 24 and 26, however, the Russians annihilated the bulk of the Turkish fleet at Scio and Chesme (Tchesme) and won a decisive victory, one that has often been compared to that at Lepanto. This triumph produced a great impression in Europe. Orlov was a novice in naval warfare, and even after full credit is given to the English naval officers under his command, Greig and Elphinston, his unexpected victory would seem to have been due to the ineptitude of the Turks rather than to the skill and daring of their enemies. Catherine was overjoyed, and honors and distinctions were showered upon the "hero

---

[4] How little was known in St. Petersburg about the territories coveted by Russia is disclosed by a memorandum of the empress which pointed out, among other things, that the important city of Tiflis appeared on some maps on the Black Sea, on others on the Caspian Sea, and on still others far inland.

of Chesme"; but the practical military effects of his victory proved surprisingly slight, and the rumored forcing of the Dardanelles, which the empress prematurely reported to Panin, never took place. A new Russian naval expedition left Reval in July, 1770, but achieved little, and the campaign of 1771 in Turkish waters was limited to coastal raids of local significance. In 1773 Catherine had to admit reluctantly that "the fleet is doing nothing."

The land campaign opened in January, 1769, with the invasion of southern Russia by the Crimean Tartars—an expedition which proved to be the last of its kind. Throughout the first eight months of the year the army of Prince Alexander Golitsin, handicapped by lack of artillery and the disorganization of the supply service, was marking time on the Dniester. Golitsin was relieved of his command in August, at the very time when he was beginning to make progress against the Turks, and his successor, Count Peter Rumiantsev, occupied within the next few weeks the undefended fortress of Khotin (Chocim), Jassy, and Bucharest, while the army of the grand vizier withdrew behind the Danube. Early in the same year the Russian troops took the unfortified ports of Azov and Taganrog and proceeded to build a fleet on the Sea of Azov preparatory to the dispatch of naval expeditions, advocated by Gregory Orlov, to the Caucasus and to Constantinople. In 1770 Rumiantsev, after withdrawing from Bucharest, resumed the offensive, and in July inflicted defeats on the Turks on the Larga and at Kagul. In November he took Brailov and reoccupied Bucharest. Izmail, Kilia, and Akkerman passed into Russian hands, and in September Peter Panin took Bender by assault. In 1771 the Russian army on the Danube experienced difficulties and made little progress, but the campaign in the Crimea was successful. In the course of the summer Prince Vasili Dolgoruky, who had succeeded Peter Panin, occupied all the important strategic points on the peninsula and initiated negotiations for the establishment of an "independent" Crimean state. In the meantime Suvorov had dealt some terrible blows to the Polish confederates. Early in 1772 military activities were temporarily suspended, an armistice was signed in May, and at the end of July the peace delegations of Russia and Turkey met at Fokshany.

In spite of the tone of frivolous detachment and forced optimism in which Catherine discussed the war with her correspondents, and notwithstanding her endorsement of Orlov's fanciful schemes for an expedition against Constantinople, the government of St. Petersburg was anxiously exploring the avenues for peace. The campaign of 1771 had been disappointing, except in the Crimea; economic and financial resources were strained almost to the breaking point; and, to make things worse, an epidemic of the plague which broke out in the Danubian army in 1770 had spread to Moscow. In the summer of the following year nearly one thousand people died daily in the capital, and in September artillery had to be used to suppress a huge popular uprising which was disgraced by the murder of an archbishop. The international situation was fraught with the gravest danger. France was hostile and supported Turkey and the Polish confederates. England, although she showed no animosity towards the Russian naval expedition to the Archipelago, viewed with disapproval St. Petersburg's plans for the dismemberment of the Ottoman empire. Austria, alarmed by Russia's domination in Poland and by her designs on the Danubian principalities of Moldavia and Wallachia, drew closer to Turkey. While the agreement between the two governments concluded in June, 1771, provided merely for Austria's good offices in bringing about a satisfactory termination of the Russo-Turkish War, it was feared in St. Petersburg that this *rapprochement* might develop into a military alliance. Frederick never failed to congratulate Catherine on her real or imaginary victories, yet he worked secretly for the speedy liquidation of the Turkish war, by which he had nothing to gain and which he had found costly, since, under the terms of the Russo-Prussian alliance, he had paid substantial subsidies to the government of St. Petersburg. On the one hand he urged Austria to resist any change in the status of the Danubian principalities, and on the other he endeavored to impress his Russian ally with the danger of a war with Austria and, perhaps, with other states, unless moderation was displayed in dealing with Turkey. Catherine, however, insisted that Russia was entitled to all the fruits of her victories.

The dismemberment of Poland provided a solution that satisfied the conflicting claims and ambitions of the eastern Powers. The idea of the partition of Poland was by no means novel: it had been discussed at the European courts for about a century. This policy, which had been urged on the Russian government by Count Zakhary Chernyshev in 1763 and in later years favored by Gregory Orlov, was at first mildly opposed by Panin, who felt uneasy about a violation of Catherine's promises to safeguard the integrity of Poland. Such scruples, however, were not permitted to interfere with the exigencies of *Realpolitik*.

The annexation by Austria, in 1769, of the Polish district of Zips, on the ground of "ancient rights," provided a suitable precedent. In 1770–1771 Prince Henry of Prussia, the king's brother, at the invitation of Catherine spent several months in St. Petersburg, and it was during this visit that the partition of Poland was for the first time officially discussed. There followed protracted and tortuous negotiations, but with the renunciation by Russia of all claims to Moldavia and Wallachia the chief obstacle was removed. A Russo-Prussian agreement in February, 1772, was followed by the signature by Russia, Prussia, and Austria of the partition treaties on August 5, 1772, N.S. The occupation of the annexed territories was carried out at once, the impassioned protests of Poniatowski were ignored, and in September, 1773, the Polish diet was partly coerced and partly bribed into acceptance of the dismemberment of the country. This action was ratified in 1775. By the first partition, Poland was deprived of about one-third of her territory and more than one-third of her population. The Russian share embraced the White Russian districts of Polotsk, Vitebsk, and Mogilev and a strip of Livonia, that is, an area of some 36,000 square miles with a population of about 1,800,000. The inhabitants of these territories, over which the Kievan and Muscovite grand dukes had once exercised a vague jurisdiction, were largely of Russian stock and belonged to the Greek Orthodox Church.

The partition of Poland had repercussions not only in Turkey, whose resistance was stiffened by the belief that a similar plan for her dismemberment had been agreed upon by the neighboring Powers, but also in Sweden. In August, 1772, the young King Gustavus III, with the assistance of France, executed a *coup d'état*, abolishing the vicious constitution of 1720 and restoring to the Swedish Crown most of its ancient rights and prerogatives. Gustavus and his followers felt that the consolidation of royal authority, which had been nil under the old constitution, was essential to save Sweden from the fate of Poland and to prevent foreign intervention. The Swedish constitution of 1720, however, had been guaranteed by Russia, Prussia, and Denmark, and the events in Stockholm produced consternation in St. Petersburg. In spite of the critical position of the Russian Danubian army, which suffered from an acute shortage of men, partly because of epidemics, several regiments were hastily withdrawn from the Turkish front and moved to Pskov. War with Sweden appeared to be a distinct possibility.

In the meantime peace negotiations between Turkey and Russia, the latter represented by Gregory Orlov and Obrezkov, just released from Turkish captivity, opened at Fokshany at the end of July, 1772. The insistence of St. Petersburg on the independence of the Crimea, and also, according to Panin, "the rage and fantasies" of Orlov (whom Catherine amorously described in a contemporary letter to Frau Bielke as her "angel of peace" and "the most beautiful man of his time"), led to the breakdown of the negotiations three weeks later. Orlov, having learned that he had been superseded in the affections of the empress by Vasilchikov, made a dash for the capital only to discover that his political career was practically closed. In October negotiations with Turkey were resumed in Bucharest, but these were interrupted early the following year, when the Porte rejected the Russian demand for the annexation of the Crimean ports of Kerch and Enikale.

After an interval of almost a year, military operations were resumed in the spring of 1773. Disregarding the cautious advice of Rumiantsev, Saltykov, Potemkin, and Frederick, Catherine insisted that Russian troops should cross the Danube. Initial successes against the Turks, in which the army of Suvorov distinguished itself, were followed by the abortive attempts of Rumiantsev to take the fortress of Silistria and by the withdrawal, at the end of June, of the Russian forces to the left bank of the Danube, a move that distressed the empress. Although the outlook was bleak and the peasant uprising led by Pugachev had assumed threatening dimensions, Catherine refused to yield to her generals and political advisers who urged the abandonment of some of the Russian demands on Turkey; she rejected the repeatedly proffered offers of mediation by Austria, Prussia, and France, and insisted on peace with victory. Her determination and persistence brought their reward. Turkey was even more exhausted and disorganized than Russia. The death of Sultan Mustapha in January, 1774, contributed to the weakening of Turkish resistance, and a series of Russian victories in the spring and early summer of the same year basically changed the military situation. Direct negotiations between Russia and Turkey were instituted at the village of Kuchuk-Kainardzhi, and a peace treaty was signed on July 10 (July 21, N.S.), 1774. Under the provisions of this treaty the Crimea became an independent state; Russia annexed Kerch and Enikale in the Crimea, Kinburn and the territories between the Bug and the Dnieper, and the Great and Little Kabarda, that is, a part of the Kuban and Terek districts. Russia's right to Azov was confirmed "in perpetuity," and the 1739 prohibition to fortify Azov and Taganrog was terminated by an ingenious invocation of "natural law" which entitles a country to build and maintain fortresses within its borders. Russia received the privilege of free navigation for her merchant fleet in the Black Sea and the right of passage through the Bosphorus and the Dardanelles. Turkey paid an indemnity of 4,500,000 rubles but retained Moldavia, Wallachia, and the islands of the Archipelago. Russia, moreover, secured some ill defined rights to protect the Christian subjects of the Porte, a provision which offered a convenient pretext for further interference in the domestic affairs of Turkey. All things considered, the Treaty of Kuchuk-Kainardzhi was exceptionally favorable to Russia, even though it fell short of Catherine's original program for the destruction of the Ottoman empire. The Crimean Tartars, however, according to Rumiantsev, received the news of their independence with "extreme repugnance": they felt, as did European statesmen, that this was a prelude to the annexation of the Crimea by Russia, which they frankly hated.

DIPLOMACY AND WAR, 1775–1796

The Polish and Turkish questions continued to dominate Russian foreign policy until the death of Catherine. Panin's academic scheme of a "Northern Accord," which was rejected by Prussia and Sweden and was treated with more or less polite indifference by the other governments concerned, had been put aside even before the first partition of Poland. The Russo-Prussian alliance concluded originally in 1764 for eight years was renewed in 1769 for another eight years (that is, until March, 1780); it was extended again in 1777, but was permitted to lapse at the expiration of its term on March 31, 1788, N.S. Russia rendered an important service to her Prussian ally by mediating, at the request of both Berlin and Vienna, the War of Bavarian Succession, which broke out in 1778, after the death of the Elector Maximilian Joseph. The Treaty of Teschen (May 13, 1779, N.S.), which terminated the war and which Frederick acclaimed as a great triumph for the Russian empress and himself, was negotiated with the participation of Prince Nicholas Repnin, and secured for Russia protective rights over the Germanic imperial constitution, thus gratifying Catherine's ambition to become the arbiter of the inner affairs of the Holy Roman

Empire. However, the formation in July, 1785, of the *Fürstenbund,* a confederation of fifteen German governments led by Prussia and directed to the defense of the constitutional rights of the empire against encroachments by Vienna, prevented Catherine from effectively exercising in Germany the hegemony to which she had aspired. For several years before the creation of the *Fürstenbund* Russia and Prussia had been drifting apart. The ascendancy of Potemkin and the eclipse of Panin in 1780 marked the beginning of the estrangement between St. Petersburg and Berlin and of the *rapprochement* between Russia and Austria.

The eccentric and unpredictable Potemkin, who surrounded himself both in the capital and at army headquarters with regal splendor which became the talk of Europe, had gained a better understanding of the character of his imperial mistress than had any other of her many favorites. Realizing the empress's predilection for breath-taking plans of conquest, he adopted and developed the somewhat shapeless scheme of Gregory Orlov for the expulsion of the Turks from Europe. The "Greek project" associated with Potemkin's name envisaged the restoration of the Byzantine empire under the rule of Catherine's grandson, who was born in 1779 and appropriately named Constantine. Moldavia, Wallachia, and Bessarabia were to constitute the independent "kingdom of Dacia," with Potemkin as its most likely monarch, although at various times he had coveted the thrones of Courland and Poland and had considered the possibility of ruling over Ukraine, which was to be raised to the status of an independent state. Although these plans appealed to Potemkin's romantic imagination, they were not, in all probability, divorced from certain practical considerations. He was ten years younger than Catherine and was cordially hated by the Grand Duke Paul and by the latter's son, Alexander. The acquisition of a sovereign domain outside the Russian frontiers might well have appeared to him as a safeguard against the fate of the fallen favorites of previous reigns. It was this "Greek project" that increasingly occupied the mind of the empress in the years following the first Turkish war and that shaped the foreign policy of St. Petersburg.

A notable manifestation of Russia's ambition to play a leading part in international affairs was the Armed Neutrality declaration in 1780. This celebrated document, which was directed primarily against England, laid down the principle that a neutral flag offered protection to enemy cargoes on the seas. Catherine despised George III of England

and, much as she hated the American "rebels" and the Declaration of Independence, she refused his request to send Russian troops to North America. Armed Neutrality was resented in England, but the controversy had no serious repercussions on the relations between the two countries: although Pitt opposed Catherine's eastern policy in later years, powerful interests were not prepared to jeopardize the extensive English trade with Russia which, moreover, was the chief source of maritime supplies.

The "Greek project" which Catherine and Potemkin had so much at heart could not be carried out without cooperation with Austria. Emperor Joseph II, eager to weaken the ties between St. Petersburg and Berlin and to win Russian support against Prussia, visited Mogilev and St. Petersburg in 1780. The opportune death of Maria Theresa (November 29, 1780, N.S.), who disliked the Russian empress, facilitated subsequent negotiations leading to the conclusion, in May, 1781, of a secret alliance between the two imperial courts. Directed primarily against the Porte, the alliance provided also for the maintenance of tranquillity in Poland and guaranteed the Polish constitution as revised by the diet of 1773–1775. In the course of the following two years Catherine and Joseph discussed detailed plans for the partition of Turkey without being able to reach an agreement. In the meantime Russia decided to proceed with the annexation of the Crimea.

The "independent" state of the Crimean Tartars established by the Treaty of Kuchuk-Kainardzhi was inexorably moving to its doom amidst bloody feuds between the supporters of Turkey, on the one hand, and those who had succumbed to the persuasive power of Russian bribes, promises, and threats, on the other. A native government, hostile to Russia, was ejected by Suvorov, and the economic structure of the Crimea was shattered in 1778–1779 by the removal, on the orders of St. Petersburg, of the entire Christian population of the peninsula. Potemkin, the all-powerful governor of the southern territories, characteristically referred to the "independent" Tartar state as "a pimple on Russia's nose." Under pressure exerted by him, the last puppet native ruler of the Crimea abdicated in favor of the Russian Crown and the annexation of the long-coveted region was proclaimed by a decree of April 8, 1783. St. Petersburg was jubilant; without firing a shot Russia had resumed her southward expansion in the fulfillment of her "historic mission." Austria, anticipating her share of the spoils, declared herself satisfied; Prussia, Sweden, England, and France were alarmed; Turkey was outraged, recalcitrant, and vindictive; and the Tartars were supremely unhappy.

Turkish and Russian policies continued to clash in the Danubian principalities and in the Caucasus, where Georgia had accepted a Russian protectorate in 1783. Rumors of Russia's aggressive intentions and warlike preparations were circulated in Constantinople and were exploited by the representatives of France, England, and Prussia. Early in 1787 Catherine, accompanied by a large suite which included several ambassadors, undertook a spectacular journey down the Dnieper and throughout the Crimea. Although officially a pleasure party and a tour of inspection of the newly acquired provinces, the empress's journey, which remains unique in Russia's annals for the elaborate splendor of the arrangements, was regarded abroad as pregnant with political significance. The presence among Catherine's guests of Emperor Joseph, whose reluctance to accept the invitation had been overcome by Kaunitz, emphasized the anti-Turkish character of the demonstration. At Kanev, Catherine received King Stanislas Poniatowski, but the brief meeting of the former lovers after a lapse of thirty years failed to produce any tangible results. Potemkin outdid himself to dazzle the empress and her companions by the miracles he had accomplished within the few years of his administration. Some of them were merely impudent stage setting—the famous "Potemkin villages" which were nothing but sham. Others seemed real enough, for instance, the imposing display of Russia's newly built Black Sea fleet in the harbor of Sevastopol. The crop of alarming rumors sown by Catherine's triumphant progress moved the Porte to overcome its hesitation and indecision, although St. Petersburg ascribed the sudden show of energy in Constantinople to the intrigues of England and Prussia. In August, 1787, the divan accused Russia of violating the Treaty of Kuchuk-Kainardzhi, demanded the restoration of the Crimea, and ordered the incarceration in the Seven Towers Castle of the Russian envoy, Jacob Bulgakov. Russia once more found herself at war with Turkey. Emperor Joseph recognized at once a *casus foederis* for Austria (September 10, 1787, N.S.), and early in 1788 declared war on Turkey.

Notwithstanding all the glib and frivolous talk about the ejection of the Turks from Europe and the restoration of the Byzantine empire, Russia was unprepared for the war. Some of her regiments existed merely on paper, artillery and fortifications were inadequate, the personnel of the fleet was poorly trained, and many of the ships were unseaworthy. There was much animosity and rivalry among the Russian generals—Potemkin, Rumiantsev, Suvorov, Repnin. Fortunately for Russia, Turkey, as in 1768–1774, was even less well prepared. The early stage of the hostilities was indecisive. An attempt by the Turks to capture the fortress of Kinburn in October, 1787, was successfully resisted, but shortly afterwards a storm in the Black Sea inflicted heavy losses on the Russian fleet. Potemkin, in despair, wanted to withdraw from the Crimea, and only Catherine's firmness prevented him from carrying out his plan. The Russian navy won two victories over the Turks in July, 1788, and after a protracted siege the fortress of Ochakov was taken by Potemkin in December. This victory, however, was purchased at an exceptionally heavy cost in men and material. Rumiantsev in Bessarabia experienced difficulties because of lack of supplies and munitions, and it was only in August that he succeeded in taking Jassy. The Austrians, after some initial successes, suffered heavy defeats at the hands of the Turks.

In spite of the many disappointments of the campaign of 1787–1788, Catherine was making preparations for the execution of the "Greek project." She counted on a general uprising of the Balkan Christians and a holy war against Islam. A naval expedition under Admiral Greig was to sail from the Baltic to the Archipelago with orders to destroy the Turkish fleet and to supply the insurgents with arms. The Russian squadron was to carry a large delegation of the Orthodox clergy, who were to foster the zeal of the new crusaders by the distribution of icons, church bells, and inflammatory manifestoes. England, however, remembering Russia's unfriendly attitude during the war with the American colonies, Armed Neutrality, and also mindful of a commercial treaty concluded in 1787 between Russia and France much to the annoyance of London, was no longer in favor of the Russian naval venture, as she had been in 1769–1770. The government of George III did everything in its power to hinder Catherine's plan, a policy of obstruction that found considerable support in Prussia, Holland, Spain, and even in France. Vexatious negotiations concerning the Mediterranean expedition were finally abandoned when in the summer of 1788 Sweden declared war on Russia.

Relations between Russia and Sweden had been strained ever since the *coup d'état* of August, 1772, which resulted in the revision of the Swedish constitution of 1720 and the strengthening of the position of the Crown. Catherine, like her predecessors, was in favor of maintaining the constitutional arrangements of 1720 which had reduced Sweden to a state of impotence similar to that of Poland. Personal interviews between Gustavus and Catherine at St. Petersburg in 1777 and in Finland in 1783 led to much social amenity but had no appreciable effect on the relations between the two countries. The Russian ambassador at Stockholm not only kept in close touch with the circles that disapproved of the reforms of 1772 but also financed and directed their activities, while Gustavus, who was determined to defend the new constitution, was looking for an opportunity to recover some of the territories lost to Russia in 1721 and in 1743. The Russo-Turkish War created an international situation which the king deemed propitious for the execution of his plans. Although France, abandoning her traditional attitude, counseled caution and moderation, aggressive action was urged by Prussia and England in pursuance of their anti-Russian policy. A defensive alliance concluded between Sweden and Turkey in 1739 and ignored during the Russo-Turkish War of 1768–1774 offered a thin legal pretext for Swedish intervention. Relations between St. Petersburg and Stockholm deteriorated, and in the early summer of 1788 Gustavus demanded the recall of the Russian ambassador, Count Cyril Razumovsky, the restoration of Finland and Karelia to Sweden and of the Crimea to the Porte, and immediate negotiations for the termination of the Russo-Turkish War. St. Petersburg, of course, could not accept these demands. In a declaration of July 21, N.S., Gustavus denounced Russia's policy in Courland, Poland, and the Crimea and warned Europe of the peril of Muscovite expansion. Catherine was much perturbed by the outbreak of the Swedish war: there were practically no Russian troops in the north, and St. Petersburg appeared at the mercy of the Swedish fleet and army. Naval and military operations began in June, 1788, and lasted through the summer of 1790. Both sides had their share of victories and defeats, but on the whole the young Russian fleet did uncommonly well against the navy of an old maritime nation like Sweden. Gustavus was handicapped from the very beginning by the revolt of some of his officers who refused to recognize the legality of a war not sanctioned by the diet. The rebels ("confederation of Anjala") entered with Russia into negotiations for the establishment of an independent Finland. The king, however, succeeded in carrying out early in 1789 a new political *coup d'état* which further increased the legislative and executive powers of the Crown, abolished most of the privileges of the nobility, and made commoners eligible for all, or nearly all, offices of state. These constitutional changes and the daring fashion in which they were imposed on a reluctant nobility, as well as the support given to the king by the other "estates," strengthened his hand in the struggle with Russia and at the peace conference. At Svensksund, on July 9–11, 1790, moreover, the Swedish fleet inflicted a defeat on the Russians, who lost fifty-three ships and almost 10,000 men. In spite of this victory the lack of support from Prussia and England made it difficult for Gustavus to continue warlike operations, while Catherine, increasingly absorbed in the Turkish campaign and developments in Poland, was longing for peace. The Treaty of Verelä (August 14, 1790, N.S.) terminated the war on the basis of the territorial *status quo ante bellum*. Gustavus had failed to capture St. Petersburg or to recover the lost provinces, but Russia had been forced to abandon her former claims to the control of Swedish constitutional arrangements and the new Russian ambassador to Stockholm, Pahlen, was instructed to "use his eyes and ears but not to mix in anything." This revolutionary departure from St. Petersburg's traditional policy was followed by the conclusion of a defensive Russo-Swedish alliance (October 19, 1791, N.S.), which, however, did not prevent the recurrence of serious friction between the two countries even before the end of Catherine's reign.

Although war with Sweden complicated the diplomatic and military position of Russia, it did not interfere with the course of the Turkish campaign. The capture of Ochakov in December, 1788, heartened Catherine and strengthened her determination to see her grandson on the throne of the emperors of Byzantium. The campaign of 1789 was on the whole remarkably successful in spite of serious quarrels between Austrian and Russian generals. The allies won an important victory over the Turks at Fokshany (August 1, N.S.), Belgrade was occupied by the Austrians, Suvorov dealt a shattering blow to the enemy at Rymnik (September 22, N.S.), Potemkin took Bender, and the Russian troops captured Akkerman and the fort of Gadzhibei. This fort, which four years later was renamed Odessa, eventually became the principal Russian merchant port on the Black Sea.

The international situation was less satisfactory. The French Revolution had put an end to the *rapprochement* between Paris and St. Petersburg which might have led to a political alliance. Frederick William II of Prussia (Frederick II had died in August, 1786), who was allied with England and Holland, supported Sweden and Turkey and pursued an anti-Russian policy in Poland. The energetic diplomatic intervention of Prussia and England, accompanied by threats of the occupation of Holstein by Prussian troops, prevented Denmark from giving Russia effective military assistance in the Swedish war in accordance with the terms of the Danish-Russian treaty of 1773.[5] The disastrous Turkish defeat involving the loss of the Danubian principalities (1789) prompted Frederick William to enter with the Porte into an alliance (January 31, 1790, N.S.) binding Prussia to declare war on both imperial courts in the spring and not to lay down arms until the territories occupied by Russia and Austria, as well as the Crimea, had been restored to the rule of the sultan. Two months later Frederick William concluded a military alliance with Poland. The revolt of the Austrian Netherlands, which led to the proclamation of the independence of "The United States of Belgium" in January, 1790, and the threatening revolt in Hungary and Galicia seemed to endanger the existence of the Hapsburg Monarchy and diverted the depleted resources of Vienna to objects other than the Turkish war. The death of Emperor Joseph II (February 20, 1790, N.S.) deprived Catherine of a trusted ally. Leopold II, Joseph's brother and successor, entered into negotiations with Prussia in spite of the opposition of Kaunitz. By the convention of Reichenbach (July 27, 1790, N.S.) Austria consented to the principle of *status quo ante bellum*, to an immediate armistice with the Porte, and to the summoning of a peace congress under the mediation of England, Prussia, and Holland. Leopold had thus withdrawn from the Turkish war; but the negotiations proved difficult, and the Peace of Sistova, which formally terminated the state of war, was not signed until August 4, 1791, N.S.

Although Catherine was left alone to fight the Turks, the convention of Reichenbach was not without its advantages from Russia's point of view because it prevented an outbreak of hostilities with Prussia, whose army had been mobilized and posted on the Russian and Austrian frontiers. The Peace of Verelä, moreover, had removed anxieties regarding Sweden; and while the military campaign of 1790 had been far less successful than that of the previous year, Suvorov had won new

[5] The treaty of alliance concluded between Russia and Denmark in March, 1765, contained a secret provision binding the two courts to maintain the Swedish constitution of 1720. The Treaty of May 21, 1773, N.S., signed by the Grand Duke Paul in his capacity of duke of Holstein, transferred Schleswig-Holstein to Denmark in exchange for Oldenburg and Delmenhorst.

laurels in December by taking Izmail by storm. The offers of England and Prussia to mediate the Russo-Turkish War on the basis of *status quo ante bellum* were rejected in St. Petersburg. Catherine in her correspondence poured scorn on the two kings, whom she designated by a composite name of her invention: "Gegu," that is, Georges and Guillaume. Though she had reluctantly shelved the "Greek project," she was determined to annex Ochakov and the adjoining territory which commanded the mouth of the Dnieper and of the Bug. Pitt took exception to this program, and in March, 1791, decided to send to Russia an ultimatum in the name of England and Prussia (whose consent he had obtained) demanding the acceptance of the principle of *status quo* and the renunciation of territorial acquisitions at the expense of Turkey. He planned a naval demonstration in the Baltic, which, if carried out, would in all probability have led to war. Parliament and public opinion in England, however, refused to endorse this adventurous policy. Pitt, therefore, bowing to a determined opposition, accepted defeat, and both England and Prussia withdrew their objections to Catherine's program of expansion. Throughout the crisis the Russian empress displayed remarkable fortitude and refused to yield to British and Prussian threats and to the councils of moderation tendered by her ministers, including Potemkin. Russian victories on land and sea in 1791, but especially the defection of England and Prussia, made the Porte more amenable to the peace offers of St. Petersburg. Military operations were suspended in August, negotiations followed, the Treaty of Jassy (January 9, 1792, N.S.) transferred to Russia Ochakov and the territory between the Dniester and the Bug, recognized the annexation of the Crimea, and confirmed the Treaty of Kuchuk-Kainardzhi. The Peace of Jassy is considered as a great triumph for Catherine, although it fell short of the avowed object of the war. The empress herself never abandoned the "Greek project"; in a draft testament written in 1792 she expressed her intention of putting Constantine on the throne of the "Greek eastern empire." Secret provisions dealing with the dismemberment of Turkey were included in the Austro-Russian agreement of January 3, 1795, N.S., and a new war for the conquest of Constantinople was prevented only by Catherine's death.

Poland was less fortunate than Turkey because her territory was coveted not only by Russia and Austria but also by Prussia. Between the first partition and the outbreak of the Russo-Turkish War in 1787, the greatly reduced realm of King Stanislas experienced a period of relative quiet. Although Russian troops were not withdrawn and the Russian ambassador, Count Stackelberg, was regarded as enjoying greater powers than the king, the government of St. Petersburg was satisfied with the existing Polish regime and did not unduly interfere with the domestic affairs of Poland so long as this regime was not challenged. The king and the ruling class had apparently learned their lesson and treated Catherine and her representative with all the external signs of utmost deference. In this atmosphere of political *détente* the Polish government succeeded in enacting a number of administrative, financial, military, and educational measures which removed some of the abuses of the old order and were beneficial, even though Polish historians have overemphasized their importance. There were welcome signs of economic and intellectual renaissance, and the brilliant court of King Stanislas became the center of arts and letters. The movement for political reform developed along the same lines as in Sweden, that is, it favored the strengthening of the powers of the Crown, and it was natural, therefore, that the king should be identified with some of the groups advocating constitutional changes. It was a program embodying this principle that he had begged Catherine to accept during their brief interview at Kanev in May, 1787, in exchange for his promise of Polish support in the impending struggle with the Porte.

Russia's involvement in the war with Turkey and Sweden and the manifest hostility of Prussia and England towards Catherine unexpectedly confronted Poland with the possibility of throwing off the hated Muscovite shackles. The so-called "Four Years' Diet" ("confederated" by consent of all parties, a device which enabled the adoption of reforms by a simple majority) met in October, 1788, and became the instrument of the anti-Russian revolt. The king's cautious and unheroic program of an alliance with Russia, which would have involved Poland in the Turkish war but might have protected her against the annexation of her territories by Prussia, had no chance of success in the exalted nationalistic atmosphere prevailing in Warsaw. Although the ultimate object of Prussia was the acquisition of Danzig, Thorn, and other Polish provinces, these selfish designs were concealed for a time by Frederick William. The Prussian envoys Buchholz and Lucchesini posed as champions of Poland's liberation from the heavy rule of the Muscovites. Their appeal to the nation's ardent desire for real independence triumphed both over the passionate warning of Stanislas to hold fast to Russia and over Stackelberg's threats of Russian vengeance. On November 20, N.S., Frederick William came forth with a liberal and generous interpretation of the guaranty of the Polish constitution by the neighboring Powers, and the diet proceeded, with the approval of Prussia, to demolish the existing political institutions, an action which Stackelberg considered a challenge to Russia. To the general surprise the demand of the Poles for the immediate withdrawal of Russian troops was speedily and courteously granted by Catherine (May, 1789). Anxious to avoid a war with Prussia at a time when Russia was fighting the Turks and the Swedes, the empress overcame her sense of indignation and seemingly resigned herself to abdicate for a time Russia's hegemony at Warsaw in favor of Berlin. The true intentions of Frederick William did not become apparent until February, 1790, when the annexation of Danzig and Thorn was demanded as the price of the proposed alliance and commercial treaty with Poland. In view of the opposition of the diet and of Polish public opinion, these demands were temporarily dropped and the treaty of alliance was signed on March 29, 1790, N.S. It provided that any attempt by Austria or Russia to revive their rights, as grantors of the Polish constitution, "to interfere in the internal affairs" of the republic should be recognized as a *casus foederis* by Prussia. Poland had thus repudiated Russia's unwelcome hegemony and had put all her hopes of independent existence in the alliance with Frederick William.[6]

This momentous change in the international orientation of Warsaw was followed by an overhauling of the political regime. Among scenes of delirious enthusiasm the diet, this time led by the king, on May 3, 1791, N.S., adopted a new constitution, a step which is held by Polish historians as one of the greatest events in the annals of the country. The constitution abolished elections to the throne, the *liberum veto*, and the "confederations." Succession to the throne was assured to the House of Saxony, the powers of the Crown were vastly increased,

---

[6] Only a veiled reference to Danzig and Thorn was made in the treaty. Professor Lord, in his admirable study of the second partition, expresses the opinion that for all the Machiavellian flavor of Prussian policy in Poland, the alliance, at the time when it was concluded, corresponded to the vital interests of the two countries: to the Poles it appeared as the only possible safeguard against Russian vengeance and reprisals; and Frederick William desired a strong independent Poland as an ally in the coalition he was organizing against Austria. "The alliance," Lord writes, "was made, then, by both sides in good faith, for precise, practical reasons."

the functions of parliament and of the administrative departments were carefully delimited. Although some representation was conceded to the burghers, the *szlachta* (nobility) retained its privileges, and the peasantry, "from under whose hands flows the richest source of national wealth," continued to be denied political rights and was merely taken "under the protection of the law." The constitution of May 3 unquestionably marked an important step forward, but Edmund Burke, who described it as the noblest benefit received by any nation at any time, was guilty of almost as gross an exaggeration as was Voltaire when he acclaimed the first partition of Poland as a triumph of tolerance over fanaticism. Frederick William and Leopold expressed their approval of Poland's new constitutional charter, but Catherine was mortified and eventually refused to recognize it on the ground that it was "revolutionary" and had been passed by the diet in the absence of the majority of the deputies.

The intoxication of the Polish *szlachta* with their newly acquired liberty lasted for only a few months. The Peace of Verelä and the Peace of Jassy set the armies of Catherine free to deal with the Poles. The elector of Saxony, fearful of Russia's attitude, declined the proffered Polish Crown. The progress of the French Revolution and the danger it presented to the monarchical principle in Europe brought about the Austro-Prussian alliance (February 7, 1792, N.S.) and the outbreak of war between France, on the one hand, and Austria and Prussia, on the other (April, 1792). A few weeks earlier (March 1, 1792, N.S.) the death of Emperor Leopold deprived Poland of a real friend; his young and inexperienced successor, Francis II, had neither the vision nor the means to intervene effectively on behalf of Poland.

War in the west was what Catherine had been praying for, although it was not responsible for her decision to chastise Poland: she had made up her mind on the subject weeks before the news of the declaration of war by France on Austria reached St. Petersburg. A small band of malcontent Poles, whose leaders (among them the magnates Potocki, Rzewuski, and Branicki) had been in close touch with St. Petersburg, proclaimed a "confederation" at Targowica, Poland (May 14, 1792, N.S.). The act of "confederation" denounced the constitution of May 3, which was linked with the revolutionary legislation of the French National Assembly, demanded the restoration of ancient Polish "liberties," and appealed for aid to "the great Catherine." Two weeks later some 100,000 Russian troops crossed the Polish frontier. Zubov played an important part in the machinations that led to this new invasion of Poland. The war of Austria and Prussia against France and the Russian onslaught on Poland were represented by subtle diplomats as two manifestations of the same "counter-revolutionary" policy designed to restore order and stability in Europe, although the French Revolution swept away the monarchical principle which the constitution of May 3 endeavored to preserve and strengthen.

The refusal of Frederick William to honor the obligations of his Polish alliance and the indifference showed by other Powers sealed the fate of Poland. After a military campaign of a few weeks, Polish resistance broke down. Stanislas submitted to the wishes of Catherine and subscribed to the "confederation" of Targowica (July, 1792), while the supporters of the constitution of May 3 fled abroad. In the meantime the affairs of the allies on the French front had taken an unfortunate turn. The Prussians suffered a defeat at Valmy (September 20, 1792, N.S.) and the whole of Belgium was occupied by the French. Frederick William viewed with awe the triumphant return of Russian influence to Poland and sought to obtain a share of Polish territory as a compensation for the losses he had suffered in fighting revolutionary France. A new partition of Poland had been under discussion for some time between Berlin and Vienna as part of a general plan of annexations and exchanges of territories—in the worst tradition of eighteenth century diplomacy. The idea of the dismemberment of Poland had had its supporters in the Russian capital, among them the late Potemkin and Bezborodko. Highly secret Russo-Prussian negotiation in St. Petersburg culminated in the signature of the convention of January 23, 1793, N.S., which provided for the second partition of Poland. The action taken by the two governments was officially justified, not by any reference to "ancient and legitimate rights" invoked during the first partition, but by the necessity of fighting "the same spirit of insurrection and dangerous innovation" that had engulfed France and "was ready to break out in the kingdom of Poland." The share of Russia, through the second partition, comprised the districts of Vilna and Minsky and the eastern regions of Podolia and Volynia, an area of some 89,000 square miles with an estimated population of over 3,000,000 people; Prussia acquired Greater Poland, with the cities of Danzig, Thorn, Posen, and Kalisz, an area of some 23,000 square miles with an estimated population of about 1,000,000. Poland lost altogether about 54 per cent of her territory and more than half of her population. Prussia was bound by the convention to continue war against revolutionary France. Austria had no share in the second partition, but the contracting parties undertook to assist her in acquiring Bavaria. Vienna, indeed, was not informed of the Russo-Prussian agreement until March, 1793. Prussian troops had occupied Greater Poland in January, and in April the annexations were announced by the partitioning Powers. The new Russian ambassador to Warsaw, Baron Sievers, assisted by the Prussian envoy Buchholz, cheerfully assumed the unenviable task of clothing the forcible dismemberment of Poland with a transparent veil of legality. The diet which met at Grodno in June, 1793, although packed with Sievers's creatures, manifested a surprisingly rebellious spirit, but the mild-mannered, soft-spoken, and genial Russian ambassador forced it into submission by a timely display of firmness in the tradition of Repnin, von Saldern, and Stackelberg. At the point of Russian bayonets the diet ratified partition by two separate treaties, with Russia (July 22, N.S.) and with Prussia (September 25, N.S.). The Prussian treaty was formally accepted at the famous "mute session" of the diet (September 23, N.S.), when the motion of ratification was declared carried because all the deputies remained silent. A Russo-Polish treaty of "perpetual alliance" of October 14, N.S., made Poland virtually a Russian protectorate by handing over to the government of St. Petersburg the unrestricted control of her army and foreign relations. The constitution of May 3 and the laws passed by the Four Years' Diet were annulled, and Poland returned to the constitutional regime of 1775. In London and Paris the rape of Poland produced a deep impression and also some admirable speeches extolling liberty and denouncing the predatory methods of Catherine and Frederick William, but no action was taken to save Poland from her doom.

It would have been too much to expect that Poland would submit to the second partition without a movement of revolt. A wave of indignation swept the country and led to the appearance of various disaffected groups which found their leader in the person of Thaddeus Kosciuszko, the well known general in the American War of Independence. An uprising against the partitioning Powers broke out in March, 1794; and in April, after a massacre of the Russian troops, Warsaw and Vilna passed into the hands of the insurgents. Kosciuszko's appeal to the peasantry (manifesto of May 7, N.S.), to whom he promised land and freedom, met with considerable, although by no means unanimous, response. The Polish army, poorly equipped and consisting largely of partisans, inflicted several defeats on the Russians and the Prussians: these two Powers had concluded a new alliance on August 7, 1792, N.S., and were once more fighting side by side. After an unsuccessful siege of Warsaw, which lasted for two months (July to September), Frederick William was forced to withdraw ingloriously behind the Prussian frontier. Europe, however, and especially France, on whose support the insurgents had counted, remained aloof, and Polish victories proved ephemeral. In the battle of Maciejowice (October 10, N.S.) the Russian general Fermor decisively defeated the Poles, taking prisoner Kosciuszko, who had been severely wounded in action. Suvorov occupied Warsaw early in November, and by the middle of the month Polish resistance had collapsed. Victory was won entirely by the Russian troops, and the triumph of Catherine could not have been greater.

From the outbreak of the insurgent movement, St. Petersburg, Berlin, and Vienna had been engaged in complex negotiations concerning the future of Poland. While the Prussian king and Catherine's advisers—Zubov, Bezborodko, and Ostermann—favored partition, Austria was torn between the desire to preserve an independent Poland and the fear of being left out of the final settlement (as she was at the time of the second partition). By the end of June, however, Vienna was won over to the idea of partition, and subsequent negotiations centered on the delimitation of the respective shares of the three Powers. Prussian demands having proved unacceptable, an Austro-Russian agreement, commonly known as "the third partition treaty," was signed on January 3, 1795, N.S. It embodied the program of annexation previously outlined by Catherine and justified the dismemberment of Poland on the ground that she had become infected with "views most pernicious and most dangerous to the tranquillity of the neighboring Powers." In the meantime Frederick William, anticipating war with Russia and Austria over Poland, had withdrawn from the anti-French coalition and had entered into negotiations with France. This diplomatic step led to the Peace of Basel (April 5, 1795, N.S.). Although indignation in St. Petersburg and Vienna was great, and preparations were made for war with Prussia, the storm blew over, and after some more diplomatic wrangling Frederick William acceded to the Austro-Russian partition agreement after it had undergone some slight revision (October 24, 1795, N.S.). The act of delimitation was formally accepted on December 5, 1796, N.S. and the final convention for the partition of Poland was concluded on January 26, 1797. By the third partition Russia acquired Courland, Lithuania, and the western portions of Podolia and Volynia; Austria obtained Little Poland with Cracow; and Prussia took the remaining Polish territories with Warsaw. The annexation of Courland by Russia had been proclaimed somewhat earlier, on April 15, 1795, after the abdication of the last duke, Peter Biron. King Stanislas, too, abdicated in November, 1795, and later went to St. Petersburg, where he died in 1798. By a curious turn of fortune, the fate Catherine had planned for Turkey befell Poland: she was erased from the map of Europe.

The lust of the empress for territorial acquisition and military laurels was not satiated with Polish victories and was not dampened by old age. The "Greek project" was revived, in a truly fantastic form, in 1796, the closing year of her reign. Platon Zubov, Catherine's youthful lover, conceived the grandiose plan, sometimes known as the "Oriental project," which provided for a Russian invasion of the Caucasus and Persia and the occupation of all important trade stations between Turkey and Tibet, thus establishing a direct link with India and isolating Constantinople from the east. Simultaneously an army under Suvorov was to cross the Balkans and reach the Turkish capital from the north, while the Black Sea fleet, led by the empress in person (she was then sixty-seven), was to force the straits of Constantinople. Valerian Zubov, a youth of twenty-four, and the younger brother of the favorite, was appointed commander of the Persian expedition. Catherine imagined that this extraordinarily handsome young man was the greatest general in Europe, an opinion which she based partly on the fact that he had lost a leg in the Polish war of 1794. Valerian Zubov left St. Petersburg in February and in May occupied Derbent and, later, Baku, both cities offering no resistance. No further progress was made, and it soon became clear that the execution of the extravagant plan devised by the "charming children," as Catherine affectionately called the Zubov brothers, would have required hundreds of thousands of troops and millions of rubles, neither of which were available. The death of Catherine in November, 1796, saved Russia from the embarrassment and probable disaster of this preposterous venture. Emperor Paul ordered the suspension of hostilities and the withdrawal of the troops from the Caucasus.

The foreign policy of Catherine is traditionally considered by Rus-

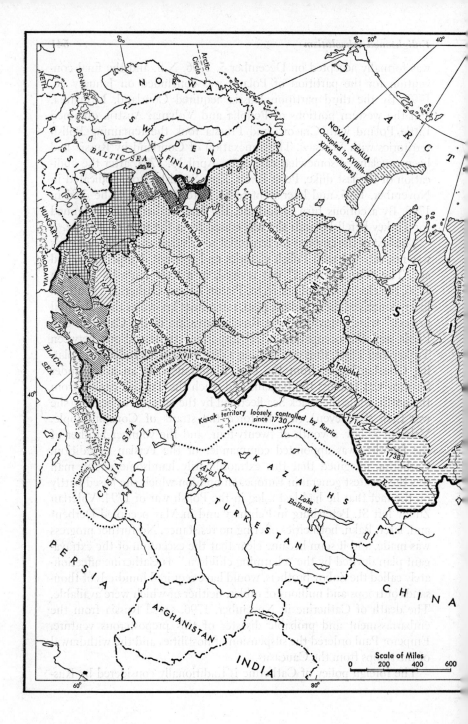

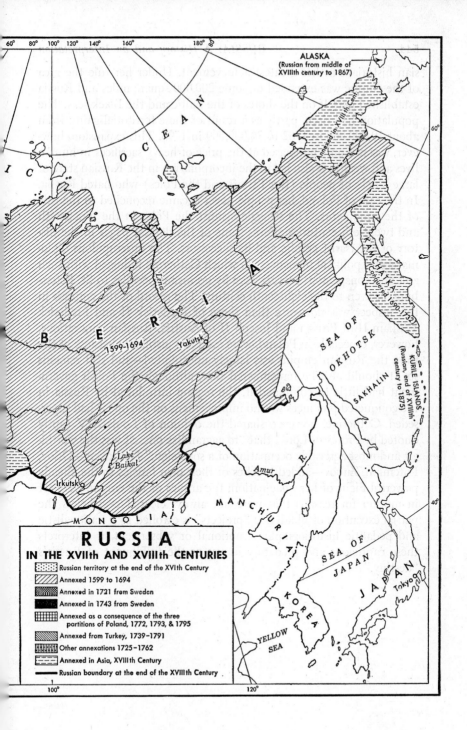

ALASKA
(Russian from middle of
XVIIIth century to 1867)

O C E A N

I C

S I B E R I A

Lena River

1599-1694

Yakutsk

Lake
Baikal

Irkutsk

MONGOLIA

MANCHURIA

Amur R.

SEA OF
OKHOTSK

SAKHALIN

KURILE ISLANDS
(Russian, end of XVIIIth
century to 1875)

KAMCHATKA
conquered 1690/1732

SEA OF
JAPAN

KOREA

YELLOW
SEA

J A P A N

Tokyo

R U S S I A
IN THE XVIIth AND XVIIIth CENTURIES

Russian territory at the end of the XVIth Century
Annexed 1599 to 1694
Annexed in 1721 from Sweden
Annexed in 1743 from Sweden
Annexed as a consequence of the three
    partitions of Poland, 1772, 1793, & 1795
Annexed from Turkey, 1739–1791
Other annexations 1725–1762
Annexed in Asia, XVIIIth Century
Russian boundary at the end of the XVIIIth Century

sian historians as her greatest achievement. Under her rule the area of the empire was extended by some 200,000 square miles and Russia established herself on the shores of the Baltic and the Black seas. The population had risen, partly as a result of these territorial gains, from about 19,000,000 in 1762 to 36,000,000 in 1796. This expansion, however, was not only purchased at the price of heavy sacrifices in human lives and wealth; it also led to the incorporation in the Russian state of large blocks of people (the Tartars and the Poles) who hated Russia. In the case of Poland, her people never became reconciled to the rule of the conquerors. The struggle against the Poles in the nineteenth and twentieth centuries affords some of the darkest pages in the history of the tsarist empire and its successors. The unscrupulous diplomatic and political maneuvers in which Catherine indulged with such zest and conspicuous success were by no means peculiar to St. Petersburg, or even to the eighteenth century. The record of the empress in this respect was no worse than those of Frederick II and Frederick William II of Prussia and Joseph II of Austria. Russian annexations, however, especially in Poland, were even less justifiable because at the time the Russian empire was largely unexploited—and still remains so. It should also be remembered that, although the Polish government had little to commend it, the regime introduced by Russia in the conquered provinces was no improvement on the one it had superseded. Catherine, however, shared the opinion of Louis XIV (aptly quoted by Professor Lord) that "to aggrandize oneself was the worthiest and most agreeable occupation of a sovereign." Her lovers—Orlov, Potemkin, Zubov—added touches of their own fancies to the already powerful flight of her imagination; the armies of the empire were set in motion for reasons that were not always clear. Nevertheless the partial execution of ill advised "projects" is extolled by a nationalistic and pedantic historiography; emotional or subservient, it interprets these capricious and predatory moves as the fulfillment of Russia's "destiny."

CHAPTER XXI

ENLIGHTENED ABSOLUTISM

Administrative Reforms, Industry, Trade, and Finance

———————— ✳ ————————

THE LEGISLATIVE COMMISSION, 1767–1768

There is a certain parallelism between the trends of Catherine's domestic reforms and of her foreign policy. In both, the vivid imagination of the empress was responsible for high-sounding and much-advertised schemes seemingly pregnant with momentous consequences for the future of the empire and of Europe. But her proposals for reform —nebulous and divorced from Russian realities—proved even more difficult of accomplishment and less fruitful than were her far-fetched "projects" for the redrafting of the map of Europe and Asia. The position of Catherine on the throne was too precarious, her liberalism too confused, superficial, and shallow, and the obstacles confronting any enlightened policy in eighteenth century Russia too formidable to permit any significant change in the political, social, and economic structure.

It will be remembered that from the days of Peter I successive legislative commissions had vainly tackled the problem of revising and amending the hopelessly inadequate Code of 1649 and that Empress Elizabeth, shortly before her death, had drawn a dreary picture of the state of lawlessness and misgovernment prevailing in every branch of the administration.[1] Catherine, with characteristic optimism and disregard for practical difficulties, addressed herself to the task which had defied the efforts of her predecessors. Her object, however, was not a mere revision of existing legislation but the preparation of an entirely new code embodying the most advanced legal theories of the

[1] See p. 494.

age. The famous *Instruction*, which she wrote for the guidance of the new Legislative Commission, was not a concrete program of legislative action—Catherine knew little about the Russian law—but, as has been pointed out, a restatement of general principles borrowed chiefly from Montesquieu and Beccaria.[2] The ideas of the distinguished foreign authors on whose writings Catherine leaned so heavily suffered, in the process of recapitulation, considerable distortion, partly at the hands of the empress herself and partly at those of her advisers who had censored and condensed the original text before it was permitted to appear in print. The expurgated version, comprising twenty chapters subdivided into 526 sections, dealt with the historical development of Russia, monarchical absolutism, the nature and the form of laws, punishments, industry and commerce, education, jurisprudence, codification, social structure, freedom of worship. Two supplements (February 28, 1768, and April 8, 1768) treated of "the police" and of "expenditure, revenue, and state administration" bringing the total number of sections to 653.

Catherine's political philosophy—if political philosophy is the appropriate term—was built around the proposition that Russia was a European Power and therefore should have a constitutional and legislative system based on "European principles." These principles, as she understood them, were those of an absolute monarchy, the only form of government suitable for a country as vast as Russia. "Any other form of government," the empress wrote, "would be not only harmful to Russia, but would lead to her utter ruin." Absolute monarchy, however, should be based on strict observance of the law, of which the sovereign was the fountain. "The intention and aim of absolute government," according to the *Instruction*, "is the glory of the citizens, of the state, and of the monarch." The social program of Catherine was in no sense revolutionary. She upheld the privileges of the nobility and intimated her intention to improve the legal and economic status of the peasantry. Most of her observations on serfdom were omitted from the official text, but what has been preserved, as well as the available fragments of the suppressed version, indicates that she did not contemplate emancipation. Section 260 states that "one should not suddenly and by legislative action create a large number of emancipated serfs." What the empress had in mind was the elimination of

[2] See pp. 510–511.

the most flagrant abuse—the definition by law of the relationship between the serfs and their masters—and the granting to the servile population of limited proprietary rights. These modest proposals were not easily reconcilable with some of the sweeping humanitarian ideas of the Enlightenment generously scattered through the pages of the *Instruction*. The empress was emphatic in her condemnation of the use of tortures as both ineffective and inhuman. The text of the *Instruction* was replete with illustrations drawn from ancient and contemporary European history, a literary device which did not render any easier the arduous task of grasping the elusive thought of its author. Of the momentous difficulties of her enterprise Catherine was hardly aware. "God forbid," she wrote in one of the closing sections, "that after the completion of the [proposed] legislation any other nation on earth shall enjoy greater justice and, therefore, greater well-being [than Russia]; [in such an eventuality] the object of the legislation would not have been achieved, a misfortune I do not wish to live to see."

The Legislative Commission which was to prepare the new code was summoned by a manifesto of December 14, 1766. This body consisted of elected representatives of central government departments and various social, ethnic, and religious groups: the nobility, the cities and towns, the peasants living on state-owned land, other specified groups of small landowners, the Cossacks, the non-nomadic native tribes, including Mohammedans and heathens. Serfs living on privately owned estates, that is, the largest single group of the population, were not represented and, curiously, the Church had merely one delegate, sent by the Holy Synod. The composition of the Commission, as Kliuchevsky has made clear, closely followed the precedents set by similar bodies in the earlier part of the century, although its membership was larger. The deputies enjoyed certain privileges and immunities, they received allowances which varied according to their status, and they were supplied with written mandates embodying the wishes of the electors. It appears that in numerous instances the voters, both in St. Petersburg and in the provinces, showed little interest in the elections, and the number of signatures on some of the mandates which the electors were requested to sign was surprisingly small. Not a few of the mandates were purely perfunctory and dealt with petty local grievances or even voiced complete satisfaction with the existing order.

Open opposition to the elections developed only in Ukraine, where it was feared that imperial legislation might lead to the abolition of local institutions, customs, and privileges.

Of the total number of 564 deputies, 28 were sent by government departments, 161 by the nobility, 208 by the urban population, and 167 by the rural communities, including the Cossacks and native tribes. The proceedings were formally opened in Moscow in the presence of the empress on July 30, 1767, when the bewildered and enthusiastic deputies reverently listened to a flowery oration by the Metropolitan Dimitry, who somewhat imaginatively linked Catherine to Justinian. In December the Commission, which carried on its work partly in plenary sessions and partly in numerous committees, took a recess and reassembled in February, 1768, in St. Petersburg. After holding altogether 203 sessions, it was adjourned *sine die* on December 18, 1768. The outbreak of the Russo-Turkish War had furnished the government with a convenient pretext to get rid of an assembly whose practical usefulness was open to doubt and whose deliberations had caused annoyance in influential circles. Several of the committees continued to meet until the end of 1774, but they failed to complete the drafting of any section of the code. The Commission was never reconvened, and the code which—as some in St. Petersburg pretended to believe—was to usher in an era of felicity for Russia and humanity remained unwritten.

The lamentable failure of the Commission would seem to have been inevitable. The assembly was far too numerous, and its members, with rare exceptions, unqualified for legislative work. The *Instruction*, with its involved and unfamiliar phraseology and glittering generalities, offered no practical assistance to the deputies in mastering the intricacies of lawmaking. The nature of the debates and the provisions of the mandates had disclosed, moreover, a sharp divergency of views on basic issues among the deputies and just as sharp a conflict between the intentions of the empress and the wishes of some of the delegates. Most of the representatives of the nobility demanded the preservation and extension of the exclusive privileges of the *dvorianstvo*; merchants, priests, and even the Cossacks clamored for the right to own serfs; but there were some deputies (among them representatives of the nobility) who criticized the existing social order and condemned the practice of serfdom. Such criticism, which in influential quarters was deemed dangerous, especially when viewed in the light of incessant peasant uprisings, was in part responsible for the inglorious demise of the Commission. Its work, however, had not been entirely futile, for it provided the government with information that was to prove useful in framing the administrative reforms of the latter part of the reign.

ADMINISTRATIVE REFORMS

On her accession Catherine, like Elizabeth some twenty years earlier, intended to abrogate the legislation enacted by her predecessor. The proposed legislative revision, however, did not go very far, and affected merely some of the minor measures of Peter III; for instance, the private chapels closed by his orders were reopened. By a decree of August 12, 1762, Catherine repealed the regulations of the former emperor concerning the secularization of ecclesiastical estates, but it soon became clear that the reprieve granted to the Church was temporary. After some preliminary measures which left no doubt as to the real intentions of the empress, ecclesiastical properties were finally taken over by the government by virtue of a decree of February 26, 1764, and were put under the administration of a lay institution, the college of economy; thenceforth Church dignitaries and monasteries were provided for from appropriations the amount of which was determined by secular authorities, that is, the pertinent legislation of Peter III was revived with minor modifications. The dispossession of the Church, which was accompanied by the closing down of a large number of monasteries, was received with consternation in Orthodox circles, but open opposition was effectively silenced by the ruthless, vindictive, and cruel persecution of Arseni Matseevich, archbishop of Rostov, who had attempted a crusade against impending secularization, anathematized the secular power for harboring evil designs against Church property, and had showed little respect for the person of the empress. The archbishop was tried by the Synod, deprived of his rank, officially dubbed "the liar" (*Vral*), and spent the remaining years of his life in prison, where he died in 1772.

No systematic reform of the institutions of the central government was attempted in the reign of Catherine, although their imperfections were flagrant and many. Desnitsky, professor of the University of Moscow, who had studied in England, submitted a project for the reorganization of the Senate as an elective legislative assembly of 600 or 800 members. This proposal had little in common with Catherine's conception of enlightened absolutism and had no chance of being accepted. Less revolutionary was the plan of Nikita Panin, a warm admirer of the aristocratic constitution of Sweden, who urged the appointment of a small permanent "Imperial Council" to advise the empress on all questions of state policy and thus eliminate irresponsible influences such as had flourished under Elizabeth. Yielding to Panin's arguments, Catherine signed, on December 28, 1762, a manifesto creating the council, whose members had already been nominated. But she soon changed her mind, presumably because she felt that the proposed institution might lead to the curtailment of the absolute powers of the Crown. The manifesto was never promulgated and the whole matter was dropped. In November, 1768, however, following the outbreak of the Russo-Turkish War, Catherine appointed a council of nine members chosen from among the higher officials. Formally inaugurated by a decree of January 17, 1769, the council was to function "at the imperial court and in the presence of Her Majesty," that is, it was to be a purely advisory body and, unlike the cabinet of Empress Anne, was not to enjoy the power of issuing decrees and orders except under the signature and in the name of the empress. Appointed originally as an emergency measure for the duration of the war, the council was retained after hostilities were over and became a permanent institution, but its position in the constitutional framework was not clearly defined until the reforms of Alexander I early in the nineteenth century. It did not succeed in eliminating the influence of the favorites, which Panin so rightly dreaded.

A reform of the provincial administration which was no less overdue than was that of the central government, had from the point of view of Catherine the advantage that it did not endanger the sacrosanct principle of autocracy. It will be remembered that the institutions of local government established by Peter I had proved unworkable and that soon after his death provincial Russia largely returned to the administrative practice of the seventeenth century. This state of affairs was maintained throughout the reigns of Anne and Elizabeth. The manifesto of February 18, 1762, which freed the *dvoriane* from the obligation of compulsory service, was followed by a mass return of noble landlords to their estates, where they had formerly made but rare appearances. The situation in the provinces was thus radically changed, and the proceedings of the Legislative Commission of 1767–1768 disclosed the desire of the nobility, as well as that of other social groups, to take a larger part in the conduct of local affairs. The ineptness of local authorities, moreover, had been demonstrated during the great peasant uprising of 1773–1774. The pressure of the *dvoriane* for local government reform, backed by considerations of expediency, was not unwelcome to the empress, because it offered an opportunity for practical application of the principles of government she had learned from Montesquieu, and more recently from Blackstone, whose celebrated treatise appeared in a French translation in 1774. As early as 1764 she had ordered the direct subordination of provincial governors to the Senate, to the exclusion of intermediate administrative organs. The Law on the Administration of the Provinces of the Russian Empire of November 7, 1775, the Charter of the Nobility (*Zhalovannaia gramota*), and the Charter of the Cities (both charters dated April 21, 1785) basically altered the territorial-administrative framework and introduced novel principles in local government.

A preamble to the law of 1775 singled out two chief defects of the then existing administrative order: (1) the unwieldy size of some of the provinces and the numerical insufficiency of available officials; and (2) the confusion resulting from the concentration of varied functions in one agency. To remedy the former evil the number of provinces (*guberniia*), which was fifteen in 1762, had been increased to forty by 1781 and reached the number of fifty towards the end of the reign. Theoretically, each province contained a population of 300,000 to 400,000 and was subdivided into counties or districts (*uezd*) with a population of 20,000 to 30,000 each. The provinces, the basic administrative units, were grouped together under an appointed governor-general. This territorial-administrative scheme, which took no account of historical development and local ties, remained in force until the advent of the Soviets.

The revised administrative structure embodied the following principles: (1) decentralization through the delegation of comprehensive power to provincial agencies acting under the direct control of the Senate; (2) separation of powers (or, rather, functions) inside the local government, that is, the administration by separate agencies of the police, finance, justice, education, public health, and poor relief; (3) the filling of administrative and judicial offices partly by appointment and partly by election; (4) impartment of a class character to the administrative and judicial organs through the granting of a predominant position in some of these bodies to the representatives of one social class or "estate" (*soslove*)—the nobility, the merchants and burghers, and the "free peasants" (chiefly those living on state-owned land)—and the creation of special agencies to deal exclusively with matters concerning the members of the respective "estates." The above principles were carried out with varying degrees of thoroughness. Officers appointed by the Crown, such as the governor of the province and the members of the provincial board (*gubernskoe pravlenie*) and of the financial board (*kazennaia palata*) were given a predominant place in provincial government, while the elected representatives of the nobility—especially the district police captain (*kapitan ispravnik*) —were largely in charge of the affairs of the county (*uezd*), although they were, of course, subordinate to the governor and other provincial authorities. Students of Russian constitutional law (Korkunov, Lazarevsky) agree that the participation of representatives of the "estates" in local administration did not lead to the establishment of self-government. The elected officials were assigned a subordinate position and enjoyed none of that independence which is the very essence of autonomy. The social standing and authority of the governor or even of his attachés, moreover, was so far above that of such officials as, for instance, the district police captain, that any show of independence on the part of the latter was out of the question. With the exception of the marshal of the nobility, all offices filled through election by the *dvoriane* carried little social prestige and were shunned by the influential and wealthy landlords, who abandoned participation in local government to the poorer and least distinguished members of their class, those incapable of opposing the wishes of the bureaucracy. The officials elected by the merchants, burghers, and peasants carried on their duties under legal and social handicaps that were even greater than those of the nobility, and they played no independent part in the affairs of local government.

The municipal institution introduced by Peter I never functioned properly, and the 1785 Charter of the Cities endeavored to rebuild them from the ground. Under this act urban population was divided into six groups, each endowed with a semblance of corporate organization: (1) "true city dwellers" (*nastoiashchie gorodovye obyvateli*), that is, owners of real estate; (2) merchants;[3] (3) artisans; (4) non-

---

[3] The merchants were subdivided into three "guilds" according to the amount of their declared business capital. A manifesto of March 17, 1775, had freed the merchants from the poll tax, for which was substituted a tax of 1 per cent on busi-

resident (*inogorodnie*) and foreign merchants; (5) "distinguished citizens" (*imenitye grazhdane*), a quaint group which comprised former municipal officials, holders of university diplomas, artists, owners of capital of 50,000 rubles or more, bankers, wholesale merchants, and shipowners; (6) unskilled workers and small traders (*possadskie*). The six groups elected a municipal council (*obshchaia duma*) which met at long intervals. The actual business of city government was entrusted to an executive board of six members (*shestiglasnaia duma*), one from each of the six subdivisions of the population, chosen by the municipal council. The police powers, however, were vested in an appointed official, the *gorodnichii*. The municipal institutions of 1785 proved stillborn. The corporate organization, foreign to Russian historical tradition, remained largely a dead letter; the municipal councils and executive boards exercised no real influence and in numerous instances were not even elected. City government was conducted, as in the past, by appointed officials headed by the *gorodnichii*. Nevertheless the municipal administration created by the Charter of 1785 remained the law of the land for eighty-five years, until the reform of Alexander II.

The reform of 1775–1785 greatly added to the cost of administration by creating a multitude of new agencies,[4] but it is less certain that it contributed to the efficiency of government or improved the ethical standards of local officials. Indirectly, the reform enhanced the position of the landed nobility, although the elected officials, as already stated, were relegated to a subordinate place. The governors and other appointed officials, however, were drawn from the ranks of the *dvorianstvo*; they understood and shared the aspirations of the noble landlords, lived among them as members of one privileged class, and found it easy to cooperate with them on all important issues.

The introduction of institutions of local government extended over a period of twenty years and led to a piecemeal reorganization of the central administration. The delegation to the newly created local organs of powers formerly exercised by the central departments and the subordination of the local officials directly to the Senate rendered useless most

ness capital arbitrarily declared by the owners of commercial establishments, provided that it was not less than 500 rubles.

[4] The cost of administration, according to Chechulin, increased from 4 million rubles in 1763 and 5 million rubles in 1773 to 18 million rubles in 1781 and 30 million rubles in 1796. The territorial expansion of the empire was in part responsible for the higher cost of government.

of the old central agencies. A decree of October 24, 1780, ordering their liquidation, was not put into effect at once. The department of state expenditure (*shtats-kontora*) was closed in 1781; the department of state revenue (*kammer kollegiia*) in 1786; the department of financial control (*revizion kollegiia*) in 1788; the department of justice (*iustits kollegiia*) was shorn of some of its functions in 1784 and abolished two years later. The department of manufactures (*manufaktur kollegiia*) was discontinued in 1780 as a consequence of the newly adopted policy of non-intervention in industrial activities, and the college of economy, which had administered the former ecclesiastical estates, was closed in 1786, after its functions had been taken over by the provincial financial boards (*kazennaia palata*). Only three central departments—the colleges of foreign affairs, army, and the admiralty—retained their position unimpaired.

The effect of these changes on the status of the Senate is of particular interest. A manifesto of December 15, 1763, decreed an internal reorganization of the Senate in accordance with a plan submitted by Nikita Panin.[5] In spite of the elimination of most of the central government departments and notwithstanding the important place the law of 1775 assigned to the Senate as the chief organ of administrative and judicial control, the position of that institution was weakened rather than strengthened under the rule of Catherine. Professor Chechulin, co-author of the official history of the Senate (1911), has made it clear that the empress, carried away by theoretical schemes, failed to comprehend the grave consequences of the wholesale destruction of the machinery, however imperfect, of central government. The inconvenience of complete decentralization was first felt in the field of public finance. As early as 1773 there was attached to the Senate a department (*ekspeditsiia*) of public revenue which largely duplicated the functions performed by other agencies. In 1780 this department was vested with comprehensive powers and was transferred to the direct control of the procurator-general of the Senate. This official, rather than the Senate, inherited many of the functions formerly exercised by the defunct institutions of central government. In the second half of Catherine's reign, according to Chechulin, the

[5] The manifesto also ordered a substantial increase both in the number of government employees and in their emoluments. The latter measure, which aimed at the eradication of the deep-rooted system of graft, cost the treasury 620,000 rubles a year, a sum equivalent to 5 per cent of the total state expenditure, but corrupt practices continued unabated.

procurator-general became an independent organ of state administration and no longer functioned as an officer of the Senate, but side by side with that body. For all practical purposes he combined the duties of the ministers of finance, justice, and the interior. There was nothing in the law to justify this broad authority. It must be explained by the fact that the office of procurator-general was held from 1764 to 1792 by Prince Alexander Viazemsky, a favorite collaborator of the empress and one of her most trusted "pupils." The official standing of the Senate was undermined not only by the enhanced independence and authority of the procurator-general, but also by the influence that the advisory council of 1768 exercised upon the monarch. In spite of the plethora of governmental agencies created by Catherine, Russia continued to be ruled, as under Elizabeth, not by "the authority of state institutions," but by "the power of persons."

Probably the most lasting, albeit negative, contribution made by Catherine to the theory and practice of Russian government was the forcible enunciation and vigorous enforcement of the principle of administrative unification and "Russification." In an instruction given to Prince Viazemsky in 1764, the empress, referring to Ukraine, the Baltic provinces, and Finland, observed that although these territories enjoyed special administrative privileges confirmed by the Russian Crown, "to call them foreign and to treat them as such would be more than a mistake; it would be, indeed, plain stupidity. These provinces . . . should be easily reduced to a condition where they can be Russified and no longer, like wolves, look for the woods. This can be achieved without effort if reasonable men are put in charge." Ukraine was the first victim of this clear-cut policy. In 1764 Cyril Razumovsky, who had held the office of hetman since 1750, was forced to resign, and the government of Ukraine was entrusted to a commission of eight members headed by General Rumiantsev. A decree of October 27, 1781, divided Ukraine into three provinces and substituted for her autonomous institutions the imperial provincial administration provided by the law of November 7, 1775. By a decree of May 3, 1783, the freedom-loving people of the steppes were made subject to the poll tax and were merged with the mass of Russian bondsmen.

The turn of the Baltic provinces came next. The insistence of their representatives in the Legislative Commission of 1767–1768 on the preservation of their autonomous institutions and special privileges had greatly irritated the empress. By a series of decrees issued in 1782–

1786, all legislation providing for such institutions and privileges was repealed and the Baltic provinces were incorporated in the administrative, financial, and social framework of the empire. Russian Finland suffered a like fate. By a decree of May 3, 1783, the poll tax was introduced in Finland, as it had been in Ukraine and the Baltic provinces, and local government on the Russian model by a decree of July 25, 1793. The territories annexed from Poland under the three partitions received no autonomous government and were administered in the same way as the other provinces. Although in the 120 years between the death of Catherine and the revolution of 1917 there were some notable departures from the practice of administrative unification and Russification—in the case of Poland and especially of Finland—her successors on the throne (with the exception of Emperors Paul and Alexander I), remained on the whole faithful to the program inaugurated in 1764.

ECONOMIC AND FINANCIAL POLICIES

Catherine's economic policies, like her administrative reforms, were determined by expediency, tradition, and the influence of liberal ideas. Two of the more important measures of the early part of her reign— land surveying and the creation of colonies of foreign settlers—were a continuation of the administrative action taken by the government of Elizabeth. In 1751 several hundred Serbs, driven away from their native land by Magyar persecution, migrated to Russia and settled along the Polish frontier, between the Dnieper and the Bug. New Serbia, as the colony was called, was organized along military lines, and its leader, Ivan Khorvat, received the rank of major-general in the Russian army. The Serbs were followed by a small group of Montenegrins, who were given land in the province of Orenburg. The colonists had the backing of the Russian government, and their transfer was at first authorized by Vienna. When it appeared, however, that the migration was threatening to assume larger dimensions than was originally anticipated, the Austrian government withdrew the authorization. There followed acrimonious and inconclusive negotiations between the two courts. Turkey, alarmed by the probable effect of Russian policy upon the Christian subjects of the Porte and by the creation of a military colony in the vicinity of her frontier, raised strong objections to the action of St. Petersburg. There also developed complications with Poland when, in 1754, Khorvat carried on raids across the

Polish border. The result of the experiment was not encouraging. Although their number remained small, the settlers proved unruly and unmanageable. Khorvat was eventually found guilty of misappropriation of funds and in 1762 was deprived of his rank and command. Early the following year New Serbia was reorganized as the province of Novorossisk and put under the rule of a Russian governor.

In spite of the failure of the Elizabethan venture in foreign colonization, the policy was revived by Catherine on a grander scale. The settlement of the border regions was desirable both from the political and from the economic standpoint, and since the movement of the native population was precluded by the attachment of the peasants to the land an appeal to foreigners appeared—in theory—the logical solution. A decree of October 15, 1762, threw the unpopulated expanses of the empire open to settlement by foreigners irrespective of race and religious denomination, "except for the Jews." A decree of July 22, 1763, created the Office of Foreign Settlers (*Kantseliariia Opekunstva Inostrantsev*) under Gregory Orlov and granted to the immigrants freedom of worship, exemptions from taxation and from obligatory service, and the right of self-government. Subsequent regulations provided for the free distribution of land which would eventually become the hereditary property of the colonists. The majority of the immigrants, as contemplated by a project prepared towards the end of the reign of Elizabeth, came from Germany. Actual enlistment and settlement were conducted through the offices of French concessionaires. The whole enterprise was lacking in proper organization, brought about conflicts between the Germans and the native population, which resented their privileges, and imposed a heavy burden on the treasury. The budgetary appropriation under this heading which in 1766 was 200,000 rubles was increased to 440,000 rubles in 1796. Further outlays were involved in the termination of the concessions in 1779, when the administration of the colonies was taken over by the government. The 104 colonies, with a population of some 23,000, which by 1768 had been established on the lower Volga around Saratov and Tsaritsin gave proof of remarkable vitality in spite of their unpromising start, and survived until World War II. For a century and a half these settlers have retained to a surprising degree their language, religion, and customs. Under the Soviet regime the colonies were merged into the Autonomous Soviet Socialist Republic of the Volga Germans, which, according to the census of January 17, 1939, had a population of 605,500. In 1941, however, the republic of the Volga Germans was dissolved and its population "resettled elsewhere."

The necessity of bringing some order out of the chaos in land relations had been long recognized by the Russian government. The most recent general land survey was made in 1680–1686, and in the subsequent years the distribution of landed estates had proceeded in a haphazard manner with the result that boundaries between many holdings were drawn in an arbitrary fashion. Large tracts of land had been unlawfully appropriated by individual owners; land deeds, when they existed at all, were lacking in precision. In the hands of wealthy and unscrupulous landlords such deeds tended to become powerful weapons for the dispossession of their weaker neighbors. This chaotic situation led to endless litigation, accompanied at times by bloody feuds, murder, and arson. Curiously, even the national frontiers were not definitely traced: in 1757, for instance, St. Petersburg accused Poland of the unlawful occupancy of hundreds of square miles of allegedly Russian territory. The necessity of a general land survey had been vainly urged by Vasili Tatishchev as far back as 1719. His proposal was revived in 1752 by Peter Shuvalov; an appropriate commission, appointed in 1754, accomplished little and was discontinued in 1761 for lack of funds. The task was resumed in 1765 with the appointment of a commission on land surveying (*kommissiia gosudarstvennago mezhevaniia*) and the preparation of a new instruction which dropped some of the rigid formal requirements of the earlier legislation and provided greater latitude for the fixing of boundaries by agreement of the parties concerned. Although land surveying, which involved the most vital interests of the landlords, did not proceed smoothly, by the end of Catherine's reign the work had been completed over an area of 141 million dessiatines (381 million acres) comprising some twenty provinces. The total cost was 5.4 million rubles; of this amount 2.5 million rubles were defrayed from the proceeds of a special tax and 2.9 million rubles were contributed by the treasury. The surveying of the other provinces was not completed until the middle of the nineteenth century.

The regime of industrial and trading companies endowed with monopolistic privileges, which had been maintained from the days of Peter I, underwent a great deal of criticism towards the end of the reign of Elizabeth. It became apparent that monopolies stifled the development of independent enterprises without improving the technique of production and that they had proved injurious to the progress of the peasant cottage industry, which, in spite of all obstacles, played an increasingly important part in supplying the market with a wide range of commodities. Peter III, it will be remembered, enacted several measures for the liberation of trade and commerce. The proceedings of the Legislative Commission of 1767–1768 disclosed widespread dissatisfaction with the monopolies and a desire for greater economic freedom. This demand was in general agreement with the views expressed by Catherine in her *Instruction:* the empress was familiar with the writings of the Physiocrats, professed to share their admiration for the toilers of the soil, and voiced her predilection for small artisans who combined farming with industrial pursuits. But although the *dvoriane*, merchants, and "free peasants" agreed in condemning monopolies, they were at odds as to the remedy to be applied. By a decree of March 29, 1762, Peter III had prohibited the purchase of serfs for employment in factories, and this rule was confirmed by Catherine (August 8, 1762). The use of servile labor in industry was thus reserved to the nobility, except in the possessionary works already owned by the non-*dvoriane*.[6] The representatives of the nobility in the Legislative Commission insisted that the provisions of the decree of March 29, 1762, should be strictly enforced, while the merchants and burghers clamored for repeal of the decree and for the exclusion of the nobles from participation in industrial and commercial activities.[7] The merchants, even more bitter in their attack on the peasants, demanded that all industrial and commercial pursuits should be closed to them. To this program not only the peasants but also the nobles were opposed because the serfowners were unwilling to permit a reduction of the earning capacity of their serfs on which their own economic well-being depended. The peasants were on the whole against the ownership of industrial enterprises by the *dvoriane*, experience having taught them that such enterprises were not vastly different from penal institutions.

[6] See pp. 389–390.

[7] There was no unanimity among the spokesmen of the nobility. The *dvoriane* of Shuia, for instance, were against the ownership of factories by noble landlords. The *dvoriane* of Voronezh petitioned for the prohibition of iron foundries and glassworks in their province on the ground that they "serve no useful purpose and merely lead to the destruction of forests." The *dvoriane* of Kashin, on the other hand, held that merchants should not be permitted to own factories and that promotion of industry should be reserved exclusively to noble landlords.

It was not an easy matter to reconcile these incompatible claims. Beginning in 1762, the government proceeded with a series of measures directed towards the curtailment of monopolistic privileges, and a manifesto of March 17, 1775, did away with them altogether by providing that the establishment and ownership of industrial enterprises were free to all and required no special authorization. This rule was confirmed by a decree of November 22, 1779, ordering the closing down of the department of manufactures. The chief gainers by this liberal economic policy were the noble landlords. The Charter of the Nobility (1785) specifically provided that they should be entitled to sell wholesale the produce of their estates and to own factories. The merchants, on the other hand, had failed to obtain from Catherine the repeal of the decree of March 29, 1762. The right of the non-*dvoriane* to purchase serfs for employment in industrial enterprises was not restored until 1798, in the reign of Emperor Paul; it was finally abolished in 1816 by Emperor Alexander I. No legislative attempt was made to define the proprietary rights of the serfs, as owners of industrial establishments; their legal status therefore, as will appear later, remained highly anomalous.

The economic liberalism of Catherine did not mean the abandonment of government intervention. Foreign entrepreneurs were still encouraged to come to Russia, especially in the early years of her reign, and a manifesto of 1763 conferred upon them the right to purchase serfs for employment in factories, a right denied only a year earlier to domestic manufacturers. Subsidies and exemptions from taxation continued to be granted to the promoters of new industries, export of certain raw materials needed by domestic producers was prohibited, and a few government-owned enterprises were established, for instance, the large woolen mills in Ekaterinoslav. Such measures, however, played a subordinate part, and the general trend was in the direction of greater economic liberalism.

A similar tendency was observable in tariff policies. The tariff act of 1766 was moderate; the rates of duty on most manufactured goods did not exceed 20 or 30 per cent ad valorem, and the list of articles subject to prohibitive duties or exclusion was unimportant. By the act of 1782 the tariff rates were on the whole increased, but the degree of protection they offered was not yet excessive. The situation was changed in 1793–1796, when for political and financial reasons the government adopted protectionist and prohibitive measures. The manifesto of April 8, 1793, directed primarily against revolutionary France, ordered the suspension of all commerce with that country, including trade carried through the intermediary of any third state. At the same time St. Petersburg was deeply concerned about the progressive depreciation of the ruble on the international market, a process that was due to the introduction of paper currency and the immoderate use of the printing press. The restrictive measures of 1793–1796 had as one of their objects the strengthening of the position of the national currency through the creation of a "favorable" balance of trade. This consideration was particularly important in view of the rapid growth of the foreign debt, which involved large payments abroad.[8]

An evaluation of the progress of Russian industry in the second half of the eighteenth century meets with considerable difficulties. It is usually stated (Tugan-Baranovsky, Miliukov, Tarle, Rozhkov) that between 1762 and 1796 the number of large industrial enterprises had substantially increased. According to Tugan-Baranovsky, the respective figures were 984 and 3,161, that is, the number of "factories" had more than trebled. This rapid industrial expansion is often linked with the development of new sources of industrial labor: (1) urban population, which grew from 328,000 in 1724 to 1.3 million in 1796 (Miliukov),[9] and, especially, (2) serfs on *obrok*, that is, bondsmen who paid their lord a specified annual tribute (*obrok*) and earned their living by working in factories. In contrast with the practice in the earlier part of the century, it is held that under Catherine industry was substantially dependent on hired, and not on compulsory or servile, labor. Professor Kulisher, a thoughtful student of economic history, takes a less favorable view. He rightly observes that in the eighteenth century the term "factory" (*fabrika*), used to describe industrial enterprises, had no precise meaning and that the estimated number of such establishments given in contemporary sources shows a surprising variation. It is not improbable, according to Kulisher, that in some of the more impressive estimates of the number of "factories" are included not

---

[8] Officially, the tariff act of 1782 remained in force until the end of the reign of Catherine. On Sept. 16, 1796, the empress appended her signature to a new tariff act which was to become effective on Jan. 1, 1797, but Emperor Paul ordered its suspension (Nov. 18, 1796), and a new tariff act was issued on Oct. 12, 1797. This was almost identical with the tariff of 1782.

[9] A. G. Rashin in a recent study (Moscow, 1940) challenges Miliukov's widely accepted figures of urban population. According to Rashin, urban population in 1794 was 2.3 million. The discrepancy between the two estimates emphasizes the unreliability of Russian population statistics.

only large industrial establishments but also small shops employing only a few men. In the eighteenth century concentration of productive processes under one roof was still uncommon, and work was carried on in small shops or in the workers' own cottages. This, Kulisher believes, might have been another source of confusion. Estimates of the number of industrial workers towards the end of Catherine's reign vary from 100,000 to as many as 500,000. The higher figure comprises, presumably, small artisans who are not included in the more conservative estimates. Under these conditions it is difficult to express a definite opinion on the development of large-scale industry during this period, but it would seem to have been far less impressive than these questionable statistics would indicate. There is much evidence, however, to show that the operation of small establishments of the cottage-industry type, which were carried on by peasants chiefly as a part-time occupation subsidiary to farming, was making good progress. Official reports confirm the impression that the technical levels of the old-established government-sponsored manufacturers, such as woolen mills, remained deplorably low.

Throughout the second half of the eighteenth century no important change took place in the direction and composition of Russian foreign trade. England and, to a lesser degree, Holland retained the position of predominance on the Russian market they had already achieved. English merchants were largely responsible for the promotion of Russian exports, carried chiefly in English bottoms, except in the southern European trade, where the Dutch took the leading part. Russian exports to England, in addition to commodities intended for consumption in that country—especially maritime supplies needed by the navy and the merchant marine—were comprised of goods that were to be reexported to other European states, to British colonies, and to Spanish America. English purchases in Russia were considerably in excess of their sales there, and in an age when the mercantilist doctrines were in vogue this "favorable" balance of trade made the Anglo-Russian trade particularly attractive from the Russian point of view. Commercial relations between the two Powers were regulated by the important treaty of 1734, probably the first purely commercial agreement concluded by Russia with any other nation. This treaty, which was on the whole favorable to England, remained in force for thirty years; its provisions were reproduced with but minor modifications in the Anglo-Russian commercial treaty of 1766, which was permitted to lapse in 1786 at the expiration of its twenty-year term. The estrangement between Russia and England brought about by the Declaration of Armed Neutrality (1780) and the disapproval in London of Russian aggressive policies in Poland and Turkey were not allowed, however, to interfere unduly with the flow of the mutually profitable and old-established trade. In 1789 Catherine expressed her willingness to negotiate an Anglo-Russian commercial agreement from which reference to the "neutrality rules" would be omitted. The rapid pace of events in revolutionary France made St. Petersburg and London forget their political differences, and in 1793 the two governments reached a preliminary agreement for the renewal of the treaty of 1766. In 1797, under Emperor Paul, this was superseded by a new Anglo-Russian commercial treaty which retained all the essential features of the earlier agreements and was concluded for a period of eight years. Thus, in spite of the stormy international atmosphere of the eighteenth century, Anglo-Russian trade suffered no serious dislocation. Trade with France, which was carried on almost exclusively through English and Dutch intermediaries, was far less important, and the outbreak of the French Revolution deprived the elaborate Franco-Russian commercial treaty of 1787 of all usefulness.[10]

The southward expansion of Russia under the Treaty of Kuchuk-Kainardzhi (1774), followed by the annexation of the Crimea (1783), the acquisition of Ochakov (1792), and the building of the port of Odessa (1794), revived the dreams of an extensive Black Sea trade that had once haunted Peter I. In 1775 the rates of duty chargeable on goods imported through Russian Black Sea ports were reduced by one fourth and in 1784 a manifesto of Catherine announced that the ports of Sevastopol, Kherson, and Theodocia were open to the commerce of all Powers, which could send their ships to these waters "freely, safely, and without fear of obstruction." The illusions of Catherine in this respect were shared by the French, who imagined that the annexation of the Crimea and the Franco-Russian treaty of 1787 offered them the opportunity to supersede the Dutch as intermediaries in the commerce between Russia and southern Europe. Such sanguine expectations failed to take into account the fact that the Straits were controlled, as in the past, by Turkey. Although the Treaty of Kuchuk-Kainardzhi conceded to Russian merchant vessels

---

[10] Commercial treaties were concluded also with Denmark (1782), Austria (1785), Portugal (1787), and the kingdom of Naples (1787).

the right of navigation in Turkish waters, passage through the Dardanelles and the use of Turkish ports,[11] the Sublime Porte showed no
disposition to open the Black Sea to the merchantmen of other nations. The privilege was granted to Austria in 1784 but her Black
Sea trade remained insignificant. Commerce in these waters was almost
exclusively in the hands of Turkish nationals, although some of the
vessels were operated under the Russian flag.

Statistics of Russian foreign trade in the eighteenth century are
notoriously untrustworthy. Moreover, in interpreting the figures
quoted below one should keep in mind that the ruble began to de-
preciate in 1771 and that by 1796 it had lost, in terms of foreign cur-
rencies, about one-third of its nominal value. According to the data
of Storch quoted by Kulisher, the value of the total Russian foreign
trade increased from the annual average of 29.4 million rubles in
1773–1777 to 81.6 million rubles in 1793–1797, while the respective
figures of overland trade were only 1.6 million rubles and 4.7 million
rubles. Of the total annual sea-borne trade, which in 1773–1776
averaged 27.8 million rubles, 25.5 million rubles went through the
ports of the Baltic Sea and 1.9 million rubles through those of the
White Sea. In 1793–1797, when the value of Russia's total annual
sea-borne trade reached 76.9 million rubles, the share of the Baltic
Sea was 71.3 million rubles; of the White Sea 3.7 million rubles; and
of the Black Sea and Sea of Azov 1.9 million rubles. Thus, through the
latter part of the eighteenth century almost 90 per cent of Russian
foreign trade was centered in the Baltic ports, and approximately two-
thirds of the sea-borne trade went through St. Petersburg (an average
of 51 million rubles in 1793–1797).[12]

[11] These provisions were further elaborated in the Russo-Turkish convention of
1779 and the commercial treaty of 1783. The privilege was limited to Russian
merchant vessels "similar" to those of England and France. In virtue of the
"capitulations," British and French merchant ships enjoyed the right of using
western Turkish ports but were not permitted to penetrate the Bosphorus.

[12] The following figures of Russian foreign trade quoted by Professor Miliukov
are not strictly comparable with those of Storch and Kulisher:

Annual average:	1759–1763	1774–1778	1794–1798
	(in million rubles)		
Exports	11	19	57
Imports	8	13	39

An investigation held by the department of commerce in 1794 reached the conclusion that official returns of foreign trade presented a grossly distorted picture.
According to the department's report, dutiable imports had been systematically
undervalued for customs purposes with the result that the actual balance of trade

The chief articles of export were hemp and flax, flat iron, rough linen cloth (for reexport to the West Indies and South America), sail cloth, timber, cordage, bristles, hides, and furs. The export of grain, which went chiefly through Riga but later also through Taganrog, increased considerably (from an average of 32,000 chetvert [13] in 1717–1719 to 400,000 chetvert in 1793–1795), but the great expansion of grain exports did not take place until the nineteenth century. Principal imports were woolen cloth for army uniforms and luxury articles such as wines and spirits, cane sugar, silks, cottons, dyestuffs, tea, coffee, and fruit.

The promotion of merchant shipping by a variety of measures inspired by the Navigation Acts was inaugurated in Russia by Peter I and was continued under his successors. Substantial rebates on import and export duties were granted to goods which entered or left the country in vessels of Russian registry. The average number of such ships in Russian ports was 227 in 1773–1777 and increased to 350 in 1793–1797. According to Kulisher, however, Russian registry in the majority of cases meant little. It was acquired either by the naturalization of foreign owners or by taking advantage of a provision of the law which extended the protection of the Russian flag to any vessel with a specified percentage of Russian subjects in its crew. These subterfuges deprived the treasury of legitimate revenue and in no way contributed to the promotion of national shipping. All special privileges enjoyed by Russian merchantmen were revoked by Emperor Paul in 1797.

The foreign wars of Catherine imposed on public finance a burden which was further aggravated by costly administrative reforms, lavish court expenditure, and the munificence displayed by the empress towards her many favorites. The disorder of the financial administration under Elizabeth and the huge cost of her campaigns against Prussia had brought Russia to the verge of bankruptcy. Catherine did not exaggerate the situation when on July 14, 1762, she wrote to her ambassador in Warsaw, Count Kayserling: "I shall tell you the plain truth: my treasury is empty and will remain empty until I put some order in public finance, which cannot be done at a moment's notice." This commendable intention, like so many others, was never realized, and at Catherine's death Russia not only had a large budget deficit

---

was in all probability adverse, and not favorable to Russia, as it had been made to appear by official statistics.

[13] One chetvert = 5.8 bushels.

but was also saddled with a substantial foreign and domestic debt.

In studying Russian public finance during this period, it must be emphasized again that available data, like those on industry and foreign trade, are incomplete, unreliable, and at times hopelessly contradictory. According to the instruction of the Senate to its deputy on the Legislative Commission of 1767–1768, "Sources of state revenue are so ill defined and confused (*sputany i zameshany*) that up to the present time it has been impossible to ascertain what they actually are." The table of state revenue (*okladnaia kniga*) compiled in 1769 by Prince Viazemsky and Alexis Melgunov, and similar surveys prepared in later years, meritorious as they were, failed to produce a clear picture of the financial situation, and returns of the yield of certain taxes for a number of years are not available. Professor Chechulin, author of the leading study on public finance under Catherine, and his penetrating but not unfriendly critic Lappo-Danilevsky are emphatic in pointing out how untrustworthy were contemporary estimates both of revenue and of expenditure. "The determination of deficits, for instance," writes Chechulin, "always involves so many assumptions, reservations, and qualifications, that it is almost impossible to state their actual amounts."

According to the computations of Chechulin, the net state revenue increased from 14.5 million rubles in 1763 to 55.4 million rubles in 1796.[14] The chief sources of revenue were the poll tax, which over the whole period provided more than 33 per cent of the total receipts (5.7 million rubles in 1763 and 24.7 million rubles in 1796); spirits 25 per cent (4.4 million rubles and 15.0 million rubles); salt 7 to 10 per cent (1.5 million rubles and 5.2 million rubles); customs 10 per cent (2.0 million rubles and 6.5 million rubles). Expenditure, however, increased more rapidly than revenue,[15] and the government endeavored to bridge the gap by the issuance of paper money and by foreign borrowing. The possibilities of paper currency had attracted some attention in Russia from the days of Peter I, who sought to induce John Law to come to St. Petersburg after he had suffered disaster in France. Peter III, by a decree of May 25, 1762, provided for the establishment of a state bank for the issue of assignats (bank notes), but this order was

---

[14] The net revenue is obtained by deducting the cost of collection from the gross revenue. The gross revenue was 18.6 million rubles in 1763 and 73.1 million rubles in 1796.

[15] The total expenditure was 17.2 million rubles in 1763 and 78.2 million rubles in 1796.

repealed after the revolution of June 28. The outbreak of hostilities with Turkey and the need of funds to meet war expenditure, however, forced the government to change its mind. A decree of December 29, 1768, established two banks for the issue of assignats, one in St. Petersburg and one in Moscow. The issue of bank notes was originally limited to one million rubles, convertible on demand, but it was not long before these restrictions were dropped. By 1774 the circulation of bank notes had increased to 20 million rubles; by 1785 to 45–46 million rubles; and the manifesto of June 28, 1786, raised the limit of issue to 100 million rubles.[16] The latter measure was due to the exigencies of the impending war with Turkey and the heavy drain suffered by the treasury as a consequence of the introduction of new and costly institutions of local government. In spite of the solemn and explicit promise of the manifesto that the limit of 100 million rubles would "never" be exceeded, the printing of bank notes was resumed in 1790, and by 1796 the volume of paper currency in circulation reached 156 million rubles. The immoderate use of the printing press had its inevitable consequences. The depreciation of the assignats began, according to Lappo-Danilevsky, in 1771; convertibility into silver was suspended in 1777; and by 1796 the actual value of the paper ruble had declined to 68 per cent of its nominal value.

The international position of the ruble was further weakened by foreign borrowing, which required annual payments abroad because of interest and amortization. Foreign borrowing was inaugurated in 1769, simultaneously with the issue of paper money. During the reign of Catherine the Russian government negotiated sixteen foreign loans, chiefly in Holland, to the total amount of 93 million gulden (approximately 52.7 million rubles). About one-third of this sum was used for purposes of conversion and amortization, and by the end of the reign the total net foreign indebtedness was 62 million gulden, or at the then prevailing rate of exchange, 35.4 million rubles. There also came into existence a domestic debt of some 24.5 million rubles, which consisted of sums owed by the treasury to various firms and those borrowed by the government from the deposits of the state-owned banks. According to Khodsky, the total foreign and domestic indebtedness (including the assignats in circulation) had reached towards the end

---

[16] Lappo-Danilevsky quotes interesting archive documents which prove that the decision to increase the issue of paper currency to 100 million rubles was reached by the government as early as Jan. 30, 1785.

of the reign of Catherine 215 million rubles, that is, it was roughly equal to the cumulative budget deficit, which Chechulin estimated at some 200 million rubles. The annual payments on account of interest and amortization of the foreign debt were fixed in January, 1797, at 6 million rubles, with the expectation that the debt would be extinguished not later than 1809. This plan, however, was almost immediately abandoned.

Little can be said in favor of the financial policy of Catherine. Chechulin rightly speaks of the "ineptness of the financial administration, the flagrant inability of the ruling group to deal with current problems, the absence of skilled financiers among the members of the government." The economic advancement of Russia during the eighteenth century, according to the same author, was practically nil, and the sources of state revenue were the same as those of a hundred years before. "The growth of state revenue was in no way due to greater economic activity," writes Chechulin, "but must be explained by the higher rates of taxes and the natural accretion of the population; no new sources of revenue had appeared because nothing new took place in the economic life of the nation. . . . The extreme overburdening of the taxpayers clearly emerges as the inevitable result of financial maladministration and economic stagnation; over a period of thirty years the burden of the taxpayer increased two and a half times; the actual increase in the burden would have been less than is indicated by this figure had the country experienced some economic revival; in the absence of any such development the doubling of the tax payments accurately reflects the twofold increase of the actual tax burden." This gloomy picture drawn by one of Russia's most authoritative historians may be accepted as a fair summary of the economic results of a superficially brilliant reign.

CHAPTER XXII

ENLIGHTENED ABSOLUTISM

The Nobility and the Peasants

------------------------------ ✳ ------------------------------

"THE GOLDEN AGE OF THE NOBILITY"

The second half of the eighteenth century brought to the *dvoriane* the fulfillment of most of their wishes. The manifesto of February 18, 1762, by which Peter III freed them from the obligation of compulsory service, remained in force after the palace revolution of June 28, although the government was uneasy about its probable repercussions in the army and in the civil administration. The report of a commission of high officials appointed early in 1763 to devise suitable measures for encouraging the nobles to enroll voluntarily in government service was deemed unsatisfactory, and no action was taken until 1785. In the meantime the *dvoriane* flocked to their country estates, this time not as mere visitors but as a privileged group eager to stay and to assume the direction of local affairs. This attitude was clearly expressed in the Legislative Commission of 1767–1768 by the spokesmen of the nobility, whose pronouncements, while free from any pretense at imposing constitutional restrictions on the powers of the Crown (such as had confronted Empress Anne in 1730), voiced the desire for a larger share in local government and for the organization of the *dvorianstvo* into autonomous corporations. These aspirations, as has already been pointed out, were partially met by the reform of local government in 1775. A corporate organization nucleus was provided in 1767, when the *dvoriane* of each county (*uezd*) were directed to choose a representative to supervise the election of deputies to the Legislative Commission; this official, who was known as the county marshal of the nobility (*uezdnyi predvoditel dvorianstva*), continued to act as the leader of the local nobles after the elections were over.

The local government act of 1775 provided for the election of the county marshals of the nobility, and since this act introduced the election of various officials by the *dvoriane* of each province (*guberniia*), provincial marshals of the nobility (*gubernskii predvoditel dvorianstva*) made their appearance, although their legal status was not officially recognized until the publication of the Charter of the Nobility, on April 21, 1785. The Charter, a loosely worded and verbose document, recapitulated and expanded the privileges of the *dvoriane* and established the framework of their corporate organization. No nobleman, according to the Charter, could be deprived of his "honor," life, property, and title of nobility (which was hereditary except in the case of "personal nobles," to be discussed below) without a trial by his peers. The Charter confirmed the right of the nobles to resign at will from government service, to travel abroad, and to enter the service of friendly foreign states. They were to be free to dispose of the property they had acquired, but were forbidden to transfer hereditary estates in contravention of the law. If a nobleman was convicted on a serious charge, his hereditary estates passed to his heirs instead of being confiscated, as had previously been customary. The *dvoriane* were exempted from corporal punishment, the poll tax, and the billet. They enjoyed the right to own populated estates and houses in urban localities; to sell wholesale, both at home and abroad, the produce of their estates; to own industrial enterprises and to maintain fairs; and to exploit the mineral and forest resources of their landed properties.

The Charter granted the *dvoriane* of each province the right to form a corporation headed by a general assembly and by a provincial marshal of the nobility. The general assemblies, which were held in the provinces (*guberniia*) and counties (*uezd*) at three-year intervals, consisted of hereditary nobles. They elected the provincial and county marshals and the officials provided for by the act of 1775. The powers of the corporations were strictly limited. The provincial marshal of the nobility acted as chairman of a board of deputies of the nobility, one from each county, a body whose principal function consisted in keeping an up-to-date register of local nobles and in passing on the qualifications of prospective members. The officers of the corporation administered certain funds, raised for professional and cultural purposes, as well as the estates of widows and orphans. The corporations were entitled to petition the Crown, the Senate, the governors-general, and the governors, but only concerning matters of immediate interest to the nobles. Since petitions deemed contrary to the law and therefore "unreasonable" (*nedelnyia*) were punishable by fines (Article 49), this right was seldom used and played no part in the political and constitutional history of Russia. The Charter made no provision for a national organization of the nobility, and the corporations it established dealt exclusively with local matters. They were formed, moreover, only in provinces which had an "adequate" number of noble landowners. On the eve of the revolution of 1917 such corporations were functioning in thirty-nine provinces; none were ever organized in the northern and northeastern provinces of European Russia or in Siberia.

Like the reform of 1775, the Charter of 1785 failed to produce real self-government. All officials elected by the nobles were subject to confirmation by the governor-general or by the governor; although the provincial and county marshals played an important part in local administration, this was rather in their capacity as officers of the Crown than in that of representatives of local interests. The bureaucratic character of the reform was emphasized by a provision (Article 64) which disqualified for holding an elective office or voting in the assembly any nobleman who had never been in government service or who had failed to attain a specified rank in the official hierarchy. The Charter, moreover, repeated the provisions of the Table of Ranks of 1722 which conferred the dignity of hereditary nobility on all army officers and on civil servants who had reached Rank 8 in the hierarchy established by the Table; civil servants of lower ranks were granted the status of "personal nobles." "Personal nobility" (*lichnoe dvorianstvo*) —a quaint and elusive notion—was not hereditary and did not entitle to participation in the corporate activities of the nobility. Government service was thus retained as the normal and chief source of *anoblissement*, much to the disgust of the supporters of the aristocratic principle, such as Prince Michael Shcherbatov.

If the self-government of the nobility had little practical effect, the privileges of the nobles could not have been more tangible and real. The political and economic power of the *dvorianstvo* rested on its exclusive right to own populated landed estates and on the practically unlimited authority it exercised over the servile population. By the middle of the eighteenth century serfdom had reached its full development, and the legislation of Catherine entrenched it even more completely. The noble landowners had gradually acquired the power, which was not clearly vested in them by any law, to dispose of their serfs as they pleased, to move them from one part of the country to another (after notifying a local court, whose approval, however, was not requested), to sell them with or without land, to mortgage them, to give them away as dowry, gift, or in settlement of card debts. The sale of serfs apart from the land often led to the breaking up of peasant families, a practice that was condemned by Peter I in 1721. Fifty years later, in 1771, a decree of Catherine provided merely that such sales should not be made at public auctions, and a decree of 1792 confirmed the rule that while serfs could be sold apart from the land in settlement of their owners' debts the gavel should not be used on these occasions. The sale of serfs as if they were chattels continued until the emancipation of 1861. The owners, moreover, had the power to remove the serfs from the land and to assign them to jobs in their own households. The domestic establishment of a wealthy landowner comprised hundreds of men and women, from stableboys, cooks, footmen, gardeners, tailors, and bootmakers to secretaries, artists, actors, musicians, poets, and even astronomers. They were known as household serfs (*dvorovye*).

The judicial authority of the landowner over his servile population extended to all crimes except murder and robbery. The Elizabethan decree of December 13, 1760, gave the owner power to deport delinquent serfs for settlement in Siberia on condition that the deportees be not older than forty-five and that they be accompanied by their wives, although not necessarily by their children. The exiles were credited towards the owners' quota of army recruits and were freed from any further obligations towards their master. In actual practice the above conditions were often violated, old and decrepit men were sent to Siberia and their wives were prevented from accompanying them. By 1772 over 20,000 former serfs of both sexes were settled in Siberia under the provisions of the decree of 1760, but the actual number of deportees was presumably much larger: mortality among them was extraordinarily high, and there is evidence that only about one-fourth of the persons deported reached their destination. Although some of Catherine's advisers (among them Sievers) urged the repeal of the decree of 1760 as unduly severe, a decree of January 17, 1765, made the law even more stringent. It gave owners the power to sentence serfs to penal servitude in Siberia and then to claim them back whenever they pleased. Although the decree of 1765 would seem to have been repealed in 1773 (Semevsky), the deportation of serfs to Siberia by order of their owners continued unchecked and was specifically confirmed during the reign of Alexander I. Other punishments inflicted by owners upon their serfs included forced enrollment in the army, confinement in a public jail (the owner, however, was to bear the cost of the prisoner's maintenance), detention in chains, and a large assortment of corporal chastisements: rods, lashes, cudgels, and the knout. The selection of the appropriate weapon from this formidable arsenal was left to the discretion of the master. "The punishment of slaves [*sic*]," wrote a keen contemporary French observer, Passenans, "varies according to the frame of mind and disposition of their lord or of his deputy."

This comprehensive authority invited abuse which the law did little to prevent. A decree of 1719 empowered the Senate to remove an owner who mistreated his serfs and to appoint his wife or children administrators of his estate, but this provision was rarely, if ever, invoked. The local government act of 1775 directed provincial governors "to stop all abuse, especially immeasurable and ruinous luxury, to check excesses, immorality, extravagance, tyranny, and cruelty," a well meaning provision which offered no practical protection to the serf. Local administration and the courts, it will be remembered, were in the hands of the *dvoriane*, who displayed unbounded leniency towards evils condoned by an influential body of public opinion. The notorious case of Daria Saltykov (known as "Saltychika"), a bigoted and perverse female monster who was accused of having tortured to death seventy-five of her serfs, was unsuccessfully brought before the courts twenty-one times before it was thoroughly investigated by order of Empress Catherine, and then the case dragged on for six years, from 1762 to 1768. Daria Saltykov, deprived of her title of nobility, publicly exhibited in Moscow as a "torturer and murderer," spent the rest of her life in the prison cell of a convent, where she had a child by one of her guards and where she died in 1801. Her case, however, was quite exceptional. The law was silent on the punishment of landlords guilty of causing the death of their serfs, and of the twenty known instances in the reign of Catherine when action was taken on such charges, only six resulted in sentences of forced labor and two in deportation to Siberia; in the other cases punishment was incarceration in convents or monasteries for terms which varied from one week to twelve months. Of the twenty landlords convicted of cruelty resulting in the death of serfs, nine were women.

In the absence of any legal protection against exploitation and inhuman treatment, the serfs had to rely exclusively on petitions to the Crown. This right, as has been noted, rested on a flimsy legal foundation, but the practice was nevertheless tolerated. It frequently ended, however, in the punishment, not of the landowner, but of the petitioners. Several decrees issued in the early years of the reign of Catherine prohibited the serfs, under the threat of cruel penalties, from petitioning the empress directly. Nevertheless, during a spectacular journey along the Volga in the spring of 1767, Catherine was approached by delegations of serfs seeking redress of their grievances against their masters. These appeals to imperial clemency brought an unexpected response: a decree of August 22, 1767, prohibited *all* complaints by the serfs against their lords; the infringement of the decree was made punishable by the knout and penal servitude for life, the guilty serfs being credited to the owner towards his quota of army recruits. This Draconian edict was issued at the very time when the humanitarian views of Catherine were being aired before the Legislative Commission.

The economic relations between masters and serfs were not regulated by the law, except for the obligation imposed on the owners to provide for their serfs in years of famine and thus prevent them from turning to beggary.[1] This rule, which was repeated in 1767 and in 1772, when the landed proprietors were made subject to a fine of five rubles for each of their serfs found begging, might have had a salutary effect on a small group of wealthy owners, but the majority of the *dvoriane* were much too poor to take care of their destitute serfs in times of stringency even if they had wished to do so. Under serfdom the financial status of a nobleman was reckoned in terms of the "registered souls" (*revizorskaia dusha*) he owned, that is, the number of male serfs credited to him by the last census (*reviziia*). In the second half of the eighteenth century, according to the avowedly incomplete data collected by Semevsky, the leading authority on the peasants in the reign of Catherine II, 59 per cent of the landed proprietors owned less than 21 male serfs each; 25 per cent from 21 to 100; and 16 per cent over 100. It is impossible to determine from contemporary data

[1] See p. 485.

the distribution of the servile population among these three groups of landed proprietors. In 1834, however, according to the computation of Koeppen quoted by Semevsky, 5 per cent of the total number of male serfs belonged to "small" proprietors (less than 21 male serfs each); 15 per cent to the "medium" proprietors (21 to 100 male serfs each); and 80 per cent to the "big" proprietors (over 100 male serfs each). The actual concentration of wealth was even greater than is suggested by these striking figures. In 1834, in Great Russia (*Veliko-rossiia*) the 3 per cent of the landowners having in their possession over 500 male serfs each owned 45 per cent of the total servile population, and 870 magnates (about 1 per cent of the landed proprietors) owned 2,038,000 male serfs, or 30 per cent of the total. Although the above computations, which do not include Ukraine, have no claim to mathematical exactness, one may agree with Semevsky that they probably present a reasonably accurate picture of the distribution of servile labor among the *dvoriane*, not only in 1834 but also in the second half of the eighteenth century.

THE PEASANTS

The term "peasants" (*krestiane*) was used in eighteenth and nineteenth century Russia to denote the entire rural population subject to the poll tax. According to the third census (1762–1766) there were 7.2 million male peasants in Great Russia and Siberia, a territory which did not include Ukraine. Of this number 2.8 million, or 39.2 per cent, were state peasants (*gosudarstvennye* or *kazennye krestiane*) [2] and 3.8 million, or 53.2 per cent, were serfs, that is, peasants in the possession of the nobility. Four hundred and ninety-five thousand peasants (6.9 per cent) lived on the domains of the Crown and the imperial family (*dvortsovye* and *gosudarevy krestiane*), and there was a small group of some 48,000 "possessionary" peasants (0.7 per cent).[3] Throughout the second half of the eighteenth century the above distribution of the peasants remained practically unchanged. In 1794–1796, when the fifth census was taken, the 5.7 million serfs represented 53.1 per cent of the male peasant population, which had risen to 10.7 million. Catherine's lavish gifts of populated estates to generals and to her favorites

---

[2] Before the secularization of 1764, the number of state peasants was 1.8 million; in 1764 it was increased to 2.8 million after the taking over by the state of the 992,000 male peasants living on the former ecclesiastical estates.

[3] See pp. 389–390, 559.

had no appreciable effect upon the onward march of serfdom in Great Russia because such grants were made chiefly in Ukraine and in the territories annexed from Poland. At the beginning of her reign, according to Semevsky, serfs constituted about 45 per cent of the total population of Great Russia and Siberia.[4]

The territorial distribution of the various groups of the peasantry was uneven and, roughly, the percentage of serfs declined in the east and in the north. According to the fourth census (1781–1783), in the province of Kaluga 83 per cent of the peasants were serfs; in Smolensk and Tula 80 per cent; in Riazan 75 per cent; in Moscow 66 per cent; in Novgorod 55 per cent; in Tambov 45 per cent; in Vologda 34 per cent; in Perm 33 per cent; in Ufa 21 per cent; in Kazan 18 per cent; in Olonetsk 6 per cent; in Viatka 2 per cent. In the province of Archangel and in Siberia there were practically no serfs. This distribution of the servile population explains why the corporations of the nobility created by the Charter of 1785 were never organized in the northeastern provinces and in Siberia.

There was a basic difference in the legal status of the serfs and that of all other groups of the peasantry. Serfs, as has already been stated, could be sold with the land or apart from it; the state peasants, as well as the peasants settled on the estates of the Crown and of the imperial family, were regarded as permanently attached to the land, and they could not be sold. The importance of this safeguard, which eliminated some of the worst features of serfdom (such as the breaking up of peasant families), was minimized by the fact that the populated estates held by the state, the Crown, and the imperial family were not infrequently made over to members of the nobility, with the result that the population of such estates was reduced to the status of serfs. Some of the state peasants, moreover, were compulsorily attached to government-owned and privately owned mines, ironworks, quarries, factories, distilleries, lumber mills, and shipyards, where they worked a part of the year in fulfillment of their obligations towards the state. The wages of these forced laborers were extremely low, the discipline cruel and ruthless, and the unfortunate men had occasionally to travel hundreds of miles to their place of employment. In the 1760's some 100,000 state peasants were attached to privately owned enterprises in the Urals. Towards the end of the reign of Catherine the total num-

---

[4] It is estimated that serfs constituted 45 per cent of the population of European Russia in 1836, and 37.5 per cent in 1859.

ber of men engaged in compulsory work of this type was estimated at nearly 500,000. The truly atrocious conditions of their employment were made abundantly clear in the authoritative firsthand reports of Prince Viazemsky (1762) and Volkov, governor of Perm (1792). Nothing, however, was done to improve their position.

The financial obligations of the state peasants consisted of the poll tax and the *obrok*, which was a rent payable to the state for the use of land allotments. The poll tax was 70 copecks a year per male peasant in 1760, and this was increased to one ruble in 1794. The *obrok*, which was 40 copecks a year per male peasant in 1723 when it was first introduced, was raised to one ruble in 1761, to two rubles in 1768, and to three rubles in 1783. A revealing memorandum submitted to the empress in April, 1783, by Prince Viazemsky and his associates advocated an increase in the *obrok* of the state peasants on the ground that their financial burden was lighter than that of the serfs and that the resulting inequality incited the latter to "disobedience to their masters and to various acts of insubordination." The memorandum argued, not very convincingly, that "light taxes lead to idleness just as an excessive tax burden discourages honest endeavor." In addition to their financial obligations the state peasants were required to provide recruits for the army, to repair roads, and so on.

Although the state peasants were, in theory, permanently attached to their allotments, there developed among them the practice of disposing of the land they occupied as if it were their private property. Allotments were leased out, mortgaged, given as dowry, and sold not only to other state peasants but to outsiders, such as merchants, burghers, and the clergy. The unrestricted transfer of land led to the accumulation of considerable landed properties in the hands of some of the state peasants, while others were greatly impoverished and found it difficult or impossible to meet their tax obligations. The resulting desire of the holders of small allotments for an equalitarian distribution of land among the inhabitants of rural communes coincided with the interests of the government, always mindful of the needs of the treasury. The 1766 instruction for land surveying ordered the restitution, without compensation, to the communes of state peasants of land that had been transferred to the ownership of members of other social groups; further transfers of land to outsiders as well as among the state peasants were prohibited except with the permission of the authorities. Although this measure was not always enforced, it deprived the state peasants of much of the economic freedom they had traditionally enjoyed. Moreover, the instruction of 1766 was followed by several decrees which had for their object the promotion among the state peasants of communal land tenure based on the equalitarian principle. Under this system the land of a peasant commune was periodically redistributed among its members on the basis either of the labor power (number of adult males) or of the consumption needs (number of people receiving maintenance) of each household. In the administration of their communal affairs the state peasants enjoyed some degree of self-government, electing their own officials, whose activities, needless to say, were carried on under the close supervision of Crown officers, especially of the police.

The eighteenth century brought no improvement in the legal status of the state peasants; their tax burden was increased manyfold, and their customary right to dispose of their land allotments was restricted. Their general status, however (with the exception of peasants attached to mines and factories), was probably more favorable than that of the majority of the serfs. The state peasants could not be removed from the land; their tax burden was lighter and their allotments, as a rule, larger than those of the serfs; they enjoyed a greater degree of self-government, and—last but not least—they were not exposed to daily arbitrary interference by landed proprietors vested with almost unlimited powers. They were, however, practically defenseless against the unlawful exactions and misrule of police and other officials.

The legal and economic status of the peasants living on the estates owned by the Crown and by the imperial family or on estates formerly belonging to the Church was not very different from that of the state peasants. Secularization, therefore, might be considered a measure beneficial to the peasantry, especially since the Church was among the harshest landlords, even with powers less comprehensive than those of private owners. Monasteries and ecclesiastical dignitaries, for instance, could not sell their peasants or remove them from the land, and the power to deport undesirable men to Siberia by virtue of the decree of December 13, 1760,[5] was in this case conditional on the confirmation of this verdict by the village assembly and peasant officials. After secularization the portions of the estates formerly farmed directly by ecclesiastical owners were transferred to the local peasants and their allotments were thus increased.

[5] See p. 485.

The relatively liberal treatment of the peasants emancipated from the stern rule of the Church provoked much uneasiness among serf-owners. Even Sievers, a critic of many aspects of serfdom, urged Catherine to lease the former ecclesiastical estates to private persons, while Prince Shcherbatov, that staunch advocate of the exclusive privileges of the nobility, favored the more drastic plan of transferring such estates to private hands by selling them at low prices. The empress, who had long resisted the pressure of reactionary elements, appeared to be on the point of yielding, but her death saved the former Church peasants from their impending doom.

The serfs, like the state peasants, paid the poll tax, provided recruits for the army, repaired roads, and performed other services required by the state. In this respect they differed from the slaves (*kholopy*) in old Muscovy who were rated as chattels and were therefore exempted from direct taxation and from the performance of state-imposed services. The cultivation of the estates of the *dvoriane* was carried on under the system of either *obrok* or *barshchina*. Under the *obrok* system most or all of the land of an estate was farmed on their own account by the serfs, who paid the owner an annual amount known as *obrok*. Under the *barshchina* system only a portion of the land of an estate, and usually the smaller portion, was farmed by the serfs on their own account, while the bulk of the land was managed directly by the owner and was cultivated by compulsory servile labor (the French *corvée*). Under *barshchina* the serfs paid no monetary tribute to the owner but discharged their obligations towards him by working on his fields and by rendering other services. The amount of the *obrok* paid by a male serf increased, according to Semevsky, from the annual average of between one and two rubles in the 1760's, to from two to three rubles in the 1770's, four rubles in the 1780's and five rubles in the 1790's.[6] The amount of the *obrok* being determined by the owners, there was a great variety in the actual sum exacted. Moreover, the *obrok* of the serfs, like the poll tax and the *obrok* of state peasants, belonged to the "apportioned" type of taxation, that is, every rural community was assessed a sum which was usually arrived at by multiplying the per capita rate of the *obrok* (or poll tax) by the number of male inhabitants as determined by the latest census. The actual apportioning of the levy among the serfs was sometimes influenced by their

[6] It should be noted that during the same period the price of bread increased approximately three times.

economic status; invalids and indigent householders might obtain a partial or complete exemption, while well-to-do villagers paid a great deal more than their proportional share. The *obrok* of some of the wealthy serfs reached the impressive figure of several hundred rubles. It was customary to supplement the monetary *obrok* by deliveries in kind which comprised every type of farm produce: hay, oats, firewood, sheep, fowl, game, pork, butter, eggs, cucumbers, cabbage, berries, turnips, mushrooms, homespun cloth, and so on. The transportation of these supplies to the sometimes distant residence of the owner put the serfs to much expense and inconvenience. Although it is hazardous to venture an even approximate estimate of the monetary value of the deliveries in kind and of the occasional services performed by the serfs under the *obrok* system, Semevsky has tentatively evaluated them at one-third of their average money payments. Many of the owners, moreover, exacted no deliveries in kind and others reduced the amount of the money *obrok* to compensate their serfs for such deliveries and for the occasional services they were called upon to render.

Under the *barshchina* system the number of days the serfs were required to work for their master was left to his discretion except for the provision of the Code of 1649 which prohibited work on Sundays and holidays. The prevailing custom was for the serfs, both male and female, to work three days a week for their lord and three days on their allotments. There were, of course, many departures from this arrangement, and the petitions of the serfs and other contemporary documents disclose that some of the bondsmen were forced to work for their masters four, five, six, and even seven days a week. The serfs, much to the detriment of their own farms, were required to give an exceptionally heavy share of their time during the harvest. The length of the working day varied from eleven to as much as sixteen hours. The serfs on the *barshchina* estates, like those under the *obrok* system, supplied the owner with specified quotas of agricultural produce and, in addition to the cultivation of his fields, performed for him other services, but they were seldom called upon to make supplementary money payments. The removal of the serfs from the land and their assignment to jobs in their master's household (which put them in the class of landless household serfs—*dvorovye*) was relatively rare, but a large number of serfs were compulsorily attached as part or full-time workers to industrial enterprises owned by their masters, a most unpopular form of employment against which the serfs vainly protested. The land allotments of serfs on the *barshchina* estates were, as a rule, smaller than those under the *obrok* system, and the exactions of the owners were heavier. In Great Russia, according to Semevsky, the total payments of the *barshchina* serfs were probably twice as large as the payments of the *obrok* serfs. With the purpose of attracting settlers and discouraging the flight of the servile population to near-by Poland, the economic position of the serfs in Ukraine had been made more favorable.

The serfs, like the state peasants, traditionally enjoyed a limited right of self-government; this they exercised under the control of their master or his representative. The owner had power to set aside any decision of the village assembly, to remove elected officials, and to appoint new ones. In practice such interference was rare, and in the great majority of cases village authorities were permitted to function unmolested, provided state taxes and the tributes exacted by the owner were forthcoming. The superintendent of an estate (*prikashchik*) was always appointed by the owner, to whom he was personally responsible. The chief organ of peasant self-government was the village assembly, which consisted of adult male householders. The normal functions of the assembly comprised the election of village officials (the elder, assistant elder, treasurer, collector of revenue, bookkeeper, policemen); participation in the administration of justice and in the determination of punishments; apportionment of taxes and tributes among the householders; selection of recruits for the army; administration of funds raised for communal purposes such as wages of village officials, relief of the poor, bribing of authorities; administration of the equalitarian distribution of land among the households on those estates where communal land tenure was in force. As a rule, serfs under the *obrok* system enjoyed greater autonomy than did those on the *barshchina* estates, and their general status was not very different from that of state peasants, although their financial burden was appreciably greater. Above all, they were largely immune from that curse of serfs under *barshchina*, arbitrary interference by the owner. In eighteenth century Russia, as in other countries of continental Europe, it became customary to submit the everyday life of the serfs to meticulous regulations which only too often degenerated into petty tyranny. Resident owners were tempted to duplicate on a small scale on their estates that regime of "enlightened absolutism" of which Catherine was so outspoken a champion. Paternalistic rule, however, seldom took the form of providing for the real economic and educational needs of the bondsmen. A few of the landed magnates maintained homes for their aged and indigent serfs and established schools, but such enlightened policies were rare exceptions and, according to Semevsky, all village schools had ceased to function before the end of the century. The ministration to the spiritual needs of the serfs expressed itself more frequently in such measures as the imposition of heavy penalties on bondsmen who absented themselves from Church services or became converted to the "heresy" of the old-believers; and the munificence of the masters seldom went further than the distribution of occasional glasses of vodka and beer and the convocation of villagers to more or less copious meals on Church holidays.

In view of the difference in the position of the serfs under *obrok* and under *barshchina*, the proportional distribution of the servile population between these two groups is of importance. A careful analysis of the pertinent source material has led Semevsky to the conclusion that in the second half of the eighteenth century 44 per cent of the serfs in Great Russia lived under the *obrok* system and 56 per cent under the *barshchina* system. The *obrok* system was prevalent in the areas where conditions were less favorable to agriculture and on the estates of the big landowners; the *barshchina* system, on the other hand, was commonly found in the fertile black-soil zone and on the estates of the smaller owners.[7] From the standpoint of the landed proprietors the *obrok* system had the advantage of reducing the administration of their estates to the relatively simple operation of collecting tributes. In spite of the influx of the *dvoriane* into the countryside after the manifesto of February 18, 1762, which freed them from the obligation of compulsory service, absentee landownership continued to be common. The *dvoriane* had grown accustomed to the greater amenities and comforts of city life, government service remained the chief road

----

[7] These conclusions are not generally accepted. Catherine in her *Instruction* maintained that "practically all villagers are under the *obrok* system." This opinion was shared by the eighteenth century writers Storch and Rychkov and has been endorsed by Kliuchevsky. "From the middle of the eighteenth century . . ." writes Kliuchevsky, "it became clear that the *obrok* system definitely predominated on the estates of the *dvoriane*." He supports this statement by references to the views of Catherine, Storch, and Rychkov, which Semevsky has shown to be over-optimistic. Incidentally, Catherine, Storch, and Rychkov believed that while the *obrok* system was advantageous from the point of view of individual owners, it was detrimental to agriculture because it offered the serfs an opportunity to seek outside employment and thus induced them to neglect their farms.

to social advancement and government salaries an often essential supplement to the meager revenue of small proprietors, and—last but not
least—frequent peasant uprisings, especially the wholesale slaughter
of the noble landlords during the peasant war of 1773–1774, acted as
a powerful deterrent, causing many squires to hesitate about establishing their residence in isolated manor houses.

The economic position of the serfs was anomalous because of the
many limitations on their right to own private property. Their movable property was not protected by law against appropriation by their
lord, but it was customary to grant them the enjoyment of such property provided they had met their financial obligations towards both
the state and their owner. A decree of 1730 specifically provided that
serfs might not own real estate in urban localities, and a decree of
August 1, 1737, allowed them to purchase agricultural land only in
the name of their lord and with his permission. In spite of these restrictions serfs owned town houses, populated estates, and industrial
enterprises which were registered in the name of their masters. Cotton
mills, one of the most prosperous branches of Russian industry in the
first half of the nineteenth century, were founded and owned largely
by the serfs of Count Sheremetev. Some of the serfs accumulated fortunes that ran into hundreds of thousands of rubles, and they enjoyed
the *de facto* right to dispose of them as they pleased, subject to the
formal consent of their owner. Infringements of this customary rule,
although not unknown, were rare: serfowners usually shared in the
prosperity of their serfs, thus deriving considerable personal benefits.
Populated estates, as well as individual serfs, were sometimes purchased by peasant communes in the name of the owner. In 1794, on
some of the estates of Count Sheremetev, one-seventh of the entire
servile population was the *de facto* property of the other serfs. One
of the reasons for the purchase of serfs by serfs was the desire to escape
military service, an obligation that the peasants dreaded even more
than they hated serfdom. As the date of the levy of recruits drew
nearer, village communes—sometimes with the financial assistance
of the owner—raised the funds to buy the number of able-bodied
men necessary to meet their quota of recruits. The demand was brisk,
and the price of a man fit for the army rose from 150 rubles in the
1760's to 300 rubles in the 1770's and to 400 rubles in the 1780's.[8] The

---

[8] This was considerably higher than the average price of a male serf. The price
of a landed estate, including the value of the land, was reckoned in terms of male

practice of purchasing recruits, which was also common among state peasants, was among the most obnoxious features of serfdom, and a decree of 1766 made a half-hearted attempt to discourage it by prohibiting, during a period of three months preceding the army draft, the sales of able-bodied men apart from the land. This, incidentally, was the only restriction (and one that proved ineffective) on the right of the owners to sell their serfs without the land.

Serfdom was a hereditary status, transmitted by a serf to his children. It could be terminated by enrollment in the army, by deportation to Siberia under the terms of the decree of December 13, 1760, or by emancipation voluntarily granted by the owner. In the first two cases the cure was probably worse than the disease; moreover, the selection of recruits was decided not by the men themselves, but by the owner and superintendent of the estate or by the village assembly. Even the more enlightened landed proprietors, such as the Sheremetev, were reluctant to emancipate their serfs, and Catherine had refused to follow the advice of Sievers, who urged that the price at which serfs should be entitled to purchase their freedom be fixed by law. A decree of 1775 prohibited the emancipated serfs from resuming their former servile status. However, since eighteenth century Russia, like the Muscovy of the seventeenth century, would not tolerate citizens who were not definitely affiliated with one of the social and legal groups into which the population was subdivided, the freemen were ordered to join the ranks of the merchants, burghers, or state peasants.

An important landmark in the development of serfdom was its formal introduction in Ukraine and the regions of southeastern Russia. The position of the once-free peasantry in Ukraine had progressively deteriorated from the time of its annexation by Russia in 1654. Nevertheless, in the middle of the eighteenth century Ukrainian peasants still enjoyed the theoretical right to give up their tenancy and move from one landlord to another, although the practical exercise of this right was hindered by various restrictions. In 1763 a change of tenancy was made subject to written permission from the landlord, and freedom of movement was formally abolished in some of the Ukrainian provinces in 1765 and in the whole of the land in 1783. By a decree of

---

serfs, that is, of the entire male population (which included not only able-bodied men but also children, invalids, and old people), as determined by the latest census. The average price of a male serf as defined above was 30 rubles at the beginning of the reign of Catherine, 80 rubles in the 1780's, and 200 rubles in the 1790's.

December 12, 1796, issued by Emperor Paul but presumably prepared during Catherine's lifetime, the attachment of peasants to their allotments was extended to the remaining southeastern regions, including the Caucasus and the territory of the Don. The poll tax, as already stated, was introduced in Ukraine by a decree of May 3, 1783. The combined effect of these measures was to reduce the peasantry in the regions affected to the status of Russian serfs and to eliminate the last area within the empire where rebellious bondsmen could still hope to make a living as free men.

It is difficult to find a more striking contrast than that offered by the glorification of the ideas of the Enlightenment and human rights in the writings and pronouncements of Catherine and her practical policies in the peasant question. Great pressure, no doubt, was brought to bear upon her by the reactionary landed interests to which she owed her Crown. Not all of the landed proprietors, however, were blind to the realities of the peasant problem and the dangers it presented. In 1763 General Peter Panin, a man of conservative views, submitted to the empress a memorandum in which he proposed the enactment of legislation defining the rights of the landowners over the serfs and removing at least some of the more flagrant inequities of serfdom, such as the sale of individual serfs without the land and the breaking up of peasant families. Sievers, an outstanding administrator and diplomat, advanced a somewhat similar view in 1765, and on numerous occasions pleaded with the empress for legislative intervention on behalf of the serfs. The records of the Legislative Commission of 1767–1768 bear evidence that a measure of support for a more liberal policy towards the peasantry was not lacking among the rank and file of the *dvoriane*. None of these proposals was in any sense revolutionary, nor did they contemplate the abolition of serfdom, but merely the granting to the servile population of minimum legal protection against the cupidity and capricious rule of the landed proprietors. Catherine invariably turned a deaf ear to these councils of decency, moderation, and common sense, and at the end of her reign the institution of serfdom was more formidable, ruthless, and firmly entrenched than it had ever been before. The theories of Voltaire and Montesquieu, which lent so pleasing a flavor of intellectual distinction and liberalism to the conversation of the polished courtiers who surrounded the empress and the favorite of the day in the elegant salons of the Winter Palace and in the exquisite gardens of the summer residences, were confined to this charmed circle and left no imprint on the social legislation of what the historians like to call the enlightened age of Catherine.

THE PEASANT WAR, 1773–1774

The emancipation of the *dvoriane* from compulsory service and the increased rigor of serfdom contributed to the social unrest that forms the background of Russian history in the seventeenth and eighteenth centuries. Unfounded rumors that the manifesto of February 18, 1762, would be followed by the emancipation of the serfs were widely circulated and were given credence by the masses of the peasantry. The endeavor of the government to discourage such hopes (for instance, the manifesto of June 19, 1762, which ordered the serfs to render complete obedience to their masters) failed to check the sanguine expectations that had been generated by a spontaneous protest against increased hardships.

The flight of the serfs, so frequently mentioned in these pages, continued undiminished, and led to much repetitious legislation designed to bring about, by a combination of threats and promises of forgiveness and special privileges, repatriation of the fugitives and return to their abandoned villages. Poland, until her extinction as a sovereign state, was one of the favorite havens of the discontented Russian peasantry, especially those from the border provinces. This is why the partition of Poland and the extension of serfdom to Ukraine and to those southeastern territories that had also attracted large numbers of fugitive serfs were received with profound satisfaction by the serfowners: if the government of Catherine did nothing to remove the conditions that prompted the flight of the bondsmen, it effectively closed all avenues of escape.[9]

The same factors that caused the flight of the serfs were behind the ominous spread of popular uprisings and the outbreak of the Peasant War of 1773–1774. A peculiar set of circumstances permitted a rebellion led by an obscure Cossack, Emelian Pugachev, to assume dimensions unprecedented since the great upheaval of the Time of Troubles

[9] The mass flight of the serfs was of vital concern to the owners; not only did it deprive them of free labor or the revenue it represented, but it also increased the burdens of the remaining serfs, who were responsible for the share of taxes and the quotas of recruits that should have been borne by the fugitives. Increased burdens fostered discontent and incited the remaining serfs to desertion or rebellion.

and to threaten the very foundation of Catherine's rule. Some of the conditions explaining the temporary success of Pugachev were general, while others were local. Persistent rumors of the impending emancipation of the serfs were revived with new force in 1767–1768, in connection with the much-advertised activities of the Legislative Commission, only to be dashed to the ground by measures of repression, such as the decree of August 22, 1767, prohibiting all complaints by the serfs against their masters, and by the dissolution of the Commission itself. The palace revolutions, which had decided the succession to the throne since the death of Peter I, had undermined the traditional prestige of the Crown, and the murders of Peter III in 1762 and of the deposed Ivan VI in 1764 brought forth the usual crop of crude impostors claiming to be one or the other of the former tsars who had miraculously escaped assassination. At least half a dozen pretenders masquerading as Peter III made their appearance in various parts of the country between 1762 and 1772 and gained some local recognition, but were quickly suppressed by government action. Insignificant in themselves, the pretenders served as a rallying point of the forces of discontent and of the hopes of the masses that they might achieve through direct action the relief denied to them by a weak but obstinate government. "Everyone was angry," wrote a contemporary observer (Pospelov), "and merely waited for a pretext for rebellion; this pretext was furnished by Pugachev." According to Bibikov, commander of the government troops sent against the insurgents, "Pugachev himself is unimportant; what is important is general indignation."

Emelian Pugachev, a Don Cossack born in 1726, had served with some distinction in the Russian army during the Seven Years' War. His life story previous to 1773 is a bewildering saga of military campaigns in foreign lands, desertion, imprisonment, escape, and wanderings, an Odyssey typical of the experiences of many frontiersmen. A timely escape from a Kazan jail in May, 1773, saved him from the usual flogging and from a sentence of forced labor at Pelym. In September, 1773, he raised the banner of rebellion in the territory of the Yaik (later Ural) Cossacks east of the Volga and definitely assumed the name of Peter III, which he had occasionally used since November, 1772.

The general situation in the provinces of Orenburg and Kazan, where the Pugachev movement originated, was favorable to the uprising. The scattered population of these vast regions numbered many who nursed against the government old grudges that had been aggravated by recent vexations. The Yaik Cossacks, who formed the nucleus of the insurgent movement, in January, 1772, had murdered a general sent from St. Petersburg to arbitrate their quarrels, and in the summer of the same year they suffered cruel reprisals at the hands of a punitive expedition. The Cossacks of the Urals and the Don, moreover, were alarmed by the reorganization of their force which had been decided upon by the central government. The old-believers, numerous and influential in the Volga region, revered the memory of Peter III for having removed some of their disabilities, and they supported Pugachev, who showed respect for the "old faith" although he did not himself belong to the dissenters. The nomadic native tribes—the Bashkirs, Tartars, Kirghizes, and others—had lost, through distribution to Russian settlers, much of the land they considered their own, and they were incensed both by the ruthless methods of the missionaries who forced them to embrace Christianity and by the exactions and misrule of government officials. The tens of thousands of forced laborers in the mines and works of the Urals had invariably exhibited a rebellious spirit, easily explained by the inhuman conditions of their employment. The provinces of Orenburg and Kazan, moreover, were teeming with fugitive serfs and escaped convicts ready to join any subversive movement. In the city of Kazan alone the number of convicts, eventually released by Pugachev, is said to have been about four thousand. It was the enthusiastic support of these groups, as well as the general sympathy of the peasantry, that was largely responsible for the temporary success of the insurrection. On the other hand, the progress of Pugachev was favored by the weakness of local authorities, the lack of reliable troops, and the unpreparedness and ineptitude of the central government, which was severely handicapped by its involvement in the first partition of Poland and by the Turkish war.

Pugachev's following, which when he opened his campaign in September, 1773, did not exceed eighty men, increased by leaps and bounds, and it is said that at times he had under his command as many as twenty or even thirty thousand irregular troops. They did not constitute an organized army, but were rather large groups of guerrillas who occasionally fought with desperate courage but were incapable of a sustained effort and had no proper leadership. Hence the peculiar character of the campaign, with the columns of Pugachev moving about over the immense area along the Volga, from Perm to

Tsaritsin, with government troops in close pursuit. The inherent weakness of the insurgents became apparent every time they met with organized resistance. They won several important victories, occupied Saratov and Kazan, but were unable to take Ufa and Orenburg, which they besieged for several months. The military success of Pugachev was particularly impressive in the autumn of 1773 and in the early summer of 1774, when it was believed that the road to Moscow was open to him.

The political program of Pugachev was indefinite, vague, and somewhat contradictory. He promised his followers freedom from the rule of the landowners, the restoration of the "old faith," prohibition of shaving beards and of wearing foreign clothes, an equitable administration, and prosperity and happiness for all. He did not wish to rule the country himself, but spoke of removing Catherine as a usurper and of placing on the throne the Grand Duke Paul. His immediate entourage was a crude parody of the court and government of St. Petersburg. A truly revolutionary movement was thus carried on under a banner calling for the restoration of the legitimate monarch. The practical policies of Pugachev were those of a reign of terror. The noble landlords bore the brunt of the insurgents' wrath, but no mercy was shown to opponents belonging to other social groups, including the Cossacks and the peasantry. In view of the nature of the struggle, with government troops most of the time on the heels of the rebels and cities and villages changing hands at frequent intervals, the unhappy population of the area affected found itself on the horns of a dilemma: if they refused to submit to Pugachev, they were faced with the knout and gallows; if they submitted the same fate was likely to befall them should government forces retake the place, and vice versa.

The outbreak of the insurrection was at first taken lightly by the local authorities. The news of Pugachev's early successes was not received in St. Petersburg until October, 1773, where it produced the impression of a bombshell in the midst of the elaborate festivities on the occasion of the marriage of the Grand Duke Paul with the Princess of Hesse-Darmstadt. Dreading the effect of the news abroad and its repercussions on the delicate international situation and on that pleasing fiction of a Russia prospering under the benevolent rule of a beloved and enlightened empress, which Catherine had so painstakingly endeavored to build up in Europe with the assistance of Voltaire, Diderot, Grimm, and Madame Geoffrin, the government decided at first to suppress all information about the rebellion. By the middle of December, 1773, however, the situation had taken so serious a turn that the policy of secrecy had to be abandoned. Alexander Bibikov, one of Catherine's trusted advisers, was put in command of the troops sent against Pugachev, and an official announcement of the outbreak of the insurrection was made in a manifesto of December 23. It was feared that the movement might spread to other parts of the country, especially to Moscow, where Prince Michael Volkonsky, commander of the local garrison, anticipated serious disturbances. The situation was well summed up in a letter written by Paul Potemkin to his cousin, the favorite Gregory Potemkin: "*Le peuple n'est pas sûr.*" Nevertheless, Catherine, in her letters to her foreign correspondents, did everything in her power to belittle the importance of the insurrection and facetiously referred to its leader as "le Marquis Pugacheff." But when the news of the capture of Kazan by Pugachev on July 12, 1774, was received in St. Petersburg, the empress could conceal her anxiety no longer and expressed the desire to go to Moscow to assume in person the conduct of the operations against the rebels. She was dissuaded by Nikita Panin from taking a step he considered politically inadvisable. Instead, General Peter Panin, hero of the capture of Bender from the Turks, was appointed to succeed Bibikov, who had died in April. This was no small concession on the part of Catherine, who mistrusted and disliked Peter Panin because of his critical attitude towards the regime and his support of Grand Duke Paul's candidacy for the throne.

She had no reason, however, to regret her choice. The interests of the serfowners were in this case, as in many others, identical with those of the government, and Panin acted with skill and ruthless energy. His task was simplified by the conclusion in July, 1774, of the Russo-Turkish peace, which released for service on the domestic front regular troops and some of the ablest Russian generals, including Suvorov. In spite of wide popular support, the poorly armed, undisciplined, and unorganized bands of Pugachev were unable to offer adequate resistance to government forces, even though some of the latter went over to Pugachev. An insurrection of the Don Cossacks on which Pugachev had counted failed to materialize, and his military following melted away, vanishing as rapidly and spontaneously as it had flocked to his banners. On September 15 Pugachev was surrendered by some of his former supporters to an officer of the imperial army and on November 4 was brought to Moscow. After a searching investigation conducted by Sheshkovsky, head of the security police, Pugachev was tried in the Palace of the Kremlin by an extraordinary court which consisted of the Senate, the Holy Synod, and the higher government officials. On January 11, 1775, he was executed in Moscow, his head was exhibited on a pole, and in four suburbs of the capital parts of his dismembered body were publicly broken on the wheel and then burned. The Synod anathematized Pugachev and his followers, his house in his native village was razed to the ground, and the village itself was moved to the opposite bank of the Don River and renamed. On January 15, 1775, the Yaik Cossacks, who had taken so prominent a part in the movement, were reorganized and given the name of Ural Cossacks. The government did everything in its power to destroy every tangible reminder of the Peasant War and its leader. The nature of the punishment meted out to Pugachev and his followers had, of course, little in common with the humanitarian theories of Beccaria, for which Catherine professed so deep an attachment. Government reprisals were as savage and bloody as the uprising itself. Like its numerous forerunners, the Peasant War of 1773–1774 failed to achieve any constructive purpose; it merely emphasized the inequities of Russia's social and economic order.

==

ENLIGHTENED ABSOLUTISM

Schools, Literature, and Art

———————————— ❊ ————————————

SCHOOLS

The government of Catherine was too absorbed in international wars, administrative reforms, and the suppression of peasant revolts to give practical consideration to the advancement of popular education, a policy that was hardly compatible with the expansion and strengthening of the institution of serfdom. State revenue, it will be remembered, was for the most part inadequate to meet the expenditures for the army, the bureaucracy, and the court, and left no surplus for cultural activities. The upper classes had not yet overcome their aversion to government-sponsored schools, and the few existing schools (with the exception of the St. Petersburg military academy, which offered its graduates important advantages in securing lucrative positions) experienced great difficulty in securing the prescribed number of students. The educational standards of the University of Moscow and of the university attached to the Academy of Science in St. Petersburg—the only two institutions of higher learning—remained deplorably low, and their contribution to the enlightenment of the country was negligible. According to Kliuchevsky, the University of Moscow conferred one degree of doctor of medicine during the entire reign of Catherine. In 1786 a plan was prepared for the founding of three new universities—in Pskov, Chernigov, and Pensa—but no steps were taken to put it into effect.

A gradual infiltration of new educational ideas owed much to the enthusiasm, zeal, and devotion of Ivan Betsky (1704–1795), an illegitimate son of Prince Ivan Trubetskoy, who after his capture in the battle of Narva in 1700 was detained for eighteen years in Sweden as a prisoner of war. Betsky was educated abroad, had traveled extensively in Germany, Holland, Italy, and France, was a close friend of the Russian poet Antiokh Kantemir, had frequented the Paris salon of Madame Geoffrin, and knew the Encyclopedists and Jean Jacques Rousseau. After the accession of Catherine he was appointed president of the Academy of Arts and director of the St. Petersburg military academy. His views on education expressed in his *Report on the Education of Young People of Both Sexes* and his *Plan for the Moscow Orphanage* were inspired by the theories of Rousseau, Locke, and Fénelon. Betsky believed that the chief object of schools was to build up character rather than to impart knowledge; he argued that since environment was the determining factor in molding the minds and hearts of the young people a "new breed of humanity" could be obtained by submitting children, from an early age, to proper influences and by excluding pernicious outside contacts, including those of the family. Betsky, therefore, favored boarding schools as the best method of protecting the young from traditional attitudes and prejudices. Much as Catherine disliked the political views of Rousseau, the idea of changing and improving human nature strongly appealed to her, and she enthusiastically endorsed Betsky's somewhat nebulous theories. The practical results of these policies were not striking. In 1763 the Moscow Orphanage (*Vospitatelnyi dom*) was founded and a similar institution was established in St. Petersburg in 1772. The former inmates of orphanages supported by private contributions were expected eventually to fill the ranks of Russia's practically non-existent middle class (*srednii rod liudei*). The first government-sponsored school for girls of noble families was opened at the Smolny (then Voskresenky) Convent in St. Petersburg in 1764, and a school for girls of the non-privileged class (except serfs) was opened in 1765. Schools for boys of this class (except serfs) were established in 1764 under the auspices of the Academy of Arts and the military academy. Through the generosity of Prokofy Demidov, the Moscow Orphanage was endowed in 1772 with a school of commerce which was moved to St. Petersburg in 1779. The curriculums of the two sets of schools—for children of noble parentage and for all other children—differed in that the former had a broad educational program while the latter put the emphasis on professional training. A significant and welcome innovation was the prohibition of corporal punishment. That system was abolished in the military academy in 1766 and was not officially tolerated in the new schools. Betsky's project for the establishment of boarding schools in the principal cities was never realized. The romantic idea of "breeding a new type of humanity" gradually faded away, but it survived, in a perverted form, in the Smolny school for girls of noble descent, whose graduates gained a proverbial reputation for affected gentility. By 1780 Catherine, sobered by experience, lost confidence in the magic-working power of boarding schools, and the aged and ailing Betsky went into retirement.

A more matter-of-fact, if no less ambitious, attempt at providing Russia with an adequate school system was inspired by the Austrian school reform of 1774, which was based on the Prussian model. The guiding spirit of the Russian reform was Theodor Yankovich-de-Mirievo, a graduate of the University of Vienna and a participant in the reorganization of the Austrian schools. Yankovich, a Serb who spoke Russian and belonged to the Greek Orthodox Church, came to St. Petersburg in September, 1782, and was at once made a member of the school commission newly appointed under the chairmanship of Count Peter Zavadsky. The industrious and learned Serb was chiefly responsible for the drafting of the Statute of Popular Schools (*Ustav narodnykh uchilishch*), which was confirmed by the empress on August 5, 1786. The plan of the commission provided for three types of schools: elementary (*malyia*), intermediate (*sredniia*), and high (*glavnyia*). The course of instruction in the elementary schools lasted for two years, and their curriculum included reading, writing, catechism, Church history, Russian grammar, a text on "the duties of man and citizen," calligraphy, and drawing. The intermediate schools added to the two years of the elementary school a third year with more thorough instruction in the above-mentioned subjects as well as in European and Russian history and Russian geography. The high schools, which consisted of the three-year intermediate school plus a fourth year, provided instruction, in addition to the above subjects, in the basic principles of mechanics, geometry, physics, natural history, and civil architecture. The proposal for intermediate schools was dropped at an early stage, and the reform, in its practical application, was limited to the introduction of the two-year elementary schools and the four-year high schools. Following the Austrian model, the plan of the Russian commission banished corporal punishment and assigned the teachers a more active and responsible part in the classroom than had been customary in the past. The schools were open to all children irrespective of the status of their parents, but the majority of the students came from families of merchants, burghers, artisans, and minor government officials.

The reform, which if carried out would have marked an important step forward, demanded textbooks and teachers. By 1786 some twenty-seven textbooks were printed, chiefly translations and adaptations of Austrian texts prepared under the supervision of Yankovich. A teachers' college founded in 1786 supplied the school system up to 1801 with 425 teachers drawn mostly from the ranks of the lower clergy. Towards the end of 1786 high schools were established in the principal cities of twenty-six provinces, and a decree of November 3, 1788, ordered the opening of such schools in other provinces. In spite of this promising beginning progress was slow and disappointing. The law, as Miliukov points out, made no provision for the maintenance of the new schools, whose expenses were to be met from the already inadequate funds of the provincial social relief boards (*prikazy obshchestvennago prizreniia*). Parents obstinately refused to send their children to school, and zealous administrators had to use high-handed methods to enforce enrollment and attendance. An official investigation in 1789 disclosed that the curriculum of the high schools was generally considered too advanced. This probably explains, according to Miliukov, why of the 1,432 students who between 1786 and 1803 were admitted to the high school in Archangel only fifty-two completed the course and received their diplomas.

According to the same author, elementary schools which it was proposed to establish in the chief town of each county (*uezd*) encountered even greater difficulty. Local authorities often found the cost of school maintenance both excessive and unwarranted, and by 1790 in a number of localities the newly established schools had closed their doors. Student attendance was most unsatisfactory. In the town of Tikhvin, for instance, of the sixty-eight students enrolled in the elementary school in 1788 fifty-four vanished and were not heard of again. The general effect of the reform is indicated by the following figures, which are quoted by Miliukov with the warning that they are not too reliable. In 1786 Russia had forty lay schools (including village and private schools) with 136 teachers and 4,398 students; in 1796 there were 316 schools with 744 teachers and 17,341 students. While this was an improvement, the fact remains that in 1790, when the total school enrollment was 16,525, there was only one student per

1,573 inhabitants.[1] Between 1782 and 1800, girls accounted for about 7 per cent of the student body.

Nothing was done about village schools, although a subcommittee of the Legislative Commission in 1770 produced a project for compulsory education of the entire male population. Based on the Prussian model, the plan recommended the opening of one village school for each 100 to 250 peasant households, the cost of maintenance to be borne by the parishioners. This project, which was buried in the archives of some government department, merely bears evidence that popular education in the eighteenth century had a few friends, although its opponents were numerous and the obstacles formidable.

In spite of the practically total absence of schools, the age of Catherine is rightly regarded as something of a turning point in the intellectual history of the country. French influence, which had been strong under Elizabeth, reigned supreme, and the ability to speak the language of Voltaire and to exhibit at least some knowledge of French literature became a coveted mark of social distinction and the prerequisite of a successful career. Hence the popularity among the well-to-do *dvoriane* of French tutors and of private schools maintained by foreigners. Some of these imported pedagogues were as ignorant as their Russian colleagues, and there are many amusing stories of Parisian barbers and coachmen from Marseilles, sometimes with a criminal record, whose inexperienced and unclean hands guided the scions of Russian nobility along the thorny path of knowledge and virtue. But there were also among them men of erudition capable of leaving a lasting imprint on the minds of their pupils. Political radicalism was the fashion in court circles until almost the very end of Catherine's reign, and the example set by the empress in appointing the "Jacobin" La Harpe tutor of her grandsons had many imitators. The education of the children of Count Saltykov, for instance, was entrusted to a brother of Jean Paul Marat (member of the Paris commune and editor of *L'ami du peuple*) and himself an outspoken supporter of the French Revolution. Emancipation from compulsory service and the right to travel abroad, granted to the *dvoriane* by Peter III and confirmed by Catherine, for the first time offered the Russian nobility the opportunity, unhampered by official supervision, to gain a first-

---

[1] According to Miliukov, the number of students in parish and other ecclesiastical schools was 11,329 in 1783 and 24,167 in 1807.

hand knowledge of western Europe. A rapidly growing number of noble Russian pilgrims hastened to take the road to Paris, where many Muscovite fortunes were dissipated in fashionable gambling dens, restaurants, cafés, dressmaking establishments, tailor shops, and brothels. Contemporary satirical journals were unanimous in ridiculing this aspect of the experience of Russians abroad, but there were Russian travelers who visited literary and political salons, museums and picture galleries, attended lectures, and took a keen interest in the constitutional system, social conditions, and intellectual life of foreign countries, where they stayed sometimes for months or even years. Not a few of them brought home from their travels observations and disturbing new ideas which did not fit into the Russian environment.

LITERATURE AND ART

A certain stimulus to intellectual activity and economic thought was given by the founding in 1765 of the Free Economic Society (*Volno-Ekonomicheskoe Obshchestvo*), which inaugurated its work by offering a prize for the best monograph on serfdom. This society eventually assembled a great deal of information on rural Russia and did much to encourage the study of economics.

In 1783 the Russian Academy for the advancement of literature and linguistic studies was opened, but under the leadership of its president, Princess Dashkov, a truly insufferable prig, its record was undistinguished. It was not the fault of the academy, however, that Russian literature of the second half of the eighteenth century was distressingly mediocre. Literary works followed slavishly the stale pattern of the pseudo-classical school, which had taken firm root in Russia in the reign of Elizabeth, and their contents—with rare exceptions—were uninspiring. The two favorite themes elaborated in verse and prose were exaggerated eulogy of the wisdom, virtue, and charm of the empress, and timid, cautious criticism, kept strictly within prescribed limits, of contemporary social evils. Poetry became the usual means of winning the patronage of powerful Maecenases, and the tenor of many odes—the then most popular form of versification—could not have been more vile, loathsome, and ridiculous. According to Pypin, the only redeeming features of literature during this period were a certain improvement in style and language, which cleared the way for later writers, and the contributions of a few men, especially Radishchev and Novikov, who displayed courageous disregard for tradition and

gave expression to vigorous ideas which their more circumspect con-
freres would have deemed it wise to leave unsaid.

Among the better known authors of the later eighteenth century
were Denis Von-Vizen (1745–1792), Gabriel Derzhavin (1743–1816),
Michael Kheraskov (1733–1807), Hippolyte Bogdanovich (1743–
1803), Ivan Khemnitser (1745–1784), and Jacob Kniazhin (1742–
1791). Von-Vizen was primarily a dramatist and his most popular works
were the comedies *Brigadier* and, especially, *Nedorosel* (The Minor),
which created a sensation when it was first produced in 1783. The political orthodoxy of Von-Vizen, however, was soon questioned, and in
1788 the publication of his new journal (*Starodum*, named after one of
the characters of *The Minor*) was prevented by the police. Derzhavin,
"the bard of Catherine," was not only a poet but also a quarrelsome
administrator who held several important offices under Catherine and
who was for a short time minister of justice under Alexander I. Not
devoid of poetical talent, Derzhavin owed his literary reputation to the
numerous odes in which he sang the glory of Catherine, her favorites,
and her generals, and extolled the victories of Russian arms. Kheraskov,
a prolific author, wrote poems, lyrics, comedies, tragedies, and novels.
His chief claim to fame rested on his two epic poems *Rossiada* and
Vladimir, dealing, respectively, with the conquest of Kazan by Ivan
IV and the conversion of Russia to Christianity. Although contemporary opinion saw in him a "Russian Homer," he had no poetical
gift, his interpretations of history were fanciful, and his characters
combined in an unpalatable fashion traits borrowed from Homer,
Vergil, Tasso, and the Bible. Today the once much admired poems
of Kheraskov appear at best as odd museum pieces. Bogdanovich, who
like the other versifiers of his time wrote odes, hymns, fables, and
lyrics, became famous as the author of the poem *Dushenka* (The
Darling), a heavy-footed adaptation of La Fontaine's *Les Amours de
Psyché et de Coupidon*, in which Russian opinion chose to see a model
of elegance and wit, although it was just as pedestrian and clumsy as
the offerings of Kheraskov. The fables of Khemnitser, translator of La
Fontaine, bore evidence of greater literary skill and provided instances
of a felicitous use of the popular language. Kniazhin was a dramatist
in the worst tradition of Sumarokov,[2] and his tragedies and comedies,
although immensely successful at the time, were no improvement on
the work of his predecessor.

[2] See p. 492.

The tone of this literature was didactic: vice was exposed and virtue invariably triumphed. However, the list of contemporary evils the castigation of which was not only allowed but was obligatory was limited. It included misbehavior of unworthy landowners; the corruption of judges and minor officials; the immorality of the younger generation excessively devoted to French clothes and French manners; the ignorance, bigotry, and superstition of the adherents of the old Russian way of life. These themes were elaborated *ad nauseam* in the writings of Catherine and her contemporaries, but criticism and satire merely touched the surface; they were not permitted to attack the foundations of the existing social order, where might have been found the roots of the evil. To make things even less palatable, the pseudo-historical writings of the period were imbued with a spirit of crude and aggressive nationalism in agreement with the historical views held by the empress.

Of greater value than these humble efforts were the translations of foreign authors ranging from Greek and Latin classics to Milton, Shakespeare, Tasso, Lessing, Klopstock, Voltaire, and the Encyclopedists. If not all the translations did justice to the originals, they nevertheless made available to the Russian reading public the masterpieces of the past and the outstanding foreign contributions to contemporary thought.

A special place in the intellectual history of the later eighteenth century is occupied by the work of Radishchev and Novikov. Alexander Radishchev (1749–1802) studied at the University of Leipzig, traveled extensively abroad, and was a disciple of Voltaire, Holbach, Helvetius, Rousseau, and De Mably. His volume *Journey from St. Petersburg to Moscow*, which was inspired by *A Sentimental Journey* of Laurence Sterne, offered a bitter, eloquent, and deeply moving indictment of serfdom, of the misrule of the bureaucracy and—*horribile dictu*—of the sacred principle of monarchical absolutism. Passed by the censor and published in 1790, the *Journey from St. Petersburg to Moscow* came to the attention of the empress and threw her into a state of indescribable rage. The unhappy author was tried and received a death sentence; this, however, was commuted to exile for ten years in eastern Siberia. After the accession of Emperor Paul, Radishchev was permitted to live on his estates, and in 1801 he was called by Emperor Alexander I to St. Petersburg, where he committed suicide a year later.

No less tragic, and even less deserved, was the fate of the leader of Russian Freemasonry, Nicholas Novikov (1744–1818). Novikov, who had had no formal schooling—he was expelled in 1760 from the secondary school attached to the University of Moscow—entered the literary field in St. Petersburg in 1769 as editor and principal contributor of a satirical journal which attracted considerable attention by its skirmishes with the journal *Vsiakaia vsiachina* (This and That), a mouthpiece of Catherine. A believer in the greatness and nobility of the Russian national tradition, Novikov, from 1772 on, combined his journalistic activities with the publication of several works devoted to Russian history, among them the first—and highly eulogistic—biographical dictionary of Russian authors. In 1775 Novikov joined the Freemasons and in 1779 he moved from St. Petersburg to Moscow. Freemasonry was introduced in Russia about 1730, and made numerous converts among the upper classes. During the earlier years of his association with the Freemasons, Novikov was particularly interested in the humanitarian and philanthropic aspects of their vague doctrine, and it was only after his release from the fortress of Schlüsselburg that he definitely espoused the mystical teaching of the lodges. After 1775 there was a change in the character of the Novikov publications and journals, which followed one another in rapid succession. Satire and historical studies were abandoned in favor of a philosophical discussion of great moral issues. The essence of the philosophy expounded by Novikov and his friends was a plea for moral self-improvement, an argument tinged with pietism combined with a protest against the materialistic attitude of French rationalism. The fact that the inspiration of the movement came largely from Germany is partly explained by the close association of Novikov with a distinguished German expatriate and enthusiastic Freemason, Johann Georg Schwartz (died in 1784).

Novikov had come to the ancient capital in order to take over the management of the printing press of the University of Moscow. Under his administration there was remarkable progress, and in six years the university issued some four hundred titles, that is, more than it had published during the entire period from its founding to 1779. Availing himself of a law of 1783 which allowed private persons to own printing establishments, Novikov acquired several printing presses in his own name, in those of his associates, and in the name of a company of which he was the founder. He thus became the head of the greatest publishing enterprise Russia had ever known. Simultaneously Novikov continued his journalistic activities and acted as editor of several journals. Not satisfied, however, with being a publicist, editor, and publisher, he invaded other fields of educational and philanthropic endeavor. The proceeds of the journals he had published in St. Petersburg and funds raised privately were used to establish and maintain two elementary schools for underprivileged children. These activities were expanded after Novikov moved to Moscow. He became, with Schwartz, the guiding spirit of the Friendly Learned Society, which raised funds for educational purposes, provided scholarships, and sent deserving students abroad. The printing company of which Novikov was the head maintained a hospital and dispensary for its employees and distributed medicines free of charge to those who could not afford to pay for them. Many of the books he published were distributed free to schools and other institutions. During the famine of 1787 Novikov organized the relief work among the sufferers. His sterling honesty, enthusiasm, and devotion to the cause of social betterment and education won him a large following, and some of his supporters not only contributed generously to his campaigns but put at his disposal their entire fortunes (for instance, Pokhodiashin).

The extraordinary and unprecedented success of the many enterprises directed by Novikov and his rapidly growing influence proved his undoing. Catherine mistrusted Freemasonry, and her comedies, in which she ridiculed, among other things, the philanthropic work of the lodges, proved that she had an erroneous notion of the real objects of the organization. Enlightened absolutism, as she understood it, was essentially totalitarian and would tolerate no educational or social movement that was not fully under its control. Novikov was suspected of heresy, fraud, treasonable relations with German courts, and of agitation on behalf of the Grand Duke Paul. It was in vain that Platon, archbishop of Moscow, attested that "in the whole world one could not find a better Christian than Novikov." In 1791 his publishing activities were suspended by order of the government. The investigation of his alleged crimes was conducted by the dreaded Sheshkovsky, head of the security police, but the evidence obtained proved so inadequate that the proposed trial by "trustworthy men" originally contemplated by the empress was abandoned. Novikov was arrested and sentenced, by the imperial decree of August 1, 1792, to detention in the fortress of Schlüsselburg for fifteen years. It is noteworthy that no action was taken against his associates. Four years later, on the accession of Emperor Paul, Novikov was pardoned and received by the new emperor, who is said to have begged his forgiveness for the injustice perpetrated by Catherine; but he emerged from prison a prematurely aged and broken man. It seems difficult not to agree with Pypin that in the closing years of her reign Catherine was destroying with her own hands the tender growths of culture that she had once endeavored to implant.

As has already been noted, the latter part of the eighteenth century witnessed a considerable revival of interest in Russian history. The most prominent historian of this period was Prince Michael Shcherbatov (1733–1790), offspring of an ancient boyar family. His six-volume history of Russia from ancient times to the accession of Michael Romanov made use, for the first time, of archive materials instead of blindly following the chronicles. Miliukov has proved that Karamzin, often regarded as the founder of modern Russian historiography, owed much to the spadework of Shcherbatov, whose *magnum opus* was severely criticized by nineteenth century historians as a clumsy and tasteless compilation of official texts. It is seldom consulted today except by the most conscientious students. Very different in character, and probably of greater interest, was Shcherbatov's treatise *On the Decline of Morals in Russia*, in which the author extolled the virtues of old Muscovy and traced an unflattering picture of the moral decadence he believed had taken place after Peter I, and especially under Catherine II. Shcherbatov wisely refrained from publishing this curious study at the time, and it first appeared in print in London in 1858. Much revealing information is given in the memoirs of Princess Dashkov, Derzhavin, Andrew Bolotov, Simon Porshin, and in the diary of Alexander Khrapovitsky, secretary to Catherine from 1782 to 1793, but these memoirs were not made available to the public until the nineteenth century.

Little need be said about Russian art. The pseudo-classical tradition which dominated Russian literature was even more in evidence in architecture and painting. Catherine, her favorites, and the wealthy members of the nobility spent large sums on the construction of sumptuous palaces, churches, and public buildings and on the assembling of imposing art collections. The galleries of the Ermitage, an annex of the Winter Palace built by the Frenchman Lamothe, housed a vast collection of cameos, statues, and drawings and paintings by such masters as Raphael, Murillo, Guido Reni, Salvator Rosa, Poussin, Van Dyck, Schidoni, Carlo Lotti, Rembrandt, Wouwerman, Teniers, Van Loo, and many others. The nucleus of the Ermitage collection was formed by the acquisition of the admirable collections of Baron de Thiers, Count Heinrich Brühl, and Sir Robert Walpole, but it was greatly extended by later purchases. By the end of the century St. Petersburg had established its claim as one of the treasure-houses of European art.

Most of the artists and architects whose genius added luster to the rule of the Semiramis of the North came from foreign lands. Outstanding among them were Giacomo Trombara, Giacomo Quarenghi, Cameron, Clérisseau, Lamothe, Valois, Lorrain, Lagrenée, Doyen, Falconet, Houdon, Benner, Lampi, Brompton, König, Madame Vigée-Lebrun. To this galaxy of foreign celebrities and near celebrities must be added some Russian names. The outstanding Russian architects were V. I. Bazhenev (1737–1799), originator of a striking plan for the reconstruction of the Kremlin (this, however, was never adopted); M. F. Kazakov (1733–1812), who designed the Administration Building in the Kremlin and the building of the University of Moscow; and I. E. Starov (1743–1808), creator of the Alexander Nevsky Cathedral in St. Petersburg and of the magnificent Taurida Palace built for Prince Potemkin and eventually the seat of the Russian parliament (State Duma). F. I. Shubin (1740–1805), F. F. Shchedrin (1751–1825), and M. I. Kozlovsky (died in 1802) were talented sculptors, and F. S. Rokotov (1730–1810), D. G. Levitsky (1735–1822), and V. L. Borovikov (1757–1825) won a deserved reputation as portrait painters. The work of these Russian masters, however, showed little originality, and it was dominated by the influence of western art. It was in the latter part of the eighteenth century that the classical style of architecture—Greek porticoes supported by columns—became increasingly popular; later known as "the Russian *empire*," the Russian version is reminiscent in many ways of the colonial style of architecture in the United States.

There were no new developments in the field of music. Although Catherine, as she candidly admitted, was incapable of identifying or remembering a tune, she duly patronized the opera and found some pleasure in the lighter forms of musical entertainment, such as the works of Paisiello, which the maestro in person conducted at the Ermitage theater. Foreign operas, of course, were accessible to only a small group among the upper class. No Russian composer worthy of the name appeared before the nineteenth century.

THE BALANCE SHEET OF ENLIGHTENED ABSOLUTISM

At the time of Catherine's sudden death following a stroke of apoplexy (November 6, 1796), the empire she left to her son was different in many essential respects from the Russia of the middle of the eighteenth century. One feature of her reign which stands out, although the empress would never have admitted it, is the sharp contrast—in every field of endeavor—between the avowed objects and the results achieved. The foreign policy of Catherine, which constitutes her chief claim to fame, led to vast territorial expansion and to the acquisition of the littoral of the Black Sea and of new outlets on the Baltic, but it did not bring about the destruction of the Ottoman Porte, which was her declared aim, to say nothing of her other truly fanciful schemes.[3] Military laurels are always costly; the onerous wars of the second half of the eighteenth century not only greatly retarded the economic development of Russia but extended the rule of St. Petersburg to the Polish provinces, which never became reconciled to Muscovite domination and carried on the struggle for independence until they finally achieved it 150 years later. The much-publicized Legislative Commission proved incapable of producing even a draft of the code that the empress imagined was to make Russia the envy of the civilized world. Autocracy, in which Catherine so firmly believed, was retained unimpaired; her administrative reforms, however, contributed to the decay of the central government, while the multiplication of costly local agencies failed to produce self-government or to raise the deplorably low standards of honesty among government officials. There was economic stagnation, the burden of taxation increased manyfold, the currency was debased, and there was a large foreign debt. The ideas of the Enlightenment remained an exotic adornment of court life, with little practical effect on the policies of the regime. Moreover, the outbreak of the French Revolution (and, probably, the influence of Platon Zubov) caused Catherine to repudiate

---

[3] "Could I live for two hundred years," Catherine told Derzhavin, according to his memoirs, "the whole of Europe would be brought under the Russian rule"; and "I shall not die before I have ejected the Turks from Europe, have broken the insolence of China, and have established trade relations with India."

many of her former views, and by an ironical turn of fortune she forbade the *dvoriane* to travel in France at the very time when the younger generation, brought up by foreign tutors and governesses, spoke far better French than Russian. In religious matters there was greater tolerance than during the reign of Elizabeth, and the persecutions of the dissenters subsided, although their legal disabilities were not removed. As a result of the annexation of the Polish provinces, with their large Jewish population, the position of the Jews was legalized, but the solution adopted had little in common with the principles of the Enlightenment. The Jews, who had formerly been prohibited from residing in Russia (except, after 1769, in the province of Novorossisk), were permitted to settle in specified areas, subject to the payment of taxes higher than those borne by the Christian population. There thus came into being the "Jewish pale," which remained a distinct feature of Russian constitutional arrangements until the end of the empire.[4]

It was in the social texture of Russia that the most significant changes took place. The *dvorianstvo* had long enjoyed important privileges but until the middle of the eighteenth century it was subject to the obligation of government service, borne in some form or other by all social classes. Peter III and Catherine II, by removing the obligation of compulsory service, by conferring upon the *dvoriane* new privileges and immunities, and by tightening at the same time the noose of serfdom, basically altered the character of the social structure that had evolved in the course of the preceding centuries. Serfdom had its historical explanation and theoretical justification in the fact that it permitted the *dvoriane* to devote their time and energies to the service of the state. In practice, however, the system led to gross abuse and assumed forms that cannot be condoned. The manifesto of February 18, 1762, and the 1785 Charter of the Nobility created for the first time a social group with many valuable privileges and with no direct personal obligations towards the state. Russian

---

[4] The first comprehensive enactment dealing with the position of the Jews was the decree of Jan. 1, 1773. The decrees of May 3, 1783, and of Dec. 23, 1791, which allowed the Jews to reside in the provinces of White Russia, Ekaterinoslav, and Taurida, contained no provision for discriminatory taxation. A decree of June 23, 1794, however, while extending the "pale" to three more Ukrainian provinces, ordered the Jews to pay taxes at double the normal rate; those who were dissatisfied were "free to leave the empire after they had paid the double tax for three years."

peasants, of course, knew no history, but they had a crude, inborn sense of justice which made them feel that the emancipation of the *dvoriane* should be followed by the abolition of serfdom; but instead of the expected liberation came greater restrictions, heavier exactions, and closer supervision of the bondsmen by the landowners, who were then free to settle on their estates. Hence the successive waves of popular uprisings which culminated in the Peasant War of 1773–1774.

The emancipation of the nobility had other important repercussions. In spite of all its privileges, the *dvorianstvo* lacked the essential characteristics of aristocracy as it was understood in western Europe. Hereditary titles of nobility continued to be automatically conferred on all army officers and on government officials who had reached a specified grade in the official hierarchy, and the functions and powers of the corporations of the nobility were so limited as to deprive them of any real autonomy. The influence of the *dvoriane* rested largely on the fact that they filled the ranks of the office-holders; conversely, government service led to the acquisition of the coveted title of nobility. The emancipation of the *dvoriane*, therefore, far from weakening the sway of the bureaucratic machine tended to enhance the position of the bureaucracy, which, indeed, was to rule the empire in the name of the tsar until the revolution of 1917. The persistence of this bureaucratic tradition has had an important bearing upon the administrative methods of the U.S.S.R.

In spite of the sterility of the half-hearted effort to improve educational standards, the consequences of the infiltration of new ideas were making themselves felt. The popularization of the views of the Encyclopedists, Voltaire, Montesquieu, Rousseau, and others, stimulated independent thought and prepared the ground for the radical intellectual and political movements that were soon to make their appearance. But there was a reverse side to the medal. The adoption by the *dvoriane* of the French language, Parisian fashion, and outlandish theories widened the gulf between the privileged few and the illiterate serfs over whom they ruled. The fatal cleavage between the thin layer of the educated classes, on the one hand, and the sullen masses, on the other, grew wider as decades rolled by, and proved to be a probably decisive factor in determining the character of the revolution of 1917.

CHAPTER XXIV

THE TURN OF THE CENTURY

Paul I

━━━━━━━━━━━━━━━━━━━━ ❊ ━━━━━━━━━━━━━━━━━━━━

THE SON OF CATHERINE

Few scholarly studies of the brief reign of Emperor Paul I (1796–1801) have been made by Russian historians, whose attempts at lifting the veil of prejudice and mystery which shrouds this period have, until recently, been effectively discouraged by censorship. The numerous accounts of the rule of Paul I have, with rare exceptions, been based on contemporary memoirs, many of them emanating from avowed opponents of the emperor and some written long after the event. These highly colored narratives were not scrutinized in the light of archive documents, but they were accepted as giving an authentic picture of the reign of the imperial madman whose murder in a palace conspiracy was made to appear both as a historical necessity and as an act of divine grace. History, as Shumigorsky put it, thus tended to become a political pamphlet. The prevailing attitude of Russian historiography towards Paul was epigrammatically summed up by Kliuchevsky. "The entire democratic program [of Paul] was broken up into unconnected and capricious trifles," he writes; "in fits of the emperor's temper—cruel or benignant—this program degenerated into mere anecdotes, and except for anecdotes we know nothing about his reign." An objective documentary study of the reign of Paul did not become feasible until the closing years of the empire. In 1907 Professor V. F. Chizh, a psychiatrist, expounded the view that Paul was not suffering from any mental ailment. Of much greater value to historians is the study by E. S. Shumigorsky (1907) and especially the admirable monograph by Professor M. V. Klochkov (1916) in which was presented a closely documented survey of the program and policies of the ill fated emperor. Klochkov definitely lifted the discussion from the level of "anecdotes" and brought out the deeper significance of the tragedy that befell the son of Catherine.

Paul was born on September 20, 1754, and was removed from the care of his parents by Empress Elizabeth, who insisted on assuming personal responsibility for the upbringing of the heir to the throne. She entrusted the supervision of his education to the enlightened guidance of the astute Nikita Ivanovich Panin, eventually Catherine's chief diplomatic adviser. Nikita Panin, until his death in 1784, remained Paul's mentor and trusted friend, and he and his brother, General Peter Panin, exercised considerable influence upon the political ideas of the future emperor. Under the direction of a carefully selected group of teachers, Paul acquired a good knowledge of geography, history, and mathematics, and became an accomplished linguist. He spoke Russian, French, and German well, was conversant with Church Slavonic, and wrote fluently in these languages, although his spelling and grammar were often defective. He was thoroughly familiar with the literature of the Enlightenment and he owned a sizable library which, as evidenced by numerous annotations and excerpts copied in his hand, was extensively used. At the age of nineteen Paul married Wilhelmina, daughter of the landgrave of Hesse, but this union was a short and unhappy one. The grand duchess had a liaison with Count Andrew Razumovsky, one of her husband's closest friends, and died in childbirth in April, 1776. In September, 1776, less than half a year after the death of his wife, Paul married again. His second bride was Sophie Dorothy, princess of Württemberg, who on her conversion to Greek Orthodoxy assumed the name of Maria Fedorovna. Frederick II of Prussia, an uncle of the princess, took a part in arranging the match, and it was in Berlin, under the auspices of the man Peter III had so deeply admired, that Paul first met his future wife. This visit to Berlin contributed to the grand duke's already pronounced predilection for Prussia and especially for the Prussian army, which was then rated one of the best in Europe. The second matrimonial venture of Paul appeared to be successful. For over twenty years he was a model husband, and between 1777 and 1798 Maria Fedorovna bore him four sons and six daughters. In the autumn of 1781 the grand-ducal couple left St. Petersburg for a fourteen months' tour which took them to Austria, Italy, France, the Netherlands, Switzerland, and southern Germany. Although Paul and his wife traveled incognito as Count and Countess du Nord, they were received at European courts with all the attention and pomp befitting their exalted rank. The grand duke proved a keen and intelligent observer, and the favorable impression he left abroad offers a striking contrast to the memories in European capitals of his illustrious ancestor, Peter I. Personal contact with the western world provided the future monarch with much food for thought and confirmed him in the conviction that Russia was sadly in need of administrative and social reform.

In view of the conditions under which Catherine assumed power, it was probably inevitable that the relations between mother and son should be lacking in harmony. Waliszewski is technically right when he holds that since the law of 1722 gave the occupant of the throne the power to nominate his successor, Paul owed his Crown to Catherine who after her accession made him heir apparent. Legality, however, had little to do with the order of succession in eighteenth century Russia and, as already stated, an influential body of public opinion clung to the traditional view that the father should be succeeded by the son and that Catherine was entitled, at the utmost, to regency during the minority of Paul. Fully aware of this trend of thought and of the danger it presented to her own position, the empress not only refused to step down and make room for her son but deliberately eliminated him from participation in the business of government. The ambitious and active grand duke, who was forced to be satisfied with the empty title of grand admiral, had no effective voice in the deliberations on affairs of state, and he was even kept in ignorance of some of Russia's international alliances. The overbearing insolence displayed by some of the favorites towards the son of their mistress widened the gulf between Catherine and Paul, whose private life at the time was above reproach. Catherine, moreover, assumed control over the education of Alexander and Constantine, the two elder sons of Paul, and for years the parents of the boys were not permitted to see them except by appointment.

In 1783 Catherine gave Paul Gatchina, an estate formerly owned by Gregory Orlov in the neighborhood of St. Petersburg. The grand duke spent the following thirteen years in the semi-retirement of this pleasant country residence, where he led the life of a country squire and garrison commander, making only rare appearances at the imperial court. A diligent, benevolent, and generous landlord, he did much to improve the lot of his serfs, opened hospitals and schools, established several industrial enterprises and, being both tolerant and deeply religious, built Greek Orthodox, Roman Catholic, and Lutheran churches. The real passion of Paul, however, was the army, and he showed much pride in the Gatchina garrison, whose soldiers he dressed in Prussian uniforms, and he himself drilled the troops in the art of warfare, in accordance with the army regulations of Frederick II. Maria Fedorovna was no less active. Both at Gatchina and in the nearby less pretentious residence of Pavlovsk, she presided over a perhaps not very brilliant literary and artistic salon; she organized theatricals, of which her husband was very fond, and took a real interest in charitable and social work. The ill concealed hostility with which Catherine viewed the "young court" necessarily restricted the entourage of the grand-ducal couple. Some of those who braved Catherine's displeasure by close association with her son were men of sinister reputation, for instance, Alexis Arakcheev and Ivan Kutaisov; others, however, were enlightened and by no means unprincipled men, such as Serge Pleshcheev, a naval officer educated in England, and an ardent Freemason. Paul, who had been introduced to Freemasonry by Nikita Panin, was much impressed by the mystical aspects of its doctrine. He followed with close and sympathetic interest the work of the lodges and the activities of Novikov, and he had many supporters among the Freemasons.

The mystical leanings of the future tsar assumed a peculiar form which played havoc with the peaceful and well ordered existence of Gatchina. Around 1785 Paul developed a romantic and chivalrous attachment for Catherine Nelidov, a lady-in-waiting to the grand duchess. Mademoiselle Nelidov, although not pretty, was mystically inclined, romantic, and unusually high-minded, and she is said to have exercised a benevolent and soothing influence upon Paul, who was subject to fits of uncontrollable temper, especially when confronted with real or imaginary breaches of military discipline. Although the relationship between Mademoiselle Nelidov and her admirer remained within the bounds of propriety, the marks of affection Paul showered upon the object of his passion created a scandal, outraged Maria Fedorovna, and divided the small world of Gatchina into warring camps. In 1793 Mademoiselle Nelidov, finding her position intolerable, withdrew to the Smolny Convent, but she continued to pay frequent visits to the grand-ducal court. After the accession of Paul, Maria Fedorovna made peace with her rival and they solemnly promised to use their influence over Paul "for the good of the tsar and of the empire." The infatuation of Paul with Mademoiselle Nelidov lasted until 1798, when he became obsessed with a less eerie passion for the nineteen-year-old Anne Lopukhin, who married Prince Paul Gagarin and became the emperor's official mistress.

THE POLITICAL PROGRAM OF PAUL

Paul had no illusions about the perils that darkened his political horizon. He knew that Catherine had made up her mind to disinherit him and to appoint his elder son, the Grand Duke Alexander, as her successor. The fateful announcement was expected to follow the marriage (September 28, 1793) of Alexander at the unusually early age of sixteen to Louise, princess of Baden, who on her admission to the Greek Orthodox Church assumed the name of Elizabeth (Elizaveta Alekseevna). It is believed that the postponement of this plan was due to the stern opposition of La Harpe, whose influence with Alexander was great. Consulted by the empress, the Swiss tutor of the young grand duke not only refused to lend his support to Catherine's scheme but gave a warning to Paul and exerted himself to bring about a *rapprochement* between the father and son. In 1795 Alexander and his younger brother Constantine were often seen on the drilling ground of Gatchina, and in 1796 they were daily visitors to the residence of their parents. At the end of 1794 La Harpe was summarily dismissed and left early the following year for Switzerland, where he was destined to play an important political role.

In spite of the sword of Damocles hanging over his head, Paul carefully prepared himself for the duties of kingship. His program of domestic reforms, to which he remained faithful until the end, was influenced by the views of Nikita Panin, an admirer of the aristocratic constitution of Sweden; by his predilection for things Prussian, which was fostered by both Panin and Maria Fedorovna; by the absolutist theories of Catherine (although he was critical of many of her practical policies); and by his aversion, which he shared with his mother, to the French Revolution. The political credo of Paul was expounded in his correspondence, especially in his letters to Panin, in a political testament or instruction (*nakaz*) he wrote for his wife in 1788,[1] and in the official acts passed after his accession. In agreement with the

---

[1] After the outbreak of the Russo-Turkish War in 1787, Paul vainly petitioned his mother for permission to join the army as a volunteer. Fearing that the presence

accepted theory of the eighteenth century, Paul held that the object of the state was "the happiness of each and all." He believed, with Catherine, that this high aim could be best achieved through the monarchic form of government which, by vesting the sovereign both with legislative and with executive powers, guaranteed the rule of law combined with speedy administrative action. Paul, however, was not blind to the limitations of absolutism which he saw in the human fallibility of the monarch. He was opposed to the republican form of government, especially after the outbreak of the French Revolution, but he also hated despotism in any guise. He pictured the monarch, not as a figurehead, but as the actual ruler with whom rest all important decisions; advised by the higher officers of state, he exercises his powers through a closely knit system of judicial and administrative organs with clearly delimited functions. Rigid centralization and the personal responsibility of higher officials for the work of their departments were the logical corollaries of this political philosophy. Absolutism, as conceived by Paul, was to rest on the immutable foundation of the law, a principle advocated by Panin and espoused by Catherine, at least in theory. Laws were to be equally obeyed by all subjects of the Crown, irrespective of birth or official position. Hence the emphasis on discipline both in the army and in civil service. A firm believer in the aristocratic principle, Paul, reverting to the tradition of Peter I, interpreted it in terms of duties rather than of privileges. He was genuinely concerned with the promotion of education and social welfare, as evidenced, for instance, by his activities at Gatchina, and he often spoke of the necessity of bettering the position of the peasants. His concept of the state was heavily colored by a certain romantic mysticism. He dreamed of a thoroughly disci-

---

of the grand duke at the front might enhance his popularity and embarrass Potemkin, Catherine, after many delays, answered with a curt refusal. Paul and his Gatchina battalions were, nevertheless, permitted to take part in the war with Sweden which began in 1788. The grand duke reached Viborg on July 1 but saw little action because the Swedish war was fought largely on the high seas. He found much to criticize in the organization of the Russian army and in the conduct of its leaders, and on September 18 returned to St. Petersburg bitterly disappointed with his short experience in active service. No publicity was given to the presence of Paul among the troops and, contrary to custom, he received no reward. Before leaving for the army he wrote his political testament and the draft of the act regulating succession to the throne, which was promulgated after he had become emperor.

plined polity over which a wise absolute monarch exercised a quasi-paternalistic rule within the framework of the law.

GOVERNMENT REFORMS

It was this program, which on the whole compared not unfavorably with what his predecessors had offered, that Paul endeavored to put into effect after the death of Catherine (November 6, 1796) placed the helm of the ship of state in his eager but inexperienced hands. He was in his forty-third year, and decades of uncertainty, vexation, and forced inactivity had accentuated his inborn disposition towards eccentricity, irritability, impetuosity, and suspicion. Nevertheless the early measures of his regime were surprisingly free from vindictiveness. In some of his decrees, it is true, there is revealed an unflattering picture of the preceding reign; but his criticism has been subsequently endorsed by many historians, and the sharply worded manifesto written by Count Peter Panin years before the accession of Paul and containing an indictment of the rule of Catherine was never promulgated. Paul ordered the exhumation of the body of his father from its sepulchre at the Alexander Nevsky Monastery, had the coffin placed next to that of Catherine, and then the remains of the imperial couple were interred side by side in the cathedral of the fortress of Peter and Paul, the resting place of the Romanov. At this unprecedented and sinister ceremony the aged and ailing Count Alexis Orlov carried the imperial Crown behind the coffin of the man he had murdered. Yet Paul showed little ill will towards the participants in the tragedy of Ropsha or towards his mother's favorites. Princess Dashkov was exiled to a remote estate, but Alexis Orlov was merely ordered to go abroad, where he led a life of pleasure and luxury. Clemency rather than persecution appeared to be the leitmotiv of the new regime. Novikov, Radishchev, and all persons detained by the security police were freed. The Polish prisoners were released, and Kosciuszko was the recipient of generous presents and special marks of attention. Titles, decorations, and lavish gifts of money and populated estates went not only to Paul's friends and supporters but also to men who had been close to his mother, for instance, Platon Zubov and Alexander Bobrinsky, an illegitimate son of Catherine by Gregory Orlov. There were, of course, many newcomers in high places, but dismissals were at first few and some of the former advisers of Catherine (Bezborodko, Dimitry Troshchinsky, Nicholas Arkharov) retained their influence under the rule of the new monarch.

One of Paul's first legislative measures was the abolition of the arbitrary power of the occupant of the throne to nominate his successor, a power which greatly contributed to political instability in eighteenth century Russia. A law promulgated on April 5, 1797, the day of Paul's coronation, made the Crown hereditary in the house of Romanov and defined the order of succession. Klochkov has made it clear that, contrary to prevalent opinion, Paul introduced no drastic change in the functioning of the three principal agencies of central government: the council of the sovereign, the Senate, and the procurator-general. The council, which was established by Catherine in 1769 and continued to act as the chief advisory body to the monarch, consisted of higher officers of state and dealt with a wide range of questions, especially with financial matters.[2] The Senate retained its place as the higher court and the supreme organ of administrative control. Internal reorganization, the temporary doubling of the number of senators, and the substantial increase in its clerical staff added to the efficiency of this body.[3] The procurator-general continued, as under Catherine, to exercise the duties of the minister of the interior,

---

[2] Since the council functioned in an advisory capacity, its actual participation in the conduct of public affairs depended on the sovereign's pleasure. The ebb and flow of the council's influence is suggested by fluctuations in the frequency of its sessions. In the calendar year 1796 the council met 17 times. In the first year of the reign of Paul it was convened 58 times; in the second, 24; in the third, 22; in the fourth, 14; in the four months of the fifth year, 6. Klochkov has demonstrated that the popular theory concerning the drastic curtailment of the jurisdiction of the council under Paul is unwarranted. Far from being limited during the closing year of the reign to the function of censorship, as is often alleged, the council did not discuss censorship from the middle of April, 1800, to March, 1801; during the same period it examined the state budget and dealt with other important financial and administrative problems.

[3] There were 46 senators at the end of the reign of Catherine; their number, increased to 90 early in 1797, was reduced to 50 in 1800. Baron A. E. Nolde, the official historian of the Senate, rightly points out that the number of cases awaiting decision decreased but slightly, from some 11,000 (actually over 14,000 according to official data) at the end of 1796 to a figure over 10,000 four years later. The unfavorable conclusions drawn by Nolde from these data ignore the fact that the number of cases brought annually before the Senate had risen from an average of 10,000 to 13,000 in the reign of Catherine to 44,000 in 1800. The average yearly number of decisions rendered by the Senate under Catherine was about 10,000; it rose to 31,000 in the four years of the rule of her son, a record which suggests that the drive of Paul for administrative efficiency was not the failure it is usually represented to be.

justice, and finance, and for all practical purposes was the tsar's prime minister. But while Prince Alexander Viazemsky held this position for nearly thirty years (1764–1792), Russia had four procurators-general during the brief reign of Paul. Among these officials the longest term was that of Prince Alexis Kurakin, who remained in office two years and eight months. These frequent changes, the impetuous interference of the tsar with the work of his chief official adviser, the creation in December, 1796, of the office of state treasurer (*gosudarstvennyi kaznachei*), and the reorganization of central government departments under heads responsible directly to the monarch—all these factors tended to minimize the influence of the procurator-general.

Paul was concerned about the breakdown of the machinery of central government which followed the local administration reform under the act of 1775. Among his early measures was the restoration of the colleges (central departments) of extractive industry (*berg kollegiia*), manufactures (*manufaktur kollegiia*), commerce (*kommerts kollegiia*), and state revenue (*kammer kollegiia*) (decrees of November 19, 1796, and February 10, 1797). The reversion to the tradition of Peter I, however, was nominal. The collegial principle, so dear to the tsar-reformer, remained a dead letter, and the restored colleges were administered by "general directors" solely responsible to the emperor for the work of their respective departments. The head of the college of commerce received the title of minister; the newly created agency for the administration of the properties of the imperial family (April 5, 1797) was called the ministry of appanages (*ministerstvo udelov*); its charter contained no provision for a collegial controlling body. The new department of water transportation was organized along similar lines. The result of these measures and of the intensive work for the reconstruction of central agencies, in accordance with the principle of greater centralization and of the clearer delimitation of their functions, was the building up of a fairly coherent bureaucratic machine of central government. Although Paul did not succeed in putting into effect his plan for the concentration of the executive work of central administration in seven ministries whose heads were to form the council of ministers, he provided a foundation for the reforms undertaken by Emperor Alexander soon after the latter's accession.

The reform of local government, which followed somewhat similar lines, was guided by a desire for economy and greater centralization;

the latter, however, was mitigated by the restoration of some of the institutions formerly in operation in the border regions. A decree of December 12, 1796, ordered revision of the administrative-territorial structure, and in the course of the next year the number of provinces (*guberniia*) into which Russia was subdivided was reduced from fifty to forty-one. The over-elaborate and cumbersome machinery of the judiciary created by the act of 1775 was simplified by the abolition of several courts, and the number of judicial officers, especially those attached to the office of the provincial public prosecutor (*prokuror*), was cut down. The cost of local government, which at the end of the reign of Catherine was about 8 million rubles, was thus reduced to about 6 million rubles (Klochkov). The treasury derived further relief from the imposition of a tax, amounting annually to 1,744,000 rubles, on the landed estates of the nobility; the proceeds of this tax were earmarked for the maintenance of certain local officials (decree of December 18, 1797, and resolution of the emperor of July 12, 1798). The burghers, too, were called upon to contribute to the maintenance of municipal administration (law of December 31, 1796) and, more specifically, to the support of the police (decree of December 18, 1797); but the amount of their assessment was not stated, and their participation in financing local government—if it was forthcoming at all—was on a more modest scale than that of the *dvoriane*.

The filling of many offices of local government by election, an essential feature of the legislation of Catherine, was sacrificed to the principle of bureaucratic centralization. Beginning early in 1797, elections in certain provinces were replaced by appointment; and a decree of May 14, 1800, abolished them altogether (although the *dvoriane* continued to elect the marshals of the nobility and other officers of their corporations) and provided that in the future all local officials were to be appointed by the Senate. In seemingly sharp contrast to the general tendency towards administrative unification and centralization was the treatment of the northwestern, western, and southwestern provinces, that is, Finland, the Baltic provinces, Russian Poland, and Ukraine. After his accession Paul ordered the restoration of "all institutions based on local rights and privileges" in force in those territories prior to the application of the local government act of 1775. In spite of the liberal and comprehensive terms of this declaration, the process of restoration had little effect except upon the judiciary. The uniform system of taxation introduced by Catherine and the general framework of provincial government established by the act of 1775 were everywhere retained, and appointed governors and other officials continued to exercise wide powers in administrative and financial matters, much to the detriment of the often ill defined ancient "rights and privileges."

FOREIGN POLICY

The foreign policy of Paul displayed none of the unity of purpose and inner consistency that some of the students of Russian government have observed in his administrative reforms. Following the tradition of Catherine, her son took a decisive part in the conduct of foreign affairs. He was critical of the military ventures of his mother, and held that the country had been exhausted by decades of almost uninterrupted warfare. A circular note sent to Russian representatives abroad after the accession of the new emperor proclaimed his intention of following a policy of peace; at the same time it voiced his abhorrence of the French Revolution, in which he saw a revolt of the rabble against legitimate rulers and against an order established by divine Providence. The mysticism of Paul gradually assumed a messianic complexion; he dreamed of uniting under his leadership all enemies of "fashionable philosophical systems," and of heading a crusade for the destruction of the revolutionary hydra. The early diplomatic moves of the tsar, however, had as their object keeping the country out of war. Russian troops were recalled from Georgia and Persia; the Russian squadron, which was cooperating with the British in the Northern Sea, was withdrawn, and the plan of Catherine for sending an army to the Rhine was abandoned. These policies, which permitted the cancellation of a draft of recruits announced during the preceding reign, were received with a general sigh of relief. The attachment of Paul to the idea of a "Northern Accord," so dear to his late mentor, Nikita Panin, was shattered by the final collapse of the negotiations for a marriage between the emperor's daughter, Alexandra, and King Gustavus Adolphus of Sweden; [4] the subsequent en-

[4] Negotiations for this dynastic alliance were opened by Catherine and were proceeding smoothly when they were suddenly broken off over the question of the retention by the bride of her membership in the Greek Orthodox Church. The rupture came dramatically after court and state dignitaries had assembled at the St. Petersburg Winter Palace for the ceremony of formal betrothal. The disappointment experienced by Catherine is believed to have been in part re-

gagement and marriage of Alexandra to Joseph, prince palatine of Hungary (a union sponsored by the empress and the Grand Duke Alexander) contributed to a new temporary *rapprochement* with Austria. After the Franco-Austrian Peace of Campo Formio (October 17, 1797, N.S.), which crowned the Italian campaign of Bonaparte, the French *émigré* corps of Prince Condé, formerly in the service of Austria, found in Russia generous hospitality and financial support. In February, 1798, Louis XVIII, who had come to reside in Mittau in the palace of the dukes of Courland, which Paul put at his disposal, accepted from the Russian government a pension of 200,000 rubles. The triumphant inroads of the revolutionary movement in Holland, Switzerland, and Italy, and rumors of the alleged plan of Bonaparte to restore Poland led the emperor to renounce his former policy of non-intervention in France. His reactionary tendencies and messianic zeal were fostered by the enemies of the French Revolution among the members of his immediate entourage: the Empress Maria and her German relatives, the British ambassador Lord Whitworth, and the French royalist *émigrés*.

Oddly, one of the decisive factors that led to the participation of Russia in the new anti-French coalition was the involvement of the tsar in the affairs of the Maltese Order of the Knights of St. John of Jerusalem. Russia had maintained relations with Malta from the days of Peter I, and in 1770 Catherine had negotiated with the knights an abortive agreement for joint action against Turkey. In 1792 Count Jiulio Litta, a former admiral in the Russian navy and a high official of the order, came as Maltese envoy to St. Petersburg, where his efforts on behalf of the knights were seconded by his brother Lorenzo, the papal nuncio at the Russian court. After Paul's accession, the brothers Litta not only succeeded in securing a highly advantageous settlement of the proprietory claims of the grand priory of the order in Volynia (first established in 1775, under the guarantee of the courts of St. Petersburg, Berlin, and Vienna), but had no difficulty in persuading the tsar to accept the title of "protector" of the order (November, 1797). In June, 1798, Bonaparte occupied Malta on his way to Egypt and endeavored to justify his action by pleading the necessity of sav-

---

sponsible for the stroke of apoplexy from which she died shortly after. Negotiations with Sweden were resumed in March, 1797, but came to naught. The Russian ambassador to Stockholm and the Swedish ambassador to St. Petersburg were recalled.

ing the island from Russian domination. The Russian grand priory retorted by deposing the grand master of the order, Baron Ferdinand de Hompesh. On September 10 Paul announced that he had taken the order under his supreme direction, and on October 27 he was elected grand master by the knights of the Russian grand priory, who were chiefly Poles and French *émigrés*. Although election by the Russian grand priory alone was of questionable constitutional validity, Paul accepted the title; thus, incongruously enough, an ardent member of the Greek Orthodox Church became the head of a Roman Catholic knightly order. A manifesto of December 28, 1798, established a Greek Orthodox grand priory in Russia and officially transferred the capital of the Order to St. Petersburg. Pope Pius VI at first refused to recognize the election but is said to have changed his mind under the pressure of the brothers Litta, who worked assiduously (and as they imagined successfully) for the reunion of the eastern and western Churches. Persuasion and intimidation (in the case of Bavaria) induced the non-Russian grand priories to accept the grandmastership of the tsar. The practical consequence of these strange maneuvers was that the liberation of Malta from the "ungodly" rule of the French—and later of the British—became an immediate concern of the Russian Crown.

From a maze of diplomatic negotiations there gradually emerged in 1798 and 1799 an anti-French coalition which comprised Russia, England, Austria, Turkey, and the kingdom of Naples. Prussia, in spite of Paul's persistent efforts to involve her in the struggle, wisely remained on the side line. In July, 1798, a Russian squadron sailed from Kronstadt to Yarmouth with orders to cooperate with the British fleet under Lord Duncan in operations along the coast of Holland. In September, October, and November, 1798, a joint Russo-Turkish naval expedition occupied the Ionian Islands, which had been held by the French, and in February, 1799, Admiral Fedor Ushakov took possession of Corfu. Suvorov, Russia's eccentric military genius, called from semi-voluntary retirement, was created field marshal of the Austrian army, and was appointed commander in chief of the allied expeditionary force in southern Europe. In the conduct of his Italian and Swiss campaigns he wrote some of the most brilliant, albeit futile, pages in the military history of Russia. Leaving Vienna at the head of his troops early in April, 1799, he moved with lightning speed, inflicted a defeat on General Moreau on the Adda and at the end of the month made a triumphant entry into Milan. After dealing further blows to the French on the Trebbia in June and at Novi early in August, Suvorov was planning a march on Paris by way of Genoa and the Dophiné when he received the unwelcome order to proceed instead to Switzerland and effect a junction with the corps of General Alexander Rimsky-Korsakov, who was advancing from the Rhine Valley. Suvorov's crossing of the Saint Gotthard Pass is rated among the outstanding feats in world history, but the untold sacrifices it required proved to have been in vain: at the end of September, while the field marshal was threading his way through the Alpine mountain paths, Rimsky-Korsakov and the Austrians were defeated near Zurich. Although Suvorov succeeded in extricating his depleted army from a situation that might well have been considered desperate, the political consequences of the lack of Austro-Russian cooperation disclosed by the Swiss campaign proved fatal. Suvorov nursed grudges of long standing against the Vienna *Hofkriegsrat* and complained about the difficulties created for him by the Austrian authorities. In June, 1799, Paul was still sufficiently devoted to the cause of the allies to declare war on Spain because of her unwillingness to break off relations with France, but by the autumn he had changed his mind. It was not only in Switzerland that the allies suffered reverses. The Anglo-Russian expeditionary force in Holland had met with no success, and in October, 1799, the Russian army was forced to capitulate. Friction with Austria increased, the exactions and the objectionable conduct of the troops of Suvorov in Switzerland and Bohemia, where the Russians established their winter quarters, added to the strain, and in January, 1800, the field marshal and his army were finally recalled.

Anglo-Russian relations, too, deteriorated. England was blamed in St. Petersburg for the failure of the Dutch venture, and Russia's suspicion of the British was fostered by the continuation of friendly relations between London and Vienna. It was the Maltese question, however, that proved the chief source of discord. In September, 1799, Admiral Ushakov was prevented by England from carrying out his instructions for an attack on Malta, and a year later (September 5, 1800, N.S.) the British themselves occupied the island and refused to surrender it to Paul. This attitude of London dealt the *coup de grâce* to the moribund Anglo-Austro-Russian coalition. Paul, who had never completely abandoned the idea of a "Northern Accord," had signed in October, 1799, a treaty of alliance with Sweden; a visit to St. Petersburg a year later by King Gustavus Adolphus led to the organization of the second Armed Neutrality League (December, 1800), uniting Russia, Sweden, Prussia, and Denmark for the common purpose of defending the freedom of the seas. Based on the 1780 declaration of Armed Neutrality, the provisions of which were somewhat expanded and made more stringent, the League was directed primarily against England. In August, September, and October Paul imposed an embargo on British shipping, and some 1,100 British seamen were arrested in Russian ports and interned. After the formation of the League, London retaliated by proclaiming an embargo on the merchantmen of the "neutral" Powers (with the exception of Prussia). The Russian ambassador to the Court of St. James's and the British ambassador to St. Petersburg were recalled, and the two former allies were rapidly drifting towards a state of war.

Paul simultaneously revised his French policy. The *coup d'état* of Brumaire 18 (November 9, 1799) which overthrew the Directory and established the Consulate was rightly interpreted in St. Petersburg as the abandonment by Paris of the Jacobin revolution principles and a step towards the restoration of monarchy. Bonaparte appeared no longer as usurper and dangerous demagogue but as the probable savior of France and Europe from the rule of the revolutionary rabble. The victory of Marengo (June, 1800) added to the prestige he already enjoyed at the court of St. Petersburg, and the *rapprochement* between France and Russia was facilitated by the friendly and conciliatory manner in which the first consul responded to Russian advances. He agreed to cede Malta to Paul at the very moment when the island was about to be occupied by the British, and he ordered the unconditional release, with full military honors, of Russian prisoners of war detained in France. Rostopchin, head of the Russian department of foreign affairs, and then still an admirer of Bonaparte, prepared a plan for the destruction of the might of England and the partition of Turkey in agreement with France, Prussia, and Austria. Paul enthusiastically approved this fanciful project, which provided for the annexation by Russia of Constantinople, Bulgaria, Rumelia, and Moldavia (October 2, 1800). As early as March, 1800, the French corps of Prince Condé was dismissed from Russian service, and in January, 1801, Louis XVIII was curtly invited to leave Mittau. The speedy and smooth progress of the Franco-Russian negotiations for a military alliance encouraged Paul to take the path of territorial expansion. On January 18,

1801, Russia formally annexed Georgia, over which she had exercised a vague suzerainty after the Peace of Jassy; a few days earlier (January 12) the government of the tsar had decided to embark on the conquest of India. The hastily improvised expedition, comprised of some 23,000 Cossacks under Vasili Orlov, was expected to reach the Ganges by way of Khiva and Bokhara. The murder of Paul (March 11, 1801) and the subsequent recall of Orlov and his men brought to an end this preposterous and reckless venture, however, not before the nearly impassable roads and the rigors of the climate had worked frightful ravages among the Cossacks.[5] With the accession of Alexander the foreign relations of Russia entered upon a new phase.

THE COUP D'ÉTAT OF MARCH 11, 1801

Paul, as has already been pointed out, was in no sense revolutionary, and had probably a more exalted conception than had any of his predecessors of the place occupied by an aristocracy in the framework of the state. It was, nevertheless, his attitude towards the nobility which offers a clue to the palace conspiracy which terminated his reign. Paul had never contemplated the abolition of serfdom, and although his pronouncements and legislation reveal a desire to improve the lot of the peasantry his practical measures for the achievement of this object were few and the results negligible. Reverting to a practice prevalent before the reign of Elizabeth, Paul, on his accession, ordered the serfs to take the oath of allegiance. He restored the right of the serfs to petition the Crown, but limited the scope of this measure by providing that collective petitions (which were customary) should no longer be permitted and that complaints might be presented only by individual serfs (decree of December 12, 1796). A manifesto of April 5, 1797, prohibited the landowners from forcing their serfs to work on Sundays on the ground that the remaining six days of the week, equally divided between the cultivation of the fields of the owners and those of the serfs, were adequate to meet the needs of good husbandry. The Sunday-rest rule was a recapitulation of an often violated provision of the Code of 1649; the loose wording of the manifesto ruling allegedly restricting to three days per week the servile labor to which the owners were entitled has been the source of much confusion. The majority of Russian historians and constitutional lawyers regard it as a binding

[5] The leader of the expedition, for instance, was not provided with maps of the territories he was expected to conquer.

legal rule, and this interpretation was officially sanctioned by the Code of 1832 (Volume IX, Articles 589 and 590). Paul and some of his principal advisers (Kurakin, Bezborodko) took a similar view, but the Senate in its official exposé of the manifesto ignored the three-days-a-week provision and referred exclusively to the prohibition of Sunday work (decree of April 6, 1797). This was also the construction put on the manifesto, at the time of its promulgation, by the organs of local administration. Whatever might have been the real intention of Paul, the manifesto was consistently disregarded, not only in his reign and in that of Alexander I but even after the disputed provision definitely became the law of the land in 1832. There is much evidence to support the opinion of more recent students (Klochkov, Kornilov) that the three-days rule, as stated in the manifesto of 1797, was not a legislative enactment but the announcement of a policy the government considered desirable. Free from ambiguity but of minor practical significance was a decree prohibiting the sale in Ukraine of serfs without the land (October 16, 1798), as were also various measures for the improvement of the economic well-being and promotion of self-government among the state peasants and the "appanage" peasants (as the peasants formerly owned by the imperial family became known after the formation of the ministry of appanages). The policies of Paul, however, were not uniformly favorable to the peasantry. Merchants were again granted the privilege of purchasing serfs for employment in industrial enterprises (decree of March 16, 1798); the *obrok* [6] of the state peasants was increased, and it varied, according to the locality, from 3.5 rubles to 5 rubles (decree of December 18, 1797); a large number of state peasants, estimated at 500,000, were distributed to private owners and became serfs; and, last but not least, the government took stern measures for the suppression of sporadic peasant uprisings. A manifesto of January 29, 1797, enjoined the serfs, under threat of severe punishment, to show complete obedience to their masters. All things considered, there was little in the peasant policies of Paul to disturb the peace of mind of the most conservative serf-owners.

The real source of the disaffection among the *dvoriane* was the attitude of the tsar towards their recently won privileges. The Russian nobility, having finally escaped the strait-jacket of compulsory service, treasured its hard-earned immunities and special rights. Paul, however,

[6] See p. 577.

considered that the privileges of the aristocracy were not a gift, but a reward for services rendered to the state. He did not formally repeal the provision of the Charter of the Nobility (1785), which reaffirmed the right of the *dvoriane* to enter and resign government service at will, but in operation his administrative practice made service, especially military service, compulsory for every *dvorianin*. The imposition of a tax on the estates of the nobility [7] violated another provision of the Charter by which the *dvoriane* were exempted from direct taxation. It became customary, moreover, to "invite" the noble landowners to finance certain public enterprises, such as the building of army barracks, and since the "invitation" could not be refused without dire consequences the *dvoriane* had no choice but to foot the bill. Immunity from corporal punishment, a cherished privilege, received a restrictive although not illogical interpretation. In a decision of January 3, 1797, the emperor enunciated the doctrine that a nobleman convicted of a crime involving the loss of his legal status was to be no longer a member of the privileged class and, therefore, had no claim to exemption from flogging. This ruling was of considerable practical importance, since the loss of a title of nobility, which had been a rare occurrence under Catherine, became much more frequent under Paul. The emperor held that his interpretation served the interests of the aristocracy by removing from its midst unworthy members, but this line of thought did not commend itself to the more practical-minded *dvoriane*.

The right of corporate self-government, so parsimoniously measured out by Catherine, suffered further curtailment. In view of the subordinate position assigned by the legislation of Catherine to the local officials elected by the *dvoriane* (except the marshals of the nobility), the substitution of appointment for election (decree of May 14, 1800), unpopular as it was, was nevertheless of relatively minor practical importance. The very structure of corporate self-government, however, underwent far-reaching changes. The provincial assemblies of the nobility were discontinued (decree of October 14, 1799), thus depriving the *dvoriane* of a province as a whole (county assemblies were not affected by the order) of the only opportunity, limited as it was, for exchanging views and devising common policies. The provincial marshals of the nobility were no longer elected by the provincial assemblies but by the county marshals of the nobility from

[7] See p. 616.

among their own numbers; the election was carried out not at a meeting, but by correspondence and written ballots (decree of October 24, 1800). Those among the *dvoriane* who had been dishonorably discharged from army and government service (and their number increased rapidly in the closing years of the reign of Paul) were debarred from participation in corporate activities, and the already comprehensive control by the governors over such activities was made even more stringent. The pomp and circumstance customarily displayed during the assemblies of the nobility were discouraged; the emperor, indeed, curtly declined to receive loyal addresses from the *dvoriane*, a ritual which both the nobility and Catherine relished but which her son regarded as a mere waste of time. The practical measures of Paul to enhance the position of the nobility, such as the establishment of a credit bank for their exclusive use (1797) and greater opportunities for promotion in the army, proved inadequate to stem the rising tide of disaffection. This feeling of discontent, rampant in the ruling class, provided the background for the tragedy of March 11. One of the first measures of the successor of Paul was to restore the Charter of the Nobility and the local government act of 1775.

No less detrimental to the position of the tsar was his army reform and his attitude towards the guards. Historians who have studied these aspects of his policy (D. Miliutin, P. S. Lebedev, A. Petrushevsky, and especially S. A. Panchulidzev) are in general agreement that many of his innovations were of lasting value. The army regulations of Paul, modeled on those of Prussia, provided each branch of the service with a clear-cut organization based on strict subordination and designed to eliminate the arbitrary rule of commanding officers. The efficiency of the troops was promoted by rigorous drilling. The introduction of a strict system of accounting did much to eradicate the spoliation and misappropriation of funds prevalent in the military establishment under Catherine. Paul particularly insisted that the legitimate needs of the common soldier should be properly taken care of by his superiors. These reforms, beneficial in themselves, disturbed the complacency of the officers' corps, which had grown accustomed to the easy-going ways and paternalism of the era of Catherine. Paul, moreover, showed none of his mother's predilection for the guards, whom he contemptuously called *"la troupe dorée."* Officers in the guards resented the inclusion in the ranks of their exclusive body of Paul's Gatchina battalions, the introduction of Prussian uniforms, the prohibition of costly and elaborate army dress, and above all the discipline ruthlessly applied to every soldier, from field marshals to privates. The lists of the aristocratic regiments were purged of officers whose connection with the service was nominal (a common practice at that time). Almost overnight the holding of a commission in the guards, which was traditionally regarded as a sinecure and the necessary preliminary to a comfortable career, became an exacting full-time occupation fraught, moreover, with considerable peril, since nothing was more likely to provoke the wrath of the emperor and bring severe penalties than an infringement, however trivial, of army regulations. If the impartiality with which discipline was enforced made it appear somewhat more palatable to the rank and file, the officers—especially the higher officers—may be forgiven for having failed to perceive the advantage.

Insistence on discipline and conformity with the law, so alien to Russia's tradition, extended to the civil service and to practically every manifestation of national life. Paul issued orders prohibiting certain fashions in dress which, in his opinion, suggested sympathy with revolutionary France; decreed the type of carriages and the number of horses by which they were to be drawn (varying according to the official rank of the owners); and introduced a rigid court etiquette. With the ascendancy of Mademoiselle Lopukhin (later Princess Gagarin) and the estrangement of the tsar from Mademoiselle Nelidov and the Empress Maria (1798), the political regime which in theory was to be the rule of law became *de facto* more and more arbitrary and capricious. The declaration of war on France accentuated the repressive character of the government: the importation of foreign books, journals, and even music was prohibited; Russians were no longer permitted to travel abroad; censorship became more stringent and extended to private correspondence; dismissals of officials, sometimes accompanied by degradation and deportation, were numerous, and although often followed by immediate forgiveness made the tenure of higher offices precarious. The feeling of insecurity and irritation prevailing in court, military, and governmental circles was fostered by the many eccentricities of the tsar's demeanor and by his quaint sense of humor, of which those close to him were the defenseless victims. Paul was aware of the spread of disaffection and discontent among the social groups on which rested the power of the Crown —the *dvoriane*, the officers' corps, and the bureaucracy—he remembered the fate of his father, and was increasingly suspicious of the members of his entourage, including his wife and his sons.

Rumors about a conspiracy for the overthrow of Paul were reported by the Swedish ambassador to St. Petersburg towards the end of 1797. So far as can be ascertained from contradictory accounts, the actual plot originated in the autumn of 1799, when it took shape in the discussions between three men who all enjoyed the confidence of the emperor: Count Nikita Petrovich Panin (son of General Peter Panin and nephew of Paul's former tutor, Nikita Ivanovich Panin), then vice chancellor; Joseph Ribas, a Spanish soldier of fortune born in Malta and an admiral in the Russian navy; and Count Peter Pahlen, military governor of St. Petersburg. Neither Panin nor Ribas took an active part in the events of March 11: the former was dismissed in November, 1800, and deported to one of his estates, and the latter died in December of the same year. The role of Panin was nevertheless highly important: he disclosed to the Grand Duke Alexander the existence of a conspiracy for the deposition of his father. Alexander had good reasons for hesitating: he had been proclaimed heir apparent upon the accession of Paul, his right to the throne was established by the law of succession of April 5, 1797, he held various high civil and military offices, and he took an active part in the conduct of affairs of state. It does not seem likely, therefore, that he would have put much credence in the rumors of his impending disgrace which were circulated in St. Petersburg. There is no doubt, nevertheless, that he gave his assent to the proposed *coup d'état*, and it is difficult to believe, as it is often alleged, that he merely envisaged the establishment of a regency and that he did not anticipate the murder of his father.

The final and decisive stage of the conspiracy was engineered by Pahlen with the support of a small band of officers of the guards, among them Count Leon Bennigsen and the three brothers Zubov—Platon, Valerian, and Nicholas—who had only recently returned from exile. In the night of March 11 (March 23, N.S.), 1801, the conspirators gained admission to the bedchamber of the tsar in the newly built Mikhailovsky Castle, to which he had only recently transferred his residence, and brutally murdered him. The question whether the assassination was premeditated or merely an accident cannot be answered with any degree of finality, but the former hypothesis seems more plausible. Pahlen did not reach the scene of the regicide until after the death of Paul. It is believed that this delay was intentional and that the cautious and scheming courtier was preparing an avenue of retreat in case the conspiracy proved a failure. Alexander, greatly shaken and on the verge of a nervous breakdown, was proclaimed emperor, but the assembled troops received the announcement with a marked absence of enthusiasm and insisted on viewing the body of the deceased emperor, who, according to the official version, had died from a stroke of apoplexy. There was, however, no opposition and much rejoicing in court circles and among the nobility. The last palace revolution in the history of Russia had run true to form.

INDEX

Abo, Peace of (1743), 468

Absolutism, Russian, roots of, 63; foundation of, 98, 100, 108, 110, 180-181; Metropolitan Macarius on, 184-185; Ivan IV on, 185-187; triumph of, 208; maintained under Shuisky, 230; maintained on accession of Michael Romanov, 245-246, 250; Theophan Prokopovich on, 413; formulation of, in Army Regulations and Church Statute, 426; limitations of, imposed on Empress Anne, 441; restored, 444-445; Catherine II on, 510, 546, 601; Paul I on, 612

Academy of Arts, 493, 593

Academy of Science, 13, 404, 408-409, 471, 492-493, 505, 510, 592

Adashev, A. F., 189, 191-192, 199-200

Adrian, Patriarch, 326, 409-410

Adrianople, Treaty of (1713), 345 n.

Aix-la-Chapelle, Peace of (1748), 473-475

Akhmad, Khan, 64, 68-69, 160, 165

Aksakov, Ivan, 427

Aland Islands, Conference of (1718–1719), 350-351

Alexander, Grand Duke. See Alexander I, Emperor

Alexander, Grand Duke of Lithuania, 157-158

Alexander, Grand Duke of Tver and Vladimir, 87

Alexander IV, Pope, 175

Alexander I, Emperor, 527, 550, 556, 598-599, 609, 615, 623; expected to succeed Catherine II, 611; approved conspiracy to overthrow Paul I, 627; proclaimed emperor, 628

Alexander II, Emperor, 553

Alexander Nevsky, 61, 80-84

Alexandra, daughter of Paul I, 617

Alexandra Fedorovna, wife of Nicholas II, 134

Alexis, Metropolitan, 93, 96, 104, 139, 141

Alexis, Tsar, 129, 249, 251-253, 261-262, 267-268, 270-272, 277, 280, 283-284, 286, 297-298, 300, 307, 314-315, 317, 385, 403; and Patriarch Nikon, 287-292, 409-410

Alexis, son of Peter I, 320, 323, 325, 328, 330-333, 346, 404, 411, 413, 426-427, 434-435, 437, 439

Alphabet, Slavonic, 128, 142, 300, 401

Anastasia, wife of Ivan IV, 188, 191, 199, 220

Anastasius, Metropolitan, 184

Andrew, brother of Vasili III, 182

Andrew II, Grand Duke of Vladimir, 61, 80

Andrew III, Grand Duke of Vladimir, 82-83

Andrew Bogoliubsky, 31, 40, 48-54, 115

Andrew Junior, brother of Ivan III, 159-160

Andrew Senior, brother of Ivan III, 159-160

Andronov, Fedka, 239

Andrusovo, Armistice of (1667), 263-264

Anglo-Russian Convention (1755), 475

Anhalt-Zerbst, Princess of, mother of Catherine II, 467, 471

Anhalt-Zerbst, Sophie Augusta Frederica, Princess of. See Catherine II, Empress

i